Victorian Dramatic Criticism

Victorian Dramatic Criticism

Selected and Introduced by
George Rowell

720699

Methuen & Co Ltd
11 New Fetter Lane London EC4

First published 1971
by Methuen & Co Ltd
11 New Fetter Lane London EC4
© 1971 Methuen & Co Ltd
Printed in Great Britain by
Richard Clay (The Chaucer Press) Ltd
Bungay, Suffolk

SBN hardbound 416 12320 1

SBN paperback 416 30010 3

Distributed in the U.S.A.
by Barnes & Noble Inc.

Contents

Acknowledgements

The editor and publishers wish to express their thanks to the following for permission to reproduce the articles listed:

Mrs Rose Elton and Chatto & Windus Ltd for 'The Art of Mr Poel' by C. E. Montague from *Dramatic Values* (London, Chatto & Windus, 1910).

Mrs D. W. Finley for the following articles by William Archer: '*A Doll's House*' ('Ibsen and English Criticism') from *The Fortnightly Review*, July 1889; '*A Woman of No Importance*' and '*The Second Mrs Tanqueray*' from *The Theatrical World of 1893* (London, Walter Scott, 1894); '*Arms and the Man*' and '*The Case of Rebellious Susan*' from *The Theatrical World of 1894* (London, Walter Scott, 1895); '*The Importance of Being Earnest*' and '*Trilby*' from *The Theatrical World of 1895* (London, Walter Scott, 1896); 'Forbes Robertson as Hamlet' ('*Hamlet*') from *The Theatrical World of 1897* (London, Walter Scott, 1898).

Granada Publishing Ltd for the following articles by Max Beerbohm from *Around Theatres* (London, Rupert Hart-Davis, 1953): '*The Devil's Disciple*' ('"G.B.S." at Kennington'), 'Benson as Henry V' (extract from 'Two Performances of Shakespeare'), '*The Admirable Crichton*' ('A Welcome Play'), '*Letty*' ('A Magnificent Dis-Play'), 'The Older and Better Music Hall', 'Dan Leno', '*Peter Pan*' ('The Child Barrie'), '*The Voysey Inheritance*', 'In the Pit', '*The Passing of the Third Floor Back*' ('A Deplorable Affair'), 'At the Gaiety' and '*Justice*'.

Hutchinson Publishing Group Ltd for '*Trelawney of the "Wells"*' and '*The Only Way: A Tale of Two Cities*' by J. T. Grein from *Dramatic Criticism* (London, John Long, 1899).

Mr Michael MacCarthy for the following articles by Desmond MacCarthy: 'The Influence of Dramatic Criticism' and '*John Bull's Other Island*' from *The Court Theatre 1904–1907* (London, A. H. Bullen, 1907), and 'Granville Barker's Production of *A Midsummer Night's Dream*' ('The Production of Poetic Drama') from *Theatre* (London, MacGibbon & Kee, 1954).

The Society of Authors, for and on behalf of the Bernard Shaw Estate, for the following articles by G. B. Shaw: 'Problems of Dramatic Criticism' (extract from *The Quintessence of Ibsenism*, 1891 edition) from *Shaw on Theatre* (London, MacGibbon & Kee, 1958); *'Guy Domville* and *An Ideal Husband'* ('Two New Plays') and *'The Notorious Mrs Ebbsmith'* ('Mr Pinero's New Play') from *Our Theatres in the Nineties* (London, Constable, 1932), vol. I; *'The Sign of the Cross'*, *'True Blue'* ('Boiled Heroine'), 'Irving's Production of *Cymbeline'* ('Blaming the Bard') and *'Little Eyolf'* from *Our Theatres in the Nineties*, vol. II; 'At the Pantomime', 'Her Majesty's', *'John Gabriel Borkman'*, 'Tree's Production of *Julius Caesar'* ('Tappertit on Caesar') and 'The Drama in Hoxton' from *Our Theatres in the Nineties*, vol. III.

Our thanks are also due to the Raymond Mander and Joe Mitchenson Theatre Collection for their advice and assistance in obtaining the illustration featured on the cover, 'A First Night at the Theatre' by Alfred Stevens.

Introduction

The Victorian age was an era of essentially popular theatre and increasingly popular journalism. One manifestation of this journalism was the emergence of the dramatic critic from the anonymity and brevity which had previously characterized periodical treatment of the theatre. That Victorian dramatic criticism should be prolific was therefore predictable; what was less expected, though doubly welcome in a century of pot-boiling playwrights, was the high quality of its critics, particularly at the start and end of the era. If the Victorian theatre may be regarded as existing to all intents and purposes thirty years before Victoria acceded, and surviving until the outbreak of the Great War, the roll of Victorian dramatic criticism is enhanced by the names of Lamb, Leigh Hunt and Hazlitt at one end, and of the mature Beerbohm and MacCarthy at the other. Even if we interpret the term Victorian precisely, its theatre boasted Lewes, James, Archer, Walkley, Shaw and Montague among its critics. All these writers, and others less famous, are represented in this selection.

Since, however, the Victorian theatre was distinguished by its acting rather than its drama, the selection has been made on the basis of the play in performance, rather than the play as literature. Such a principle rules out the work of several significant writers, notably Coleridge, who (despite penning perhaps the century's most quoted piece of dramatic criticism: 'To see Kean act is like reading Shakespeare by flashes of lightning') never served as a dramatic critic; and it may be argued that the Romantics are already well represented in collections of literary criticism. The extracts have also been arranged according to various aspects of the theatrical process and not around each critic in turn. The aim is therefore to build up a picture of the theatre at work in the words of its leading commentators, and to sustain the personal note unsigned contributions have been excluded, even when the importance of the occasion tempts an editor to break his own rules. Other principles of selection include limitation to the original production (of new plays) and to British actors and playwrights, although an exception has been made in the case of Ibsen, whose significance in the theatrical climate of the 1890s brought about his virtual naturalization in the eyes of his advocates!

The publication in 1807 of Leigh Hunt's *Critical Essays on the Performers of the London Theatres* reflects a new era in both the theatre and dramatic criticism. Theatrical activity in London had become diversified enough to inspire this comprehensive account of its actors and to foster the calling of theatrical journalist, whose craft Leigh Hunt mocks so mercilessly in his 'Rules for the Theatrical Critic of a Newspaper'. When Hunt became dramatic critic of the *News* in 1805 (at the age of twenty-one) he adopted a tone which several of his most readable successors, notably Lewes and Shaw, were to emulate: colloquial, informed, iconoclastic, above all concerned with the technical processes of the actor as he strove to adjust himself to the vast amphitheatres of a nation in the grip of the Industrial Revolution, where 'To gain the attention of an audience is always in some degree to gain their applause.'

As a young man Hunt took something of the urchin's delight in thumbing his nose at the great, even those like Garrick whom he had never seen. His account of John Philip Kemble is too professional to withhold praise where praise is due, but it is always grudging praise; whereas if faults could be found (and Kemble's acting provided plenty of such opportunities), Hunt would fall to with a will. Although his tone mellowed later, when he wrote for his own paper, the *Examiner*, and for the *Tatler*, so that he could hail Kean's Othello as 'the masterpiece of the living stage', his youthful impudence provided a dangerous precedent for less gifted critics. His radical sympathies, too, give his account of the notorious 'Old Price' Riots a manifest bias. But if he was often disenchanted by actors, he was never disenchanted by the theatre, and one of his last pieces, 'Christmas and the Theatre', shows his appreciation of those humble contributors to the playgoer's pleasure, the scene-shifter, the candle-snuffer, the musician and the fruit-seller.

While Hunt's work looks forward to modern dramatic criticism, Lamb's writing on the theatre seems to hark back to the eighteenth-century essayist. Only occasionally did he undertake to review a particular performance. More often he was concerned to communicate his delight in an actor's playing or personality, and sometimes (as with his accounts of Elliston) it is impossible to distinguish between the two. Lamb does not analyse the performer's technique, as Leigh Hunt did with such accuracy; instead he recreates the effect of his acting by the exercise of his own literary skill, so that the performance is really Lamb's, rather than Munden's or Elliston's.

But if Lamb the playgoer delighted in the theatre, Lamb the scholar distrusted it, condemning the distortion which the highest drama seemed to him to suffer in performance. Such notorious statements as 'The Lear of Shakespeare cannot be acted' must be read in the context of a corrupt text presented in a theatre aspiring to crude realism before a largely illiterate audience. Lamb's two major dramatic essays, 'On the Tragedies of Shakspeare Considered with Reference to their Fitness for Stage Representation' and 'On the Artificial Comedies of the Last Century', may therefore be interpreted as complementary expressions of the same viewpoint: Shakespeare's tragedies should only be judged off the stage, Congreve's comedies should only be judged on the stage, lest their airs and graces perish in the cold climate of reality and morality.

William Hazlitt's dramatic criticism covered a wider field than Hunt's or Lamb's. At various dates between 1813 and 1830 he wrote for the *Morning Chronicle*, the *Champion*, *The Times*, the *London Magazine* and, most importantly, the *Examiner*. In 1818 he published a selection of his criticism as *A View of the English Stage*. He was also stricter with himself than Hunt and sterner towards his subject than Lamb: his regret that Mrs Siddons should continue to act beyond her prime contrasts strongly with Lamb's indulgence towards his old favourites.

Hazlitt's immediate recognition of Kean's gifts contributed greatly to that actor's unique triumph, but he was never preoccupied with the technique of acting. In a single article he can denounce the slovenly standards of the transpontine Coburg and write affectionately of the country strollers from his youth. Perhaps it was this wide-ranging interest which prompted him to make the first analysis in English of the actor's public and private *persona* in the essay: 'On Actors and Acting'. In the theatre it was the actor's interpretation of the text that provided Hazlitt's grounds for judgement. Of Kean at his finest, as Othello, he suggests: 'His lips might be said less to utter words, than to bleed drops of blood gushing from his heart', and later describes 'I cannot think but Desdemona's honest' as 'irradiating his countenance with joy, like sudden sunshine', while his careful assessment of Kemble's career distinguishes between those parts he could interpret acceptably (Coriolanus, Cato, Penruddock) and those in which he failed the author (including some of Kemble's favourite roles: Hamlet and even Macbeth).

Hazlitt and Leigh Hunt were fortunate in their era, dominated as it was by two great exponents of strongly contrasted acting styles, Kemble and Kean. George Henry Lewes's debut as a dramatic critic occurred some ten months before Macready's farewell performance, and the leading classical actors on the London stage during his comparatively brief term of office were Charles Kean and Samuel Phelps, men more noted for their high principles of management than for their tragic powers. Consequently when in 1875 Lewes published a distillation of his dramatic criticism under the title *On Actors and the Art of Acting*, he gave pride of place to foreign performers (Salvini, Ristori) or to English actors he had seen in his youth (Edmund Kean, Macready), rather than to his contemporaries.

The bantering tone Lewes adopted as 'Vivian' of the *Leader* recalls Hunt's handling of Kemble and looks forward to Shaw's treatment of Irving, characteristically claiming that Charles Kean 'makes Macbeth ignoble – one whose crime is that of a common murderer, with perhaps a tendency towards Methodism'. But behind the teasing and flights of fancy there was always the recognition of strict professionalism in an actor which prompted his verdict of 'perfection' on Charles James Mathews, a performer of extremely narrow range but impeccable within that range. Lewes came of a theatrical family, his grandfather having created the part of Young Marlow, and his views on acting were informed by inherited knowledge and first-hand experience.

His claim that Shakespeare could not have been a good actor because he was so great a writer carries the weight of one who had acted (and failed!) in his own plays, just as his contemptuous dismissal of the idea that a performance regularly repeated must become 'mechanical' (and this before the days of the modern long run) reflects his professional principles.

But if he had professional pride, he had also professional humility; he was always quick to play down the performer's contribution to a supreme theatrical experience, when compared with the playwright's, and his analysis of the actor's 'transient glory' rejects the charity Hazlitt brought to the subject. Perhaps it is Lewes's treatment of acting in general, rather than his considera-tion of any particular performer or performance, that represents his most valuable contribution to dramatic criticism. His distinction between 'reflection' and 'passion' in acting, and his insistence on the need for both, defined the boundaries within which all subsequent arguments on the subject have ranged.

Westland Marston, like Lewes, was a critic with considerable professional knowledge of the theatre, limited in his case to the playwright's contribution. His portrait gallery, *Our Recent Actors*, was published in 1888, but draws on his experience as dramatic critic of the *Athenaeum* twenty-five years earlier, and on an even longer career as a playgoer. The freshness of his memory gives immediacy to his account of some of Macready's finest performances, but he is always discriminating: if he applauds that actor's performance as Richelieu, he does not overrate the genre of the play, and his analysis of Macready's Macbeth is both critical and reasoned. It is understandable that John Forster's detailed descriptions of Macready from the *Examiner* should lack this discrimination, for he was one of Macready's closest associates.

Between Lewes's early retirement in 1854 and Archer's early emergence in 1878, English dramatic criticism displayed more respectability than dis-tinction, accurately reflecting the tone of the theatre in these years. Thus Henry Morley, Professor of English at London University, laments the fact that 'no theatrical company now in existence can speak such poetry as that of the *Midsummer Night's Dream*' and condemns the Princess's audience as 'depraved' for encoring the 'Maypole dance' in Charles Kean's production, but accepts 'Athens, a Room in the Palace of Theseus' as 'Shakespeare's direction'. Two later critics, Dutton Cook and Joseph Knight, displayed a sense of proportion, if lacking absolute standards. Cook, for example, realized the appropriateness of the modest Prince of Wales's theatre to Robertson's miniature comedies, and Knight recognized the strength (its romantic appeal) and weakness (its vocal failings) of Irving's Hamlet.

A more controversial figure is that of Clement Scott, for over a quarter of a century dramatic critic of the *Daily Telegraph*, an assiduous editor of the *Theatre* in the 1880s, and ultimately doyen of the *corps dramatique*. Scott's hysterical campaign against Ibsen and the Ibsenites has perhaps obscured the modest but real achievements of his earlier career. It was his misfortune to be chiefly concerned for dramatic literature at a time when English drama, though increasingly literate, was not yet literature. Thus his careful analysis of the first night of *The Bells* gives pride of place to the play (in fact both second-hand and second-rate) at the expense of Irving's historic performance as Matthias. Much of Scott's opposition to Ibsen sprang, not from outraged morality but from his resentment of invidious comparisons between Ibsen's plays and the native product, 'a drama that is as distinguished in literary excellence as that of any other country in the world'.

The limitations of Scott's taste were shared by the playgoer of his day, to whom his work therefore consistently appealed. The title of his book, *The Drama of Yesterday and Today*, suggests that he could judge what had happened but not what should happen, and this restricted vision applied to his handling of the performance as well as the text. Thus, writing of *Much Ado About Nothing* at the Lyceum, he notes that for 'Sigh no more, ladies' Balthazar 'did not come down to the footlights and deliver his song in a full-bodied way, as operatic tenors are wont to do, but he acted Balthazar and belonged to the scene', adding, revealingly, 'Of course the song was encored, for taste was in every note and line of it.'

It is instructive to compare Scott's attitude to Irving's productions with that of the American-born, Paris-educated Henry James. For James *Faust* at the Lyceum is full of 'importunate limelight' and 'irrepressible blue fire', and the resulting spectacle not only obscures the play but is displeasing in itself: 'The scenic effect is the ugliest we have ever contemplated.' Even the acting, or what James could detect of it through the limelight and blue fire, was second-rate; Ellen Terry's Margaret he found 'amateurish' and 'rough and ready', Faust (George Alexander) 'not in it at all', Irving himself superficial and cheap. What is worse, he committed the unforgivable sin of allowing Mephistopheles's scene with Martha to be 'the most successful of the play'. They managed things differently at the Comédie Française!

Despite the division of their worlds by the work of Ibsen, set as a flaming sword between them, there is a curious parallel between the careers of Clement Scott and William Archer, which extends to the titles of their major works: *The Drama of Yesterday and Today* and *The Old Drama and the New*. Both applauded the leading playwrights of their own day for their literacy and responsibility. Both, in recognizing these achievements, failed to recognize the striking originality of at least one contemporary giant (in Scott's case Ibsen, in Archer's Shaw). Both, by campaigning for the drama of their time, have suffered serious loss of reputation in the eyes of later generations.

Archer's role as translator of Ibsen is less relevant to his dramatic criticism than the part he played in the campaign for a National Theatre, for which he drew up with Granville Barker the first detailed scheme in 1904. His vision was of an endowed alternative to the *laissez-faire* of the actor-managers' theatre, in which the best drama of all ages and all nations could be staged without commercial pressure. In his day-by-day criticism for the *World*, the *Westminster Gazette* and other journals, he looked for worthy British contributors to such a repertory, and found them above all in Jones and Pinero. His grounds for such judgement are significant: even the epoch-making *Second Mrs Tanqueray*, he declares, 'satisfies the intelligence more completely than any other modern English play; but it is not in the least moving'. Since emotions are natural and eternal, whereas intelligence is trained and cumulative, it follows that an intelligence trained more comprehensively than Archer's is bound to find both his views and his idols badly dated.

In particular his equation of 'intelligence' with 'seriousness' blinded him to a good deal of gold among the dross, whether it was Tree's acting as Svengali ('it stands on a low plane of art, because it is not an effort of observation or composition, but of sheer untrammelled fantasy') or Shaw's promise in *Arms and the Man*: 'I begin positively to believe that he may one day write a serious and even an artistic play if only he will repress his irrelevant whimsicality.' In view of Archer's reputation as a dour, humourless Scot, however, it should be pointed out that he recognized Wilde's brilliance, and could even cap his wit: '"Nothing survives being thought of." Nothing – not even *A Woman of No Importance*.'

Shaw's own dramatic criticism needs less introduction than that of any other Victorian. He is, with Dryden, the only major English dramatist yet to make a substantial contribution to dramatic criticism, and his column from the *Saturday Review* has been more widely reprinted than even the theatrical essays of Lamb or Hazlitt. This availability is due less to Shaw's eminence as a dramatist than to his skill as an entertainer. He can immortalize the most mortal of reputations by coining the word 'Sardoodledom' for the school of Sardou, and his polemic style, in the traditions of Hunt and Lewes, has been widely followed and sometimes abused by his successors.

Moreover Shaw is his own best commentator. He succinctly describes his dramatic criticism as 'a siege laid to the theatre of the nineteenth century by an author who had to cut his way into it at the point of a pen', and explains: 'I postulated as desirable a certain kind of play in which I was destined ten years later to make my mark as a playwright . . . and I brought everybody, authors, actors, managers, to the one test: were they coming my way or staying in the old grooves?' In this respect Shaw may be regarded as his own John the Baptist. He never for one moment pretended to impartiality, and after demolishing *The Notorious Mrs Ebbsmith* he can boast: 'My criticism has not, I hope, any other fault than the inevitable one of extreme unfairness.' But he is at least impartial in his partiality; if he is unfair to *Mrs Ebbsmith*, he is no less unfair to *Cymbeline* or *True Blue*. Moreover what emerges from Shaw's collected criticism, once the effects of the bravura and the bias have worn off, is the sheer comprehensiveness of his grasp of the theatrical process. Whether he is considering actors or audiences, playwrights or scene-painters, detailed knowledge and reasoned judgement are everywhere apparent.

Doubtless Shaw applauded when, soon after succeeding him on the *Saturday Review*, Max Beerbohm declared: 'I do not much care about good criticism. I like better the opinion of strong, narrow, creative personalities.' He was probably born too close to the theatre to revere actors, whom he consistently describes as 'mimes', often in such doubly disparaging phrases as that with which he dismisses both the cricket and the acting of the Benson Company: 'The tired but victorious mimes go to doff their flannels and to don the motley.'

Where dramatists are concerned, he was no less irreverent; but while the first-rate tended to sharpen his pen, he was often kind and understanding to the second-rate. Thus his treatment of Pinero and Barrie is a good deal more constructive (if less entertaining) than his handling of Shaw and Shakespeare. To the third-rate he was unmerciful; in his column *The Passing of the Third Floor Back* constitutes death by dynamite. Beerbohm is above all the stylist among Victorian critics, and his work is more obviously a contribution to belles-lettres than to theatrical records. Viewing *The Devil's Disciple* before its publication, he composes a stage-direction for Burgoyne's entry which is far more Shavian than Shaw's. His spiritual father in the family of dramatic critics was most probably Charles Lamb; both are essentially essayists, and Beerbohm's affection for the *lions comiques* of the music hall parallels Lamb's love of the broad comedians of his day.

A. B. Walkley was dramatic critic of *The Times* from 1900 to 1926 and his career reached back to 1888, thus covering an expansive era in theatrical journalism, characterized by editorial enlightenment in the space and import-ance accorded to its critics. To this enlightenment Walkley, with his classical training and strong Aristotelian sense of dramatic form, contributed hand-somely. That he lacked confidence in his judgement of acting is apparent from his own account of the critic's difficulties in *Playhouse Impressions*, and his study of Henry Irving in that collection is a *catalogue raisonné* of the actor's career, not an analysis of the actor at work. But he invariably wrote with graceful authority on the drama as literature, a gift which puts him at an advantage over all but the finest critics of acting, since he deals at length with plays we still value and only briefly with actors we can never have known. It may be relevant to compare his work with that of J. T. Grein, whose contri-butions to the *Sunday Times* and other journals, like his encouragement of the independent theatre movement, were marked by courage and seriousness of purpose, rather than style or profundity.

C. E. Montague is the only provincial critic to figure in these pages, though his fellow-citizens, past and present, would certainly argue that Manchester is not provincial and *The Guardian* emphatically a national newspaper. Like Walkley's, his long career spanned two eras, since he served *The Guardian* from 1890 to 1925, and if Walkley was especially sensitive to the drama as literature, Montague was acutely aware of the drama's history, at a time when the theatre's stability tended to blind the public to its past. This made him a particularly perceptive observer of the work of William Poel, with its reintroduction of widely differing dramatic forms from other ages: Greek, Medieval, Elizabethan – though Montague was wholly free of historical pedantry and always tolerant of Poel's oddly eclectic approach to costume, casting and even text.

The youthful début of Desmond MacCarthy as critic of the *Speaker*, accounts for his inclusion here, although the bulk of his dramatic criticism was done between the two wars. Like most critics who are men of letters first and always, and men of the theatre incidentally, he preferred to recollect his theatrical emotions in tranquillity, rather than discharge them immediately into print. Hence the delicate savouring of an unforgettable chapter in English drama which characterizes his account of the Vedrenne-Barker seasons at the Court Theatre – 'How good they all were' is his highest, though by no means invariable, tribute to the actors – and his plea in the introduction to that book for a double time-scheme in dramatic criticism: an immediate, strictly factual report after the first night, and a later and lengthier passing of sentence. It is a plea that countless critics, as well as authors and actors, have made, only to be dismissed by the inexorable judgement of journalism: a first night is news.

Perhaps it is the immediacy and excitement of first impressions which set the tone of Victorian dramatic criticism. Whatever its early limitations, the Victorian theatre was remarkable for its abundance and vitality, and it is these qualities which are conveyed by its critics, whether they are writing of great acting, as Hunt and Hazlitt were fortunate to do, or the promise of great drama, as Archer, Walkley and Shaw had the chance to do. Of course, there were gaps between these peaks, both in theatrical achievement and critical assessment, but if all the critics here represented convey something of a theatrical era, popular, vigorous and persevering in its painful but determined struggle towards the modern theatre as we still know it, neither they nor their subjects will have been ill served.

Biographical Notes

WILLIAM ARCHER (1856–1924)
Dramatic critic of the *London Figaro*, 1879–81, of the *World*, 1884–1905, of the *Tribune*, 1905–8, and of the *Nation*, 1908–10. Five volumes of his collected criticism from the *World* were published between 1893 and 1897. Also contributed to the *Fortnightly Review*, the *Nineteenth Century Review* and other periodicals. In 1890–1 translations of all the mature plays of Ibsen then written appeared under his editorship, and a revised edition was published in eleven volumes between 1906 and 1908.

His books included *English Dramatists of Today* (1882), *About the Theatre* (1886), *Masks or Faces?* (1888), *Study and Stage* (1899), *A National Theatre – Schemes and Estimates* (with Granville Barker, 1907), *Play-Making* (1912) and *The Old Drama and the New* (1923). His play, *The Green Goddess*, was successfully produced in 1923.

MAX BEERBOHM (1872–1956)
Half-brother of Herbert Beerbohm Tree. Succeeded Shaw as dramatic critic of the *Saturday Review* in 1898 and continued in that capacity until 1910. Selections from his dramatic criticism were published as *Around Theatres* (1924), *Around More Theatres* (1969) and *Last Theatres* (1970). Many of his cartoons for *Vanity Fair* were of theatrical subjects. Author of several short plays and stories, one of which, *The Happy Hypocrite*, has been successfully dramatized. Knighted 1939.

EDWARD DUTTON COOK (1829–83)
Dramatic critic of the *Pall Mall Gazette*, 1867–75, and of the *World*, 1875–83. Collaborated with Leopold Lewis on a melodrama, *The Dove and the Serpent*, produced in 1859. Compiled several volumes of theatrical criticism, including *A Book of the Play* (1876), *Hours with the Players* (1881), *Nights at the Play* (1883) and *On the Stage* (1883). Author of various novels. Contributed theatrical biographies to the *Dictionary of National Biography*.

JOHN FORSTER (1812–76)
While still at Newcastle Grammar School published *A Few Thoughts in Vindication of the Stage* (1827) and in 1828 his play, *Charles at Tunbridge;*

or the Cavalier of Wildinghurst, was produced at the Newcastle Theatre. Dramatic critic of the *Examiner,* 1833–8, and later editor, 1847–55.

Intimate of Macready, Bulwer-Lytton and others. Acted regularly and successfully with Dickens's group, giving performances in aid of the Guild of Literature and Art at Devonshire House and elsewhere, 1844–55. Among his best parts were Ford in *The Merry Wives of Windsor* and Kitely in *Every Man in his Humour.*

JOHN ('JACK') THOMAS GREIN (1862–1935)

A Dutchman who came to London in 1885. Dramatic critic of *Life,* 1890–3. In 1891 founded the Independent Theatre, which opened with the first English production of *Ghosts.* Dramatic critic of the *Sunday Special* (which became the *Sunday Times* in 1903) from 1898 to 1918. Five annual volumes of his dramatic criticism were published between 1889 and 1905. Dramatic critic of the *Illustrated London News,* 1920–35, of the *Sketch,* 1922–35, and of the *Christian Science Monitor,* 1923–31.

WILLIAM HAZLITT (1778–1830)

Between 1813 and 1818 contributed dramatic criticism to the *Examiner,* the *Morning Chronicle,* the *Champion* and *The Times.* A selection of these reviews was published in 1818 as *A View of the English Stage.* Also wrote a series of essays on the drama in the *London Magazine,* 1820, and some dramatic criticism for the *Atlas,* 1829.

Provided the introduction to a number of plays in *Oxberry's New English Drama,* 1818–19. His books, often based on lectures, included *The Characters of Shakespeare's Plays* (1817), *The English Comic Writers* (1819) and *The Dramatic Literature of the Age of Elizabeth* (1820).

JAMES HENRY LEIGH HUNT (1784–1859)

Dramatic critic of the *News* (then edited by his brother John), 1805–7; also of the *Examiner* (which he edited with his brother), 1808–13, when he was sentenced to two years' imprisonment for publishing reflections on the Prince Regent. Contributed occasional dramatic criticism to the *Examiner* after his release, and continued to edit it until 1821. Between 1830 and 1832 edited and reviewed the theatre for the *Tatler.*

His criticism from the *News* was published as *Critical Essays on the Performers of the London Theatres* in 1807. His only play, *A Legend of Florence,* was successfully produced at Covent Garden, 1840. He edited the plays of Sheridan, Wycherley, Congreve, Vanbrugh and Farquhar in 1840, and of Beaumont and Fletcher in 1855.

Established close ties with Keats, Shelley and Byron, editing the *Liberal* with the latter at Pisa, 1822–3.

Also edited the *Indicator,* 1819–21, and *Leigh Hunt's London Journal,* 1834–5.

HENRY JAMES (1843–1916)

Born in New York, settled in England in 1876 and was naturalized in 1915. Never worked as a dramatic critic but wrote articles on dramatic subjects, chiefly for American periodicals, such as the *Nation*, the *Galaxy* and the *New York Tribune*, but also for the *Pall Mall Gazette*, and on one or two occasions the *Cornhill Magazine* and the *New Review*.

Only three of his plays were produced during his lifetime, *The American* (1891), *Guy Domville* (1893) and *The High Bid* (1909), none with commercial success, although several adaptations of his novels have subsequently proved popular.

JOSEPH KNIGHT (1829–1907)

Dramatic critic of the *Literary Gazette*, 1860, and of the *Athenaeum*, 1867–1907. A selection of his criticism was published in 1893 as *Theatrical Notes*. Also dramatic critic of the *Daily Graphic*, 1894–1906. Editor of *Notes and Queries* from 1883 until his death.

Chief contributor of theatrical biographies to the *Dictionary of National Biography*. Edited *Roscius Anglicanus* by John Downes (1883). In 1905 his status as senior English dramatic critic was recognized by a dinner in his honour at which Irving took the chair.

CHARLES LAMB (1775–1834)

Reviewed some performances for the *Morning Post* in 1802 and for other journals later, but avoided regular dramatic criticism, as he found he 'could not write to time'. Contributed essays on theatrical subjects (including 'On the Tragedies of Shakspeare . . .') to the *Reflector*, 1811–12, and to the *Examiner*, 1819. Between 1820 and 1823 contributed regularly to the *London Magazine* the articles later collected and published as *Essays of Elia* (1823) and *Last Essays of Elia* (1833). The former collection included 'On the Artificial Comedy of the Last Century'.

Employed at East India House, London, 1792–1825. Of his four plays – *John Woodvil*, *Mr H.*, *The Wife's Trial* and *The Pawnbroker's Daughter* – only *Mr H.* was produced, unsuccessfully, at Drury Lane in 1806.

His books included *Tales from Shakespeare* (with his sister Mary, 1807) and *Specimens of English Dramatic Poets Contemporary with Shakespeare* (1808).

GEORGE HENRY LEWES (1817–78)

Grandson of Charles Lee Lewes, the original Young Marlow in *She Stoops to Conquer*. Dramatic critic of the *Leader* (which he edited with Thornton Leigh Hunt), 1850–4. Contributed essays on the drama to the *Pall Mall Gazette*, 1875, which were published the same year as *On Actors and the Art of Acting*. Among his other books were a *Life of Goethe* (1855) and *Selections from Modern British Dramatists* (1867).

Acted professionally for a brief period in Manchester and elsewhere. His plays included *The Noble Heart* (Manchester, 1849, with the author as Ruy Gomez; Olympic, London, 1850); and under the pen-name Slingsby Lawrence *The Game of Speculation* (1851), *A Chain of Events* (1852) and *Sunshine through the Clouds* (1854), all adapted from the French for Charles Mathews and Madame Vestris at the Lyceum.

Separated from his wife in 1852 and in 1854 entered a life-long association with Mary Ann Evans (George Eliot).

DESMOND MACCARTHY (1877–1952)

Dramatic critic of the *Speaker*, 1904–7, and of the *New Statesman* from 1913. Editor of the *New Quarterly*, 1907–10, and of *Life and Letters*, 1928–32. In later life an influential literary critic on the *Sunday Times*. Knighted 1951.

His books included *The Court Theatre 1904–1907* (1907), *Criticism* (1932), *Drama* (1940), *Shaw* (1951) and *Theatre* (published posthumously, 1954).

JOHN WESTLAND MARSTON (1819–90)

Served as dramatic critic in the 1860s and drew on his experience in this capacity to write *Our Recent Actors* (1888). As a playwright earned recognition by his blank verse tragedy with a contemporary setting, *The Patrician's Daughter* (1842). His lead was not followed, but he wrote several costume plays, *Strathmore* (1849) and *Philip of France and Marie de Maranie* (1850); 'strong' dramas (*A Hard Struggle*, 1858); and comedies, *Donna Diana* (from Moreto, *El Desdén con el Desdén*, 1864) and *The Favourite of Fortune* (1866).

Acted with Dickens's circle at Devonshire House and elsewhere. In later life encountered hardship and was the beneficiary of a special performance of Byron's *Werner*, given by Irving and his company at the Lyceum in 1887.

CHARLES EDWARD MONTAGUE (1867–1928)

Joined the *Manchester Guardian* in 1890, married the daughter of the then editor, C. P. Scott, in 1898, and remained a leading member of its staff until 1925. Wrote dramatic criticism for the *Guardian* throughout his career, selected contributions being reprinted in *The Manchester Stage* (1900) and *Dramatic Values* (1911). Author of several successful novels, notably *A Hind Let Loose* (1910) and *Rough Justice* (1926); also collected essays, including *Disenchantment* (1922) and *A Writer's Notes on His Trade* (published posthumously, 1930).

HENRY MORLEY (1822–94)

Contributed to *Household Words* and *All the Year Round* under Dickens's editorship. Wrote on the drama for the *Examiner* and in 1866 compiled *The Journal of a London Playgoer from 1851 to 1866*, though this was not published until 1891. Edited *Morley's Universal Library* and *Cassell's National Library*.

Professor of Literature, University College, London, 1865–78, and Queen's College, London, 1878–90.

CLEMENT WILLIAM SCOTT (1841–1904)

Dramatic critic of the *Sunday Times*, 1863–5, and of the *Daily Telegraph*, 1871–98. Editor of the monthly periodical, the *Theatre*, 1877–97. Adapted a number of successful plays, mostly from the French, including two from Sardou: *Peril* (*Nos Intimes*), 1876, and *Diplomacy* (*Dora*), 1878, both in collaboration with B. C. Stephenson. His books include a survey of Irving's career at the Lyceum, *From 'The Bells' to 'King Arthur'* (1895), and *The Drama of Yesterday and Today* (1899).

GEORGE BERNARD SHAW (1856–1950)

Reviewed books for the *Pall Mall Gazette;* art critic for the *World* and *Truth*; as 'Corno di Bassetto' reviewed music for the *Star* and *World*; dramatic critic of the *Saturday Review*, 1895–8.

His dramatic criticism was collected by James Huneker and published as *Dramatic Opinions and Essays* in 1906. This was later reissued in three volumes as *Our Theatres in the Nineties* (1931).

ARTHUR BINGHAM WALKLEY (1855–1926)

Combined a career as dramatic critic with that of civil servant, holding various appointments in the Post Office from 1877 to 1919. Dramatic critic of the *Star*, 1888–1900, of the *Speaker*, 1890–9 and of *The Times* from 1900 until his death. His first collection of dramatic criticism, *Playhouse Impressions*, was published in 1892, and another, *Drama and Life*, in 1907.

In 1903 he gave three lectures to the Royal Institute on *Dramatic Criticism*, published in the same year. He inspired the character of 'Trotter' who appears in the Induction and Epilogue of *Fanny's First Play*.

In later life he contributed essays on various literary subjects to *The Times*, and these were collected and published as *Pastiche and Prejudice* (1921), *More Prejudice* (1923) and *Still More Prejudice* (1925).

1 The Actors

William Hazlitt
On Actors and Acting

Players are 'the abstract and brief chronicles of the time'; the motley repre-
sentatives of human nature. They are the only honest hypocrites. Their life
is a voluntary dream; a studied madness. The height of their ambition is to
be *beside themselves*. Today kings, tomorrow beggars, it is only when they are
themselves that they are nothing. Made up of mimic laughter and tears,
passing from the extremes of joy or woe at the prompter's call, they wear the
livery of other men's fortunes; their very thoughts are not their own. They
are, as it were, train-bearers in the pageant of life, and hold a glass up to
humanity, frailer than itself. We see ourselves at second-hand in them:
they show us all that we are, all that we wish to be, and all that we dread
to be. The stage is an epitome, a bettered likeness of the world, with the dull
part left out: and, indeed, with this omission, it is nearly big enough to hold
all the rest. What brings the resemblance nearer is that, as *they* imitate us,
we, in our turn, imitate them. How many fine gentlemen do we owe to the
stage! How many romantic lovers are mere Romeos in masquerade! How
many soft bosoms have heaved with Juliet's sighs! They teach us when to
laugh and when to weep, when to love and when to hate, upon principle and
with a good grace! Wherever there is a playhouse, the world will not go on
amiss. The stage not only refines the manners, but it is the best teacher of
morals, for it is the truest and most intelligible picture of life. It stamps the
image of virtue on the mind by first softening the rude materials of which it
is composed, by a sense of pleasure. It regulates the passions, by giving a
loose to the imagination. It points out the selfish and depraved to our
detestation; the amiable and generous to our admiration; and if it clothes
the more seductive vices with the borrowed graces of wit and fancy, even those
graces operate as a diversion to the coarser poison of experience and bad
example, and often prevent or carry off the infection by inoculating the mind
with a certain taste and elegance. To show how little we agree with the common
declamations against the immoral tendency of the stage on this score, we will
hazard a conjecture that the acting of the *Beggar's Opera* a certain number of
nights every year since it was first brought out has done more towards putting
down the practice of highway robbery, than all the gibbets that ever were
erected. A person, after seeing this piece, is too deeply imbued with a sense

of humanity, is in too good humour with himself and the rest of the world, to set about cutting throats or rifling pockets. Whatever makes a jest of vice leaves it too much a matter of indifference for any one in his senses to rush desperately on his ruin for its sake. We suspect that just the contrary effect must be produced by the representation of *George Barnwell*, which is too much in the style of the Ordinary's sermon to meet with any better success. The mind in such cases, instead of being deterred by the alarming consequences held out to it, revolts against the denunciation of them as an insult offered to its free-will, and, in a spirit of defiance, returns a practical answer to them, by daring the worst that can happen. The most striking lesson ever read to levity and licentiousness is in the last act of *The Inconstant*, where young Mirabel is preserved by the fidelity of his mistress, Orinda, in the disguise of a page, from the hands of assassins, into whose power he had been allured by the temptations of vice and beauty. There never was a rake who did not become in imagination a reformed man, during the representation of the last trying scenes of this admirable comedy.

If the stage is useful as a school of instruction, it is no less so as a source of amusement. It is a source of the greatest enjoyment at the time, and a never-failing fund of agreeable reflection afterwards. The merits of a new play, or of a new actor, are always among the first topics of polite conversation. One way in which public exhibitions contribute to refine and humanize mankind, is by supplying them with ideas and subjects of conversation and interest in common. The progress of civilization is in proportion to the number of common-places current in society. For instance, if we meet with a stranger at an inn or in a stage-coach, who knows nothing but his own affairs – his shop, his customers, his farm, his pigs, his poultry – we can carry on no conversation with him on these local and personal matters: the only way is to let him have all the talk to himself. But if he has fortunately ever seen Mr Liston act, this is an immediate topic of mutual conversation, and we agree together the rest of the evening in discussing the merits of that inimitable actor, with the same satisfaction as in talking over the affairs of the most intimate friend.

If the stage thus introduces us familiarly to our contemporaries, it also brings us acquainted with former times. It is an interesting revival of past ages, manners, opinions, dresses, persons and actions – whether it carries us back to the wars of York and Lancaster, or half-way back to the heroic times of Greece and Rome, in some translation from the French, or quite back to the age of Charles II in the scenes of Congreve and of Etherege (the gay Sir George!) – happy age, when kings and nobles led purely ornamental lives; when the utmost stretch of a morning's study went no farther than the choice of a sword-knot, or the adjustment of a side curl; when the soul spoke out in all the pleasing elegance of dress; and beaux and belles, enamoured of themselves in one another's follies, fluttered like gilded butterflies in giddy mazes through the walks of St James's Park!

A good company of comedians, a Theatre-Royal judiciously managed, is your true Herald's College; the only Antiquarian Society that is worth a rush. It is for this reason that there is such an air of romance about players, and that it is pleasanter to see them, even in their own persons, than any of the three learned professions. We feel more respect for John Kemble in a plain coat than for the Lord Chancellor on the woolsack. He is surrounded, to our eyes, with a greater number of imposing recollections: he is a more reverend piece of formality; a more complicated tissue of costume. We do not know whether to look upon this accomplished actor as Pierre, or King John, or Coriolanus, or Cato, or Leontes, or the Stranger. But we see in him a stately hieroglyphic of humanity; a living monument of departed greatness; a sombre comment on the rise and fall of kings. We look after him till he is out of sight, as we listen to a story of one of Ossian's heroes, to 'a tale of other times'!

The most pleasant feature in the profession of a player, and which, indeed, is peculiar to it, is that we not only admire the talents of those who adorn it, but we contract a personal intimacy with them. There is no class of society whom so many persons regard with affection as actors. We greet them on the stage; we like to meet them in the streets; they almost always recall to us pleasant associations; and we feel our gratitude excited, without the uneasiness of a sense of obligation. The very gaiety and popularity, however, which surround the life of a favourite performer, make the retiring from it a very serious business. It glances a mortifying reflection on the shortness of human life, and the vanity of human pleasures. Something reminds us that 'all the world's a stage, and all the men and women merely players'.

It has been considered as the misfortune of first-rate talents for the stage, that they leave no record behind them except that of vague rumour, and that the genius of a great actor perishes with him, 'leaving the world no copy'. This is a misfortune, or at least a mortifying reflection, to actors; but it is, perhaps, an advantage to the stage. It leaves an opening to originality. The *semper varium et mutabile* of the poet may be transferred to the stage, 'the inconstant stage', without losing the original felicity of the application: it has its necessary ebbs and flows, from its subjection to the influence of popular feeling, and the frailty of the materials of which it is composed, its own fleeting and shadowy essence, and cannot be expected to remain for any great length of time stationary at the same point, either of perfection or debasement. Acting, in particular, which is the chief organ by which it addresses itself to the mind – the eye, tongue, hand by which it dazzles, charms, and seizes on the public attention – is an art that seems to contain in itself the seeds of perpetual renovation and decay, following in this respect the order of nature rather than the analogy of the productions of human intellect; for whereas in the other arts of painting and poetry, the standard works of genius, being permanent and accumulating, for awhile provoke emulation, but, in the end, overlay future efforts, and transmit only their defects to those that come after; the exertions of the greatest actor die with him, leaving to his successors only the admiration of his name, and the aspiration after imaginary excellence; so that, in effect, no one generation of actors binds another; the art is always setting out afresh on the stock of genius and nature, and the success depends (generally speaking) on accident, opportunity, and encouragement. The harvest of excellence (whatever it may be) is removed from the ground, every

twenty or thirty years, by Death's sickle; and there is room left for another
to sprout up and tower to any equal height, and spread into equal luxuriance
– to 'dally with the wind, and court the sun' – according to the health and
vigour of the stem, and the favourableness of the season. But books, pictures,
remain like fixtures in the public mind, beyond a certain point encumber the
soil of living truth and nature, distort or stunt the growth of original genius.
When an author dies, there is a void produced in society, a gap which requires
to be filled up. The literary amateur may find employment for his time in
reading old authors only, and exhaust his entire spleen in scouting new ones:
but the lover of the stage cannot amuse himself, in his solitary fastidiousness,
by sitting to witness a play got up by the departed ghosts of first-rate actors;
or be contented with the perusal of a collection of old play-bills: he may
extol Garrick, but he must go to see Kean; and, in his own defence, must
admire, or at least tolerate, what he sees, or stay away against his will. If,
indeed, by any spell or power of necromancy, all the celebrated actors, for the
last hundred years, could be made to appear again on the boards of Covent
Garden and Drury Lane, for the last time, in their most brilliant parts, what a
rich threat to the town, what a feat for the critics, to go and see Betterton, and
Booth, and Wilks, and Sandford, and Nokes, and Leigh, and Penkethman,
and Bullock, and Estcourt, and Dogget, and Mrs Barry, and Mrs Montfort,
and Mrs Oldfield, and Mrs Bracegirdle, and Mrs Cibber and Cibber himself,
the prince of coxcombs, and Macklin, and Quin, and Rich, and Mrs Clive,
and Mrs Pritchard, and Mrs Abington, and Weston, and Shuter, and Garrick,
and all the rest of those who 'gladdened life', and whose death 'eclipsed the
gaiety of nations'! We should certainly be there. We should buy a ticket for
the season. We should enjoy *our hundred days* again. We should not miss a
single night. We would not, for a great deal, be absent from Betterton's
Hamlet or his Brutus, or from Booth's Cato, as it was first acted to the contend-
ing applause of Whigs and Tories. We should be in the first row when
Mrs Barry (who was kept by Lord Rochester, and with whom Otway was in
love) played Monimia or Belvidera; and we suppose we should go to see
Mrs Bracegirdle (with whom all the world was in love) in all her parts. We
should then know exactly whether Penkethman's manner of picking a chicken,
and Bullock's mode of devouring asparagus, answered to the ingenious account
of them in the *Tatler*; and whether Dogget was equal to Dowton – whether
Mrs Montfort or Mrs Abington was the finest lady – whether Wilks or Cibber
was the best Sir Harry Wildair – whether Macklin was really 'the Jew that
Shakespeare drew', and whether Garrick was, upon the whole, so great an
actor as the world would have him made out! Many people have a strong
desire to pry into the secrets of futurity; for our own parts, we should be
satisfied if we had the power to recall the dead, and live the past over again,
as often as we pleased! Players, after all, have little reason to complain of their
hard-earned, short-lived popularity. One thunder of applause from pit, boxes
and gallery, is equal to a whole immortality of posthumous fame; and when we
hear an actor (Liston), whose modesty is equal to his merit, declare that he
would like to see a dog wag his tail in approbation, what must he feel when

he sets the whole house in a roar! Besides, Fame, as if their reputation had been entrusted to her alone, has been particularly careful of the renown of her theatrical favourites: she forgets, one by one, and year by year, those who have been great lawyers, great statesmen, and great warriers in their day; but the name of Garrick still survives with the works of Reynolds and of Johnson.

Actors have been accused, as a profession, of being extravagant and dissipated. While they are said to be so, as a piece of common cant, they are likely to continue so. But there is a sentence in Shakespeare which should be stuck as a label in the mouths of our beadles and whippers-in of morality: 'The web of our life is of mingled yarn, good and ill together: our virtues would be proud if our faults whipped them not: and our crimes would despair if they were not cherished by our virtues.' With respect to the extravagance of actors, as a traditional character, it is not to be wondered at. They live from hand to mouth, they plunge from want into luxury; they have no means of making money *breed*, and all professions that do not live by turning money into money, or have not a certainty of accumulating it in the end by parsimony, spend it. Uncertain of the future they make sure of the present moment. This is not unwise. Chilled with poverty, steeped in contempt, they sometimes pass into the sunshine of fortune, and are lifted to the very pinnacle of public favour; yet even there they cannot calculate on the continuance of success, but are, 'like the giddy sailor on the mast, ready with every blast to topple down into the fatal bowels of the deep!' Besides, if the young enthusiast, who is smitten with the stage, and with the public as a mistress, were naturally a close *hunks*, he would become or remain a city clerk, instead of turning player. Again, with respect to the habit of convivial indulgence, an actor, to be a good one, must have a great spirit of enjoyment in himself – strong impulses, strong passions, and a strong sense of pleasure: for it is his business to imitate the passions, and to communicate pleasure to others.

A man of genius is not a machine. The neglected actor may be excused if he drinks oblivion of his disappointments; the successful one if he quaffs the applause of the world, and enjoys the friendship of those who are the friends of the favourites of fortune, in draughts of nectar. There is no path so steep as that of fame: no labour so hard as the pursuit of excellence. The intellectual excitement, inseparable from those professions which call forth all our sensibility to pleasure and pain, requires some corresponding physical excitement to support our failure, and not a little to allay the ferment of the spirits attendant on success. If there is any tendency to dissipation beyond this in the profession of a player, it is owing to the prejudices entertained against them – to that spirit of bigotry which in a neighbouring country would deny actors Christian burial after their death, and to that cant of criticism which, in our own, slurs over their characters, while living, with a half-witted jest. Players are only not so respectable as a profession as they might be, because their profession is not respected as it ought to be.

A London engagement is generally considered by actors as the *ne plus ultra* of their ambition, as 'a consummation devoutly to be wished', as the great prize in the lottery of their professional life. But this appears to us, who are not in the secret, to be rather the prose termination of their adventurous career: it is the provincial commencement that is the poetical and truly enviable part of it. After that, they have comparatively little hope or fear. 'The wine of life is drunk, and but the lees remain.' In London they become gentlemen, and the King's servants; but it is the romantic mixture of the hero and the vagabond that constitutes the essence of the player's life. It is the transition from their real to their assumed characters, from the contempt of the world to the applause of the multitude, that gives its zest to the latter, and raises them as much above common humanity at night as in the daytime they are depressed below it. 'Hurried from fierce extremes, by contrast made more fierce' – it is rags and a flock bed which give their splendour to a plume of feathers and a throne. We should suppose that if the most admired actor on the London stage were brought to confession on this point, he would acknowledge that all the applause he had received from 'brilliant and over-flowing audiences' was nothing to the light-headed intoxication of unlooked-for success in a barn. In towns, actors are criticized: in country places, they are wondered at, or hooted at: it is of little consequence which, so that the interval is not too long between. For ourselves, we own that the description of the strolling player in *Gil Blas*, soaking his dry crusts in the well by the roadside, presents to us a perfect picture of human felicity.

The Examiner, 15 January 1817

Leigh Hunt
Mr Kemble

Mr Kemble is a peculiar instance of almost all these essentials to good acting, and at the same time an example how much they may be injured by an indiscriminate application of study. His conceptions of character are strong where the characters themselves are strong, his attention to passions is fixed by large objects, he cannot sufficiently study the minute where minuteness is important, though, as I shall hereafter explain, he can give importance to minutenesses that mean nothing. He appears to submit everything to his judgement, and exhibits little of the enthusiasm of genius. The grander emotions are his chief study; he attaches a kind of loftiness to every sensation that he indulges, and thus conceives with much force the more majestic passions, at the same time that he is raised above the pathetic passions, which always carry with them an air of weakness and humility.

For the expression of the loftier emotions no actor is gifted by nature with greater external means. His figure, though not elegant, is manly and dignified, his features are strongly marked with what is called the Roman character, and his head altogether is the heroic head of the antiquary and the artist. This tragic form assumes excellently well the gait of royalty, the vigorous majesty of the warrior, and the profound gravity of the sage: but its seriousness is unbending; his countenance seems to despise the gaiety it labours to assume, and its comic expression is comic because it is singularly wretched. Of the passion of love he can express nothing; the reason is obvious; love from its dependent nature must always, unless associated with some other passion, betray an expression of tender feebleness, and such an expression is unknown to Mr Kemble's countenance. The attempt of Mrs Inchbald to make Mr Kemble a lover is more honourable to her partiality for the friend than to her affection for just criticism. She says that he can paint love more vigorously than any other man, though he cannot love *moderately*: in her opinion, 'sighs, soft complainings, a plaintive voice, and tender looks bespeak mere moderation; Mr Kemble', she continues, 'must be struck to the heart's core, or not at all: he must be wounded to the soul with grief, despair, or madness.' But this is mistaking the associated passion for its companion. What a lover is he who can neither speak softly nor look tenderly? No man, according to this idea, can express a perfect love, that is, a love opposed to *mere moderation*, unless he is struck with grief, or desperate, or mad: but by such an association of outrageous passions, the expression of the individual one will not be a perfect, because it is not a simple expression: the actor who cannot express an individual passion without the assistance of others can no more be said to be master of that passion, than a singer can be called a master of his art who cannot sing without an accompaniment.

It is in characters that are occupied with themselves and with their own importance, it is in the systematic and exquisite revenge of Zanga, in the indignant jealousy of Othello, and in the desperate ambition of King John, that Mr Kemble is the actor. There is always something sublime in the sudden completion of great objects, and perhaps there is not a sublimer action on the stage than the stride of Mr Kemble as Zanga, over the body of his victim, and his majestic exultation of revenge.

But if he succeeds in the prouder passions, his diligence of study has given him no less success in the expression of impressive seriousness.

The character of Penruddock in *The Wheel of Fortune* is his greatest performance, and I believe it to be a perfect one. It is admirable, not because the tenderness of his love, as Mrs Inchbald tells us, 'appears beneath the roughest manners', but because the very defect which hurts his general style of acting, that studious and important preciseness, which is affectation in all his other characters, contributes to the strength, to the nature of Penruddock. Those who can discern any peculiar expression of tenderness under the roughness of Mr Kemble's acting mistake their feelings for their observation: it is the tenderness the character is supposed to feel, not what he actually exhibits, it is the tenderness of the author not of the actor, which they discern: if there are one or two phrases of tenderness uttered by the stern recluse, they have a pathetic effect, not because they are expressed with peculiar tenderness by the actor, but because a soft emotion so unexpected in one of his appearance produces a strong effect from the strength of contrast. To give a man imaginary praise is to give him real dispraise. Mr Kemble himself would never think of valuing his own performance for its tenderness of expression; he would value it, and with justice, for its severity of expression, for its display of external philosophy, and for its contempt of everything that can no longer amuse.

Wherever this air of self-importance or abstraction is required, Mr Kemble is excellent. It is no small praise to say of an actor that he excels in soliloquies: these solitary discourses require great judgment because the speaker has no assistance from others, and because the audience, always awake to action, is inclined during a soliloquy to seek repose in inattention. Indeed to gain the attention of an audience is always in some degree to gain their applause, and this applause must cheerfully be given to Mr Kemble, who by his busy air and impressive manner always attaches importance to a speech of whatever interest or length. To this excellence in particular, and to the general action of the stage, he contributes by an exact knowledge of every stage artifice, local and temporal; and I could not but admire the judicious contrivance by which he added a considerable interest to his first appearance in the season of 1805. The curtain rose and discovered a study; it was adorned with the most natural literary disorder possible: the grave actor appeared writing at a table with open books here and there about him; the globes, the library, the furniture, everything had its use, and no doubt its effect, for an audience, though perhaps insensibly, is always pleased with a natural scene. Of another necessary stage artifice, which is called *bye-play*, and which beguiles the intervals of action by an air of perpetual occupation, he is a perfect master; he never stands feebly inactive, waiting for his turn to speak; he is never out of his place, he attends to everything passing on the stage at once, nor does he indulge himself in those complacent stares at the audience which occupy inferior actors.

This attention to the minute, however, is often employed needlessly; he has made it a study hardly less important than that of the passions, and hence arises the great fault of his acting, a laborious and almost universal preciseness. Some of the instances of this fault are so ludicrous that a person who had not seen him would scarcely credit the relation. He sometimes turns from one object to another with so cautious a circumflexion of head, that he is no doubt very often pitied by the audience for having a stiff neck. His words now and then follow one another so slowly, and his face all the while assumes so methodical an expression, that he seems reckoning how many lines he has learnt by heart. I have known him make an eternal groan upon the interjection *Oh!* as if he were determined to show that his misery had not affected his lungs; and to represent an energetical address he has kept so continual a jerking and nodding of the head, that at last, if he represented anything at all, it could be nothing but Saint Vitus's dance. By this study of nonentities it would appear that he never pulls out his handkerchief without a design upon the audience, that he has as much thought in making a step as making a speech, in short that his very finger is eloquent and that nothing means something. But all this neither delights nor deceives the audience: of an assembly collected together to enjoy a rational entertainment, the majority will always be displeased with what is irrational, though they may be unable to describe their sensations critically: irrationalities amuse in farce only. An audience when judging the common imitations of life have merely to say 'Is it like ourselves!'

Perhaps there is not a greater instance of the ill effects one bad habit like this can produce, than in Mr Kemble's delivery. No actor in his declamation pleases more at some times or more offends at others. His voice is hollow and monotonous from the malformation, as it is said, of his organs of utterance: its weakness cannot command a variety of sound sufficiently powerful for all occasions, nor is its natural extent melodious or pleasing. But a voice naturally monotonous must be distinguished from a monotony of delivery; the latter neglects emphasis and expression, the former, though it will not always obtain, may always tempt both. No player, perhaps, understands his author better, and such a knowledge will easily impart itself to others: his declamation therefore is confident and exact, he is at all times carefully distinct, and his general delivery is marked, expressive, and even powerful: the art with which he supplies the natural weakness of his voice by an energy and significancy of utterance is truly admirable. But the same affectation, which indulges itself in an indiscriminate importance of manner, the same ambition of originality where originality is least wanted, characterizes Mr Kemble's pronunciation: it has induced him to defy all orthoepy, and to allow no accent but what pleases his caprice or his love of innovation. To be novel for the mere sake of novelty belongs neither to genius nor to judgment. Mr Kemble insists that the word *rode* should be *rod, beard* is metamorphosed into *bird,* he never *pierces* the heart but *purses* it, and *virtue* and *merchant* become in the dialect of the kitchen *varchue* and *marchant.* The strong syllable *er* appears to be an abomination, and is never allowed utterance; Pope says

> To err is human, to forgive divine –

but Mr Kemble will not consent to this, he says

> To air is human –

making the moralist say that it is the nature of man to dry his clean shirt or to take a walk. *Thy* is changed into *thĕ,* probably because the sound of *my* is sometimes contracted into *mĕ*; but mutabilities of pronunciation in one word never argue for them in another; people are not accustomed to say, such a man has a *wrĕ* neck, or that it is very *drĕ* weather. Dr Johnson, who had an antipathy to the pronunciation *wĭnd,* and wished to call it *wīnd,* attacked the custom by a ludicrous assemblage and mispronunciation of other words,

in which the letter *i* is naturally long, and said with much critical gravity, –
'*I have a mind to find why you call that wind.*' But this pleasantry did not
change the pronunciation in general converse. Let us see how Mr Kemble
would improve the following lines: we will put his improvement after the
original, since the beauty of the contrast will be greater:

> Virtue, thy happy wisdom's known
> In making what we wish our own;
> Nay, e'en to wish what wishes thee
> Imparts the blest reality:
> For since the soul that pierces mine,
> Sweet Myra's soul, is full of thine,
> In my breast too thy spirit stirs,
> Since all my soul is full of her's!

Mr Kemble's improvement:

> *Varchue, the* happy wisdom's known
> In making what we wish our own;
> Nay, e'en to wish what wishes thee
> Imparts the blest reality:
> For since the soul that *purses* mine,
> Sweet Myra's soul, is full of thine,
> In my breast too thy spirit *stares*,
> Since all my soul is full of *hairs*!

This is very amusing, but there is no rule for pronunciation but custom;
as customs change, actors may change; but no individual should alter what he
has no reason for altering, or what has either a bad effect or none at all when
altered. There have been several attempts to vary the mode of spelling now
in use; the latest innovation was practised by Ritson, a man of curious and
happy research into old English literature, and one who might have boasted
a better originality than that of making his words unintelligible. Nobody has
adopted a single one of these innovations, first, because it is painful to depart
from old rules and habits, and secondly, because it is still more painful to
depart from them without a cause. For the same reasons, nobody will adopt
Mr Kemble's pronunciations; and if he were to carry his dialect into private
life, he would be either pitied or laughed at. But why place his ambition where
there are no hopes of original praise? I could mispronounce much better than
he when I was a mere infant.

Upon the whole, Mr Kemble appears to be an actor of correct rather than
quick conception, of studious rather than universal or equal judgment, of
powers some naturally defective but admirably improved and others excellent
by nature but still more so by art; in short of a genius more compulsive of
respect than attractive of delight. He does not present one the idea of a man
who grasps with the force of genius, but of one who overcomes by the toil of
attention. He never rises and sinks as in the enthusiasm of the moment; his
ascension though grand is careful, and when he sinks it is with preparation

and dignity. There are actors who may occasionally please more, but not on who is paid a more universal or profound attention.

Critical Essays on the Performers of The London Theatres, 1807

William Hazlitt
Mr Kemble's Retirement

Mr Kemble took his leave of the Stage on Monday night, in the character of Coriolanus. On his first coming forward to pronounce his Farewell address, he was received with a shout like thunder: on his retiring after it, the applause was long before it subsided entirely away. There is something in these partings with old public favourites exceedingly affecting. They teach us the shortness of human life, and the vanity of human pleasures. Our associations of admiration and delight with theatrical performers, are among our earliest recollections – among our last regrets. They are links that connect the beginning and the end of life together; their bright and giddy career of popularity measures the arch that spans our brief existence. It is near twenty years ago since we first saw Mr Kemble in the same character – yet how short the interval seems! The impression appears as distinct as if it were of yesterday. In fact, intellectual objects, in proportion as they are lasting, may be said to shorten life. Time has no effect upon them. The petty and the personal, that which appeals to our senses and our interests, is by degrees forgotten, and fades away into the distant obscurity of the past. The grand and the ideal, that which appeals to the imagination, can only perish with it, and remains with us, unimpaired in its lofty abstraction, from youth to age; as, wherever we go, we still see the same heavenly bodies shining over our heads! We forget numberless things that have happened to ourselves, one generation of follies after another; but not the first time of our seeing Mr Kemble, nor shall we easily forget the last! Coriolanus, the character in which he took his leave of the Stage, was one of the first in which we remember to have seen him; and it was one in which we were not sorry to part with him, for we wished to see him appear like himself to the last. Nor was he wanting to himself on this occasion: he played the part as well as he ever did – with as much freshness and vigour. There was no abatement of spirit and energy – none of grace and dignity: his look, his action, his expression of the character, were the same as they ever were: they could not be finer. It is mere cant, to say that Mr Kemble has quite fallen off of late – that he is not what he was: he may have fallen off in the opinion of some jealous admirers, because he is no longer in exclusive possession of the Stage: but in himself he has not fallen off a jot. Why then do we approve of his retiring? Because we do not wish him to wait till it is necessary for him to retire. On the last evening, he displayed the same excellences, and gave the same prominence to the very same passages, that he used to do. We might refer to his manner of doing obeisance to his mother in the triumphal procession in the second act, and to the scene with Aufidius in the last act, as among the most striking instances. The action with which he accompanied the proud taunt to Aufidius –

> Like an eagle in a dove-cote I
> Flutter'd your Volscians in Corioli;
> Alone I did it

gave double force and beauty to the image. Again, where he waits for the coming of Aufidius in his rival's house, he stood at the foot of the statue of Mars, himself another Mars! In the reconciliation scene with his mother, which is the finest in the play, he was not equally impressive. Perhaps this was not the fault of Mr Kemble, but of the stage itself, which can hardly do justice to such thoughts and sentiments as here occur:

> My mother bows:
> As if Olympus to a mole-hill should
> In supplication nod.

Mr Kemble's voice seemed to faint and stagger, to be strained and cracked, under the weight of this majestic image: but, indeed, we know of no tones deep or full enough to bear along the swelling tide of sentiment it conveys; nor can we conceive any thing in outward form to answer to it, except when Mrs Siddons played the part of Volumnia.

We may on this occasion be expected to say a few words on the general merits of Mr Kemble as an actor, and on the principal characters he performed; in doing which, we shall

> Nothing extenuate,
> Nor set down aught in malice.

It has always appeared to us, that the range of characters in which Mr Kemble more particularly shone, and was superior to every other actor, were those which consisted in the development of some one solitary sentiment or exclusive passion. From a want of rapidity, of scope, and variety, he was often deficient in expressing the bustle and complication of different interests; nor did he possess the faculty of overpowering the mind by sudden and irresistible bursts of passion: but in giving the habitual workings of a predominant feeling, as in Penruddock, or The Stranger, in Coriolanus, Cato, and some others, where all the passions move round a central point, and are governed by one master-key, he stood unrivalled. Penruddock, in *The Wheel of Fortune*, was one of the most perfect on the modern stage. The deeply-rooted, mild, pensive melancholy of the character, its embittered recollections, and dignified benevolence, were conveyed by Mr Kemble with equal truth, elegance, and feeling. In The Stranger, again, which is in fact the same character, he brooded over the recollection of disappointed hope till it became a part of himself; it sunk deeper into his mind the longer he dwelt upon it; his regrets only became more profound as they became more durable. His person was moulded to the character. The weight of sentiment which oppressed him was never suspended: the spring at his heart was never lightened – it seemed as if his whole life had been a suppressed sigh! So in Coriolanus, he exhibited the ruling passion with the same unshaken firmness, he preserved the same haughty dignity of demeanour, the same energy of will, and unbending sternness of temper throughout. He was swayed by a single impulse. His tenaciousness of purpose was only irritated by opposition; he turned neither to the right nor the left; the vehemence with which he moved forward increasing every instant, till it hurried him on to the catastrophe. In Leontes, also, in *The Winter's Tale* (a character he at one time played often), the growing jealousy of the King, and the exclusive possession which this passion gradually obtains over his mind, were marked by him in the finest manner, particularly where he exclaims –

> Is whispering nothing?
> Is leaning cheek to cheek? Is meeting noses?
> Kissing with inside lip? Stopping the career
> Of laughter with a sigh (a note infallible
> Of breaking honesty)? Horsing foot on foot?
> Skulking in corners? Wishing clocks more swift?
> Hours minutes? The noon midnight? and all eyes
> Blind with the pin and web, but their's; their's only
> That would unseen be wicked? Is this nothing?
> Why then the world and that's in 't is nothing,
> The covering sky is nothing, Bohemia's nothing,
> My wife is nothing, if this be nothing!

In the course of this enumeration, every proof told stronger, and followed with quicker and harder strokes; his conviction became more riveted at every step of his progress; and at the end, his mind, and 'every corporal agent' appeared wound up to a phrenzy of despair. In such characters, Mr Kemble had no occasion to call to his aid either the resources of invention, or the tricks of the art: his success depended on the increasing intensity with which he dwelt on a given feeling, or enforced a passion that resisted all interference or control.

In Hamlet, on the contrary, Mr Kemble in our judgment unavoidably failed from a want of flexibility, of that quick sensibility which yields to every motive, and is borne away with every breath of fancy, which is distracted in the multiplicity of its reflections, and lost in the uncertainty of its resolutions. There is a perpetual undulation of feeling in the character of Hamlet;

but in Mr Kemble's acting 'there was neither variableness nor shadow of turning'. He played one undeviating line, which is as remote from the natural grace and indolent susceptibility of the character, as the sharp angles and abrupt starts to produce an effect which Mr Kean throws into it.

In King John, which was one of Mr Kemble's most admired parts, the transitions of feeling, though just and powerful, were prepared too long beforehand, and were too long in executing to produce their full effect. The actor seemed waiting for some complicated machinery to enable him to make his next movement, instead of trusting to the true impulses of passion. There was no sudden collision of opposite elements; the golden flash of genius was not there; 'the fire i' th' flint was cold', for it was not struck. If an image could be constructed by magic art to play King John, it would play it in much the same manner that Mr Kemble played it.

In Macbeth, Mr Kemble was unequal to 'the tug and war' of the passions which assail him: he stood as it were at bay with fortune, and maintained his ground too steadily against 'fate and metaphysical aid'; instead of staggering and reeling under the appalling visions of the preternatural world, and having his frame wrenched from all the holds and resting places of his will, by the stronger power of imagination. In the latter scenes, however, he displayed great energy and spirit; and there was a fine melancholy retrospective tone in his manner of delivering the lines,

'My way of life has fallen into the sear, the yellow leaf', which smote upon the heart, and remained there ever after. His Richard III wanted that tempest and whirlwind of the soul, that life and spirit, and dazzling rapidity of motion, which fills the stage, and burns in every part of it, when Mr Kean performs this character. To Mr Kean's acting in general, we might apply the lines of the poet, where he describes

> The fiery soul that, working out its way,
> Fretted the pigmy body to decay,
> And o'er-inform'd the tenement of clay.

Mr Kemble's manner, on the contrary, had always something dry, hard, and pedantic in it. 'You shall relish him more in the scholar than the soldier': but his monotony did not fatigue, his formality did not displease; because there was always sense and meaning in what he did. The fineness of Mr Kemble's figure may be supposed to have led to that statue-like appearance, which his acting was sometimes too apt to assume: as the diminutiveness of Mr Kean's person has probably compelled him to bustle about too much, and to attempt to make up for the want of dignity of form, by the violence and contrast of his attitudes. If Mr Kemble were to remain in the same posture for half an hour, his figure would only excite admiration: if Mr Kean were to stand still only for a moment, the contrary effect would be apparent. One of the happiest and most spirited of all Mr Kemble's performances, and in which even his defects were blended with his excellences to produce a perfect whole, was his Pierre. The dissolute indifference assumed by this character, to cover the darkness of his designs, and the fierceness of his revenge, accorded admirably with Mr Kemble's natural manner; and the tone of morbid rancorous raillery, in which Pierre delights to indulge, was in unison with the actor's reluctant, contemptuous personifications of gaiety, with the scornful spirit of his Comic Muse, which always laboured – *invita Minerva* – against the grain. Cato was another of those parts for which Mr Kemble was peculiarly fitted by his physical advantages. There was nothing for him to do in this character, but to appear in it. It has all the dignity of still-life. It was a studied piece of classical costume – a conscious exhibition of elegantly disposed drapery, that was all: yet, as a mere display of personal and artificial grace, it was inimitable.

It has been suggested that Mr Kemble chiefly excelled in his Roman characters, and among others in Brutus. If it be meant, that he excelled in those which imply a certain stoicism of feeling, and energy of will, this we have already granted; but Brutus is not a character of this kind, and Mr Kemble failed in it for that reason. Brutus is not a stoic, but a humane enthusiast. There is a tenderness of nature under the garb of assumed severity; an inward current of generous feelings, which burst out, in spite of circumstances, with bleeding freshness; a secret struggle of mind, and disagreement between his situation and his intentions; a lofty inflexibility of purpose, mingled with an effeminate abstractedness of thought, which Mr Kemble did not give.

In short, we think the distinguishing excellence of his acting may be summed up in one word – intensity; in the seizing upon some one feeling or idea, in insisting upon it, in never letting it go, and in working it up, with a certain graceful consistency, and conscious grandeur of conception, to a very high degree of pathos or sublimity. If he had not the unexpected bursts of nature and genius, he had all the regularity of art; if he did not display the tumult and conflict of opposite passions in the soul, he gave the deepest and most permanent interest to the uninterrupted progress of individual feeling; and in embodying a high idea of certain characters, which belong rather to sentiment than passion, to energy of will, than to loftiness or to originality of imagination, he was the most excellent actor of his time. This praise of him is not exaggerated: the blame we have mixed with it is not invidious. We have only to add to both, the expression of our grateful remembrances and best wishes – Hail, and farewell!

The Times, 15 June 1817

William Hazlitt
Mrs Siddons

Players should be immortal, if their own wishes or ours could make them so; but they are not. They not only die like other people, but like other people they cease to be young, and are no longer themselves, even while living. Their health, strength, beauty, voice, fails them; nor can they, without these advantages, perform the same feats, or command the same applause that they did when possessed of them. It is the common lot; players are only not exempt from it. Mrs Siddons retired once from the stage; why should she return to it again? She cannot retire from it twice with dignity; and yet it is to be wished that she could do all things with dignity. Any loss of reputation to her, is a loss to the world. Has she not had enough of glory? The homage she has received is greater than that which is paid to queens. The enthusiasm she excited had something idolatrous about it; she was regarded less with admiration than with wonder, as if a being of a superior order had dropped from another sphere to awe the world with the majesty of her appearance. She raised Tragedy to the skies, or brought it down from thence. It was something above nature. We can conceive of nothing grander. She embodied to our imagination the fables of mythology, of the heroic and deified mortals of elder time. She was not less than a goddess, or than a prophetess inspired by the gods. Power was seated on her brow, passion emanated from her breast as from a shrine. She was Tragedy personified. She was the stateliest ornament of the public mind. She was not only the idol of the people, she not only hushed the tumultuous shouts of the pit in breathless expectations, and quenched the blaze of surrounding beauty in silent tears, but to the retired and lonely student, through long years of solitude, her face has shone as if an eye had appeared from heaven; her name has been as if a voice had opened the chambers of the human heart, or as if a trumpet had awakened the sleeping and the dead. To have seen Mrs Siddons, was an event in every one's life; and does she think we have forgotten her? Or would she remind us of herself by shewing us what *she was not*? Or is she to continue on the stage to the very last, till all her grace and all her grandeur gone, shall leave behind them only a melancholy blank? Or is she merely to be played off as 'the baby of a girl' for a few nights? – 'Rather than so,' come, Genius of Gil Blas, thou that didst inspire him in an evil hour to perform his promise to the Archbishop of Grenada, 'and champion us to the utterance' of what we think on this occasion.

It is said that the Princess Charlotte has expressed a desire to see Mrs Siddons in her best parts, and this, it is said, is a thing highly desirable. We do not know that the Princess has expressed any such wish, and we shall suppose that she has not, because we do not think it altogether a reasonable one. If the Princess Charlotte had expressed a wish to see Mr Garrick, this would have been a thing highly desirable, but it would have been impossible; or if she had desired to see Mrs Siddons *in her best days*, it would have been equally so; and yet without this, we do not think it desirable that she should see her at all. It is said to be desirable that a princess should have a taste for the Fine Arts, and that this is best promoted by seeing the highest models of perfection. But it is of the first importance for princes to acquire a taste for what is reasonable: and the second thing which it is desirable they should acquire, is a deference to public opinion: and we think neither of these objects likely to be promoted in any way proposed. If it was reasonable that Mrs Siddons should retire from the stage three years ago, certainly those reasons have not diminished since, nor do we think Mrs Siddons would consult what is due to her powers or her fame in commencing a new career. If it is only intended that she should act a few nights in the presence of a particular person, this might be done as well in private. To all other applications she should answer – 'Leave me to my repose.'

Mrs Siddons always spoke as slow as she ought: she now speaks slower than she did. 'The line too labours, and the words move slow.' The machinery of the voice seems too ponderous for the power that wields it. There is too long a pause between each sentence, and between each word in each sentence. There is too much preparation. The stage waits for her. In the sleeping scene she produced a different impression from what we expected. It was more laboured, and less natural. In coming on formerly, her eyes were open, but the sense was shut. She was like a person bewildered, and unconscious of what she did. She moved her lips involuntarily; all her gestures were involuntary and mechanical. At present she acts the part more with a view to effect. She repeats the action when she says, 'I tell you he cannot rise from his grave', with both hands sawing the air, in the style of parliamentary oratory, the worst of all others. There was none of this weight or energy in the way she did the scene the first time we saw her, twenty years ago. She glided on and off the stage almost like an apparition. In the close of the banquet scene, Mrs Siddons condescended to an imitation which we were sorry for. She said, 'Go, go', in the hurried familiar tone of common life, in the manner of Mr Kean, and without any of that sustained and graceful spirit of conciliation towards her guests, which used to characterize her mode of doing it. Lastly, if Mrs Siddons has to leave the stage again, Mr Horace Twiss will write another farewell address for her: if she continues on it, we shall have to criticize her performances. We know which of these two evils we shall think the greatest.

Too much praise cannot be given to Mr Kemble's performance of Macbeth. He was 'himself again', and more than himself. His action was decided, his voice audible. His tones had occasionally indeed a learned quaintness, like the colouring of Poussin; but the effect of the whole was fine. His action in delivering the speech, 'To-morrow and to-morrow', was particularly striking and expressive, as if he had stumbled by an accident on fate, and was baffled by the impenetrable obscurity of the future. In that prodigious prosing paper, *The Times*, which seems to be written as well as printed by a steam-engine, Mr Kemble is compared to the ruin of a magnificent temple, in which the divinity still resides. This is not the case. The temple is unimpaired; but the divinity is sometimes from home.

The Examiner, 16 June 1816

Charles Lamb
G. F. Cooke as Richard III

Some few of us remember to have seen, and all of us have heard our fathers tell of Quin, and Garrick, and Barry, and some faint traditional notices are left us of their manner in particular scenes, and their style of delivering certain emphatic sentences. Hence our curiosity is excited when a new Hamlet or a new Richard makes his appearance, in the first place, to inquire, how he acted in the Closet scene, in the Tent scene; how he looked, and how he started, when the Ghost came on, and how he cried

> Off with his head,   So much for Buckingham.

We do not reprehend this minute spirit of comparison. On the contrary, we consider it as a delightful artifice, by which we connect the recreations of the past with those of the present generation, what pleased our fathers with what pleases us. We love to witness the obstinate attachments, the unconquerable prejudices (as they seem to us), of the old men, our seniors, the whimsical gratification they appear to derive from the very refusal to be gratified; to hear them talk of the good old actors, whose race is for ever extinct.

With these impressions, we attended the first appearance of Mr Cooke, in the character of Richard the Third, last winter. We thought that he 'bustled' through the scenes with at least as much spirit and effect as any of his predecessors whom we remember in the part, and was not deficient in the delivery of any of those remarkable speeches and exclamations, which old prescription hath set up as criteria of comparison. Now that the grace of freshness is worn off, and Mr Cooke is no longer a novitiate candidate for public favour, we propose to enter into the question – whether that popular actor is right or wrong in his conception of the great outlines of the character; those strong essential differences which separate Richard from all the other creations of Shakespeare. We say of Shakespeare; for though the Play, which passes for his upon the Stage, materially differs from that which he wrote under the same title, being in fact little better than a compilation or a cento of passages extracted from other of his Plays, and applied with gross violation of propriety (as we are ready at any time to point out), besides some miserable additions, which he never could have written; all together producing an inevitable inconsistency of character, sufficient to puzzle and confound the best Actor; yet, in this chaos and perplexity, we are of opinion, that it becomes an Actor to shew his taste, by adhering, as much as possible, to the spirit and intention of the original Author, and to consult his safety in steering by the Light, which Shakespeare holds out to him, as by a great Leading Star. Upon these principles, we presume to censure Mr Cooke, while we are ready to acknowledge that this Actor presents us with a very original and very forcible portrait (if not of the man Richard, whom Shakespeare drew, yet) of the monster Richard, as he exists in the popular idea, in his own exaggerated and witty self-abuse, in the overstrained representations of the parties who were sufferers by his ambition; and, above all, in the impertinent and wretched scenes, so absurdly foisted in by some, who have thought themselves capable of adding to what Shakespeare wrote.

But of Mr Cooke's Richard:

1st, His predominant and masterly simulation.
He has a tongue he can wheedle with the DEVIL.

It has been the policy of that ancient and grey simulator, in all ages, to hide his horns and claws. The Richard of Mr Cooke perpetually obtrudes his. We see the effect of his deceit uniformly successful, but we do not comprehend how it succeeds. We can put ourselves, by a very common fiction, into the place of the individual upon whom it acts, and say, that, in the like case, we should not have been alike credulous. The hypocrisy is too glaring and visible. It resembles more the shallow cunning of a mind which is its own dupe, than the profound and practised art of so powerful an intellect as Richard's. It is too obstreperous and loud, breaking out into *triumphs* and *plaudits* at its own success, like an unexercised *noviciate* to *tricks*. It has none of the silence confidence, and steady self-command of the *experienced politician*; it possesses none of that *fine address*, which was necessary to have betrayed the heart of Lady Anne, or even to have imposed upon the duller wits of the Lord Mayor and Citizens.

2ndly, *His habitual jocularity*, the effect of buoyant spirits, and an elastic mind, rejoicing in its own powers, and in the success of its machinations. This quality of unstrained mirth accompanies *Richard*, and is a prime feature in his character. It never leaves him; in plots, in strategems, and in the midst of his bloody devices, it is perpetually driving him upon wit, and jests, and personal satire, fanciful allusions, and quaint felicities of phrase. It is one of the chief artifices by which the consummate master of dramatic effect has contrived to soften the horrors of the scene, and to make us contemplate a bloody and vicious character with delight. Nowhere, in any of his plays, is to be found so much of sprightly colloquial dialogue, and soliloquies of genuine humour as in *Richard*. This character of unlaboured mirth Mr Cooke seems entirely to pass over, and substitutes in its stead the coarse, taunting humour, and clumsy merriment, of a low-minded assassin.

3rdly, *His personal deformity*. When the Richard of Mr Cooke makes allusions to his own form, they seem accompanied with *unmixed distaste* and *pain*, like some obtrusive and haunting idea – But surely the Richard of Shakspeare mingles in these allusions a perpetual reference to his own powers and capacities, by which he is enabled to surmount these petty objections; and the joy of a defect conquered, or turned into an advantage, is one cause of these very allusions, and of the satisfaction with which his mind recurs to them. These allusions themselves are made in an ironical and good humoured spirit of exaggeration – the most bitter of them are to be found in his self-congratulating soliloquy spoken in the very moment and crisis of joyful exultation on the success of his unheard of courtship. No *partial excellence* can satisfy for this absence of a just general conception – otherwise we are inclined to admit, that, in the delivery of single sentences, in a new and often felicitous light thrown upon old and hitherto misconstrued passages, no actor that we have seen has gone beyond Mr Cooke. He is always alive to the scene before him; and by the fire and novelty of his manner, he seems likely to infuse some warm blood into the frozen declamatory style, into which our theatres have for some time past been degenerating.

The Morning Post, 4 January 1802

Charles Lamb
On the Tragedies of Shakspeare
(considered with reference to their fitness for stage representation)

Taking a turn the other day in the Abbey, I was struck with the affected attitude of a figure which I do not remember to have seen before, and which upon examination proved to be a whole-length of the celebrated Mr Garrick. Though I would not go so far with some good Catholics abroad as to shut players altogether out of consecrated ground, yet I own I was not a little scandalized at the introduction of theatrical airs and gestures into a place set apart to remind us of the saddest realities. Going nearer, I found inscribed under this harlequin figure the following lines:

> To paint fair Nature, by divine command,
> Her magic pencil in his glowing hand,
> A Shakspeare rose; then, to expand his fame
> Wide o'er this breathing world, a Garrick came.
> Though sunk in death the forms the Poet drew,
> The Actor's genius made them breathe anew;
> Though, like the bard himself, in night they lay,
> Immortal Garrick called then back to-day.
> And till Eternity with power sublime
> Shall mark the mortal hour of hoary Time,
> Shakspeare and Garrick like twin-stars shall shine,
> And earth irradiate with a beam divine.

It would be an insult to my readers' understandings to attempt anything like a criticism of this farrago of false thoughts and nonsense. But the reflection it led me into was a kind of wonder how, from the days of the actor here celebrated to our own, it should have been the fashion to compliment every performer in his turn that has had the luck to please the town in any of the great characters of Shakspeare, with a notion of possessing a *mind congenial with the poet's*; how people should come thus unaccountably to confound the power of originating poetical images and conceptions with the faculty of being able to read or recite the same when put into words; or what connection that absolute mastery over the heart and soul of man, which a great dramatic poet possesses, has with those low tricks upon the eye and ear, which a player by observing a few general effects, which some common passion, as grief, anger, etc., usually has upon the gestures and exterior, can easily compass. To know the internal workings and movements of a great mind, of an Othello or a Hamlet, for instance; the *when* and the *why* and the *how far* they should be moved; to what pitch a passion is becoming; to give the reins and to pull in the curb exactly at the moment when the drawing in or the slacking is most graceful – seems to demand a reach of intellect of a vastly different extent from that which is employed upon the bare imitation of the signs of these passions in the countenance or gesture, which signs are usually observed to be most lively and emphatic in the weaker sort of minds, and which signs can, after all, but indicate some passion, as I said before, anger, or grief generally. But of the motives and grounds of the passion, wherein it differs from the same passion in low and vulgar natures, of these the actor can give no more idea by his face or gesture than the eye (without a metaphor) can speak, or the muscles utter intelligible sounds. But such is the instantaneous nature of the impressions which we take in at the eye and ear at a playhouse, compared with the slow apprehension oftentimes of the understanding in reading, that we are apt not only to sink the playwriter in the consideration which we pay to the actor, but even to identify in our minds in a perverse manner, the actor with the character which he represents. It is difficult for a frequent playgoer to disembarrass the idea of Hamlet from the person and voice of Mr K. We speak of Lady Macbeth, while we are in reality thinking of Mrs S. Nor is this confusion incidental alone to unlettered persons, who, not possessing the advantage of reading, are necessarily dependent upon the stage player for all the pleasure which they can receive from the drama, and to whom the very idea of *what an author is* cannot be made comprehensible without some pain and perplexity of mind. The error is one from which persons otherwise not meanly lettered, find it almost impossible to extricate themselves.

Never let me be so ungrateful as to forget the very high degree of satisfaction which I received some years back from seeing for the first time a tragedy of Shakspeare performed, in which these two great performers sutained the principle parts. It seemed to embody and realize conceptions which had hitherto assumed no distinct shape. But dearly do we pay all our life afterwards for this juvenile pleasure, this sense of distinctness. When the novelty is past, we find to our cost that, instead of realizing an idea, we have only materialized and brought down a fine vision to the standard of flesh and blood. We have let go a dream, in quest of an unattainable substance.

How cruelly this operates upon the mind, to have its free conceptions thus cramped and pressed down to the measure of a straitlacing actuality, may be judged from that delightful sensation of freshness with which we turn to those plays of Shakspeare which have escaped being performed, and to those passages in the acting plays of the same writer which have happily been left out in the performance. How far the very custom of hearing anything *spouted*, withers and blows upon a fine passage, may be seen in those speeches from *Henry the Fifth*, etc., which are current in the mouths of school-boys from their being to be found in *Enfield Speakers* and such kind of books. I confess myself utterly unable to appreciate that celebrated soliloquy in *Hamlet* beginning 'To be or not to be', or to tell whether it be good, bad, or indifferent, it has been so handled and pawed about by declamatory boys and men, and torn so inhumanely from its living place and principle of continuity in the play, till it is become to me a perfect dead member.

It may seem a paradox, but I cannot help being of opinion that the plays of Shakspeare are less calculated for performances on a stage than those of almost any other dramatist whatever. Their distinguished excellence is a reason that they should be so; there is so much in them which comes not under the province of acting, with which eye and tone and gesture have nothing to do.

The glory of the scenic art is to personate passion and the turns of passion; and the more coarse and palpable the passion is, the more hold upon the eyes and ears of the spectators the performer obviously possesses. For this reason, scolding scenes, scenes where two persons talk themselves into a fit of fury, and then in a surprising manner talk themselves out of it again, have always been the most popular upon our stage. And the reason is plain, because the spectators are here most palpably appealed to – they are the proper judges in this war of words; they are the legitimate ring that should be formed round such 'intellectual prize-fighters'. Talking is the direct object of the imitation here. But in the best dramas, and in Shakspeare above all, how obvious it is that the form of *speaking*, whether it be in soliloquy or dialogue, is only a medium, and often a highly artificial one, for putting the reader or spectator into possession of that knowledge of the inner structure and workings of mind in a character, which he could otherwise never have arrived at *in that form of composition* by any gift short of intuition. We do here as we do with novels written in the *epistolary form*. How many improprieties, perfect solecisms, in letter-writing do we put up with in *Clarissa* and other books for the sake of the delight which that form upon the whole gives us!

But the practice of stage representation reduces everything to a controversy of elocution. Every character, from the boisterous blasphemings of Bajazet to the shrinking timidity of womanhood, must play the orator. The love-dialogues of *Romeo and Juliet*, those silver-sweet sounds of lovers' tongues by night; the more intimate and sacred sweetness of nuptial colloquy between an Othello or a Posthumus with their married wives; all those delicacies which are so delightful in the reading, as when we read of those youthful dalliances in Paradise –

> As beseemed
> Fair couple linked in happy nuptial league,
> Alone,

by the inherent fault of stage representation, how are these things sullied and turned from their very nature by being exposed to a large assembly; when such speeches as Imogen addresses to her lord come drawling out of the mouth of a hired actress, whose courtship, though nominally addressed to the personated Posthumus, is manifestly aimed at the spectators, who are to judge of her endearments and her returns of love.

The character of Hamlet is perhaps that by which, since the days of Betterton, a succession of popular performers have had the greatest ambition to distinguish themselves. The length of the part may be one of their reasons. But for the character itself, we find it in a play, and therefore we judge it a fit subject of dramatic representation. The play itself abounds in maxims and reflections beyond any other, and therefore we consider it as a proper vehicle for conveying moral instruction. But Hamlet himself – what does he suffer meanwhile by being dragged forth as a public schoolmaster to give lectures to the crowd! Why, nine parts in ten of what Hamlet does are transactions between himself and his moral sense; they are the effusions of his solitary musings, which he retires to holes and corners and the most sequestered parts of the palace to pour forth – or rather, they are the silent meditations with which his bosom is bursting, reduced to *words* for the sake of the reader, who must else remain ignorant of what is passing there. These profound sorrows, these light-and-noise-abhorring ruminations, which the tongue scarce dares utter to deaf walls and chambers, how can they be represented by a gesticulating actor who comes and mouths them out before an audience, making four hundred people his confidants at once? I say not that it is the fault of the actor so to do; he must pronounce them *ore rotundo*, he must accompany them with his eye, he must insinuate them into his auditory by some trick of eye, tone, or gesture, or he fails. *He must be thinking all the while of his appearance, because he knows that all the while the spectators are judging of it.* And this is the way to represent the shy, negligent, retiring Hamlet!

It is true that there is no other mode of conveying a vast quantity of thought and feeling to a great portion of the audience, who otherwise would never learn it for themselves by reading, and the intellectual acquisition gained this way may, for aught I know, be inestimable; but I am not arguing that *Hamlet* should not be acted, but how much *Hamlet* is made another thing by being acted. I have heard much of the wonders which Garrick performed in this part; but as I never saw him, I must have leave to doubt whether the representation of such a character came within the province of his art. Those who tell me of him, speak of his eye, of the magic of his eye, and of his commanding voice – physical properties vastly desirable in an actor, and without which he can never insinuate meaning into an auditory. But what have they to do with Hamlet? What have they to do with intellect? In fact, the things aimed at in theatrical representation are to arrest the spectator's eye upon the form and the gesture, and so to gain a more favourable hearing to what is spoken. It is not what the character is, but how he looks; not what he says, but how he speaks it. I see no reason to think that if the play of *Hamlet* were written over again by some such writer as Banks or Lillo, retaining the process of the story, but totally omitting all the poetry of it, all the divine features of Shakspeare, his stupendous intellect, and only taking care to give us enough of passionate dialogue, which Banks or Lillo were never at a loss to furnish – I see not how the effect could be much different upon an audience, nor how the actor has it in his power to represent Shakspeare to us differently from his representation of Banks or Lillo. Hamlet would still be a youthful accomplished prince, and must be gracefully personated; he might be puzzled in his mind, wavering in his conduct, seemingly cruel to Ophelia; he might see a ghost, and start at it, and address it kindly when he found it to be his father – all this in the poorest and most homely language of the servilest creeper after nature that ever consulted the palate of an audience; and I see not but there would be room for all the power which an actor has to display itself. All the passions and changes of passion might remain, for those are much less difficult to write or act than is thought – it is a trick easy to be attained, it is but rising or falling a note or two in the voice, a whisper, with a significant foreboding look to announce its approach; and so contagious the counterfeit appearance of any emotion is, that let the words be what they will, the look and tone shall carry it off and make it pass for deep skill in the passions.

It is common for people to talk of Shakspeare's plays being *so natural* that everybody can understand him. They are natural indeed, they are grounded deep in nature – so deep that the depth of them lies out of the reach of most of us. You shall hear the same persons say that *George Barnwell* is very natural, and *Othello* is very natural, that they are both very deep; and to them they are the same kind of thing. At the one they sit and shed tears because a good sort of young man is tempted by a naughty woman to commit a *trifling peccadillo*, the murder of an uncle or so, that is all, and so comes to an untimely end, which is so *moving*; and at the other, because a blackamoor in a fit of jealousy kills his innocent white wife – and the odds are that ninety-nine out of a hundred would willingly behold the same catastrophe happen to both the heroes, and have thought the rope more due to Othello than to Barnwell. For of the texture of Othello's mind, the inward construction marvellously laid open, with all its strengths and weaknesses, its heroic confidences and its human misgivings, its agonies of hate springing from the depths of love, they see no more than the spectators at a cheaper rate, who pay their pennies apiece to look through the man's telescope in Leicester Fields, see into the inward plot and topography of the moon. Some dim thing or other they see – they see an actor personating a passion, of grief or anger, for instance, and they recognize it as a copy of the usual external effects of such passions, or at least as being true to that symbol of the emotion which passes current at the theatre for it; for it is often no more than that. But of the grounds of the passion, its correspondence to a great or heroic nature, which is the only worthy object of tragedy; that common auditors know anything of this, or can have any such notions dinned into them by the mere strength of an actor's lungs – that apprehensions foreign to them should be thus infused into them by storm, I can neither believe, nor understand how it can be possible.

We talk of Shakspeare's admirable observation of life, when we should feel that not from a petty inquisition into those cheap and everyday characters which surround him, as they surround us, but from his own mind, which was, to borrow a phrase of Ben Jonson's, the very 'sphere of humanity', he fetched those images of virtue and of knowledge, of which every one of us, recognizing a part, think we comprehend in our natures the whole, and oftentimes mistake the powers which he positively creates in us for nothing more than indigenous faculties of our own minds, which only waited the application of corresponding virtues in him to return a full and clear echo of the same.

To return to Hamlet. Among the distinguishing features of that wonderful character, one of the most interesting (yet painful) is that soreness of mind which makes him treat the intrusions of Polonius with harshness, and that asperity which he puts on in his interviews with Ophelia. These tokens of an unhinged mind (if they be not mixed in the latter case with a profound artifice of love, to alienate Ophelia by affected discourtesies, so to prepare her mind for the breaking off of that loving intercourse, which can no longer find a place amidst business so serious as that which he has to do) are parts of his character, which, to reconcile with our admiration of Hamlet, the most patient consideration of his situation is no more than necessary; they are what we *forgive afterwards*, and explain by the whole of his character, but *at the time* they are harsh and unpleasant. Yet such is the actor's necessity of giving strong blows to the audience that I have never seen a player in this character who did not exaggerate and strain to the utmost these ambiguous features – these temporary deformities in the character. They make him express a vulgar scorn at Polonius which utterly degrades his gentility, and which no explanation can render palatable; they make him show contempt and curl up the nose at Ophelia's father – contempt in its very grossest and most hateful form; but they get applause by it: it is natural, people say – that is, the words are scornful, and the actor expresses scorn, and that they can judge of; but why so much scorn, and of that sort, they never think of asking.

So to Ophelia. All the Hamlets that I have ever seen, rant and rave at her as if she had committed some great crime, and the audience are highly pleased, because the words of the part are satirical, and they are enforced by the strongest expression of satirical indignation of which the face and voice are capable. But then, whether Hamlet is likely to have put on such brutal appearances to a lady whom he loved so dearly, is never thought on. The truth is, that in all such deep affections as had subsisted between Hamlet and Ophelia, there is a stock of *supererogatory love* (if I may venture to use the expression), which in any great grief of heart, especially where that which preys upon the mind cannot be communicated, confers a kind of indulgence upon the grieved party to express itself, even to its heart's dearest object, in the language of a temporary alienation; but it is not alienation, it is a distraction purely, and so it always makes itself to be felt by that object; it is not anger, but grief assuming the appearance of anger – love awkwardly counterfeiting hate, as sweet countenances when they try to frown. But such sternness and fierce disgust as Hamlet is made to show, is no counterfeit, but the real face of absolute aversion, of irreconcilable alienation. It may be said he puts on the madman; but then he should only so far put on this counterfeit lunacy as his own real distraction will give him leave; that is, incompletely, imperfectly, not in that confirmed, practised way, like a master of his art, or, as Dame Quickly would say, 'like one of those harlotry players'.

I mean no disrespect to any actor, but the sort of pleasure which Shakspeare's plays give in the acting seems to me not at all to differ from that which the audience receive from those of other writers; and, they being in themselves essentially so different from all others, I must conclude that there is something in the nature of acting which levels all distinctions. And, in fact, who does not speak indifferently of the *Gamester* and of *Macbeth* as fine stage performances, and praise the Mrs Beverley in the same way as the Lady Macbeth of Mrs S.? Belvidera and Calista and Isabella and Euphrasia, are they less liked than Imogen, or than Juliet, or than Desdemona? Are they not spoken of and remembered in the same way? Is not the female performer as great (as they call it) in one as in the other? Did not Garrick shine, and was he not ambitious of shining, in every drawling tragedy that his wretched day produced – the productions of the Hills and the Murphys and the Browns – and shall he have that honour to dwell in our minds for ever as an inseparable concomitant with Shakspeare? A kindred mind! Oh, who can read that affecting sonnet of Shakspeare which alludes to his profession as a player –

> Oh, for my sake do you with Fortune chide,
> The guilty goddess of my harmful deeds,
> That did not better for my life provide
> Than public means which public manners breeds,
> Thence comes it that my name receives a brand,
> And almost thence my nature is subdued
> To what it works in, like the dyer's hand,

Or that other confession –

> Alas, 'tis true, I have got here and there,
> And made myself a motley to the view,
> Gored mine own thoughts, sold cheap what is most dear,

Who can read these instances of jealous self-watchfulness in our sweet Shakspeare and dream of any congeniality between him and one that, by every tradition of him, appears to have been as mere a player as ever existed; to have had his mind tainted with the lowest player's vices – envy and jealousy and miserable cravings after applause; one who in the exercise of his profession was jealous even of the women-performers that stood in his way – a manager full of managerial tricks and strategems and finesse; that any resemblance should be dreamed of between him and Shakspeare – Shakspeare, who in the plenitude and consciousness of his own powers could with that noble modesty which we can neither imitate nor appreciate, express himself thus of his own sense of his own defects –

> Wishing me like to one more rich in hope,
> Featured like him, like him with friends possessed:
> Desiring *this man's art, and that man's scope*!

I am almost disposed to deny to Garrick the merits of being an admirer of Shakspeare. A true lover of his excellences he certainly was not; for would any true lover of them have admitted into his matchless scenes such ribald trash as Tate and Cibber and the rest of them, that

> With their darkness durst affront his light,

have foisted into the acting plays of Shakspeare? I believe it impossible that he could have had a proper reverence for Shakspeare and have condescended to go through that interpolated scene in *Richard the Third* in which Richard tries to break his wife's heart by telling her he loves another woman, and says 'If she survives this she is immortal'. Yet I doubt not he delivers this vulgar stuff with as much anxiety of emphasis as any of the genuine parts; and for acting, it is as well calculated as any. But we have seen the part of Richard lately produce great fame to an actor by his manner of playing it, and it lets us into the secret of acting, and of popular judgments of Shakspeare derived from acting. Not one of the spectators who have witnessed Mr C.'s exertions in that part but has come away with a proper conviction that Richard is a very wicked man, and kills little children in their beds with something like the pleasure which the giants and ogres in children's books are represented to have taken in that practice; moreover, that he is very close and shrewd and devilish cunning, for you could see that by his eye.

But is in fact this the impression we have in reading the Richard of Shakspeare? Do we feel anything like disgust, as we do at that butcher-like representation of him that passes for him on the stage? A horror at his crimes blends with the effect which we feel; but how is it qualified, how is it carried off, by the rich intellect which he displays, his resources, his wit, his buoyant spirits, his vast knowledge and insight into characters, the poetry of his part! – not an atom of all which is made perceivable in Mr C.'s way of acting it. Nothing but his crimes, his actions, is visible – they are prominent and staring; the murderer stands out – but where is the lofty genius, the man of vast capacity, the profound, the witty, accomplished Richard?

The truth is, the characters of Shakspeare are so much the objects of meditation rather than of interest or curiosity as to their actions that while we are reading any of his great criminal characters – Macbeth, Richard, even Iago – we think not so much of the crimes which they commit, as of the ambition, the aspiring spirit, the intellectual activity which prompts them to overlap those moral fences. Barnwell is a wretched murderer; there is a certain fitness between his neck and the rope; he is the legitimate heir to the gallows; nobody who thinks at all can think of any alleviating circumstances in his case to make him a fit object of mercy. Or to take an instance from the higher tragedy, what else but a mere assassin in Glenalvon? Do we think of anything but of the crime which he commits and the rack which he deserves? That is all which we really think about him. Whereas in corresponding characters in Shakspeare, so little do the actions comparatively affect us, that while the impulses, the inner mind in all its perverted greatness, solely seems real, and is exclusively attended to, the crime is comparatively nothing. But when we see these things represented, the acts which they do are comparatively every-thing, their impulses nothing. The state of sublime emotion into which we are elevated by those images of night and horror which Macbeth is made to utter, that solemn prelude with which he entertains the time till the bell shall strike which is to call him to murder Duncan – when we no longer read it in a book, when we have given up that vantage-ground of abstraction which reading possesses over seeing, and come to see a man in his bodily shape before our eyes actually preparing to commit a murder, if the acting be true and impressive, as I have witnessed it in Mr K.'s performance of that part, the painful anxiety about the act, the natural longing to prevent it while it yet seems unperpetrated, the too close pressing semblance of reality, give a pain and an uneasiness which totally destroy all the delight which the words in the book convey, where the deed doing never presses upon us with the painful sense of presence; it rather seems to belong to history, to something past and inevitable, if it has anything to do with time at all. The sublime images, the poetry alone, is that which is present to our minds in the reading.

So to see Lear acted – to see an old man tottering about the stage with a walking-stick, turned out of doors by his daughters in a rainy night, has nothing in it but what is painful and disgusting. We want to take him into shelter and relieve him – that is all the feeling which the acting of Lear ever produced in me. But the Lear of Shakspeare cannot be acted. The contemptible machinery, by which they mimic the storm which he goes out in, is not more inadequate to represent the horrors of the real elements than any actor can be to represent Lear; they might more easily propose to personate the Satan of Milton upon a stage, or one of Michael Angelo's terrible figures. The greatness of Lear is not in corporal dimension, but in intellectual; the explosions of his passion are terrible as a volcano – they are storms turning up and disclosing to the bottom that sea, his mind, with all its vast riches. It is his mind which is laid bare. This case of flesh and blood seems too insignificant to be thought on, even as he himself neglects it. On the stage we see nothing but corporal infirmities and weakness, the impotence of rage; while we read it, we see not Lear, but we are Lear – we are in his mind, we are sustained by a grandeur which baffles the malice of daughters and storms. In the aberrations of his reason we discover a mighty, irregular power of reasoning, immethodized from the ordinary purposes of life, but exerting its powers, as the wind blows where it listeth, at will upon the corruptions and abuses of mankind. What have looks or tones to do with that sublime identification of his age with that of the *heavens themselves*, when in his reproaches to them for conniving at the injustice of his children he reminds them that 'they themselves are old'? What gestures shall we appropriate to this? What has the voice or the eye to do with such things? But the play is beyond all art, as the tamperings with it show; it is too hard and stony – it must have love scenes, and a happy ending. It is not enough that Cordelia is a daughter, she must shine as a lover too. Tate has put his hook in the nostrils of this Leviathan, for Garrick and his followers, the showmen of scene, to draw the mighty beast about more easily. A happy ending! – as if the living martyrdom that Lear had gone through, the flaying of his feelings alive, did not make a fair dismissal from the stage of life the only decorous thing for him. If he is to live and be happy after, if he could sustain this world's burden after, why all this pudder and preparation, why torment us with all this unnecessary sympathy? As if the childish pleasure of getting his gilt robes and sceptre again could tempt him to act over again his misused station; as if at his years, and with his experience, anything was left but to die!

Lear is essentially impossible to be represented on a stage. But how many dramatic personages are there in Shakspeare which, though more tractable and feasible (if I may so speak) than Lear, yet from some circumstance, some adjunct to their character, are improper to be shown to our bodily eye. *Othello*, for instance. Nothing can be more soothing, more flattering to the nobler parts of our natures, than to read of a young Venetian lady of highest extraction, through the force of love and from a sense of merit in him whom she loved, laying aside every consideration of kindred and country and colour, and wedding with a *coal-black Moor* (for such he is represented, in the imperfect state of knowledge respecting foreign countries in those days compared with our own, or in compliance with popular notions; though the Moors are now well enough known to be by many shades less unworthy of white woman's fancy) – it is the perfect triumph of virtue over accidents, of the imagination over the senses. She sees Othello's colour in his mind. But upon the stage, when the imagination is no longer the ruling faculty, but we are left to our poor, unassisted senses, I appeal to every one that has seen *Othello* played, whether he did not, on the contrary, sink Othello's mind in his colour; whether he did not find something extremely revolting in the courtship and wedded caresses of Othello and Desdemona; and whether the actual sight of the thing did not outweigh all that beautiful compromise which we make in reading. And the reason it should do so is obvious because there is just so much reality presented to our senses as to give a perception of disagreement, with not enough of belief in the internal motives – all that which is unseen – to overpower and reconcile the first and obvious prejudices. What we see upon a stage is body and bodily action; what we are conscious of in reading is almost exclusively the mind and its movements; and this, I think, may sufficiently account for the very different sort of delight with which the same play so often affects us in the reading and the seeing.

It requires little reflection to perceive that if those characters in Shakspeare which are within the precincts of nature have yet something in them which appeals too exclusively to the imagination to admit of their being made objects to the sense without suffering a change and a diminution – that still stronger the objection must lie against representing another line of characters which Shakspeare has introduced to give a wildness and a supernatural elevation to his scenes, as if to remove them still further from that assimilation to common life in which their excellence is vulgarly supposed to consist. When we read the incantations of those terrible beings, the Witches in *Macbeth*, though some of the ingredients of their hellish compositions savour of the grotesque, yet is the effect upon us other than the most serious and appalling that can be imagined? Do we not feel spellbound as Macbeth was? Can any mirth accompany a sense of their presence? We might as well laugh under a conscious-ness of the principle of Evil himself being truly and really present with us. But attempt to bring these beings on to a stage, and you turn them instantly into so many old women that men and children are to laugh at. Contrary to the old saying, that 'seeing is believing', the sight actually destroys the faith; and the mirth in which we indulge at their expense, when we see these crea-tures upon a stage, seems to be a sort of indemnification which we make to ourselves for the terror which they put us in when reading made them an object of belief – when we surrendered up our reason to the poet, as children to their nurses and their elders; and we laugh at our fears, as children who thought they saw something in the dark triumph when the bringing in of a candle discovers the vanity of their fears. For this exposure of supernatural agents upon a stage is truly bringing in a candle to expose their own delusiveness. It is the solitary taper and the book that generates a faith in these terrors; a ghost by chandelier light and in good company deceives no spectators – a ghost that can be measured by the eye, and his human dimensions made out at leisure. The sight of a well-lighted house and a well-dressed audience shall arm the most nervous child against any apprehensions, as Tom Brown says of the impenetrable skin of Achilles, with his impenetrable armour over it, 'Bully Dawson would have fought the devil with such advantages.'

Much has been said, and deservedly, in reprobation of the vile mixture which Dryden has thrown into the *Tempest*; doubtless without some such vicious alloy, the impure ears of that age would never have sat out to hear so much innocence of love as is contained in the sweet courtship of Ferdinand and Miranda. But is the *Tempest* of Shakspeare at all a subject for stage repre-sentation? It is one thing to read of an enchanter, and to believe the won-drous tale while we are reading it; but to have a conjuror brought before us in his conjuring-gown, with his spirits about him, which none but himself and some hundreds of favoured spectators before the curtain are supposed to see, involves such a quantity of the *hateful incredible* that all our reverence for the author cannot hinder us from perceiving such gross attempts upon the senses to be in the highest degree childish and inefficient. Spirits and fairies cannot be represented, they cannot even be painted; they can only be believed. But the elaborate and anxious provision of scenery, which the luxury of the age demands, in these cases works a quite contrary effect to what is intended. That which in comedy, or plays of familiar life, adds so much to the life of the imitation, in plays which appeal to the higher faculties positively destroys the illusion which it is introduced to aid. A parlour or a drawing-room, a library opening into a garden, a garden with an alcove in it, a street, or the piazza of Covent Garden, does well enough in a scene; we are content to give as much credit to it as it demands; or rather, we think little about it, it is little more than reading at the top of a page, 'Scene, a garden', we do not imagine ourselves there, but we readily admit the imitation of familiar objects. But to think, by the help of painted trees and caverns which we know to be painted, to transport our minds to Prospero and his island and his lonely cell, or by the aid of a fiddle dexterously thrown in, in an interval of speaking, to make us believe that we hear those supernatural noises of which the isle was full – the Orrery Lecturer at the Haymarket might as well hope, by his musical glasses cleverly stationed out of sight behind his apparatus, to make us believe that we do indeed hear the crystal spheres ring out that chime which, if it were to inwrap our fancy long, Milton thinks,

> Time would run back and fetch the age of gold,
> And speckled vanity
> Would sicken soon and die,
> And leprous Sin would melt from earthly mould, –
> Yea, Hell itself would pass away,
> And leave its dolorous mansions to the peering day.

The Garden of Eden, with our first parents in it, is not more impossible to be shown on a stage than the Enchanted Isle, with its no less interesting and innocent first settlers.

The subject of scenery is closely connected with that of the dresses, which are so anxiously attended to on our stage. I remember, the last time I saw Macbeth played, the discrepancy I felt at the changes of garment which he varied – the shiftings and re-shiftings, like a Romish priest at mass. The luxury of stage-improvements and the importunity of the public eye requires this. The coronation robe of the Scottish monarch was fairly a counterpart to that which our king wears when he goes to the parliament-house – just so full and cumbersome, and set out with ermine and pearls. And if things must be represented, I see not what to find fault with in this. But in reading, what robe are we conscious of? Some dim images of royalty, a crown and sceptre, may float before our eyes, but who shall describe the fashion of it? Do we see in our mind's eye what Webb or any other robe-maker could pattern? This is the inevitable consequence of imitating everything, to make all things natural. Whereas the reading of a tragedy is a fine abstraction. It presents to the fancy just so much of external appearances as to make us feel that we are among flesh and blood, while by far the greater and better part of our imagination is employed upon the thoughts and internal machinery of the character. But in acting, scenery, dress, the most contemptible things, call upon us to judge of their naturalness.

Perhaps it would be no bad similitude to liken the pleasure which we take in seeing one of these fine plays acted, compared with that quiet delight which we find in the reading of it, to the different feelings with which a reviewer and a man that is not a reviewer reads a fine poem. The accursed critical habit, the being called upon to judge and pronounce, must make it quite a different thing to the former. In seeing these plays acted, we are affected just as judges. When Hamlet compares the two pictures of Gertrude's first and second husband, who wants to see the pictures? But in the acting, a miniature must be lugged out – which we know not to be the picture, but only to show how finely a miniature may be represented. This showing of everything levels all things; it makes tricks, bows and courtesies of importance. Mrs S. never got more fame by anything than by the manner in which she dismisses the guests in the banquet-scene in *Macbeth*; it is as much remembered as any of her thrilling tones or impressive looks. But does such a trifle as this enter into the imagination of the reader of that wild and wonderful scene? Does not the mind dismiss the feasters as rapidly as it can? Does it care about the gracefulness of the doing it? But by acting, and judging of acting, all these non-essentials are raised into an importance injurious to the main interest of the play.

I have confined my observations to the tragic parts of Shakspeare. It would be no very difficult task to extend the inquiry to his comedies, and to show why Falstaff, Shallow, Sir Hugh Evans, and the rest are equally incompatible with stage representation. The length to which this essay has run, will make it, I am afraid, sufficiently distasteful to the amateurs of the theatre, without going any deeper into the subject at present.

The Reflector, No. IV, 1812

Leigh Hunt
Mr Mathews

Those comedians are infinitely mistaken who imagine that mere buffoonery or face-making is a surer method of attaining public favour than chastened and natural humour. A monstrous grin, that defies all description or simile, may raise a more noisy laughter, but as I have before observed, the merest pantomime clown will raise a still noisier: laughter does not always express the most satisfied enjoyment, and there is something in the ease and artlessness of true humour that obtains a more lasting though a more gradual applause: it is like a rational lover, who allows confidence and extravagant mirth to catch a woman's eye first, but wins his way ultimately from the very want of qualities which please merely to fatigue. While such an actor, therefore, as Dowton will attempt buffooneries in which he neither can nor ought to succeed, it is no small credit to Mr Mathews that he had the judgment to avoid in general what he really can exhibit with the greater effect. This is the proper pride of an actor who has a greater respect for the opinion of the boxes than of the galleries; this is the laudable ambition that would rather be praised by those who are worthy of respect themselves than by a clamorous mob who, in fact, applaud their own likeness in the vulgarity and nonsense so boisterously admired.

Such a judgment is the more praiseworthy in Mr Mathews, as his principal excellence is the representation of officious valets and humourous old men, two species of character that with most actors are merely buffoons in livery and buffoons with walking-sticks. His attention to correctness, however, by no means lessens his vivacity, but it is the vivacity of the world, not of the stage; it seems rather his nature than his art, and though I dare say all actors have their hours of disquiet, and perhaps more than most men, yet he has not the air of one who elevates his sensations the moment he enters the stage and drops them the instant he departs. It is a very common and a very injurious fault with actors to come before the audience with a manner expressive of beginning a task; they adjust their neckcloths and hats as if they had dressed in a hurry, look about them as much as to say, 'What sort of a house have I got this evening?' and commence their speeches in a tone of patient weariness, as if they contemplated the future labours of the evening. This is a frequent error with Mr H. Johnston, and a most peculiar one with Mr C. Kemble, who often seems to have just arrived from a fatiguing walk. Mr Mathews makes his appearance neither with this indifference on the one hand, nor on the other with that laboured mirth which seems to have been lashed into action like a top, and which goes down like a top at regular intervals. If, therefore, he does not amaze like many inferior actors with sudden bursts of broad merriment, he is more equable and consistent in his humour, and inspires his audience with a more constant spirit of cheerfulness. Such a cheerfulness is the most desirable effect in every comic performer, and this feeling is one of the sensations which render us more truly pleased with comedy than with farce: it is more agreeable to reason, because it leaves room for thinking; it is removed from violence, which always carries a degree of pain into the more exquisite pleasures: it is more like the happiness that we may attain in real life, and therefore more fitted to dispose us to an enjoyment of our feelings.

The principal fault in the general style of Mr Mathews is a redundancy of bodily motion approaching to restlessness, which I have sometimes thought to have been a kind of nervousness impatient of public observation; but I think he has repressed this considerably within these few months, and if it be owing to want of confidence, the stage is not a place to increase any of the more bashful feelings. This fault, however, like Mr Kemble's stiffness in Penruddock, becomes a beauty in his performance of the restless *Lying Valet*, and of Risk in *Love Laughs at Locksmiths*, who are both in a perpetual bustle of cheating and contrivance. Possibly it may be the frequency of his performance in characters of intrigue that originally led him to indulge it, for there is yet another character, that of the intriguing servant in the farce of *Catch him who Can*, in which he is at full liberty to indulge it. In this servant he gives a specimen of that admirable power of mimicry, in which he rivals Mr Bannister. I believe there were many in the theatre who had much difficulty to recognize him in his transformation into the Frenchman, and for alteration of manner, tone, and pronunciation, it certainly was not inferior to the most finished deceptions of that great comedian. As this kind of deception, indeed, depends chiefly upon a disguise of the voice, one would imagine it ought not to be very difficult to be an actor, one of whose first powers should be a flexibility of tone; but this flexibility becomes valuable on our stage for its rarity, for it is curious enough to observe that we have not a single tragedian or female performer who can at all disguise the voice, and of all our comedians, who really ought to excel in this point, Mr Bannister and Mr Mathews seem the only two who can thus escape from themselves with any artifice: many of the comic actors as Munden, Simmons, Blanchard, Liston, Johnstone, Wewitzer, and particularly Fawcett, seem blessed with such honest throats as to be incapable of the slightest deception.

The old age of Mr Mathews is like the rest of his excellencies, perfectly unaffected and correct; the appearance of years he manages so well, that many of his admirers, who have never seen him off the stage, insist that he is an elderly man, and the reason of this deception is evident: most of our comedians in their representation of age either make no alteration of their voice, and, like antiquarian cheats, palm a walking-stick or a hat upon us for something very ancient, or sink into so unnatural an imbecility that they are apt on occasion to forget their tottering knees and bent shoulders, and like Vertumnus, in the poet, are young and old in the turn of a minute. Mathews never appears to wish to be old; time seems to have come to him, not he to time, and as he never, where he can avoid it, makes that show of feebleness which the vanity of age always would avoid, so he never forgets that general appearance of years, which the natural feebleness of age could not help. Our old men of the stage are in general of one unvarying age in all their various characters, as in the case of Munden, for instance, who, though he imitates the appearance of a hearty old gentleman with much nature, is seldom a jot the older or younger than his usual antiquity, whatever the author might have led us to imagine. The two characters of Don Manuel in *She Would and She Would Not* and of Old Philpot in the *Citizen* are sufficient examples of the ease with which Mr Mathews alters his years and of the general excellence of his old age. In the former piece he is a naturally cheerful old man, whose humour depends much on the humour of others, and who is overcome alternately with gaiety and with despair, as he finds himself treated by those about him. The voice of Mr Mathews, were we to shut our eyes, would be enough to convince us of his age in this character, and of his disposition, too; there is something in it unaccountably petty and confined, while at the same time it appears to make an effort of strength and jollity; and when his false pitch of spirits meets with a sudden downfall, nothing can be more natural than the total dissolution with which he yields himself to a hundred imaginary miseries. When his spirits are raised again and his excessive joy gradually overcomes itself by its own violence, the second exertion of his fatigued talkativeness and of his excessive laughter reduces him to mere impotence; he sinks into his chair; and in the last weariness of a weak mind and body, cannot still refrain from the natural loquacity of old age, but in the intervals of oppressed feeling attempts to speak when he has not only nothing to say, but when it is perfectly painful to him to utter a word. In this character, therefore, Mr Mathews exhibits all the gradations of the strength and weakness of declining years; in that of Philpot, he settles himself into a confirmed and unresisting old age: his feeble attitudes, his voice, his minutest actions, are perfectly monotonous, as becomes a money-getting dotard, whose soul is absorbed in one mean object: his limbs contracted together are expressive of the selfish closeness of the miser, and in his very tone of utterance, so sparing of its strength and so inward, he seems to retire into himself.

From the general performances, however, of Mr Mathews, I had been induced to consider him as an actor of habits rather than of passions; and as the present essay originally stood, I had classed him in a rank much inferior to Bannister and Dowton. But one of his late performances raised his genius so highly in my estimation, that I cancelled the original paragraph on purpose to do justice to his Sir Fretful Plagiary in the *Critic*, to a performance which has proved his knowledge of the human heart, has given its true spirit to one of the most original characters of the first wit of our age, and has even persuaded the ancient dramatic connoisseurs to summon up the claps of former times: nay, some of the old gentlemen, in the important intervals of snuff, went so far as to declare that the actor approached Parsons himself. We are generally satisfied when an actor can express a single feeling with strength of countenance; but to express two at once, and to give them at the same time a powerful distinctness, belongs to the perfection of his art. Nothing can be more admirable than the look of Mr Mathews when the severe criticism is detailed by his malicious acquaintance. While he affects a pleasantry of countenance, he cannot help betraying his rage in his eyes, in that feature which always displays our most prominent feelings; if he draws the air to and fro through his teeth, as if he was perfectly assured of his own pleasant feelings, he convinces everybody by his tremulous and restless limbs that he is in absolute torture; if the lower part of his face expands into a painful smile, the upper part contracts into a glaring frown which contradicts the ineffectual good humour beneath; everything in his face becomes rigid, confused, and uneasy; it is a mixture of oil and vinegar, in which the acid predominates; it is anger putting on a mask that is only the more hideous in proportion as it is more fantastic. The sudden drop of his smile into a deep and bitter indignation, when he can endure sarcasm no longer, completes this impassioned picture of 'Sir Fretful'; but lest his indignation should swell into mere tragedy, Mr Mathews accompanies it with all the touches of familiar vexation: while he is venting his rage in vehement expressions, he accompanies his more emphatic words with a closing thrust of his buttons, which he fastens and unfastens up and down his coat; and when his obnoxious friend approaches his snuff-box to take a pinch, he claps down the lid and turns violently off with a most malicious mockery of grin. These are the performances and the characters which are the true fame of actors and dramatists. If our farcical performers and farcical writers could reach this refined satire, ridicule would vanish before them, like breath from a polished knife.

Critical Essays on the Performers of the London Theatres, 1807

William Hazlitt
Mr Grimaldi

Both Pantomimes are indifferent. That at Drury-Lane consists in endless flights of magpies up to the ceiling, and that at Covent-Garden stays too long in China. The latter part was better where Mr Grimaldi comes in, and lets off a culverin at his enemies, and sings a serenade to his mistress in concert with Grimalkin. We were glad, right glad, to see Mr Grimaldi again. There was (some weeks back) an ugly report that Mr Grimaldi was dead. We would not believe it; we did not like to ask any one the question, but we watched the public countenance for the intimation of an event which 'would have eclipsed the gaiety of nations'. We looked at the faces we met in the street, but there were no signs of general sadness; no one stopped his acquaintance to say that a man of genius was no more. Here indeed he is again, safe and sound, and as pleasant as ever. As without the gentleman at St Helena, there is an end of politics in Europe; so without the clown at Sadler's Wells there must be an end of pantomimes in the country!

The Examiner, 31 December 1815

Charles Lamb
On the Acting of Munden

Not many nights ago I had come home from seeing this extraordinary performer in *Cockletop*; and when I retired to my pillow his whimsical image still
stuck by me in a manner as to threaten sleep. In vain I tried to divert myself
of it by conjuring up the most opposite associations. I resolved to be serious.
I raised up the gravest topics of life, private misery, public calamity. All would
not do:

> There the antic sat,
> Mocking our state,

his queer visnomy, his bewildering costume, all the strange things which he
had raked together, his serpentine rod swagging about in his pocket, Cleopatra's tear, and the rest of his relics, O'Keefe's wild farce, and *his* wilder
commentary, till the passion of laughter, like grief in excess, relieved itself
by its own weight, inviting the sleep which in the first instance it had driven
away.

But I was not to escape so easily. No sooner did I fall into slumbers than
the same image, only more perplexing, assailed me in the shape of dreams.
Not one Munden, but five hundred, were dancing before me, like the faces
which, whether you will or no, come when you have been taking opium – all
the strange combinations which this strangest of all strange mortals ever
shot his proper countenance into, from the day he came commissioned to dry
up the tears of the town for the loss of the now almost forgotten Edwin. Oh,
for the power of the pencil to have fixed them when I awoke! A season or two
since there was exhibited a Hogarth gallery. I do not see why there should
not be a Munden gallery. In richness and variety, the latter would not fall
far short of the former.

There is one face of Farley, one face of Knight, one (but what a one it is!)
of Liston; but Munden has none that you can properly pin down and call *his*.
When you think he has exhausted his battery of looks, in unaccountable
warfare with your gravity, suddenly he spouts out an entirely new set of
features, like Hydra. He is not one, but legion; not so much a comedian as a
company. If his name could be multiplied like his countenance, it might fill
a playbill. He, and he alone, literally *makes faces*; applied to any other person,
the phrase is a mere figure, denoting certain modifications of the human
countenance. Out of some invisible wardrobe he dips for faces, as his friend
Suett used for wigs, and fetches them out as easily. I should not be surprised
to see him some day put out the head of a river-horse, or come forth a pewit
or lapwing, some feathered metamorphosis.

I have seen this gifted actor in Sir Christopher Curry, in old Dornton,
diffuse a glow of sentiment which has made the pulse of a crowded theatre
beat like that of one man, when he has come in aid of the pulpit, doing good

to the moral heart of a people. I have seen some faint approaches to this sort of excellence in other players. But in the grand grotesque of farce, Munden stands out as single and unaccompanied as Hogarth. Hogarth, strange to tell, had no followers. The school of Munden began and must end with himself.

Can any man *wonder* like he does? Can any man *see ghosts* like he does? or *fight with his own shadow*, 'SESSA', as he does in that strangely-neglected thing, the *Cobbler of Preston*, where his alterations from the Cobbler to the Magnifico, and from the Magnifico to the Cobbler, kept the brain of the spectator in as wild a ferment as if some Arabian Night were being acted before him? Who like him can throw, or ever attempted to throw, a preternatural interest over the commonest daily life objects? A table or a joint stool, in his conception, rises into a dignity equivalent to Cassiopeia's chair; it is invested with constellatory importance. You could not speak of it with more deference if it were mounted into the firmament. A beggar in the hands of Michael Angelo, says Fuseli, rose the Patriarch of Poverty. So the gusto of Munden antiquates and ennobles what it touches. His pots and his ladles are as grand and primal as the seething-pots and hooks seen in old prophetic vision. A tub of butter, contemplated by him, amounts to a Platonic idea. He understands a leg of mutton in its quiddity. He stands wondering, amid the commonplace materials of life, like primeval man with the sun and stars about him.

The London Magazine, October 1822

Charles Lamb
Munden's Farewell

The regular playgoers ought to put on mourning, for the king of broad comedy is dead to the drama. Alas! Munden is no more! – give sorrow vent. He may yet walk the town, pace the pavement in a seeming existence, eat, drink, and nod to his friends in all the affectation of life; but Munden, *the* Munden, Munden with the bunch of countenances, the bouquet of faces, is gone forever from the lamps, and as far as comedy is concerned, is as dead as Garrick! When an actor retires (we will put the *suicide* as mildly as possible), how many worthy persons perish with him! With Munden Sir Peter Teazle must experience a shock; Sir Robert Bramble gives up the ghost; Crack ceases to breathe. Without Munden what becomes of Dozey? Where shall we seek Jemmy Jumps? Nipperkin and a thousand of such admirable fooleries fall to nothing, and the departure, therefore, of such an actor as Munden is a dramatic calamity. On the night that this inestimable humourist took farewell of the public, he also took his benefit – a benefit in which the public assuredly did not participate. The play was Coleman's *Poor Gentleman*, with Tom Dibdin's farce of *Past Ten O'Clock*. Reader, we all know Munden in Sir Robert Bramble and old tobacco-complexioned Dozey; we all have seen the old hearty baronet in his light sky-blue coat and genteel cocked hat, and we have all seen the weather-beaten old pensioner, dear old Dozey, tacking about the stage in that intense blue sea livery, drunk as heart could wish, and right valorous in memory. On this night Munden seemed, like the Gladiator, 'to rally life's whole energies to die'; and as we were present at this great display of his powers, and as this will be the last opportunity that will ever be afforded us to speak of this admirable performer, we shall 'consecrate', as old John Buncle says, 'a paragraph to him'.

The house was full. *Full*! – pshaw! that's an empty word! The house was stuffed, crammed with people – crammed from the swing-door of the pit to the back-seat in the banished *one shilling*. A quart of audience may be said (vintner-like, may it be said) to have been squeezed into a pint of theatre. Every hearty playgoing Londoner who remembered Munden years agone mustered up his courage and his money for this benefit, and middle-aged people were therefore by no means scarce. The comedy chosen for the occasion is one that travels a long way without a guard – it is not until the third or fourth act, we think, that Sir Robert Bramble appears on the stage. When he entered, his reception was earnest, noisy, outrageous; waving of hats and handkerchiefs, deafening shouts, clamorous beating of sticks – all the various ways in which the heart is accustomed to manifest its joy – were had recourse to on this occasion. Mrs Bamfield worked away with a sixpenny fan till she scudded only under bare poles. Mr Whittington wore out the ferule of a new nine-and-sixpenny umbrella. Gratitude did great damage on the joyful occasion.

The old performer, the veteran, as he appropriately called himself in the farewell speech, was plainly overcome; he pressed his hands together, he planted one solidly on his breast, he bowed, he sidled, he cried. When the noise subsided (which it invariably does at last), the comedy proceeded and Munden gave an admirable picture of the rich, eccentric, charitable old batchelor baronet who goes about with Humphrey Dobbin at his heels and philanthropy in his heart. How crustily and yet how kindly he takes Humphrey's contradictions. How readily he puts himself into an attitude for arguing. How tenderly he gives a loose to his heart on the apprehension of Frederick's due. In truth he played Sir Robert in his very ripest manner; and it was impossible not to feel in the very midst of pleasure, regret that Munden should then be before us for the last time.

In the farce he became richer and richer. Old Dozey is a plant from Greenwich. The bronzed face and neck to match, the long curtain of a coat, the straggling white hair, the propensity, the determined attachment to grog, are all from Greenwich. Munden as Dozey seems never to have been out of action, sun, and drink. He looks (alas! he *looked*) fireproof. His face and throat were dried like a raisin, and his legs walked under the rum-and-water with all the indecision which that inestimable beverage usually inspires. It is truly tacking, not walking. He *steers* at a table, and the tide of grog now and then bears him off the point. On this night he seemed to us to be doomed to fall in action; and we therefore looked at him, as some of the *Victory's* crew are said to have gazed upon Nelson, with a consciousness that his ardour and his uniform were worn for the last time. In the scene where Dozey describes a sea-fight, the actor never was greater, and he seemed the personification of an old seventy-four! His coat hung like a flag at his poop. His phiz was not a whit less highly coloured than one of those lustrous visages which generally super-intend the head of a ship. There was something cumbrous, indecisive, and awful in his veerings. Once afloat, it appeared impossible for him to come to his moorings; once at anchor, it did not seem an easy thing to get him under weigh.

The time, however, came for the fall of the curtain and for the fall of Munden. The farce of the night was finished. The farce of the long forty years' play was over. He stepped forward, not as Dozey, but as Munden, and we heard him address us from the stage for the last time. He trusted – unwisely, we think – to a written paper. He *read* of 'heartfelt recollections' and 'indelible impressions'. He stammered and he pressed his heart, and put on his spec-tacles, and blundered his written gratitudes, and wiped his eyes, and bowed and stood, and at last staggered away for ever. The plan of his farewell was bad, but the long life of excellence which really made his farewell pathetic overcame all defects, and the people and Joe Munden parted like lovers. Well! Farewell to the Rich Old Heart. May thy retirement be as full of repose as thy public life was full of excellence. We must all have our farewell benefits in our turn.

The London Magazine, July 1824
(unsigned, but attributed to Lamb by Thomas Shepherd
Munden, the actor's son and biographer)

Leigh Hunt
The Death of Elliston

We have to lament, with all the lovers of genuine comedy and fervid animal spirits, the death of our old favourite Elliston, who was carried off last Friday by apoplexy – a death not peculiar, as many suppose, to the sluggish and over-fed, but too common to those who have lived a life of excitement, and drawn much upon sanguine heads. Elliston was of no spare class of men either: he

seems to have eaten and drunk stoutly enough, perhaps too much for one who
had so much to do, and whose faculties were half made up of sanguineness.
We believe the wonder is that he lasted so long, especially as he had had severe
attacks of illness on and off for a good many years, some of them of a mortal
aspect. We remember hearing a long time back that his hands had become
useless with palsy; he recovered that shock, gesticulated as much as ever, and
not long since had another attack. He recovered again, appeared on the stage
as if nothing had happened, and was meditating, we believe, new characters,
when he was taken off. A man of a less vital order would have been killed
long ago. But the mystery of life, in some people, seems to carry itself on in
spite of obstacles. They have more of the *life* of life in them than others.
This is what is understood by the familiar but no less mysterious term, animal
spirits. We have a theory respecting the cause of it, with which we will not
trouble the reader. All we shall say is, that we take a man's parentage to have
a great deal more to do with it than his education.

The death of a comic actor is felt more than that of a tragedian. He has
sympathized more with us in our every-day feelings, and has given us more
amusement. Death with a tragedian seems all in the way of business.
Tragedians have been dying all their lives. They are a 'grave' people. But it
seems a hard thing upon the comic actor to quench his airiness and vivacity –
to stop him in his happy career – to make us think of him, on the sudden,
with solemnity – and to miss him for ever. We could have 'better spared a
better man'. It is something like losing a merry child. We have not got used
to the gravity. Mrs Siddons, the other day, was missed far less than Elliston
will be. She had withdrawn, it is true, for some time; but her life was, in a
manner, always withdrawn. She lived with the tragic pall round her. Kemble
was missed by those who had been used to him; but he was missed rather as
a picture than a man. There is something of this in the popularity of Charles
Kemble; but as the picture is of a more gallant and agreeable kind, none of
the family will have been so cordially lamented as he will be when he dies –
next century: for we suppose he does not mean even to grow old for these
forty years.

Mr Elliston was the best comedian, in the highest sense of the word, that
we have seen. Others equalled him in some particular points; Lewis surpassed
him in airiness; but there was no gentleman comedian who comprised so
many qualities of his art as he did, or who could diverge so well into those
parts of tragedy which find a connecting link with the graver powers of the
comedian in their gracefulness and humanity. He was the best Wildair, the
best Archer, the best Aranza; and carrying the seriousness of Aranza a little
further, or making him a *tragic gentleman* instead of a comic, he became the
best Mortimer, and even the best Macbeth, of any performer who excelled
in comedy. When Charles Kemble acts comedy, he gives you the idea of an
actor who has come out of the chivalrous part of tragedy. It is grace and show
that are most natural to him – the ideal of mediocrity. Elliston being naturally
a comedian, and comedy of the highest class demanding a greater sympathy
with actual flesh and blood, his tragedy, though less graceful than Charles

Kemble's, was more natural and cordial. He suffered and was shaken more. The other, in his greatest grief, is but like the statue of some Apollo Belvedere vivified, frowning in beauty, and making a grace of his sorrow. The god remains impassive to ordinary suffering. Elliston's features were nothing nearly so handsome or so finely cut as the other's, but they were more sensitive and intelligent. He had nothing of the poetry of tragedy; the other has the form of it; but Elliston, in Macbeth, could give you something of the weak and sanguine and misgiving usurper; and, in Mortimer, in the *Iron Chest*, he has moved the audience to tears. It ought not to be forgotten that he restored that character to the stage when John Kemble had killed it with his frigidity.

The tragedy of this accomplished actor was, however, only an elongation, or drawing out, of the graver and more sensitive part of his comedy. It was in comedy that he was the master. When Kean appeared and extinguished Kemble, Elliston seems prudently to have put out his tragic lamp. In comedy, after the death of Lewis, he remained without a rival. He had three distinguished excellencies – dry humour, gentlemanly mirth, and fervid gallantry. His features were a little too round, and his person latterly became a great deal too much so. But we speak of him in his best days. His face, in one respect, was of that rare order which is peculiarly fitted for the expression of enjoyment: it laughed with the eyes as well as mouth. His eyes, which were not large, grew smaller when he was merry, and twinkled with glee and archness; his smile was full of enjoyment, and yet the moment he shook his head with a satirical deprecation, or dropped the expression of his face into an innuendo, nothing could be drier or more angular than his mouth. There was a generosity in his style, both in its greater and smaller points. He understood all the little pretended or avowed arts of a gentleman, when he was conversing or complimenting, or making love – everything which implied the necessity of attention to the other person, and a just, and as it were, mutual consciousness of the graces of life. His manners had the true *minuet dance* spirit of gentility – the knowledge how to give and take, with a certain recognition of the merits of either side, even in the midst of raillery. And then his voice was remarkable for its union of the manly with the melodious; and as a lover nobody approached him. Certainly nobody approached a woman as he did. It was the reverse of that preposterous style of *touch and avoid* – that embracing at arm's length, and hinting of a mutual touch on the shoulders – by which the ladies and gentlemen of the stage think fit to distinguish themselves from the characters they perform, and even the Pollys and Macheaths propitiate our good opinion. Elliston made out that that it was no shame to love a woman, and no shame in her to return his passion. He took her hand, he cherished it against his bosom, he watched the moving of her countenance, he made the space less and less between them, and as he at length burst out into some exclamation of 'Charming!' or 'Lovely!' his voice trembled, not with the weakness, but with the strength and fervour of its emotion. All the love on the stage, since this (with the exception of Macready's domestic tenderness), is not worth two pence, and fit only to beget waiters.

The Tatler, 10 July 1831

Charles Lamb
Ellistoniana

My acquaintance with the pleasant creature, whose loss we all deplore, was but slight. My first introduction to E., which afterwards ripened into an acquaintance a little on this side of intimacy, was over a counter in the Leamington Spa Library, then newly entered upon by a branch of his family. E., whom nothing misbecame – to auspicate, I suppose, the filial concern, and set it a-going with a lustre – was serving in person two damsels fair who had come into the shop ostensibly to inquire for some new publication, but in reality to have a sight of the illustrious shopman, hoping some conference. With what an air did he reach down the volume, dispassionately giving his opinion of the worth of the work in question, and launching out into a dissertation on its comparative merits with those of certain publications of a similar stamp, its rivals! His enchanted customers fairly hanging on his lips, subdued to their authoritative sentence. So have I seen a gentleman in comedy *acting* the shopman. So Lovelace sold his gloves in King Street. I admired the histrionic art by which he contrived to carry clean away every notion of disgrace from the occupation he had so generously submitted to; and from that hour I judged him, with no after repentance, to be a person with whom it would be a felicity to be more acquainted.

To descant upon his merits as a comedian would be superfluous. With his blended private and professional habits alone I have to do – that harmonious fusion of the manners of the player into those of everyday life which brought the stage-boards into streets and dining-parlours, and kept up the play when the play was ended. 'I like Wrench', a friend was saying to him one day, 'because he is the same natural, easy creature on the stage that he is *off*.' 'My case exactly,' retorted Elliston, with a charming forgetfulness that the converse of a proposition does not always lead to the same conclusion; 'I am the same person *off* the stage as I am *on*.' The inference at first sight seems identical; but examine it a little, and it confesses only that the one performer was never, and the other always, *acting*.

And in truth this was the charm of Elliston's private deportment. You had spirited performance always going on before your eyes, with nothing to pay. As where a monarch takes up his casual abode for the night, the poorest hovel which he honours by his sleeping in it becomes *ipso facto* for that time a palace, so wherever Elliston walked, sat, or stood still, there was the theatre. He carried about with him his pit, boxes, and galleries, and set up his portable play-house at corners of streets and in the market-places. Upon flintiest pavements he trod the boards still; and if his theme chanced to be passionate, the green baize carpet of tragedy spontaneously rose beneath his feet. Now, this was hearty, and showed a love for his art. So Apelles *always* painted – in thought. So G.D. *always* poetizes. I hate a lukewarm artist. I have known actors – and some of them of Elliston's own stamp – who shall have agreeably been amusing you in the part of a rake or a coxcomb, through the two or three hours of their dramatic existence; but no sooner does the curtain fall with its leaden clatter, but a spirit of lead seems to seize on all their faculties. They emerge sour, morose persons, intolerable to their families, servants, etc. Another shall have been expanding your heart with generous deeds and sentiments till it even beats with yearnings of universal sympathy: you absolutely long to go home and do some good action. The play seems tedious till you can get fairly out of the house and realize your laudable intentions. At length the final bell rings, and this cordial representative of all that is amiable in human breasts steps forth, – a miser. Elliston was more of a piece. Did he *play* Ranger, and did Ranger fill the general bosom of the town with satisfaction? Why should *he* not be Ranger, and diffuse the same cordial satisfaction among his private circles? With *his* temperament, *his* animal spirits, *his* good-nature, *his* follies, perchance, could he do better than identify himself with his impersonation? Are we like a pleasant rake, or coxcomb, on the stage, and give ourselves airs of aversion for the identical character presented to us in actual life? Or what would the performer have gained by divesting himself of the impersonation? Could the man Elliston have been essentially different from his part, even if he had avoided to reflect to us studiously, in private circles, the airy briskness, the forwardness, the scape-goat trickeries of the prototype?

'But there is something not natural in this everlasting *acting*; we want the real man.'

Are you quite sure that it is not the man himself, whom you cannot, or will not, see under some adventitious trappings, which, nevertheless, sit not at all inconsistently upon him? What if it is the nature of some men to be highly artificial? The fault is least reprehensible in *players*. Cibber was his own Foppington, with almost as much wit as Vanbrugh could add to it.

'My conceit of his person' – it is Ben Jonson speaking of Lord Bacon – 'was never increased towards him by his *place* or *honours*. But I have and do reverence him for the *greatness* that was only proper to himself; in that he seemed to me ever one of the *greatest* men that had been in many ages. In his adversity I ever prayed that Heaven would give him strength; for *greatness* he could not want.'

The quality here commended was scarcely less conspicuous in the subject of these idle reminiscences than in my Lord Verulam. Those who have imagined that an unexpected elevation to the direction of a great London theatre affected the consequence of Elliston, or at all changed his nature, knew not the essential *greatness* of the man whom they disparage. It was my fortune to encounter him near St Dunstan's Church (which, with its punctual giants, is now no more than dust and a shadow), on the morning of his election to that high office. Grasping my hand with a look of significance, he only uttered, 'Have you heard the news?' Then, with another look following up the blow, he subjoined, 'I am the future manager of Drury Lane Theatre.' Breathless as he saw me, he stayed not for congratulation or reply, but mutely stalked away, leaving me to chew upon his new-blown dignities at leisure. In fact, nothing could be said to it. Expressive silence alone could muse his praise. This was in his *great* style.

But was he less *great* (be witness, O ye powers of Equanimity that supported in the ruins of Carthage the consular exile, and more recently transmuted, for a more illustrious exile, the barren constableship of Elba into an image of Imperial France) when, in melancholy after-years, again, much near the same spot, I met him when that sceptre had been wrested from his hand, and his dominion was curtailed to the petty managership and part proprietorship of the small Olympic, *his Elba*? He still played nightly upon the boards of Drury, but in parts, alas! allotted to him, not magnificently distributed by him. Waiving his great loss as nothing, and magnificently sinking the sense of fallen *material* grandeur in the more liberal resentment of depreciations done to his more lofty *intellectual* pretensions, 'Have you heard' (his customary exordium) – 'have you heard', said he, 'how they treat me? They put me in *comedy*.' Thought I – but his finger on his lips forbade any verbal interruption – 'Where could they have put you better?' Then, after a pause – 'Where I formerly played Romeo, I now play Mercutio;' and so again he stalked away, neither staying nor caring for responses.

Oh! it was a rich scene – but Sir A—— C——, the best of storytellers and surgeons, who mends a lame narrative almost as well as he sets a fracture, alone could do justice to it – that I was a witness to in the tarnished room (that, had once been green) of that same little Olympic. There, after his deposition from Imperial Drury, he substituted a throne. That Olympic Hill was his 'highest heaven', himself 'Jove in his chair'. There he sat in state, while before him, on complaint of prompter, was brought for judgment – how shall I describe her? – one of those little tawdry things that flirt at the tails of choruses, a probationer for the town in either of its senses, the pertest little drab, a dirty fringe and appendage of the lamp's smoke, who, it seems, on some disapprobation expressed by a 'highly respectable' audience had precipitately quitted her station on the boards, and withdrawn her small talents in disgust.

'And how dare you', said her manager, assuming a censorial severity which would have crushed the confidence of a Vestris, and disarmed that beautiful Rebel herself of her professional caprices – I verily believe he thought *her* standing before him – 'how dare you, madam, withdraw yourself, without a notice, from your theatrical duties?' 'I was hissed, sir.' 'And you have the presumption to decide upon the taste of the town?' 'I don't know that, sir, but I will never stand to be hissed', was the subjoinder of young Confidence. When, gathering up his features into one significant mass of wonder, pity, and expostulatory indignation, in a lesson never to have been lost upon a creature less forward than she who stood before him, his words were these: 'They have hissed *me*.'

'Twas the identical argument *a fortiori* which the son of Peleus uses to Lycaeon trembling under his lance, to persuade him to take his destiny with a good grace. 'I too am mortal'. And it is to be believed that in both cases the rhetoric missed of its application for want of a proper understanding with the faculties of the respective recipients.

'Quite an Opera pit', he said to me as he was courteously conducting me over the benches of his Surrey Theatre – the last retreat and recess of his every-day waning grandeur.

Those who knew Elliston, will know the *manner* in which he pronounced the latter sentence of the few words I am about to record. One proud day to me he took his roast mutton with us in the Temple, to which I had super-added a preliminary haddock. After a rather plentiful partaking of the meagre banquet, not unrefreshed with the humbler sort of liquors, I made a sort of apology for the humility of the fare, observing that for my own part I never ate but of one dish at dinner. 'I too never eat but one thing at dinner,' was his reply; then, after a pause, 'reckoning fish as nothing.' The manner was all. It was as if by one peremptory sentence he had decreed the annihilation of all the savoury esculents which the pleasant and nutritious-food-giving Ocean pours forth upon poor humans from her watery bosom. This was *greatness*, tempered with considerate tenderness to the feelings of his scanty but welcoming entertainer.

Great wert thou in thy life, Robert William Elliston! and *not lessened* in thy death, if report speak truly, which says that thou didst direct that thy mortal remains should repose under no inscription but one of pure *Latinity*. Classical was thy bringing up! and beautiful was the feeling on thy last bed, which, connecting the man with the boy, took thee back to thy latest exercise of imagination, to the days when, undreaming of Theatres and Managerships, thou wert a scholar, and an early ripe one, under the roofs builded by the munificent and pious Colet. For thee the Pauline Muses weep. In elegies, that shall silence this crude prose, they shall celebrate thy praise.

The Englishman's Magazine, August 1831

William Hazlitt
Liston

The Taming of the Shrew was revived here* on Wednesday, with the original words and additional songs. We however missed Christopher Sly, that supreme dramatic critic, who should have sat in lordly judgment on the piece, and given a drunken relief to it. This representing of a play within a play (of which Shakspeare was fond) produces an agreeable theatrical perspective – it is like painting a picture in a picture – and intimates pointedly enough that

* Drury Lane.

all are but shadows, the pageants of a dream. We also missed Mr Liston in this part; for we understand that he has some good quips and crotchets about it. Unless we saw him, we cannot pretend to say how he would do it; for we consider Mr Liston in the light of an author rather than of an actor, and he makes his best parts out of his own head or face, in a sort of *brown study*, with very little reference to the text. He has nevertheless more comic humour oozing out of his features and person than any other actor in our remembrance, or than we have any positive evidence of since the time of Hogarth. No one is *stultified*, no one is *mystified* like him – no one is so deep in absurdity, no one so full of vacancy; no one puzzles so over a doubt, or goes the whole length of an extravagance like him – no one chuckles so over his own conceit, or is so dismayed at finding his mistake: the genius of folly spreads its shining gloss over his face, tickles his nose, laughs in his eyes, makes his teeth chatter in his head, or draws up every muscle into a look of indescribable dullness, or freezes his whole person into a lump of ice (as in Lubin Log) or relaxes it into the very thaw and dissolution of all common sense (as in his Lord Grizzle). Munden's acting (which many prefer, and in this number may be included Mr Liston himself) was external, overdone, and aimed at the galleries – it was a sort of prodigious and inspired *face-making* – Liston's humour bubbles up of itself, and runs over from the mere fulness of the conception. If he does not go out of himself, he looks into himself, and ruminates on the idea of the idle, the quaint, and the absurd, till it does his heart good within him, and makes 'the lungs of others crow like chanticleer'. Munden's expressions, if they could have been taken off on the spot, would have made a capital set of grotesque masks: Liston's would make a succession of original comic sketches, as rich as they are true: – Mr Wilkie failed in attempting one of them – his pencil was not oily and unctuous enough. We have seen many better comedians, that is, better imitators of existing or supposed characters and manners – such as Emery, Little Simmons, Dowton, and others – we know no other actor who has such a fund of drollery in himself, or that makes one laugh in the same hearty unrestrained manner, free from all care or controul, that we do with Sancho Panza or Parson Adams. We have heard a story of Mr Liston being prevented by some accident from attending his professional duties, and wrapping himself up in a flannel gown and heart's-content over a winter fire, to read our good old English novelists for a fortnight together. What fine marginal notes his face would make! Which would he enjoy most, the blanket falling and discovering philosopher Square behind it, or the drawing up of the curtain and the broad laugh of the pit? We will answer that question for him. The meanest apprentice that sees a play for the first time from the gallery, has more pleasure than the most admired actor that ever trod the stage: there is more satisfaction in reading one page of a sterling author with good faith and good will, than the writer had in the composition or even the success of all his works put together. The admiration we bestow on others comes from the heart; but never returns back to it. Vanity closes up the avenues, or envy poisons it.

The Examiner, 18 May 1828

William Hazlitt
Kean as Shylock

Mr Kean (of whom report had spoken highly) last night made his appearance at Drury-Lane Theatre in the character of Shylock. For voice, eye, action, and expression, no actor has come out for many years at all equal to him. The applause, from the first scene to the last, was general, loud, and uninterrupted. Indeed, the very first scene in which he comes on with Bassanio and Antonio, shewed the master in his art, and at once decided the opinion of the audience. Perhaps it was the most perfect of any. Notwithstanding the complete success of Mr Kean in the part of Shylock, we question whether he will not become a greater favourite in other parts. There was a lightness and vigour in his tread, a buoyancy and elasticity of spirit, a fire and animation, which would accord better with almost any other character than with the morose, sullen, inward, inveterate, inflexible malignity of Shylock. The character of Shylock is that of a man brooding over one idea, that of its wrongs, and bent on one unalterable purpose, that of revenge. In conveying a profound impression of this feeling, or in embodying the general conception of rigid and uncontroul-able self-will, equally proof against every sentiment of humanity or prejudice of opinion, we have seen actors more successful than Mr Kean; but in giving effect to the conflict of passions arising out of the contrasts of situation, in varied vehemence of declamation, in keenness of sarcasm, in the rapidity of his transitions from one tone and feeling to another, in propriety and novelty of action, presenting a succession of striking pictures, and giving perpetually fresh shocks of delight and surprise, it would be difficult to single out a competitor. The fault of his acting was (if we may hazard the objection), an over-display of the resources of the art, which gave too much relief to the hard, impenetrable, dark groundwork of the character of Shylock. It would be endless to point out individual beauties, where almost every passage was received with equal and deserved applause. We thought, in one or two instances, the pauses in the voice were too long, and too great a reliance was placed on the expression of the countenance, which is a language intelligible only to a part of the house.

The rest of the play was, upon the whole, very respectably cast. It would be an equivocal compliment to say of Miss Smith that her acting often reminds us of Mrs Siddons. Rae played Bassanio; but the abrupt and harsh tones of his voice are not well adapted to the mellifluous cadences of Shakespear's verse.

The Morning Chronicle, 27 January 1814

Mr Kean appeared again in Shylock, and by his admirable and expressive manner of giving the part, fully sustained the reputation he had acquired by his former representation of it, though he laboured under the disadvantage of a considerable hoarseness. He assumed a greater appearance of age and feebleness than on the first night, but the general merit of his playing was the same. His style of acting is, if we may use the expression, more significant, more pregnant with meaning, more varied and alive in every part, than any we have almost ever witnessed. The character never stands still; there is no vacant pause in the action; the eye is never silent. For depth and force of conception, we have seen actors whom we should prefer to Mr Kean in Shylock; for brilliant and masterly execution, none. It is not saying too much of him, though it is saying a great deal, that he has all that Mr Kemble wants of perfection. He reminds us of the descriptions of the 'far-darting eye' of Garrick. We are anxious to see him in Norval and Richard, and anticipate more complete satisfaction from his performance of the latter part, than from the one in which he has already stamped his reputation with the public.

Miss Smith played Portia with much more animation than the last time we saw her, and in delivering the fine apostrophe on Mercy, in the trial-scene, was highly impressive.

The Morning Chronicle, 2 February 1814

Leigh Hunt
Kean as Richard III

The Editor for the first time since his imprisonment went to the Theatre on Monday last, when he saw Mr Kean; and it must not be imputed to the fastidiousness of criticism, if he confesses that upon the whole he was disappointed. Indeed it is but proper, and may in some measure perhaps account for the disappointment, to mention that his expectations had been raised to a very high pitch by the reports in favour of that performer, expectations to which he gave way the more readily, inasmuch as he had been in the habit, for years, of objecting to the artificial style of the actors lately in vogue; so that he had enthusiastically concluded that he was now going to realize, on the sudden, all that had ever appeared to him natural and desirable in theatrical representation. It is right to mention also (thanks to the magnificent inconvenience of these fine theatres!) that he was not as near to the stage as he ought to have been; and it should not be omitted that many of the most intelligent as well as ardent admirers of this gentleman think him much fallen off from what he was the last season.

Neither of these circumstances, however, can account, in his mind, for the *sort* of deficiency which Mr Kean appeared to exhibit. It was not that the actor seemed to want only to be perfectly seen and heard, or to be inferior in degree to what he might have been a season before; but that the general run of his style was not of the cast that we had been led to anticipate. It seemed too artificial to be a mere falling off from nature. It was artificial in the general, and natural only in the particular; its native parts were the exceptions; in other words, and to state at once our conclusion respecting him, as far as this one character can enable us to come to any, Mr Kean appeared to us, during the greater part of his performance, to be nothing but a first-rate actor of the ordinary, stagy class, and to start only occasionally into passages of truth and originality.

To come a little more to particulars. We expected to find no declamation, no common rant, no puttings forth of the old oratorical right hand, no speech-making and attitudinizing at one, no implication, in short, of a set of spectators; but something genuine and unconscious, something that moved, looked, and spoke solely under the impulse of the immediate idea, something as natural in its way, with proper allowance, of course, for the gravity of the interests going forward, as the man who enters his room after a walk, takes off his hat, pinches off one glove and throws it into it, gives a pull down to his coat or a pull up to his neckcloth, and makes up the fireplace with a rub of his hands and a draught of the air through his teeth. If this should be thought too much to demand in tragedy, it is only because we have been accustomed to the reverse – to art instead of nature. We are persuaded that it is quite practicable, that it would take, as the phrase is, immediately, and that it wants only a daring genius, with the genuine boldness and unaccommodating self-respect of enthusiasm, to push it to its utmost.

Such was the actor we expected to find in Mr Kean; but his Richard, for one character at least, does not prove him to be the person. In the ordinary scenes, for instance, such as those with Buckingham, with his mother, with the young Princes, and in all the more level parts of the dialogue, he was no better than Mr Kemble; that is to say, without meaning any invidious allusion to that gentleman, he was no better than the best kind of actor in the artificial style; he dealt out his syllables, and stood finely, and strutted at the set off of a speech, just as other well-received performers do; and he is much farther gone in stage trickery than we supposed him to be, particularly in the old violent contrasts when delivering an equivoque, dropping his voice too consciously from a serious line to a sly one, and fairly putting it to the house as a good joke.

On the other hand, he has occasional bursts, and touches of nature, such as might be expected from the actor we had fancied to ourselves, and such as would go near to make us think that the general run of his style was really different from what it used to be, were those who are once in love with nature, genuinely and heartily, apt to let an inferior habit get the better of them. We wish the reader to keep in mind that we look upon him to be equal, at all times, to the best actors in vogue; but in particular passages, he undoubtedly goes far beyond any of them, and makes us regret that he who can be so natural, so nobly familiar, in half a dozen instances, should not conduct himself with the same nativeness throughout. Nothing, for example, can take leave, with better effect, of the usual solemn pedantry of the stage than that action of rubbing his hands, to which he gives way occasionally in his part when he thinks his views are succeeding. In some characters there might be a vulgarity and an over-excitement in it; but people of Richard's cast of ambition are seldom very refined, and their joy is not bound to be philosophical. His other gestures too, now and then, and the turns of his countenance, tend in a very happy manner to unite common life with tragedy – which is the great stage-desideratum; and it would be impossible to express in a deeper manner the intentness of Richard's mind upon the battle that was about to take place, or to quit the scene with an abruptness more self-recollecting, pithy, and familiar, than by the reverie in which he stands drawing lines upon the ground with the point of his sword, and his sudden recovery of himself with a 'Good night'.

The more we think on his passages of this description the more we regret our disappointment upon the whole, and the happier we should be to unsay any of our unfavourable remarks upon seeing him in another character. Of his bad voice, we should think little or nothing if he met our wishes in other respects, though, to say the truth, it grew deplorable enough towards the conclusion, and resembled a hackney-coachman's at one o'clock in the morning. It is not, we suspect, essentially bad; and it is to be wished he could find some means of keeping it in proper tone. While he was about mending himself in this particular, we would also suggest that he ought not to get under such a large hat and feathers as he seems fond of; and it might be as well also, if he would contrive to get a little handsomer deformity – to inflict a reasonable lump on his leg – instead of the enormous and holster-like pad which he puts into his stocking for that purpose.

The Examiner, 26 February 1815

William Hazlitt
Kean as Othello

Othello was played here on Saturday to a crowded house. There were two new appearances – Mr Maywood as Iago, and a young lady as Desdemona. The name of this young debutante is not announced; but her reception was exceedingly flattering. Her face is handsome, her person elegant, her voice sweet, and her general deportment graceful and easy. There was also a considerable portion of tenderness and delicacy of feeling in several of the passages; but perhaps less than the character would bear. The only faults which we think it necessary to mention in her performance were, a too continual movement of the hands up and down, and sometimes a monotonous cadence in the recitation of the blank verse. Mr Maywood's Iago had some of the faults which we have noticed in his former characters; but in the most trying scenes in the third act with Othello, we thought him exceedingly happy and successful. His conception was just, and his execution effective. There was a cold stillness in his manner which was more frightful than the expression of the most inveterate malignity. He seemed to crawl and watch for his prey like the spider, instead of darting upon it like the serpent. In the commencement of the part his timidity appeared to prevent him from doing justice to his intention, and once or twice his voice grew loud and unmanageable, so as to excite some marks of disapprobation. Mr Kean's Othello is, we suppose, the finest piece of acting in the world. It is impossible either to describe or praise it adequately. We have never seen any actor so wrought upon, so 'perplexed in the extreme'. The energy of passion, as it expresses itself in action, is not the most terrific part; it is the agony of his soul, showing itself in looks and tones of voice. In one part, where he listens in dumb despair to the fiend-like insinuations of Iago, he presented the very face, the marble aspect of Dante's Count Ugolino. On his fixed eyelids 'Horror sat plumed'. In another part, where a gleam of hope or of tenderness returns to subdue the tumult of his passions, his voice broke in faltering accents from his over-charged breast. His lips might be said less to utter words, than to bleed drops of blood gushing from his heart. An instance of this was in his pronunciation of the line 'Of one that loved not wisely but too well'. The whole of this last speech was indeed given with exquisite force and beauty. We only object to the virulence with which he delivers the last line, and with which he stabs himself – a virulence which Othello would neither feel against himself at that moment, nor against the turbaned Turk (whom he had slain) at such a distance of time. His exclamation on seeing his wife, 'I cannot think but Desdemona's honest', was 'the glorious triumph of exceeding love'; a thought flashing conviction on his mind, and irradiating his countenance with joy, like sudden sunshine. In fact, almost every scene or sentence in this extraordinary exhibition is a masterpiece of natural passion. The convulsed motion of the hands, and the involuntary swellings of the veins of the forehead in some of the most painful situations, should not only suggest topics of critical panegyric, but might furnish studies to the painter or anatomist.

The Times, 27 October 1817

Leigh Hunt
Kean as Othello

Mr Kean has returned from his tour to France and Italy – a very proper relaxation for a man of his talents – and has performed in the course of the week *Richard the Third* and *Othello*. We saw the latter on Thursday evening; and with all our experience of the stage, and with all our scepticism as to the powers of the very best actors in characters from Shakespeare, we never witnessed a performance that struck us so forcibly. It brought back upon us the earnestness and implicit attention of our younger days. We have admired Mrs Siddons, been infinitely amused with Lewis, been sore with laughing at Munden, been charmed with Mrs Jordan; but we never saw anything that so completely held us suspended and heart-stricken, as Mr Kean's Othello. In all parts it is as complete as actor can shew it – in the previous composure of its dignity, in its soldier-like repression of common impulse, in the deep agitation of its first jealousy, in the low-voiced and faltering affection of occasional ease, in the burst of intolerable anguish, in the consciousness that rage has hurt its dignity and ruined the future completeness of its character, in the consequent melancholy farewell to its past joys and greatness, in the desperate savageness of its revenge, in its half-exhausted reception of the real truth, and lastly, in the final resumption of a kind of moral attitude and dignity, at the moment when it uses that fine deliberate artifice and sheathes the dagger in its breast.

If we might venture to point out any parts the most admirable in this performance, it would be the low and agitated affectation of quiet discourse, in which he first canvasses the subject with Iago, the mild and tremulous farewell to 'the tranquil mind, the plumed troop', etc., in which his voice occasionally uttered little tones of endearment, his head shook, and his visage quivered, and thirdly, those still more awfully mild tones in which he trembles and halts through those dreadful lines beginning –

> Had it pleased heaven
> To try me with affliction; had he rained
> All kind of sores and shames on my bare head.

His louder bitterness and his rage were always fine; but such passages as these, we think, were still finer. You might fancy you saw the water quivering in his eyes.

And here two things struck us very forcibly; first, how impossible it is for actor and audience to be both as they ought to be in such large theatres, since Mr Kean's quietest and noblest passages could certainly not have been audible in the galleries; and second, how much an actor's talent must be modified by his own character off the stage, an observation we may reasonably make when it leans to the favourable side; for we conjecture from anecdotes that are before the public, that Mr Kean's temper is hasty, and his disposition excellent and generous; and it is of passion and natural generosity that Othello's character is made up. For this reason we can never help being sceptical about Garrick's excellence in characters of deep and serious interest; since off the stage, he was little better than a quick-eyed trifler, full of phrases of garbling jargon, and coarse-minded withal.

Of the two performers – Mrs West who repeated Desdemona and Mr Clary, who changed from Othello to Iago – we have nothing to add to our former observations, except that the lady performed still better than before. There is a new afterpiece here, which is below criticism. Mr Kean's Othello is the masterpiece of the living stage.

The Examiner, 4 October 1818

G. H. Lewes
Edmund Kean

The greatest artist is he who is greatest in the highest reaches of his art, even although he may lack the qualities necessary for the adequate execution of some minor details. It is not by his faults, but by his excellences, that we measure a great man. The strength of a beam is measured by its weakest part, of a man by his strongest. Thus estimated, Edmund Kean was incomparably the greatest actor I have seen, although even warm admirers must admit that he had many and serious defects. His was not a flexible genius. He was a very imperfect mime – or more correctly speaking, his miming power, though admirable within a certain range, was singularly limited in its range. He was tricky and flashy in style. But he was an actor of such splendid endowments in the highest departments of the art, that no one in our day can be named of equal rank, unless it be Rachel, who was as a woman what he was as a man. The irregular splendour of his power was felicitously characterized in the saying of Coleridge, that 'seeing Keen act was reading Shakspeare by flashes of lightning', so brilliant and so startling were the sudden illuminations, and so murky the dull intervals. Critics who had formed their ideal on the Kemble School were shocked at Kean's want of dignity, and at his fitful elocution, sometimes thrillingly effective, at other times deplorably tame and careless; in their angry protests they went so far as to declare him 'a mere mountebank'. Not so thought the pit; not so thought less biased critics. He stirred the general heart with such a rush of mighty power, impressed himself so vividly by accent, look and gesture, that it was as vain to protest against his defects as it was for French critics to insist upon Shakspeare's want of *bienséance* and *bon goût*. Could audiences have remained unmoved, they might have lent a willing ear to remonstrances, and laughed at or hissed some grave offences against taste and sense. But no audience could be unmoved; all defects were overlooked or disregarded, because it was impossible to watch Kean as Othello, Shylock, Richard, or Sir Giles Overreach, without being strangely shaken by the terror, and the pathos, and the passion of a stormy spirit uttering itself in tones of irresistible power. His imitators have been mostly ridiculous, simply because they reproduced the manner and the mannerism, but could not reproduce the power which made these endurable. It is a fact little understood by imitators that the spots on the sun in nowise warm the world and that a deficiency in light and heat cannot be replaced by a prodigality of spots.

Although I was a little boy when I first saw Kean, in 1825, and but a youth when, in 1832, he quitted the stage for ever, yet so ineffaceable are the impressions his acting produced, that I feel far more at ease in speaking of his excellences and defects than I should feel in speaking of many actors seen only a dozen years ago. It will be understood that I was in no condition then to form an estimate of his qualities, and that I criticize from memory. Yet my memory of him is so vivid that I can see his looks and gestures and hear his thrilling voice as if these were sensations of yesterday. Perhaps the defects which I now recognize would be more salient were I now to witness the performances. There is a softening, idealizing tendency in memory which may exaggerate the degree of excellence. Still these are only matters of degree; and I think that my appreciation of the actor is on the whole little disturbed by such influences. At any rate, I will try to set down fairly what a retrospect discloses.

Kean's range of expression, as already hinted, was very limited. His physical aptitudes were such as confined him to the strictly tragic passions; and for these he was magnificently endowed. Small and insignificant in figure, he could at times become impressively commanding by the lion-like power and grace of his bearing. I remember, the last time I saw him play Othello, how puny he appeared beside Macready, until in the third act, when roused by Iago's taunts and insinuations, he moved towards him with a gouty hobble, seized him by the throat, and, in a well-known explosion, 'Villain! Be sure you prove', etc., seemed to swell into a stature which made Macready appear small. On that very evening, when gout made it difficult for him to display his accustomed grace, when a drunken hoarseness had ruined the once matchless voice, such was the irresistible pathos – manly, not tearful – which vibrated in his tones and expressed itself in look and gestures, that old men leaned their heads upon their arms and fairly sobbed. It was, one must confess, a patchy performance considered as a whole; some parts were miserably tricky, others misconceived, others gabbled over in haste to reach the 'points'; but it was irradiated with such flashes that I would again risk broken ribs for the chance of a good place in the pit to see anything like it.

Even in earlier and better days there was much in his performance of Othello which was spasmodic, slovenly, false. The address to the Senate was very bad. He had little power of elocution unless when sustained by a strong emotion; and this long simple narrative was the kind of speech he could not manage at all. He gabbled over it, impatient to arrive at the phrase, 'And this is all the witchcraft I have used. Here comes the lady, let her witness it.' His delivery of this 'point' always startled the audience into applause by its incisive tone and its abrupt transition; yet nothing could be more out of keeping with the Shakspearian character. Othello might smile with lofty disdain at the accusation of witch-craft, or rebut it calmly, but not make it the climax of a withering sarcasm – attacking the word 'witchcraft' with high and sudden emphasis, and dropping into an almost disrespectful colloquialism as the lady appeared. Indeed, throughout the first and second acts, with the exception of occasional flashes (as in the passionate fervour with which he greets Desdemona on landing at Cyprus), Kean's Othello was rather irritating and disappointing – arresting the mind, but not satisfying it. From the third act onwards all was wrought out with a mastery over the resources of expression such as has been seldom approached. In the successive unfolding of these great scenes here presented with incomparable effect the lion-like fury, the deep and haggard pathos, the forlorn sense of desolation, alternating with gusts of stormy cries for vengeance, the misgivings and sudden reassurances, the calm and deadly resolution of one not easily moved, but who, being moved, was stirred to the very depths.

Kean was a consummate master of passionate expression. People generally spoke of him as a type of the 'impulsive actor'. But if by this they meant one who abandoned himself to the impulse of the moment, without forethought of pre-arranged effect, nothing could be wider from the mark. He was an artist, and in Art all effects are regulated. The original suggestion may be, and generally is, sudden and unprepared – 'inspired', as we say; but the alert intellect recognizes its truth, seizes on it, regulates it. Without nice calculation no proportion could be preserved; we should have a work of fitful impulse, not a work of enduring art. Kean vigilantly and patiently rehearsed every detail, trying the tones until his ear was satisfied, practising looks and gestures until his artistic sense was satisfied; and having once regulated these he never changed them. The consequence was that, when he was sufficiently sober to stand and speak, he could act his part with the precision of a singer who has thoroughly learned his air. One who often acted with him informed me that when Kean was rehearsing on a new stage he accurately counted the number of steps he had to take before reaching a certain spot, or before uttering a certain word; these steps were justly regarded by him as part of the mechanism which could no more be neglected than the accompaniment to an air could be neglected by the singer. Hence it was that he was always the same; not always in the same health, not always in the same vigour, but always master of the part, and expressing it through the same symbols. The voice on some nights would be more irresistibly touching in 'But, oh! the pity of it, Iago!' – or more musically forlorn in 'Othello's occupation gone' – or more terrible in

'Blood, Iago; blood, blood!' – but always the accent and rhythm were unchanged; as a Tamberlik may deliver the C from the chest with more sonority one night than another, but always delivers it from the chest, and never from the head.

Kean was not only remarkable for the intensity of passionate expression, but for a peculiarity I have never seen so thoroughly realized by another, although it is one which belongs to the truth of passion, namely, the expression of *subsiding emotion*. Although fond, far too fond, of abrupt transitions – passing from vehemence to familiarity, and mingling strong lights and shadows with Caravaggio force of unreality – nevertheless his instinct taught him what few actors are taught – that a strong emotion, after discharging itself in one massive current, continues for a time expressing itself in feebler currents. The waves are not stilled when the storm has passed away. There remains the ground-swell troubling the deeps. In watching Kean's quivering muscles and altered tones you felt the subsidence of passion. The voice might be calm, but there was a tremor in it; the face might be quiet, but there were vanishing traces of the recent agitation.

One of his means of effect – sometimes one of his tricks – was to make long pauses between certain phrases. For instance, on quitting the scene, Sir Edward Mortimer has to say warningly, 'Wilford, remember!' Kean used to pause after 'Wilford', and during the pause his face underwent a rapid succession of expressions fluently melting into each other, and all tending to one climax of threat; and then the deep tones of 'remember!' came like muttered thunder. Those spectators who were unable to catch these expressions considered the pause a mere trick; and sometimes the pauses were only tricks, but often they were subtle truths.

Having been trained to the stage from his childhood, and being endowed with a remarkably graceful person, he was a master of scenic effect. He largely increased the stock of 'business', which is the tradition of the stage. Hamlet, Othello, Richard, Shylock, Lear, Sir Giles Overreach, or Sir Edward Mortimer have been illuminated by him in a way neither actors nor play-goers commonly suspect. It is his reading of the parts, his 'points', that we applaud. He was a real innovator, but the parts he could play were few. He had no gaiety; he could not laugh; he had no playfulness that was not as the playfulness of a panther showing her claws every moment. Of this kind was the gaiety of his Richard III. Who can ever forget the exquisite grace with which he leaned against the side-scene while Anne was railing at him, and the chuckling mirth of his 'Poor fool! what pains she takes to damn herself!' It was thoroughly feline – terrible yet beautiful.

He had tenderness, wrath, agony, and sarcasm at command. But he could not be calmly dignified; nor could he represent the intellectual side of heroism. He was nothing if not passionate. I never saw his Hamlet, which, however, was never considered one of his successes, though parts were intensely admired. He must have been puzzled what to do with many of the long speeches and the quiet scenes, and could have had no sympathy with the character. Yet Hamlet is the easiest of all Shakspeare's great parts for an actor of moderate ability. Othello, which is the most trying of all Shakspeare's parts, was Kean's masterpiece. His Shylock was freer from fault, and indeed was a marvellous performance. From the first moment that he appeared and leant upon his stick to listen gravely while moneys are requested of him, he impressed the audience, as Douglas Jerrold used to say, 'like a chapter of Genesis'. The overpowering remonstrant sarcasm of his address to Antonio, and the sardonic mirth of his proposition about the 'merry bond', were fine preparations for the anguish and rage at the elopement of his daughter, and for the gloating anticipations of revenge on the Christians. Anything more impressive than the passionate recrimination and wild justice of argument in his 'Hath not a Jew eyes?' has never been seen on our stage.

On Actors and the Art of Acting, 1875

William Hazlitt
Miss O'Neill as Juliet

We occasionally see something on the stage that reminds us a little of Shakespear. Miss O'Neill's Juliet, if it does not correspond exactly with our idea of the character, does not degrade it. We never saw Garrick; and Mrs Siddons was the only person who ever embodied our idea of high tragedy. Her mind and person were both fitted for it. The effect of her acting was greater than could be conceived before-hand. It perfectly filled and overpowered the mind. The first time of seeing this great artist was an epoch in everyone's life, and left impressions which could never be forgotten. She appeared to belong to a superior order of beings, to be surrounded with a personal awe, like some prophetess of old, or Roman matron, the mother of Coriolanus or the Gracchi. Her voice answered to her form, and her expression to both. Yet she was a pantomime actress. Her common recitation was faulty. It was in bursts of indignation, or grief, in sudden exclamations, in apostrophes and inarticulate sounds, that she raised the soul of passion to its height, or sunk it in despair.

We remember her manner in the *Gamester*, when Stukely (it was then played by Palmer) declares his love to her. The look, first of incredulity and astonishment, then of anger, then passing suddenly into contempt, and ending in bitter scorn, and a convulsive burst of laughter, all given in a moment, and laying open every movement of the soul, produced an effect which we shall never forget. Her manner of rubbing her hands, in the night scene in Macbeth, and of dismissing the guests at the banquet, were among her finest things. We have, many years ago, wept outright during the whole time of her playing Isabella, and this we take to have been a higher employment of the critical faculties than doubling down the book in dog-ears to make out a regular list of critical common-places. To the tears formerly shed on such occasions, we may apply the words of a modern dashing orator, 'Sweet is the dew of their memory, and pleasant the balm of their recollection.'

We have, we believe, been betrayed into this digression, because Miss O'Neill, more than any late actress, reminded us in certain passages, and in a faint degree, of Mrs Siddons. This young lady, who will probably become a favourite with the public, is rather tall; and though not of the first order of fine forms, her figure is of that respectable kind, which will not interfere with the characters she represents. Her deportment is not particularly graceful: there is a heaviness, and want of firmness about it. Her features are regular, and the upper part of her face finely expressive of terror or sorrow. It has that mixture of beauty and passion which we admire so much in some of the antique statues. The lower part of her face is not equally good. From a want of fulness or flexibility about the mouth, her laugh is not at any time pleasing, and where it is a laugh of terror, is distorted and painful. Her voice, without being musical, is distinct, powerful, and capable of every necessary exertion. Her action is impressive and simple. She looks the part she has to perform, and fills up the pauses in the words, by the varied expression of her countenance or gestures, without any thing artificial, pointed, or far-fetched.

In the silent expression of feeling, we have seldom witnessed any thing finer than her acting, where she is told of Romeo's death, her listening to the Friar's story of the poison, and her change of manner towards the Nurse, when she advises her to marry Paris. Her delivery of the speeches in the scenes where she laments Romeo's banishment, and anticipates her waking in the tomb, marked the fine play and undulation of natural sensibility, rising and falling with the gusts of passion, and at last worked up into an agony of despair, in which imagination approaches the brink of frenzy. Her actually screaming at the imaginary sight of Tybalt's ghost, appeared to us the only instance of extravagance or caricature. Not only is there a distinction to be kept up between physical and intellectual horror (for the latter becomes more general, internal, and absorbed, in proportion as it becomes more intense), but the scream, in the present instance, startled the audience, as it preceded the speech which explained its meaning. Perhaps the emphasis given to the exclamation, '*And Romeo banished*', and to the description of Tybalt, '*festering in his shroud*', was too much in that epigrammatic, pointed style, which we think inconsistent with the severe and simple dignity of tragedy.

In the last scene, at the tomb with Romeo, which, however, is not from Shakespear, though it tells admirably on the stage, she did not produce the effect we expected. Miss O'Neill seemed least successful in the former part of the character, in the garden scene, etc. The expression of tenderness bordered on hoydening, and affectation. The character of Juliet is a pure effusion of nature. It is as serious, and as much in earnest, as it is frank and susceptible. It has all the exquisite voluptuousness of youthful innocence. There is not the slightest appearance of coquetry in it, no sentimental languour, no meretricious assumption of fondness to take her lover by surprise. She ought not to laugh, when she says, 'I have forgot why I did call thee back', as if conscious of the artifice, nor hang in a fondling posture over the balcony. Shakespear has given a fine idea of the composure of the character, where he first describes her at the window, leaning her cheek upon her arm. The whole expression of her love should be like the breath of flowers.

Mr Jones's Mercutio was lively farce. Of Mr Conway's Romeo, we cannot speak with patience. He bestrides the stage like a Colossus, throws his arms into the air like the sails of a windmill, and his motion is as unwieldly as that of a young elephant. His voice breaks in thunder on the ear like Gargantua's, but when he pleases to be soft, he is 'the very beadle to an amorous sigh'. Mr Coates's absurdities are tame and trifling in comparison. *Quere*, Why does he not marry?

The Champion, 16 October 1814

William Hazlitt
Macready as Orestes

A Mr Macready appeared at Covent Garden Theatre on Monday and Friday, in the character of Orestes, in the *Distressed Mother*, a bad play for the display of his powers, in which, however, he succeeded in making a decidedly favourable impression upon the audience. His voice is powerful in the highest degree, and at the same time possesses great harmony and modulation. His face is not equally calculated for the stage. He declaims better than any body we have lately heard. He is accused of being violent, and of wanting pathos. Neither of these objections is true. His manner of delivering the first speeches in this play was admirable, and the want of increasing interest afterwards was the fault of the author, rather than the actor. The fine suppressed tone in which he assented to Pyrrhus' command to convey the message to Hermione was a test of his variety of power, and brought down repeated acclamations from the house. We do not lay much stress on his mad-scene, though that was very good in its kind, for mad-scenes do not occur very often, and when they do, had in general better be omitted. We have not the slightest hesitation in saying, that Mr Macready is by far the best tragic actor that has come out in our remembrance, with the exception of Mr Kean. We however heartily wish him well out of this character of Orestes. It is a kind of forlorn hope in tragedy. There is nothing to be made of it on the English stage, beyond experiment. It is a trial, not a triumph. These French plays puzzle an English audience exceedingly. They cannot attend to the actor, for the difficulty they have in understanding the author.

We think it wrong in any actor of great merit (which we hold Mr Macready to be) to come out in an ambiguous character, to salve his reputation. An actor is like a man who throws himself from the top of a steeple by a rope. He should chuse the highest steeple he can find, that if he does not succeed in coming safe to the ground, he may break his neck at once, and so put himself and the spectators out of farther pain.

Ambrose Phillips's *Distressed Mother* is a very good translation from Racine's *Andromache*. It is an alternation of topics, of pros and cons, on the casuistry of domestic and state affairs, and produced a great effect of ennui on the audience. When you hear one of the speeches in these rhetorical tragedies, you know as well what will be the answer to it, as when you see the tide coming up the river – you know that it will return again. The other actors filled their parts with successful mediocrity.

The Examiner, 22 September 1815

John Forster
Macready as Lear

What we ventured to anticipate when Mr Macready assumed the management of Covent Garden Theatre, has been every way realized. But the last of his well-directed efforts to vindicate the higher objects and uses of the drama, has proved the most brilliant and the most successful. He has restored to the stage Shakespeare's true *Lear*, banished from it, by impudent ignorance, for upwards of a hundred and fifty years.

A person of the name of Boteler has the infamous repute of having recommended to a notorious poet laureate, Mr Nahum Tate, the new modelling of *Lear*. 'I found the whole', quoth Mr Tate, addressing the aforesaid Boteler in his dedication, 'to answer your account of it; a heap of jewels unstrung and unpolished, yet so dazzling in their disorder, that I soon perceived I had seized a treasure.' And accordingly to work set Nahum, very busily indeed; strung the jewels and polished them with a vengeance;

omitted the grandest things, the Fool among them, polished all that remained into commonplace; interlarded love-scenes; sent Cordelia into a comfortable cave with her lover, to dry her clothes and get warm, while her distracted and houseless old father was still left wandering without, amid all the pelting of the pitiless storm; and finally rewarded the poor old man in his turn, and repaid him for all his suffering, by giving him back again his gilt robes and tinsel sceptre!

Betterton was the last great actor who played Lear before the commission of this outrage. His performances of it between the years 1663 and 1671, are recorded to have been the greatest efforts of his genius. Ten years after the latter date Mr Tate published his disgusting version, and this was adopted successfully by Boheme, Quin, Booth, Barry, Garrick, Henderson, Kemble, Kean. Mr Macready has now, to his lasting honour, restored the text of Shakespeare, and we shall be glad to hear of the actor foolhardy enough to attempt another restoration of the text of Tate! Mr Macready's success has banished that disgrace from the stage for ever.

The Fool in the tragedy of *Lear* is one of the most wonderful creations of Shakespeare's genius. The picture of his quick and pregnant sarcasm, or his loving devotion, of his acute sensibility, of his despairing mirth, of his heart-broken silence – contrasted with the rigid sublimity of Lear's suffering, with the huge desolation of Lear's sorrow, with the vast and outspread image of Lear's madness – is the noblest thought that ever entered into the mind and heart of man. Nor is it a noble thought alone. Three crowded audiences in Covent Garden Theatre have now proved by something better than even the deepest attention that it is for action – for representation: that it is necessary to an audience as tears are to an overcharged heart; and necessary to Lear himself as the recollection of his kingdom, or as the worn and faded garments of his power. We predicted some years since that this would be felt, and we have the better right to repeat it now. We take leave again to say that Shakespeare would have as soon consented to the banishment of Lear from the tragedy, as to the banishment of his Fool. We may fancy him, while planning his immortal work, feeling suddenly, with an instinct of divinest genius, that its gigantic sorrows could never be presented on the stage without a suffering too frightful, a sublimity too remote, a grandeur too terrible – unless relieved by quiet pathos, and in some way brought home to the apprehensions of the audience by homely and familiar illustration. At such a moment that Fool rose to his mind, and not till then could he have contemplated his marvellous work in the greatness and beauty of its final completion.

The Fool in *Lear* is the solitary instance of such a character, in all the writings of Shakespeare, being identified with the pathos and passion of the scene. He is interwoven with Lear – he is the link that still associates him with Cordelia's love, and the presence of the regal state he has surrendered. The rage of the wolf Goneril is first stirred by a report that her favourite gentleman had been struck by her father 'for chiding of his fool' – and the first impatient questions we hear from the dethroned old man are 'Where's my knave – my fool? Go you and call my fool hither.' – 'Where's my fool? ho! I think the world's asleep.' – 'But where's my fool? I have not seen him this two days.' – 'Go you and call hither my fool.' All which prepare us for that affecting answer stammered forth at last by the Knight in attendance – 'Since my young Lady's going into France, sir, the fool hath much pined away.' Mr Macready's manner of turning off at this with an expression of half impatience, half ill-repressed emotion – 'No more of that – *I have noted it well*' – was inexpressibly touching. We saw him, in the secret corner of his heart, still clinging to the memory of her who used to be his best object, the argument of his praise, balm of his age, 'most best, most dearest'. And in the same noble and affecting spirit was his manner of fondling the Fool when he sees him first, and asks him with earnest care – 'How now, my pretty knave? *How dost thou?*' Can there be a doubt, after this, that his love for the Fool is associated with Cordelia, who had been kind to the poor boy, and for the loss of whom he pines away? And are we not even then prepared for the sublime pathos of the close, when Lear, bending over the dead body of all he had left to love upon the earth connects with her the memory of that other gentle, faithful, and loving being who had passed from his side – unites, in that moment of final agony, the two hearts that had been broken in his service – and exclaims – 'And my poor fool is hanged!'

Mr Macready's Lear, remarkable before for a masterly completeness of conception, is heightened by this introduction of the Fool to a surprising degree. It accords exactly with the view he seeks to present of Lear's character. The passages we have named, for instance, had even received illustration in the first scene, where something beyond the turbulent greatness or royal impatience of Lear had been presented – something to redeem him from his treatment of Cordelia. The bewildered pause giving his 'father's heart' away – the hurry yet hesitation of his manner as he orders France to be called – 'Who stirs? Call Burgundy' – had told us at once how much consideration he needed, how much pity, of how little of himself he was indeed the master, how crushing and irrepressible was the strength of his sharp impatience. We saw no material change in his style of playing the first great scene with Goneril, which fills the stage with true and appalling touches of nature. In that scene he ascends indeed with the heights of Lear's passion; through all its changes of agony, of anger, of impatience, of turbulent assertion, of despair, and mighty grief; till on his knees, with arms upraised and head thrown back, the tremendous curse bursts from him amid heaving and reluctant throes of suffering and anguish. The great scene of the second act had also its old passages of power and beauty – his self-persuading utterance of 'hysterica passio' – his anxious and fearful tenderness to Regan – the elevated grandeur of his appeal to the Heavens – his terribly suppressed efforts, his pauses, his reluctant pangs of passion, in the speech 'I will not trouble thee, my child' – and surpassing the whole, as we think, in deep simplicity as well as agony of pathos, that noble conception of shame as he *hides his face* on the arm of Goneril and says –

I'll go with thee –
Thy fifty yet doth double five and twenty,
And thou art twice her love!

The Fool's presence then enabled him to give an effect, unattempted before, to those little words which close the scene, when, in the effort of bewildering passion with which he strives to burst through the phalanx of shaking, and suddenly exclaims, 'O, Fool! I shall go mad!' This is better than hitting the forehead and ranting out a self-reproach.

But the presence of the Fool in the storm-scene! The reader must witness this to judge its power, and observe the deep impression with which it affects the audience. Every resource that the art of the painter and the mechanist can afford is called in aid in this scene – every illustration is thrown on it of which the great actor of Lear is capable – but these are nothing to that simple presence of the Fool! He has changed his character there. So long as hope existed he had sought by his hectic merriment and sarcasm to win Lear back to love and reason – but that half of his work is now over, and all that remains for him is to soothe and lessen the certainty of the worst. Kent asks who is with Lear in the storm, and is answered –

> None but the *Fool*, who labours to outjest
> His heart-struck injuries!

When all his attempts have failed, either to soothe or outjest these injuries, he sings, in the shivering cold, about the necessity of 'going to bed at noon'. He leaves the stage to die in his youth, and we hear of him no more till we hear the sublime touch of pathos over the dead body of the hanged Cordelia.

The finest passage of Mr Macready's scenes upon the heath is his remembrance of the 'Poor naked wretches', wherein a new world seems indeed to have broken upon his mind. Other parts of these scenes wanted more of tumultuous extravagance, more of a preternatural cast of wildness. We should always be made to feel something beyond physical distress predominant here. The colloquy with Mad Tom, however, was touching in the last degree – and so were the two last scenes, the recognition of Cordelia and the death, which elicited from the audience the truest and best of all tributes to their beauty and pathos. Mr Macready's representation of the father at the end, broken down to his last despairing struggle, his heart swelling gradually upwards till it bursts in its closing sigh, completed the only perfect picture that we have had of Lear since the age of Betterton.

The Examiner, 4 February 1838

John Forster
Macready as Coriolanus

The presentation of this play at Covent Garden Theatre on Monday night last may be esteemed the worthiest tribute to the genius and fame of Shakespeare that has been yet attempted on the English stage. We have had nothing to compare with it, even in Mr Macready's management. Magnificent as the revivals of *Hamlet*, *Othello*, *Lear* and *Macbeth* have been, this of *Coriolanus* surpasses them all, in the opportunity it has afforded of presenting together upon the stage those striking characteristics, material no less than intellectual, which render a correct knowledge of great times past superior to every other sort of knowledge – not less an instructive picture of noble or heroic manners, that an exercise of reason, and a school of philosophy.

Rome has been presented on the theatrical scene before, but never this Rome; the rude city of the rude age of the Conqueror of Corioli. That is the first distinction which claims notice. The pictures which Kemble gave when he revived the play might be splendid, but they were utterly unreal – they clustered fine buildings together with equal disregard to the proprieties of place or time – the arch of Severus or Constantine, the Coliseum, the pillar of Trajan, all the grandeurs of imperial Rome, flaunted away within three hundred years of the first birth of the city – and even men of scholarship could find no bounds to the satisfaction they expressed. We can scarcely blame them. It was natural that they should prefer even that to the wilder absurdity of a picture of Grosvenor Square; and it must be confessed that the effect of solid long lines and triumphant-looking arches is so very Roman, generally speaking, and the idea of Rome in the mind of posterity possesses so mighty and enduring a grandeur analagous to its stone and marble, that one of these Kemble misrepresentations might be almost hailed as even the just substitution of a general truth for a particular one – a moral and characteristic, if not a chronologic truth. Nevertheless, truth itself, as a plain-spoken old Roman would have said, is the best of all truths; and upon this wiser principle Mr Macready has proceeded; with what effect let the reader judge who goes to see the play. To what infinitely higher purpose is the moral grandeur of the place and of the men set off by a comparatively rude and barren city!

The first scene (all are painted with consummate skill and exactness) presents Rome from the skirt of Mount Aventine across a bend of the Tiber (which would bear, by-the-bye, an additional tinge of yellow) – taking in a view of the Capitoline hill, a glimpse of the porticoes of the forum, the temple of Vesta, the Cloaca Maxima, and the Palatine covered with its patrician dwellings. It is by an exquisite arrangement of art that, throughout the play, and in the rudest streets of the city, the Capitol is kept in view, and still presents, under varying aspects, the never-changed old Roman form (no matter that the materials were afterwards more splendid) of the three temples to Jupiter, Juno, and Minerva. As a chord in music pervading the entire composition, this awakens and sustains in the spectator's mind grand associations of the later with those of the earlier Rome. The second scene is the interior of the house of Coriolanus, with its earthen vases, its bronze candelabra, its exquisite and almost pathetic simplicity. We have then pictures of the country between Rome and the Volscian territory – a distant view of the square camp entrenched – a field of battle covered with dead, and in the distance Corioli. We are afterwards brought back to Rome, and placed in the interior of the forum, with, above, a glimpse of the still proud Capitol, and the little 'thatched house of Romulus', while on our right stands the rostrum, and terrifying us even yet from the very thought of litigation, the transfixed and ghastly image of the miserable Marsyas. Then follows Coriolanus' triumphant entrance into Rome. The emotion of the vast crowds as the passage of the procession through the gate brings nearer and nearer its renowned hero – the forest of laurel boughs rustling through the air as each hand seeks to contribute something to the glory of the scene – the 'stalks, bulks, windows' of the old and rude brick buildings of the city 'smother'd up' –

> Leads fill'd and ridges hors'd
> With variable complexions, all agreeing
> In earnestness to see him –

and more touching still, the triumph, surpassing all this, of the mother and wife of the great soldier, as standing apart in the crowd (not coldly and absurdly, as in Kemble's time, arranged as figures in the procession) they see him enter at last covered with the light purple and crowned with the oaken garland – these were the elements of a picture of life and excitement at once the noblest, and produced by the simplest and most striking means, we ever witnessed in a theatre. Every attempt at a stage 'triumph' we happen to have seen before, compared with this, was as the gilt gingerbread of a Lord Mayor's show – the gorgeous tinsel of an ill-imitated grandeur. *This* was the grandeur itself, the rudeness and simplicity, the glory and the truth of Life. The next scene was that of the assembled senate of Rome, and perhaps in simple and majestic beauty this scene surpassed every other. The senators, in number between one and two hundred, occupy three sides of the stage in triple rows of benches – all in their white robes; with every point of the dress, no less than of the grave and solemn bearing, that distinguished the Roman senator, duly and minutely rendered. The Consul occupies the chief seat in the middle of the back row – before him burns the sacred fire on an altar – and behind him, overhead, is the only other ornament of the place, the famous brazen wolf suckling Romulus and Remus. We defy any one, scholar or not, to look at this scene without emotion. It is not simply the image of power, but a reflection of the great heart, of Rome. It does not strike the senses, but appeals at once to the imagination. It breathes into the cold and statue-like associations of our youthful studies the passionate spirit of humanity and life. It is, as it were, the actual presence of the *genius* of Rome – not of her turbulent and wilful days, nor of those grim, ghastly, long-robed heartless figures, that too often usurp her memory – but of that high-souled thought and temper, which, whenever the few great minds of the earth have since her fall made a stand against violence and fraud in the cause of liberty and reason, has still in the midst of them conjured up her image – the comfort of the battlefield of Hampden, the glory and consolation of the scaffolds of More and Vane and Sydney!

When Kemble played Coriolanus, his first appearance after his banishment was under worthy James Thomson's statue of Mars in the house of Aufidius. This was to the text of Shakespeare as a declamation to a feeling. When the curtain withdrew upon the first scene of the fourth act on Monday night, it disclosed a view of the city of Antium, by starlight – a truly grand and imaginative yet real scene – and in the centre of the stage Macready stood alone, the muffled, disguised, banished Coriolanus. This realized Shakespeare and Plutarch. Behind him were the moles running out into the sea, and at the back of the scene the horizon drawn beyond the sea in one level line, interrupted only by a tall, solitary tower, the pharos, or watch-tower of Antium. The strict truth, and lofty moral effect, of this scene, are surpassingly beautiful. Its wide and barren aspect presents the simplicity and large-minded poverty of those old times, and the tower looks like Coriolanus himself in a less mortal shape, rising in lonely grandeur, but with still unextinguished light, above the melancholy of his exile and the level sternness of his contemporaries. The pathetic effect is suddenly and startlingly increased by the intrusion of music on the air, as the door of Aufidius' house, where the General feasts his nobles, opens on the left of the stage. The next scene shows Coriolanus (an image of Themistocles) seated by the wide hearth of Aufidius, around which are the household gods, and in its centre a burning fire. In all this Shakespeare's text is illustrated by the text of Shakespeare's own original, North's Plutarch. 'It was even twi-light when he entered the city of Antium, and many people met him in the streets, but no man knew him. So he went directly to Tullus Aufidius' house, and when he came thither, *he got him up straight to the chimney harth, and sate him downe*, and spake not a word to any man, his face all muffled over. They of the house spying him, wondred what he should be, and yet they durst not bid him rise. For il favouredly muffled and disguised as he was, yet there appeared a certaine maiestie in his countenance, *and in his silence.*'

The last scene was worthy climax to this series of triumphant effects (among which, by the way, we should have mentioned the striking simplicity of the tent of Coriolanus). The entire Volscian army is shown under the walls of Rome, which are presented, with the proud Capitol still visible above them, in the distance, while we see in various moving towers and battering-rams vivid preparations for a siege. The number of brilliantly equipped soldiers on the stage in this scene is truly startling, and as their serried ranks open for the advance of the suppliants from Rome, we might fancy them thousands instead of hundreds. The appearance – the black apparition rather – of Coriolanus' mother and family with the other Roman matrons, stretching obliquely across the stage, in the midst of these brilliant warrior-files, one long, dreary, sable line of monotonous misery – was in the best and deepest taste. The last effect of all is a simple adherence to Shakespeare's own stage directions.

The tragedy, as it were, does not end. Its action is only removed to Antium or Rome. 'Exeunt, bearing the body of Coriolanus'. As Aufidius mourns his treachery, the warriors around lift up the dead body of the conqueror on their shields, hang around it the splendidest trophies of war, and trailing their steel pikes in sorrow, move with it slowly up the stage to the sound of mournful music. The curtain falls, and, thinking of the scene about to be enacted in Antium, we imagine the sorrow which will break some hearts in Rome!

Such are the pictorial effects alone in this magnificent revival, in themselves most beautiful always, and yet in every case kept strictly subservient to the conduct of the action and story of Coriolanus – not standing, as it were, apart from it, picture like – but forming an actual portion of the lofty purposes and passions of the play. This profoundest effect of all is created throughout by the masterly arrangement and grouping of the persons engaged in each scene, and above all by the management of the formidable mob of the tragedy, the starving, discontented, savage, cowardly, fickle, tumultuous Roman people. The last alone would have sufficiently demonstrated the power of the artist-actor to grasp the entire conception of the poet's genius. The mob in *Coriolanus* were now for the first time shown upon the stage, on a level with the witches in *Macbeth*, as agents of the tragic catastrophe. 'First mob' (as the list of dramatis personae calls a plebeian speaker with his 'Many') was personated with singular skill and energy by Mr Meadows, and never before, we dare assert, felt himself in such lively and multitudinous condition. He was something like a mob. His numerousness gave due effect to his will. He was not the one, or two, or halfdozen inefficient *sawnies* of former times, when John Kemble stalked and *thin-voiced* it among them, like the ghost of the Roman State; but a proper massy crowd of dangerous, violent fellows, fit to hustle Macready's flesh and blood. Those first and second mobs hitherto proper to the stage, and whose 'voices' Coriolanus might reasonably scorn to ask for, were fitter to have represented the nine tailors who make one married man in Mr Beresford's laughable appendix to his *Miseries of Human Life*; where *their wife* hearing *him-them* coming upstairs, meets him on the stair-case, and says, 'I knew it was you, my love; for I heard your *voices*.' It was really formidable to see these Covent Garden mobs of Monday night. They fluctuated to and fro, as their violent assent or dissent impelled them, with a loud and overwhelming suddenness, and one-minded ponderosity, truly fearful to think of encountering; and the mere recollection of which gives more heroic breadth to the courage of Coriolanus. Their dresses, we may add, varying in every degree from the complete toga to the savage strip, were in the highest degree accurate and effective, as indeed the dresses were throughout. Old Menenius, who, when his zeal has betrayed him on one occasion into an appearance in armour, complains that he can hardly bear it, does not, as in Kemble's time, wear nothing else throughout the tragedy; nor does Coriolanus himself (wisely recollecting the Tarpeian rock) venture out in the fluttering scarlet which Kemble took such perverse delight in.

We have left ourselves less room than we could have wished, in closing our notice of this memorable revival, to speak of what has equal beauty, though less novelty, with these noble illustrations we have so long dwelt upon. Mr Macready's Caius Marcius (we do not express this opinion for the first time) makes what we believe to be the nearest approach the stage has ever presented to the intention Shakespeare had in view. Coriolanus is not an ideal abstraction of the dignities and graces, but a soldier of the early republic of Rome, a man of rough manners, but of fiery and passionate sincerity. His friends are driven in the course of the tragedy to find many excuses for his unaccommodating temper and style of language in the rudeness of military habits, and it must be admitted that his style and temper are much the same, whether he addresses Patricians or People. He objects that the senate should 'monster' his nothings, and he begs of the Consul Cominius, 'for that he hath not wash'd his nose that bled', that he will not diet the little he has been able to accomplish 'in praises sauc'd with lies'. Plutarch (after whom Shakespeare modelled his tragedy) observes distinctly of him that for 'lack of education' he was 'so cholericke and impatient, that he would yeeld to no living creature: which made him churlish, *uncivill*, and altogether unfit for any man's conversation.' And again, the historian observes of him: '*He was a man too ful of passion and choller*, and too much given over to selfe-wil and opinion, and *one of a high mind* and great courage, that *lacked the gravitie and affabilitie* that is gotten with iudgment of learning and reason.' This is the original sketch which Shakespeare has filled up with so much power and grandeur, with all the truth, the greatness, and the majesty of man. It is the silliest of mistakes to suppose that Coriolanus is an abstraction of Roman-nosed grandeur – an embodiment of signified contempt against the poor common people. Let not aristocrats suppose it. The scorn which he gives vent to, wrong and misplaced as it often is, has its unfailing source in what his own heart believes to be noble in thought and just in action. He has none of the characteristics of an oppressor or scorner of the poor. 'He would not', as his friend tells us, 'Flatter Neptune for his trident, or Jove for his power of thunder.' A thing has no charms for him because it is a thing of custom – for of 'Custom' he holds 'mountainous Error' to have been born. He opposed the people because he does not believe them to be trustworthy – he sides with the Patricians, only (as Plutarch says) because he hopes to persuade them to 'show themselves no lesse forward and willing to fight for their country, than the common people were: and to let them know by their deeds and acts, *that they did not so much passe the people and riches, as they did exceed them in true nobility and valiantnesse*' – and not succeeding in this, he stigmatizes them as 'dastard nobles'. Yet were all these glorious gifts made vain by an unhappy temper, and an education still more unhappy – his own strong natural passions and intense sensibility thwarted every way by the Spartan severity of Volumnia, his mother. The people had their faults no less, and as the passionate soldier refused to acknowledge the fairness of their simple claim, of exacting as the price of the Consulship that it should be asked for kindly – so, on the other hand, they would not see an anti-patrician simplicity and beauty in the claim of Coriolanus from *them*, that they should account him the more virtuous that he had not been common in his love and attachment to men.

This is the Coriolanus of Mr Macready – not merely an ideal picture of one intense sentiment, but the reality of various and conflicting passion. He does not work up dignified contempt to an extraordinary pitch of intensity with a view to have it on the minds of the audience as one great ideal abstraction – he gives nature full and various play; he calls in other passions to harmonize and redeem; he suffers as much as he sways, and conflicting with opposite emotions in his soul, sinks at last beneath the struggle. After the preternatural excitement in the quarrel with Aufidius we feel that he is for the Earth no more. His scene with his mother and friends in the third act – his banishment in the forum – the claim of protection from Aufidius – the agonies of his yielding resolution in the last scene – all are exquisite illustrations of the view of the character we have attempted to describe. He was well supported by Miss Huddart in Volumnia (who was only a little too vehement sometimes) and by Mr Anderson and Mr Warde in Aufidius and Cominius. Mr Bartley's Menenius is well known as an accurate and delightful picture of that honest and humourous patrician.

The Examiner, 18 March 1838

Westland Marston
Macready as Macbeth

Of all Macready's representations, that of Macbeth probably most satisfied himself. He had performed no Shaksperian character more frequently; it was that, moreover, in which he took his leave of the stage. Though it never realized my ideal, I learned, as I grew in years, to appreciate its many excellences. After the departure of the witches, in the first act, the air of brooding reverie in the soliloquy, with a strange sense conveyed in the fixed and fateful gaze of impending evil, the insidious encroachment of evil, spite of brief but terrible recoil, and afterwards the overdone warmth with which he excuses his abstraction to Rosse and Angus, were rendered with consummate skill and effect. In the scenes where Lady Macbeth prompts him to the murder, his resistance seemed somewhat too feeble for the remorse he has afterwards to display. 'One of John Kemble's most effective passages', said that fine critic, W. J. Fox, 'was the one beginning –

We will proceed no further in this business,

which he uttered with such a sigh of relief and thankfulness, it seemed to bear away with it a crushing load and to leave him renewed and hopeful.' The apostrophe to the 'air-drawn dagger', as given by Macready, was a triumph of discrimination and emphasis. The transitions from amazement and awe to reviving reason – once more staggered by the growing force of his terrors, and again reasserting itself to dispel them – could not have been more judiciously marked. And yet – to me, at least – there seemed a want. Reasoning carried it over intuition; all had been too obviously reasoned out. The thoughts did not sufficiently hurry upon and partly confuse each other, as they do in real tumults of the soul. The crouching form and stealthy, felon-like step of the self-abased murderer, as he quitted the scene, made, however, a picture not to be forgotten.

In contrast with the erect, martial figure that entered in the first act, this change was the moral of the play made visible. The acting of Macready, after the murder, has been so generally extolled, that I rather state as a personal feeling than as a critical opinion that here again various mental states seemed too sharply defined and separated. The emotions of shame, terror, remorse, momentary despair, and selfish fear, might, I fancied have more often flowed into each other, as when, in real life, some fatal act almost at the same moment excites and yet paralyses apprehension by the sense that it is irretrievable. I thought of Hazlitt's description of Edmund Kean at this point. 'The hesitation, the bewildered look, the coming to himself when he sees his hands bloody; the manner in which his voice clung to his throat and choked his utterance; his agony and tears, the force of nature overcome by passion – beggared description.' Something of this I missed in Macready, though his entire performance was probably finer and more suggestive than that of Kean. But Macready's final waking to the full conviction of the gulf between the past and the present was one of his grandest moments. I still vividly recall the terrible agony of his cry –

Wake Duncan with thy knocking; I would thou couldst!

as, with his face averted from his wife, and his arms outstretched, as it were, to the irrecoverable past, she dragged him from the stage.

The entrance of Banquo's ghost in the third act gives an opportunity to a tragic actor of which Macready fully availed himself. His great merit, however, in this act, was the force with which he previously brought out the gnawings of conscience and the insecurity of ill-gotten power. In his haggard aspect, in his restless movements, it seemed as if the curse, 'Macbeth shall sleep no more', had taken visible effect. What misery pierced through his hollow mirth when he exclaimed –

But let the frame of things disjoint, both the worlds suffer,
Ere we will eat our meal in fear,

feigning so quickly by his tones of hopeless yearning in the words –

Duncan is in his grave,
After life's fitful fever he sleeps well.

When his wife questioned him as to Banquo, the furtive look with which he turned from the very partner of his crime bore terrible witness to the isolation of guilt. The sinister, ill-suppressed laugh which accompanied his answer –

> Be innocent of knowledge, dearest chuck,
> Till thou applaud the deed!

marked, I thought, a new and dreadful stage in the usurper's experience. What a revelation in the words, *dearest chuck*! She whose spirit had so dominated his in the early scenes was now his mere half-trusted accomplice. His misery had cast off awe; he was become grimly familiar with her. His much applauded transition in the last act, from the impetuous command to Seyton, 'Give me mine armour', to the ultra-colloquial, 'How does your patient, doctor?' never appeared to me a beauty. It was a telling stage-contrast, but so extreme as to be factitious. His closing scenes could not have been surpassed. His physical energy was terrific, and took grandeur from the desperate mind. He turned upon Fate and stood at bay.

Our Recent Actors, Vol. I, 1888

Westland Marston
Macready as Richelieu

In March 1839, I fought my way with another young enthusiast to the pit door of old Covent Garden, on the first night of Bulwer's *Richelieu*. What a human sea it was, and how lit up by expectation, that surged and roared for two hours against that grim, all-ignoring barrier! But its stubborn resistance, and the dense pressure which, at last, almost wedged out the breath of every unit in the crowd, gave an almost stern delight, a zest of contest for a prize, of which the lounger into a reserved box or seat has no conception. The interest connected with a new play was increased by the fact that Bulwer was the author, for with us young critics his epigrams, his rhetorical flashes, and, let it be said, a vein of aspiration and generous feeling, rarely absent from his later works, had made him a favourite. We had an impression, moreover, that he was hardly dealt with by a portion of the press, on account of his politics. The future Lord Lytton of Lord Derby's Government was at that time a liberal.

To return to *Richelieu*, in which Macready was perfection. I think I shall probably best help my readers, not only to form an estimate of his excellence in that play, but to gain a general insight into his mind and method, if I try to live over with them my old impressions on the eventful first night of *Richelieu*, from the rise to the fall of the curtain. This method of criticism is far too elaborate to be generally employed, but for once I will have recourse to it, and fancy that I am still fresh from the scene, while describing to the listener an event nearly fifty years old.

Suppose, then, the thronged house hushed, the curtain raised, the gay scene of the conspirators and gamesters going forward beneath the roof of Marion de L'Orme. Even amidst the interest of this opening scene, the thought of the house escapes to Macready. Will he be discovered with all the insignia of his rank and power? Will he be closeted with Louis, or giving audience to a spy? Will his manner have the pride of the churchman, or the smoothness of the diplomatist? The first scene is over, and we have our answer.

Macready, as the Cardinal, enters, followed by the Capuchin Joseph, and the coming revelation – signal, and in some respects new – of the actor's powers is at once foreshadowed by his appearance. How full of individuality are the whitening hair, the face sharpened to the utmost expression of subtlety and keenness, the gait somewhat loose with age, but now quick and impulsive, now slow or suddenly arrested, which seems to give a rhythm to the workings of his brain – to his swift, contemptuous penetration of the schemes against him, on the one hand, or, on the other, to his suspense, his caution, or his rapid decision. Soon followed one of those 'ultra-colloquialisms' which, when first reading the play, he had thought incompatible with Richelieu's dignity, but which, with the dry, caustic humour he gave them, were not only very telling, but seemed natural reliefs to the strained mind of the statesman. 'Orleans heads the traitors' says Father Joseph: 'A very wooden head, then!' exclaims Richelieu; and, though the sarcasm was threadbare, it had all the force of novelty and wit. Examples of the actor's unrivalled power in familiar touches abounded through the performance. His manner of exposing the strategy of Baradas to De Mauprat blended with contempt an easy penetration, an amused superiority which was quite irresistible –

> Where was thy wit, man? Why, these schemes are glass;
> The very sun shines through them!

Early in the play were encountered some of those dazzling, but rather forced metaphors, which the author's better judgment afterwards cancelled. Amongst these, however, was one which, as Macready gave it, drew great applause –

> From rank showers of blood
> And the red light of blazing roofs you build
> The rainbow, Glory, and to shuddering Conscience
> Cry – Lo the Bridge to Heaven!

Soon after this example of poetic pyrotechnics, Richelieu charges De Mauprat with fraud. The indignant young man advances upon his accuser with an air and tone of menace when, it will be remembered, Huguet, one of Richelieu's guard, who waits armed behind a screen to intercept any possible violence to the Cardinal, raises his carbine to fire. Richelieu, with a wave of his hand, exclaims –

> Not so quick, friend Huguet;
> The Sieur de Mauprat is a patient man,
> And he can wait.

The dry, parenthetical utterance of these words, with the careless accompanying gesture, had in them the secret of a terrible humour, and the proud assurance of a 'charmed life' that no succeeding impersonator of Richelieu has discovered. The whole of this first act is rich in those contrasts of feeling and character in which Macready delighted. The fervour with which, after finding De Mauprat worthy of his confidence, he asserts the justice of his rule, had in it all the passionate earnestness and dignity of a man who, long scornfully silent under misconception and calumny, at last relieves his heart and vindicates himself to an honourable judge. Soon follow the lines in which, under pretence of dismissing De Mauprat to death, he causes him to be conducted to the presence of the woman for whose sake he has braved it, this act, of course, implying Richelieu's consent to their union. 'Huguet,' says he,

> To the tapestry chamber
> Conduct your prisoner. (*To De Mauprat*) You will there behold
> Your executioner. Your doom be private,
> And Heaven have mercy on you.

The rapidity and sternness with which these lines were pronounced, as if only by hurry and a forced overdoing of severity he could prevent himself from giving way to the benevolent enjoyment of his device, showed one of the actor's characteristic merits – his just perception of the right note of feeling even to a semi-tone. The look of sly and eager anticipation with which he followed De Mauprat, as he retired, had in it all the *bonhomie* which Bulwer, rather than history, ascribes to the Cardinal, and the zest with which the sceptical mind of a diplomatist may for once taste pure pleasure in bestowing it.

In the second act, the contrast between Richelieu's usual scornful levity in dismissing the schemes of his enemies, and the composed but grave attention which denotes real peril, was strikingly marked. With rapid step and hands carelessly knotted behind him, he had paced to and fro, listening to Father Joseph's rumours of plots with incredulity or with smiling confidence in his power to baffle them. But when Marion de L'Orme entered with news of the conspiracy headed by Orleans, every trace of caustic mirth or easy, exulting contempt at once disappeared. Of course, all actors would at this point have made a transition of manner; few, indeed, would have made it with Macready's arresting effect. He questioned Marion in tones the lowness of which expressed the intensity of his interest. His trust in his own resources was still unshaken, but he felt that they might now be taxed to the utmost. The breathless audience listened to the words, 'Now there is danger', as if each man had his personal stake in the crisis. It was felt that if Richelieu could apprehend danger, there must be danger indeed. The tone of gay flattery to Marion de L'Orme at that moment of peril –

What an eye you have,
And what a smile, child . . . 'tis well I'm old,

and the ringing exhortation to the page François, when sent on his critical mission – 'Never say fail again; that's my young hero!' – were brilliant examples of the actor's variety and quick self-adaptation to his instruments. The fascination which illustrious old age has for the young and aspiring could never have been better justified than by Macready's cheery laugh and look, full of kind encouragement, with which he uttered these words to the page. I have before me a copy of *Richelieu*, marked from the tragedian's acting copy of 1843 (four years after the production of the play), in which the compliment to Marion de L'Orme is cut out – a mistake, I think, for his delivery of it was certainly one of the brilliant facets which his genius exhibited in this manifold character.

So full of fine variety was his delineation at the close of this second act, as almost to atone for its want of incident. His momentary distrust of Huguet, as he noted 'he bowed too low' (some Richelieus have so overemphasized this trait of minute observation, that they should, to be consistent, have discharged the guardsman on the spot); his brief lapse into melancholy, as he reflects on the snares that beset his bed and board and his friendlessness at the height of power; his proud rally from these thoughts to faith in the indomitable heart of Armand Richelieu, and the quaint Bonhomie, strangely compounded of archness, good-feeling, and dissimulation, with which he addresses Joseph – all received their just proportion. Each trait harmonized with, and flowed into its fellow. There was no hard line to divide, or even to distinguish, diplomacy from sentiment or sentiment from humour, but a living man in whom all these qualities naturally blended.

The third act gave scope for the excellences already noted, and with yet higher development. The Richelieu who waited, with breathless eagerness, from François the proofs that should convict Baradas; the Richelieu who, minutely observant, even in his excitement, could pause to note the small number of the conspirators – who, learning that the despatch which would have secured his triumph had been wrested from François, one moment sternly warned him to see his face no more till he had regained it, and the next relented into smiling encouragement – 'Away! Nay, cheer thee; thou hast not failed yet; there's no such word as fail!' – was, in these various aspects, not only the same man but so happy in expressing them that each new trait seemed to complete and enhance the others.

This third act contains the scene in which De Mauprat, duped into the belief that Richelieu in causing him to marry, has made him a mere pander to the King, seeks the Cardinal's life in revenge. When Macready, personating the old and feeble man, encountered, without recognizing him, the armed figure whose very visor was closed, and learned his deadly purpose, nothing could be more intense and life-like, nothing freer from inflation, than the glorious arrogance with which he exclaimed –

> Earth has no such fiend –
> No – as one parricide of his fatherland,
> Who dares in Richelieu murder France!

It should be noticed here that Macready carefully avoided the error into which some of his successors have fallen – that of over-idealizing Richelieu, by delivering his patriotic speeches in such tones of exalted devotion as might have befitted Brutus. Macready's apostrophes to France, on the contrary, were given with a self-reference, sometimes fierce in its expression, that showed her triumphs to be part of his own. Her glory was the object of his ambition, for it made him great, while the thought that he laboured for her consciously ennobled his ambition. Thus his haughty boast in the foregoing lines was no expression of abstract and ideal patriotism (of which the Cardinal was incapable), but of passionate and practical sympathy. How fine, again when De Mauprat, still unrecognized, betrays that the dishonour put upon him has made him an avenger, were the sudden gleam in the eye, and the hushed tones of relief which showed the statesman's sleepless vigilance at that crisis –

> I breathe – he is no hireling!

When, in this scene, De Mauprat reveals himself, and Richelieu arrests his dagger by showing the arts that have deluded him, the actor produced one of those massive effects which make the fortune of a drama. His commanding air, as he motioned the dupe to his knees; his rapid energy, blent with a look of lofty pity, as he proclaimed that, instead of planning dishonour for Mauprat's wife, he had saved her from it; his indignant look as, with tottering but imperial step, he hurried to the door, and, summoning Julie, confronted De Mauprat with the living proof of his truth – all this caused an excitement which I have rarely seen equalled. It was surpassed, however, by that supreme moment, in the fourth act, when the might of Rome seemed to pass into the sick man's frame, as he sprang up, dominant and terrible, to shield Julie from the King with the aegis of the Church. At this point the vast pit seemed to rock with enthusiasm, as it volleyed its admiration in rounds of thunder. In the final scene of the fifth act, where the Cardinal, apparently on the verge of death, attends the King to resign, and to 'render up the ledgers of a realm', words can but faintly hint the excellence of the performance. How touching was the proud humility of the weak old man as he relinquished, seemingly for ever, the splendid cares of State; how arresting the sight of him as, supported in his chair, his face now grew vacant, as if through the feebleness of nature, now resumed a gleam of intelligence, which at times contracted into pain, as he gathered the policy of his rivals – a policy fatal to France! One noted the uneasy movements of the head, the restless play of the wan fingers, though the lips were silent, till at last the mind fairly struggled awhile through its eclipse, as, in a loud whisper, he warned the King his succours would be wasted upon England. Then came the moment when, recovering the despatch which convicted his foes of treason, he caused it to be handed to the King, and sank supine with the effort. Slowly and intermittently consciousness returned, as Louis thrice implored him to resume his sway over France. So naturally marked were the fluctuations between life and death, so subtly graduated (though comprised within a few moments) were the signs of his recovery, that the house utterly forgot its almost incredible quickness when, in answer to the King's apprehensive cry as to the traitors –

Where will they be next week?

Richelieu springs up resuscitated, and exclaims –

There, at my feet!

But it was not alone by acting, however fine, in this particular situation, that his triumph over probability was obtained. He had from the beginning of the play so seized every opportunity of identifying his fortunes with the greatness of his country, that when the King besought him to live for France, it seemed quite in the order of nature such an adjuration should have magical force. Who can forget the electrical rapidity and decision with which Macready, as the revivified minister cut the Gordian knots of policy? The waiting envoys shall now have their answer. Chavigny, halting not for sleep or food, shall 'arrest the Duc de Bouillon at the head of his armies'. Baradas, who has 'lost the stake', shall pay it and go out under guard. The barque of the State, but now tossing and plunging, a waif on the bosom of chance, has once more a helmsman, knows a course, and, through the sheer waters, bears on. And interests, dear though minor, confess the sudden change. Poor Julie, lately trembling for her husband's life, seeks in his death writ but 'parchment for battledores'. The epicure and traitor, De Berrighen, scents danger to his dear health in the air of Paris. On François, the page who regained the despatch, again falls the smile that cheered and now rewards him. 'He will never say fail again!' Ah, Joseph, trusty Joseph, bishop to be! The minister's policy – prompt action, daring and retribution – the old man's fondness, the cynic's raillery, the patron's indulgence and humour – this brilliant résumé of Richelieu throughout the play was so given, flash after flash, that its various effects seemed simultaneous rather than successive. Thus it was an audience dazzled, almost bewildered by the brilliancy of the achievement, that, on the instant fall of the curtain, burst into a roar of admiration that, wild, craving, unappeasable, pursued, like a sea, the retreating actor, and swept him back to the front.

Our Recent Actors, Vol. I, 1888

G. H. Lewes
Macready

In Edmund Kean and Rachel we recognize types of genius; in Macready I see only a man of talent, but of talent so marked and individual that it approaches very near to genius; and, indeed, in justification of those admirers who would claim for him the higher title, I may say that Tieck, whose opinion on such a matter will be received with great respect, told me that Macready seemed to him a better actor than either Kean or John Kemble; and he only saw Macready in the early part of his long and arduous career.

Of John Kemble I cannot, of course, speak. And with respect to Kean, while claiming for him the indisputable superiority in the highest reaches of his art, I should admit that he was inferior to Macready in that general flexibility of talent and in that range of intellectual sympathy which are necessary to the personation of many and various parts. In this sense Macready was the better actor. And he showed it also in another striking difference. Kean created scarcely any new parts: with the exception of Bertram, Brutus and Sir Edward Mortimer, all his attempts with modern plays were more or less failures. He gave the stamp of his own great power to Shylock, Othello, Sir Giles Overreach and Richard; but he could not infuse life into Virginius or Tell, nor would he, perhaps, have succeeded with Werner, Richelieu, Claude Melnotte, Ruy Gomez and the fifty other parts which Macready created. It is worthy of note that Kean was greatest in the greatest parts, and seemed to require the wide range of Shakspearian passion for his arena; whereas Macready was greatest in parts like Werner, Richelieu, Iago, or Virginius, and always fell short when representing the great Shakspearian hero.

Macready had a voice powerful, extensive in compass, capable of delicate modulation in quiet passages (though with a tendency to scream in violent passages), and having tones that thrilled and tones that stirred tears. His declamation was mannered and unmusical; yet his intelligence always made him follow the winding meanings through the involutions of the verse, and never allowed you to feel, as you feel in the declamation of Charles Kean and many other actors, that he was speaking words which he did not thoroughly understand. The trick of a broken and spasmodic rhythm might destroy the music proper to the verse, but it did not perplex you with false emphasis or intonations wandering at hazard. His person was good, and his face expressive.

We shall perhaps best understand the nature of his talent by thinking of the characters he most successfully personated. They were many and various, implying great flexibility in his powers; but they were not characters of grandeur, physical or moral. They were domestic rather than ideal, and made but slight appeals to the larger passions which give strength to heroes. He was irritable where he should have been passionate, querulous where he should have been terrible.

In Macbeth, for example, nothing could be finer than the indications he gave of a conscience wavering under the influence of 'fate and metaphysical aid', superstitious, and weakly cherishing the suggestions of superstition; but nothing could have been less heroic than his presentation of that great criminal. He was fretful and impatient under the taunts and provocations of his wife; he was ignoble under the terrors of remorse; he stole into the sleeping-chamber of Duncan like a man going to purloin a purse, not like a warrior going to snatch a crown.

In Othello, again, his passion was irritability, and his agony had no grandeur. His Hamlet I thought bad, due allowance being made for the intelligence it displayed. He was lachrymose and fretful: too fond of a cambric pocket-handkerchief to be really affecting; nor, as it seemed to me, had he that sympathy with the character which would have given an impressive unity to his performance – it was 'a thing of shreds and patches', not a whole. In King John, Richard II, Iago, and Cassius all his great qualities were displayed. In Werner he represented the anguish of a weak mind prostrate, with a pathos almost as remarkable as the heroic agony of Kean's Othello. The forlorn look and wailing accent when his son retorts upon him his own plea, 'Who taught me there were crimes made venial by the occasion?' are not to be forgotten. Nor was the fiery impatience of his Cassius less remarkable; it was just the kind of passion he could best express.

In tenderness Macready had few rivals. He could exhibit the noble tenderness of a father in Virginius, as well as the chivalrous tenderness of a lover. None of the young men whom I have seen play Claude Melnotte had the youthfulness of Macready in that part; you lost all sense of his sixty years in the fervour and resilient buoyancy of his manner; and when he paced up and down before the footlights, describing to the charming Pauline with whom his Melnotte is memorably associated – Helen Faucit – the home where love should be, his voice, look, and bearing had an indescribable effect. It was really a rare sight to witness Claude Melnotte and Lear played by the same actor in the same week. The fretful irritability of the senile king was admirably rendered; he *almost* succeeded in making the character credible; and although the terrific curse was probably delivered by Kean with incomparably more grandeur, the screaming vehemence of Macready was quite in keeping with the irritability of the earlier scenes.

He was a thorough artist, very conscientious, very much in earnest, and very careful about all the resources of his art. Hence he was always picturesque in his costume. Often, indeed, his 'get up' was such that, to use a common phrase, he seemed to have stepped from the canvas of one of the old masters.

Compared with anyone we have seen since upon our stage, Macready stands at such an immeasurable height that there must needs be a strange perplexity in the minds of his admirers on learning that while Kean and Young were still upon the stage, Macready was very frequently called 'a mere melodramatic actor'. In any sense which I can affix to this phrase it is absurd. He was by nature unsuited for some great tragic parts; but by his intelligence he was fitted to conceive, and by his organization fitted to express *characters,* and was not like a melodramatic actor – limited to *situations*. Surely Lear, King John, Richard II, Cassius, and Iago are tragic parts? In these he was great; nor could he be surpassed in certain aspects of Macbeth and Coriolanus, although he wanted the heroic thew and sinew to represent these characters as wholes.

He did not belong to the stately declamatory school of Kemble, but in all parts strove to introduce as much familiarity of detail as was consistent with ideal presentation. His touches of 'nature' were sometimes a little out of keeping with the general elevation of the performance, and he was fond of making a 'point' by an abrupt transition from the declamatory to the conversational; but whenever he had an emotion to depict, he depicted it sympathetically and not artificially; by which I mean that he felt himself to be the person, and having identified himself with the character, sought by means of the symbols of his art to express what that character felt; he did not stand outside the character and try to express its emotions by the symbols which had been employed for other characters by other actors. There is a story told of him which may be exaggerated, or indeed may not be true of him, but which at any rate illustrates so well the very important point now under notice that it may be repeated here. In the great scene of the third act of the *Merchant of Venice*, Shylock has to come on in a state of intense rage and grief at the flight of his daughter. Now it is obviously a great trial for the actor to 'strike twelve at once'. He is one moment calm in the green-room, and the next he has to appear on the stage with his whole nature in an uproar. Unless he has a very mobile temperament, quick as flame, he cannot begin this scene at the proper state of white heat. Accordingly, we see actors in general come bawling and gesticulating, but leaving us unmoved because they are not moved themselves. Macready, it is said, used to spend some minutes behind the scenes, lashing himself into an imaginative rage by cursing *sotto voce*, and shaking violently a ladder fixed against the wall. To bystanders the effect must have been ludicrous. But to the audience the actor presented himself as one really agitated. He had worked himself up to the proper pitch of excitement which would enable him to express the rage of Shylock.

I have heard Madame Vestris tell a similar story of Liston, whom she overheard cursing and spluttering to himself, as he stood at the side scene waiting to go on in a scene of comic rage.

* * *

Let me add to this estimate of Macready's powers the brief account I wrote in 1851 of his farewell performance.

On Wednesday night this expected 'solemnity', as the French phrase it, attracted an audience such as the walls of Drury have not enclosed for many a long year. Fortunately, the most rigorous precautions had been taken against overcrowding and occasion for disputes, so that the compact mass of beings was by no means chaotic. Every seat in stalls boxes and slips had been taken long before. Only the pit and galleries had to scramble for places, and by two o'clock the most patient and provident were waiting outside. Fancy the weariness of those four hours' attendance! Vinegar-yard and Little Russell street were dense with masses of expectant, jubilant, sibilant, 'chaffing', swearing, shouting men; and there was no slight crowd to *see* the crowd.

As an immense favour, I was offered two places in the 'basket' (as they call it), at the back of the uppermost boxes; and, in the innocence of my heart, I paid for those places, into which I would not have crammed a dog of any gentility. But I was rescued from this rehearsal of purgatory without its poetry, by the beneficence of a friend whose private box was almost as capacious as his generosity; so that, instead of an imperfect view of the scene, I commanded the whole house. And what a sight that was! How glorious, triumphant, affecting, to see every one starting up, waving hats and handkerchiefs, stamping, shouting, yelling their friendship at the great actor, who now made his appearance on that stage where he was never more to reappear! There was a *crescendo* of excitement enough to have overpowered the nerves of the most self-possessed; and when after an energetic fight – which showed that the actor's powers bore him gallantly up to the last – he fell pierced by Macduff's sword, this death, typical of the actor's death, this last look, this last act of the actor, struck every bosom with a sharp and sudden blow, loosening a tempest of tumultuous feeling such as made applause an ovation.

Some little time was suffered to elapse wherein we recovered from the excitement, and were ready again to burst forth as Macready the Man, dressed in his plain black, came forward to bid 'Farewell, a long farewell, to all his greatness'. As he stood there, calm but sad, waiting till the thunderous reverberations of applause should be hushed, there was one little thing which brought the tears into my eyes, viz, the crape hat-band and black studs, that seemed to me more mournful and more touching than all this vast display of sympathy; it made me forget the paint and tinsel, the artifice and glare of an actor's life, to remember how thoroughly that actor was a man – one of us, sharer of sorrows we all have known or all must know!

Silence was obtained at last; and then in a quiet, sad tone, Macready delivered this address:

'My last theatrical part is played, and, in accordance with long-established usage, I appear once more before you. Even if I were without precedent for the discharge of this act of duty, it is one which my own feelings would irresistibly urge upon me; for, as I look back on my long professional career, I see in it but one continuous record of indulgence and support extended to me, cheering me in my onward progress, and upholding me in most trying emergencies. I have, therefore, been desirous of offering you my parting acknowledgments for the partial kindness with which my humble efforts have uniformly been received, and for a life made happy by your favour. The distance of five-and-thirty years has not dimmed my recollection of the encouragement which gave fresh impulse to the inexperienced essays of my youth, and stimulated me to perseverance when struggling hardly for equality of position with the genius and talent of those artists whose superior excellence I ungrudgingly admitted, admired and honoured. That encouragement helped to place me, in respect to privileges and emolument, on a footing with my distinguished competitors. With the growth of time your favour seemed to grow; and undisturbed in my hold on your opinion, from year to year I found friends more closely and thickly clustering round me. All I can advance to testify how justly I appreciated the patronage thus liberally awarded me is the devotion throughout those years of my best energies to your service. My ambition to establish a theatre, in regard to decorum and taste, worthy of our country, and to leave in it the plays of our divine Shakspeare fitly illustrated, was frustrated by those whose duty it was, in virtue of the trust committed to them, themselves to have undertaken the task. But some good seed has yet been sown; and in the zeal and creditable productions of certain of our present managers we have assurance that the corrupt editions and unseemly presentations of past days will never be restored, but that the purity of our great poet's text will henceforward be held on our English stage in the reverence it ever should command. I have little more to say. By some the relation of an actor to his audience is considered slight and transient. I do not feel it so. The repeated manifestation, under circumstances personally affecting me, of your favourable sentiments towards me, will live with life among my most grateful memories; and, because I would not willingly abate one jot in your esteem, I retire with the belief of yet unfailing powers, rather than linger on the scene, to set in contrast the feeble style of age with the more vigorous exertions of my better years. Words – at least such as I can command – are ineffectual to convey my thanks. In offering them, you will believe I feel far more than I give utterance to. With sentiments of the deepest gratitude I take my leave, bidding you, ladies and gentlemen, in my professional capacity, with regret and most respectfully, farewell.'

This was received with renewed applause. Perhaps a less deliberate speech would have better suited the occasion; a few words full of the eloquence of the moment would have made a deeper and more memorable impression; but under such trying circumstances a man may naturally be afraid to trust himself to the inspiration of the moment. Altogether I must praise Macready for the dignity with which he retired, and am glad that he did not *act*. There was no ostentation of cambric sorrow; there was no well got-up broken voice to simulate emotion. The manner was calm, grave, sad, and dignified.

Macready retires into the respect of private life. A reflection naturally arises on the perishableness of an actor's fame. He leaves no monument behind him but his name. This is often thought a hardship. I believe that great confusion exists in the public mind on this subject.

It is thought a hardship that great actors in quitting the stage can leave no monument more solid than a name. The painter leaves behind him pictures to attest his power; the author leaves behind him books; the actor leaves only a tradition. The curtain falls – the artist is annihilated. Succeeding generations may be told of his genius: none can test it.

All this I take to be a most misplaced sorrow. With the best wishes in the world I cannot bring myself to place the actor on a level with the painter or the author. I cannot concede to the actor such a parity of intellectual greatness;

while, at the same time, I am forced to remember that, with inferior abilities, he secures far greater reward, both of pudding and praise. It is not difficult to assign the causes of an actor's superior reward, both in noisy reputation and in solid guineas. He amuses. He amuses more than the most amusing author. And our luxuries always cost us more than our necessities. Taglioni or Carlotta were better paid than Edmund Kean or Macready; Jenny Lind better than both put together.

But while the dramatic artist appeals to a larger audience, and moves them more forcibly than either painter or author, owing to the very nature of his art, a very slight acquaintance with acting and actors will suffice to show there can be no parity in the rank of a great painter and a great actor. Place Kean beside Caravaggio (and, though I select the greatest actor I have known, I take a third-rate painter, not wishing to overpower the argument with such names as Raphael, Michel Angelo, Titian), and ask what comparison can be made of their intellectual qualifications! Or take Macready and weigh him in the scale with Bulwer or Dickens.

The truth is, we exaggerate the talent of an actor because we judge only from the effect he produces, without enquiring too curiously into the means. But, while the painter has nothing but his canvas and the author has nothing but white paper and printer's ink with which to produce his effects, the actor has all other arts as handmaids: the poet labours for him, creates his part, gives him his eloquence, his music, his imagery, his tenderness, his pathos, his sublimity; the scene-painter aids him; the costumes, the lights, the music, all the fascinations of the stage – all subserve the actor's effect: these raise him upon a pedestal; remove them, and what is he? He who can make a stage mob bend and sway with his eloquence, what could he do with a real mob, no poet by to prompt him? He who can charm us with the stateliest imagery of a noble mind, when robed in the sables of Hamlet, or in the toga of Coriolanus, what can he do in coat and trousers in the world's stage? Rub off the paint, and the eyes are no longer brilliant! Reduce the actor to his intrinsic value, and then weigh him with the rivals whom he surpasses in reputation and in fortune.

If my estimate of the intrinsic value of acting is lower than seems generally current, it is from no desire to disparage an art I have always loved; but from a desire to state what seems to me the simple truth on the matter, and to show that the demand for posthumous fame is misplaced. Already the actor gets more fame than he deserves, and we are called upon to weep that he gets no more. During his reign the applause which follows him exceeds in intensity that of all other claimants for public approbation; so long as he lives he is an object of strong sympathy and interest; and when he dies he leaves behind him such influence upon his art as his genius may have effected (true fame!) and a monument to kindle the emulation of successors. Is not that enough? Must *he* weep because other times will not see his acting? Must *we* weep because all that energy, labour, genius, if you will, is no more than a tradition? Folly! In this crowded world how few there are who can leave even a name, how rare those who leave more. The author can be read by future ages! Oh! yes he *can* be read: the books are preserved; but *is* he read? Who disturbs them from their repose upon the dusty shelves of silent libraries? What are the great men of former ages, with rare, very rare, exceptions, but *names* to the world which shelves their well-bound volumes!

Unless some one will tell me in sober gravity (what is sometimes absurdly said in fulsome dinner speeches and foolish dedications) that the actor has a 'kindred genius' with the poet, whose creations he represents, and that in sheer intellectual calibre Kean and Macready were nearly on a par with Shakspeare, I do not see what cause or complaint can exist in the actor's not sharing the posthumous fame of a Shakspeare. His fame while he lives surpasses that of almost all other men. Byron was not so widely worshipped as Kean. Lawrence and Northcote, Wilkie and Mulready, what space did they fill in the public eye compared with Young, Charles Kemble, or Macready? Surely this renown is ample?

If Macready share the regret of his friends, and if he yearn for posthumous fame, there is yet one issue for him to give the world assurance of his powers. Shakspeare is a good raft whereon to float securely down the stream of time; fasten yourself to that and your immortality is safe. Now Shakspeare must have occupied more of Macready's time and thought than any other subject. Let fruits be given. Let us have from him an edition of Shakspeare, bringing all his practical experience as an actor to illustrate this the first of dramatists. We want no more black letter. We want no more hyperboles of admiration. We want the dramatic excellence and defects illustrated and set forth. Will Macready undertake such a task? It would be a delightful *object* to occupy his leisure; and it would settle the question as to his own intellectual claims.

The foregoing was written in 1851. This year, 1875, the *Reminiscences and Diaries of Macready* have been given to the world by Sir Frederick Pollock, and they strikingly confirm the justice of my estimate, which almost reads like an echo of what Macready himself expressed. In those volumes we see the incessant study which this eminently conscientious man to the last bestowed on every detail connected with his art; we see also how he endeavoured by study to make up for natural deficiencies, and how conscious he was of these deficiencies. We see him oversensitive to the imaginary disrespect in which his profession is held, and throughout his career hating the stage, while devoting himself to the art. But although his sensitiveness suffered from many of the external conditions of the player's life, his own acceptance by the world was a constant rebuke to his exaggerated claims. He was undeniably a cultivated, honourable, and able man, and would have made an excellent clergyman or member of Parliament; but there is absolutely no evidence that he could have made such a figure either in the Church or Senate as would compare with that which he made upon the stage.

On Actors and the Art of Acting, 1875

Henry Morley
Helen Faucit as Imogen

5 NOVEMBER 1864

At Drury Lane the reappearance of Miss Helen Faucit brought us *Cymbeline*; for Imogen, the most beautiful of Shakespeare's female characters, is that in which this lady seems most to delight and to excel, and with this she desired, in returning to the London stage of which she was some years since a chief ornament, to make her first impression. The play had been formerly acted at Drury Lane with very good scenery of its own, so that on its recent revival it was found to be in all respects well mounted, and the acting did not greatly impede the sense in following the exquisite freedom of the poet's fancy through the swiftly changing scene of British court and Roman camp and royalty of man in savage mountain life. No mortal actors, perhaps, can fitly speak the lament of Guiderius and Arviragus over the body of Fidele. There was inevitably much that jarred in the representation. But Miss Faucit was on the whole well supported, and she had Mr Phelps for Posthumus and Mr Creswick for Iachimo, parts that no living actors could have better filled. In its tenderness and grace of womanhood, in the simple piety that looks to the gods when Imogen commits herself to rest or is about to read a letter from her husband, in the wife's absolute love and perfect innocence, void of false shame, slow to believe ill, strong to resist it, Miss Faucit's Imogen is eloquent to our eyes, even when she fails, now and then, to satisfy our ears. She is an actress trained in the school of the Kembles, careful to make every gesture an embodiment of thought, too careful sometimes, as when, after the cry, 'What ho, Pisanio!' she remains with upraised arm throughout half the speech of Iachimo that begins 'O happy Leonatus!' There is a graver fault of excess in the first part of the representation of womanly fear when, as Fidele, she calls at the mouth of the unoccupied cavern, and runs from the sound herself had made. The warning of her error might be found in the fact that her pantomime here excites rather general laughter, where surely Shakespeare never meant that even the dullest boor should grin. But that short sin of excess is followed by the entry into the cavern, which is made most charmingly.

Miss Faucit's voice is more often at fault; it fails her whenever she has a violent emotion to express, and passion sounds often like petulance. The voice may not obey the prompting of the will, or there may be defect of that higher dramatic genius which can make words sound as 'thoughts that breathe'. Whatever be the cause, she fails to express by voice such phases of the character of Imogen as we have in the scene with Pisanio near Milford Haven. Yet where the mere emotion to be expressed is more tender than violent she attains often – though even then, perhaps, with a too visible art – to the utmost delicacy of expression. An example of this is in her picture to Pisanio of how she would have strained her eye to look on her departing lord,

till he had melted from
The smallness of a gnat *to air; and then*
Have turned mine eye and wept.

The sense of the final vanishing, and of the tears that follow it, is here exquisitely rendered by the actress.

The Journal of a London Playgoer, 1891

G. H. Lewes
Charles James Mathews

It has long been the opinion of playgoers and critics that Charles Mathews might fairly be classed with the best French actors in his own line; and the success which during two seasons he has achieved on the French stage is a striking confirmation of that opinion. Although he has been a great favourite with our public from the first night through the whole of his career, it is only of late years that he has displayed remarkable powers as a comedian. He was admired for his grace and elegance, his ease and pleasant vivacity, and for a certain versatile power of mimicry: but critics denied that he was a comedian, and I do not think the critics were unjust, so long as he confined himself to what are called 'character pieces', and did not show his powers in 'character parts'. The difference between his performances in *He Would be an Actor* or *Patter versus Clatter*, and in *The Game of Speculation* or *The Day of Reckoning*, is all the difference between a clever mimic and a fine comedian – between a lively caricaturist and a skilful portrait-painter.

I have followed the career of this actor with delight. His first appearance, in *Old and Young Stagers*, forms a pleasant landing-place in my memory as I wander backwards. The incomparable Liston delayed his departure from the stage in order to protect the début of the son of his old colleague and friend, and there have been few débuts more curiously expected and more cordially welcomed. It was known to 'the boxes' that Charles Mathews had been made a pet of in many aristocratic families, and had acted in private circles at Rome, Florence, and Naples with singular success. It was known to 'the pit' (in those days there were no stalls) that the son of the public favourite, though trained as an architect, had resolved to quit Pugin for Thespis; and as the

Olympic, under the management of Madame Vestris, was the theatre of the elegances and the home of pleasant mirthfulness, the appearance of the young artist at this theatre was in itself an event. But expectations such as these are as perilous to weak pretensions as they are encouraging to real talent; and if Charles Mathews triumphed it was in virtue of very undeniable qualities. Anything so airy and fascinating as this young man had not been seen upon our stage. In general, theatres feel that the *jeune premier* is their weak point. He is bad enough in fiction; but in fiction we do not *see* him, whereas on the stage the weakness of the character is usually aggravated by a 'bend in the back' and an implacable fatuity.

It is a rare assemblage of qualities that enables an actor to be sufficiently good-looking without being insufferably conceited, to be quiet without being absurdly insignificant, to be lively without being vulgar, to look like a gentleman, to speak and move like a gentleman, and yet to be as interesting as if this quietness were only the restraint of power, not the absence of individuality. And the more pronounced the individuality, that is, the more vivacious, the character represented, the greater is the danger of becoming offensive by exaggeration and coarseness.

Charles Mathews was eminently vivacious: a nimble spirit of mirth sparkled in his eye, and gave airiness to every gesture. He was in incessant movement without ever becoming obtrusive or fidgety. A certain grace tempered his vivacity; an innate sense of elegance rescued him from the exaggerations of animal spirits. 'He wanted weight', as an old playgoer once reproachfully said of him; but he had the qualities of his defects, and the want of weight became delightful airiness. Whether he danced the Tarantella with charming Miss Fitzpatrick, or snatched up a guitar and sang, he neither danced like a dancer, nor sang like a singer, but threw the charm of a lively nature into both. I think I see him now in *One Hour* seated opposite Madame Vestris, and made to subdue his restless impatience while he held her skeins of silk – a *very* drawing-room version of Hercules at the feet of Omphale – and I picture to myself how the majority of *jeunes premiers* would comport themselves in that position.

In our juvenile apprehensions he was the beau-ideal of elegance. We studied his costumes with ardent devotion. We envied him his tailor, and 'made him our patron to live and to die'. We could see no faults in him; and all the criticisms which our elders passed on him grated harshly in our ears as the croaking of 'fogies'. As a proof of my enthusiasm I may mention that I wrote a one-act comedy for him, at an age when anything less than five acts and blank verse seemed beneath the dignity of an aspiring author (I will do him the justice to say that he did not accept it).

But if no faults were discernible then, I now see, in retrospect, that it was the charm of the man rather than any peculiar talent in the actor which carried him so successfully through those little Olympic pieces; and that when he began to try his powers in more exacting parts – such as Charles Surface, for instance – there was still the old elegance but not the old success. Practice and study, however, made him an accomplished comedian within a certain range,

the limits of which are determined by his singular want of passionate expression. No good actor I have ever seen was so utterly powerless in the manifestation of all the powerful emotions: rage, scorn, pathos, dignity, vindictiveness, tenderness and wild mirth are all beyond his means. He cannot even
laugh with animal heartiness. He sparkles, he never explodes. Yet his keen
observation, his powers of imitation, and a certain artistic power of preserving
the unity of a character in all its details, are singularly shown in such parts as
Lavater, Sir Charles Coldstream, Mr Affable Hawk, and the villain in *The
Day of Reckoning*.

This last mentioned part was, unfortunately for him, excluded from his
habitual repertory by the disagreeable nature of the piece. A French melodrama,
never worth much even on the Boulevards, and still less adapted to the Lyceum
audiences, afforded him an opportunity which I think is unique in his varied
career, the opportunity of portraying a melodramatic villain: and he showed
himself a great comedian in the way he portrayed it. Imagine a Count D'Orsay
destitute alike of principle and of feeling, the incarnation of heartless elegance,
cool yet agreeable, admirable in all the externals which make men admired in
society, and hateful in all the qualities tested by the serious trials of life; such
was the Count presented by Charles Mathews. Instead of 'looking the villain',
he looked like the man to whom all drawing-rooms would be flung open.
Instead of warning away his victims by a countenance and manner more
significant of villainy than the description of the 'Hue and Cry', he allured
them with the graceful ease of a conscience quite at rest, and the manner of
an assured acceptance. Whether the pit really understood this presentation,
and felt it as a rare specimen of art, I cannot say; but I am sure that no critic
capable of ridding himself of conventional prepossession would see such a
bit of action and forget it.

It is needless to speak of his performance in *The Game of Speculation*, the
artistic merit of which was so great that it almost became an offence against
morality, by investing a swindler with irresistible charms, and making the very
audacity of deceit a source of pleasurable sympathy. Enough to say that all
who had the opportunity of comparing this performance with that of the
original actor of the part in France, declared that the superiority of Charles
Mathews was incalculable (I have since seen Got, the great comedian of the
Théâtre Français, in this part, yet I prefer Charles Mathews).

The multitude of characters, some of them excellent types, which he has
portrayed, is so great that I cannot name a third of them. They had all one
inestimable quality, that of being pleasant; and the consequence is that he is
a universal favourite. Indeed, the personal regard which the public feels for
him is something extraordinary when we consider that it is not within the scope
of his powers to *move* us by kindling any of our deeper sympathies. And it is
interesting to compare this feeling of regard with its absence in the case of
Farren. Farren was assuredly a finer actor, and held a more undisputed position on the stage, for he had simply no rival at all. His career was long, and
unvaryingly successful. Yet the public which applauded him as an actor did
not feel much personal regard for him as a man; whereas for Charles Mathews

the feeling was not inaptly expressed by an elderly gentleman in the boxes of the Lyceum on the fall of the curtain one night after *The Game of Speculation*: 'And to think of such a man being in difficulties! There ought to be a public subscription got up to pay his debts.'

* * *

The reappearance of Charles Mathews in one of his favorite parts, in *Used Up*, after having played that part with great success in Paris, naturally attracts large audiences to the Haymarket; and as I had not seen him play it for many years it drew me there, that I might enjoy what now becomes more and more of a rarity, a really fine bit of acting. Nor was my enjoyment balked, as far as he was concerned, although it would have been greater had there been a little more attention paid to the mounting of the piece. The Haymarket Theatre is, or rather pretends to be, our leading theatre for comedy. And on such a stage, or indeed on any stage, the insolent disregard of all artistic conditions which could permit such a performance as that of Sir Adonis Leech by Mr Rogers (an actor not without merit in certain characters), and which could allow a valet to be dressed like Mr Clark, implies a state of facile acquiescence on the part of the public which explains the utter decay of the drama. As long as critics are silent and the groundlings laugh, such things will continue. If Mr Rogers can be accepted as the representative of an English gentleman of our day, if aspect and bearing such as his can pass without protest, what can be the peculiar delight received from the exquisite elegance and verisimilitude of Charles Mathews? My private conviction is that the majority of the audience enjoyed the fun of the *part* with very little enjoyment of the *acting*; and what deepens this conviction is that there was more applause in the second act, where the fun 'grows fast and furious', and where the acting is indifferent, than in the first act, where the acting is perfect and the fun mild. As the languorous man of fashion Charles Mathews is faultless. There is an exquisite moderation in his performance which shows a nice perception of nature. The coolness is never overdone. The languor is never obtruded. When the blacksmith is threatening him, there is nothing to suggest that he is assuming an attitude of indifference. From first to last we have a character the integrity of which is never sacrificed to isolated effects.

But in the second act, where the man of fashion appears as a plough-boy, all sense of artistic truth is wanting. There are two methods of carrying out the dramatic conception of this act – one which should present a plough-boy, with enough verisimilitude to deceive the farmer and delight the audience; the other, which should present a gentleman acting the plough-boy, and every now and then overacting or forgetting the part, and always when alone, or with Mary, relapsing into his native manner. Now Charles Mathews misses both these. He is not at all like a plough-boy, nor like Sir Charles Coldstream acting the plough-boy. So little regard has he to truth, that he does not even remove the rings from his white fingers, although a jewelled hand is not usually seen directing a plough. Nor when the farmer is absent does the removal of such a constraint make any change in his voice and bearing. The situations of this act are funny, and the amused spectators perhaps enjoy the broad contrast between the elegance of Sir Charles and the homeliness of the plough-boy; but an accomplished comedian like Charles Mathews ought to have seized such an opportunity of revealing the elegance and refined coolness of the man under the necessary coarseness of his assumed character. The alterations are just the sort of effects which one could fancy must be tempting to an artist conscious of his powers. It is, however, plain to anyone who is sufficiently critical to discriminate between the acting and the situation, that Charles Mathews has no distinct conception in his mind of any character at all placed in this difficult situation, but that he abandons himself to the situation, and allows the fun of it to do his work. In other words it is farce, not comedy: whereas the first act is comedy, and high comedy.

As I did not see what the French critics wrote about his performance, I cannot say what effect this act had on them. And, indeed, as, according to my experience, the French critics usually confine their remarks to the general impression of a performance, and seldom analyse it, they may have contented themselves with eulogies varied by allusions to Arnal, who created the part. Yet I am much mistaken if they also did not perceive the glaring discrepancy between the first and second acts; and whatever Arnal may have done, I feel persuaded that Bouffé or Got (supposing them to have played the parts) could have made the second act quite as remarkable for its representation of character as the first act.

After *Used Up* came the burlesque of *The Golden Fleece*, with Compton delightfully humorous as the King, and Charles Mathews inimitably easy as the Chorus. Compton's burlesque seems to me in the very finest spirit of artistic drollery, and as unlike what is usually attempted as true comedy is unlike efforts to be funny. Bad actors seem to imagine that they have only to be extravagant to be burlesque; as bad comedians think they have only to make grimaces to be comic. But Robson and Compton, guided by a true artistic sense, show that burlesque acting is the grotesque personation of a character, not the outrageous defiance of all character; the personation has truth, although the character itself may be preposterously drawn.

A similar remark may be made of the acting of Charles Mathews as the Chorus. He is assuredly not what would be called a burlesque actor in the ordinary acceptation of the term, nor would any one familiar with his style suppose him capable of the heartiness and force usually demanded by burlesque; and yet, because he is a fine actor, he is fine also in burlesque, giving a truthful and easy personation to an absurd conception. Another actor in such a part as Chorus would have 'gagged' or made grimaces, would have been extravagant and sought to startle the public into laughter at broad incongruities. Charles Mathews is as quiet, easy, elegant, as free from points and as delightfully humorous as if the part he played and the words he uttered belonged to high comedy; he allows the incongruity of the character and the language to work their own laughable way, and he presents them with the gravity of one who believed them. Notice also the singular unobtrusiveness of his manner, even when the situation is most broadly sketched. For example, when the King interrupts his song by an appeal to Chorus, Charles Mathews steps forward, and, bending over the footlights with that quiet gravity which has hitherto marked his familiar explanations of what is going on, begins to sing *fol de riddle lol*. There is not one actor in a score who would not have spoiled the humour of this by a wink or grimace at the audience, as much as to say, 'Now I'm going to make you laugh.' The imperturbable gravity and familiar ease of Mathews give a drollery to this *fol de riddle lol* which is indescribable. Probably few who saw Charles Mathews play the Chorus consider there was any art required to play it; they can understand that to sing patter songs as he sings them may not be easy, but to be quiet and graceful and humorous, to make every line tell, and yet never show the stress of effort, will not seem wonderful. If they could see another actor in the part it would open their eyes.

On Actors and the Art of Acting, 1875

G. H. Lewes
Charles Kean as Macbeth

I should like to write an essay on *Macbeth*, but journalistic necessities compel me to confine myself to the two leading characters, and of them to speak only in hints.

Macbeth himself admits of two different conceptions. He may be represented as 'bloody, bold, and resolute' – a border chieftain in a turbulent and incult period – a man of the dark ages, rushing onwards with reckless impetuosity – murdering his royal host, seizing the crown, and accomplishing his *coup d'état* without respect to persons. In this view, all the metaphysical meshes which entangle him would be but the excuses of his conscience, or the instruments used to serve his purpose; they would be to him what 'Socialism' and 'saving society' were to that more ignoble usurper who snatched a crown in 1852. I do not think this the Shakespearian Macbeth; but I think it is a conception of the character which might be very dramatic and effective. The other and the truer conception would represent a wild, rude, heroic nature, hurried by his passions into crime, but great even in crime – severed from the rectilinear path of honour by the horrible suggestions of the Witches coming upon him in the flush and exaltation of victory, and playing on his active imaginations, making him its slave. For Macbeth is distinctively a bold soldier, and a man of most impressible imagination. He is intensely superstitious: in those days all men were, but the imaginative were so to an inordinate degree. He *sees* a dagger in the air; he *hears* the sleeper say, 'Macbeth doth murder sleep; Macbeth shall sleep no more.' He tells us how

> The time has been my senses would have cool'd
> To hear a night-shriek; and my fell of hair
> Would at a dismal treatise rouse and stir
> As life were in't.

(By the way, is 'fell of hair' the correct phrase, and what can it mean? May not one suggest 'fall of hair' – i.e. the hair which naturally falls on his shoulders would rise up in horror.) So that when the Witches prophesy that he shall be king, he is moved deeply, his active imagination shaping possibilities –

> My thought, whose murder yet is but fantastical
> Shakes so my single state of man, that function
> Is smothered in surmise.

But Banquo, to whom the greatness of a line of kings is promised, is not moved at all, disbelieves, in fact, the diabolical suggestion. Thus, we see, Macbeth is represented as more imaginative than the common run of men. He is good, too; full of the milk of human kindness. He would be great, is not without ambition, but is without the illness which should attend it. He desires highly, but would win holily. He has a moral conscience. And here lies the tragedy. He is no common murderer; he is criminal because great temptations overcome great struggles; the tragic collision of antagonistic principles – Ambition and Conscience – take him from the records of vulgar crime, and raise him into a character fitly employed by Art. One might enlarge here upon the manner in which Shakespeare's own intense reflectiveness is allowed to shine through his varied creations. He cannot even take this wild, feudal chief, without making him nearly as metaphysical as Hamlet. I hint this view, and pass on.

All through the play we see him as one made irresolute by conscience, but resolute and terrible in act – when roused to action – because his nature is that of a brave onrushing soldier. His hands once reddened by murder, he pursues with vigour the murderer's career. He is bold, even in the very face of his superstition. What though Birnam wood *be* come to Dunsinane, and what though Macduff be not of woman born, the soldier fights like a desperate man, defiant of the metaphysical terrors that shake him.

Does Charles Kean represent either of these characters? He does not. He cannot be said to take any view of the *character* at all; he tries to embody the various feelings of each situation; taking, however, the literal and unintelligent interpretation, so that almost every phase of the character is falsified. We see neither the gallant soldier, nor the imaginative man. His bearing is neither warrior-like nor reflective. The wondrous touches with which Shakespeare illuminates the character are all slurred over by hin. When the witches accost him, his only expression of 'metaphysical influence' is to stand still with his eyes fixed and his mouth open, in the way you know. The *fluctuating* emotions which Macbeth must be undergoing all that time are expressed by a *fixed* stare. And the profound art of Shakespeare, shown in Macbeth's *tentative* appeals to Banquo – avoiding all mention of what the witches promised him, yet trying to get at Banquo's thoughts by alluding to Banquo's children – these touches, which an actor of intelligence could not, one would think, fail to make impressive, are passed over by Charles Kean, as if they were ordinary lines of the text. As a palpable illustration of his unintelligent reading of the character, let me refer to what I have before called his *literal* interpretation (it is of that kind which always supposes that the words 'tears' must be uttered in a tearful voice). In that famous dagger soliloquy, will it be credited that he does not rise to a crescendo of horrible amazement at the words –

Thou marshall'st me the way that I was going!

but at the superfluous fact that –

Such an instrument I was to use;

and again he flies into a paroxysm of horror at seeing 'on its blade and dudgeon gouts of blood'. Now, considering that he has already determined on murdering Duncan, and the dagger has marshalled him the way, the horror at gouts of blood is ludicrous; the horror is the parent, not the child of his blood; it precedes, it does not succeed it. Let me call attention to one egregious and constant mistake Charles Kean commits in this as in other parts – viz, the alternation of explosive rant with calmness. One moment he is ranting till his voice is hoarse, and the next he is as quiet as a melancholy recluse. Now every one knows that even in the subsidence of rage there is peculiar agitation; and although the voice may be low, its tones are tremulous.

In Charles Kean's Macbeth all the tragedy has vanished; sympathy is impossible, because the mind of the criminal is hidden from us. He makes Macbeth ignoble – one whose crime is that of a common murderer, with perhaps a tendency towards Methodism.

I believe my readers by this time are pretty well assured of my impartiality, and that the opinions I utter are irrespective of personal considerations; they may be erroneous, but they are mine. Moreover, I have praised Charles Kean enough on other occasions to be allowed, without suspicion, to say how poor his performance of Macbeth seems to me. And for that opinion I have assigned the reasons. If any one seeing Macbeth can discover in Charles Kean either the heroic soldier or the imaginative man; if he can say that the reading of the character as a whole, or of individual passages, was such as embodied the plain text, then let what I have written go for nothing.

Let me add, however, that bad as the performance was, it had fine points. The weariness of guilt was tragically, and even imaginatively, portrayed, the terror after the deed *was* terror, although I think it had more the aspect of a house-breaker's fear of the police than of Macbeth's agitated conscience; and the desperation at the close *was* desperation. At times Charles Kean does things so well, that one is at a loss to conceive how it is he can have been acting fine parts so many years, and yet fall short of what every one demands in a Shakespearian character.

It is now some twenty years since Mrs Charles Kean first attempted the character of Lady Macbeth in London. She was then a charming actress of comedy and the lighter parts of tragedy; her very charmingness was an obstacle to her representation of Lady Macbeth, according to the received notion in England; and she failed in it. I do not remember her performance; but I suspect that it was much better than the public, accustomed to the Siddons type, would accept. Indeed, I am very much of Mrs Siddons's opinion, that Lady Macbeth was a fair, delicate, *womanly* woman; capable of great 'valour of the tongue'; capable of nerving herself for any one great object, but showing by her subsequent remorse and broken heart that she had been *playing* a part. Be this as it may, Mrs Charles Kean was not successful then, and is successful now. I do not accept her view of the part, but at any rate she *has* a view, and realizes it with a vulture-like ferocity. In no sense was she weak; in the sleep-walking scene she was terrific.

It is not, however, so much the acting as the 'getting up' of Macbeth which will attract the public. In some respects the *mise en scène* is worthy of loud praise, and makes one almost forget the bad taste of the play-bill, whereof a whole page is devoted to an exposition of the authorities of the costumes adopted. Charles Mathews has set a wretched example, and one may now expect all managers to make the play-bill a fly-sheet of criticism and erudition, unless a little timely ridicule warn them of their danger. Charles Kean makes a formidable display; talks familiarly of Diodorus Siculus, Pliny, Strabo, Xiphilin, and the Eyrbyggia Saga. Xiphilin! he read Xiphilin! What a name to fling at the pit! How many of his public ever turn over the leaves of that abbreviator of Dion Cassius? And the manager himself, does he *really* read Xiphilin? 'A question not to be asked', for listen to his preface, written in the choicest English –

> The success which attended the production of *King John* last season at this theatre has encouraged me to attempt another Shakespearian revival on the same scale. The very uncertain information, however, which we possess respecting the dress worn by the inhabitants of Scotland in the eleventh century, renders any attempt to present the tragedy of *Macbeth* attired in the costume of that period a task of very great difficulty. I hope, therefore, I may not be deemed presumptuous if I intrude a few words upon the subject, and endeavour to explain upon what authorities I have based my opinions.

Could he have heard the 'guffaws' which saluted that bill, he would have fervently wished it unwritten. It was praiseworthy in him to take so much pains about his costume; but suppose Mr Smith were to follow this example, and tell the public all the books on the Australian diggings he *might* have read before producing *Gold* or Mr Webster were to tell us all the authorities upon which he based his *opinions* before he produced *Masks and Faces*!

This is a digression. Let me return to the *mise en scène*, which really does display research and ingenuity. All the old stage 'business' has been altered, and mostly improved. Thus, the wounded soldier, instead of coming on as if he had run all the way from the battlefield, is brought in on a litter. The banquet scene, again, has a most lifelike and picturesque aspect – it is a real glimpse into feudal times. The appearances of Banquo's ghost are admirable, and ghostly. The scenery throughout is both pictorial and historical. For a spectacle, one cannot desire anything more animated, varied, imposing. It shows – what I have always said – that Charles Kean has a real appreciation of artistic *mise en scène*, and that whatever one may think of him as an actor, he deserves public support as a manager. But there is a want perceptible through it all – the want of poetical mind. Melodramatic effects he can reach – he falls short of poetry. Thus, the least effective portion of the present *mise en scène* is the witch portion. In the first place, for one who pretends to care for Shakespeare, it is a gross violation of the poet's meaning to multiply the three weird sisters – those Parcae of the north – into some fifty absurdly attired witches, called it managerial English 'the vocal *strength* engaged for this occasion' (and strength of lungs they did display!). How much effect is lost by this need only be hinted. In the next place, these witches exhibit a fatiguing unanimity: they all simultaneously throw their arms up and down, again, as an expression of rejoicing, till one thinks they are puppets moved by mechanism – living marionettes. The same mistake is committed by the other crowds upon the stage – they throw themselves into the *same* attitude at given signals, thereby destroying the peculiarity of a mob of individuals.

These are but small deductions from the general effect, which is, assuredly, very remarkable; and for those who want to see *Macbeth* arranged as a spectacle – indifferent whether it be Shakespearian or not – I can promise them that a visit to the Princess's will be a treat. Indeed, I am anxious that all my readers should go, if only to test the accuracy of what is here written on the acting.

The Leader, 19 February 1853

G. H. Lewes
Charles Kean in *The Corsican Brothers*

Charles Kean, after vainly battling with fate so many years, seems now, consciously or unconsciously, settling down into the conviction that his talent does not lie in any Shakespearian sphere whatever, but in melodrames, such as *Pauline* or his last venture, *The Corsican Brothers*, where, as high intellect is not *de rigueur*, he is not restricted by its fastidious exigencies. It is certainly worth a passing remark, to note how bad an actor he is in any part requiring the expression of intellect or emotion – in any part demanding some sympathy with things poetical – in any part calling for *representative* power, and how impressive, and, I may say, *unrivalled*, he is in gentlemanly melodrama. The successful portions of his tragic characters are all melodramatic; and in *Pauline* and *The Corsican Brothers* he satisfies all the exigencies of criticism. I shall not be suspected of partiality, and I beg the reader not to suppose any latent irony in my praise (for I am *not* afraid to praise Kean when that praise is due), and with this preface, let me say that *The Corsican Brothers* is the most daring, ingenious, and exciting melodrama I remember to have seen; and is mounted with an elegance, an accuracy, an ingenuity in the mingling of the supernatural with the real, and an artistic disposition of effects, such as perhaps no theatre could equal, certainly not surpass.

The first act sets forth Corsican life in its wildness, its superstitions, and its *vendetta*. An excellent scene is that of the reconciliation of the Orlandos and the Colonnas, and their relinquishment of the *vendetta* – a scene both fresh and effective, and capitally played by Ryder; but it has nothing to do with the piece, and surprises by its presence in a French drama, where construction is always so careful. Its only office is to bring visibly before us the Corsican feeling about *la vendetta*. Besides this feeling, there is another indicated in this act – viz, the mysterious affinity of the twin brothers, Louis and Fabian, through which they communicate at whatever distance. Fabian is now restless and uneasy, convinced that something has happened to his brother Louis; and, while he writes to him, to learn the truth, the spectre of his brother, with blood on his breast, appears to him. Nothing can exceed the art with which this is managed; with ghostly terror, heightened by the low tremolos of the violins, and the dim light upon the stage, the audience, breath-suspended, watches the slow apparition, and the vision of the duel which succeeds; a scenic effect more real and terrible than anything I remember.

By a daring novelty of construction, the second act is supposed to go on simultaneously with the first, so that at the end of the second, the two are blended in one vision. The second act opens with a gay and brilliant scene of a *bal de l'opéra* wonderfully well done – the groups animated and life-like, the dresses splendid and various, and the drama naturally issuing out of the groups in the most unforced manner. The *action* of this act is simply the entanglement of Louis in the circumstances which lead to the duel wherein he is killed, as the vision of Act I exhibited to us. The third act is brief, and is little more than the duel with Fabian, come from Corsica to avenge his brother; but it is surrounded with a number of superstitious circumstances that give a shuddering anxiety to every passage. Fabian and Chateau Renaud fight; during the pause, the latter leans upon his sword, and breaks it. Fabian, to equalize the combat, snaps his sword also, and both then take the broken halves, and fastening them in their grasp by cambric handkerchiefs, *they fight as with knives*. This does not *read* as horrible, perhaps; but to see it on the stage, represented with minute ferocity of detail, and with a truth on the part of the actors, which enhances the terror, the effect is so intense, so horrible, so startling,

that one gentleman indignantly exclaimed *un-English*! It was, indeed, gra-
tuitously shocking, and Charles Kean will damage himself in public estimation
by such moral mistakes, showing a vulgar lust for the lowest sources of excitement – the tragedy of the shambles! But it is the fatality of melodrama to
know no limit. The tendency of the senses is *downwards*. To gratify them
stimulants must be added and added, chili upon cayenne, butchery upon
murder, 'horrors on horrors' head accumulated!' And herein lies the secret
weakness and inevitable failure of Melodrama; the secret of the failure of
Le Théâtre Historique, in spite of Dumas, in spite of Melingue, in spite of
the concentration of 'effects', in spite of vogue, scenery, dresses, acting, terrors,
tears, laughter, the clash of swords, the clatter of spurs, the spasms of agony,
the poniards, the poisons, the trap-doors, and moonlight effects – bankruptcy
was the goal to which all tended! The secret, as I said, lies in the fact that
Melodrama appeals to the lowest faculties, the avenues to which are very
limited, consequently the influence is soon exhausted; whereas Drama appeals
to the higher faculties, and *their* avenues are infinite.

But I will not philosophize; enough for the present that the *Corsican
Brothers* is a Melodrame, full of invention, riveting in interest, put on the stage
with immense variety and splendour, and very finely acted. Leave the aesthetic
question aside, and consider the Melodrame *as* a Melodrame, and, short of
the horrible termination, I say we have had nothing so effective for a long
while.

Charles Kean plays the two brothers; and you must see him before you
will believe how well and how *quietly* he plays them; preserving a gentlemanly
demeanour, a drawingroom manner very difficult to assume on the stage,
if one may judge from its rarity, which intensifies the passion of the part,
and gives it a terrible reality. Nothing can be better than the way he steps
forward to defend the insulted woman at that supper; nothing can be more
impressive than his appearance in the third act as the avenger of his brother.
The duel between him and Wigan was a masterpiece on both sides: the Bois
de Boulogne itself has scarcely seen a duel more real or more exciting. Kean's
dogged, quiet, terrible walk after Wigan, with the fragment of broken
sword in his relentless grasp, I shall not forget. Nor can I forget Wigan's
performance. In 'make-up', in demeanour, in look, in tone, he was perfect –
the type of a French duellist.

The Leader, 28 February 1852

Henry Morley
Charles Kean's Production of
A Midsummer Night's Dream

25 OCTOBER 1856

The beautiful mounting of the *Midsummer Night's Dream* at the Princess's Theatre attracts and will attract for a long time crowded audiences. The words of the play are spoken agreeably, some of the sweetest passages charmingly, and much of Shakespeare's delicate pleasantry is made to tell with good effect upon its hearers. The *Midsummer Night's Dream* is full of passages that have only to be reasonably well uttered to be enjoyed even by the dull; and with so fair a Hermia as Miss Bufton, so whimsical a Bottom as Mr Harley, who seems to have no particular conception of the part, but nevertheless makes it highly amusing – with a generally good delivery of words and songs – the play speaks for itself in a great measure.

The one defect in the mounting of the *Midsummer Night's Dream* is that which has lessened the value of many former efforts made at this house to produce Shakespeare with every accessory of scenic decoration. I do not think money ill spent upon stage-furniture, and certainly can only admire the exquisite scenery of the play now being presented at the Princess's; but there may be a defect of taste that mars the effect of the richest ornament, as can best be shown by one or two examples.

Shakespeare's direction for the opening scene of the *Midsummer Night's Dream* is: 'Athens, a Room in the Palace of Theseus'. For this, is read at the Princess's Theatre: 'A Terrace adjoining the Palace of Theseus, overlooking the City of Athens'; and there is presented an elaborate and undoubtedly most beautiful bird's-eye view of Athens as it was in the time of Pericles. A great scenic effect is obtained, but it is, as far as it goes, damaging to the poem. Shakespeare took for his mortals people of heroic times, Duke Theseus and Hippolyta, and it suited his romance to call them Athenians; but the feeling of the play is marred when out of this suggestion of the antique mingled with their fairy world the scene-painter finds opportunity to bring into hard and jarring contrast the Athens of Pericles and our own world of Robin Goodfellow and all the woodland elves. 'A Room in the House of Theseus', left that question of the where or when of the whole story to be touched as lightly as a poet might desire; the poetry was missed entirely by the painting of the scene, beautiful as it is, which illustrates the first act of the *Midsummer Night's Dream* at the Princess's.

In the second act there is a dream-like moving of the wood, beautifully managed and spoilt in effect by a trifling mistake easily corrected. Oberon stands before the scene waving his wand, as if he were exhibitor of the diorama, or a fairy conjurer causing the rocks and trees to move. Nobody I believe, ever attributed to fairies any power of that sort. Oberon should either be off the stage or on it still as death, and it should be left for the spectators to feel the dreamy influence of wood and water slipping by their eyes unhindered and undistracted. This change leads to the disclosure of a fairy ring, a beautiful scenic effect, and what is called in large letters upon the play-bills, 'Titania's Shadow Dance'. Of all things in the world, a shadow dance of fairies! If anything in the way of an effect of light was especially desirable, it would have been such an arrangement as would have made the fairies appear to be dancing in a light so managed as to cast no shadow, and give them the true spiritual attribute. Elaborately to produce and present, as an especial attraction, fairies of large size, casting shadows made as black and distinct as possible, and offering in dance to pick them up, as if even they also were solid, is as great a sacrifice of Shakespeare to the purposes of the ballet-master, as the view of Athens in its glory was a sacrifice of poetry to the scene-painter. Enough has been said to show the direction in which improvement is necessary to make the stage-ornament at the Princess's Theatre as perfect as it is beautiful. The Puck is a pretty little girl, belted and garlanded with flowers! From the third act we miss a portion of the poem most essential to its right effect – the quarrel between Hermia and Helena; but we get, at the end, a ballet of fairies round a maypole that shoots up out of an aloe, after the way of a transformation in a pantomime, and rains down garlands. Fairies, not airy beings of the colour of the greenwood, or the sky, or robed in misty white, but glittering in the most brilliant dresses, with a crust of bullion about their legs, cause the curtain to fall on a splendid ballet; and it is evidence of the depraved taste of the audience to say that the ballet is encored.

I make these comments in no censorious mood. It is a pleasure to see Shakespeare enjoyed by the large number of persons who are attracted to the Princess's Theatre by the splendours for which it is famous. I do not wish the splendour less, or its attraction less, but only ask for more heed to the securing of a perfect harmony between the conceptions of the decorator and those of the poet.

The Journal of a London Playgoer, 1891

Henry Morley
Phelps's Production of
A Midsummer Night's Dream

15 OCTOBER 1853

Every reader of Shakespeare is disposed to regard the *Midsummer Night's Dream* as the most essentially unactable of all his plays. It is a dramatic poem of the utmost grace and delicacy; its characters are creatures of the poet's fancy that no flesh and blood can properly present – fairies who 'creep into acorn-cups', or mortals who are but dim abstractions, persons of a dream. The words they speak are so completely spiritual that they are best felt when they are not spoken. Their exquisite beauty is like that of sunset colours which no mortal artist can interpret faithfully. The device of the clowns in the play to present Moonshine seems but a fair expression of the kind of success that might be achieved by the best actors who should attempt to present the *Midsummer Night's Dream* on the stage. It was, therefore, properly avoided by managers as lying beside and above their art; nor was there reason to be disappointed when the play some years ago furnished Madame Vestris with a spectacle that altogether wanted the Shakespearean spirit.

In some measure there is reason for a different opinion on these matters in the *Midsummer Night's Dream* as produced at Sadler's Wells by Mr Phelps. Though stage fairies cannot ride on bluebells, and the members of no theatrical company now in existence can speak such poetry as that of the *Midsummer Night's Dream* otherwise than most imperfectly, yet it is proved that there remains in the power of the manager who goes with pure taste and right feeling to his work, enough for the establishment of this play as a most charming entertainment of the stage.

Mr Phelps has never for a minute lost sight of the main idea which governs the whole play, and this is the great secret of his success in the presentation of it. He knew that he was to present merely shadows; that spectators, as Puck reminds them in the epilogue, are to think they have slumbered on their seats, and that what appeared before them have been visions. Everything has been subdued as far as possible at Sadler's Wells to this ruling idea. The scenery is very beautiful, but wholly free from the meretricious glitter now in favour; it is not so remarkable for costliness as for the pure taste in which it and all the stage-arrangements have been planned. There is no ordinary scene-shifting; but, as in dreams, one scene is made to glide insensibly into another. We follow the lovers and the fairies through the wood from glade to glade, now among trees, now with a broad view of the sea and Athens in the distance, carefully but not at all obtrusively set forth. And not only do the scenes melt dream-like one into another, but over all the fairy portion of the play there is a haze thrown by a curtain of green gauze placed between the actors and the audience, and maintained there during the whole of the second, third, and fourth acts. This gauze curtain is so well spread that there are very few parts of the house from which its presence can be detected, but its influence is everywhere felt; it subdues the flesh and blood of the actors into something more nearly resembling dream-figures, and incorporates more completely the actors with the scenes, throwing the same green fairy tinge, and the same mist over all. A like idea has also dictated certain contrivances of dress, especially in the case of the fairies.

Very good taste has been shown in the establishment of a harmony between the scenery and the poem. The main feature – the Midsummer Night – was marked by one scene so elaborated as to impress it upon all as the central picture of the group. The moon was just so much exaggerated as to give it the required prominence. The change, again, of this Midsummer Night into morning, when Theseus and Hippolyta come to the wood with horn and hound, was exquisitely presented. And in the last scene, when the fairies, coming at night into the hall of Theseus, 'each several chambers bless', the Midsummer moon is again seen shining on the palace as the curtains are drawn that admit the fairy throng. Ten times as much money might have been spent on a very much worse setting of the *Midsummer Night's Dream*. It is the poetical feeling prompting a judicious but not extravagant outlay, by aid of which Mr Phelps has produced a stage spectacle more refined and intellectual, and far more absolutely satisfactory, than anything I can remember to have seen since Mr Macready was a manager.

That the flesh and blood presentments of the dream-figures which constitute the persons of the play should be always in harmony with this true feeling, was scarcely to be expected. A great deal of the poetry is injured in the speaking. Unless each actor were a man who combined with elocutionary power a very high degree of sensibility and genius, it could hardly be otherwise. Yet it cannot be said even here that the poet's effects entirely failed. The *Midsummer Night's Dream* abounds in the most delicate passages of Shakespeare's verse; the Sadler's Wells pit has a keen enjoyment for them; and pit and gallery were crowded to the farthest wall on Saturday night with a most earnest audience, among whom many a subdued hush arose, not during but just before, the delivery of the most charming passages. If the crowd at Drury Lane is a gross discredit to the public taste, the crowd at Sadler's Wells more than neutralizes any ill opinion that may on the score be formed of playgoers. The Sadler's Wells gallery, indeed, appeared to be not wholly unconscious of the contrast, for, when Bottom volunteered to roar high or roar low, a voice from the gallery desired to know whether he could 'roar like Brooke'. Even the gallery at this theatre, however, resents an interruption and the unexpected sally was not well received.

A remarkably quick-witted little boy, Master F. Artis, plays Puck, and really plays it with faithfulness and spirit as it has been conceived for him by Mr Phelps. His training has evidently been most elaborate. We see at once that his acts and gestures are too perfect and mature to be his own imaginings, but he has been quick-witted enough to adopt them as his own, and give them not a little of the charm of independent and spontaneous production. By this thoughtfulness there is secured for the character on the stage something of the same prominence that it has in the mind of closet-readers of the play.

Of Miss Cooper's Helena we cannot honestly say very much. In that as in most of the other characters the spirit of the play was missed, because the arguing and quarrelling and blundering that should have been playful, dreamlike, and poetical, was much too loud and real. The men and women could not fancy themselves shadows. Were it possible so far to subdue the energy of the whole body of actors as to soften the tones of the scenes between Theseus, Hippolyta, Lysander, Demetrius, Hermia, and Helena, the latter character even on the stage might surely have something of the effect intended by the poem. It is an exquisite abstraction, a pitiful and moving picture of a gentle maid forlorn, playfully developed as beseems the fantastic texture of the poem, but not at all meant to excite mirth; and there was a very great mistake made when the dream was so worked out into hard literalness as to create constant laughter during those scenes in which Helena, bewildered by the change of mood among the lovers, shrinks and complains, 'Wherefore was I to this keen mockery born?' The merriment which Shakespeare connected with those scenes was but a little of the poet's sunlight meant to glitter among tears.

It remains for us only to speak of the success of Mr Phelps as Bottom, whom he presented from the first with remarkable subtlety and spirit, as a man seen in a dream. In his first scene, before we know what his conception is, or what spirit he means the whole play to be received, we are puzzled by it. We miss the humour, and get a strange, elaborate, and uncouth dream-figure, a clown restless with vanity, marked by a score of little movements, and speaking ponderously with the uncouth gesticulation of an unreal thing, a grotesque nightmare character. But that, we find, is precisely what the actor had intended to present, and we soon perceive that he was right. Throughout the fairy scenes there is a mist thrown over Bottom by the actor's art. The violent gesticulation becomes stillness and the hands are fixed on the breast. They are busy with the unperceived business of managing the movements of the ass's head, but it is not for that reason they are so perfectly still. The change of manner is a part of the conception. The dream-figure is dreaming, there is dream within dream, Bottom is quiet, his humour becomes more unctuous, but Bottom is translated. He accepts all that happens, quietly as dreamers do; and the ass's head we also accept quietly, for we too are in the middle of our dream, and it does not create surprise. Not a touch of comedy was missed in this capital piece of acting, yet Bottom was completely incorporated with the *Midsummer Night's Dream*, made an essential part of it, as unsubstantial, as airy and refined as all the rest. Quite masterly was the delivery by Mr Phelps of the speech of Bottom on awakening. He was still a man subdued, but subdued by the sudden plunge into a state of unfathomable wonder. His dream slings about him, he cannot sever the real from the unreal, and still we are made to feel that his reality is but a fiction. The pre-occupation continues to be manifest during his next scene with the players, and his parting 'No more words; away; go away', was in the tone a man who had lived with spirits and was not yet perfectly returned into the flesh. Nor did the refinement of this conception, if we except the first scene, abate a jot of the laughter that the character of Bottom was intended to excite. The mock-play at the end was intensely ludicrous in the presentment, yet nowhere farcical. It was the dream. Bottom as Pyramus was more perfectly a dream-figure than ever. The contrast between the shadowy actor and his part, between Bottom and Pyramus, was marked intensely; and the result was as quaint a phantom as could easily be figured by real flesh. Mr Ray's Quince was very good indeed, and all the other clowns were reasonably well presented.

It is very doubtful whether the *Midsummer Night's Dream* has yet, since it was first written, been put upon the stage with so nice an interpretation of its meaning. It is pleasant beyond measure to think that an entertainment so refined can draw such a throng of playgoers as I saw last Saturday sitting before it silent and reverent at Sadler's Wells.

The Journal of a London Playgoer, 1891

Henry Morley
Phelps as Timon of Athens

18 OCTOBER 1856

Timon of Athens has been reproduced again by Mr Phelps, with even more pains than were bestowed upon his former revival of that play, which, when he first produced it, had been acted but a few times since the days of Shakespeare. As now performed it is exceedingly effective. A main cause of the success of Mr Phelps in his Shakespearean revivals is, that he shows in his author above all things the poet. Shakespeare's plays are always poems, as performed at Sadler's Wells. The scenery is always beautiful, but it is not allowed to draw attention from the poet, with whose whole conception it is made to blend in the most perfect harmony. The actors are content also to be subordinated to the play, learn doubtless at rehearsals how to subdue excesses of expression that by giving undue force to one part would destroy the balance of the whole, and blend their work in such a way as to produce everywhere the right emphasis. If Mr Phelps takes upon himself the character which needs the most elaborate development, however carefully and perfectly he may produce his own impression of his part, he never by his acting drags it out of its place in the drama. He takes heed that every part, even the meanest, shall have in the acting as much prominence as Shakespeare gave it in his plan, and it is for this reason that with actors, many of whom are anything but 'stars', the result most to be desired is really obtained. Shakespeare appears in his integrity, and his plays are found to affect audiences less as dramas in a common sense than as great poems.

This is the case especially with *Timon*. It may be that one cause of its long neglect, as potent as the complaint that it excites no interest by female characters, is the large number of dramatis personae, to whom are assigned what many actors might consider parts of which they can make nothing, and who, being presented in a slovenly way, by a number of inferior performers, would leave only one part in the drama, and take all the power out of that. Such an objection has not, however, any weight at Sadler's Wells, where every member of the company is taught to regard the poetry he speaks according to its nature rather than its quantity. The personators of the poet and the painter in the first scene of the *Timon*, as now acted, manifestly say what Shakespeare has assigned to them to say with as much care, and as much certainty that it will be listened to with due respect, as if they were themselves Timons, Hamlets, or Macbeths. Nobody rants – it becomes his part that Alcibiades should be a little blustery – nothing is slurred; a servant who has anything to say says it in earnest, making his words heard and their meaning felt; and so it is that, although only in one or two cases we may have observed at Sadler's Wells originality or genius in the actor, we have nevertheless perceived something like the entire sense of one of Shakespeare's plays, and have been raised above ourselves by the perception.

It is not because of anything peculiar in the air of Islington, or because an audience at Pentonville is made of men differing in nature from those who would form an audience in the Strand, that Shakespeare is listened to at Sadler's Wells with reverence not shown elsewhere. What has been done at Islington could, if the same means were employed, be done at Drury Lane. But Shakespeare is not fairly heard when he is made to speak from behind masses of theatrical upholstery, or when it is assumed that there is but one character in any of his plays, and that the others may be acted as incompetent performers please. If *The Messiah* were performed at Exeter Hall, with special care to intrust some of the chief solos to a good bass or contralto, the rest being left to chance, and members of the chorus allowed liberty to sing together in all keys, we should enjoy Handel much as we are sometimes asked to enjoy Shakespeare on the London stage. What Signor Costa will do for an orchestra, the manager must do for his company, if he would present a work of genius in such a way as to procure for it a full appreciation.

Such thoughts are suggested by the effect which *Timon of Athens* is producing on the audiences at Sadler's Wells. The play is a poem to them. The false friends, of whom one declares, 'The swallow follows not summer more willingly than we your lordship', and upon whom Timon retorts, 'Nor more willingly leaves winter', are as old as the institution of society. Since men had commerce first together to the present time, the cry has been 'Such summer birds are men'. The rush of a generous impulsive nature from one rash extreme into the other, the excesses of the man who never knew 'the middle of humanity', is but another common form of life; and when have men not hung – the poets, the philosophers, the lovers, the economists, men of all habits – over a contemplation of the contrast between that soft town-life represented by the luxury of Athens in its wealth and its effeminacy, and the life of a man who, like Timon before his cave's mouth, turns from gold because it is not eatable, and digs in the wood for roots? With a bold hand Shakespeare grasped the old fable of Timon, and moulded it into a form that expresses much of the perplexity and yearning of our nature. He takes up Timon, a free-handed and large-hearted lord, who, though 'to Lacedaemon did his lands extend', found them too little to content his restless wish to pour himself all out in kindness to his fellows. He leaves him dead by the shore of the mysterious eternal sea.

I do not dwell upon the play itself, for here the purpose only is to show in what way it can be made, when fitly represented – and is made at Sadler's Wells – to stir the spirit as a poem. Mr Phelps in his own acting of Timon treats the character as an ideal, as the central figure in a mystery. As the liberal Athenian lord, his gestures are large, his movements free – out of himself everything pours, towards himself he will draw nothing. As the disappointed Timon, whose love of his kind is turned to hate, he sits on the ground self-contained, but miserable in the isolation, from first to last contrasting with Apemantus, whom 'fortune's tender arm never with favour clasped', who is a churl by the original sourness of his nature, hugs himself in his own ragged robe, and worships himself for his own ill manners. Mr Marston's Apemantus is well acted, and helps much to secure a right understanding of the entire play.

The Journal of a London Playgoer, 1891

Westland Marston
Phelps as Falstaff and Bottom

This actor's Falstaff hardly conformed to the general ideal. In the first place, he lacked unction. Capons had not mollified him into lazy enjoyment, and, to judge from his humour, his sack must have been extra dry. On the other hand, there was a pith, a touch of Yankee 'cuteness in the delivery of the fat knight's dialogue, that in time began to tell. If much of Falstaff's self-enjoyment was missing, it was atoned for by so much phlegm, by such an air of caustic shrewdness in his comments, and of ease and conviction in his mendacity, that, by the time the Prince and Poins tear to pieces his bragging lies, and expose his cowardice, Phelps's dry, self-possessed effrontery convulsed his hearers as much as if it had been the overflow of animal spirits and humour. His answer to the Prince's charge of running away from the attack – 'by the Lord, I knew ye as well as he that made ye', given with a cool, matter-of-fact expectation that the monstrous lie would at once be swallowed, was as mirth-provoking as the air of triumph in ready resources which other Falstaffs have displayed in this emergency. In the last act, the dissertation on the worthlessness of honour, and the conclusion that 'discretion is the better part of valour', though wanting in self-complacency, seemed to emanate from a mind so penetrated by their truth, that the gravity of their delivery was probably more mirth-provoking than obvious honour would have been. Jovial, luxurious, lazily delighting in jest and in creature comforts, or exulting in braggadocio and quick expedients, the Falstaff of Phelps was not, or, at least, not more than the language of Shakspere forced him to be; but, as a shrewd soul who has mastered what he deems the truth – that self-interest is everything – who has an unbounded invention in extolling or excusing himself, a fairly sociable turn, with not an atom of ill-nature, the same amount of conscience, and a large proportion of Dutch phlegm in his system, this Falstaff was as effective as it was unique. Nevertheless, it is probable that the admirers of an 'unctuous Falstaff' would greatly exceed those of Phelps's dry and somewhat sarcastic exposition.

To some other characters, however, his dryness of treatment was admirably suited. The calm self-conceit of his Bottom, who finds so many things within his range, because his ignorance conceals their difficulties, was far more humourous than if his vanity had been made broader and more boisterous. His absolute insensibility to the ridiculous was more mirth-moving than the most grotesque means by which inferior actors would have italicized the absurd conceit of the character. His quiet, matter-of-course belief that the parts of Thisbe and the Lion are equally within his grasp, and that, as to the latter, he could roar, with equal success, either 'terribly' or 'as gently as any sucking dove', was more telling than would have been a violent and highly-coloured expression of his self-complacency. The same may be said of his air of contented superiority in contriving means to protect the ladies from fears of the drawn sword and of the lion in the play, of his ready assumption of the ass's head, of his light fingering of it, as if it had been the most natural of head-gears, and his satisfaction with his own wit in fathoming and baffling the designs of Puck, who had imposed it. In all this, the sense of acquiescence in the absurd was far more ludicrous than extreme wonder or excitement would have been. As a picture of intense self-conceit, expressed generally rather by signs of inward relish of his acuteness than by more open display – of ridiculous fastidiousness and equally ridiculous devices to satisfy it – as a parody of sense and ingenuity by a shallow brain, – Bottom must be ranked as one of this actor's most original conceptions.

Our Recent Actors, Vol. II, 1888

Henry Morley
Sothern as David Garrick

18 JUNE 1864

Mr Sothern has considered his dignity by discarding the mere nonsense of Bunkum Muller, and sustaining a character in a play which demands alternation of serious and comic acting. The play is a translation from the French drama of *Sullivan*, and I wish, though probably Mr Buckstone's Chancellor of the Exchequer has his reasons for differing from me, that the translator, Mr T. W. Robertson, had not taken the liberty of considering *Sullivan* the French for *David Garrick*. The play-bill does, indeed, append to the name of the piece a note, saying, 'This play is founded on an incident said to have occurred to Garrick, but which has no pretension to biographical accuracy'; euphemism for 'This play is called *David Garrick*, but has nothing on earth to do with Garrick'. But why should English actors deal so lightly with the memory of their great chief, that, for the sake of so poor and false an effect as the placarding of Sothern as Garrick, they should falsify and confuse the memory of Garrick's life? Mr Sothern, we think, should have resisted the temptation to have his name brought into such apposition; for he is not a Garrick; he is a very long way indeed from being a Garrick, excellent as he is in his own way of art. If he could act Abel Drugger, he could not act Macbeth; and his serious passages in this French-English drama, though they are well felt, are delivered with a heaviness of intensity remarkable in one whose touch as a comedian is so light. He is cleverly supported. Miss Nelly Moore is the heroine, a young lady whom I remember having seen two or three years ago in some small farce at the St James's Theatre, and having liked much as a genuine young English actress of the class which the French call *ingénue*, and which is on the French stage my particular aversion. She vanished almost immediately into the provinces, but has come back to London with a Haymarket engagement, and quite justifies the good hope of her I formed when she was first seen upon the stage. Let me not forget to record of *David Garrick* that it is so very moral as to proceed in the last act to the delivery of a long exhortation, unbroken by dialogue, which Mr Sothern preaches with such quiet seriousness that we are almost invited to look under his chin for the band and bibs. In the main, however, it is comic, and it is now followed by a new and rapid act of Dundrearyism, written by Mr H. J. Byron, entitled *Lord Dundreary Married and Done For*, in which Mr Sothern's Lord Dundreary is amusing still, and the nonsense, though it *is* nonsense, is rather smarter than it was in the original piece, and so we laugh heartily and do not despise ourselves for laughing. We check the sense that will rise sometimes of flagging in the imitator's strain at a worn theme, while we appreciate the skill with which Mr Byron has caught and repeated, and even mellowed with another humanizing touch or two, all the characteristics of Dundreary as we knew him in his days of bachelorhood.

The Journal of a London Playgoer, 1891

Joseph Knight
Ellen Terry as Portia

24 APRIL 1875

In passing from the domain of realistic comedy to that of the comedy of manners, the management of the Prince of Wales's Theatre attempted a march of no ordinary difficulty and danger. Recognizing the efforts that had been made to give completeness in respect to external details, sensible of the merits of portions of the performance, and pleased with a series of bright and life-like pictures, the public accepted a representation of the *School for Scandal* which effected a rupture with tradition, and a complete severance of modern art from that of past days. Now, however, when a further step is taken, and the *Merchant of Venice* is produced in the same style as the *School for Scandal*, a like display of clemency or favour is not to be expected. What respect for dramatic art still exists in England clings to Shakspeare; and an attempt to convert his plays into spectacular entertainments, however it may suit the ignorant pleasure seekers who, flocking to Drury Lane, have turned what should be a national theatre into something not widely different from a circus, is not likely to find acceptance from a more enlightened public. In spite, accordingly, of a lavish, and in its way judicious expenditure, the result of the experiment appears in this case to be failure. Superb views of Venice are presented. The gay, idle, *insouciante*, and withal mysterious life of the Queen of the Adriatic, is depicted with as much truth and colour as in the pages of Consuelo. Cavaliers and rufflers, 'witty as youthful poets in their wine', play in the street jests that may lead to 'cracked crowns', or whisper beneath half-opened lattices vows that may bring a dagger slit in the doublet. Music of endless serenades rings through streets ignorant of all noise of traffic. The idlers upon the quays and banks rouse themselves from their slumbers to hurl execrations at the passing Jews, and the busy masque of medieval Venice defiles with marvellous fidelity before our eyes. These things are good enough in themselves, and form an agreeable and appropriate background to a picture. Unfortunately, however, in the present case, these are the picture. To accept as a performance of the *Merchant of Venice* such a representation as took place in these surroundings would involve a complete abandonment of all that has been held indispensable to histrionic art. 'The world is still deceived with ornament', says Bassanio, before he chooses the leaden casket. This view, apparently, has prevailed with the management. In the present instance, however, the later lines of the same speech will, we think, supply the lesson –

> Thus ornament is but the guiled shore
> To a most dangerous sea.

Mr Coghlan, under whose direction the whole has, to some extent, been produced, and who himself plays Shylock, has sought to divest the performance of rant. In itself the endeavour is creditable. He has, however, sunk it to the level of a recitation. Few plays require more careful treatment than this. A central interest, which deepens almost into tragedy, is framed in scenes of delicious comedy. In the present performance the serious interest of the piece disappeared, buried in spectacle, and that the lighter scenes escaped the same fate was due to the genius of one actress. A more remarkable instance of collapse has seldom been witnessed. Mr Coghlan is an intelligent man, who can point to many successes in a short career. So completely did he fail, however, to grasp the part, or to render intelligible his conception, that during the trial scene the audience scarcely seemed conscious of his existence, and the proceedings might almost have continued without his presence. Against this regrettable miscarriage must be placed the triumph of Miss Terry, whose Portia revealed the gifts which are rarest on the English stage. More adequate expression has seldom been given to the light-heartedness of maidenhood, the perplexities and hesitations of love, and the ineffable content of gratified aspirations and ambitions. Not less successful were the scenes of badinage. Portia's address before the court was excellent, and the famous speech on mercy assumed new beauties from a correct and exquisite delivery. A very noteworthy point in the performance was the womanly interest in Shylock – the endeavour to win him, for his own sake, from the pursuit of his grim resolve. The delivery of the lines –

> Shylock, there's thrice thy money offered thee,

and –

> Have by some surgeon, Shylock, on your charge,
> To stop his wounds, lest he do bleed to death,

were dictated by sublime compassion. Beside Miss Terry's performance most of the other impersonations seemed weak. The most satisfactory were the Duke of Mr Collette, and the Antonio of Mr Archer; Mr Bancroft contented himself with the small part of the Prince of Morocco, of which he gave a picturesque representation; Mr A. Wood was Launcelot Gobbo; Miss C. Addison was Nerissa, and Miss A. Wilton Jessica.

Theatrical Notes, 1893

Clement Scott
Irving in *The Bells*

We have so recently sketched the literary and dramatic history of that extraordinary psychological study, *Le Juif Polonais*, by M. M. Erckmann-Chatrian, on the occasion of the production of Mr Burnand's version, called *Paul Zegers*, at the Alfred Theatre, that it only becomes necessary to note the different treatment by Mr Leopold Lewis, in his drama of *The Bells*, which was received on its first production with the most gratifying enthusiasm. We have before remarked upon the fact that the weird story, though written in dramatic form, was not originally intended for stage representation, and have given our opinion that, without picturesque scenery and detail, coupled with powerful acting, the study is comparatively worthless for histrionic purposes. Mr Burnand departed widely from the author's intention, and by adding a prologue and toning down many of the terrible details, gave us more of a stage play, and much less of a psychological study. Mr Leopold Lewis, on the other hand has more faithfully followed the lead of the authors, has preserved the poetical pictures of Alsatian life, and, with one conspicuous and most important exception, gives us the idea of M. M. Erckmann-Chatrian. The exception in question must be recognized, because, as it seems to us, Mr Lewis has, for the sake of a beautiful stage picture, sacrificed the most important dramatic point in the tale. We take it the intention of the authors was to represent the outward and inner life of a man whose conscience is burdened with the hideous weight of a murder committed fifteen years ago – of a crime, by means of which he obtained capital, success, and the best prizes the world can bestow. The fact of the murder having been committed by Mathias, the respected burgomaster, is only to be suggested to the audience by his uneasiness and trouble when alone. In society he is to be the most genial and charming of men; in private he is to be torn with an agony of grief. The first act is artistically contrived to show this double life.

The scene is Christmas Eve, an occasion consecrated to domesticity. Though the snow is deep and blinding without, the hearth of the burgomaster is bright, and sorrow is unknown in the happy household. The wife is anxiously awaiting her lord's return; the daughter, happy in the love of a young and honourable man, has still a warm corner in her heart for the father she idolizes. In comes Mathias from the cold, apparently the picture of health and happiness. He brings with him kisses for his wife, and a bridal present for the pretty daughter. He sits down to his supper as hungry as a hunter, and the first glass is raised to his lips to toast his family and his friends, when an accidental remark of one of the guests recalls the murder of a Polish Jew, who on this very night, at this very hour, started from this very inn, fifteen years ago, and was never seen again. The wine-cup is put down untasted, and for an instant a cloud comes over the happy face of Mathias. It is well to notice how the dramatic interest increases. Suddenly a noise of bells is heard across the snow, a sledge stops at the door, a man in Polish costume stands on the threshold, asking a blessing on the assembled family, and craving hospitality. Mathias, horrified at this terrible coincidence; it is not the murdered Jew, nor the murdered Jew's brother, but merely a chance visit of another wanderer, similarly apparelled, to the inn – falls down in a fit, and the act concludes with the cry, 'Le médecin! courez chercher le médecin!' Strange to say, this double Jew has been objected to by those who most admire and appreciate the story. 'Who is he? and what is he?' they say, failing to see that he is merely introduced in order to re-enact, by a strange fatality, the same scene of fifteen years ago.

Be this as it may, Mr Leopold Lewis has dismissed the second Jew; he has omitted the original termination of the act; he has given a wrench to the quietly revolving wheels of the story, and he supplies, instead of the tragic incident, a picture of the actual murder supposed to be seen by Mathias during his delirium. The illusion is admirably contrived, and most effective. It called down shouts of applause from the audience; but it has just this ill effect, it tells the listeners unhesitatingly that Mathias is a murderer, and this is scarcely what M. M. Erckmann-Chatrian desired to do at this moment. It is only in this instance Mr Lewis departs from the French play in any important manner, though we own we could have wished the concluding lines of the original drama could have been preserved, which show that, in spite of all, the Alsatian family are unshaken in their confidence in the beloved burgomaster. The death of Mathias is ascribed by the kindly old doctor to the poor fellow's habit of drinking too much white wine. His family believe him to be an honest, upright fellow to the last.

We have before commented upon the extraordinary difficulty attending the proper representation of the character of Mathias, the murderer, particularly in the overlong dream scene, in which the guilty man is brought before his judges, and under mesmeric influences, re-enacts the murder. It must be unanimously granted that Mr Henry Irving's performance is most striking, and cannot fail to make an impression. There are possibly very few who were aware that this actor possessed so much undeveloped power, and would be capable in such a character, of succeeding so well. His notion of the haunted man is conceived with great cleverness, and though, here and there, there are apparent faults, there are points of detail which are really admirable. The study, to begin with, is one eminently picturesque. Mr Irving was never less mannered. The two most striking points in the performance are the powerful acting as the poor frenzied creature dozes off at the will of the mesmerizer, and the almost hideously painful representation of death at the end of the play. The gradual stupefaction, the fixed eye, the head bent down on the chest, and the crouching humility before a stronger will in the one scene; and the ugly picture of a dead man's face, convulsed after a dream, in which he thought he was hanged, are touches of genuine art, which, while they terrify, cannot fail to be admired. Almost as telling was the low, terrified wail as the awful sentence is being pronounced, and Mathias sinks kneeling to the floor of the court. Vivid and picturesque as is Mr Irving's art, he somehow failed to convey the genial side of the character of the man. The colouring in the first two acts was of too sombre a tone, and the requisite contrast was, therefore, not given. We believe that M. Talien made his best point by deceiving the audience, and taking it off its guard by his extreme geniality. Mr Irving's strength also failed him more than once. The monologue in the dream act is far too long, and Mr Irving has not the power to carry it through to the entire satisfaction of those in front. The light and shade disappear when the actor has overtaxed his strength. But, taking the bad with the good, the performance is highly satisfactory, and by it, Mr Irving has unquestionably increased his reputation. In such a character as this, trick and artifice are of no avail. It requires acting out, and cannot be played with. We have no desire to recall our opinion that such a part demands the genius of a Garrick or a Robson; but it is a subject for congratulation that Mr Irving is able by it to do himself and the Stage such infinite credit. The other characters are comparatively subordinate; but cheerful assistance was given by Miss Pauncefort as the wife; by Mr Herbert Crellin as the lover, who both looked and acted well; and by Miss Fanny Heywood, who, at the end of the second act, sang the touching 'Air de Lauterbach' with delightful expression.

Even in these days of scenic splendour and taste in decoration, we seldom see a play so unexceptionally mounted. The interior of the inn in the first act, with its quaint furniture, its shelves of queer crockery, and its thoroughness from end to end, is a picture well worth study; and most striking are the frescoes on the walls of the court of justice, and the general arrangement of this scene. The management has evidently spared no trouble, and grudged no expense, to aid the tragedy and preserve the idyllic character of the story. Messrs Hawes, Craven and Cuthbert are the scenic artistes. The chef d'orchestre of the Théâtre Cluny, M. Pingla, has been borrowed from Paris on purpose to conduct and give his assistance in the rehearsals; and with regard to this last subject, we may remark, and it is a point worth noting, that the play was rehearsed to perfection. There was not a hitch or a contretemps of any kind, and it went as well on the first night as it doubtless will when the representations are reckoned by hundreds. Weird enough is the story to be sure, but there is a strange fascination about horrible things, and for many reasons, *The Bells* is a play, which those interested in the drama as an art should not fail to see. After every act, Mr Henry Irving was called, and when the usual compliment had been paid to all at the end of the performance, another shout was raised, and Mr Bateman led on Mr Irving, shaking him by the hand and patting him on the back. Without a doubt, the audience was much impressed by the new drama.

From 'The Bells' to 'King Arthur', 1897

Joseph Knight
Irving and Ellen Terry in *Hamlet*

4 JANUARY 1879

How firm a faith in Mr Irving inspires a large section of the public was testified on Monday night, when that actor made his first appearance in a theatre under his own management. The occasion is not to be forgotten by those who were present. In a house which may now claim to be one of the handsomest in London, and in presence of a thoroughly representative audience, Mr Irving received such manifestations of delight and approval as recall the most brilliant triumphs of the tragedians of past time. It is impossible to doubt the sincerity of the convictions that found expression in ringing cheers and shouts of affectionate welcome. No amount of care or expense could have organized a demonstration of the kind; nothing short of spontaneous and overmastering enthusiasm could have produced it. The most severely critical estimate of Mr Irving's powers does not involve any scepticism as to the value of a demonstration like this. While successive governments, with a timidity and mistrust of the people which speak little for their intelligence, leave all questions of literature and art to look after themselves, the public recognizes a debt of gratitude to those who endeavour by private action to make up for national shortcoming. To present a Shakspearian masterpiece under favourable conditions, with an adequate cast and artistic surroundings, is a work of no small difficulty or importance. In saying, as he did in a short address to the public after the performance, that the dream of his life had been to do this, Mr Irving obtained implicit credence. It has, indeed, required years of preparation to bring about the result. As some motive of personal ambition is sure to colour most private effort, it was necessary for the actor to win acceptance for his own conception of Hamlet or some other leading Shakspearian character. This in itself means delaying an experiment until the top of an arduous profession is reached. A theatre has then to be obtained, and actors, seldom too amenable to discipline, have to be drilled until they become parts of one harmonious whole. This triumph Mr Irving has obtained. The representation of *Hamlet* supplied on Monday night is the best the stage during the last quarter of a century has seen, and it is the best also that is likely under existing conditions to be seen for some time to come. Scenic accessories are explanatory without being cumbersome, the costumes are picturesque and striking and show no needless affectation of archaeological accuracy, and the interpretation has an *ensemble* rarely found in any perform- ance and never during recent years in a representation of tragedy. Here is much for which to be grateful. The points raised call for a few further words. As regards scenery, successful attempt is made to add to the impressiveness and intelligibility of the action. The 'more remote part of the platform', to which the Ghost draws Hamlet, presents that 'dreadful summit of the cliff' which Horatio shrinkingly describes. Very impressive is the effect of the ghostly figure, erect, with a background of sea, and with an unearthly light falling upon his helmet. The play scene is well arranged, though there is nothing in it calling for special notice; the scene of Ophelia's interment gives an imposing representation of Catholic ceremonial, and furnishes Hamlet and Horatio with satisfactory means of escaping observation. Perhaps, however, the best arrangement of all is that in the closing scene, in which the King's death is brought about. This, if not perfect, is a great improvement on anything previously seen. To avoid the extreme improbability of a man standing, like Claudius, to hear himself defied and outraged, and to wait for his death-blow, the King should be so absorbed in the death of the Queen as to be scarcely conscious of the surrounding circumstances; and the accusation of Laertes, made with failing breath, should only reach him when the final words are uttered: 'The King knows all'. In the present case the action becomes, however, intelligible on the exercise of slight powers of imagination on the part of the audience.

It is, of course, an anomaly to show early Danish soldiers wearing chain armour. All, however, that is necessary in the case of a play like this is to give a species of picturesque antiquity to the attire. Shakspeare has, as Mr Marshall says in his preface to the acting version now employed, been hampered by 'no formal respect for geographical or historical accuracy', and has introduced, in a period which is almost fabulous, references to 'partisans', 'cannons', 'rapiers', and 'hangers'. One or two things may, indeed, be mentioned at which no stickler for accuracy has ever arrived. When the players came on the stage, the player queen should in fact, be a boy. Up to Shakspeare's time women had taken no part in dramatic representation, and Hamlet when he says: 'What, my young lady and mistress! By'r lady, your ladyship is nearer to heaven than when I saw you last, by the altitude of a chopine', may be supposed to indicate that he recognizes the player of women under his female disguise. A second alteration that regard for historical accuracy would suggest is that, according to early custom, the play before the King should be presented in the afternoon by daylight. Plays were thus given in early days, and in the century in which the action is supposed to pass, the means of lighting would not be adequate to an evening entertainment of the class. Hamlet shortly afterwards, says: "Tis now the very witching time of night'. This, however, does not, as might easily be shown, disprove our assertion. These suggestions are not intended for acceptance. They aim only at showing how hopeless a matter is the struggle after absolute accuracy.

Of Mr Irving's Hamlet we have already spoken. It is not greatly changed. The outline is distinctly the same as before, though much pains have been bestowed on the filling up. We do not accept as new readings the delivery while sitting of speeches formerly spoken standing, or other like alterations in arrangement. Nor do we feel that changes of method as regards matters of detail call for special comment. The one vital alteration of conception appears to consist in presenting Hamlet as under the influence of an overmastering love for Ophelia. A knowledge of his own weakness seems to inspire him when, subsequently addressing Horatio, he says:

> Give me that man
> That is not passion's slave, and I will wear him
> In my heart's core, ay, in my heart of heart.

The chief grace in the new representation consisted in the delivery of the speeches to Ophelia in the third act. In this the mocking tone did not for a moment hide the profound emotion under which Hamlet laboured, and the hands which repulsed her petitioning hands trembled with passionate longing. That this view of Hamlet is correct will scarcely be disputed. That he loved Ophelia he declares over her grave; that he felt it his duty, under the influences of a task such as that enjoined him, to erase from the table of his memory all 'trivial fond records', he also states. The indications of the pain it costs a nature such as this, quick in resolution and shrinking and incapable in action, to inflict on the woman he loves the grief it is yet necessary she should sustain, are well conceived. That they were effective in action was ascribable to a great extent to the admirable acting of Miss Terry. Picturesque, tender, and womanly throughout, Miss Terry on one or two occasions gave an inspired rendering of Ophelia. The support she afforded Mr Irving was of the utmost importance, and the scene before the play has probably never been so well rendered. An attempt to dignify the character of Polonius, to which most are prompted who see how wise midst his sententiousness he appears in the early scenes, is made in the interest of Mr Chippendale, who plays the character. In order to bear out this, portions of the speech to Claudius and Gertrude, which elicit from the latter the rebuke: 'More matter, with less art', are omitted. Mr Forrester's King and Miss Pauncefort's Queen are worthy of notice, as is also the Ghost of Mr T. Mead.

It is impossible to regard this performance with disfavour, and it would be ungracious as well as tedious, to expatiate upon defects. As regards interpretation, it is possible to point out many passages in which a different reading might with advantage be adopted. The most noteworthy defect on the part of the principal actor consists in a tendency to deprive vowels of their value, and pronounce, for instance, *ghost* as though it rhymed to lost instead of host.

Theatrical Notes, 1893

Clement Scott
Irving's Production of
Much Ado About Nothing

Benedick and Beatrice, the blessed (benedictus) and the blesser – what shall
be said at the outset of the hero and heroine conceived by Shakespeare in the
very zenith of his dramatic and poetic powers? Are they, indeed, the hero and
heroine at all of that enchanting comedy, *Much Ado About Nothing*, and not
mere subordinate actors in a simple story that is spun from the sentimental
loves of Claudio and Hero? Is it true that the spectator is alone concerned
with a vain, chattering, 'marriage-hating Benedick', and the attention solely
aroused by a 'furiously anti-nuptial Beatrice'? Had Shakespeare no deeper
design, no truer insight into human character than the stage figures as they
are ordinarily presented to us – the talkative misogynist and the terrible
termagant that have been tacitly accepted through want of thought or the
influence of an unyielding tradition? The greater part of the first night's
brilliant audience must have been puzzled with some such reflections as
these before they took their seats to watch carefully and wait for the result
of Mr Henry Irving's last, and, in many respects, most remarkable, Shakespearean revival.

There has been no manager in our time – and we say it with all respect to
the memories of Macready, Charles Kean, and Samuel Phelps – who, having
got the ear of the public, was so determined as has been Mr Irving to take
Shakespeare as his text, in preference to tradition. The Shakespeare of the
stage is not the Shakespeare of the poet. Thanks to Mr Irving, in this period
of greater intellectual thought, we have seen on the Lyceum stage the explosion of many dramatic heresies. He has cut himself adrift from the fantastic
improvements of David Garrick and saved us from the remorseless editings
of Colley Cibber. The changes effected in the long list of Lyceum acting
editions have not been for the mere love of change; they have not been due to
the vanity of the actor, or the unwholesome pandering to theatrical effect.

We may think what we like of the new Hamlet, Richard, Macbeth,
Shylock, Othello, Iago and Romeo; but at least this may be said that one and
all are more intelligible beings in action and in impulse when read by the light
of Shakespeare than when distorted and disfigured by the clumsiness of
editors, and the cheap fireworks of tradition. Mr Irving has, at any rate, decided
the question whether Shakespeare should be for the study or the stage by
bringing the student's Shakespeare as near to the footlights as practical considerations would allow. No enthusiast could do more, no ardent lover of
Shakespeare could desire less.

Who and what, then, are this Benedick and Beatrice, as designed by
Shakespeare, and evidenced by the text? Is the one a mere conceited, self-
sufficient woman-hater, and the other, as Campbell calls her, 'an odious
woman', a lady scold, a termagant, a Tartar, and a shrew? Is it not possible

to find in the play, with all its enchanting variety, incidents bringing out by distinct and natural gradations a profound seriousness lying beneath all the superficial levity seen at first in the hero and heroine? Is there not, in the development of the characters of Beatrice and Benedick 'a partial antipathy converted into a perfect sympathy', a war between a man and woman who 'all but' liked one another at the outset, and ended by marrying and living happily ever afterwards?

Did Shakespeare mean what he said when he described his Beatrice as 'a merry-hearted, pleasant-spirited lady', never 'sad but when she sleeps, and not ever sad then; for I have heard my daughter say she hath often dreamed of unhappiness, and waked herself with laughing'; or was she the 'odious' and 'insolent' woman that the stage has decided her to be? Is it to be held true that 'there is a kind of merry war betwixt Signor Benedick and her; they never meet but there is skirmish of wit between them'; or do the spectators merely behold a cat-and-dog fight, ending in a union that will only result in a 'predestinate scratched face'? Is the purpose of the dramatist confined to illustrating a nagging brawl between two commonplace people, or to showing the 'whole ardour and ingenuity of a clever, bright-witted woman, exerting themselves to humble silence, if possible, the satirical loquacity of a vivacious cavalier'?

Pressing as these contradictory views must have been to the anxious and interested spectator who came to enjoy, and in enjoying to learn, the curtain had scarcely risen before all doubts about the matter were immediately solved. That Mr Irving would invest Benedick with a curious and fantastic humour, and that Miss Ellen Terry would endow Beatrice with singular charm and gaiety, were foregone conclusions. The comedy of the one and the other must be familiar to most playgoers by this time – a comedy as rich as it is refined. But few except those who have waited, and waited in vain, for Mr Irving's Jacques and Miss Terry's Rosalind, could have hoped for more intellectual enjoyment than is contained in their Benedick and Beatrice.

The sumptuous revival by Mr Henry Irving of this wise and witty comedy has, at any rate, proved to the public satisfaction that Shakespeare, if properly understood, is an evergreen. The simile is surely not inapt or strained. We shut up a green fir tree in a box-room, lumber-place, or garret, the very tree round which the children had danced at Christmas time, the bush just borrowed from the young plantation, and what comes to it? It browns, it saddens, it withers, and it dies. But plant it out, give it light and air, return it to its native soil, and it recovers its freshness. It is this light and air that has been given to *Much Ado About Nothing*, and persuaded us of its everlasting vitality; it is this harmonizing of the play to modern taste and sentiment that causes its wit and wisdom to fall upon the ear as if it were written but yesterday for our enjoyment; it is this careful study of the highest principles of dramatic effect that sets idea into action and invigorates the imagination. How often has not Shakespeare suffered for sins both of omission and commission on the part of his interpreters and exponents.

We throw away his beauties on ignorant and indifferent performers; we mumble and de-poetize his text; we fail to apply him to modern taste and circumstance; we blindly follow traditions, often as senseless as they are ugly; we take him up with half-hearted energy, and relinquish him with a sigh of relief, and then it is considered wonderful that Shakespeare spells ruin and bankruptcy as well. What author, living or dead, would not spell ruin under similar conditions? Like other everlastings and evergreens, Shakespeare wants light and air. Apply them, and what follows? The poet's vitality surprised no one more than his most reverent worshippers. Take this play of *Much Ado About Nothing*, seen on our stage many a time and often, acted for benefits, familiar enough to leading actors and actresses, who have a theatrical and superficial admiration for Benedick and Beatrice; and when before, may we ask, have so many beauties and ideas been unfolded from the text? Who could have imagined that so many deep and pressing thoughts of solemn meaning could have come from the picture of the grand old cathedral at Messina, charging the mind with love and hate, and pity and despair, as we watch and understand the crushed heart of the tender Hero, the eloquent indignation of the misguided Claudio, the pathetic devotion of the grand old father Leonato, the comfort of trust in those last beautiful words of the Friar, 'have patience and endure', and, most important of all, the presence of a great and common grief, that turns the partial antipathy of Benedick and Beatrice into a perfect sympathy?

How is it, then, that this one scene of all, representing the Sicilian cathedral, so deeply impresses the spectator, and is suddenly found to be such a faithful aid to the imagination? Why do we discover new beauties in a dramatic position familiar to every Shakespearean student? Because for the first time, at any rate in our day, it has been approached with sympathy, and guided by a refined and artistic mind. One false step, one little error of taste, one pardonable moment of zeal in excess would have ruined the whole conception. It is the one solemn and serious moment in the play, and the danger is to treat it realistically and still with reverence. This cathedral scene seems to an imaginative playgoer the very triumph of artistic effect pushed to the nicest point of refinement and good taste. The art here is to impress and not to shock the spectator – to soothe the mind and not disturb it. It is needless to point out the dangers ready to the hand of any one arranging such a scene for the stage. A red lamp burning before the altar, a crucifix, the use of vestments by the officiating friar, any of the determined signs of a nuptial mass, an excess of genuflexions, would have shipwrecked the whole idea and seriously endangered the beautiful in art.

But what do we get instead? The symbols severed from the soul; the suggestion without the reality. There can be no harm in the incense that fills the air as the bridal processions file to the appointed spot; in the plaintive wail of the organ, with its soft and persuasive reed stop, contrasted with the secular music attendant on the bride; there can be no danger in the admirable and effective contrast of the major and the minor keys throughout this extraordinary scenic composition; a contrast of priests and courtiers, of ecclesiastical ritual and courtly solemnity; of organ and stringed band; of religion and the world. And the consequence is that there is left impressed on the memory all that is beautiful and nothing that is distasteful. That surely is the highest mission of art.

We recall old Leonato, with a look of tender love upon his face, guiding his daughter into the cathedral sanctuary; we see her crushed under the heel of a cruel suspicion, a 'broken blossom, a ruined rhyme'; we hear the passionate cry of Claudio, 'O, Hero! What a Hero hadst thou been', and, old play as it is, know full well how many Heros and Claudios are about us in the life of today. We are conscious of the sudden change from gay to grave, from lively to severe, as that one sudden, impulsive, and womanlike command, 'Kill Claudio!' changes the purpose of the unreflective Benedick, and causes him to sacrifice friendship on the altar of love.

It will be found that Mr Irving has succeeded in persuading us of three cardinal truths in connection with this most interesting play. First, that the complete unfolding of the characters of Beatrice and her lover is the mainstay of the whole plot; secondly, that between Beatrice and Benedick there is a close affinity, that each is the other's counterpart, that they are echoes of one another as much at the outset as when they are discovered at the close writing verses to one another in secret, that the antipathy which exists in partial, and is changed by the humour of their friends to a sympathy that is real; and lastly, most important fact of all, that in this merry and enchanting comedy, a 'profound seriousness lies beneath all the superficial levity seen at first in the hero and heroine', or, as a clever critic has put it, 'the very pair who have given the most decidedly comic character to the outset of the play, are found on the point of giving it the most tragic turn towards its close.' It is impossible to study Mr Irving's acting as Benedick, or to sympathize fully with his masterly direction of the scene without being persuaded that he has grasped these three most important truths.

Much has been said already of the admirable humour of the new Benedick, of his inimitable delivery of Shakespeare's witty phrases, bringing them home to the dullest intelligence by the slyness of his artistic method; of his soliloquies, that seem to us masterpieces of comic expression, as full of thought, and intention, and earnestness as the thinking aloud of Hamlet himself. But there is much more than this in Mr Irving's Benedick. There is expression – and the kind of expression may be seen by those who noticed that comical shrug of the shoulders and air of martyred resignation when the tamed Beatrice begins her old habit of chattering – but there is also seriousness.

When the cathedral scene has filled the eyes of Beatrice with tears, and Benedick has been accepted as her protector, the whole man changes. There is a moment of revolt at the words, 'Kill Claudio!' he answers, 'Ha! not for the wide world', and Benedick means it. But he is over-persuaded, and love masters him. All the gentlemen and soldier comes out in the now accepted lover. 'Think you, in your soul, that Count Claudio hath wronged Hero?' asks this fine-spirited and noble-hearted gentleman. 'Yes! as sure as I have a thought or a soul.' That assertion from his mistress is enough for Benedick. 'Enough; I am engaged. I will challenge him.' And he never breaks his word;

he assumes the quarrel in all honour and honesty. Mr Irving's Benedick is not a mere mountebank railer against womankind, not a swaggering, self-sufficient egotist; but a soldier first, a lover next, and always a gentleman. This most comprehensive study will go far to remove many of the prejudices that have sprung from the actor's popularity, and in a measure explain that very popularity itself. Mr Irving has never played a part without impressing the audience with his personal influence and his nature, and here these qualities are seen at their very best.

Merriment is the abiding quality of Miss Ellen Terry's Beatrice. She is Shakespeare's 'pleasant-spirited lady'; she was born in a 'merry hour'; we know that a 'star danced, and under that she was born'; she has a 'merry heart', and the actress leans charmingly on this view of the character. All the people about the court love Beatrice, as well they may. They know her antipathy to the rougher sex is only skin deep, and they trick her into matrimony. She is no virago or vixen, but a smiling, chaffing, madcap girl, whose laughter and high spirits are next door to tears. How true this is of life! Laughter and tears are only divided by the narrowest channel, and the art with which Miss Ellen Terry expresses this in the scene after the cruel condemnation of her cousin is quite admirable. She wants to laugh with Benedick, but she must weep for Hero.

Most daring and original of all is her reading of the well-known outburst, 'O! God, that I were a man! I would eat his heart in the market-place.' We hold it, novel as it is, to be perfectly correct and natural in such a woman. It is not the scornful rage of a vixen, or the scream of a vulgar shrew, but a sudden, passionate sob of suppressed emotion. 'O God, that I were a man! I would –', and then there is a long pause, as if the woman were too passionately indignant to give her thoughts utterance, but soon, with a wounded cry, and with rage expressed in the scarcely suppressed tears, come the words, 'I would eat his heart in the market-place.' When we object to unconventional readings we must remember the kind of woman presented to us.

There are many Beatrices who could not speak those lines in that particular way. But such a Beatrice as Miss Ellen Terry must have spoken them so. All who understand and have studied the style of this gay and sportive actress will guess how she could say such words as, 'No, my lord, unless I might have another for working days: your grace is too costly to wear every day', or her answer to the question if she were born in a merry hour, 'No, sure, my lord, my mother cried.' Such sentences as these are received with a veritable shout of applause. But the audience was scarcely prepared for so excellent a delivery of the rhymed and lyrical soliloquy, 'What fire is in mine ears? Can this be true? Stand I condemned for pride and scorn so much?'; and how true is the well-known Shakespearian simile as applied to this actress. 'For look where Beatrice, like a lapwing, runs close by the ground.' This is exactly how Miss Ellen Terry does run, on or off the stage.

At once both Mr Irving and Miss Ellen Terry caught the spirit of the play; they filled it with gaiety and with humour, and every line of the text fell upon eager and appreciative ears. How often have we heard Shakespeare of late mouthed and mumbled over, distorted and twisted out of all shape! Here, then, was a sudden revelation. It was the very light breath and fragrance of true comedy. Beatrice was no shrew, but the most light-hearted, pleasant-spirited lady in the world. Benedick was no boor, but a refined, whimsical, humour-loving gentleman, whose every utterance was taken up with a hearty laugh even to the uttermost parts of the distant gallery. Surely this is a subject for congratulation, when, through the skill of the artists, the comedy of Shakespeare can amuse – honestly amuse – and when the bantering scenes between Benedick and Beatrice are so gay and radiant that poor Dogberry and Verges, when they appeared upon the scene, were literally snuffed out. On ordinary occasions these comic characters come as a relief; this time they were felt to be a hindrance.

The point most admired – as a rule – apart from the fantastic beauty of the scene, that put the whole attention in a period and so continually delighted the eye, was the thoroughly sound and excellent way that the comedy was being spoken. To elegance and taste was added expression, and it was Benedick himself who set the good example. So much has been said about Mr Irving's manner and artistic method that it is only right and just to point to his Benedick as a model of good accent and expressive delivery. This quality was even more strongly felt later on, particularly in the soliloquies, which will be remembered as Mr Irving's most successful efforts in comedy.

The first scene of the second act introduced another welcome surprise in the Don John of Mr C. Glenny. Now, Don John is not considered a very telling or welcome part, but instantly this young actor made his mark, not by overdoing the villain, but by making him a plausible and possible man. The speech, 'I had rather be a canker in a hedge', roused the attention of the audience, because it was understood by the actor and intelligently delivered; with the slighest effort and in the smallest possible space Don John made his mark.

As the play proceeded the Beatrice rose gradually with the occasion. She had already shown she was Shakespeare's Beatrice, or something very like it, and there was no attempt to make acting points or to obtrude the virago. 'No, uncle, I'll none: Adam's sons are my brethren, and truly I hold it a sin to match in my kindred.' To hear Miss Terry speak that one sentence was enough to know that she understood the gay spirit of Beatrice. And it was a struggle in more senses than one for the mastery between the hero and heroine of the play. Mr Irving and Miss Terry appeared to be vying with one another who should act the best; and though, in all probability, the prize will be awarded to the former, there was not much to choose between them until the test scene came after Hero's denunciation.

Such sentences as Benedick's 'Why, that's spoken like an honest drover: so they sell bullocks', made the house laugh as uproariously as it is sometimes inclined to do over far less pregnant and witty matter; and even louder applause fell to Benedick's avowal, 'I would not marry her though she were endowed with all that Adam had left him before he transgressed', charged with infinite cynicism by Mr Irving, as well as to Miss Terry's arch answer to Don Pedro's bantering request, 'Will you have me, lady?' 'No, my lord, unless I might have another for working-days.' What wonder then, that the second act went even better than the first, and was rewarded with another loud summons for all the performers?

In the third act, the scene in Leonato's garden was lovely in itself, both in arrangement and in colour, with its yellowing brown foliage, dim arcades of green, and old marble moss-eaten seat; but it was more remarkable still for Mr Irving's soliloquy, in which the hesitating Benedick rails at love and lovers in general. The manner in which the actor gave a world of expression to such sentences as 'But, till all graces be in one woman, one woman shall not come in my grace', and 'Of good discourse, an excellent musician, and her hair shall be of what colour it please God', can only be understood by those who see and appreciate Mr Irving's rich flow of sly humour. The audience had been presented with comedy at last and sincerely appreciated it. The introduction of Balthazar, with his song, 'Sigh no more, ladies; sigh no more', was extremely welcome for it introduced a young singer, Mr J. Robertson, brother of two charming sisters well-known in the musical world, who has not only a sweet and expressive voice, but well understood the grace and delicacy of this charming lyric. He did not come down to the footlights and deliver his song in a full-bodied way, as operatic tenors are wont to do, but he acted Balthazar and belonged to the scene. Of course the song was encored, for taste was in every note and line of it.

There is one scene of comedy in this play as good, surely, as can be desired. We allude to the trick played upon Benedick by Leonato, Don Pedro and Claudio. It is worthy the closest and most minute study, and is sustained throughout in the gayest and most laughter loving spirit. Would indeed that the correlative scene between Beatrice and the girl could have been played so well. The manly, hearty, outspoken style of Mr W. Terriss is of the greatest value to the play, and gives to Don Pedro an importance that cannot be overvalued. Mr Terriss is popular with a Lyceum audience, because they can hear him, and they like his spirit. The play moves – any play must move – when life and energy are given to it. This is of more serious consequence with Don Pedro, because he has to tell the story of the play. Once miss that, and down goes the comedy several tones. If young actors would only follow the advice of Mr Terriss and put their heart in their work, they would be more appreciated. The radical fault of modern acting is dropping the voice at the end of every sentence. The audience cannot hear, and consequently they yawn.

To the Don Pedro of Mr Terriss, Mr Forbes Robertson as Claudio makes an admirable contrast. The young man is in love, but he is never affected, he can be gay and bright in his comedy, and in pathos he feels the scene and the position. In the cathedral scene the passionate, nervous acting of the Claudio was just the note that was wanted in this very beautiful harmony of ideas. There is heart in Mr Forbes Robertson's acting. Mention has already been made of Mr Glenny's Don John, a nicely-conceived and artistic little bit, and what better or more picturesque Antonio could be found than Mr H. Howe?

But a second visit to the play – but, in my humble opinion, it is not necessary – to confirm the good impressions formed of the Leonato of Mr Fernandez, as fine and firm, as varied and picturesque a performance as any Shakespearean enthusiast could desire. He is light and full of humour in the comedy scenes, and when called upon for pathos is as firm as a rock, giving eloquence to the poetry and passion to the scene. The Leonato is as impressive as any figure in the play, and as acted by Mr Fernandez, he is one of the strong pivots on which the structure rests.

Dogberry and his companions fail to attract any interest whatever, but it is not the fault of Shakespeare. As usual, the public is inclined to visit the poet with the sins of the performers. A Dogberry with more pronounced humour; a Hero who should add idealism to her prettiness and more poetry to her promise; and a less modern Ursula in voice and style, would remove the only blots on a performance of singular interest and magnificent moment.

One more word about Dogberry. 'I don't think very much about Shakespeare's humour', is the contemptuous opinion of the crowd when a Dogberry has no sententiousness, and laughs at his own jokes. And yet we have an actor, who, I suppose, would make the most ideal Dogberry the stage has ever seen. I allude to Mr Harry Paulton. He is, so far as his humour is concerned, Dogberry himself. He has just the face, just the voice, just the manner for Dogberry. If Mr Paulton played the part, it is not likely that we should hear that Shakespeare had no humour, or that his jokes were out of colour.

From 'The Bells' to 'King Arthur', 1897

Henry James
The Acting in Mr Irving's *Faust*

As an assistance to making clear to ourselves some of the questions suggested by the wonderful modern art of 'staging' a piece, and in particular the effect that traps and panoramas, processions and coloured lights, may have in their exuberance, their obtrusiveness upon the personal interpretation, the manner in which, at the Lyceum, Mr Henry Irving has produced a version of Goethe's *Faust* (for which he has been indebted to the fruitful pen of Mr Wills) is greatly to be welcomed. Nothing lights up a subject like a good example, Mr Irving's examples are always excellent. His production of *Faust* has been largely acclaimed and still more largely witnessed; it has had one of the longest of long runs, which, at the moment these words are written, shows no signs of abating. To the richness and ingenuity of the spectacle, unnumerable pens will have testified. The critic gives his impression, and that impression has been abundantly uttered. There is another one which also naturally has its turn. The *mise-en-scène* in the light of the acting, and the acting in the light of the *mise-en-scène*, are the respective halves of the interesting question. It is with the second half only that we ourselves are concerned.

In this connection the first thing that strikes us is a certain perversity in the manner in which Mr Irving has approached and regarded his task, a perversity most singular on the part of a manager to whom the interests of the dramatic art have long appeared to be so dear. Saying to himself that he would give great attention to the machinery of the piece, he omitted to indulge at the same time in this indispensable reflection – that to prevent the impression of triviality which might easily arise from an abuse of pantomimic effects, he should take care to put at the service of the great story a consummate interpretation; to see that Faust and Margaret and Martha, as well as Mephistopheles, were embodied in such a manner as to enable them to hold up their heads and strike their respective notes in the midst of the wilderness of canvas and paint. To the canvas and paint – since he feels Goethe's poem, or indeed simply the wondrous legend, in that way; or even, as we may say, since he feels in that way the manner in which Mr Wills feels Goethe and the legend – he was perfectly welcome; but surely he ought to have perceived that, given the grandly poetic, ironic, but at the same time very scantily dramatic nature of his drama; given the delicacy and subtlety of a work of genius of the complexion of *Faust*, special precautions should be taken against the accessories seeming a more important part of the business than the action. Evidently, however, Mr Irving argued in directly the opposite way. It is as if he had said that he would pile the accessories so high that the rest of the affair wouldn't matter, it would be regarded so little.

It wouldn't matter, in the first place, that Mr Wills should have turned him out an arrangement of Goethe so meagre, so common, so trivial (one really must multiply epithets to express its inadequacy), that the responsibility of the impresario to the poet increased tenfold, rather than diminished, with his accepting it, there being so much more, as it were to make up for. It wouldn't matter that from the beginning to the end of the play, thanks to Mr Wills's ingenious dissimulation of the fact, it might never occur to the auditor that he was listening to one of the greatest productions of the human mind. It wouldn't matter that Mr Irving should have conceived and should execute his own part in the spirit of somewhat refined extravaganza; a manner which should differ only in degree from that of the star of a Christmas burlesque – without breadth, without depth, with little tittering effects of low comedy. It wouldn't matter that Faust should be represented by a young actor, whose general weakness should prevent him, in spite of zealous effort, from giving stature and relief to his conception of the character, and whose unformed delivery should interfere in the same degree with his imparting variety of accent to his different speeches. It wouldn't matter that, with Mr Wills's version and such an interpretation, the exquisite episode of the wooing of Margaret should hold no place in the play – should literally pass unperceived. It wouldn't matter that Miss Ellen Terry, as picturesque and pleasing a figure as usual, should give perhaps a stranger exhibition than she has ever given before of her want of art and style, and should play the divine, still, concentrated part of Margaret without apparently a suspicion of what it consists. If it wouldn't matter that Mr Irving himself should be thin, that Mr Alexander should be insignificant, that Miss Terry should be rough, and that Mr Wills should be all three, of course it would matter still less that the two extremely mature actresses who were successively to attempt Martha should give the English public (so far at least as represented at the Lyceum) a really rare opportunity to respond to bad taste with bad taste, to greet with artless and irrepressible glee the strange gruntings and snortings with which the performers in question have seen fit to enrich the character. All these things, to our sense, *should* have mattered; it was far better that the overtopping scenery should have been sacrificed than that a concession should have been made in regard to the personal rendering of the piece. It was far better that the 'points' should remain the points that Goethe made, even if the background had to be bare for it; that the immortal group of the scholar with his passions rekindled; the girl who trusts and suffers, and the mocking, spell-weaving fiend should hold itself well together, detach itself, and stamp itself strongly, even if the imagination had to do the work of putting in the gardens and spires of the German city, the mist and goblins of the Brocken, and the blue fire that plays about Mephistopheles. Of course if Mr Irving could both have mounted the play and caused the acting of it to be an equal feature, that would have been best of all; but since the personal representation of a work at once so pregnant poetically and so faulty as a dramatic composition was the problem to challenge by its very difficulties an artist of his high reputation – an artist universally acclaimed as leading the public taste, not as waiting behind its chair – he would have consulted best the interests of that reputation by 'going in' for a dramatic as distinguished from a spectacular success.

We may as well confess frankly that we attach the most limited importance to the little mechanical artifices with which Mr Irving has sought to enliven *Faust*. We care nothing for the spurting flames which play so large a part, nor for the importunate limelight which is perpetually projected upon somebody or something. It is not for these things that we go to see the great Goethe, or even (for we must, after all, allow for inevitable dilutions) the less celebrated Mr Wills. We even protest against the abuse of the said limelight effect: it is always descending on some one or other, apropos of everything and of nothing; it is disturbing and vulgarizing, and has nothing to do with the author's meaning. That blue vapours should attend on the steps of Mephistopheles is a very poor substitute for his giving us a moral shudder. That deep note is entirely absent from Mr Irving's rendering of him, though the actor, of course, at moments presents to the eye a remarkably sinister figure. He strikes us, however, as superficial – a terrible fault for an archfiend – and his grotesqueness strikes us as cheap. We attach also but the slenderest importance to the scene of the Witches' Sabbath, which has been reduced to a mere bald hubbub of capering, screeching, and banging, irradiated by the irrepressible blue fire, and without the smallest articulation of Goethe's text. The scenic effect is the ugliest we have ever contemplated, and its ugliness is not paid for by its having a meaning for our ears. It is a horror cheaply conceived, and executed with more zeal than discretion.

It seems almost ungracious to say of an actress usually so pleasing as Miss Terry that she falls below her occasion, but it is impossible for us to consider her Margaret as a finished creation. Besides having a strange amateurishness of form (for the work of an actress who has had Miss Terry's years of practice), it is, to our sense, wanting in fineness of conception, wanting in sweetness and quietness, wanting in taste. It is much too rough-and-ready. We prefer Miss Terry's pathos, however, to her comedy, and cannot but feel that the whole scene with the jewels in her room is a mistake. It is obstreperous, and not in the least in the poetic tone. If the passages in the garden fail of their effect, the responsibility for this is not, however, more than very partially with the Margaret. It is explained in the first place by the fact that the actor who represents Faust is, as we have hinted, not 'in it' at all, and in the second by the fact that the conversation between Mephistopheles and Margaret is terribly overaccented – pushed quite out of the frame. Martha's flirtation, especially as Mrs Stirling plays it, becomes the whole story, and Faust and Margaret are superseded. What can have beguiled Mr Irving into the extraordinary error of intrusting the part of Martha first to one and then to another of (on this occasion at least) signally little temperance and taste? The fault has been aggravated by being repeated; the opportunity of retrieving it might have been seized when Mrs Stirling laid down her task. But Mrs Chippendale has even a heavier hand. We should be sorry to fail of respect to the former actress, who, today full of years and honours, has always shown an eminent acquaintance with her art and has been remarkable for a certain old-fashioned richness of humour. As such matters go, on the English stage, she is supposed to have the 'tradition'. It is to be hoped, however, for the tradition's sake, that she violates it today by her tendency to spread, to 'drag', as the phrase is, to take too much elbow room. This defect was sufficiently marked when a year or two ago she played the Nurse of Juliet, whom she put sadly out of focus. It is manifested in an even greater degree by her Martha, and it must be said that if she renders the part in the spirit of the tradition, the traidition will on this occasion have been strangely coarse. Yet Mrs Stirling is distinction itself compared with the displeasing loudness to which her successor treats us; and of this latter lady's acting, it is enough to say that it compelled us to indulge in a melancholy 'return' on an audience moved by such means to such mirth. The scene between Mephistopheles and Martha is the most successful of the play, judged by the visible appreciation of the public – a fact which should surely minister to deep reflection on the part of those who, as artists, work for the public. All the same, Mr Irving would have been well advised, from the artistic point of view, in causing Martha, by contact and example, to be represented in a higher style of comedy.

We shall not attempt to point out still other instances in which, as it seems to us, he would have been well advised; we have said enough to substantiate our contention that it is not for the interest of the actor's art that it should be too precipitately, or too superficially, assumed that the great elaboration of a play as a spectacle is a complete expression of it – a complete solution of the problem.

The Century Magazine, December 1887

G. B. Shaw
Irving's Production of *Cymbeline*

I confess to a difficulty in feeling civilized just at present. Flying from the country, where the gentlemen of England are in an ecstasy of chicken-butchering, I return to town to find the higher wits assembled at a play three hundred years old, in which the sensation scene exhibits a woman waking up to find her husband reposing gorily in her arms with his head cut off.

Pray understand, therefore, that I do not defend *Cymbeline*. It is for the most part stagey trash of the lowest melodramatic order, in parts abominably written, throughout intellectually vulgar, and, judged in point of thought by modern intellectual standards, vulgar, foolish, offensive, indecent, and exasperating beyond all tolerance. There are moments when one asks despairingly why our stage should ever have been cursed with this 'immortal' pilferer of other men's stories and ideas, with his monstrous rhetorical fustian, his unbearable platitudes, his pretentious reduction of the subtlest problems of life to commonplaces against which a Polytechnic debating club would revolt, his incredible unsuggestiveness, his sententious combination of ready reflection with complete intellectual sterility, and his consequent incapacity for getting out of the depth of even the most ignorant audience, except when he solemnly says something so transcendently platitudinous that his more humble-minded hearers cannot bring themselves to believe that so great a man really meant to talk like their grandmothers. With the single exception of Homer, there is no eminent writer, not even Sir Walter Scott, whom I can despise so entirely as I despise Shakespear when I measure my mind against his. The intensity of my impatience with him occasionally reaches such a pitch, that it would positively be a relief to me to dig him up and throw stones at him, knowing as I do how incapable he and his worshippers are of understanding any less obvious form of indignity. To read *Cymbeline* and to think of Goethe, of Wagner, of Ibsen, is, for me, to imperil the habit of studied moderation of statement which years of public responsibility as a journalist have made almost second nature in me.

But I am bound to add that I pity the man who cannot enjoy Shakespear. He has outlasted thousands of abler thinkers, and will outlast a thousand more. His gift of telling a story (provided someone else told it to him first); his enormous power over language, as conspicuous in his senseless and silly abuse of it as in his miracles of expression; his humour; his sense of idiosyncratic character; and his prodigious fund of that vital energy which is, it seems, the true differentiating property behind the faculties, good, bad, or indifferent, of the man of genius, enable him to entertain us so effectively that the imaginary scenes and people he has created become more real to us than our actual life – at least, until our knowledge and grip of actual life begins to deepen and glow beyond the common. When I was twenty I knew everybody in Shakespear, from Hamlet to Abhorson, much more intimately than I knew my living contemporaries; and to this day, if the name of Pistol or Polonius catches my eye in a newspaper, I turn to the passage with more curiosity than if the name were that of – but perhaps I had better not mention any one in particular.

How many new acquaintances, then, do you make in reading *Cymbeline*, provided you have the patience to break your way into it through all the fustian, and you are old enough to be free from the modern idea that Cymbeline must be the name of a cosmetic and Imogen of the latest scientific discovery in the nature of a hitherto unknown gas? Cymbeline is nothing; his queen nothing, though some attempt is made to justify her description as 'a woman that bears all down with her brain'; Posthumus, nothing – most fortunately, as otherwise he would be an unendurably contemptible hound; Belarius, nothing – at least, not after Kent in *King Lear* (just as the Queen is nothing after Lady Macbeth); Iachimo, not much – only a *diabolus ex machina* made plausible; and Pisanio, less than Iachimo. On the other hand, we have Cloten, the prince of numbsculls, whose part, indecencies and all, is a literary masterpiece from the first line to the last; the two princes – fine presentments of that impressive and generous myth, the noble savage; Caius Lucius, the Roman general, urbane among the barbarians; and, above all, Imogen. But do, please, remember that there are two Imogens. One is a solemn and elaborate example of what, in Shakespear's opinion, a real lady ought to be. With this unspeakable person virtuous indignation is chronic. Her object in life is to vindicate her own propriety and to suspect everybody else's, especially her husband's. Like Lothaw in the jeweller's shop in Bret Harte's burlesque novel, she cannot be left alone with unconsidered trifles of portable silver without officiously assuring the proprietors that she has stolen naught, nor would not though she had found gold strewed i' the floor. Her fertility and spontaneity in nasty ideas is not to be described: there is hardly a speech in her part that you can read without wincing. But this Imogen has another one tied to her with ropes of blank verse (which can fortunately be cut) – the Imogen of Shakespear's genius, an enchanting person of the most delicate sensitiveness, full of sudden transitions from ecstasies of tenderness to transports of childish rage, and reckless of consequences in both, instantly hurt and instantly appeased, and of the highest breeding and courage. But for this Imogen, *Cymbeline* would stand about as much chance of being revived now as *Titus Andronicus*.

The instinctive Imogen, like the real live part of the rest of the play, has to be disentangled from a mass of stuff which, though it might be recited with effect and appropriateness by young amateurs at a performance by the Elizabethan Stage Society, is absolutely unactable and unutterable in the modern theatre, where a direct illusion of reality is aimed at, and where the repugnance of the best actors to play false passages is practically insuperable. For the purposes of the Lyceum, therefore, *Cymbeline* had to be cut, and cut liberally. Not that there was any reason to apprehend that the manager would flinch from the operation: quite the contrary. In a true republic of art Sir Henry Irving would ere this have expiated his acting versions on the scaffold. He does not merely cut plays: he disembowels them. In *Cymbeline* he has quite surpassed himself by extirpating the antiphonal third verse of the famous dirge. A man who would do that would do anything – cut the coda out of the first movement of Beethoven's Ninth Symphony, or shorten one of Velasquez's Philips into a kitcat to make it fit over his drawing room mantelpiece. The grotesque character tracery of Cloten's lines, which is surely not beyond the appreciation of an age educated by Stevenson, is defaced with Cromwellian ruthlessness; and the patriotic scene, with the Queen's great speech about the natural bravery of our isle, magnificent in its Walkürenritt swing, is shorn away, though it might easily have been introduced in the Garden scene. And yet, long screeds of rubbish about 'slander, whose edge is sharper than the sword', and so on, are preserved with superstitious veneration.

This curious want of connoisseurship in literature would disable Sir Henry Irving seriously, if he were an interpretative actor. But it is, happily, the fault of a great quality – the creative quality. A prodigious deal of nonsense has been written about Sir Henry Irving's conception of this, that, and the other Shakespearean character. The truth is that he has never in his life conceived or interpreted the characters of any author except himself. He is really as incapable of acting another man's play as Wagner was of setting another man's libretto; and he should, like Wagner, have written his plays for himself. But as he did not find himself out until it was too late for him to learn that supplementary trade, he was compelled to use other men's plays as the framework for his own creations. His first great success in this sort of adaptation was with the *Merchant of Venice*. There was no question then of a bad Shylock or a good Shylock: he was simply not Shylock at all; and when his own creation came into conflict with Shakespear's, as it did quite openly in the Trial scene, he simply played in flat contradiction of the lines, and positively acted Shakespear off the stage. This was an original policy, and an intensely interesting one from the critical point of view; but it was obvious that its difficulty must increase with the vividness and force of the dramatist's creation. Shakespear at his highest pitch cannot be set aside by any mortal actor, however gifted; and when Sir Henry Irving tried to interpolate a most singular and fantastic notion of an old man between the lines of a fearfully mutilated acting version of *King Lear*, he was smashed. On the other hand, in plays by persons of no importance, where the dramatist's part of the business is the merest trash, his creative activity is unhampered and uncontradicted; and the author's futility is the opportunity for the actor's masterpiece. Now I have already described Shakespear's Iachimo as little better than any of the lay figures in *Cymbeline* – a mere *diabolus ex machina*. But Irving's Iachimo is a very different affair. It is a new and independent creation. I knew Shakespear's play inside and out before last Tuesday; but this Iachimo was quite fresh and novel to me. I witnessed it with unqualified delight: it was no vulgar bagful of 'points', but a true impersonation, unbroken in its life-current from end to end, varied on the surface with the finest comedy, and without a single lapse in the sustained beauty of its execution. It is only after such work that an artist can with perfect naturalness and dignity address himself to his audience as 'their faithful and loving servant'; and I wish I could add that the audience had an equal right to offer him their applause as a worthy acknowledgment of his merit. But when a house distributes its officious first-night plaudits impartially between the fine artist and the blunderer who roars a few lines violently and rushes off the stage after compressing the entire art of How Not to Act into five intolerable minutes, it had better be told to reserve its impertinent and obstreperous demonstrations until it has learnt to bestow them with some sort of discrimination. Our first-night people mean well, and will, no doubt, accept my assurance that they are donkeys with all possible good humour; but they should remember that to applaud for the sake of applauding, as schoolboys will cheer for the sake of cheering, is to destroy our own power of complimenting those who, as the greatest among us, are the servants of all the rest.

Over the performances of the other gentlemen in the cast let me skate as lightly as possible. Mr Norman Forbes's Cloten, though a fatuous idiot rather than the brawny 'beef-witted' fool whom Shakespear took from his own Ajax in *Troilus and Cressida*, is effective and amusing, so that one feels acutely the mangling of his part, especially the cutting of that immortal musical criticism of his upon the serenade. Mr Gordon Craig and Mr Webster are desperate failures as the two noble savages. They are as spirited and picturesque as possible; but every pose, every flirt of their elfin locks, proclaims the wild freedom of Bedford Park. They recite the poor maimed dirge admirably, Mr Craig being the more musical of the twain; and Mr Webster's sword-and-cudgel fight with Cloten is very lively; but their utter deficiency in the grave, rather sombre, uncivilized primeval strength and Mohican dignity so finely suggested by Shakespear, takes all the ballast out of the fourth act, and combines with the inappropriate prettiness and sunniness of the landscape scenery to handicap Miss Ellen Terry most cruelly in the trying scene of her awakening by the side of the flower-decked corpse; a scene which, without every accessory to heighten its mystery, terror, and pathos, is utterly and heart-breakingly impossible for any actress, even if she were Duse, Ristori, Mrs Siddons and Miss Terry rolled into one. When I saw this gross and palpable oversight, and heard people talking about the Lyceum stage management as superb, I with difficulty restrained myself from tearing out my hair in handfuls and scattering it with imprecations to the four winds. That cave of the three mountaineers wants nothing but a trellised porch, a bamboo bicycle, and a nice little bed of standard roses, to complete its absurdity.

With Mr Frederic Robinson as Belarius, and Mr Tyars as Pisanio, there is no reasonable fault to find, except that they might, perhaps, be a little brighter with advantage; and of the rest of their male colleagues I think I shall ask to be allowed to say nothing at all, even at the cost of omitting a tribute to Mr Fuller Mellish's discreet impersonation of the harmless necessary Philario. There remains Miss Geneviève Ward, whose part, with the Neptune's park speech lopped off, was not worth her playing, and Miss Ellen Terry, who invariably fascinates me so much that I have not the smallest confidence in my own judgment respecting her. There was no Bedford Park about the effect she made as she stepped into the King's garden; still less any of the atmosphere of ancient Britain. At the first glance, we were in the Italian fifteenth century; and the house, unversed in the cinquecento, but dazzled all the same, proceeded to roar until it stopped from exhaustion. There is one scene in *Cymbeline*, the one in which Imogen receives the summons to 'that same blessed Milford', which might have been written for Miss Terry, so perfectly does its innocent rapture and frank gladness fit into her hand. Her repulse of Iachimo brought down the house as a matter of course, though I am convinced that the older Shakespeareans present had a vague impression that it could not be properly done except by a stout, turnip-headed matron, with her black hair folded smoothly over her ears and secured in a classic bun. Miss Terry had evidently cut her own part; at all events the odious Mrs Grundyish Imogen had been dissected out of it so skilfully that it went into a single jar. The circumstances under which she was asked to play the fourth act were, as I have explained, impossible. To wake up in the gloom amid the wolf and robber-haunted mountain gorges which formed the Welsh mountains of Shakespear's imagination in the days before the Great Western existed is one thing: to wake up at about three on a nice Bank-holiday afternoon in a charming spot near the valley of the Wye is quite another. With all her force, Miss Terry gave us faithfully the whole process which Shakespear has presented with such dramatic cunning – Imogen's bewilderment, between dreaming and waking, as to where she is; the vague discerning of some strange bedfellow there; the wondering examination of the flowers with which he is so oddly covered; the frightful discovery of blood on the flowers, with the hideous climax that the man is headless and that his clothes are her husband's; and it was all ruined by that blazing, idiotic, prosaic sunlight in which everything leapt to the eye at once, rendering the mystery and the slowly growing clearness of perception incredible and unintelligible, and spoiling a scene which, properly staged, would have been a triumph of histrionic intelligence. Cannot somebody be hanged for this? Men perish every week for lesser crimes. What consolation is it to me that Miss Terry played with infinite charm and delicacy of appeal, made up her lost ground in other directions, and had more than as much success as the roaring gallery could feel the want of?

A musical accompaniment to the drama has been specially composed; and its numbers are set forth in the bill of the play, with the words 'LOST PROPERTY' in conspicuous red capitals in the margin. Perhaps I can be of some use in restoring at least some of the articles to their rightful owners. The prelude to the fourth act belongs to Beethoven – first movement of the Seventh Symphony. The theme played by 'the ingenious instrument' in the cave is Handel's, and is familiar to lovers of *Judas Maccabeus* as 'O never bow we down to the rude stock or scultured stone'. J.F.R. will, I feel sure, be happy to carry the work of identification further if necessary.

Sir Henry Irving's next appearance will be on Bosworth Field. He was obviously astonished by the startling shout of approbation with which the announcement was received. We all have an old weakness for Richard. After that, *Madame Sans-Gêne*, with Sardou's Napoleon.

The Saturday Review, 26 September 1896

A. B. Walkley
Henry Irving

It is no longer modish to deal in universal categories. Time was when you commenced aphorist by compelling the whole human race to choose alternatives of your invention. 'All men, are either –', you began brazenly, and tossed up a coin to determine the predicate. Born Aristotelians or Platonists, said one; borrowers or lenders, said another. Fools or d——d fools, suggested the undergraduate. Of such dead-and-gone dichotomies there is one, a favourite with the French Romanticists of the Thirties, which might well be revived. Théophile Gautier and his generation divided mankind into the great classes of *flamboyant* and *drab*. Don Quixote, Diderot, Shelley, the Devil (Milton's, of course), and Mr Henry Irving, are all flamboyant. Sancho Panza, Voltaire, Wordsworth, the 'magnified Lord Shaftesbury' of Matthew Arnold, the British Public, are all drab. It is the glory of Mr Irving that he gives the world the spectacle, all too rare, of the two classes in their proper relationship; that is, the second subservient to the first. A flamboyant of the flamboyants, he has conquered the drab public. Don Quixote has brought Sancho to heel.

In the great Reckoning Day of the arts, this shall be counted unto him for righteousness. He has vindicated the supremacy of Romance in the face of all Philistia. The assertion is not to be carped at as only a roundabout way of saying that he is a romantic actor who has won the favour of the pit. Merely to call him a romantic actor might mean little enough; the phrase has been too often used on the stage – where even the great name of romance has not escaped degradation – for some little extra smirching of red ochre and burnt cork; a mere difference between 'twopence coloured' and 'penny plain'. The point is that he is a flamboyant, a romantic in the grand style, drums beating and colours flying. He is a dreamer of dreams, the Alnaschar of the stage – yet happier than Alnaschar in that his most splendid visions, 'the cloud cap't towers, the gorgeous palaces', become for us all, in due time, waking realities on the Lyceum stage. Like his own Charles, in Marvel's verse, he nothing common does nor mean upon that memorable scene. At his worst, as at his best, he ever touches the imagination. Now, to touch the imagination in the playhouse world of Romance, and, withal, to bring the great outer Philistine world to its knees – to set our ears ringing with the 'chink-chink' of the Polish Jew's sleigh-bells, and to get elected to the Athenaeum Club *honoris causa* – is an achievement verging on the paradoxical; it is running with the hare and hunting with the hounds. Alone among actors, Mr Irving has taken this double-first: a success on the stage and off it – *in republica tanquam in scena*, as Lord Coleridge once said of him in the words of the great Roman orator. Of his predecessors, Macready came near doing it, but failed. For Macready was a bit of a Philistine – was, in fact, among the drabs. He was ashamed of his profession. Mr Irving is proud of it, feeling a stain on its honour 'like a wound'. Burke's phrase comes naturally to the mind, for there is something chivalric in the man as in the player – a dignity, a gust, a touch of the hidalgo.

When a quarter of a century ago Henry Irving, after ten year's rustication, was permanently enrolled in a London company, the prospects of the English stage were, as Mr Stevenson would say, aleatory. The die might have come down drab; our next great actor might have been a John Kemble, or an elder Farren, a classic, a depositary of 'correctness' and the traditions. Like every other young actor, Irving began by doing what Theodora, in Sardou's play, says her imperial husband does – *un peu de tout*. Of these miscellaneous experiments, our elders still profess to remember with gratitude the actor's Richard Chevenix, his Rawdon Scudamore, his Jeremy Diddler, his Bill Sykes. He was by no means an ideal Claude Melnotte. Then he fell to playing Doricourt, Charles Surface, Young Marlow, Captain Absolute, drab heroes to a man. But this was only a trial of the die; the gambler's first throw 'for love'. When it was finally cast, it came down flamboyant. The actor approached his proper goal of the romantic, the fantastic, in Digby Grant, in Jingle, and reached it, amid a roar of astonished applause from the crowd, in Burgomaster Mathias. This was his first great assault on Philistia. It roused the average sensual man to the disquieting consciousness of a nervous system. Contrast it with M. Coquelin's impersonation of the same part, and you have the pass-key to Mr Irving's method. The one is of imagination all compact, a common Alsation inn-keeper, transfigured by romance, seen, as it were, by flashes of lightning; the other is plausible, logical, correct; a figure of cold daylight, leaving you as cold. In a word, the one is flamboyant; the other only drab.

It was evident from the first that he had not the fluid or ductile temperament which makes your all-round actor, your Betterton, your Garrick. His mind was not like Squire Brooke's, a jelly which ran easily into any mould. Here again his method is antithetic to M. Coquelin's. Universality is the foible of M. Coquelin, who – in defiance of a nose suggesting obvious limitations – thinks with Colley Cibber that 'anything naturally written ought to be in every one's way that pretends to be an actor'. Mr Irving's individuality is too strongly marked to let him fall into that heresy. As soon as he attacked Shakespeare we saw that he was not going to sweep the board. He began – of course, they all do – with Hamlet. It is a part in which no actor has ever been known entirely to fail; but it will never be linked with Mr Irving's name as it is, for all time, with Betterton's – the classic impersonation, 'the best part, I believe', says Pepys, 'that ever man acted'. His Othello, his Richard, were only half-successes. One still prefers to read how Edmund Kean did them. Over the recollection of his Romeo one passes hastily, suppressing a chuckle. His Macbeth, even in its second version, revised and improved, was rather romantic than tragic. So it was in the romantic rather than the tragic repertory of Shakespeare, in the figures painted from the rich fantastic palette of the Italian Renaissance, that one waited for him confidently. Shylock, Iago, Malvolio, Benedick, these are all flamboyant parts, and he took possession of them by right of temperament. To say that his 'was the Jew that Shakespeare drew' would be to quote Pope's doggerel inopportunely. It was the Jew idealized in the light of the modern Occidental reaction against the *Judenhetze*, a Jew already conscious of the Spinozas, the Sidonias, the Disraelis, who were to issue from his loins. His Iago was daringly Italian, a true compatriot of the Borgias, or rather better than Italian, that 'devil incarnate, an Englishman Italianate'. The remembrance of those grapes which he plucked and slowly ate still sets the teeth of Philistia on edge. His Malvolio had an air of *hidalguia*, something of Castilian loftiness, for all the fantasy of its cross-gartering; Don Quixote turned Major Domo. Quite the best of his Renaissance flamboyants is his Benedick, as gallant a picture of the courtier-scholar-soldier as anything in the pages of Cellini, or the canvases of Velasquez. But, grateful as we are for these things, his greatest services to Shakespeare, most of us will think, have been less immediate than mediate, less as actor than as manager. Nero did not surpass, nor the late M. Perrin equal, him as a *metteur en scène*. His series of Shakespearean land and seascapes, Veronese gardens open to the moonlight, a Venice unpolluted by Cook's touristry, groves of cedar and cypress in Messina, Illyrian shores, Scotch hillsides, and grim castle, Bosworth Field – what a panorama he has given us! The sensuous, plastic, pictorial side of Shakespeare had never been seen before he showed it. Here you have the flamboyant artist outdoing Delacroix on his own ground.

Nevertheless, man cannot live by Shakespeare alone, least of all this man. His most pertinent triumph has been in melodrama – which is Philistia's name for the stage-flamboyant expressed in prose. His prototype in this was

Lemaître; and his conquest of the Lemaîtrist repertory is complete. His Robert Macaire, his Dubosc, are the most effective of stage sudorifics. French melodramas, too, have yielded him Louis XI, the two Dei Franchi, while two of Macready's great parts – played in a manner widely different from Macready's – have furnished him with Richelieu and Werner. These are all studies in the lurid, the volcanic, and they are among his strongest; but two at least of his best things are figures of repose, if not of still life – his Charles I and his Dr Primrose. Over them all, the just and the unjust, his romance has gleamed impartially.

But, as Sainte-Beuve somewhere says, *L'écueil particulier du genre romanesque, c'est le faux*, and this romantic actor could not hope to escape the special danger of his temperament. Like the Don Quixote with whom I have compared him, he has now and then mistaken spavined hacks for Rosinantes and flocks of sheep for armies. His Vanderdecken, his Eugene Aram, perhaps his Philip, and his Count Tristan, were among these errors. His Mephistopheles, too, and, as some think, his Edgar of Ravenswood. The fault was not all his own. His authors played him false. There one touches him between the joints of his harness; he has failed to create a great modern playwright. Let him crown his career by doing that, and I, for one, will vote for his canonization. Where is he to find the playwright? Well, at the risk of passing for a Curious Impertinent, I will hint that a great artist in fiction is to be found under the shadow of a certain hill in Surrey. Only to think what the creator of those princely flamboyants, Old Mel and Richmond Roy, might have done – might, surely, still do – for Henry Irving! As George Tesman says, 'fancy that!'

Playhouse Impressions, 1892

William Archer
Forbes Robertson as Hamlet

First-night applause may be roughly classified under three heads. There is first the applause due to mere politeness, friendship, and thoughtless good nature, proceeding from people who do not ask themselves whether a piece of acting is good or bad, whether it has or has not given them pleasure, but simply clap because it is expected of them and because it is pleasanter to approve than disapprove. Secondly, we have the applause of personal fanatics (often quite disinterested in their mania) who think this actor or that the greatest genius that ever lived, and bellow themselves hoarse whatever he does and however he does it. The third and rarest sort of applause, easily distinguishable from the other two, is that in which the spontaneous and irrepressible delight of the whole audience finds utterance; in which intelligent appreciation chimes in with fanaticism and good-nature; in which the actor, if he have any delicacy of ear, can detect the tribute of the few amid the facile plaudits of the many. Such was the applause which at many points greeted Mr Forbes Robertson's Hamlet on Saturday night – notably at the end of the second act, and at the close of the play. It was indeed an admirable performance, falling short in only one respect of what may be called a reasonable ideal. The grace and distinction of Hamlet, his affability (to use a needlessly degraded word), his melancholy, his intellectual discursiveness – all these aspects of the many-sided character Mr Robertson brought out to perfection. He shone especially in the monologues. I have never heard any similar passage of Shakespeare better delivered than the 'Oh, what a rogue and peasant slave am I' soliloquy, as treated by Mr Robertson. His method of introducing it, while conning a prompt-book of the play handed him by the First Actor, is at once ingenious and unforced; and the way in which he graduates and varies it is quite masterly. He makes it a little drama in itself. Not quite so happy is his treatment of the 'To be or not to be' speech. His face seems to light up at the phrase 'To sleep – perchance to dream!' – whereas the thought should clearly overcloud the momentary serenity with which Hamlet has been contemplating the 'consummation devoutly to be wished'. On the whole, however, Mr Robertson's handling of the meditative passages could scarcely have been improved. It was so good that one doubly regretted the omission of the 'Now could I do it pat' speech. Having restored Fortinbras at the close, moreover, Mr Robertson might surely have managed to get in the soliloquy 'How all occasions do inform against me', hitherto omitted along with the 'occasion' which inspires it. As it is, the introduction of Fortinbras lends dignity and picturesqueness to the final scene, but is of no literary value. The only point in which Mr Robertson's performance is notably defective happens, unfortunately, to be a rather important one: he slurs and almost ignores that nervous excitability on Hamlet's part which merges so naturally, nay, almost indistinguishably, into his pretended madness. We do not nowadays waste time in arguments about Hamlet's sanity. If Hamlet is mad, which of us shall 'scape Hanwell? He deliberately puts on an 'antic disposition' to serve him at once as a mask and a weapon – to protect him from his uncle's malice and at the same time to further his revenge. But there can be no doubt that the assumption of lunacy is congenial to him, and that he uses it as a safety-valve for pent-up emotion. He is in a state of nervous overstrain which finds relief in fantastic ejaculations, scathing ironies, wild and whirling words of every sort, quite apart from their calculated effect upon others. Now Mr Forbes Robertson makes, one may almost say, as little as possible of Hamlet's assumed lunacy and real hysteria. It was probably this side of the character that chiefly appealed both to actors and audiences, in Shakespeare's own day. Our forefathers took a delight in the contemplation of insanity which we no longer feel, and it is evident that their actors revelled in exhibitions of mopping, mowing and gibbering, such as would merely inspire us with disgust. But the very fact that Hamlet's madness is assumed makes it quite endurable even to modern nerves, and I can conceive no reason, whether of art or expediency, for the exceeding tameness of Mr Forbes Robertson's acting in such passages as the end of the first act (after the departure of the Ghost) and the great scene with Ophelia. He omits a good many of the wild and whirling words, and he puts no force or gusto into those he utters. Such a phrase, for instance, as 'Aha, boy, art thou there!' addressed to the Ghost 'in the cellarage', he speaks with respectful melancholy, instead of the feverish freakishness which is surely the keynote of this scene. I cannot but hope that Mr Robertson will reconsider these scenes, which are certainly well within his compass. Artistic self-restraint is a very good thing, but in this case it verges on timidity. One or two individual readings I would gladly discuss with Mr Robertson if space permitted. As it is, I can only refer him to *Dramatic Essays* by George Henry Lewes (ed. 1896, p. 176) for proof that the strain by which 'Neméan' can be got into the metre is not only uncalled for but positively wrong. Shakespeare scanned the word as Virgil did – 'Némean'.

The other parts are not very fortunately cast. Mrs Patrick Campbell's Ophelia cannot rank among her successes; Mr Barnes is a far too robust and solid Polonius; Miss Granville, as the Queen, looks absurdly young, and shows a total lack of experience in this class of work; no one, in short, except Mr Forbes Robertson, rises above mediocrity. But he rises so far above it as to make the revival interesting and memorable.

The World, 15 September 1897

G. B. Shaw
Tree's Production of *Julius Caesar*

The truce with Shakespear is over. It was only possible whilst *Hamlet* was on the stage. *Hamlet* is the tragedy of private life – nay, of individual bachelor-poet life. It belongs to a detached residence, a select library, an exclusive circle, to no occupation, to fathomless boredom, to impenitent mugwumpism, to the illusion that the futility of these things is the futility of existence, and its contemplation philosophy: in short, to the dream-fed gentlemanism of the age which Shakespear inaugurated in English literature: the age, that is, of the rising middle class bringing into power the ideas taught it by its servants in the kitchen, and its fathers in the shop – ideas now happily passing away as the onslaught of modern democracy offers to the kitchen-taught and home-bred the alternative of achieving a real superiority or going ignominiously under in the class conflict.

It is when we turn to *Julius Caesar*, the most splendidly written political melodrama we possess, that we realize the apparently immortal author of *Hamlet* as a man, not for all time, but for an age only, and that, too, in all solidly wise and heroic aspects, the most despicable of all the ages in our history. It is impossible for even the most judicially minded critic to look without a revulsion of indignant contempt at this travestying of a great man as a silly braggart, whilst the pitiful gang of mischief-makers who destroyed him are lauded as statesmen and patriots. There is not a single sentence uttered by Shakespear's Julius Caesar that is, I will not say worthy of him, but even worthy of an average Tammany boss. Brutus is nothing but a familiar type of English suburban preacher: politically he would hardly impress the Thames Conservancy Board. Cassius is a vehemently assertive nonentity. It is only when we come to Antony, unctuous voluptuary and self-seeking sentimental demagogue, that we find Shakespear in his depth; and in his depth, of course, he is superlative. Regarded as a crafty stage job, the play is a triumph: rhetoric, claptrap, effective gushes of emotion, all the devices of the popular playwright, are employed with a profusion of power that almost breaks their backs. No doubt there are slips and slovenliness of the kind that careful revisers eliminate; but they count for so little in the mass of accomplishment that it is safe to say that the dramatist's art can be carried no further on that plane. If Goethe, who understood Caesar and the significance of his death – 'the most senseless of deeds' he called it – had treated the subject, his conception of it would have been as superior to Shakespear's as St John's Gospel is to the Police News, but his treatment could not have been more magnificently successful. As far as sonority, imagery, wit, humor, energy of imagination, power over language, and a whimsically keen eye for idiosyncrasies can make a dramatist, Shakespear was the king of dramatists. Unfortunately, a man may have them all, and yet conceive high affairs of state exactly as Simon

Tappertit did. In one of the scenes in *Julius Caesar* a conceited poet bursts into the tent of Brutus and Cassius, and exhorts them not to quarrel with one another. If Shakespear had been able to present his play to the ghost of the great Julius, he would probably have had much the same reception. He certainly would have deserved it.

When it was announced that Mr Tree had resolved to give special prominence to the character of Caesar in his acting version, the critics winked, and concluded simply that the actor-manager was going to play Antony and not Brutus. Therefore I had better say that Mr Tree must stand acquitted of any belittlement of the parts which complete so strongly with his own. Before going to Her Majesty's I was curious enough to block out for myself a division of the play into three acts; and I found that Mr Tree's division corresponded exactly with mine. Mr Waller's opportunities as Brutus, and Mr McLeay's as Cassius, are limited only by their own ability to take advantage of them; and Mr Louis Calvert figures as boldly in the public eye as he did in his own production of *Antony and Cleopatra* last year at Manchester. Indeed, Mr Calvert is the only member of the company who achieves an unequivocal success. The preference expressed in the play by Caesar for fat men may, perhaps, excuse Mr Calvert for having again permitted himself to expand after his triumphant reduction of his girth for his last appearance in London. However, he acted none the worse; in fact, nobody else acted so skilfully or originally. The others, more heavily burdened, did their best, quite in the spirit of the man who had never played the fiddle, but had no doubt he could if he tried. Without oratory, without style, without specialized vocal training, without any practice worth mentioning, they assaulted the play with cheerful self-sufficiency, and gained great glory by the extent to which, as a masterpiece of the playwright's trade, it played itself. Some small successes were not lacking. Caesar's nose was good: Calpurnia's bust was worthy of her: in such parts Garrick and Siddons could have achieved no more. Miss Evelyn Millard's Roman matron in the style of Richardson – Cato's daughter as Clarissa – was an unlooked-for novelty; but it cost a good deal of valuable time to get in the eighteenth century between the lines of the first B.C. By operatic convention – the least appropriate of all conventions – the boy Lucius was played by Mrs Tree, who sang Sullivan's ultra-nineteenth-century 'Orpheus with his Lute', modulations and all, to a pizzicato accompaniment supposed to be played on a lyre with eight open and unstoppable strings, a feat complexly and absurdly impossible. Mr Waller, as Brutus, failed in the first half of the play. His intention clearly was to represent Brutus as a man superior to fate and circumstance; but the effect he produced was one of insensibility. Nothing could have been more unfortunate; for it is through the sensibility of Brutus that the audience have to learn what they cannot learn from the phlegmatic pluck of Casca or the narrow vindictiveness of Cassius: that is, the terrible momentousness, the harrowing anxiety and dread, of the impending catastrophe. Mr Waller left that function to the thunderstorm. From the death of Caesar onward he was better; and his appearance throughout was effective; but at best his sketch was a water-colour one. Mr Franklyn

McLeay carried off the honours of the evening by his deliberate staginess and imposing assumptiveness: that is, by as much of the grand style as our play-goers now understand; but in the last act he was monotonously violent, and died the death of an incorrigible poseur, not of a noble Roman. Mr Tree's memory failed him as usual; and a good deal of the technical part of his work was botched and haphazard, like all Shakespearean work nowadays; nevertheless, like Mr Calvert, he made the audience believe in the reality of the character before them. But it is impossible to praise his performance in detail. I cannot recall any single passage in the scene after the murder that was well done: in fact, he only secured an effective curtain by bringing Calpurnia on the stage to attitudinize over Caesar's body. To say that the demagogic oration in the Forum produced its effect is nothing: for its effect is inevitable, and Mr Tree neither made the most of it nor handled it with any pretence of mastery or certainty. But he was not stupid, nor inane, nor Bard-of-Avon ridden; and he contrived to interest the audience in Antony instead of trading on their ready-made interest in Mr Beerbohm Tree. And for that many sins may be forgiven him nowadays, when the playgoer, on first nights at all events, goes to see the cast rather than the play.

What is missing in the performance, for want of the specific Shakespearean skill, is the Shakespearean music. When we come to those unrivalled grandiose passages in which Shakespear turns on the full organ, we want to hear the sixteen-foot pipes booming, or, failing them (as we often must, since so few actors are naturally equipped with them), the ennobled tone, and the tempo suddenly steadied with the majesty of deeper purpose. You have, too, those moments when the verse, instead of opening up the depths of sound, rises to its most brilliant clangour, and the lines ring like a thousand trumpets. If we cannot have these effects, or if we can only have genteel drawing room arrangements of them, we cannot have Shakespear; and that is what is mainly the matter at Her Majesty's: there are neither trumpets nor pedal pipes there. The conversation is metrical and emphatic in an elocutionary sort of way; but it makes no distinction between the arid prairies of blank verse which remind one of *Henry VI* at its crudest, and the places where the morass suddenly piles itself into a mighty mountain. Cassius in the first act has a twaddling forty-line speech, base in its matter and mean in its measure, followed immediately by the magnificent torrent of rhetoric, the first burst of true Shakespearean music in the play beginning –

> Why, man, he doth bestride the narrow world
> Like a Colossus, and we petty men
> Walk under his huge legs and peep about
> To find ourselves dishonourable graves.

I failed to catch the slightest change of elevation or reinforcement of feeling when Mr McLeay passed from one to the other. His tone throughout was dry; and it never varied. By dint of energetic, incisive articulation, he drove his utterances harder home than the others; but the best lines seemed to him no more than the worst: there were no heights and depths, no contrast of black thunder-cloud and flaming lightning flash, no stirs and surprises. Yet he was not inferior in oratory to the rest. Mr Waller certainly cannot be reproached with dryness of tone; and his delivery of the speech in the Forum was perhaps the best piece of formal elocution we got; but he also kept at much the same level throughout, and did not at any moment attain to anything that could be called grandeur. Mr Tree, except for a conscientiously desperate effort to cry havoc and let slip the dogs of war in the robustious manner, with no better result than to all but extinguish his voice, very sensibly left oratory out of the question, and tried conversational sincerity, which answered so well that his delivery of 'This was the noblest Roman of them all' came off excellently.

The real hero of the revival is Mr Alma Tadema. The scenery and stage coloring deserve everything that has been said of them. But the illusion is wasted by want of discipline and want of thought behind the scenes. Every carpenter seems to make it a point of honor to set the cloths swinging in a way that makes Rome reel and the audience positively seasick. In Brutus' house the door is on the spectator's left: the knocks on it come from the right. The Roman soldiers take the field each man with his two javelins neatly packed up like a fishing rod. After a battle, in which they are supposed to have made the famous Roman charge, hurling these javelins in and following them up sword in hand, they come back carrying the javelins still undisturbed in their rug-straps, in perfect trim for a walk-out with the nursery maids of Philippi.

The same want of vigilance appears in the acting version. For example, though the tribunes Flavius and Marullus are replaced by two of the senators, the lines referring to them by name are not altered. But the oddest oversight is the retention in the tent scene of the obvious confusion of the original version of the play, in which the death of Portia was announced to Brutus by Messala, with the second version, into which the quarrel scene was written to strengthen the fourth act. In this version Brutus, already in possession of the news, reveals it to Cassius. The play has come down to us with two alternative scenes strung together; so that Brutus' reception of Messala's news, following his own revelation of it to Cassius, is turned into a satire on Roman fortitude, the suggestion being that the secret of the calm with which a noble Roman received the most terrible tidings in public was that it had been carefully imparted to him in private beforehand. Mr Tree has not noticed this; and the two scenes are gravely played one after the other at Her Majesty's. This does not matter much to our playgoers, who never venture to use their common sense when Shakespear is in question; but it wastes time. Mr Tree may without hesitation cut out Pindarus and Messala, and go straight on from the bowl of wine to Brutus' question about Philippi.

The music, composed for the occasion by Mr Raymond Roze, made me glad that I had already taken care to acknowledge the value of Mr Roze's services to Mr Tree; for this time he has missed the Roman vein rather badly. To be a Frenchman was once no disqualification for the antique, because French musicians used to be brought up on Gluck as English ones were brought up on Handel. But Mr Roze composes as if Gluck had been supplanted wholly in his curriculum by Gounod and Bizet. If that prelude to the third act were an attempt to emulate the overtures to *Alceste* or *Iphigenia* I could have forgiven it. But to give us the soldiers' chorus from *Faust*, crotchet for crotchet and triplet for triplet, with nothing changed but the notes, was really too bad.

The Saturday Review, 29 January 1898

Max Beerbohm
Benson as Henry V

Mr F. R. Benson is an Oxford man, and he is in the habit of recruiting his company from his university. Insomuch that, according to the *Daily Chronicle*, 'the influence of university cricket has been seen in the cricket fields of many provincial towns visited by Mr Benson's company, as well as that of university culture on the boards of the local theatres. In the summer months cricket by day and dramatic art in the evening is a rule which he follows as far as possible.' A delightful existence! The stumps are drawn, the curtain is rung up. All day long the sun shines while Mr Benson and his merrymen wring from the neighbourhood respectful admiration of university cricket. But, when the shadows of the wickets lengthen across the pitch, the call-boy appears, and the tired but victorious mimes go to doff their flannels and to don the motley. I repeat, a delightful existence! But one cannot help wondering what Mr Vincent Crummles would have thought of it. 'Trace the influence of university cricket and university culture on histrionic art at the close of the nineteenth century' is likely to be a favourite question when the Drama, at length, gets its chartered Academy, with power to set examination papers. University culture imbues the mime with some sense of blank verse, and saves him from solecisms in pronunciation. University cricket keeps his body in good training, enables him to move on the stage with the more agility and to posture with the more grace. In the old days, before the cult of athletics, and before acting was regarded as a genteel art, the strolling mimes were mostly illiterate, and mostly fat. They knew little of anything but their art, and they spent their days in drinking, and smoking and talking about their performances. They were not gentlemen, and as men they were very poor creatures indeed, vastly inferior to their successors. But as artists? That is another matter. The better man is not necessarily the better mime, nor does even gentility carry one very far in art. Art is a mysterious thing, in which cads and weaklings may often excel, and gentlemanly athletes may often fail. The old strollers lived a life of degradation; but it does not follow that their excess in alcohol and nicotine hurt them as mimes. The new strollers play cricket and other games, and are healthy and reputable fellows; but they do not necessarily act the better for that. Indeed, I should say (though it is a hard saying) that the old method was better than the new. The art of acting, more even than any other art, demands that the artist live on his nerves: the more highly-strung his nerves, the better he will act. The old stroller, living a sedentary life and indulging overmuch in stimulants, was a bundle of nerves. The new stroller is a bundle of muscles. Of course, as I have suggested, muscles are a very good thing for a mime to have. The ideal mime would be a bundle of nerves *and* muscles. But alas! the two things do not go together, and nerves are infinitely the more important of the two. The old stroller would cut a sorry figure on the cricket pitch: he would muff all his catches and be bowled out first ball. But on the wooden boards, behind the footlights, he seems to us more admirable than the members of Mr Benson's eleven – company, I mean.

Alertness, agility, grace, physical strength – all these good attributes are obvious in the mimes who were, last week, playing *Henry the Fifth* at the Lyceum. Every member of the cast seemed in tip-top condition – thoroughly 'fit'. Subordinates and principals all worked well together. The fielding was excellent, and so was the batting. Speech after speech was sent spinning across the boundary, and one was constantly inclined to shout 'Well *played*, sir! Well played *indeed*!' As a branch of university cricket, the whole performance was, indeed, beyond praise. But, as a form of acting, it was not impressive. Not one of the parts was played with any distinction. There was not one that stood out at the time or was remembered later. Everyone rattled along and bustled about and gave one the impression that he was a jolly, modest, high-spirited, presentable young fellow in private life; and there one's impression of him ended. The whole thing was very pleasant, but it was not Shakespearian acting. It had neither the sonorous dignity of the old school, nor the subtle intelligence of the modern metropolitan school. It was simply what the dramatic critics call 'adequate', meaning 'inadequate'. Now, there are some Shakespearian plays of which 'adequate' performances are tolerable. But *Henry the Fifth* is not one of them. It should be done brilliantly, splendidly, or not at all. Only the best kind of acting, and the best kind of production, could make it anything but tedious. Except a few purple patches of poetry, it contains nothing whatsoever of merit. It is just a dull, incoherent series of speeches, interspersed with alarums and excursions. As a spectacle, it might be made much of. Mimes might, by exercise of much imagination, make the speeches interesting and impressive. With a very keen sense of character, they might give life and individuality to the puppets. But, since Mr Benson's system precludes spectacle, and since cricket tends to exhaust in its devotees the energy which might otherwise be spent in cultivating imagination and sense of character, those members of the public who forgot to visit the Lyceum last week lost very little and (I am tempted to say) escaped much. Before these words appear, Mr Benson will have produced *A Midsummer Night's Dream*. That will be quite another matter. It is, in itself, a play of surpassing beauty. So are *The Tempest* and *Antony and Cleopatra*, and other Shakespearian plays which Mr Benson is to produce in due course. Even if the performances of them be not better than the performance of *Henry the Fifth*, they will be well worth seeing. I trust that Mr Benson will have a successful season. His enthusiasm for Shakespeare is very laudable and attractive. No one could help wishing him well. But – he must, really, break himself and his company of this fatal cricketing-habit.

The Saturday Review, 24 February 1900

C. E. Montague
The Art of Mr Poel

Hearing *Samson Agonistes* played in the new great hall of the University of Manchester, in the twilight and first darkness of a December evening, a new pleasure possessed you. One seemed to be in at the birth of a thing that some day might be valued for ancientry. Great buildings are furnished in that way, in youth, with treasures for their old age: the resonance does not die out; and today, in the Hall of the Middle Temple, it is part of a diner's pleasure that *Twelfth Night* was first acted there, and Shakspere's voice, it may well be, rang in the rafters you sit under. Old fiddles, people say, keep in them something of all the music that ever was made on them. So many old rooms. The paintings that hang in them sucked in the light one century after another, to hoard up the lustre you see; it seems as if timber and glass, like oil paint, must have their physical memory of all the waves of sound that have broken upon them. At least, it is easily fancied. In Christ Church Hall or the Hall of Gray's Inn imagination does not need much stirring to feel the Holbeins giving out rays saved on days of Tudor sunshine, or the panels echoing more genially, when people laugh, for some unspent vibrations from the first-night mirth about *The Comedy of Errors*. All new great halls, you may feel, ought to be stored in that way, in good time, that when they are old, and their builders long dead they may light imagination in the eager minds of people then young, like some cathedrals where, to be heard, the organ scarcely needs to be played, or those rooms of pictures where, on the wettest English day, Venetian or Florentine sunlight does not fail.

Then came other pleasures – these also, perhaps, not strictly pleasures of the theatre. In a play that is good as a play your eye and ear together are kept in a state of expectancy constantly piqued and then satisfied, repiqued and resatisfied. Sir Arthur Pinero will keep your mind craning, on tip-toe, for hours to know what will A say to this, what will B do on hearing of that, what dress will C wear when next she comes in, and how will D act when he sees it. *Samson* does not keep you asking these questions and taking in savoursome answers. Nor, surely, did Milton study Greek playcraft as he studied Greek poetry, or he would have felt one difference grievous that there is between *Samson* and a good Greek play. The long narrative speech is, it is true, chracteristic of Greek tragedy, but even more characteristic of it is the long bout of one-line dialogue, where speech clicks in on speech, as foil on foil, so pat and nervous as almost to outpace the fencing rhymes of French comedy. Can Milton have consciously thought that he alone among playwrights on the Greek model could keep an audience animated and expectant without any of these rallies of volleying at the net? Certainly *Samson*, Chorus and all, is made almost wholly of such mighty allocutions as French actors call generically *récits de Théramène*, in honour of the vasty specimen entrusted to that person in the *Phèdre* of Racine. They are magnificent, but not drama. An apt ear, of course, is kept happy, merely by the august loveliness of the verse; a reader's mind may find extrinsic poignancy in the poem as a 'last sunset cry' of Milton's wounded spirit; but the eye, the playgoer's change-seeking and incident-loving eye, is apt to have poor sport of it among these wide expanses of still rhetoric, in which the one shrewd touch of stagecraft, the finely announced entry of Dalila, shines like a good deed in a naughty world. Here, to the vacant eye's rescue, came in the genius of Mr William Poel, the master of this revel.

Mr Poel began by planting the whole visible action of the play not on the horizontal plane – the floor of the stage – but on the vertical plane – its back wall. He built up this back wall into something like the semi-circular tribuna at the east end of an early Christian basilica; travellers in Italy will remember one in the cathedral at Torcello, with the priests' seats rising in steps, tier above tier, culminating in the bishop's throne, at the top in the middle. In the seat corresponding to this episcopal throne Mr Poel planted Samson for almost the whole time that he was on the stage. The remaining characters were repeatedly grouped and regrouped so as, in the aggregate, to present a triangular mass of colour receding and tapering as it rose, like one side of a pyramid. Thus, in an early group, Samson was at the apex of this pyramid, one of its bounding lines was formed by the Chorus, and the other marked out by Dalila in the middle of the line and by her attendants at its base. At her exit the composition of the picture dissolved for a few moments; the Chorus gesticulated, huddled, swarmed, and then, like swallows re-perching after a moment's scare, resumed their place in the pyramidal formation, Harapha and his followers now forming the other side line of the triangle, precisely as Dalila and hers had done. Again the composition melted away for some minutes; the Chorus declaimed and pattered, twittered and crooned and keened, and then it settled again as before, with the Public Officers in Harapha's and Dalila's place, and his guard of soldiers in that of their attendants.

In each of these groupings Samson was seen full length, his feet higher than the head of the person next below, and this person in turn was seen, clear from head to foot, above the group below; and this mode of presentation was singularly pleasing to the eye, for reasons not explicable here, but good enough, as it would seem, to have made Raphael adopt it almost exactly, steps and all, in the so-called 'School of Athens' and in the 'Incendio del Borgo' at the Vatican. And not Raphael only; the pyramidal formation is perhaps the most familiar of all beautiful patterns of pictorial grouping; it is the pattern of the Ansidei Madonna in the National Gallery, and of the Giorgione altar-piece at Castelfranco; and two or three times in the playing of *Samson* the design of this last painting was recalled by a grouping of the three persons forming for the moment the apex of the larger pyramid – Samson at the top, his green-clad attendant below him on his right, where St Liberalis is in the picture, and Manoa or Dalila in the place of St Francis. We are not in Mr Poel's secrets, but to an uninformed spectator it looked as if he had had every one of his groupings painted to a finish in his mind and then transferred it, touch by touch, to its place on the purple background, all under the strong influence of Italian medieval and Renaissance theories of pictorial design. Whatever the words that were spoken, it would have been good to sit for two hours and stare at the spectacles painted upon the end wall of the hall. Their colour was choice; they had line and structure enough for cathedrals. Not strict play-going, perhaps, all this, but quite strict pleasure; the play-going eye was at least triumphantly pacified.

There was a famous medley of dresses – Samson's attendant in something quite Greek, Dalila, we believe, in the best clothes of a Cretan lady – we know not of what date; the soldiers in Roman uniform; Harapha in something barbarian, and so on. No doubt the aim was to represent the way in which the seventeenth century might probably have dressed the play, had it played it at all – that is, without the faintest interest in our modern hobbies of local colour and general exactitude in unessentials. Anyhow, for this or some other good reason, Mr Poel gave himself a fine free hand in colour for his pictures. The united wardrobes of the Greeks, the Romans, the Cretans, and the Germans or Scandinavians afford, between them, a liberal palette for studies in Philistian genre, and handsomely he used it.

The same resources were used, to a slightly different end, when Mr Poel put upon a stage the fifteenth-century Morality of *Everyman*. To see what his task in this was, you have to tell yourself first what the place of *Everyman* was in the life of the stage. When the Roman theatre, heir to the Greek, had gone to the bad and then died, there came a long blank gap. By the year A.D. 500 plays were no longer being written or acted in Europe. Six hundred years later the stage was being rediscovered. It was no mere taking up of a dropped thread; it was a re-invention of an old invention long lost. The Greek drama had been born in church, and our modern drama was born there too.

The germ of it was, perhaps, this: After Mass on an eleventh-century saint's day three priests would put on albs and give the people a *tableau vivant* of the three Marys announcing the Resurrection to the disciples. Today it would be called a 'P.S.A. Movement'. It drew crowds, and to keep them songs were added and lengthening pieces of dialogue, and the whole Bible was searched for subjects. Then the church became too small for the congregation, and the stage had to be moved into the churchyard, and then into some roomy field outside, and then into the market-place. There, as a Church institution, it died of its success. Priests could not gad about the streets acting; laymen had to do it. But most laymen did not know Latin, so Latin was given up for English; new subjects, not drawn straight from the Bible came in – the strife of good and evil in the mind, the pleasant exterior and disappointing interior of vice, the snares of the world for young men, the discomfiture of hypocrites, at last even of clerical hypocrites. As the thing grew, actors became professional, theatres permanent, performances continuous. Finally, at the Renaissance, there burst in on this raw, half-grown theatre, as it existed in England, the whole flood of artistic influences, of stored-up achievement and experience, that had been frozen in and unavailable throughout the Middle Ages. The gifted, vigorous, bungling native drama bound itself apprentice to Plautus and produced *Ralph Roister Doister*, to Seneca and produced *Gorboduc*, till Marlowe and Shakspere came to unite in the Elizabethan theatre all that was alive in the raw native drama with all that the revival of learning had yet shown to be worth copying from classical models. Now *Everyman*'s historical interest is this: it is the best piece surviving in English from the time when the reborn stage had generally passed from the hands of the priests to those of trade guilds, had dropped Latin for English, and had gone beyond the Bible for its characters, but had not yet come into its estate as heir of the Greek and Roman theatres. *Everyman* is of the Middle Ages.

One might be hard set to define the medieval spirit, but Mr Poel and his friends had not been playing *Everyman* for many minutes before you felt that your mind was being adroitly filled with reminiscences of everything that at other times had brought it nearest to late medieval ways of looking at life and death – reminiscences mainly Italian. The Messenger who spoke the Prologue was a study in the ascetic's waxlike anticipation, in living flesh, of that fine austerity of death which is perhaps most fully expressed by another art in the sculptured tombs on the floor of Santa Croce at Florence. The decoration of the canopied recess from which God spoke the opening lines was a typical landscape background of Giovanni Bellini, with topped trees and a distance of mountains. The angel sitting on the steps was in every detail, if memory did not mislead us, the angel of Botticelli's 'Tobit'. Everyman, in his graveclothes, seemed to come straight from the 'Last Judgment' of Orcagna, where the grave is giving up its dead; the figure of Confession was, to the life, one of the blithely angelic monks who looked so much like happy, serious, pretty, and good children, with tonsures, on tombs sculptured by Mino da Fiesole. All out of place, somebody might say, in acting an English play ascribed by some to the early fifteenth century, and not placed later than that century's end by any one fitted to judge. In one sense – a narrow one – yes, but not in another. Most of those English people whose imaginations have conceived with any energy the frames of mind that distinguish the later Middle Ages have come at this through Italy, at Florence, Assisi, Padua, Venice; and what are dozens of anachronisms so long as one is helped to come as near as one's ignorance permits to a right mood for listening to a play?

In such a case 'the right mood' does not necessarily mean the mood of an audience of the play's own date. It is too clear that the ordinary medieval audience listening to Moralities, and even to Mysteries, with their more official sacredness, was not as their authors would have had it. Their extant texts are like gramophones, in which the chatter of the medieval playgoer is preserved, or, rather, a kind of 'negative' or death mask of it – the correlative entreaties of the actors for a little silence. 'Doulces gens, un pou de silence!' – 'Nun schweiget still!' – 'Each man has but his own tongue to hold!' From all the medieval stage of Europe there rose the polyglot entreaty to the public to be quiet. One of the Towneley Mysteries opens with Pilate bawling for silence in the name of the devil and of Mahomet's blood. Jörg Wickram of Colmar craftily begins his *God-fearing Tobias* by putting on the stage a messenger from Lucifer to ask those present to interrupt and misbehave, and the messenger will take down for his master the names of those who misbehave the best. Besides browbeating and threatening, the medieval dramatists would give their restless audiences enormous and unseemly bribes of comic digression. The executioners in the Towneley Mysteries jest lengthily over the nailing of Christ to the cross, and Pilate, in a scene of low comedy, cheats them at dice for Christ's coat. Blind and halt men, miraculously restored, complain comically of the loss of their easy livelihood as beggars. Perhaps our inveterate English habit of mixing 'comic relief' with tragedy – a habit that has given scandal to all the bigwigs of classical tradition from Ben Jonson to Sarcey – took its rise in the medieval practice of bringing in a supposed madman to rave or drivel for some minutes in the middle of a Nativity or Passion play, in order to put the audience into enough good humour to tide them over the serious part safely. As a whole, a medieval audience at a Mystery or a Morality performance seems to have been rather like a young child in church – half awed, half bored, wholly un-critical, sometimes frightened, sometimes touched, sometimes tickled, never far from being naughty.*

That audience and its temper even Mr Poel's reconstructive genius could not bring back. His audiences for *Everyman* were made up of hardened play-goers seeking new thrills, of devout persons casting back to pick up the authentic scent of medieval devout thought, of literary students improving an oppor-tunity, of archaic sentimentalists projecting themselves into the dear, delightful Middle Ages, of theatrical craftsmen edified by the cunning simplicity of the business with the bells 'off' and the electrifying patness of the successive exits of Everyman's friends. Most of the assemblage might be unaccepting

---

* It is a common mistake to suppose that medieval audiences generally resembled the comparatively modern type of audience created for themselves by post-medieval religious dramas like that of Oberammergau.

and unawed, part of it might be fiercely repugnant against much that the play holds up to be admired, but all of it was breathlessly quiet, polite, respectful. We may not believe, but we can sit still; we are working out the monkey.

Besides, Mr Poel knows how to absorb us in acting. 'He reads the Bible', an amazed fellow undergraduate once said of Arnold Toynbee, 'as if he liked it – as if it were any other book.' His acting and the acting that he taught made many people listen to that grave, drastic, fifteenth-century 'play with a purpose' as if they liked it – as if it were some other play. There are many theatrical curios – academic revivals of Greek tragedies, for instance – which people contrive to enjoy as antiquaries, as friends of the cast, or as champions of culture. One might, as a gymnast, enjoy a play that one witnessed while hanging by the legs from a horizontal bar. But at *Everyman*, acted this way, you could easily and strongly be stirred simply as a playgoer who wanted his money's worth in emotions. The acting had a maintained ecstasy of simple seriousness, every actor seemed to have the same grave, thrilled sense of the momentous of what they were all handling; it was a kind of animated awe. They spoke like people who felt they were bringing tremendous news.

There was a rare and curious pleasure to be had from Marlowe's *Doctor Faustus*, too, when Mr Poel gave it; but the pleasure was different. With all its magnificence *Doctor Faustus* is not a good play, at least not to us who live now. Compared with *Everyman*, time has clawed it terribly in his clutch. The Morality may be two centuries older, and yet in a way it is the more modern of the two, modern in the vital sense in which *The Pilgrim's Progress* comes more excitingly close to a modern man than *Sir Charles Grandison*, though Bunyan did write so long before Richardson. The older play, like the older story, goes straighter to feelings that do not change from age to age, whereas, in spite of all its imperishable single lines, whole tracts or aspects of *Doctor Faustus* were of their own time solely, and now are dead as door-nails – the keen Renaissance relish, for example, for a certain kind of bookishness. And yet the show had its flavours. There was the pleasure of comparing the dramatic value of Marlowe's technics in the final scene, where Faustus has one hour to live, with the treatment of the same idea by a modern poet, in Mr Yeats's *Hour-Glass*, and by a modern play-manufacturer, M. Sardou, in his *Dante*. There was the interest of seeing whether delivery on a stage could add anything to the worth of some of the most beautiful and famous verses ever written:

> Was this the face that launched a thousand ships
> And burned the topmost towers of Ilium?
> O, thou art fairer than the evening air.
> Clad in the beauty of a thousand stars.

There was, again, the pleasure of seeing what it was – as near as we can go – that gave people the pleasure of the theatre in Shakspeare's youth. However much we may have lost of the power to take the play in, or to be taken in by it, in the same way as they, that way and the external means to it are piquant for us to see, just in proportion as they are alien and surprising. Here Mr Poel spread a banquet of tit-bits of antiquarian research and acute conjecture. The stage set up was a copy of that of the Fortune Theatre built by Henslowe and Alleyn, outside Cripplegate, north of London, partly to be out of range of the City Corporation, partly to escape the competition of the Burbages, who had just plumped down the new and fine Globe Theatre beside Henslowe and Alleyn's old house, the Rose, south of the river. Of course, it would have been better still if we could have had the very stage – probably that of the Curtain Theatre – where *Doctor Faustus* was first acted, about 1588, for the Fortune was only built in 1600. No doubt it weighed with Mr Poel that the Fortune is one of the most possible of Tudor theatres to reproduce rightly, because it is, we fancy, almost the only one for which we still have the text of the builder's contract, with specifications of the house's shape, dimensions, and arrangement, down to provision for tiling and guttering the roof of the stage so as not to let rain water slop over on to the heads of the pit, who, of course, were exposed to the sky.

Some of us, perhaps, were a little troubled by Faustus' clothes. The part, as first played by Alleyn, is one of the few Elizabethan parts still to be known by sight. On the title-page of the 1616 edition of the play there is a woodcut of Alleyn's Faustus invoking a squat and stubby heraldic-looking Devil with a pug nose. The Faustus has a sort of ruff and what seems like an academic robe, very long and lined or bordered with white fur, with puffy, almost episcopal, sleeves that might be lawn. Then there is a chance note of Alleyn's costume in Samuel Rowlands's contemporary play, *The Knave of Cards*:

> The gull gets on a surplice
> With a cross upon his breast.
> Like Alleyn playing Faustus,
> In that manner was he dressed.

We looked to Mr Poel for these garments, but did not exactly find them as one usually finds in his doings all that research could furnish. No doubt he had some other records in mind, or some very good reason for not going precisely by these.

A keen pleasure was this – that, at least while it lasted, the acting kept you in something of that state of grave and childlike absorption, and of freedom from our modern affliction of knowingness, which simple and enthusiastic souls can achieve in Florence while looking at Giotto's tower with an unclouded faith in Ruskin. The Pope at dinner was a masterpiece of well-conceived naïveté; the bell, book and candle business was in delicious contrast with a recent commination service at Drury Lane, and the set, mortified countenance of the Duchess's one waiting woman was worth whole retinues of the wheeling and countermarching stage Abigails of our years. The Méryon devil from Notre Dame, the quaintly trapesing and trolloping Seven Deadly Sins, the Michaelangelically sinewy Lucifer were all delectable inventions in a most difficult kind, for the least slip in judgment was sure to raise laughter, and nobody laughed. Everyone's mind for the moment was simplified, not, indeed, to the point of sharing Elizabethan joy in such a play, but to the point of a stirred interest in that joy and a hope of partial comprehension of it.

In *Measure for Measure*, arranged for Miss Horniman's actors at Manchester, Mr Poel was tackling greater stuff. No play has been more full of challenge to choice spirits. It stirred Pater to his best and Tennyson almost to his. Mariana and her moated grange have become part of the received landscape and figures of the English romantic imagination. The song sung to Mariana is a possible candidate for the place of finest lyric in the English language. Claudio's 'thrilling regions of thick-ribbed ice' speech might run Macbeth's 'To-morrow and to-morrow and to-morrow' speech and Prospero's 'insubstantial pageant faded' speech close for the place of finest speech in Shakspere, were such competitions decent. The grisly humour of Barnardine and Pompey jesting at the dawn with death is the prototype of who knows how many modern essays in the macabre, and none of them touches it. On the other hand the means taken to dish Angelo are pretty nasty; the liquidation of the whole imbroglio by the Duke is lethally slow and wordy; the Duke himself, for whom our respect is seemingly invited, is a sad skulker, who shirks the odium of his own decrees; the final pairing-off is a sorry business all round; and the steepness of some of the things we are asked to believe – Isabella's assent to the stratagem for instance – approaches the vertical.

In staging this jumble of beauties and uglinesses Mr Poel's Elizabethanism went about as far as it could without rebuilding the Gaiety Theatre. For the essence of the Elizabethan theatre was the fusion of interpenetration of stage and auditorium, and the essence of the modern theatre is their separation by the proscenium arch. The Elizabethan theatre was a deliberate reproduction of the accidental conditions of the previous performances of strolling players in inn yards, like the well-known yard of the Tabard. The players would rig up on trestles, against one wall of the quadrangle, a platform to play on. It did not run the whole length of the wall, but jutted out from its centre into the yard, and so the crowd in the yard (the modern 'pit'), could look on from the sides as well as from in front; and the guests of the inn, standing on the continuous balconies of each floor (the originals of our 'dress circle', 'upper circle', and 'gallery') could watch the play from at least three sides. The post-Restoration importation of the proscenium arch from the Continent, and afterward the gradual drawing back of almost the whole stage to within it, were, together, a deep-going change. Instead of being looked at and heard from three sides at once, the actor is now only seen and heard from in front. Instead of being presented to the spectator like a statue, 'in the round', he is presented like a picture, in perspective and with a frame.

Mr Poel did wonders, but he could not get rid of the proscenium arch. What he gave us was not an Elizabethan stage as it was to Elizabethan playgoers, but a picture of an Elizabethan stage seen through the frame of a modern proscenium. So we gained a good visual idea of a Shaksperean stage, but not the Elizabethan sensation of having an actor come forward to the edge of a platform in the midst of ourselves and deliver speeches from a position almost like that of a speaker from a pulpit or from a front bench in Parliament, with only the narrowest scope for theatrical illusion, with no incentive to naturalism, and with every motive for putting his strength into sheer energy and beauty of declamation, giving his performance the special qualities of fine recitation, as distinct from those of realistic acting. But, without that, we got a good deal. We saw better than ever the needlessness, as well as the destructiveness, of the quite modern method of taking Shakspere's shortest scenes.

They are usually scurried through by actors who maintain a precarious footing on a strip of boarding between the footlights in front and a bellying sail painted with landscape, which swells out at them from behind. In Mr Poel's Elizabethan arrangement a roomy front portion of the stage is divisible from the rest by a curtain which can be either passed through at its middle or walked around at its ends; the rear portion of the stage is in turn divisible into two or more planes of distances as it retreats into the 'tiring house' at the very back. With this arrangement those short scenes and the long ones flow into one another without the slightest jolt or scrappiness. The use of the upper stage, too, was surprisingly effective and undisturbing; it made you see why Shakspere's stage directions so often bring in people 'above', 'on the walls', or otherwise aloft. But in fact the whole performance threw 'side-lights on Shakspere' by the dozen, while – just cause for thanksgiving – it never froze up the imagination of us ordinary, half-instructed persons, as reconstructive sholarship often does. As for scenery, one did not think about it, either in the way of missing it, or of being glad it was away. But if any people did imperatively need to be distracted from the play, they could look at the dresses, which were quaint and rich to admiration, and, we understood, prodigies of historical accuracy – only another Mr Poel should venture to speak more dogmatically.

Last, and very large, there was the pleasure of the acting of Angelo by Mr Poel himself, an actor who did not wait for Irish amateurs or Sicilian peasants to teach him to act as if he meant it. Whatever he may be doing at the moment, the consuming energy with which he conceives a part communicates itself to the spectator; the character is so vehemently imagined by the artist that its expression seems almost independent of the ordinary symbolism of tones and looks. Or, rather, while he uses just the means which other actors use, they mean more to him; they stand for a more ardent realization, by him, of the idea, say, of an Angelo. When once the spectator is caught up into itself by this authentic heat of passionate imagination in an actor, the actor can then do nothing wrong; thenceforth his technics seem scarcely to matter; you feel as if you had got past all that, as you get past any little inexpressivenesses in a friend. So Mr Poel's acting seizes you up and makes you more intimate with the character than its own speeches are.

Dramatic Values, 1910

Desmond MacCarthy
Granville Barker's Production of
A Midsummer Night's Dream

THE PRODUCTION OF POETIC DRAMA

Before criticizing the performance at the Savoy Theatre I must (I apologize) discourse on the production of poetic drama in general.

A Midsummer Night's Dream is a difficult play to produce so that everybody shall find in it satisfaction, and it is hard to find out what one wants. In the theatre that each playgoer carries under his own hat, it has already been performed, perhaps several times and in several ways. We are our own scene makers and shifters in that theatre, and what easy miracles we perform! The action takes place amidst surroundings more vague and changeable than clouds; the scenery paints itself, as we read, upon the darkness of the mind, a more suggestive background for beauty than any decorative curtain. Indeed, can we even say that anything definite is painted on the darkness at all? We *feel* as we read; we have hardly time to see. Did we see anything when we read, for instance:

> Met we on hill, or dale, forest or mead,
> By paved fountain or by rushy brook,
> Or in the beached margent of the sea,
> To dance our ringlets to the whistling wind?

We were charmed, but did we *see* what charmed us? Now you put the question to yourself you may, at the words 'rushy brook', see rushes and water for a hundredth of a second; and 'the beached margent of the sea' may call up for an instant a scene before you. Indeed, as I wrote down the above lines they called up one for me: the moon is up, but it is not night; a sea, green as the stalks of daffodils, spills softly wave after wave over smooth white sand. But how utterly irrelevant such details are! Next time I may see a different shore or nothing at all, I can even trace to their sources these particular irrelevancies. I happen to have spent a month this summer on the coast of Wexford; 'rushy' in the previous line must have lingered in my mind and made me think of the reedy grasses which grow on the dunes there, and then of the magic emptiness of that beach one evening, and the little, tossing fringes of fresh foam running in, more frailly white than snow, one after the other. How recklessly the imagination picks and jumps and chooses! There was not a suggestion of 'the whistling wind' in my picture, on the contrary, a warm stillness; though the dancing and the fairies and their ringlets were somehow there – in the foam.

Again, what different dawns the following lines will call up to different minds, at different times:

> Even till the Eastern gate, all fiery red,
> Opening in Neptune with fair blessed beams
> Turns into yellow gold his salt green streams.

In my picture there may be a headland – I may be seeing England on a summer morning from the sea; you may be looking upon a broad restless circle of empty water, a path of gold across it to the rising sun; another reader, a green swell heaving against the sky, catching on its side a golden light. And another may see nothing at all.

The poet has written what he has written, and we have all found different things upon the page. But our various experiences have this in common: a *feeling* of morning and the sea. It does not matter that this feeling should be centred in one case upon one detail, in another upon another. The important fact is that each vision has a certain consonance with sea and morning and that the poetry has created in us a capacity to feel (this is the only test of poetry) the beauty of whatever picture or idea the words happened to call up.

Such psychological facts are not unrelated to the art of the theatre. They suggest the limits of the art of interpreting poetry with dress and scenery on the stage, and a standard by which to criticize it. They suggest that this art, like the art of words, should leave us to a great extent fancy free. What scenery should aim at is the expression of a beauty consonant with the underlying emotion which runs through the poetry of a scene, act or play.

There are, of course, some people whose imaginations demand absolute freedom. To them any attempt to express emotion visibly is irksome; and they, too, go to Shakespeare performances sometimes, sitting through them with resigned patience. Perhaps, for their benefit, goggles might be procurable for a shilling in the slot, as opera-glasses are now for others. Certainly the producer can do nothing more for them than that; he cannot be expected to consider people who want *only* to use their ears in the theatre.

But, clearly if we are to be left to a great extent fancy free, the staging of poetic drama should not tie or direct our imaginations too definitely. That it should be beautiful in itself no producer denies; but if it is added that it must also possess a beauty consonant with the spirit of the act or the scene, they are all at sixes and sevens – at any rate in their practice. And well they may be. For what is meant by the beauty of stuffs, colours, forms and light being consonant with the beauty of the poetry is something extremely vague. Suggestion of place, of night or day, is another matter and a simpler one. The scene must always be laid somewhere, and this must be indicated, if only by a symbol or an announcement. The attitude towards scenery of different schools of producers are discussed and distinguished in Mr Palmer's *Future of the Theatre*. Beauty in the setting of a play must, he asserts, detract from dramatic art, which is 'the realization through the living player of the conceptions of a dramatic poet'. 'It is psychologically impossible', he says, 'to receive more than one appeal at a time.' I deny this generalization, and with an energy which, if he could see my gesture, he might mistake for personal animosity. He appeals to our experience, and instances Purcell's setting of one of Shakespeare's songs. *Santo Diavolo*! I am unconvinced! I will appeal to his experience. Has he never been glad a beautiful song has been sung in an unintelligible language, not because the poetry was too good, but because it was too bad? Has he never glanced at a programme translation afterwards with a sense of relief at what he had providentially missed?

I know a man who heard a lady sing a pretty song he thought was about an Indian potentate called Sir Cusha Sweesong Twar. Unfortunately, when he discovered that the refrain was '*Ce que je suis sans toi*', I neglected to ask him if the song appealed to him more, but probably, in this instance, on either alternative his answer would have been another nail in the coffin of Mr Palmer's theory that good words and good music inevitably spoil each other. And as for his twin theory that what delights the eye and charms the fancy in stage settings must subduct from the poetry of drama, and his deduction from it that the scenery for Shakespeare must be so conventional, so much in every detail a matter of course as to become psychologically invisible like Mr Chesterton's postman in his detective story, they leave us in a pretty quandary. For it follows that it is impossible to produce Shakespeare at all. As he points out, Mr Poel's more or less archaeological method of staging the plays, though it may get near the bare stage conventions of Shakespeare's time, is so strange to ours that it needs a 'complicated mental gymnastic' on our part 'before we can begin to see and appreciate the play'. We must, however – this is granted – indicate time and place on the stage. But then what hopeless difficulty we are in! If we have no scenery, then we cannot attend to the play, if we have elaborate naturalistic scenery we are distracted; and if the producer 'decorates', instead of 'illustrates', he is calling in a conflicting element of beauty.

How can we establish a convention as stable, and therefore as unnoticeable, as the Greek stage was to the Greeks? If we build a Shakespeare theatre for that purpose, would not its bare, unchanging platform prove also distracting to an audience which frequented other theatres in which every degree of realism and abstract decoration was in vogue? I know I am pressing Mr Palmer's theory in a way which will suggest to those who have not read his book that it contains extravagant theories, instead of being remarkable for good sense and even knife-like discriminations. But seeing eye to eye with him at so many points, I want him to admit that he has overstated his theory, and that he would accept as the description of the kind of scenery appropriate to poetic drama that it should be unobtrusive and beautiful with a beauty consonant with the spirit of the play performed.

All producers are agreed that it should be beautiful; where they differ is in what they consider to be consonant beauty. Sir Herbert Tree considers any picture which may be called up by the poetry (just as the empty beach rose in my mind while copying the quotation from Titania's speech) to be relevant provided that it can be reconciled with the stage directions; and even if it cannot be, he often puts it in. I remember in his *Antony and Cleopatra* in the middle of the play the lights went down, and as if there was not enough witchery and mystery in Cleopatra herself, a symbolic transformation scene was introduced; a sphinx loomed out of the darkness to die into it again, while, a thrumming, vibrating, aromatic kind of music fell on our ears, to suggest the maddened luxury of the East and the exasperating, enigmatic attraction of the queen. This tableau was greeted, I remember, with louder applause than any part of the play. The scenery at His Majesty's is sometimes charming and beautiful, but, as everybody has been saying for years, amazing, amusing as the scenic effects often are, Shakespeare on that stage is smothered in scenery.

To Mr Poel it is the atmosphere of the Elizabethan playhouse which is always relevant whatever the time and place at which the action nominally takes place. He has taught us much. The beauty and spirit of Shakespeare's age, at any rate, does seem the right inspiration for the consonant setting of some of the plays, but not, I think, of all. Parts of Mr Granville Barker's *Twelfth Night* must have convinced people of this. Mr Gordon Craig often writes as though his chief difficulty would be not to find decorations and schemes of movement which would produce an effect of beauty consonant with a play, but a play which would prove duly subordinate to them. Dr Reinhardt (but I have only seen two of his productions and am generalizing chiefly from his *Oedipus*) seems to hold that if only an effect is impressive and beautiful it cannot be too strong. He dismisses, it seems to me, the principle of consonance and subordination as flimsy and unimportant compared with producing a vivid effect to the eye. He, too, tethers our imagination like Sir Herbert. Mr Granville Barker – but I am to criticize him in detail next week. I could not do it without explaining from what point of view I approached the *Midsummer Night's Dream* – namely, that the setting of poetic drama should be beautiful but not compete with it, lead our fancies in the direction of the spirit of the scene but leave them free.

* * *

Last week I wrote about the art of producing poetic drama. The reaping machine went clattering round and round, diminishing with each circuit the standing corn till it was a mere island in a shaven field, and when the game did come out, it was only a small rabbit. The only generalization which bolted at last was that the setting of such plays should be beautiful yet undistracting, leading our fancies in the direction of the spirit of each scene, yet leaving them free.

Had space permitted, I should have gone on to say of the performance of *A Midsummer Night's Dream* that I did not think Mr Norman Wilkinson's scenery beautiful, that it was distracting and not in harmony with the spirit of the play. I am glad I had the sense to go again before writing my criticism. I strongly recommend everyone who, while enjoying the performance, felt dissatisfied with it on such general grounds to go again. They will enjoy it a great deal more the second time. The merits of this production come out clearer when surprise at the scenic effects, the golden fairies, and the red-puppet-box Puck has subsided.

Mr Granville Barker has said in his preface that he wished people were not so easily startled. If you are among such people you ought certainly to go twice. The producer has always two choices open to him in such cases. He can employ methods which disconcert at first sight, but when familiar serve his purpose best, or others, not in the end so serviceable, which on first acquaintance are not so likely to attract disproportionate attention. Mr Granville Barker chose the first alternative. I am sure (the newspaper criticisms confirm this) that the majority of the audience thought as much about scenery at the Savoy Theatre as ever did an audience at His Majesty's. It was a different kind of scenery, but just as distracting to most people.

When, however, your astonishment at the ormolu fairies, looking as though they had been detached from some fantastic, bristling old clock, no longer distracts, you will perceive that the very characteristics which made them at first so outlandishly arresting now contribute to make them inconspicuous. They group themselves motionless about the stage, and the lovers move past and between them as casually as though they were stocks or stones. It is without effort we believe these quaintly gorgeous metallic creatures are invisible to the human eyes. They, therefore, possess the most important quality of all from the point of view of the story and the action of the play. Dramatically, they are the most convincing fairies yet seen upon the stage. Whether their make-up is the best for making the peculiar poetry of Shakespeare's fairies felt is another question. Personally, I do not think it is.

In this case, as throughout this production, Mr Granville Barker has chosen to bring out the dramatic quality of the scene before the poetic one. He seems to have said to himself, 'I am staging a work written for the stage. It is my business to look after the drama; the poetry can look after itself.' The production is primarily a dramatist's production, not a poet's. You may be thinking, remembering the stuff out of which the play is woven, that this implies a condemnation. As a reader I am with you. I have always enjoyed *A Midsummer Night's Dream* as a poem, not as a play. What is remarkable about Mr Granville Barker's production is that it shows as has never been shown before, how dramatic also passages and scenes are which seem to the reader to be entirely lyrical. This is a very considerable achievement. There are consequent losses, and these were what at first I felt most; on a second visit to the Savoy it was the positive achievement which impressed me.

People are always wondering whether it is true or not that first judgements of others are most trustworthy. First impressions of people often seem to tell one most, and yet one finds one is always going back on them afterwards. The truth is we are often aware of the *temperament* of a person we meet for the first time more acutely than we are afterwards aware of it again; his character, intellect, etc., we judge of far better on closer acquaintance, so that those we liked at first we often cease to like, and vice versa. If a play can be said to have a temperament, and I don't see why it shouldn't, the temperament of Mr Granville Barker's production was not one which attracted me; but on nearer acquaintance, as might be the case with a human being, I began to be immensely impressed by admirable qualities.

I missed poetry at all sorts of points. Puck was a shock to me. I kept staring at Mr Norman Wilkinson's arrangements in green and red and blue and gold and asking myself if each moment were a picture should I like to buy it, and answering emphatically, 'No'. The scene upon the stage was so absorbing that I did not think of it as a background for acting and judged it solely on its own merits. But the second time I was not so attentive to it, and began to notice instead that it served excellently as a generalized background against which any sort of figure, Greek, gilded or bucolic, was more or less congruous. I had ceased to wonder if there were too many silver stars on the curtain of night, or if they were cunningly placed.

I had given up my Puck, a phantom born of reading, a bundle of glorious inconsistencies, and began to wonder, since he must be materialized on the stage, if Mr Calthrop were quite so impossible. Puck is at once will-o'-the-wisp, Oberon's jester, and a rowdy imp; he touches Nature on one side, and on the other country superstitions about poltergeists. Mr Granville Barker has decided, with that peremptoriness which is responsible at once for the merits and the shortcomings of the whole production, that he must be either one or the other, and he has made him a buffoon-sprite. There is nothing of Nature in him, nothing of Ariel, nothing of Loki; he is a clowning bogey. Much of the poetry of Puck is therefore lost. When Puck says, 'I'll put a girdle round the earth in a minute', Mr Calthrop (quite consistently) pronounces these words as a piece of fantastic bombast, and off he struts extravagantly kicking out his feet in a comic swagger. It is true that Puck is a creation of English folk-lore, but he is English folk-lore transmuted by Shakespeare's imagination, and by turning him again into Robin Goodfellow we lose the effects of that wonderful alchemy. On the other hand all in Puck that is represented in his exclamation 'Lord, what fools these mortals be!' that is to say, all that tells dramatically in such situations as the quarrel between Hermia and Helena and the rivalry between the two lovers, was excellently brought out. Whenever the presence of Puck as a spirit of unmalevolent mischief on the scene adds to the piquancy of the situation Mr Calthrop succeeds. He was very good in this scene, and it was also one of the very best in the performance.

Hermia and Helena (Miss Cowie and Miss Lillah McCarthy) were admirable. Hermia's vindictive, suspicious fury, her gradual transformation into a spiteful little vixen, and the fluttering, frightened indignation of Helena were excellent. The acting revealed more dramatic comedy in the situation than any reader, however imaginative, is likely to feel in it.

Everyone has praised Bottom and his friends. The fussy, nervous, accommodating Quince, the exuberant Bottom, poor timid old Starveling, Snout with his yokel's grin, and Flute with the meek blankness which marks him out for the lady's part, the laconic and cautious Snug – they were perfect.

The performance of Pyramus and Thisbe was the great success of the production; for the first time the presence of an audience, of Theseus and his court, on the stage was a sounding-board for fun. Mr Dennis Neilson-Terry was a graceful and dignified Oberon. His movements, his stillness were delightful to watch. In some passages his elocution was excellent, but his voice – a fine one in timbre – is not yet completely under his control. He fails when the passage demands rapidity of utterance (just, by the by, where Miss McCarthy as a speaker succeeds most), and there is a curious kind of expression of composed surprise in his voice which often suits the lines ill and becomes monotonous. Miss Silver was a delicious Titania. She spoke her first long speech beautifully, or rather the first part of it, losing her art, it seemed to me, over the description of the floods and frosts, recovering it again in her second speech – and delivering perfectly the lines at the close:

> But she, being mortal, of that boy did die;
> And for her sake do I rear up that boy,
> And for her sake I will not part with him.

Theatre, *1954*

II The Theatres and Audiences

Leigh Hunt
The 'O.P.' Riots at Covent Garden

It was ardently hoped by all the lovers of the Theatre, that the Managers of Covent-Garden, in shewing their taste for the fine arts would have shewn also a liberality worthy of the taste, and thus increased the respectability and the true interest of the stage: but people, it seems, are destined to be disappointed, who expect from these men anything but the merest feelings of tradesmen. The new theatre opened on Monday night with the increased prices of 4s. to the Pit, and 7s. to the Boxes, and if the town at least expected an increase of comfort on the occasion it was to be disappointed even in that respect.

The *appearance*, indeed, was classical and magnificent throughout. On your entrance through the portico, you turn to the left, and pay your money at the top of a short flight of steps, adorned on each side by a bronze Grecian lamp on a tripod: immediately beyond this is the grand staircase, rising through a landing place adorned on each side with large Ionic pillars in imitation of porphyry, between each of which hangs another lamp of bronze: this brings you directly opposite Mr Rossi's statue of Shakespeare in the ante-room; it stands in an easy assured attitude, making a sling of its cloak with its left arm, and holding a scroll in the other; its countenance does not much remind you of any of the faces attributed to the Great Poet, nor was it desirable that it should, for of the two commonly received likenesses, the Chandos and the Felton, the former is the head of a coxcomb, and the latter that of a dolt; but Mr Rossi has very poorly supplied what was deficient in dignity and genius; the poet merely looks as if he good-humouredly enjoyed his elevation, an expression certainly very distant from the noble simplicity of the antique, and in short, the figure altogether exhibits the usual feebleness of this artist, resulting from want of invention. This ante-room leads to the principal lobby, which disappoints one at first sight with regard to size, but it is quite large enough for the proper purposes of ingress and egress, and is very classically adorned with eight casts from the antique, among which are *Minerva, Venus*, and *Bacchus*, the *Apollo de Medicis*, and the *Farnesian Flora*, so justly celebrated for its magnificent breadth of drapery. These entrances are certainly worthy of introducing you to a stage over which Shakespeare presides.

In the audience part of the theatre, *appearances* are still as magnificent, but there is a sad abridgement of comfort. Those who had obtained seats in the lower boxes or pit might certainly feel themselves comfortable enough to look about and admire the aspect of the place. It is of a chaste and classical elegance. The boxes are of a dove-colour ground in front, the lower circle ornamented with a simple Etruscan border in gold, and the rest with the Grecian honey-suckle alternately upright and inverted. The light pillars that support them remind you of Drury-Lane Theatre; they are of a gold colour, and furnished with superb chandeliers, which, however, do not shew the backs of the boxes to advantage, smeared as they are with glaring red, and abruptly patched with doors of new mahogany that look like common unfinished wood: the slips and galleries are improved in *appearance* by being formed into a row of semi-circular arcades, and the arched front of the stage is adorned at top by a short curtain like the Greek peplum, festooned at intervals, and ornamented in each festoon by an Apollo's wreath: the pilasters at the side are in imitation of yellow stained marble, but unaccountably supported upon bases of most evident wood. The drop-scene is worthy the general classicality, and repre-sents a temple dedicated to Shakespeare, who stands in the vista in his usual attitude, while your eye approaches him through two rows of statues, con-sisting of the various founders of the drama in various nations, Aeschylus, Menander, Plautus, Lope de Vega, Ben Jonson, Molière, etc. They seemed to be looking over the way at each other with surprise to find themselves on a spot so new to a set of wits.

But the Managers, in all this display of taste, seem to have had no eye to the improvement of the public taste, but to have obeyed a certain aristocratic impulse of their pride and consulted little but the accommodation of the higher orders. The people felt this immediately. It is certainly monstrous to pay seven shillings for admission to the garrets at the top of the house, where you can neither see nor hear, and still more monstrous, when you see a whole circle taken from the public by way of private boxes with ante-chambers, to make room for which the places and comforts of the lower orders have been so circumscribed: that old nuisance, the basket, as it is called, has been pre-served to give the usual effect to the noise and interruption of the lobbies, and thus, if the accommodations are confined in some respects, the theatre is altogether as large in others as the avarice of the Managers and their contempt for a real taste in the drama could make it. In no such theatre can a true taste be excited, because a true drama, which requires nicety of expression in the voice and countenance, cannot be felt in it: Shakespeare may be played to the pit and side boxes, but he will be little better than dumb and blind shew to the people in the basket, who pay seven shillings to hear nothing but noise, or to those in the upper boxes, who pay seven shillings to see nothing but indecency. Naturally therefore the rise of the old prices entirely disgusted the public, and their disgust was increased by various attempts on the part of the Managers and their friends to plead the excuse of *necessity*. It was stated at one time that the Managers could not reimburse the expenses of rebuilding the theatre without raising the prices; at another, that their profits have lately been only six per cent; and the Editor of *Bell's Weekly Messenger* gravely desires us to 'look round and point out any one who has been enriched by a patent.' 'Is *Colman* rich?' he asks—'Is *Sheridan* rich? Is *Harris* rich? In the course of nearly one hundred years,' he continues, '*Garrick* will be found to be the only man who was enriched by a theatre. But Garrick was at once actor and proprietor', and the writer should have added, an economist and no debauchee. The Proprietors he has named would not thank him for obtruding the causes of their poverty on the public recollection. Mr Harris, however, as we see by the papers, keeps his country house, and can entertain Madame Catalani there, and Mr Kemble, besides his reputation as a bon-vivant, can afford to throw away his fifty and a hundred pounds upon old black-letter books which no man of taste would read. The public therefore neither does nor will believe a syllable respecting any plea of necessity, or rather they will treat it as ridiculous and contemptible, till they are convinced of its truth by inspection of the theatrical accounts.

With these impressions, people went to the new Theatre on Monday night, and though by a stratagem as barbarous as it was mean, numbers had been admitted into the house before the doors were regularly opened, the public feeling most decidedly predominated, and obtained the general voice of the audience.

On Mr Kemble's appearance in the dress of *Macbeth*, the character he was about to play, he was received with a partial applause, which was instantly drowned in a torrent of execration, and after plaintively bowing, and looking as tenderly disconsolate as he could, for a minute or two, he was compelled to retire. The curtain then drew up, and the noise and outcry that followed were continued with an energy truly terrific the whole evening. It was impossible that more determined resistance could be displayed on any occasion, and as it consisted entirely of noise, it was gratifying to see how much the audience felt themselves in the right by abstaining from every other mode of opposition. Every species of vocal power was exercised on the occasion, and some persons seemed to pride themselves in shewing their invention at making a noise: in one corner of the pit you had a heap of groans, in another a combination of hisses, in a third a choir of yells, in a fourth a doleful undulating moaning, which, mingling with the other sounds, reminded you of infernal regions, when in an instant the whole house seemed about to be rent asunder with a yah! of execration, whenever Mr Kemble presented himself from the side-scenes. When Mrs Siddons appeared, and seemed to petition for a little compassion, there was a general groan of disgust; but the death of her brother in the last act was followed by triumphant shouts of exultation, as if the spectators congratulated themselves on this temporary demise. After the farce, some persons, said to be magistrates, appeared on the stage, but soon vanished before the general indignation; and it was not till two o'clock that the audience retired, growling as they went, like Homer's lions, at those who had laid toils for them.

' 'Twas the same the next night, and the next, and the next', as Mr Colman says in a production much superior to the Prologue which he gave Mr Kemble to gesticulate on the present occasion. Each succeeding evening increased in noise: to cat-calls were added horns and trumpets; and to a placard or two,

banners all over the house covered with proverbs, lampoons, and encourage-
ments to unanimity. An attempt on Tuesday night to fasten one of these
placards on the stage-curtain at the end of the performances, which closed at
half past nine, produced a whole regiment of Bow-street officers, constables,
and bruisers on the stage, the trap-doors were opened to guard against
approach, and when all this was found to be no intimidation, a noise of pump-
ing was heard by way of innuendo, and one or two engine pipes were insinu-
ated through the stage door, a threat that served no purpose but to make the
indignation of the audience ten times hotter. A respectable gentleman of the
name of Leigh then addressed them, and exhorted them to a proper perseverance, a lesson which they put in practice the next night, Wednesday, with
unabated energy. The actors by this time had become the audience, and the
audience the actors, and Mr Kemble, seeing no probable termination of the
tragedy, again presented himself and begged to know in the usual frigid way
which he mistakes for dignity, '*of what the House had to complain?*' This ludicrous piece of affectation produced the usual burst of impatience and
execration, but after another very temperate and strenuous exhortation from
Mr Leigh, the Manager again made his appearance; he stated that 'for the
last ten years the Proprietors have not received for their capital more than
six per cent', and talked of 'the exigencies of dress and scenery', having
'doubled, trebled, and quadrupled', besides other expenses 'too numerous to
mention', and 'with which he was in fact *unacquainted*'. This egregious trifling
produced nothing but laughter: the same indignant vociferation was kept up
all Thursday evening and on Friday Mr Kemble once more presented himself
'to submit a proposal'. This proposal was to submit the decision of the question to a few great men, such as the 'Governor of the Bank of England', the
'*Attorney-General of England*', etc., etc., but it said nothing about lowering
the prices till the question *should be* decided. Of course, the speaker met with
his usual reception. The audience, less molested than before with the interference of the peace officers, were left to amuse their lungs to their hearts'
content, and so they were doing last night when this paper went to press. It
is evident that the managers cannot proceed in their plan of obstinacy much
longer, if such a determined system of opposition be continued, for they must
be losing a good deal by it already, in consequence of the temporary retainers
they keep about the theatre, and the orders that they scatter by hundreds
through the hands of their friends and tradesmen. If it is true, that they have
made only six per cent of their property no reasonable person can deny them
the advance of price, but when Mr Kemble talks of *average*, and tells us
nothing of the deductions, hazards, crosses, and losses, unconnected with the
people's responsibility on these occasions, he must not be surprised that his
speeches are treated as so many evasions, and that the people will believe
nothing till they can inspect his accounts through an *open and popular medium*.
Till then, it is to be hoped that they will repeat and invigorate their efforts,
and that, whenever the word necessity is mentioned, they will only answer
that they see no necessity why Mr Harris or Mr Kemble should grow
immensely rich, or why that grave actor should be so pathetic upon his

necessities, when he carries hundreds of pounds on his back in *Macbeth*, and has the face to make pitiful bows to the poor fellows cooped up in the galleries.

The Examiner, 24 September 1809

Leigh Hunt
The 'O.P.' Riots Continued

There has been nothing material for criticism during the past week; and I willingly turn to a subject which demands the attention of every friend of humanity and good morals. The impolite and brutal conduct of the Managers of this Theatre has reached its climax. It is impossible that the public should ever forget the time, when to go to the play was to endanger one's liberty and very life. To seizures and skirmishes has now succeeded an unmixed brutality on the part of the retainers. These men, consisting of the lowest ruffians collected from every pot-house about the place, enter the pit with avowed purposes of malice, some of them with their sticks furnished with spikes; the company are wounded in the face, have their hands run through, and are trodden down beneath the feet of the wretches; and finally, one gentleman of the name of Cowlam, who neither hissed nor wore a placard, but had brought an action against one of the Manager's friends, was assaulted on Wednesday last by a particular gang, and malignantly thrown down and trampled upon in such a manner that he has been confined to an excruciating bed in danger of his life. When people hear of these proceedings, they know not what to think of the apparent apathy of the Lord Chamberlain. With regard to the prices of admission, there are certainly many persons who upon their own calculations, and out of regard for the Theatre, are willing to allow the rise; but nobody who converses on the subject, whether for or against the Manager in this respect, looks upon the theatrical statement as anything but a list of mere *assertions*, which, in stating only a vague expenditure, and not its *causes* or *items*, have no pretence whatever to determine the question. With regard to the private boxes, I have heard but one opinion even from those who are disposed to allow the new prices; and with respect to the policy and brutality of the Managers, everybody unites in laughing at the one and execrating the other. The private boxes are certainly the most obnoxious part of the whole managerial alterations; the lovers of the Theatre are not, generally speaking, of a temper to begrudge the advance of sixpence or a shilling, abstracted from any imposition; and even in the latter case, time, and good-nature, and in-dolence, and perhaps the proverbial credulity of Englishmen, might have given the matter up; but a whole circle of the Theatre taken from them to make privacies for the luxurious great is a novelty so offensive to the national habits, both on account of its contemptuous exclusions, and the ideas of accommodation it so naturally excites, that the Managers, granting that they suffer a great loss, deserve to suffer still more for their mercenary and ob-sequious encouragement of pride and profligacy. In truth, there is not the shadow of a pretence for this foreign piece of indulgence. In Spain, people may want to smoke and drink coffee; and in Italy, they may have such places for a thousand purposes of abandonment; but in an English Theatre, the only object is, or ought to be, to see the play; and plays are seen much better in an open box than behind the best wall in Europe. 'Oh,' say the Managers, 'but the Ladies and Gentlemen can refresh themselves between the acts.' Can they indeed? But so they could, as well as the rest, in open boxes; and what kind of refreshment can people want, who dine at five or six, drink their coffee directly, and then go to the Theatre to sit upon easy cushions? 'Oh, but they may be ill.' Then let them stay at home. 'Oh, but they may be *taken* ill.' Then let them be taken home. 'Oh, but if a new play happen to be dull, they can retire a-while.' Really! They can retire a-while, if the play happen to be dull! Delicate and dignified souls! The rest of the boxes must sit still and wait patiently for their seven shillings' worth of common-sense, and probably not hear it after all, while these nice-judging and nice-feeling personages are to draw in their horns and retire a-while! And to what purpose are they to retire? *At best*, to lounge, and trifle with a jelly, and drawl a little with Mr SK-G-A-EFINGTON, and talk nonsense instead of hearing it: but these are not the innocent amusements of *all* the great persons who lounge at Theatres, and who come there to get rid of the fumes of wine, to idle about after idle acquaintances, and to *intrigue*! These persons will take advantage of every facility offered them; they themselves will enjoy the Private Boxes and intro-duce of course whom they please. Could there possibly be easier opportunities for the whole progress of seduction and sensuality – for vanquishing the weak, and rioting with the abandoned? Ovid, in the depravity of his heart, takes great pains to teach the art of making love at Theatres; but had he addressed himself to Private Boxes, he would have needed but a word or two. 'Oh,' cry the Managers, 'but really the thing is mistaken: the Private Boxes are to accommodate – they are certainly to accommodate – but they are for none of the vile uses you mention!' Are they not? Then the answer is plain: Do away with them entirely – they have no use at all if they have no such uses; and if they have, they are a thousand times worse than useless.

The Examiner, 19 November 1809

Leigh Hunt
Drury-Lane Redecorated

Drury-Lane Theatre was to open last night, and Covent-Garden opens to-morrow. The improvements or alterations which the former has been making we saw on Friday evening, and can promise our Readers much satisfaction with the gas-lights, which are introduced not only in front of the stage, but at the various compartments on each side: Their effect as they appear suddenly from the gloom, is like the striking of daylight; and indeed, it is in its re-semblance today that this beautiful light surpasses all others. It is as mild as it is splendid – white, regular, and pervading. If the Italian Ambassador, as he entered London in the evening, took the ordinary lamps in the street for an illumination and an elegant compliment, what would he have thought had he passed through the lustre which is shed at present from so many of our shops? In some of them, where the gas is managed with taste and shot out from a slender pipe, it is no extravagance to say that it puts one in mind of what one fancies in poetry, of the flamy breath at the point of a Seraph's wand:

> And in his hand a reed
> Stood waving, tipt with fire.

The Theatre has not the advantage of this part of the beauty, as the lights are enclosed in glasses and blinded from the audience by side-scenes and reflectors; but the result in every other respect is excellent, and a very great improvement; and, if it is managed as well as we saw it on Friday, will enable the spectator to see every part of the stage with equal clearness. If the front light could be thrown as day-light is, from above instead of below (and we should like to hear the reasons why it cannot) the effect would be perfect.

The rest of the house (always excepting the bad gilt figures on the stage boxes, which spoil a pleasant subject) is very neatly coloured and ornamented, and maintains the old reputation of this theatre for a certain airy elegance, a something of the lightness of comedy in its very appearance.

But we protest vehemently against the Saloon. They have absolutely filled it with Chinese pagodas and lanthorns, a series of the former occupying the middle, and a profusion of the latter being hung up on all sides, *adorned* with monsters and mandarins, and shedding a ghastly twilight! Nothing can be more puerile or tasteless. All the world knows that though the Chinese are a shrewd people in some things, they are very stupid and disgusting in others, matters of taste included; and if all the world did not know it, yet as it is of course to go and see the new Saloon, these Chinese lanthorns would be sufficient to enlighten it. What mummeries and monstrosities! On one lant-horn, a man like a watchman; on another, a dragon or some unintelligible compound of limbs; on another, some Chinese pot-hooks and hangers! Then the pagodas rise one over the other, like the card-houses of the little boys; and as if there were not monsters enough on the lanthorns, a set of huge tyger busts, or some such substitutes for Grecian sculpture, gape down upon you from the sides of the ceiling, and only want some puppet-shew men to ventriloquize for them and make them growl, to render this exquisite attraction complete. What is the meaning? Some libelous fellows say that it is a complimentary imitation of the Prince Regent, who it is averred, has whole rooms full of such lumber in his palaces, and holds Phidias exceedingly cheap and illegitimate. Others suspect that the light has been made thus coy and shadowy, to save the blushes of such Ladies as may chance to look in, and might feel their conscious modesty disturbed by too great a glare –

> Illa verecundis lux est praebenda puellis,
> Qua timidus latebras speret habere pudor.

Others conclude that the seductive horrors are intended to rival the more natural though less wealthy novelty at the Lyceum; and others again, who are attached to the doctrine of mixed motives, have made up their mind that all these reasons co-operate more or less. Be they what they may, there never was a more graceless or absurd piece of business. It is really humiliating to the national taste. If the Prince Regent or the loungers put up with the compliment, we cannot imagine any other human being within the civilized pale who would admire it, except indeed the Chinese themselves, who hustled us out of doors the other day.

Now the Saloon at the Lyceum, though a poor business compared with what a shrubbery ought to be, and much humbler of course in point of size, is really, in our eyes, a thousand times more attractive; that is to say, there is something attractive in the very idea of green leaves and walks, in the least piece of nature, and nothing but what is repulsive in these monstrous abuses of art. But Mr Arnold, if he is not rich enough to make his shrubbery as good as we would have it, or to treat us with a regular greenhouse, should contrive to let his plants have some means of keeping themselves alive; for though young trees are much cheaper than many imagine (and how infinitely cheaper than they imagine is *real* taste, of all sorts), yet the recurrence of dusty and dying plants every season would subject him to something of a losing nature – which is ridicule. Above all, he ought not to puff so, and make so many pompous announcements. The shrubbery, for instance, about which he so repeatedly flourished his trumpets, is in fact nothing more than some ranges of shrubs in pots on each side of the saloon, pleasing enough certainly when fresh, and much better than Chinese deformities, but nothing to warrant such exceeding proclamations on the house-tops. Well, suddenly, amidst his eternal announcements, he informs us of 'a novel and interesting feature', or some such thing, which is the delight of all beholders: the readers of the play-bill are kept in attractive suspense, and then informed that this novelty is a 'Chinese walk'; and what is the Chinese walk? Nothing but the usual walk up the saloon, with a trumpery Chinese tap-room or tea-room at the *end* of it, over which is daubed on a board 'Thé à-la-Chinoise', and where (stupendous to think of!) you can buy cakes.

The sage Fum Hoams who contrived the Drury-Lane Saloon, moved admiringly, we suppose, towards this 'interesting feature', and passing by the firs and poplars, emulated the pagoda! They will find their account in it, we dare say, at first; but surely there is too much taste diffused now-a-days not to make them repent it ultimately. Now if they would emulate the Lyceum in a *shrubbery*, and adorn it with a few specimens (which they might do very cheaply) of ancient sculpture, or take the opportunity of encouraging modern, they would do themselves a lasting service, and give the public a pleasure full of the most beautiful associations both of Nature and Art.

We know not whether anything has been done with the Saloon at Covent-Garden; but we trust when we see it to find that the taste of Siddons and Kemble has not departed with their persons.

The Examiner, 7 September 1817

William Hazlitt
Minor Theatres

This is a subject on which we shall treat, with satisfaction to ourselves, and, we hope, to the edification of the reader. Indeed, we are not a little vain of the article we propose to write on this occasion; and we feel the pen in our hands flutter its feathered down with more than its usual specific levity, at the thought of the idle, careless career before it. No Theatre-Royal oppresses the imagination, and entombs it in a mausoleum of massy pride; no manager's pompous pretensions choak up the lively current of our blood; no long-announced performance, big with expectation, comes to nothing, and yet compels us gravely to record its failure, and compose its epitaph. We have here 'ample scope and verge enough'; we pick and chuse as we will, light where we please, and stay no longer than we have a mind – saying 'this I like, that I loathe, as one picks pears': hover over the Surrey Theatre; or snatch a grace beyond the reach of art from the Miss Dennetts at the Adelphi; or take a peep (like the *Devil upon Two Sticks*) at Mr Booth at the Cobourg – and one peep is sufficient – or stretch our legs and strain our fancies (as a pure voluntary exercise of dramatic faith and charity) as far as Mr Rae and the East London, where Mrs Gould (late Miss Burrell) makes fine work with Don Giovanni and the Furies! We are not, in this case, to be 'constrained by mastery'. Escaped from under the more immediate inspection of the Lord Chamberlain's eye, fastidious objections, formal method, regular details, strict moral censure, cannot be expected at our hands: our 'speculative and officed instruments' may be well laid aside for a time. At sight of the purlieus of taste, and suburbs of the drama, criticism 'clappeth his wings, and straitway he is gone!' In short, we feel it as our bounden duty to strike a truce with gravity, and give a furlough to fancy; and, in entering on this part of our subject, to let our thoughts wander over it, sport and trifle with it at pleasure, like the butterfly of whom Spenser largely and loftily sings in his Muiopotmos –

> There he arriving, round about doth fly
> From bed to bed, from one to other border,
> And takes survey, with curious busy eye,
> Of every flower and herb there set in order;
> Now this, now that he tasteth tenderly,
> Yet none of them he rudely doth disorder,
> Nor with his feet their silken leaves deface,
> But pastures on the pleasures of each place.
>
> What more felicity can fall to creature
> Than to enjoy Delight with Liberty,
> And to be lord of all the works of Nature,
> To reign in th' air from earth to highest sky:
> To feed on flowers, and weeds of glorious feature,
> To take whatever thing doth please the eye?
> Who rests not pleased with such happiness,
> Well worthy he to taste of wretchedness!

If we could but once realize this idea of a butterfly-critic extracting sweets from flowers and turning gall to honey, we might well hope to soar above the Grub-Street race, and confound, by the novelty of our appearance, and the gaiety of our flight, the idle conjectures of ignorant or malicious pretenders in entomology!

Besides, having once got out of the vortex of prejudice and fashion, that surrounds our large Winter Theatres, what is there to hinder us (or what shall) from dropping down from the verge of the metropolis into the haunts of the provincial drama – from taking coach to Bath or Brighton or visiting the Land's End, or giving an account of Botany-Bay theatricals, or the establishment of a new theatre at Venezuela? One reason that makes the Minor Theatres interesting is, that they are the connecting link that lets us down, by an easy transition, from the highest pomp and proudest display of the Thespian art, to its first rudiments and helpless infancy. With conscious happy retrospect, they lead the eye back, along the vista of the imagination, to the village barn, or travelling booth, or old-fashioned town-hall, or more genteel assembly-room, in which Momus first unmasked to us his fairy revels, and introduced us, for the first time in our lives, to that strange anomaly in existence, that fanciful reality, that gay waking dream, *a company of strolling players*! Sit still, draw close together, hold in your breath – not a word, not a whisper – the laugh is ready to start away, 'like greyhound on the slip', the big tear of wonder and expectation is ready to steal down 'the full eyes and fair cheeks of childhood', almost before the time. Only another moment, and amidst blazing tapers, and the dancing sounds of music, and light throbbing hearts, and eager looks, the curtain rises, and the picture of the world appears before us in all its glory and in all its freshness. Life throws its gaudy shadow across the stage; Hope shakes his many-coloured wings, 'embalmed with odours'; Joy claps his hands, and laughs in a hundred happy faces. Oh childish fancy, what a mighty empire is thine; what endless creations thou buildest out of nothing; what 'a wide O' indeed, thou chusest to act thy thoughts, and unrivalled feats upon! Thou art better than the gilt trophy that decks the funeral pall of kings; thou art brighter than the costly mace that precedes them on their coronation-day. Thy fearfullest visions are enviable happiness; thy wildest fictions are the solidest truths. Thou art the only reality. All other possessions mock our idle grasp: but thou performest by promising; thy smile is fruition; thy blandishments are all that we can fairly call our own; thou art the balm of life, the heaven of childhood, the poet's idol, and the player's pride! The world is but thy painting; and the stage is thine enchanted mirror. When it first displays its shining surface to our view, how glad, how surprised are we! We have no thought of any deception in the scene, no wish but to realize it ourselves with inconsiderate haste and fond impatience. We say to the air-drawn gorgeous phantom, 'Come, let me clutch thee!' A new sense comes upon us, the scales fall off our eyes, and the scenes of life start out in endless quick succession crowded with men and women actors, such as we see before us – comparable to 'those gay creatures of the element, that live in the rainbow, and play i' th' plighted clouds!' Happy are we who look on and admire; and happy, we think, must they be who are so looked at and admired; and sometimes we begin to feel uneasy till we can ourselves mingle in the gay, busy, talking, fluttering, powdered, painted, perfumed, peruked, quaintly-accoutred throng of coxcombs and coquettes – of tragedy heroes or heroines – in good earnest; or turn stage-players and represent them in jest, with all the impertinent and consequential airs of the originals!

It is no insignificant epoch in one's life the first time that odd-looking thing, a play-bill, is left at our door in a little market-town in the country (say W—m in S—shire). The Manager, somewhat fatter and more erect, 'as Manager beseems', than the rest of his Company, with more of the man of business, and not less of the coxcomb, in his strut and manner, knocks at the door with the end of a walking cane (a badge of office!) and a bundle of papers under his arm; presents one of them printed in large capitals, with a respectful bow and a familiar shrug; hopes to give satisfaction in the town; hints at the liberal encouragement they received at W——ch, the last place they stopped at; had every possible facility afforded by the Magistrates; supped one evening with the Rev. Mr J——s, a dissenting clergyman, and really a very well-informed, agreeable, sensible man, full of anecdote – no illiberal prejudices against the profession: then talks of the strength of his company, with a careless mention of his own favourite line – his benefit fixed for an early day, but would do himself the honour to leave farther particulars at a future opportunity – speaks of the stage as an elegant amusement, that most agreeably enlivened a spare evening or two in the week, and, under proper management (to which he himself paid the most assiduous attention), might be made of the greatest assistance to the cause of virtue and humanity – had seen Mr Garrick act the last night but one before his retiring from the stage – had himself had offers from the London boards, and indeed could not say he had given up all thoughts of one day surprising them – as it was, had no reason to repine – Mrs F. – tolerably advanced in life – his eldest son a prodigious turn for the higher walks of tragedy – had said perhaps too much of himself – had given universal satisfaction – hoped that the young gentleman and lady, at least, would attend on the following evening, when the *West-Indian* would be performed at the market hall, with the farce of *No Song No Supper* – and so, having played his part, withdraws in the full persuasion of having made a favourable impression, and of meeting with every encouragement the place affords! Thus he passes from house to house, and goes through the routine of topic after topic, with that sort of modest assurance, which is indispensable in the manager of a country theatre. This fellow, who floats over the troubles of life as the froth above the idle wave, with all his little expedients and disappointments, with pawned paste-buckles, mortgaged scenery, empty exchequer, and rebellious orchestra, is not of all men the most miserable: he is little less happy than a king, though not much better off than a beggar. He has little to think of, much to do, more to say; and is accompanied, in his incessant daily round of trifling occupations, with a never-failing sense of authority and self-importance, the one thing needful (above all others) to the heart of man. This however is their man of business in the company; he is a sort of fixture in their little state; like Nebuchadnezzar's image, but half of earth and half of finer metal: he is not 'of imagination all compact': he is not, like the rest of his aspiring crew, a feeder upon air, a drinker of applause, tricked out in vanity and in nothing else; he is not quite mad, nor quite happy. The whining Romeo, who goes supperless to bed, and on his pallet of straw dreams of a crown of laurel, of waving handkerchiefs, of bright eyes, and *billets doux* breathing boundless love: the ranting Richard, whose infuriate execrations are drowned in the shouts of the all-ruling pit; he who, without a coat to his back, or a groat in his purse, snatches at Cato's robe, and binds the diadem of Caesar on his brow; these are the men that Fancy has chosen for herself, and placed above the reach of fortune, and almost of fate. They take no thought for the morrow. What is it to them what they shall eat, or what they shall drink, or how they shall be clothed? 'Their mind to them a kingdom is.' It is not a poor ten shillings a week, their share in the profits of the theatre, with which they have to pay for bed, board, and lodging, that bounds their wealth. They share (and not unequally) in all the wealth, the pomp, and pleasures of the world. They wield sceptres, conquer kingdoms, court princesses, are clothed in purple, and fare sumptuously every night. They taste, in imagination, 'of all earth's bliss, both living and loving': whatever has been most the admiration or most the envy of mankind, they, for a moment, in their own eyes, and in the eyes of others, become. The poet fancies others to be this or that; the player fancies himself to be all that the poet but describes. A little rouge makes him a lover, a plume of feathers a hero, a brazen crown an emperor. Where will you buy rank, office, supreme delights, so cheap as at his shop of fancy? Is it nothing to dream whenever we please, and *seem* whatever we desire? Is real greatness, is real prosperity, more than what it seems? Where shall we find, or where shall the votary of the stage find, Fortunatus' Wishing Cap, but in the wardrobe which we laugh at: or borrow the philosopher's stone but from the *property-man* of the theatre? He has discovered the true Elixir of Life, which is freedom from care: he quaffs the pure *aurum potabile*, which is popular applause. He who is smit with the love of this *ideal* existence, cannot be weaned from it. Hoot him from the stage, and he will stay to sweep the lobbies or shift the scenes. Offer him twice the salary to go into a counting-house, or stand behind a counter, and he will return to poverty, steeped in contempt, but eked out with fancy, at the end of a week. Make a laughing-stock of an actress, lower her salary, tell her she is too tall, awkward, stupid and ugly; try to get rid of her all you can – she will remain, only to hear herself courted, to listen to the echo of her borrowed name, to live but one short minute in the lap of vanity and tinsel shew. Will you give a man an additional ten shillings a week, and ask him to resign the fancied wealth of the world, which he 'by his so potent art' can conjure up, and glad his eyes, and fill his heart with it? When a little change of dress, and the muttering of a few talismanic words, make all the difference between the vagabond and the hero, what signifies the interval so easily passed? Would you not yourself consent to be alternately a beggar and a king, but that you have not the secret skill to be so? The player has that 'happy alchemy of mind' – why then would you reduce him to an equality with yourself? The moral of this reasoning is known and felt, though it may be gainsayed. Wherever the players come, they send a welcome before them, and leave an air in the place behind them. They shed a light upon the day, that does not very soon pass off. See how they glitter along the street, wandering, not where business but the bent of pleasure takes them, like mealy-coated butterflies, or insects flitting in the sun. They seem another, happier, idler race of mortals, prolonging the carelessness of childhood to old age, floating down the stream of life, or wafted by the wanton breeze to their final place of rest. We remember one (we must make the reader acquainted with him) who once overtook us loitering by 'Severn's sedgy side', on a fine May morning, with a score of play-bills streaming from his pockets, for the use of the neighbouring villages, and a music-score in his hand, which he sung blithe and clear, advancing with light step and a loud voice! With a sprightly *bon jour*, he passed on, carolling to the echo of the babbling stream, brisk as a bird, gay as a mote, swift as an arrow from a twanging bow, heart-whole, and with a shining face that shot back the sun's broad rays! What is become of this favourite of mirth and song? Has care touched him? Has death tripped up his heels? Has an indigestion imprisoned him, and all his gaiety, in a living dungeon? Or is he himself lost and buried amidst the rubbish of one of our larger, or else of one of our Minor Theatres.

> Alas! how changed from him,
> That life of pleasure, and that soul of whim!

But as this was no doubt the height of his ambition, why should we wish to debar him of it?

This brings us back, after our intended digression, to the subject from whence we set out – the smaller theatres of the metropolis; which we visited lately, in hopes to find in them a romantic contrast to the presumptuous and exclusive pretensions of the legitimate drama, and to revive some of the associations of our youth above described. The first attempt we made was at the Cobourg, and we were completely balked. Judge of our disappointment. This was not owing, we protest, to any fault or perversity of our own; to the crust and scales of formality which had grown over us; to the panoply of criticism in which we go armed, and which made us inaccessible to 'pleasure's finest point'; or to the *cheveux-de-fris* of objections, which cut us off from all cordial participation in what was going forward on the stage. No such thing. We went not only willing, but determined to be pleased. We had laid aside the pedantry of rules, the petulance of sarcasm, and had hoped to open once more, by stealth, the source of sacred tears, of bubbling laughter, and concealed sighs. We were not formidable. On the contrary, we were 'made of penetrable stuff'. Stooping from our pride of place, we were ready to be equally delighted with a clown in a pantomime, or a lord-mayor in a tragedy. We were all attention, simplicity, and enthusiasm. But we saw neither attention, simplicity, nor enthusiasm in any body else; and our whole scheme of voluntary delusion and social enjoyment was cut up by the roots. The play was indifferent, but that was nothing. The acting was bad, but that was nothing. The audience were low, but that was nothing. It was the heartless indifference and hearty contempt shown by the performers for their parts, and by the audience for the players and the play, that disgusted us with all of them. Instead of the rude, naked, undisguised expression of curiosity and wonder, of overflowing vanity and unbridled egotism, there was nothing but an exhibition of the most petulant cockneyism and vulgar slang. All our former notions and theories were turned topsy-turvy. The genius of St George's Fields prevailed, and you felt yourself in a bridewell, or a brothel, amidst Jew-boys, pickpockets, prostitutes, and mountebanks, instead of being in the precincts of Mount Parnassus, or in the company of the Muses. The object was not to admire or to excel, but to vilify and degrade everything. The audience did not hiss the actors (that would have implied a serious feeling of disapprobation, and something like a disappointed wish to be pleased) but they laughed, hooted at, nick-named, pelted them with oranges and witticisms, to show their unruly contempt for them and their art; while the performers, to be even with the audience evidently slurred their parts, as if ashamed to be thought to take any interest in them, laughed in one another's faces, and in that of their friends in the pit, and most effectually marred the process of theatrical illusion, by turning the whole into a most unprincipled burlesque. We cannot help thinking that some part of this indecency and licentiousness is to be traced to the diminutive size of these theatres, and to the close contact into which these unmannerly censors come with the objects of their ignorant and unfeeling scorn. Familiarity breeds contempt. By too narrow an inspection, you take away that fine, hazy medium of abstraction by which (in moderation) a play is best set off: you are, as it were, admitted behind the scenes; 'see the puppets dallying'; shake hands across the orchestra, with an actor whom you know, or take one you do not like by the beard, with equal impropriety: you distinguish the paint, the individual features, the texture of the dresses, the patch-work and the machinery by which the whole is made up; and this in some measure destroys the effect, distracts attention, suspends the interest, and makes you disposed to quarrel with the actors as impostors, and 'not the men you took them for'. You here see Mr Booth, in Brutus, with every motion of his face *articulated*, with his under-jaws grinding out sentences, and his upper-lip twitching at words and syllables, as if a needle and thread had been passed through each corner of it, and the *gude wife* still continued sewing at her work – you perceive the contortion and barrenness of his expression (in which there is only one form of bent brows, and close pent-up mouth for all occasions), the parsimony of his figure is exposed, and the refuse tones of his voice fall with undiminished vulgarity on the pained ear: you have Mr Higman as Prior Aymer in Ivanhoe, who used to play the Gipsey so well at Covent Garden in Guy Mannering, and who certainly is an admirable bass singer: you have Mr Stanley, from the Theatre-Royal, Bath, and whom we thought an interesting actor there (such as poor Wilson might have been who trod the same boards, and with whom our readers will remember that Miss Lydia Melford, in Humphrey Clinker, fell in love): you have Mr Barrymore, that old and deserving favourite with the public in the best days of Mrs Siddons and of John Kemble, superintending, we believe, the whole, from a little oval window in a stage-box, like Mr Bentham eyeing the hopeful circle of delinquents in his Panopticon: and, to sum up all in one word, you have here Mr H. Kemble, whose hereditary gravity is put to the last test, by the yells and grins of the remorseless rabble.

'My soul turn from them!' – 'Turn we to survey' where the Miss Dennetts, at the Adelphi Theatre (which should once more from them be called the Sans Pareil), weave the airy, the harmonious, liquid dance. Of each of them it might be said, and we believe has been said –

> Her, lovely Venus at a birth
> With two Sister Graces more
> To ivy-crowned Bacchus bore.

Such figures, no doubt, gave rise to the fables of ancient mythology, and might be worshipped. They revive the ideas of classic grace, life, and joy. They do not seem like taught dancers, Columbines, and figurantes on an artificial stage; but come bounding forward like nymphs in vales of Arcady, or, like Italian shepherdesses, join in a lovely group of easy gracefulness, while 'vernal airs attune the trembling leaves' to their soft motions. If they were nothing in themselves, they would be complete in one another. Each owes a double grace, youth, and beauty, to her reflection in the other two. It is the principle of proportion, or harmony personified. To deny their merit or criticize their style, is to be blind and dead to the felicities of art and nature. Not to feel the force of their united charms (united, yet divided, different, and yet the same), is not to see the beauty of 'three red roses on a stalk' – or of the mingled hues of the rainbow, or of the halcyon's breast, reflected in the stream – or 'the witchery of the soft blue sky', or grace in the waving of the branch of a tree, or tenderness in the bending of a flower, or liveliness in the motion of a wave of the sea. We shall not try to defend them against the dancing-school critics; there is another school, different from that of the *pied à plomb* and *pirouette* cant, the school of taste and nature. In this school, the Miss Dennetts are (to say the least) delicious novices. Theirs is the only performance on the stage (we include the Opera) that gives the uninitiated spectator an idea that dancing can be an emanation of instinctive gaiety, or express the language of sentiment. We might shew them to the Count Stendhal, who speaks so feelingly of the beauties of a dance by Italian peasant girls, as our three English Graces; and we might add, as a farther proof of national liberality and public taste, that they had been discarded from one of the larger, to take refuge in one of our petty theatres, on a disagreement about a pound a week in their joint salaries. Yet we suppose if these young ladies were to marry, and not volunteer to put ten thousand pounds in the pockets of some liberally disposed manager, we should hear a very pitiful story of their ingratitude to their patrons and the public. It is the way of the world. There is a Mr Reeve at this theatre (the Adelphi in the Strand) of whom report had spoken highly in his particular department as a mimic, and in whom we were considerably disappointed. He is not so good as Matthews, who, after all, is by no means a *fac-simile* of those he pretends to represent. We knew most of Mr Reeve's likenesses, and that is the utmost we can say in their praise; for we thought them very bad ones. They were very slight, and yet contrived to be very disagreeable. Farren was the most amusing, from a certain oddity of voice and manner in the ingenious and eccentric original. Harley, again, was not at all the thing. There was something of the external dress and deportment, but none of the spirit, the frothy essence. He made him out a great burly swaggering ruffian, instead of being what he is – a pleasant, fidgetty person, pert as a jack-daw, light as a grasshopper. In short, from having seen Mr Reeve, no one would wish to see Mr Harley, though there is no one who has seen him but wishes to see him again; and, though mimicry has the privilege of turning into ridicule the loftier pretensions of tragic heroes, we believe it always endeavours to set off the livelier peculiarities of comic ones in the most agreeable light. Mr Kean was bad enough. It might have been coarse and repulsive enough, and yet like; but it wanted point and energy, and this was inexcusable. We have heard much of ludicrous and admirable imitations of Mr Kean's acting. But the only person who ever caricatures Mr Kean well, or from whose exaggerations he has anything to fear, is himself. There are several other actors at the Adelphi who are, and must continue to be, nameless. There are also some better known to the town, as Mr Wilkinson, Mrs Alsop, etc. This lady has lost none of her exuberant and piquant vivacity by her change of situation. She also looks much the same: and as you see her near, this circumstance is by no means to her advantage. The truth is, that there are not good actors or agreeable actresses enough in town to make one really good company (by which we mean a company able to get up any one really good play throughout) and of course there are not a sufficient number (unless by a miracle) to divide into eight or ten different establishments.

'The Drama', No. III, *The London Magazine*, March 1820

Charles Lamb
Playhouse Memoranda

I once sat in the Pit of Drury Lane Theatre next to a blind man, who, I afterwards learned, was a street musician, well-known about London. The play was *Richard the Third*, and it was curious to observe the interest which he took in every successive scene, so far more lively than could be perceived in any of the company around him. At those pathetic interviews between the Queen and Duchess of York, after the murder of the children, his eyes (or rather the places where eyes should have been) gushed out tears in torrents, and he sat entranced in attention, while every one about him was tittering, partly at him, and partly at the grotesque figures and wretched action of the women, who had been selected by managerial taste to personate those royal mourners. Having no drawback of sight to impair his sensibilities, he simply attended to the scene, and received its unsophisticated impression. *So much the rather her celestial light shone inward.* I was pleased with an observation which he made, when I asked him how he liked Kemble, who played Richard. I should have thought (said he) that that man had been reading something out of a book, if I had not known that I was in a play-house.

I was once amused in a different way by a knot of country people who had come to see a play at that same Theatre. They seemed perfectly inattentive to all the best performers for the first act or two, though the piece was admirably played, but kept poring in the play-bill, and were evidently watching for the appearance of one, who was to be the source of supreme delight to them that night. At length the expected actor arrived, who happened to be in possession of a very insignificant part, not much above a mule. I saw their faint attempt at raising a clap on his appearance, and their disappointment at not being seconded by the audience in general. I saw them try to admire and to find out something very wonderful in him, and wondering all the while at the moderate sensation he produced. I saw their pleasure and their interest subside at last into flat mortification, when the riddle as at once unfolded by my recollecting that this performer bore the same name with an actor, then in the acme of his celebrity, at Covent-Garden, but who lately finished his theatrical and mortal career on the other side of the Atlantic. They had come to see Mr C——, but had come to the wrong house.

Is it a stale remark to say, that I have constantly found the interest excited at a play-house to bear an exact inverse proportion to the price paid for admission? Formerly, when my sight and hearing were more perfect, and my purse a little less so, I was a frequenter of the upper gallery in the old Theatres. The eager attention, the breathless listening, the anxiety not to lose a word, the quick anticipation of the significance of the scene (every sense kept as it were upon a sharp look out), which are exhibited by the occupiers of those higher and now almost out of sight regions (who, going seldom to a play, cannot afford to lose any thing by inattention), suffer some little diminution, as you descend to the lower or two-shilling ranks; but still the joy is lively and unallayed, save that by some little *incursion of manners*, the expression of it is expected to abate somewhat of its natural liveliness. The oaken plaudits of the trunk-maker would here be considered as going a little beyond the line. In the pit first begins that accursed critical faculty, which, making a man the judge of his own pleasure, too often constitutes him the executioner of his own and others! You may see the jealousy of being unduly pleased, the suspicion of being taken in to admire; in short, the vile critical spirit, creeping and diffusing itself, and spreading from the wrinkled brows and cloudy eyes of the front row sages and newspaper reporters (its proper resident), till it infects and clouds over the thoughtless, vacant countenance of John Bull tradesmen, and clerks of counting-houses, who, but for that approximation, would have been contented to have grinned without rule, and to have been pleased without asking why. The sitting next a critic is contagious. Still now and then, a genuine spectator is to be found among them, a shopkeeper and his family, whose honest titillations of mirth, and generous chucklings of applause, cannot wait or be at leisure to take the cue from the sour judging faces about them. Haply they never dreamed that there were such animals in nature as critics or reviewers; even the idea of an author may be a speculation they never entered into; but they take the mirth they find as a pure effusion of the actor-folks, set there on purpose to make them fun. I love the unenquiring gratitude of such spectators. As for the Boxes, I never can understand what brings the people there. I see such frigid indifference, such unconcerned spectatorship, such impenetrability to pleasure or its contrary, such being *in the house* and yet not *of it*, certainly they come far nearer the nature of *the Gods*, upon the system of Lucretius at least, than those honest, hearty, well-pleased, unindifferent mortals above, who, from time immemorial have had that name, upon no other ground than situation, assigned them.

Take the play-house altogether, there is a less sum of enjoyment than used to be. Formerly you might see something like the effect of novelty upon a citizen, his wife and daughters, in the Pit; their curiosity upon every new face that entered upon the stage. The talk of how they got in at the door, and how they were crowded upon some former occasion, made a topic till the curtain drew up. People go too often now-a-days to make their ingress or egress of consequence. Children of seven years of age will talk as familiarly of the performers, aye and as knowingly (according to the received opinion) as grown persons; more than the grown persons in my time. Oh when shall I forget first seeing a play, at the age of five or six? It was *Artaxerxes*. Who played, or who sang in it, I know not. Such low ideas as actors' names, or actors' merits, never entered my head. The mystery of delight was not cut open and dissipated for me by those who took me there. It was *Artaxerxes* and *Arbaces* and *Mandane* that I saw, not Mr Beard, or Mr Leoni, or Mrs Kennedy. It was all enchantment and a dream. No such pleasure has since visited me but in dreams. I was in Persia for the time, and the burning idol of their devotion in the Temple almost converted me into a worshipper. I was awe-struck, and believed those significations to be something more than elemental fires. I was, with Uriel, in the body of the sun – What should I have gained by knowing (as I should have done, had I been born thirty years later) that that solar representation was a mere painted scene, that had neither fire nor light in itself, and that the royal phantoms, which passed in review before me, were but such common mortals as I could see every day out of my father's window? We crush the faculty of delight and wonder in children, by explaining everything. We take them to the source of the Nile, and shew them the scanty runnings, instead of letting the beginnings of that sevenfold stream remain in impenetrable darkness, a mysterious question of wonderment and delight to ages.

The Examiner, 19 December 1813

Leigh Hunt
The Play-Bills

The *Tatler* in future will contain the play-bills of the evening. They will be printed in an open and distinct manner, to suit all eyes, and, it is hoped may serve as companions to the theatre, like the regular bills that are sold at the doors. The measure has been adopted on the friendly suggestion of a Correspondent, who thinks that the public will not be sorry for this union of a paper with a play-bill; and that by and by, to use his pleasant quotation, *Tatlers* will be 'frequent and full' in the pit and boxes. We shall be glad to see them. Nothing will give us greater pleasure than to find ourselves thus visibly multiplied, and to see the ladies bending over us. Happy shall we be, to be pinned to the cushions for their sakes.

Without a play-bill, no true play-goer can be comfortable. If the performers are new to him, he cannot dispense with knowing who they are; if old, there are the names of the characters to learn, and the relationships of the dramatis personae: and if he is acquainted with all this, he is not sure that there may not be something else, some new play to be announced, or some new appearance. The advertisements in the papers will not supply him with the information, for they are only abridgments: and he cannot try to be content with a look at the play-bills at the door, for then he would grudge his pence: and he that grudges his pence, cannot be a genuine play-goer. How would he relish a generous sentiment, or presume to admire a pretty face? There is a story, in the tales of chivalry, of a magic seat which ejected with violence any knight who was not qualified to sit down in it. If the benches at the theatre could be imbued with the noble sentiments that abound on the stage, thus would they eject the man who was too stingy to purchase a play-bill.

But the above are not the only reasons for the purchase. The *Tatler* for instance, will in future be sold at the play-house doors, as well as by the news-men. They must be so, or they would not be play-bills. Now the poor people who sell the play-bills deserve all the encouragement that can be given them, for they prefer industry to beggary, and go through a great deal of bad weather and rejection. We may suppose that people who do this, do it for very good reasons. They look as if they did, for they are a care-worn race; they defy rain and mud, and persevere in trying to sell their bills with importunity that makes the proud angry, and the good-tempered smile. If you look into the face that is pursuing at your elbow, or jogging at the window of your coach, you would often see cause to pity it. However, not to dwell upon this point, or to make a sad article of one that is intended to be merry, on every *Tatler* which these poor people sell, they will get a half-penny. When we consider the stress which great statesmen lay upon pence and pots of beer, in their financial measures, we hope this will not have 'a mean sound', except in the ears of the mean passions of pride and avarice. For our part we affect to despise nothing that represents the food and raiment of mothers and children; though we often wonder how great statesmen can lay as much stress upon the pence they dole out and so little upon the thousands they receive. But we shall be stopping too long at the doors.

If a playgoer has a party with him, especially ladies, the purchase of a bill gives him an opportunity of shewing how he consults their pleasure in trifles. If he is alone, it is a companion. He has also the glory of being able to lend it – though with what face anyone can borrow a play-bill, thus proclaiming that he has not had the heart to buy one, is to *us* inconceivable. We grant that it may be done, once or so, out of thoughtlessness, particularly if the borrower has given away his pence for nothing; but *after the present notice*, we expect that nobody will think of making this excuse. It is better to purchase a bill than to give money, even to the sellers, for you thus encourage the sale, give and receive a pleasure, and save the venders from the temptation of begging.

A *Tatler*, we allow, costs two pence, whereas the common play-bill is a penny. But if the latter be worth what it costs, will it be too great a stretch of modesty to suppose that our new play-bill is worth it also? Our criticisms, we will be sworn, have, at all events, a relish in them: they are larger; and then there is the rest of the matter, in the other pages, to vary the chat between the acts. There will even be found, we presume, in the whole paper, something not unworthy of the humanities taught on the stage. Now as to the bills that are sold at the doors, we have a respect for the common 'housebill' as it is called, that is to say, the old unaffected piece of paper that contains nothing but the usual announcements – the play-bill of old, or 'bill o' the play', which has so often rung its pleasing changes in our ears, with the 'porter, or cyder, or ginger-beer'. Formerly the cry used only to be 'porter or cyder': previously to that it was 'oranges': and lately we have heard 'apples'. There is a fellow in the gallery at the English Opera, who half bawls and half screams a regular quick strain, all in one note, as if it were a single word, of 'bottled-porter-apples-ginger-beer'. It is as if a parrot were shouting it.

This old play-bill is a reverend and sensible bit of paper, pretends to no more than it possesses, and adds to this solid merit an agreeable flimsiness in its tissue. But there are two rogues, anticipators of us respectable interlopers, of whom we must say a word, particularly one who has the face to call himself the *Theatrical Examiner*. This gentleman, not having the fear of our reputation before his eyes sets out, in his motto, with claiming the privilege of a free speaker. 'Let me', says he, quoting Shakespeare, 'be privileged by my place and message, to be a speaker free.' Accordingly his freedom of speech consists in praising everybody as hard as he can, and filling up one of his four pages with puffs of the exhibitions. The rogue is furthermore of a squalid appearance, 'shabby' without being 'genteel': and so is his friend the *Theatrical Observer*. The following is a taste of his quality. The analysis which is given of Mr Power's style of humour will convey a striking sense of it to the reader: and the praises of the singers are very particular. 'Power's Paddy O'Rafferty', says he, 'was a performance exceedingly rich, and abounded with those exquisite displays of humour which has always characterized his representation of the part. The piece was throughout well cast, and very well supported. Melrose as Captain Coradino, introduced a song composed by Lee, "Can I my love resign", which he sung with great sweetness and effect, and was loudly applauded. Mrs Chapman, as Margaritta, introduced sweetly, "On the wings of morning", from Hoffer, which she sung very effectively. Mrs Weston of Covent Garden, made her first appearance as the Countess, and gave excellent effect to the character.' How judiciously, in this criticism, are our reflections aroused by the emphatic word *Those* and how happily are they realized! How full of *effect* also are the remaining six lines! We hope these remarks will not be reckoned invidious. If the hawkers are the critics, we are sorry; but then they should put their names, and the matter would become proper.

We must not forget one thing respecting the 'house-bill', which is that, agreeably to its domestic character, it rises in value by being within doors: costing but a penny outside the house, and two-pence in; so that no attention ought to be paid to those insidious decencies of fruit-women, who serious and elderly, dressed in clean linen, and renouncing the evil reputations of their predecessors, charge high for the honour they do you in being virtuous, and will fetch you a glass of water for a shilling. The two-pence of these people's play-bills ought to retire before the sincere and jovial superabundance of the *Tatler*, the more virtuous because it does not pretend to be so.

We must add that in our play-bill the names of the *authors* will, we hope, be inserted. The printer also has suggested another refinement, which in this Anglo–Gallic age we hope will be duly appreciated; to wit, the precedence now for the first time given to the ladies.

The Tatler, 17 September 1830

Leigh Hunt
Christmas and the Theatre

As the Theatres are closed for two nights, we have no play to criticize for two whole days, an extraordinary event for this journal: nay, we shall be at home for two whole evenings; shall have no mud at six, shall not be living for hours together with our eyes fixed upon people we never spoke to, nor breathe a yard of cold air before us on our return home, nor see the saloup-men dancing and hugging the tips of their fingers under their arms, nor eternally mystify the watchman, who wonders what can induce us to be out 'at that time of night every morning', and unquestionably takes us for a spy, or a coiner, or a lover, or a 'French foreigner', or the man that sets fire to the ricks in Norfolk, or somebody who is 'shown' and so cannot walk by day, or a Jesuit, or the 'gentleman that's missing', or one whose cloak knows more of lace than it appears to do, or some miserly proprietor going to see that his men are up, or a poet (meaning a man avoiding bailiffs) or 'some actor-man', or a tavern-keeper, or the old bachelor who always keeps them up at the Southampton Arms, or 'Mr Smith', or somebody who has something to do with some curious business, or lastly (now he has it, and draws himself up respectfully) the commissioner of police, who goes about to see that the men do their duty.

Watchman: Good morning, Sir.
The Mystery: Good morning. Terribly cold!
Watchman: Terrible, indeed, Sir. (Aside) It can't be the Commissioner. He wants dignity, like. He's too civil-spoken.

The performers cannot know the pleasure of a holiday, as we daily critics do. They have intervals – repeated gaps; and besides, they can be ill. But the scene-shifter must enter into our comforts. To have two whole evenings to himself, not Sunday ones, must be a novelty to him. Suddenly meditative in the midst of his children's gaiety, he thinks how pleasant it is to be sitting there by the fire, instead of thrusting cold summer-bowers upon the stage, or running with one half of a house at his shoulder, to meet Jenkins with the other. The candle-snuffer too must be glad not to enlighten the stage. And the musicians, who nightly warm the feelings of the audience with their charming passages and cold fingers, they too must feel with the critic in this matter, especially if he likes an orchestra as we do, and loves to be near it.

Then there are the poor people who sell fruit out of doors, and the play-bills. They work so hard, and get buffeted by such cruel bleak winds that they must surely look to have their solace on Christmas night. We asked one of them the other evening, who was standing against a corner of the theatre hopping on either foot and wrapping a bit of cloak about her, whether she was not cold. 'Sir,' said she looking us earnestly in the face, 'I am *downright* cold.' Her manner said as much as her simple words. She felt too much to exaggerate. How these people stand it, we can hardly think, but especially the old watchmen, who must feel the cold pierce their bones through and through. They must get into bed (when they do get) like withered bits of ice. And Christmas night, to them, is no Christmas! Thaw them, dear readers, with a cup of your best.

The Tatler, 25 December 1830

Leigh Hunt
Bonnets at the Theatre

In default of having anything better to write about in our present number, we beg leave to remonstrate with certain bonnets, and other enormities, with which the ladies put out our eye-sight in the theatres. The bonnet is the worst. If you sit right behind it, it shall swallow up the whole scene. It makes nothing of a regiment of soldiers, or a mountain, or a forest, or a rising sun, much less of a hero, or of so insignificant a thing as a cottage, and a peasant's family. You may sit at the theatre a whole evening, and not see the leading performer. Liston's face is a glory obscured. The persons in your neighbour-hood provided they have no bonneted ladies before them, shall revel in the jocose looks of Farren or Downton, and provokingly reflect the merriment in their own countenances, while you sit and rage in the shade. If you endeavour to strain a point, and peep by the side of it, ten to one (since Fate notoriously interferes in little things, and delights in being 'contrary', as the young ladies say) – ten to one but the bonnet seizes that very opportunity of jerking side-ways, and cutting off your resources. We have seen an enthusiastic play-goer settle himself in his seat, and evidently congratulate himself at the evening he was about to enjoy, when, a party of ladies swimming into the seats before him, one of them has been the ruin of all his prospects. Even a head-dress, without a bonnet, shall force you to play at bo-peep with the stage half the evening; now extinguishing the face of some favourite actress, and now abolishing a general or a murder. The other night, at the Queen's Theatre, we sometimes found ourselves obliged to peep at the Freemasons in a very symbolical manner, through the loops of a lady's bows. But the bonnet is the enormity. And we are sorry to say that the fair occupants who sit inside them, like the lady in the lobster, too often shew a want of gallantry in refusing to take them off, for, as we have said more than once, we hold gallantry, like all the other virtues, to be a thing mutual, and of no sex; and that a lady shews as much want of gallantry in taking advantage of the delicacies observed towards her by the gentleman as a man does who presumes upon the gentleness of a lady. We felt, the other night, all the reforming spirit of our illustrious predecessors of the *Tatler* and *Spectator* roused within us and in the same exact proportion to our regard for the sex, upon witnessing the following prodigious fact: a lady who came with a party into one of the boxes at Covent-Garden, joined very heartily in expressing her disapprobation of some person in a seat below her, who was dilatory in taking off his hat. It chanced that this lady got into the very seat that he had occupied, and her bonnet turning out to be a much greater blind than the hat, what was the astonishment and the merriment of the complainants, upon finding that she was still less accommodating than the gentleman? Nothing could induce her to perform the very same piece of justice which she had joined in demanding from the other.

We are aware that in modern, as in ancient theatres, ladies come to be seen as well as to see:

Spectatum veniunt, veniunt spectentur ut ipsae.

But we are desirous that they should not pay themselves so ill a compliment as to confound their dresses with themselves; it is the bonnets that are seen, in these cases, and not the ladies. When seen themselves, they make a part of the spectacle, but who cares to look upon these great lumps of gauze and silk? Something we grant, is to be allowed to fashion, but the wearers might be content with showing that their heads could be as absurd as other people's, and then lay aside the absurdity, and show that they understood the better part of being reasonable. They urge, when requested to take their bonnets off, that they 'cannot' do it; meaning, we suppose, besides the will not, which cannot so often signifies, that their heads are not prepared to be seen – that their hair is not dressed in the proper manner; but it would be easy to come with it so dressed; the bonnet is not the only head-dress in fashion; and above all, it would be a graceful and a sensible thing in them to remember that, in coming to a place where the object is to enjoy pleasure, their own capability of pleasure is interested in considering that of others. We never feel angry with a woman, except when she persists in doing something to diminish the delight we take in complimenting the sex.

The Tatler, 23 March 1831

Leigh Hunt
Late Hours at the Theatre

It was our intention to see Mr Reeve in the character of Brutus Hairbrain last night, in the farce of the *Middle Temple*, which was announced in the first instance to be performed between the play and another after-piece;* but as it was afterwards put last, we thought proper to waive the entertainment. It turns out that theatrical readers are not the best patrons of this paper; and we decline killing ourselves with late hours, even for the honour of dying in the service.

Everybody complains of the late hours to which theatrical performances are protracted. The weekly papers complain, the daily papers complain; yet the managers go on, heaping one piece upon another, and sometimes, as in the present instance keeping the best for the last, as if to bribe people to stay. We are to open our mouths, *and shut our eyes*, and see what twelve o'clock will send us. It is like keeping a child up at a late visit, by thrusting another bit of cake into his hand.

What is the reason for this passion for heaping one's plate whether we desire it or not; this loading us, like pretty dears, with five apples to the penny, and a grin of complacency to see how we carry them? We do not complain of Mr Arnold though we suppose he means to load us like the rest, by his saying nothing to the contrary. It was his putting his best attraction last that led us to speak on the subject; and this is the next bad thing to his giving us four pieces for three. Three pieces are often a whole one too many. The Haymarket and other theatres are sometimes not over now-a-days till a good bit past midnight. There is a first piece 'after which' comes another, 'to which will be added' another, and 'to conclude' with a fourth. The linking phrases are varied with all the ingenuity of experience. By and by, we suppose, we shall have 'to be further concluded' by a fifth, 'subsequent to which' a sixth, 'to be followed' by a seventh, and 'the whole to be wound up' with an eighth. 'N.B.: Night-caps and breakfast in the lobbies'.

This dire advantage, or supposed advantage, taken of the English propensity to have enough for their money, originated, there is reason to believe, in the practice that came up at the Haymarket, of giving us three of their small farces for the old stock play and after-piece. The practice was followed by other minor theatres, in order that they might not be outdone in the show of abundance; and at length it increased to its present overwhelming pitch. Each shop was afraid of being out-bid by the others, if it did not clap a fresh piece of cheese on its pennyworth.

Madame Vestris, with the shrewd tact of a woman, was the first to innovate on this custom. She knew that three or four hours of good sprightly entertainment, with the eyes open, was better than pretending to pleasure, half asleep. She announced that her theatre would close at a reasonable hour. It did so;

* At the English Opera House.

and it is understood that she had a remarkably successful season. We are persuaded that if the other theatres would do as much the result would be the same. The young and the old alike both of whom were play-goers twenty years ago, are almost equally shut out from the theatres, when they are so late. The late hours frighten mothers and grandmothers. It is not pleasant to take children away before the entertainments are over, and it is impossible to keep them up till one or two o'clock.

There is a notion perhaps with managers that, because hours in general are thrust forward, and people dine so much later than formerly, they like to find as much for their money when they arrive at the theatres as they used when they dined sooner. But if you look round at theatrical audiences now-a-days, it will be pretty evident that they do not consist of very fashionable people. The lateness of modern hours has indeed been injurious to theatres: and this brings us to another question, upon which we shall say a few words – the supposed decline of a taste for the drama.

We call the decline a supposed one because we cannot think that the taste is less than it was, numerically speaking, though we grant it has shifted quarters. To those who talk of the diminished number of play-goers, it is enough surely to point to the increased number of theatres. We lay little stress upon the causes usually assigned for the decline of play-going, where it has declined – such as high prices, bad plays, bad acting, etc., and, least of all, the immoral state of the lobbies. High prices are not considered by people of fashion; the plays and the acting are both good enough, considering what was tolerated, and even liked, twenty years back, and as to the sights in the lobbies, fashionable eyes are not so squeamish as people fancy them. They would have to differ too often with their own looking-glasses.

The whole secret of the matter we take to be this: first, that the richer classes, besides the drawback of late hours and the diminution of tavern habits on the part of the gentry, have so abounded of late years in the luxuries of new books, music, and visiting, that they have outgrown a disposition to go to the theatre; and, second, that the diffusion of knowledge has been bringing up the uneducated classes to the point where the others left off, and giving them an increase in all sorts of intellectual pleasures, previous to their having anything like a critical knowledge of them, or care for criticism. Ten years hence, perhaps, the trade of a theatrical critic will be better than it is now, and over the water, in preference to the once witty neighbourhood of Covent-Garden. The best thing said by a manger in his playbills, for many years, is what Mr Davidge of the Coburg has said, relative to the classical ground of Southwark, the scene of the triumphs of Shakspeare and Ben Jonson, where Mr Kean is now performing. And this reminds us, that if Mr Davidge will send us tickets, we will go to see his theatre, and give a report of the renewed honours of the neighbourhood.

The Tatler, 7 July 1831

Westland Marston
Play-Going at Sadler's Wells

Sadler's Wells opened, under the management of Mr Phelps and Mrs Warner, on May 27, 1844, with the tragedy of *Macbeth*. Phelps, of course appeared as the guilty Thane, and Mrs Warner as Lady Macbeth. Mr H. Marston was the Macduff, Mr T. H. Lacy the Banquo; while for so small a part as that of 'The Gentlewoman attending Lady Macbeth', the services of that sterling actress, Mrs H. Marston, were secured. A week later *Othello* was performed, with Phelps as the Moor, Mr H. Marston as Iago, Miss Cooper (Mrs T. H. Lacy) as Desdemona, and Mrs Warner as Emilia. In course of time the strength of the Sadler's Wells staff was importantly increased; but even at the outset, it presented a combination of ability to which the Islingtonians had, up to that period, been strangers. A company by which standard plays could be satisfactorily performed, a *mise en scène* emulating that of Macready at the large houses – picturesque and suggestive, but never obtrusively asserting itself over the acting – soon riveted the attention of the Northern suburb and gradually that of entire London. The Islington paterfamilias perceived that he had at his door a source of healthy and intellectual pleasure which the West End could not rival – nay, which at that date it could scarcely be said to present. As one great legitimate work followed another, the attractions of the little theatre spread, until it became a sort of pilgrim's shrine to the literary men of London, to the younger members of the Inns of Court, and to those denizens of the West in whom poetic taste still lingered. In the audience itself there seemed a parallel, in those dark days of the drama, between the adherents of the poetic school and the adherents of a proscribed faith of religion. A respectful, almost solemn hush pervaded the house during the less exciting scenes of a play, while the applause when a telling situation occurred conveyed something far beyond the usual tribute to an actor's skill. There was a fervour of demonstration to the chief performers (especially in the case of Phelps) which meant the recognition of great services. I have heard the execution of some passage in a tragedy hailed with something of the excitement which might have followed a political manifesto. The tenants of the pit would spring up from their seats, gaze at each other in delight, and gesticulate their admiration. It was felt that there was a *Cause*, scarcely less than sacred, to support, and that Phelps was its apostle. At times, though rarely, the enthusiasm of the gallery or the pit found vent in apostrophes, such as, 'Splendid, Phelps – splendid!' or, in later times, when a rival tragedian had assumed rule at the Princess's, 'Ah! where's Charlie Kean now?'

Our Recent Actors, Vol. II, 1888

Henry James
The London Theatres in 1877

. . . The first step in the rather arduous enterprise of going to the theatre in London is, I think, another reminder that the arts of the stage are not really in the temperament and the manners of the people. The first step is to go to an agency in an expensive street out of Piccadilly, and there purchase a stall for the sum of eleven shillings. You receive your ticket from the hands of a smooth, sleek, bottle-nosed clerk, who seems for all the world as if he had stepped straight out of a volume of Dickens or of Thackeray. There is almost always an old lady taking seats for the play, with a heavy carriage in waiting at the door; the number of old ladies whom one has to squeeze past in the stalls is in fact very striking. 'Is it good?' asks the old lady of the gentleman I have described, with a very sweet voice and a perfectly expressionless face (she means the play, not the seat). 'It is thought very good, my lady', says the clerk, as if he were uttering a 'response' in church; and my lady being served, I approach with my humbler petition. The dearness of places at the London theatres is sufficient indication that play-going is not a popular amusement; three dollars is a high price to pay for the privilege of witnessing any London performance that I have seen (one goes into the stalls of the Théâtre Français for eight francs). In the house itself everything seems to contribute to the impression which I have tried to indicate – the impression that the theatre in England is a social luxury and not an artistic necessity. The white-cravatted young man who inducts you into your stall, and having put you in possession of a programme, extracts from you, masterly but effectually, a sixpence which, as a stranger, you have wondered whether you might venture to give him, and which has seemed a mockery of his grandeur – this excellent young man is somehow the keynote of the whole affair. An English audience is as different as possible from a French, though the difference is altogether by no means to its disadvantage. It is much more 'genteel'; it is less Bohemian, less *blasé*, more *naïf*, and more respectful – to say nothing of being made up of handsomer people. It is well dressed, tranquil, motionless; it suggests domestic virtue and comfortable homes; it looks as if it had come to the play in its own carriage, after a dinner of beef and pudding. The ladies are mild, fresh-coloured English mothers; they all wear caps; they are wrapped in knitted shawls. There are many rosy young girls, with dull eyes and quiet cheeks – an element wholly absent from Parisian audiences. The men are handsome and honourable looking; they are in evening dress; they come with the ladies – usually with several ladies – and remain with them; they sit still in their places, and don't go herding out between the acts with their hats askew. Altogether they are much more the sort of people to spend a quiet evening with than the clever, cynical, democratic multitude that surges nightly out of the brilliant Boulevards into those temples of the drama in which MM. Dumas, *fils*, and Sardou are the high priests. But you might spend your evening with them better almost anywhere than at the theatre.

As I said just now, they are much more *naïf* than Parisian spectators – at least as regards being amused. They cry with much less facility, but they laugh more freely and heartily. I remember nothing in Paris that corresponds with the laugh of the English gallery and pit – with its continuity and simplicity, its deep-lunged jollity and its individual guffaws. But you feel that an English audience is intellectually much less appreciative. A Paris audience, as regards many of its factors, is cynical, sceptical, indifferent, it is so intimately used to the theatre that it doesn't stand on ceremony; it yawns, and looks away and turns its back; it has seen too much, and it knows too much. But it has the critical and the artistic sense, when the occasion appeals to them; it can judge and discriminate. It has the sense of form and of manner; it heeds and cares how things are done, even when it cares little for the things themselves. Bohemians, artists, critics, connoisseurs – all Frenchmen come more or less under these heads, which give the tone to a body of Parisian spectators. They do not strike one as 'nice people' in the same degree as a collection of English patrons of the drama – though doubtless they have their own virtues and attractions; but they form a natural, sympathetic public, while the English audience forms only a conventional, accidental one. It may be that the drama and other works of art are best appreciated by people who are not 'nice'; it may be that a lively interest in such matters tends to undermine niceness; it may be that, as the world grows nicer, various forms of art will grow feebler. All this *may* be; I don't pretend to say it is; the idea strikes me *en passant*. . . .

The Galaxy, May 1877

G. B. Shaw
Her Majesty's

When Mr Beerbohm Tree is called to his last audit by the Recording Angel, the account will shew two prominent items on opposite sides. The credit one will be Her Majesty's Theatre; the debit, Falstaff. And we can imagine Mr Tree thereupon exclaiming, 'You are a pretty sort of Recording Angel. Why, everybody – except one fool of a Saturday Reviewer – is agreed that my Falstaff was a masterpiece, whereas that theatre nearly ruined me and brought me no more thanks than if I had built a new shop in Oxford Street.' I may be in too great a hurry in anticipating such public ingratitude; but I have a very poor opinion of London in its collective capacity. It is alike incapable of appreciating a benefit and of resenting an outrage. For example, one of the finest views in the world is within a minute's walk of Charing Cross. Go down Villiers Street and ascend the first stairs to your right after you pass the music-hall. This brings you into the loggia attached to the wall of the South-Eastern terminus, and leading to the Hungerford footbridge. He who designed this loggia was no Orcagna, though he had such a chance as Orcagna never had in Florence. It is a dismal square hole in a mass of dirty bricks, through which men hurry with loathing. Yet if you look out through one of the holes – preferably the last but one – made for the convenience of the east wind, you will find the view magnificent. Right into one of the foci of that view, London, without a murmur, permitted Mr Jabez Balfour to dump the building which is now the Hotel Cecil, just as it allowed the London Pavilion Music Hall to spoil Piccadilly Circus. If that building had darkened the smallest window of a rag and bone shop, the proprietor thereof would have been supported by all the might of the State in maintaining his 'ancient lights'. But because all London – nay, all the world that visits London – was injured, there was no placard with 'Ancient View' on it put up in that grimy loggia. If the malefactor had confined himself to injuring the public collectively, he would by this time have been one of our most eminent citizens. Unfortunately, he trifled with private property; and we instantly stretched out our hand to the uttermost parts of the earth whither he had fled; seized him; and cast him into prison. If the question had been one of beneficence instead of maleficence, we should have shewn the same hyperaesthesia to a private advantage, the same anaesthesia to a public one. Mr Tree has given London a theatre. There is nothing in that by itself: a theatre is rather a promising speculation just at present; and in England theatres can be built more cheaply than anywhere else in the world: in fact, calculating the cost in the usual way per head of the seating capacity of the house, we find that whereas in some Continental cities, where the theatre rivals the parliament house or the cathedral as a public building, the cost is over £300 a head, in England we have achieved the commercial triumph of getting the cost down to £7. If Mr Tree had allowed his public spirit to carry him to the length of £10 per head, and then celebrated his first night by presenting every lady in the audience with a locket and every gentleman with a cigarette case (by arrangement with the advertising agents), his munificence would have been extolled to the skies, and the compliments to his public spirit and the handsomeness of his theatre would have been word for word just as they are at present; for to the Press a manager is a manager, and whether he gives you a theatre like Terry's or one like Daly's or the Garrick or the Palace, the acknowledgments are the same.

Under these circumstances the fact that Her Majesty's is no £7 commercial affair, but quite the handsomest theatre in London, must go altogether to the credit of Mr Tree's public spirit and artistic conscience. I do not mean that more money has been spent on Her Majesty's than Mr D'Oyly Carte lavished so splendidly on his New English Opera House, now the Palace Music-hall.

I should not be surprised to hear that, if a few special items are left out of the question, Mr Tree has spent less in proportion than Mr Hare or Mr Daly. He has had the good sense – a very rare quality in England where artistic matters are in question – to see that a theatre which is panelled, and mirrored, and mantel-pieced like the first-class saloon of a Peninsular and Oriental liner or a Pullman drawing room car, is no place for Julius Caesar, or indeed for anything except tailor-made drama and farcical comedy. When you enter it you do not feel that you have walked into a Tottenham Court Road shop window or smirk with a secret sense of looking as if you kept a carriage and belonged to a smart club; you feel that you are in a place where high scenes are to be enacted and dignified things to be done. And this is the first quality a theatre should have. The old theatres, with all their false notions of splendour and their barbarous disregard of modern ideas of health, comfort, and decency, always kept this in view and that is why the best of them, when supplemented by a couple of adjacent houses and modified by a little re-arrangement and sanitary engineering, are better than the theatres of the Robertsonian era, with their first-class-carriage idealism. Nobody can say of Her Majesty's that it proclaims itself a place built by a snob for the entertainment of snobs with snobbish plays. It rises spaciously and brilliantly to the dignity of art; and if its way of doing so is still elegantly rhetorical and Renascent in conception, yet that style is not altogether the wrong one for a theatre; and it is wonderfully humanized and subtilized by the influence of modern anti-Renaissance ideas on the decoration. For this Mr Romaine-Walker cannot be too generously praised. He has stepped in just at the point where Mr Phipps might have spoiled as a decorator what he has wrought as an architect. M. Hofler's Fontainebleau chandelier fits into the decorative scheme perfectly; and Mr Dignam's stained canvas act drop, which produces the effect of an impossibly expensive Gobelins tapestry, is a convincing discovery of what an act drop ought to be, though I make no excuse for Coypel or for Dido and Eneas (Raphael's Parnassus, the act drop of the old theatre, was a much happier subject). And so we get the new beauty with the old elevation of sentiment. The Lyceum and Drury Lane, old as they are, would, if they were destroyed, be regretted as the Garrick and Daly's would never be regretted, but not more than Her Majesty's, which has as yet no associations.

Although the practical comfort of the audience has been carefully and intelligently looked after, there are one or two points in which I am not sure that I should exactly copy Her Majesty's if I were building a theatre myself. The perfectly horizontal stage is of course to be preferred for some purposes to the ordinary sloping one. Most playgoers have seen and laughed at the way in which a pencil, stick, or log of firewood accidentally dropped on the stage rolls down the stage to the footlights; but few of them understand the difficulties raised by the slope now that 'flats' stand at angles to the footlights instead of parallel to them, as in the age of 'wings'. On the other hand, the more the stage slopes, the less steeply need the auditorium be banked up to command a view of it, and it must be confessed that the view of the stage from the back rows of the gallery at Her Majesty's is as foreshortened as that from the operatic altitudes of Covent Garden with its many tiers of boxes. This gallery will not, I understand, be always used; but it seems to me that it would be better, instead of wasting it on ordinary occasions, to set it apart at a charge of sixpence or even less for such faithful supporters of high art as the working-man with a taste for serious drama – especially Shakespeare – and the impecunious student, male and female, who will go to the stalls or balcony later in life. These people would not, like the shilling god, expect the drama to be written down to them; and once they found their way to the gallery it would never be empty. For the working-man connoisseurs, though they represent a very small percentage of their class, yet belong to an enormously large class, and so are absolutely more numerous than might be expected from their relative scarcity.

Further, I would abolish all upholstery in the nature of plush and velvet. Its contact with the sitter is so clingingly intimate that it stops the circulation in the smaller vessels near the skin, so that the playgoer at last finds himself afflicted with 'pins and needles' from the small of his back to his calves. At Bayreuth there is no upholstery – only a broad, cane-bottomed seat. This gets rid of the stuffiness which makes the stalls of some theatres less wholesome than the pit; but it would prove rather Spartan accommodation after a time if the audience did not leave the theatre for an hour between each act. In London we require cushions; but they should be covered with woollen cloth, and the stuffing should be unadulterated. At Her Majesty's the three rows of stalls next the pit, which are to be had for six shillings, are not plushy; so that to the man who sits down sensitively and knows the realities of things from the conventions, they are better upholstered than the half-guinea seats covered in velvet.

The first night was exceeding glorious. Our unique English loyalty – consisting in a cool, resolute determination to get the last inch of advertisement out of the Royal Family – has seldom been better pushed. Not a man in the house but felt that the Jubilee was good for trade. Mr Tree told us that he would never disgrace the name the theatre bore; and his air as he spoke was that of a man who, on the brink of forgery, arson and bigamy, was saved by the feeling that the owner of Her Majesty's Theatre must not do such things. Mr Alfred Austin contributed as straightforward and business-like a piece of sycophancy in rhyme as ever a Poet Laureate penned; and Mrs Tree recited it with an absence of conviction that was only emphasized by her evident desire to please us all. Miss Clara Butt shewed what a Royal College of Music can make of a magnificent voice in singing 'God Save the Queen' at full length (with a new verse thrown in) alternately with the Queen's Hall choir, the whole audience standing up determinedly meanwhile, with the Prince of Wales representing Royalty at one corner, Mr Labouchere representing Republicanism at the other, and the British Public representing Good Taste (formerly known as Hypocrisy) in the middle. The contents of the pay-boxes, it was announced, amid the enthusiasm of those who, like myself, had not paid for their seats, are to be handed over to the Prince of Wales's Ratepayers' Relief Fund. The proceedings terminated with a play, in which Mr and Mrs

Tree, Miss Kate Rorke, Miss Janette Steer, Mr Lewis Waller, Mr Lionel Brough, Mr Brookfield, Mr Murray Carson, Mr Mollison, Mr Holmes-Gore, Mr Gerald Du Maurier, and about a dozen other artists had the honour of appearing.

The Saturday Review, 1 May 1897

Max Beerbohm
In the Pit

It was with much diffidence that I wrote, last week, about Mr Sutro's new play. Usually I am well up in my subject – have a vivid impression to analyse. But of *The Fascinating Mr Vanderveldt* I had only a very faint and hazy notion. Had I not happened to read a description of the play before I visited it, I could hardly have gathered any notion at all. Only through previous knowledge of what the characters were, and what they were doing, was I enabled to form enough of an opinion to write an article. A very uninteresting article I thought it when I read it last Sunday morning. I did not blame myself, though. No man can write well about a thing which he has had no chance of mastering at first hand.

How, you ask, had this chance been withheld from me? Well, three or four years ago I began to get on Mr Arthur Bourchier's nerves. He no longer wanted my hints on the art of acting, and so, as a hint on the art of criticism, he ceased to send me tickets for his theatre. Since then, I have not intruded at the Garrick Theatre, except once or twice when Mr Bourchier has produced something that I was really anxious to see. I wanted to see Mr Sutro's play; so to the Garrick again I went; but, on my arrival, found myself suffering under the disability common to lads who are going to carve out a future in this great metropolis: I had only half a crown in my pocket. To find my way to the pit entrance, thrust my coin through a pigeon-hole, clutch at a brass ticket, and descend a narrow flight of stone stairs, was for me the work of a moment. I had no misgivings. Though I had never happened to see a play from the pit, and my heart was leaping with the sense of adventure, I knew no fear. How often, passing this or that theatre, hours before the performance, had I seen a serried row of men and women doggedly waiting outside the door that led to the pit! Was it likely that they would spend their valuable time thus if there were not a great treat in store for them? The Pit? There was a certain traditional magic in the sound. There was some secret of joy that I had often wished to elucidate. 'I enclose my card, and am, Sir, your obedient servant, AN OLD PITTITE.' How often in the newspapers had I read letters with this conclusion! And such letters – so oracular, permeated with so notable a pride! It had often been borne in on me that there must be in the pit something – some mystic grace – that enables a man to judge more surely, to take himself more seriously, and to spend a happier evening, than elsewhere. . . . It was with a glad heart that I bounded down the stone steps.

Gradually my eyes accustomed themselves to the darkness, and I groped my way to a vacant space that I discovered on the backmost bench. Not until I was seated did I realize that the play had begun. Yes, there, at a distance of what seemed to be fifty dark miles or so, was a patch of yellowish light; and therein certain tiny figures were moving. They were twittering, too, these figures. I listened intently. I strained my ears, I strained my eyes. And, since both my sight and my hearing are excellent, and since, as I have told you, I had read a detailed notice of the play, I was enabled to get some sort of vague illusion – the sort of illusion that one gets from a marionette show. I felt with my hand the back of the bench in front of me, hoping to find there a steel cylinder with a slot. Perhaps, however, it is just as well that a man in the pit cannot obtain a telescope in the way he can obtain a pair of opera-glasses in the stalls. If the mimes were so clarified and magnified for him that he could realize the changing expressions of their faces, then the faintness of their voices would seem to him all the stranger – would be all the more detrimental to his illusion of reality. So intensely, at the Garrick, did I have to listen, in order not to miss what the mimes were saying, that I thought there was perhaps something peculiar in the acoustics of the Garrick pit. I have consulted several frequenters of pits, and they tell me that the Garrick pit is a rather good one. Certainly Mr Bourchier, Miss Vanbrugh, Mr Aubrey Smith and other persons engaged in *The Fascinating Mr Vandervelt* are not bad elocutionists. And yet, the other day, with all my attention, I was constantly failing to overhear them, and having to use my experience of plays in general as a means of guessing at the drift. I saw an infinitesimal miniature of Miss Vanbrugh cross the stage and lay its hands in the hands of another lady who was just visible to the naked eye. And I heard this sound: 'Want – pew'. From the context of the play, and from the deportment of the two actresses, I was able to guess that Miss Vanbrugh had just said, 'I want to help you.' Probably my guess was right. But still, it is a bore to be kept guessing; and I was kept guessing in this way, from time to time, throughout the performance. The only members of the cast who never failed to make their words audible to me were Miss Henrietta Watson and Mr Charles Goodhart. To the latter I owed another debt of gratitude, inasmuch as I could see him smile. Mr Bourchier's smile, also, I could see, quite distinctly. For the rest, no facial expression was anywhere discernible. Had I been sitting in the stalls, I should doubtless have accused Mr Bourchier of 'clowning' – of smiling more widely than he ought to in a not farcical part. You may remember that last week I complimented him on having acquired the restraint needed for comedy. But he must not preen himself overmuch on that compliment. What seems like restraint to the man in the pit may seem like violent over-acting to the man in the stalls. And what seems like restraint to the man in the stalls may be a mere blank, a vacuum, to the man in the pit. Everything depends on the point of view.

The relativity of things occupied my mind throughout the entr'actes of the play. Here was I, who am accustomed to occupy a comfortable stall without paying anything for it, and to see the mimes life-sized, and to hear them quite distinctly. And yet I seldom enjoy a play – nearly always have to console myself with the reflection that I am going to be paid by this *Review* for my presence. Here, on the other hand, were people who are accustomed to pay for their uncomfortable seats, and who are not going to receive any payment for sitting on them and straining their eyes and ears for sight and sound of distant marionettes. And these people, obviously, are not rebellious. They really are glad to be there. Strange! For the constant pittite, no doubt, the strain of eyes and ears is less than for me. His eyes and ears must have been somewhat habituated by time. Moreover, if he has never happened to sit in a stall, he will not be conscious how much of the play and of the performance he is missing. Like Plato's cavemen, who knew naught but the shadows cast against the inner wall, and who would have been sorely puzzled by the realities, the constant pittite, doubtless, accepts as real creatures the tiny puppets vouchsafed to him. He accepts them, I mean, as the nearest approach that can in a playhouse be made to reality. I imagine that as seen from the gallery, and even from the 'upper circle', the puppets must be still less life-like than as seen from the pit. And, since these three parts of the theatre hold the majority of the audience, I begin to understand why there is so little demand for dramatic truth to life. To me, sitting in the stalls, the persons of a play look very like human beings, and I want them to be allowed to behave accordingly. I am in a position to take them seriously. But to the majority of the audience they are little more than performing fleas. If I went to criticize a troupe of performing fleas, I should not write and attack their trainer because their performance had not closely tallied with my experience of human beings. I should not go to be instructed. I should go to be amused. It is in this spirit, necessarily, that the majority of people go to the play. They know that they cannot see anything that will remind them of actual life. What matter, then, how great be the degree of remoteness from reality? The marvel to me, since my visit to the pit of the Garrick, is not that the public cares so little for dramatic truth, but that it can sometimes tolerate a play which is not either the wildest melodrama or the wildest farce. Where low tones and fine shades are practically invisible, one would expect an exclusive insistence on splodges of garish colour. . . . I shall in future be less hard on the public than has been my wont.

The Saturday Review, 12 May 1906

III The Drama

Melodrama

William Hazlitt
John du Bart

John Du Bart is said to have made a great noise in his life-time; but it was nothing to the noise he makes at present at Covent-Garden Theatre, with his good ship Fame, and his gallant son Francis. We very much doubt, whether the vessel in which the great John forced his way out of Dunkirk harbour, was equal in size to the one in which Mr Farley pipes all hands on board, and assaults the chandeliers and side-boxes of the Theatre-Royal. The ladies, like so many Andromedas, were thrown into evident consternation at the approach of this sea-monster. To what a degree of perfection the useful and elegant arts must have been carried in a country, where a real ship, as large as the life, can be brought on the stage, to the amazement and confusion of the audience! Speaking within compass, the man of war which is now got up at Covent-Garden, is full as large as any of the flotilla which last year ploughed the bosom of the Serpentine River, and the sea-fight with which the Managers have favoured us before Christmas, is as interesting as that which took place in Hyde Park, between the English and American squadrons, under the tasteful direction of the Prince Regent. We pronounce this the most non-sensical farce (with the exception perhaps of the one just alluded to) we were ever present at. The utmost that the poet or the mechanist could have aspired to, must have been to produce the effects of a first sea-voyage. There lay the ship of John Du Bart for half an hour, rocking about on crape waves, with the sun rising on one side, and night coming on in a thunder-storm on the other, guns firing, and the orchestra playing; Mr Farley on board, bawling himself hoarse, looking like the master of a Dutch squabber, or still more like the figure at the mast-head; Miss Booth as busy as she could make herself; Mr Treby and Mr Truman doing nothing; Mr Hamerton with a hat and feathers, as the Crown Prince of Poland; Mr Tokely very much at home drinking punch, and Mr Liston (the only sensible man on board) wishing himself in any other situation. If any thing were wanting to complete the dizziness of brain produced by all this, it was supplied by the music of Mr Bishop, who kept firing a perpetual broadside on the ears of the audience. From the overture to the finale, we heard nothing but

Guns, drums, trumpets, blunderbuss, and thunder!

Never since the invention of French Opera was there such an explosion of dissonant sounds. If this is music, then the clashing of bells, the letting off of rockets and detonating balls, or the firing a pistol close at your ear on an illumination night, is music. *John Du Bart* is taken from the French; and from the plot and sentiments, it is not difficult to guess the date of the French piece. It turns upon the preference due to an elected over an hereditary prince; and the chief actors are made to utter such sentiments as this, that 'treason consists in supporting a monarch on the throne in opposition to the voice of the people.' We wonder it is suffered to be acted – since the hundred days are over!

The Examiner, 29 October 1815

William Hazlitt
The Vampyre

The new Dramatic Romance (or whatever it is called) of the *Vampyre** is, upon the whole, the most splendid *spectacle* we have ever seen. It is taken from a French piece, founded on the celebrated story so long bandied about between Lord Byron, Mr Shelley, and Dr Polidori, which last turned out to be the true author. As a mere fiction, and as a fiction attributed to Lord Byron, whose genius is chartered for the land of horrors, the original story passed well enough: but on the stage it is a little shocking to the feelings, and incongruous to the sense, to see a spirit in a human shape – in the shape of a real Earl, and, what is more, of a Scotch Earl – going about seeking whom it may marry and then devour, to lengthen out its own abhorred and anomalous being. Allowing for the preternatural atrocity of the fable, the situations are well imagined and supported: the acting of Mr T. P. Cooke (from the Surry Theatre) was spirited and imposing, and certainly Mrs W. H. Chatterley, as the daughter of his friend the Baron (Mr Bartley) and his destined bride, bid fair to be a very delectable victim. She is however saved in a surprising manner, after a rapid succession of interesting events, to the great joy of the spectator. The scenery of this piece is its greatest charm, and it is inimitable. We have seen sparkling and overpowering effects of this kind before; but to the splendour of a transparency were here added all the harmony and mellowness of the finest painting. We do not speak of the vision at the beginning, or of that at the

* English Opera House.

end of the piece – though these were admirably managed – so much as of the
representation of the effects of moonlight on the water and on the person of
the dying knight. The hue of the sea-green waves, floating in the pale beam
under an arch-way of grey weather-beaten rocks, and with the light of a torch
glaring over the milder radiance, was in as fine keeping and strict truth as
Claude or Rembrandt, and would satisfy, we think, the most fastidious artist's
eye. It lulled the sense of sight as the fancied sound of the dashing waters
soothed the imagination. In the scene where the moonlight fell on the dying
form of Ruthven (the Vampyre) it was like a fairy glory, forming a palace of
emerald light: the body seemed to drink its balmy essence, and to revive in it
without a miracle. The line, 'See how the moon sleeps with Endymion',
came into the mind from the beauty and gorgeousness of the picture, notwithstanding the repugnance of every circumstance and feeling. This melodrama succeeds very well: and it succeeds in spite of Mr Kean's last nights,
and without Miss Kelly!

'The Drama', No. IX, *The London Magazine*, September 1820

G. H. Lewes
The Day of Reckoning

THE PERFECTION OF ACTING

If you desire to see really perfect acting, rush to the Lyceum and be
astonished at *The Day of Reckoning*. Astonishment elevates your eyebrows at
the Lyceum venturing upon a French *drame* instead of its customary farces,
comedies, and burlesques – a drame, too, prohibited in Paris because of its
revolutionary tendency (poor Parisians!) – a drame presenting the ignoble
scenes of the *tapis franc* – a burglary – attempted assassination – scoundrelism
of various kinds – and, finally, a bloody duel, cutting short the existence
of – Charles Mathews of all persons in the world! – a drame contrasting the
blouse and the frock coat – the rich and the poor – the law's injustice and the
villainy of the great; – a drame which, in its original shape, *L'Enfant de Paris*,
excited the invective of Jules Janin through twelve columns, to the virtuous
indignation of his author, Emile Souvestre, who protested his drame was
perfectly moral; well, this drame you find altered from five acts to three, and
otherwise improved by the accomplished Planché, and presented to a thrilled
Lyceum audience! Having recovered your astonishment at this venture and

its perfect success – having been astonished at the *mise en scène* (but you are accustomed to that in this theatre) – the lasting astonishment is that Vestris should perform a pathetic, noble woman, and perform it as no actress on our stage could do it! *That* is something to marvel at. Vestris, the greatest pet of the public, will startle even her greatest admirers in this part; for, assuredly, no one ever believed her powers lay at all in that direction. Yet I assure you her acting is quite a study. My readers have learned by this time that I am not a very great admirer of modern acting, and if, when I *do* admire, I express myself enthusiastically, yet I am not easily roused to enthusiasm; and I declare to them that the acting of Vestris and Charles Mathews in the new piece gave me more unmixed delight – more exquisite enjoyment – than I have for a long while received from the English stage. All the freshness of early enjoyment came back upon me, and no boy ever relished his first play more!

The secret of all this? Nothing can be simpler. Vestris and Charles Mathews were *natural* – nothing more, nothing less. They were a lady and gentleman such as we meet in drawing-rooms, graceful, quiet, well-bred, perfectly dressed, perfectly oblivious of the footlights. He is a polished villain – a D'Orsay without conscience, and without any of the scowlings, stampings, or intonations of the approved stage villain. There are scoundrels in high life – but they are perfectly well-bred. Whatever faults there may be in their conduct, their deportment is irreproachable. This is the villain represented by Charles Mathews – a man of fashion, reckless, extravagant, heartless, but perfectly unconscious of his being worse than his neighbours. Those who are familiar with his *Used Up* will understand how he represents the quiet elegance of the part; but they must see him in this to appreciate his refined villainy, cool self-possession, and gentlemanly devilishness. In every detail of his dress, in every gesture, and in every look, I recognized an artist representing Nature. It is, of course, a higher thing to play Othello or Macbeth, and I do not wish to exaggerate the importance of this part; but I say that in this part he plays *to perfection*: a Teniers may not be a Raphael, but it is worth a hundred ambitious attempts at Raphael.

This reliance upon Nature is what touches me so in Vestris. Her character is one which in most hands would become insipid or melodramatic: a sad, neglected wife, loving another man, of whom her husband is jealous and solacing her unhappiness by constant beneficence to the poor – a noble, loving, suffering woman, she stands there represented with a truth, a grace, a gentle pathos I have no epithets to characterize. The sad dignity with which she bears her husband's insults, the terror which agitates her when that husband intimates his knowledge that her lover is in an adjoining room, and that he, the husband, is permitted by the law to kill him – these things are represented in a manner very unlike that current on the stage – and recall the finished art of French comedy. I am well aware that a little ranting and 'letting down the back hair' would have 'told' upon the audience with more noisy effect; but the difference is, that I carry away from the theatre an exquisite picture, on which it is delightful to dwell, which reflection tells me was perfect in its art; and if the audience did not shout hoarse bravos at the time, they felt it quite as vividly, and will go to see it again and again, certain of being charmed.

Oh, what a contrast between the natural manner of these two and the stage manner and stage life of all the rest! Yet the others *played* well too – notably Frank Matthews (a real bit of character!), Roxby, and George Vining. But the contrast was between sunshine and the footlights – the ruddy cheek and the rouged cheek – the grace of a graceful woman and that of an opera dancer. I insist upon this point, for the public, the critics, and the actors may here read a valuable lesson as to what constitutes acting: a thing at present they seem to have the wildest notions of, and the ignorance of the public reacts upon the performer, forcing him often to disobey his own conceptions to gain their ignorant applause.

The Leader, 7 December 1850

Joseph Knight
Drink

7 JUNE 1879

M. Emile Zola's *L'Assommoir* may be said to represent a crisis in the long struggle between Idealists and Naturalists. Great, therefore, was the excitement produced in Paris when a dramatic version of the novel was announced, a presentation of its most daring and salient features under 'the fierce light that beats upon a *stage*' being confidently expected. It can hardly be said, however, that this expectation was fulfilled in the work given at the Ambigu. The protracted fight between the rival washerwomen was reduced to the discharge of one or two pailfuls of water by each combatant, and to a single encounter with the *battoirs*, the more gross details of the engagement being necessarily suppressed. The disgusting effects of intoxication, though presented even too vividly, were curtailed and softened, and much besides that produced revulsion in the reader was most properly withheld from the spectator. *Drink*,* the version of *L'Assommoir* by Mr Charles Reade, produced on Monday, avoids still more completely the scenes that were most objected to in the book; so that neither in Paris nor in London has the question been clearly raised in a dramatic shape whether the facts of real life carry with them an inherent right to reproduction in art. Of *Drink* it may be said that it

* Princess's Theatre.

contains no scene that has not its fair vindication in the motives of the piece. The baneful effects of drunkenness cannot, of course, be set forth without some painful and offensive details, but these are no further exhibited than the necessary connection between cause and consequence makes inevitable. Mr Reade's drama resolves itself into a picture of domestic happiness invaded and ruined by a fatal propensity.

Its success was due to a combination of causes, *Drink* is not a strongly built play. It consists rather of a succession of tableaux than of a well-knit story. The persons who figure in it do not greatly engage interest either by their worth or by their individuality, nor is the interest which they do excite either of a high or subtle kind. The positions in which they appear, however, are novel and lifelike. As much may be said of the scenery, which includes some striking and characteristic views of Paris. Finally, Mr Charles Warner's rendering of Coupeau – the central figure of the group – was of marked excellence. The actor's genial tenderness and bonhomie as the husband and father, in the scene which ends with his fall from the scaffold – one of the chief effects of the piece – were delightfully easy and natural, and his picture in the closing scene of the drunkard alternately repelled and magnetized by the fatal bottle, then a prey to the terrible spectres which crowd upon his delirium, merits no common praise. Much of his acting here was as subdued and varied as it was truthful and impressive, while the climax of his terror, though appalling and necessarily repellent, was not overcharged. To Mr William Rignold fell the part of the model artisan Gouget, who rises to be a master in his craft. The Gouget of *Drink* has nothing of the shy taciturnity which in the novel half conceals his vein of tenderness. On the contrary, he is bluff and outspoken. Mr Rignold was not deficient in vigour. He delivered his temperance homilies with an energy that denotes conviction. His fault is that in his impersonation he has only one manner. Sturdy honesty of style will not cover all the requirements of a character even so much on the surface as the Gouget of *Drink*. Mr Redmund had few opportunities as the insidious rascal Lantier; he did not turn these few to the best account. A word of commendation is due to Mr T. P. Haynes, who infused into the inebriety of Mes Bottes a touch of that sly enjoyment with which M. Dailly invests the same personage in Paris. Miss Amy Roselle, capable of strong indignation, but frank, winning and devoted, was quite equal to the general claims of Gervaise; in the crisis of pathos and suffering she left, however, something to be desired. Miss Ada Murray gave such open warning of her evil dispositions by the fixed sinister look that it was marvellous Gervaise could have been deceived by her professions of forgiveness and friendship. The gay, good-hearted Phoebe Sage – an interpolation of the dramatist – was agreeably sketched by Miss Fanny Leslie. A little lady named Katie Barry represented simply and effectively the character of Nana, Coupeau's daughter. It is a relief to find that in *Drink* Nana remains a child throughout, and does not develop to the precocious vice of the grown-up girl.

Theatrical Notes, 1893

Dutton Cook
The Lights o' London

Mr Sims's *Lights o' London** is a five-act melodrama of the good old Adelphi pattern. The story deals exclusively with English life, abounds in stir and incident, blends to the audience many familiar sights and scenes. Albert Smith's playwright, Mr Glenalvon Fogg, it may be remembered, held that the secret of success in dramatic composition consisted 'in showing people what they know something about'. On the stage, indeed, it is the known rather than the unknown that is accepted as the marvellous or the admirable; our audiences love old acquaintances. Acknowledging this opinion, Mr Sims has brought into his play excellent pictures of the Borough Market on Saturday night, of the exterior of a casual ward, of the interior of a police station, of the 'slips' in Regent's Park, with the Regent's Canal and its bridges; and these exhibitions assuredly cordial recognition and applause. It must not be understood, however, that *The Lights o' London* is a mere panoramic play, dependent for its success upon two or three strong mechanical effects, or that the author is but a subaltern to such captains as the stage-carpenter or the scene-painter. Mr Sims does not simply address himself to the eyes of his public; he compels them to listen, he interests them deeply, he is now humorous and now pathetic, he persuades them to laugh and to weep alternately. It may be objected that there is nothing absolutely novel about Mr Sims's fable, and that many of his characters and his situations are rather of the conventional type. But, without doubt, the dramatist has made good use of his materials, however trite these in truth may be; has brought to bear upon his subject a force and freshness of thought and treatment peculiar to himself. The first act, which is what Mr Boucecault would call of a 'proloquial' character, seemed to me of somewhat over-artificial construction and to move stiffly; the personages of the plot appeared to suffer from the strain of dramatic exigency, to conduct themselves less according to the laws of reason and probability than in obedience to the arbitrary dictates of the author. But in the second act the comic characters arrived upon the scene, the story developed new sources of interest and excitement, and an impressive interview between an itinerant showman and an escaped convict – a very ingenious commingling of genuine pathos and broad comicality – fairly launched the play upon its very prosperous voyage. After this all was plain sailing; and the audience missed no opportunity of expressing their hearty approval of the *Lights o' London*, its author, and interpreters.

Of course one knows beforehand that for our melodramas a comfortable conclusion is always in store, and that those who wait long enough may depend upon seeing poetical or theatrical justice fully vindicated: virtue will surely triumph, while vice will be duly abased and punished. The time comes at last when the tables are turned, the suffering poor change places with the

* Princess's Theatre.

guilty rich, the mighty are put down from their seat and the humble and meek are exalted; while as matters of detail the stolen jewels revert to their lawful proprietor, the lost will comes to light, the forger is hurried away detected and punished, for the innocent convict a royal pardon is forthcoming, and the true heir obtains possession of the valuable estates he has been so long and unrighteously deprived of. But if these happy issues are invariable results, the means by which the author designs to attain them are less apparent, and the spectators are interested in the struggles of the dramatis personae to emerge from their labyrinthine difficulties and reach the rewards and the joys of the catastrophe. Mr Sims is, I think, particularly happy in what I may call masking the batteries of his invention; he supplies his story every now and then with a new impetus, and so contrives that the incidents of the drama, however expected they may be, shall yet occur with the suddenness which ensures popular admiration and applause. Of course the work is of no great pretence, is indeed a direct bid for the favour of a miscellaneous audience, and does not disdain upon occasion recourse to time-honoured clap-traps and the indulgence of various British prejudices. At the same time Mr Sims is a skilled author, who imparts an appreciable literary flavour to his productions, who writes dexterously and wittily, with abundant humour at command, and an intimate knowledge of many phases of London life, and whose sentiments and sympathies are as honestly felt as they are forcibly expressed. *The Lights o' London* pleased the audience beyond measure; was received with an extraordinary show of favour. Nor need much abatement be made because of the custom which assigns raptures always to first performances. The success was unquestionably as genuine as it was deserved. The play strikes me, indeed, as the best example of its class I have seen for many days or nights. Nor can I think that its prosperity will need much assistance from the industry of bill-stickers or advertising agents, the certificates or testimonials of clergymen, critics and others. For nowadays certain plays resemble quack medicines; sufferers are persuaded to give evidence that they have greatly benefited by their exhibition.

The performance was altogether most satisfactory. Mr Wilson Barrett proved himself very vigorous as the hero; Miss Eastlake as the heroine was energetic to excess. Mr George Barrett, who is new to London, I think, as the showman Jarvis displayed strong natural humour, obtaining good support from the efforts of Mrs Stephens and Miss Eugenie Edwards, who personated the itinerant manager's wife and son. Certain of the minor characters were particularly well sustained; I may instance the Philosopher Jack of Mr Coote, a very life like portrayal. The London street scenes were conducted with special spirit. On every side was evidence of ingenuity, painstaking, and managerial liberality.

Nights at the Play, 1883

William Archer
Trilby

A dramatic romance named *Trilby* was produced at the Haymarket Theatre last Wednesday. It is written by an American playwright, Mr Paul M. Potter, and is stated to be 'dramatized from George du Maurier's novel'. I fancy I have heard of this work, and several people in the audience seemed to have read it. A play, however, must stand or fall on its own merits, and I have not thought it necessary to acquaint myself with Mr Potter's alleged original. Not that I have any prejudice against the dramatization of novels. So far as I am concerned, the dramatist may take his material wherever he finds it; my business is with the use he makes of it. But it is my right, and my duty, to place myself in the position of the man who knows nothing beforehand of the plot and characters – an end which I can most securely attain by actually being that man.

Without hesitation, then, I can declare that Mr Potter has told his story clearly enough within the limits of his four acts. This was all the easier as he had very little story to tell. Let me briefly set down what I make of it, that those who know the book may judge for themselves how much or how little of its effect Mr Potter has got over the footlights. Trilby O'Ferrall, the daughter of a drunken Irish Bohemian, is cast adrift at an early age in the students' quarter of Paris. She has a nature of gold, and passes unsullied through the trials and temptations of a model's existence. Three more or less English artists, nicknamed Taffy, The Laird, and Little Billee, fall in love with her, and she loves Little Billee, who is determined to marry her in spite of his mother's opposition. But a Franco–German–Jewish musician named Svengali sees in her an opportunity for making his fortune. She has a splendid voice, inherited from her father, but no ear for music, so that she cannot sing a note in tune. No matter! Svengali will hypnotize her, and inspire her with his own genius. In a state of hypnotic trance, she leaves Paris with him on the day before she was to have married Little Billee, and is not heard of for five years. Then, one evening, the three artists and all their friends happen to meet at a sort of Parisian Alhambra, where a new star, Madame Svengali, is to appear. They at once recognize her as Trilby; but she does not know them, for she has been all this time under the hypnotic spell of the wicked enchanter Svengali, who has beaten and ill-used her in order to make her sing. The incessant strain of hypnotizing and being hypnotized has meanwhile exhausted both his and her vitality, so that they are both at death's door. She sings one song, 'Ben Bolt', with enormous applause; but in the interval between her two 'turns' Svengali encounters the three artists, quarrels with them, and dies of heart disease. She, not knowing of his death, attempts to sing her second song, but makes only hideous noises, and is hissed off the stage. Then she has a fever, and, recovering, is once more about to marry Little Billee; but the malignant wizard, from his grave, sends her his portrait for a marriage present, and the shock of seeing his face kills her.

We have here, then, a fantastic fairy-tale – a mixture of Mürger and Hoffman. It appeals throughout to the imagination, not to the intelligence. I had almost said that it addresses itself to the child in us, not to the man; but children have a habit of asking, 'Is it true?' and that we deliberately refrain from doing. These things are told us and we listen to them, not because they pretend to be actually or symbolically true, but because they somehow or other tickle the fancy. The lighter side of the picture charms us by its very familiarity. The 'primrose by the gutter's brim', spotless and virginal in the midst of corruption, is always gratifying to our passion for antithesis (I am told that in the book she is not immaculate; but American chivalry has expunged her past). Familiar, too, are the three sworn friends, all in love with the same woman, two of whom remain her trusty champions after she has given her love to the third. These legendary figures are always agreeable to the imagination, and they are here presented with a good-humoured quaintness which lends them an air of novelty. As for the dark side of the picture, its charm is simply the sempiternal fascination of diablerie. Not for nothing does Svengali wear the features of a gargoyle from some medieval minster. He is lineally descended from the Devil of the Miracle Plays, own brother to Mephistopheles, and first cousin to the Pied Piper of Hamelin, and a whole tribe of demon musicians. Why this grotesque hocus-pocus should enchant us I really do not know, but, for my own part, I am not at all exempt from its influence. Our Gothic ancestors no doubt revive in us, and the terrors which made them what Stevenson calls 'midnight twitterers', coming down to us attenuated by scepticism, are found readily available as aesthetic motives. The Goth is not the highest element in our composition. He lives in our nerves, whereas the Greek lives in our intellect. But since the nerves respond automatically to the stimulus of theatrical effect, whereas the intellect responds only through a voluntary effort, when Goth meets Greek in the theatre there is practically no tug of war – the Goth holds the field. That is why Sir Henry Irving's *Faust* – a vulgar piece of diablerie – outstripped in popularity his most distinguished and beautiful productions. That is why Mr Tree's Svengali – a performance not vulgar, indeed, but superficial and facile – will very likely prove the great success of his life, and become as closely associated with his name as Dundreary with Sothern's or Rip Van Winkle with Jefferson's. When I add that the heroine of the nursery tale – the Beauty of this Beast – is a beauty indeed, with precisely the right quality of fresh and childlike loveliness, you will readily understand how wide, how universal, is its appeal. Its atmosphere of painting and music is also greatly in its favour. Three acts out of the four pass in a studio, than which there can be no more attractive scene – unless it be the foyer of a theatre, in which the remaining act is placed. Svengali's quality as a musician, too, makes 'slow music' an essential element in the action, and quite naturally converts a great part of the play into what the Germans call 'melodrame' – dialogue spoken through music. Thus all possible ingredients of popularity have, by chance or skill, been assembled in this play. Why, the very title, *Trilby*, with its bird-like quaver, acts as a lure to draw people together.

Let me define my meaning with respect to Mr Tree's Svengali. It is by no means a bad piece of acting – on the contrary it is quite as good as the play requires or permits. But it stands on a low plane of art, because it is not an effort of observation or composition, but of sheer untrammelled fantasy. Mr Tree is simply doing what comes easiest to him, luxuriating in obvious and violent gestures and grimaces, expending no more thought on the matter than is involved in the adroit use of his personal advantages and the mechanical resources of stage effect. Please note that I say this without reproach; Mr Tree gives the character all the thought that it requires or admits of. He makes the most of his material; but his material is second-rate at best. When I was an idle schoolboy, I remember achieving a great reputation among my class-mates by a knack of drawing just such figures as Svengali – spidery monstrosities, with flagrant hair and tentacle-limbs contorted in all sorts of extravagant postures. I had not the remotest talent for drawing, and never attempted to represent a man in natural proportions or conceivable attitudes; but by sheer unbridled whimsicality, I somehow managed to impress the schoolboy imagination and sense of humour. Mr Tree's Svengali carries this art to its highest pitch; but its highest pitch is low as compared with the summits either of poetical acting, or of such true character-acting as Mr Tree himself has sometimes given us. To revert to a former illustration, the carvers of the Gothic gargoyles were artists in their way, but we do not class them with Michael Angelo, or even with Houdon. Miss Dorothea Baird, as Trilby, is not only beautiful, but intelligent and unaffected. She is not yet an accomplished actress; there were points, notably in the third act, where one felt that a touch of real inspiration would have transmuted the fairy-tale into tragedy, and thrilled us with terror and pity; but, on the fairy-tale level, Miss Baird made an absolutely ideal Trilby. Miss Rosina Filippi was an admirable Madame Vinard. Her recognition of the three artists in the third act was the most genuine piece of acting of the whole evening. The other parts were fairly well played, but the interest of the piece would certainly be heightened by a less insignificant Little Billee than Mr Patrick Evans. Let me add – I don't know whether it is a confession or a boast – that so thoroughly did I enter into the innocent playfulness of the production that I can scarcely help laughing as I write at the recollection of the Laird's false nose.

The World, 6 November 1895

G. B. Shaw
The Sign of the Cross

Mr Wilson Barrett has given me such unbounded delight by his feat of persuading the London critics that several of the most characteristic passages in his *Sign of the Cross** are quotations from the Bible that I have nothing but praise for him. Sterne's 'tempering the wind to the shorn lamb' need never again be quoted as the champion instance of scripturization. It is true that Mr Wilson Barrett, following the universal law of art development, has founded his Sermon on the Mount to some extent on the original one; but I can assure the public that the text of *The Sign of the Cross* is essentially original; and if Mr Wilson Barrett writes to the papers to assure us, in the usual terms, that so far from his having taken his play from the Bible, he has never even read that volume, I am quite prepared to believe him. His literary style is altogether different. The play is a monument of sacred and profane history. The influence of Ibsen is apparent throughout, the Norwegian key-note being struck by Mr Barrett himself in the words: 'How many crimes are committed under the cloak of duty!' With scathing, searching irony, and with resolute courage in the face of the prejudiced British public, he has drawn a terrible contrast between the Romans ('Pagans, I regret to say', as Mr Pecksniff remarked of the sirens), with their straightforward sensuality, and the strange, perverted voluptuousness of the Christians, with their shuddering exaltations of longing for the whip, the rack, the stake, and the lions. The whole drama lies in the spectacle of the hardy Roman prefect, a robust soldier and able general, gradually falling under the spell of a pale Christian girl, white and worn with spiritual ecstasy, and beautiful as Mary Anderson. As she gradually throws upon him the fascination of suffering and martyrdom, he loses his taste for wine; the courtesans at his orgies disgust him; heavenly visions obsess him; undreamt-of raptures of sacrifice, agony, and escape from the world to indescribable holiness and bliss tempt him; and finally he is seen, calm and noble, but stark mad, following the girl to her frightfully voluptuous death. It is a tremendous moral lesson; and though I am pagan enough to dislike most intensely the flogging and racking and screaming on the stage (I really am such a bloodless creature that I take no delight in torture), yet no doubt it helps to drive the irony of the theme home.

On the intellectual side, Christianity hardly receives justice from Mr Wilson Barrett. 'Christianity is not in itself a crime', says Marcus to Nero. 'Marcus argues strongly, Caesar', is Poppea's comment. I must say I think Poppea is rather too easily satisfied. But, after all, we do not want to hear the case argued at this time of day. What we enjoy is being so familiarly in Rome that it sounds quite natural when such directions to wayfarers as 'Fourth on the right from the statue of Hercules' are given by the lictors. We come into the presence of Nero, and hear him ordering a set of living torches for that

* Lyric Theatre.

evening, and boasting of what an artist he is. We see the Roman ladies at home sticking pins into their slaves, and the Roman diner-out exhausted by his second vomit. We hear the thunder of the chariot race, and see the gladiator enter the arena. And we have, as aforesaid, whips and racks, chains and dungeons, uplifted crosses and Christian martyrs, not to mention plenty of music well handled by Mr Edward Jones, with hymns for the Christians, waltzes for the Romans, and Sullivan's 'Thou'rt passing hence, my brother', and Gounod's 'Nazareth' on the cornet and sackbut between the acts.

The mounting is handsome and the stage management good and unselfish, all the parts being played with quite extraordinary spirit, and in no way sacrificed to the actor-manager's. I have never seen better work got out of a company. Mr Wilson Barrett has honestly sunk the actor in the author and done his best for the play, instead of for himself personally. Indeed, the one conspicuous and laughable oversight is in Mr Barrett's own make-up. Instead of wearing the proper cropped Roman wig, he wears his own hair in his old familiar feminine fashion, with the result that when he first steps on the stage he presents such an amazing resemblance to Miss Victor that, instead of applauding him, I stared with a shocked conviction that I had that lady before me in the costume of a Roman warrior. The effect is amusing; but it spoils an otherwise manly picture.

The Saturday Review, 11 January 1896

G. B. Shaw
True Blue

BOILED HEROINE

I am often told by people who never go to the theatre that they like melodramas, because they are so funny. Those who do go know better than that. A melodrama must either succeed as a melodrama or else fail with the uttermost ignominies of tedium. But I am fain to admit that *True Blue** is an exception to this rule. It is funnier by a good deal than *H.M.S. Pinafore* in the absurd parts, and not bad, as melodramas go, in the presentable parts. The authorship has evidently been divided among many hands. In some of the epithets which Mrs Raleigh, as the lady matador, hurls at the villain, it is impossible not to recognize the vivid style of Mr Raleigh. One of the unnamed authors –

* Olympic Theatre.

I do not know which – is clearly an idiot; for it is not conceivable that the unspeakable fatuities of the plot can have proceeded from the same brain as the part of Strachan, or the dialogue, a good deal of which is animated and business-like. Probably the idiot was the original begetter of the drama. As I conjecture, he submitted his play to Mr Leonard Outram, who, as an experienced actor, at once fell under the spell which unredeemed literary and dramatic idiocy never fails to throw over his profession. He called in Lieutenant Stuart Gordon to look after the naval realism, and supply technically correct equivalents for the Avast Heavings, and Abaft the Binnacles, and Splicing the Main Braces which we may presume the original manuscript to have contained. The Lieutenant, not being an experienced actor, no doubt suggested that if his naval realism could be supplemented by a gleam or two of common sense, it would be all the better; and I can imagine Sir Augustus Harris, on being approached on the subject of finance, not only supporting the naval officer's view with some vehemence, but taking the dialogue in hand to a certain extent himself, with his popular collaborator, Mr Raleigh, to lend a hand when time ran short. If this hypothesis be correct, we get four authors besides the nameless idiot; and it is in no small degree remarkable that the play has succeeded because the collaborators, in a sort of inspired desperation, played up to the idiot instead of trying to reclaim him. Take for example the main situation of the piece. A British cruiser is anchored at Gibraltar. Its deck is used as a sort of dramatic exchange where villains and villainesses, heroes and heroines, stroll in, like bolts out of the blue, to hatch plots and make love. First there is the lady matador who loves the captain and hates the heroine whom the captain loves. Then there is the heroine, who also loves the captain. And there is the heroine's maid, who loves the comic sailor, who loves the bottle. Suddenly the cruiser is ordered to up anchor and sweep England's enemies from the seas. The women resolve not to desert the man they love in the hour of danger. The matadoress, a comparatively experienced and sensible woman, slips quietly into the pantry adjoining the captain's cabin. The maid gets into one of those settee music boxes which are, it appears, common objects on the decks of cruisers, and is presently carried into the captain's cabin. The heroine, taught by love to divine a surer hiding-place, gets into one of the ship's boilers. Here the hand of the idiot is apparent, striking out a situation which would never have occurred to Shakespeare. Once fairly at sea, the matadoress gives way to an inveterate habit of smoking, and is smelt out by the captain. She throws her arms boldly about him, and declares that he is hers for ever. Enter, inopportunely, the navigating officer. He is scandalized, but retires. When he thinks it safe to return, it is only to find the maid emerging from the settee to dispute possession of the captain, on behalf of the heroine, with the matadoress. Hereupon he describes the ship as the captain's harem, and is placed under arrest. Then comes the great dramatic opportunity of the matadoress. Becoming acquainted, Heaven knows how, with the hiding place of the heroine, she takes the stage alone, and draws a thrilling picture of her rival's impending doom. She describes her in the clammy darkness and dank cold of that boiler, listening to the wild beats of her own heart. Then the sensation of wet feet, the water rising to her ankles, her knees, her waist, her neck, until only by standing on tiptoe, with frantic upturned face, can she breathe. One mercy alone seems vouchsafed to her: the water has lost its deadly chill. Nay, it is getting distinctly warmer, even hot – hotter – *scalding*! Immortal Powers, it is BOILING; and what a moment ago was a beautiful English girl, in the first exquisite budding of her beautiful womanhood, is now but a boilerful of soup, and in another moment will be a condenserful of low-pressure steam. I must congratulate Mrs Raleigh on the courage with which she hurled this terrible word-picture at a house half white with its purgation by pity and terror, and half red with a voiceless, apoplectic laughter. Need I describe the following scene in the stokehold ('stokehole', it appears is a solecism) – how the order comes to fill the boiler; how the comic sailor, in shutting the manhole thereof, catches sight of the white finger of the captain's young lady; how the matadoress in disguise comes in, and has all but turned on the boiling water when the comic sailor disables the tap by a mighty blow from a sledge-hammer; how he rushes away to tell the captain of his discovery; how in his absence the fires are lighted and the cold water turned on; and how at the last moment the captain dashes in, shouting 'Draw the fires from No. 7' (the heroine is in No. 7), rushes up the ladder to the manhole, and drags out the heroine safe and sound, without a smudge on her face or a crumple in her pretty white frock, amid the delirious cheers of an audience which contemplates the descending curtain as men who have eaten of the insane root that takes the reason prisoner. Many more terrors does that melodrama contain, including the public drowning of the matadoress like a rat in a trap, but nothing quite so novel as the boiling scene. The last act degenerates into mere ordinary blood and thunder, only relieved by the touching acting of Mr Rignold on becoming suddenly penetrated for no mortal reason that anybody can discover, with a sense of his own unworthiness and the nobility of his donkey of a captain, who, though a sufficiently hand-some and pleasant fellow, displays just ability enough to justify a steamboat company in trusting him, under the guidance of an intelligent boy, with the sale of tickets for a Thames steamer. Mr Rignold, however, is not the man to allow himself to be bereaved of a bit of acting by the absence of any motive for it. He has the only real part in the play: and he makes the most of it to the end.

Nearly thirty actors and actresses, most of them capable and vigorous people, with more or less distinct stage talents, are provided with salaries by this melodrama. They have for the most part about as much to do as the hundreds of painted spectators in the first scene (which I forgot to mention, as it is only a bull fight). Mr Bucklaw, as the gallant, but brainless captain, shewed that he only needs to smarten himself a little – mostly in the way of enunciating his consonants – to become popular in such parts. Miss Laura Graves was irresistible as the parboiled heroine, being powerfully aided by the fact that the authors of the dialogue have thoroughly mastered the great Shakespearean secret of always making the woman woo the man. In actual life there is no point upon which individuals vary more widely than in the effect of publicity on the demonstrativeness of their affections. Some people would rather die than offer or receive the slightest endearment with anyone looking on. Others are stimulated to exceptional ardor by the presence of an audience; and it is a tragic fact that these diverse temperaments are rather apt to attract one another. The shy, conscious man whose impulsive and warm-hearted wife *will* caress him before a roomful of people, and the fastidious reticent woman whose husband's attitude is openly and blubberingly amorous, are familiar figures in our civilization. But I cannot recall on the stage any *ingénue* quite so reckless under the sway of the tenderer emotions as the one played by Miss Laura Graves. On all public occasions she positively showers kisses on the objects of her attachment. One wonders what a French audience would think of her. It is only when she is alone with the captain in his cabin that she subsides into something like the customary reserve of the bright and beautiful English girls of whom she is offered as an authentic type. The maid is hardly behind her mistress in respect of her indifference to publicity; but she does not take the initiative – is, in fact, more kissed against than kissing – the effect being so much worse that nobody less clever than Miss Kate Phillips could make the part popular. As it is, I congratulate the part on Miss Phillips, without in any way congratulating Miss Phillips on the part.

One of the humours of the piece is that the three stowaway ladies never enter twice in the same costume. They change as freely as if Worth had a branch establishment on board. The fact that this gross impossibility does not interfere in the least with the illusion (such as it is) of the drama is an illustration of the fact that melodramatic stage illusion is not an illusion of real life, but an illusion of the embodiment of our romantic imaginings. If melo-dramatists would only grasp this fact, they would save themselves a good deal of trouble and their audiences a good deal of boredom. Half the explanations and contrivances with which they burden their pieces are superfluous attempts to persuade the audience to accept, as reasonably brought about, situations which it is perfectly ready to accept without any bringing about whatever. The second-rate dramatist always begins at the beginning of his play; the first-rate one begins in the middle; and the genius – Ibsen, for instance – begins at the end. Nothing is odder about *True Blue* than the way in which the same authors who heroically disregard the commonest physical possibilities in the matter of boilers and millinery, timidly and superstitiously waste half the first and second acts in useless explanations of the villain's designs. The thousands of fiery Spaniards waiting for the bull to appear in the ring are repeatedly supposed to sit in respectful silence for five minutes at a stretch whilst the first and second villains stroll into the arena to discuss at great length the political situation which has led to the presence of a British cruiser at Gibraltar (as if that were the most improbable place for it in the world), and which renders it desirable, from their own point of view, that the cruiser should be sunk. Even if these explanations were intelligible or plausible, they would only waste time: as it is, they are stupid.

In looking over one or two criticisms of *True Blue* I have been astonished to find the writers complaining that there is too much realism and too little melodrama in it. When a man who has just been regaled on boiled heroine asks for more, it is only good manners to congratulate him on his appetite; but it is also well to point out that he has not the public on his side. The really entertaining part of *True Blue* is Lieutenant Stuart Gordon's part. The cooking of Alice Marjoribanks is only funny as a bogus monstrosity at a fair is funny; but the weighing of the anchor is both interesting and exciting. It is true that the interest is not strictly dramatic; it is the sort of interest that makes people visit a man-of-war at Portsmouth; but then this is the very sort of interest to which *True Blue* is addressed. The fact that I did not catch half the expository dialogue in the first act did not disappoint me in the least – quite the contrary; but I deeply resented the gruff unintelligibility of the orders by which the anchor-weighing process was directed, as I really wanted to know about that. What *True Blue* wants is more of the fresh naval routine, and less of the stale melodramatic routine. Why not allow the captain to descry the Venezuelan fleet on the horizon, and give us the process of preparing for action? Why not display in the third act a more interesting section of the ship shewing us both above and between decks? Why allow the catastrophe to be brought about by an impossible valet lamely rubbing out the pencil-marks on the captain's chart with a piece of india-rubber, instead of by a torpedo, or a hundred-ton projectile from the enemy, or – if the maximum of probability is preferable – a collision with some other British cruiser? I am convinced, with all respect to the contrary opinion of some of my colleagues, that in this play Lieutenant Gordon worked on the right lines, and his melodramatic collaborators on the wrong ones. The play is emphatically not the thing at the Olympic; and that is precisely why *True Blue* is better worth seeing than most exhibitions of its class.

The Saturday Review, 28 March 1896

J. T. Grein
The Only Way: A Tale of Two Cities

It was a plucky act of Mr Martin Harvey to assume the responsibilities of the Lyceum, and his valour has been deservedly rewarded: *The Only Way* is a success.

Whether or not the Rev. Freeman Wills's melodrama is founded on Dickens's famous novel is one question, and whether it will bear comparison with other plays inspired by the same book is another. But I am not very much concerned with either, for I admit that my memory of the novel, which belongs to my boyhood, is hazy, and I know less of the successful adaptations of a score of years ago.

The Only Way is, therefore, to me what it must be to the majority of play-goers, a new melodrama worked on an old plot, and as such I do not hesitate to pronounce it a very good, a vigorous, and a stirring tale of romance. Nor is there very much in it which betrays its bookish origin; perhaps the action is sometimes a little episodic; perhaps the main character shines out too brilliantly in comparison with all the others; perhaps there is a good deal of jerky suddenness in the culmination of events; but, perhaps, also, we should not have noticed all this if we had not been accessories before the acts.

Yet with all our prescience, I do not think that anybody failed to follow the action with interest, for it was, from the prologue in which St Evrémonde killed Defarge (and a more 'life-like' corpse than Mr Holbrook Blinn I have never seen, except at the Morgue), a very interesting story, which in the third act – the trial – grew deeply pathetic, not to say harrowing. The first two acts, which were laid in London, partly in Sidney Carton's chambers, partly in Dr Manette's delightful garden in Soho, had their weak points. There were too many long duologues in the former, and far too many rhetorical fireworks in the latter, although Mr Harvey, admirably discreet as the drunken young barrister, almost redeemed the opening scenes of the real drama. The second act also might have made a deeper impression if Mr Herbert Sleath, who improves, but is not yet a master of elocution, had been more effective and natural in his amorous protestations, and if Miss Grace Warner, charming to behold, possessed the gift of (figuratively) filling the stage and holding the audience. But let that pass, for our patience was not to go unrewarded.

In the entr'acte between the second and third acts there happened many things which we should like to have heard explained, for it was a big stride from Carton's and Darnay's (alias St Evrémonde) departure from London to the dock in the revolutionary tribunal. Such manœuvres are, however, most common in melodramas, and he who will be a wise man takes them for granted. And, to speak the truth, once we were well in the turmoil of the trial-scene, there was no time for much critical reflection, for the climax, which had now been reached, was overwhelming. The masses were most skilfully grouped, the yells and the shouts of the Jacobin mob had nothing theatrical about them, but sounded terribly genuine, the proceedings of the bench were conducted with as much dignity as one could have expected in the days of the Terror, and the accused and his bride exhibited such grief that in the auditorium ladies' handkerchiefs were furtively produced. Then came the speech which Sidney Carton delivered for the defence, and although to my ear it did not sound as passionately written as the occasion demanded, it burst from Mr Harvey's lips as a magnificent oration. Whoever doubted that Mr Harvey was not only a subtle, but also a strong actor, must now be convinced of his vigour. Of course, that remarkable touch of dreaminess, of ethereality, which was so evident in his Pelleas, was not absent, but it was wedded to a grand outburst of unbridled emotion; and as he stood there, the young advocate, his eye aflame, his features pallid, his breast heaving, his acting was so sincere, so convincing, that one cannot but predict for him a great future. Later again when the last hour had sounded, and Carton forfeited his life to save her whom he loved, Mr Harvey made a great impression, but now it was by his composure, by the sobriety of his words and the suppression of his emotions. The play should have ended when he and Mimi – acted with exquisite delicacy and tenderness by Miss de Silva (Mrs Harvey) – ascended the steps of the Conciergerie to surrender to death and the evil joy of the populace. The last tableau, the guillotine, with its gruesome knife and glittering in the rays of the lime-light, was a mistake. It was picturesque, but it was horrible, it sent us away with fears of bad dreams and hallucinations. And truly the play had been sad enough, so sad that the few flashes of humour scarcely penetrated the gloom.

Before I conclude, I must pay my tribute to Mr Ben Webster for a capital little sketch of a genuine 'Pair de France', and one more to Mr Holbrook Blinn, whose Doctor in *The Cat and the Cherub*, revealed an actor of no mean attainments. He did not seem quite familiar with the extent of the vast auditorium before him, and more than once he sank his voice so low that not even the stalls, let alone the pit, could understand him. But, apart from that, his acting was very fine indeed. What Rutland Barrington does as a comic actor, Mr Blinn practises in the serious line; he is seemingly neither emotional nor theatrical; he is altogether an ordinary human being in manner and in speech. Yet under that calm surface there lurks plenty of passion, and when it broke out in the third act, as Defarge denounced Darnay, the sentence fell like sledgehammers, forcibly, sonorously, impressively. It was a worthy pendant to the eloquence of Mr Martin Harvey. If only all the minor characters had been equally good! Where is the broadness of manner and diction, the 'grand style', upon which the triumphant career of the old melodramatic school was built? It has apparently vanished in the namby-pamby atmosphere of the modern drawing-room play, and that is a pity. However, in spite of such underacting, *The Only Way* held its own. For there is grit in the play, and there is enough panache in Mr Harvey to overcome a host of obstacles.

Dramatic Criticism, 1899

Max Beerbohm
The Passing of the Third Floor Back

A DEPLORABLE AFFAIR

In the course of a theatrical season, the critic's proud spirit is gradually subdued. Twaddling play succeeds twaddling play, and, as the wearisome procession goes by, the critic's protests become fainter: he begins to acquiesce in what cannot, apparently, be stopped. But when he comes back after a holiday, with a fresh eye, with a soul invigorated by contact with real things and lovely things and things that matter, and comes just in time to see the same old procession starting placidly forth on the same old route, then, oh then, it needs a very great effort in him to control his temper. Why should he try? I shall *not* try. All for art, and the temper well lost, I say. How can Mr Forbes-Robertson expect me to be polite about his production at the St James's? In the provinces, recently, he produced a play by Mr Henry James – a play that was reported to be a great success. It would be a privilege to produce a play by Mr Henry James, even though the play failed utterly. In its failure, it would be more interesting, and would bring higher esteem to its producer, than any number of successful plays by second-rate men. Having produced Mr James's play with success, what does Mr Forbes-Robertson do so soon as he comes to London? Apparently in doubt whether Mr James be good enough for the metropolis, he gives us Mr Jerome Klapka Jerome. This tenth-rate writer has been, for many years, prolific of his tenth-rate stuff. But I do not recall, in such stuff of his as I have happened to sample, anything quite so vilely stupid as *The Passing of the Third Floor Back*. I do not for a moment suppose that Mr Forbes-Robertson likes it one whit more than I do. And I wish his pusillanimity in prostituting his great gifts to it were going to be duly punished. The most depressing aspect of the whole matter is that the play is so evidently a great success. The enthusiasm of a first-night audience is no sure gauge of success. Nor is the proverbial apathy of a second-night audience a sure gauge of failure. It was on the second night that I saw *The Passing of the Third Floor Back*; and greater enthusiasm have I seldom seen in a theatre. And thus I am brought sharply up against that doubt which so often confronts me: what can be hoped of an art which must necessarily depend on the favour of the public – of such a public, at least, as ours? Good work may, does sometimes, succeed. But never with the degree of success that befalls twaddle and vulgarity unrelieved. Twaddle and vulgarity will have always the upper hand.

The reformation of a bad person by a supernatural visitor is a theme that has often been used. Mr Jerome, remembering the converted miser in *A Christmas Carol*, and the converted egoist in *A Message from Mars*, and many a similar convert, was struck by the bright idea that the effect would be just a dozen times as great if there were a dozen converts. So he has turned a supernatural visitor loose in a boarding-house inhabited by a round dozen of variously bad people – 'A Satyr', 'A Snob', 'A Shrew', 'A Painted Lady', 'A Cheat', and so on. Now, supposing that these characters were life-like, or were amusing figments of the brain, and supposing that we saw them falling, little by little, under the visitor's spell, till gradually we were aware that they had been changed for the better, the play might be quite a passable affair. But to compass that effect is very far beyond Mr Jerome's power. He has neither the natural talent nor the technical skill that the task requires. There is not a spark of verisimilitude in the whole dozen of characters. One and all, they are unreal. Mr Jerome shows no sign of having ever observed a fellow-creature. His characters seem to be the result solely of a study of novelettes in the penny weekly papers, supplemented by a study of the works of Mr Jerome K. Jerome. Take Major Tompkins, and his wife and daughter, for example. Could anything be more trite and crude than the presentment? Major and Mrs Tompkins are anxious to sell their daughter for gold to an elderly man. 'His very touch', says the daughter, according to custom, 'is loathsome.' The Major persists and says – what else could a stage-major say? – 'Damn your infernal impudence!' The unnatural mother tries to persuade the unwilling daughter to wear a more décolleté dress. The daughter, of course, loves a young painter in a brown velveteen jacket; but she is weak and worldly, and she is like to yield to the importunities of the elderly man. The young painter – but no, I won't bore you by describing the other characters: suffice it that they are all ground out of the same old rusty machine that has served *The Family Herald* and similar publications for so many weary years. Mr Jerome's humour, however, is his own, and he plasters it about with a liberal hand. What could be more screamingly funny than the doings at the outset? The landlady pours tea into the decanter which is supposed to hold whisky, on the chance that the drunken boarder won't notice the difference. Then she goes out, and the servant drinks milk out of the jug and replenishes the jug with water. Then *she* goes out, and the 'Painted Lady' comes in and steals a couple of fresh candles from the sconces on the piano and substitutes a couple of candle ends. Then *she* goes out, and the Major comes in and grabs the biscuits off the plate and drops them into his hat. Then *he* goes out, and the 'Cad' and the 'Rogue' come in and unlock the spiritcase with an illicit key and help themselves to what they presently find is tea. He's inexhaustibly fertile in such sequences is Mr Jerome K. Jerome. When the 'Passer-by' knocks at the front-door, and is admitted with a lime-light full on his (alas, Mr Forbes-Robertson's) classic countenance, the sequences set in with an awful severity. The beneficent stranger has one method for all evildoers, and he works it on every one in turn, with precisely the same result. He praises the landlady for her honesty; then the landlady is ashamed of her dishonesty and becomes honest. He praises the Major for his sweet temper; then the Major is ashamed of his bad temper, and becomes sweet-tempered. He praised the 'Painted Lady' for her modesty in not thinking herself beautiful without paint; then the 'Painted Lady' is ashamed of her paint, and reappears paintless. He praises – but again I won't bore you further. You have found the monotony of the foregoing sentences oppressive enough. Picture to yourselves the monotony of what they describe! For a period of time that seemed like eternity, I had to sit knowing exactly what was about to happen, and how it was about to happen, and knowing that as soon as it had happened it would happen again. The art of dramaturgy, some one has said, is the art of preparation. In that case Klapka is assuredly the greatest dramatist the world has ever known. It is hard to reconcile this conclusion with the patent fact that he hasn't yet mastered the rudiments of his craft.

The third and last act of the play, like the second, consists of a sequence of interviews – next man, please! – between the visitor and the other (now wholly reformed) persons of the play. Steadily, he works through the list, distributing full measure of devastating platitudes, all the way. The last person on the list, the Major's daughter, says, suddenly, 'Who are you?' The visitor spreads his arms, in the attitude of 'The Light of the World'. The Major's daughter falls on her knees in awe. When the visitor passes out through the front-door, a supernatural radiance bursts through the fanlight, flooding the stage; and then the curtain comes slowly down. Well, I suppose blasphemy pays.

The Saturday Review, 5 September 1908

Society Drama

A. B. Walkley
The Dancing Girl

The medieval hope that the old pagan gods are not dead but still survive, the 'hillside men' of some Venusburg, or inhabiting the island of Heine's fancy, still lingers among us moderns, not as folklore, but in novels and plays. In vain have we 'got religion', the Ten Commandments, conviction of sin, and chimney-pot hats; we yearn for the Athens of Pericles, the Greek cult of beauty, the Greek Joy of Living, *revant*, as M. Paul Verlaine sings, 'du divin Platon, et de Phidias, ... sous l'oeil clignotant des bleus becs de gaz' – in Piccadilly. So we call ourselves Neo-Hellenists, and go up and down buying first editions of Mr Pater. But this kind cometh not with prayer and fasting, the reading of many books (and the first editions are expensive), together with a good deal of Mr Richard Swiveller's 'make-believe'. Even then our modern Julians fail; the Galilean has conquered. But where we, with all our striving, fail, Nature sometimes succeeds. Now and again (if we are to believe the novelists and dramatists) a woman – it is generally a woman, the Eternal Feminine having the best of the luck, as usual – reincarnates for us the pure Pagan type. She is a creature of surpassing beauty, a tinted Venus, as Mr Anstey would say, and she has no conscience, no moral sense – that is, she is not immoral, but non-moral. Whether her birth squares with the law of heredity or not is quite a toss-up. Becky Sharp's did, for Becky was the daughter of a drunken artist and a French ballerina. Regina Engstrand, too, took after her mother. But sometimes what the biologists call 'sports' occur. Nature reverts to the ancient type capriciously, and grows figs from thistles. That is the case with Drusilla Ives, the latest feminine reincaration of Paganism, and the heroine of Mr Jones's new play, *The Dancing Girl*.* This tinted Venus is a harmony in white and grey. I mean that Drusilla is the daughter of a Quaker family, who inhabit the Cornish island of St Endellion, an island peopled entirely by Quakers – Quakers tempered by harmoniums. Here we find the Neo-Pagan Quakeress, demurely clad, 'thee'-ing and 'thou'-ing her kinsfolk, and, the moment their backs are turned, taking off her slipper to show her shapely foot to one man, or practising a 'shadow-dance' for the delectation of another.

The fact is, they do not know everything down in St Endellion. They do

* Haymarket.

not know, for instance, that the 'Christian' situation in which their Drusilla is supposed to have been serving up in London has been really of a 'Corybantic' nature, that she has fascinated 'smart' society in the character of Diana Valrose, 'the dancing girl', and become the paramour of his Scapegrace the Duke of Guisebury. The duke is a neo-Pagan like his mistress – a pagan, however, who has dipped into the Upanishads and is troubled, as his mistress is not, with obstinate questionings of invisible things. His philosophic bias, by the way, has not prevented him from wasting his substance in riotous living, or *The Trafalgar Square Gazette* from declaring that 'the spectacle of his career has shortened the future of the House of Lords by twenty years.' It is for his enjoyment (he is landlord of St Endellion and on a visit to the island) that the shadow-dance is rehearsed; and the dismay of a St Endellionite, interrupting the little performance with a thundering, 'Woman, what art thou?' provides what stage-managers call a 'good curtain' for the first act.

In the second, the dramatist's conception of the character of Drusilla is more fully developed. The modest Quaker garb has now been thrown off; she has exchanged the fig-leaf for the strawberry leaf, or, to vary the metaphor, the lilies and languor of St Endellion for the roses and rapture of a ducal villa at Richmond. But already the roses are crumpled. The duke is ruined by the extravagance of his mistress, who, a true devotee of the Joy of Living, is beginning to find an impecunious lover a bore. In desperation he offers her his coronet, which she coldly refuses. Then merely by way of pastime she exercises her fascinations upon a Quaker sweetheart, until he takes his courage in both hands and flees.

Throughout, the woman's character is consistently and firmly drawn; she is heartless, unconsciously cruel, fated to be a noxious thing to every man within her spell, what M. Dumas *fils* used to call *la bête*. It is a novel type on an English stage, and the dramatist has depicted it with consummate skill. I do not think he has been so successful with his duke. This duke philosophizes too much. The shibboleth of pessimism comes too glibly off his tongue (he even confides Schopenhauerisms to the crop-ears of his bull-dog), he patters too freely about 'Nirvana', is altogether too pedantic to carry conviction. As a reader of *The Nineteenth Century*, I know that some dukes are pedants, but I do not associate them with dancing girls. I associate this one, rather – may Mr Jones forgive me! – with the pages of Ouida. His bull-dog is Ouidaesque; his headlong extravagance is Ouidaesque; his pseudo-philosophy is Ouidaesque; he has even rescued a lady from under the hoofs of runaway horses – which is right Ouidaesque.

It is in the third act that this rescued lady shows us the real reason why she was snatched from an untimely death. The dramatist wanted her for the crisis of his play. We have had glimpses of her in the first two acts, through which she has flitted, a little cripple, half sad, half merry, acting as fairy godmother to the duke's tenantry, and as a sort of outspoken Miss Mowcher-like monitress to the duke himself. When such an apparently superfluous character as this appears in the earlier stages of a play, the experienced play-goer at once knows what to expect. He says to himself, 'You are useless now, therefore your turn will come by and by; it's no use deceiving me – I know you – your real name is *Dénouement*.' And so it is here. The duke (his allusions to 'Nirvana' in the preceding act were too significant to be missed) has determined to die, and, like Sardanapalus, he will die amid a general conflagration – that is, at the close of a magnificent entertainment, where all 'smart' society shall be gathered together to applaud the 'dancing-girl', and to admire the strange arras made specially for the occasion out of 'the funeral trappings of the Emperor of China' (Ouida again! – or is it Victor Hugo?). The evolutions of the fashionable crowd in this scene are a marvel of stage-management; the Meiningers could not have manœuvred better. In the height of the festivity, Drusilla's father appears, tears the finery off the girl's back, and 'smart' society, scandalized, rushes out pell-mell, leaving the duke to turn down the gas and take his plunge into Nirvana alone. Then comes the turn of the rescued lady, Miss Dénouement, who steals up to the duke and snatches the poison-phial from his hand as the curtain descends. The scene passes in dead silence, and is one of those triumphs of theatrical effect which reveal the born dramatist.

Up to this point the play has never once lost its grip of the audience, and if only it could end here (why not, Mr Jones? Why not take a hint from the third act of *Ghosts*?) all would be well. But there is, unfortunately, a fourth act – a fourth act as weak as the preceding three are strong. We are back in St Endellion, among the Quakers and harmoniums. Drusilla is dead. The duke is reformed, and (cruel penance for a Schopenhauerite and Anglo-Buddhist) lets Miss Dénouement, whom he is on the point of marrying, quote Herbert Spencer to him by the yard. After marriage, no doubt, she will read him whole chapters from *In Darkest England*. But before that dire consummation is reached, the curtain, luckily, descends.

Playhouse Impressions, 1892

William Archer
A Woman of No Importance

There is no such thing as 'absolute pitch' in criticism; the intervals are everything. In other words, the critic is bound to deal in odious comparisons; it is one of the painful necessities of his calling. He must clearly indicate the plane, so to speak, on which, in his judgment, any given work of art is to be taken; and the value of his terms, whether of praise or blame, must then be estimated in relation to that plane. Well, the one essential fact about Mr Oscar Wilde's dramatic work is that it must be taken on the very highest plane of modern English drama, and furthermore, that it stands alone on that plane. In intellectual calibre, artistic competence – ay, and in dramatic instinct to boot – Mr Wilde has no rival among his fellow-workers for the stage. He is a thinker and a writer; they are more or less able, thoughtful, original playwrights. This statement may seem needlessly emphatic, and even offensive; but it is necessary that it should be made if we are to preserve any sense of proportion in criticism. I am far from exalting either *Lady Windermere's Fan* or *A Woman of No Importance** to the rank of a masterpiece; but while we carp at this point and cavil at that, it behoves us to remember and to avow that we are dealing with works of an altogether higher order than others which we may very likely have praised with much less reserve.

Pray do not suppose that I am merely dazzled by Mr Wilde's pyrotechnic wit. That is one of the defects of his qualities, and a defect, I am sure, that he will one day conquer, when he begins to take himself seriously as a dramatic artist. At present he approaches his calling as cynically as Mr George R. Sims; only it is for the higher intellects, and not the lower, among the playgoing public, that Mr Wilde shows his polite contempt. He regards prose drama (so he has somewhere stated) as the lowest of the arts; and acting on this principle – the falsity of which he will discover as soon as a truly inspiring subject occurs to him – he amuses himself by lying on his back and blowing soap-bubbles for half an evening, and then pretending, during the other half, to interest himself in some story of the simple affections such as audiences, he knows, regard as dramatic. Most of the soap bubbles are exceedingly pretty, and he throws them off with astonishing ease and rapidity –

> One *mot* doth tread upon another's heels,
> So fast they follow –

but it becomes fatiguing, in the long run, to have the whole air ashimmer, as it were, with irridescent films. Mr Wilde will one day be more sparing in the quantity and more fastidious as to the quality of his wit, and will cease to act up to Lord Illingworth's motto that 'nothing succeeds like excess'. It is not his wit, then, and still less his knack of paradox-twisting, that makes me claim

* Haymarket.

for him a place apart among living English dramatists. It is the keenness of his intellect, the individuality of his point of view, the excellence of his verbal style, and, above all, the genuinely dramatic quality of his inspirations. I do not hesitate to call the scene between Lord Illingworth and Mrs Arbuthnot at the end of the second act of this play the most virile and intelligent – yes, I mean it, the most intelligent – piece of English dramatic writing of our day. It is the work of a man who knows life, and knows how to transfer it to the stage. There is no situation-hunting, no posturing. The interest of the scene arises from emotion based upon thought, thought thrilled with emotion. There is nothing conventional in it, nothing insincere. In a word, it is a piece of adult art. True, it is by far the best scene in the play, the only one in which Mr Wilde does perfect justice to his talent. But there are many details of similar, though perhaps not equal, value scattered throughout. How fine and simple in its invention, for instance, is the scene in which the mother tells her son the story of Lord Illingworth's treachery, only to hear him defend the libertine on the ground that no 'nice girl' would have let herself be entrapped! This exquisite touch of ironic pathos is worth half a hundred 'thrilling tableaux', like that which follows almost immediately upon it.

For it is not to be denied that in his effort to be human – I would say 'to be popular', did I not fear some subtle and terrible vengeance on the part of the outraged author – Mr Wilde has become more than a little conventional. How different is the 'He is your father!' tableau at the end of Act III from the strong and simple conclusion of Act II – how different and how inferior! It would be a just retribution if Mr Wilde were presently to be confronted with this tableau, in all the horrors of chromolithography, on every hoarding in London, with the legend 'Stay, Gerald! He is your father!' in crinkly letters in the corner. Then, indeed, would expatriation – or worse – be the only resource of his conscience-stricken soul. His choice would lie between Paris and prussic acid. The conventional element seems to me to come in with the character of Mrs Arbuthnot. Why does Mr Wilde make her such a terribly emphatic personage? Do ladies in her (certainly undesirable) position brood so incessantly upon their misfortune? I have no positive evidence to go upon, but I see no reason why Mrs Arbuthnot should not take a more common-sense view of the situation. That she should resent Lord Illingworth's conduct I quite understand, and I applaud the natural and dignified revenge she takes in declining to marry him. But why all this agony? Why all this hatred? Why can no 'anodyne give her sleep, no poppies forgetfulness'? With all respect for Mrs Arbuthnot, this is mere empty phrase-making. I am sure she has slept very well, say, six nights out of the seven, during these twenty years; or, if not, she has suffered from a stubborn determination to be unhappy, for which Lord Illingworth can scarcely be blamed. After all, what material has she out of which to spin twenty years of unceasing misery? She is – somehow or other – in easy circumstances; she has a model son to satisfy both her affections and her vanity; it does not even appear that she is subjected to any social slights or annoyances. A good many women have led fairly contented lives under far more trying conditions. Perhaps Mr Wilde would have us believe that she suffers from mild religious mania – that it is the gnawing thought of her unpardonable 'sin' that nor poppy nor mandragora can soothe. But she herself admits that she does not repent the 'sin' that has given her a son to love. Well then, what is all this melodrama about? Does not Mrs Arbuthnot sacrifice our interest, if not our sympathy, by her determination 'in obstinate condolement to persevere'? May we not pardonably weary a little (to adapt Lord Illingworth's saying) of 'the Unreasonable eternally lamenting the Unalterable'? Mrs Arbuthnot is simply a woman who has been through a very painful experience, who has suffered a crushing disappointment in the revelation of the unworthiness of the man she loved, but for whom life, after all, has turned out not so very intolerably. That is the rational view of her situation; and she herself might quite well take that view without the sacrifice of one scene or speech of any real value. The masterly scene at the end of the second act would remain practically intact, and so would the scene between mother and son in the third act; for the complacent cruelty of Gerald's commentary on her story could not but cause a bitter pang to any mother. It is only in the fourth act that any really important alteration would be necessary, and there it could only be for the better. The young man's crude sense of the need for some immediate and heroic action is admirably conceived, and entirely right; but how much better, how much truer, how much newer, would the scene be if the mother met his Quixotism with sad, half-smiling dignity and wisdom, instead of with passionate outcries of unreasoning horror! There is a total lack of irony, or, in other words, of commonsense, in this portion of the play. Heroics respond to heroics, until we feel inclined to beg both mother and son (and daughter-in-law, too, for that matter) to come down from their stilts and look at things a little rationally. Even Mr Wilde's writing suffers. We are treated to such noble phrases as 'I am not worthy or of her or of you', and it would surprise no one if Master Gerald were to drop into blank verse in a friendly way. How much more telling, too, would the scene between Mrs Arbuthnot and Lord Illingworth become if she took the situation more ironically and less tragically, if she answered the man of the world in the tone of a woman of the world! How much more complete, for one thing, would be his humiliation! As it is, the vehemence of her hatred can only minister to his vanity. From the point of view of vanity, to be hated for twenty years is just as good as to be loved. It is indifference that stings. It was all very well, in the second act, for Mrs Arbuthnot to be vehement in her protest against the father's annexation of the son; in the fourth act, when that danger is past, a tone of calm superiority would be ten times as effective. In short, the play would have been a much more accomplished work of art if the character of Mrs Arbuthnot had been pitched in another key. And I am not without a suspicion that Mr Wilde's original design was something like what I have indicated. The last word spoken 'A man of no importance' (which was doubtless the first word conceived) seems to belong to the woman I imagine rather than to the one who actually speaks it. I think, too, that the concluding situation would be more effective if some more definite indication of the unspeakable cad who lurks beneath Lord Illingworth's polished surface were vouchsafed us earlier in the play. True, his conduct towards the fair American was sufficiently objectionable; but I fear I, for my part, did not quite seriously believe in it, taking it rather as a mere *ficelle*, and not a very ingenious one, leading up to the startling picture-poster at the end of the third act.

Except in one scene, Mr Tree's acting was altogether admirable – thoughtful in intention, masterly in execution. The one scene excepted was the opening of the third act, in which this nineteenth-century Lord Chesterfield served out his moral maxims to his son with a curiously setentious monotony. Mrs Bernard Beere looked magnificent in her black robe and Magdalen-red hair, and played the perpetual penitent with great force and sincerity – but I think she would have played the other Mrs Arbuthnot still better. Mrs Tree was charming as a heartless woman of the world; nothing could have been better than Miss Le Thiere's rendering of a masterful matron; and Miss Rose Leclercq will doubtless make more of the excellently-drawn character assigned to her when she overcomes the nervousness which, on the first night, rendered her almost inarticulate. As the young lovers, Mr Fred Terry and Miss Neilson (both valuable artists in parts that suit them) were distinctly out of place. A much less practised actor than Mr Terry would have made a far better Gerald, if he could have brought to the part the ingenuous boyishness in which reside its meaning and its charm. When one sees two parts so miscast, one begins to wonder whether we have retained the disadvantages of the stock-company system, while sacrificing its advantages.

In this play, as in *Lady Windermere's Fan*, among many showy sayings, there is one really luminous and profound. 'Thought is in its essence destructive', says Lord Illingworth, 'Nothing survives being thought of.' Nothing – not even *A Woman of No Importance*; but then it is so very, very much better worth thinking of than the average play.

The World, 26 April 1893

William Archer
The Second Mrs Tanqueray

Well now, Mr Pinero and Mr Alexander, whatever your box-office returns may say – and I have little doubt that they will emphatically approve your action – don't you feel that you have done a fine thing, a thing really worth doing, worth suffering for if need be, a thing that enhances your self-respect, and makes you realize that 'a man's a man for a' that', and not the slave of a booking-sheet? Of course you are not going to suffer for it, even in pocket. To dare greatly is to succeed; it is the man who dares feebly that pays for his feebleness. I think it very probable, however, that *The Second Mrs Tanqueray** will not run as long as *Charley's Aunt*, and will not show, on the whole, as heavy a balance of profit as *Liberty Hall*. Perhaps it will not pay you more than a fair day's wage for a fair day's work, and I know that is not considered enough by the punters round the theatrical roulette table. But you are no common gamblers; you could not have done this at all if you had not done it for the pleasure of the thing – that is to say, in the only true artistic spirit. And in this world nothing is to be had for nothing; artistic pleasure must be paid for like any other. It is possible that *The Second Mrs Tanqueray* may bring in only (say) five per cent, on the time and money invested, whereas a piece of screaming buffoonery or trivial sentimentality might have brought in fifteen. But, frankly, isn't the pure joy of effort and triumph cheap at the money? Isn't the trumpery, facile, fifteen per cent success dear in comparison? Now that the thing is done – and not in a tentative, apologetic, afternoon fashion, but with straightforward courage and confidence – don't you feel that if art is not virile it is childish, and that virile art alone is really worth living for? I am no despiser of childish art, so long as there are brains in it, and I am far from urging that the stage should show us nothing but Second Mrs Tanquerays. I have not, thank goodness, outgrown my taste for lollipops, if only they be delicately flavoured, and not too heavily 'loaded' with plaster-of-Paris; but one cannot eat nothing but candy, year out year in, and yet preserve one's self-respect and one's digestion.

I wonder if Mr Pinero himself quite realizes what an immeasurable advance he has made in *The Second Mrs Tanqueray* on all his former works? He has written a play which Dumas might sign without a blush, and created a character very much better worthy of the art of Eleanora Duse than that paltry Fedora whom she played with rather than played the other night. It is not merely the seriousness of the subject that distinguishes this play from its predecessors. The subject of *The Profligate*, indeed, was equally serious, and even more largely important. It is the astonishing advance in philosophical insight and technical skill which places the new play in a new category. Technically, the work is as nearly as possible perfect. How masterly, for example, is the exposition – clear, simple, natural, profoundly interesting!

* St James's Theatre.

There is plenty of wit in it, without a trace of that elaborate conceit-hunting which has hitherto spoiled so much of Mr Pinero's best work. When I remember the first act of *The Profligate*, with the long arm of coincidence dropping Janet Preece in the office of Messrs Cheal and Murray, and with Hugh Murray's metaphor of the wild oats, I can scarcely believe it to be the work of the same man. It is true that we raved over *The Profligate* in its day, and Mr Pinero, remembering this, may be inclined to discount, a little sardonically, our praise of *The Second Mrs Tanqueray*. But there is no real inconsistency. Those of us who kept our heads – as I trust I did – raved with reservations. We did not declare *The Profligate* a positively good play, but only an immensely better and more interesting play than any we were in the habit of seeing. It contained, moreover, one situation which was, and remains, incomparable in its kind. It would have been high-and-mighty criticism indeed which should have failed to recognize these merits, amid all the logical inconsequences and technical defects of the play. But here the case is totally different. Here we have a positively good play. Here, without raving, we can praise almost without reservation. I do not mean that the thing is a consummate masterpiece, and that dramatic art can no further go. There is plenty of room for Mr Pinero and others to write profounder, more beautiful, more moving plays. Mr Pinero has not done everything; but what he has done he has done thoroughly well. The play suggests reflections, artistic and philosophical, enough to fill ten times the space at my command; but they would take the form of discursive commentary rather than of cavil and censure. If I had the wit, I should like to write such a preface to *Mrs Tanqueray* as Dumas is in the habit of prefixing to his own plays, not criticizing, in the narrow sense of the word, but explaining and expanding them. The limitations of *Mrs Tanqueray* are really the limitations of the dramatic form. To say that Mr Pinero has not entirely overcome them is merely to say that he has not achieved a miracle reserved for the very greatest artists in their very happiest inspirations. That is a totally different thing from saying, as in the case of *The Profligate*, 'This is false; that is feeble; here is an inconsistency, there an impossibility.' There is no illogical compromise in *Mrs Tanqueray*, nothing impossible, nothing flagrantly improbable. There is one coincidence – the fact that the man who falls in love with the step-daughter happens to be an old lover of the step-mother's – but there is nothing really unlikely in this, and it would be the merest pedantry to insist that the dramatist should altogether eliminate chance from human affairs. For the rest, the whole course of the drama is smooth, natural, life-like. There is no great situation, as in *The Profligate*, but there are a hundred dramatic moments worth all the attitudinizing situations ever conceived. In brief, the play is modern and masterly. Painful, yes – to me, I own, it is far more painful than certain works which Mr Pinero and those who think with him would not touch with the tongs. Why? Well, I think it is because there is a certain aridity in its painfulness – it feels gritty to the mental palate. Mr Pinero is a poet in his fantastic moods, with the Dickens stop on; but in *Mrs Tanqueray* he writes the sternest of prose. Frankly, it is not a play I hanker after seeing again. I want to read it, to study it – but, with Mrs Patrick Campbell in the title part, though, or because, her performance is almost perfect in its realism, the sensation it gave one could not at any point be described as pleasure. It interests and absorbs one; it satisfies the intelligence more completely than any other modern English play; but it is not in the least moving. Not once during the whole evening were the tears anywhere near my eyes. Yes, once – when Mr Pinero came before the curtain, and the house rose at him. Then I felt a thrill of genuine emotion to think that here at last, in spite of all the depressing and stunting influences of our English theatrical world, was a man who had had the will and talent to emancipate himself and give the artist within him free play – to take care of his soul, and let his pocket, for the nonce, take care of itself.

Some critics objected to Mr Pinero's *Lady Bountiful* that it was rather a novel than a play; whereupon I argued that this was, in itself, no valid objection, the real trouble being that the novel was a poor and commonplace one. It is the highest praise, then, that I can find for *Mrs Tanqueray* to say that its four scenes are like the crucial, the culminating, chapters of a singularly powerful and original novel. In the fact that we would fain see the intermediate chapters written and the characters of Tanqueray and Paula worked out in greater detail, we touch one of the aforesaid limitations of the dramatic form. Tanqueray in particular remains decidedly vague. What there is of him is excellent, but we want a good deal more. We want to understand more fully the conditions of his case. His conduct towards Paula is clearly the resultant of two factors, affectionate pity (or, in more general terms, philanthropy) and physical passion; but we want to know more clearly in what proportions these factors are operative. Neither his temperament nor his culture is very clearly indicated. Paula, again, is drawn with an admirably bold and certain touch in all that we actually see of her; but, without overstepping the limits of the dramatic form, it might surely have been possible to give us a somewhat clearer view of her antecedents. I do not mean of her life as 'Mrs Jarman' or 'Mrs Dartrey' (that we can take on trust), but of her parentage, her girlhood, her education, of the instincts and influences that have made her what she is. She talks now and again like a woman of intelligence, and even of culture, and she acts like a perverse child, so utterly incapable of self-restraint as to fly in the face of her own ambitions and interests at every second word. I do not say that this is inconsistent; on the contrary, I believe it to be absolutely true to nature; but I think a little retrospective analysis, so to speak, might have shown the underlying harmony of certain superficial discords. As the character developed in the second act, I felt for some time as though Mr Pinero had repeated the mistake he made in *The Profligate*, and failed to present a fairly typical case. Just as Dunstan Renshaw was not the ordinary loose liver, but a peculiarly heartless seducer, so it seemed to me that Paula was not the ordinary upper-class courtesan, but simply a woman of diabolical temper, with whom life would have been impossible even if she had been chaste as the icicle that hangs on Dian's temple. But I soon recognized the injustice of this view. In *The Profligate*,

Mr Pinero was bound by the conditions of the case to present an average type; in *The Second Mrs Tanqueray* he was under no such obligation. A vivid and truthful individual character-study was all we had a right to demand of him, and that he gave us. Nor was it the case that, like Mr Shaw in *Widowers' Houses*, he had complicated the problem by unnecessary and irrelevant ill-temper. Paula's irritability, though partly constitutional no doubt, is embittered and rendered morbid by social slights, isolation, idleness, and the frigid politeness of Ellean – in short, it is not only natural, but almost inevitable, and belongs to the very essence of the situation. The indications of generosity and good feeling in the later acts are lightly and skilfully touched in, and the play is nowhere marred by sentimentality. On the side of the woman, as of the man, we miss a clearer definition of the elements which go to make up their relation. How far, in the beginning, is she influenced by love, how far by ambition? Is she capable or incapable of genuine passion for her husband? And are we to understand that the breakdown of the experiment is in some measure due to the perversion of her natural sensibilities by her past life? The physical factor, in short, which in one way or another must enter largely into any such problem, is left very much in the vague; but here again the inherent limitations of the dramatic form are largely to blame, to say nothing of the statutory limitation embodied in the Censorship. Finally, I am not quite certain that Paula's suicide, though natural enough and most effectively handled, is absolutely the most artistic close to the play. It would perhaps have been bolder and better simply to have left the thing at a loose end, dropping the curtain upon Mr and Mrs Tanqueray's determination to go abroad and try to make a fresh start, and leaving the spectator to forecast for himself the course of their future life.

In Mrs Patrick Campbell, Mr Alexander has laid his hand upon the very woman for the part of Paula. Her performance was as novel and unconventional as the character itself, and her triumphant success was thoroughly deserved. Never was there a more uncompromisingly artistic piece of acting. It was incarnate reality, the haggard truth. Mr Alexander himself played Aubrey Tanqueray with his unfailing tact, elegance, and self-restraint, and Mr Cyril Maude was exceedingly good in the capital character of Cayley Drummle. Miss Maude Millett did not seem to me quite the Ellean designed by Mr Pinero, but she played the part pleasantly and intelligently. Miss Amy Roselle was good as Mrs Cortelyon; the Orreyeds were amusingly played by Miss Edith Chester and Mr A. Vane-Tempest; and Mr Ben Webster, as Captain Ardale, did well in his one scene.

The World, 31 May 1893

G. B. Shaw
Guy Domville and An Ideal Husband

TWO NEW PLAYS

The truth about Mr James's play* is no worse than it is out of fashion. Any dramatically disposed young gentleman who, cultivating sentiment on a little alcohol, and gaining an insight to the mysteries of the eternal feminine by a couple of squalid intrigues, meanwhile keeps well aloof from art and philosophy, and thus preserves his innocence of the higher life of the senses and of the intellect, can patch up a play tomorrow which will pass as real drama with the gentlemen who deny that distinction to the works of Mr Henry James. No doubt, if the literary world were as completely dominated by the admirers of Mr Rider Haggard as the dramatic world is by their first cousins, we should be told that Mr James cannot write a novel. That is not criticism: it is a mere begging of the question. There is no reason why life as we find it in Mr James's novels – life, that is, in which passion is subordinate to intellect and to fastidious artistic taste – should not be represented on the stage. If it is real to Mr James, it must be real to others; and why should not these others have their drama instead of being banished from the theatre (to the theatre's great loss) by the monotony and vulgarity of drama in which passion is everything, intellect nothing, and art only brought in by the incidental outrages upon it. As it happens, I am not myself in Mr James's camp: in all the life that has energy enough to be interesting to me, subjective volition, passion, will, make intellect the merest tool. But there is in the centre of that cyclone a certain calm spot where cultivated ladies and gentlemen live on independent incomes or by pleasant artistic occupations. It is there that Mr James's art touches life, selecting whatever is graceful, exquisite, or dignified in its serenity. It is not life as imagined by the pit or gallery, or even by the stalls: it is, let us say, the ideal of the balcony; but that is no reason why the pit and gallery should excommunicate it on the ground that it has no blood and entrails in it, and have its sentence formulated for it by the fiercely ambitious and wilful professional man in the stalls. The whole case against its adequacy really rests on its violation of the cardinal stage convention that love is the most irresistible of all the passions. Since most people go to the theatre to escape from reality, this convention is naturally dear to the world in which love, all powerful in the secret, unreal, day-dreaming life of the imagination, is in the real active life the abject slave of every trifling habit, prejudice, and cowardice, easily stifled by shyness, class feeling, and pecuniary prudence, or diverted from what is theatrically assumed to be its hurricane course by such obstacles as a thick ankle, a cockney accent, or an unfashionable hat. In the face of this, is it good sense to accuse Mr Henry James of a want of grip of the realities of life because he gives us a hero who sacrifices his love to a strong and noble vocation for the Church? And yet when some unmannerly playgoer, untouched

* St James's Theatre.

by either love or religion, chooses to send a derisive howl from the gallery at such a situation, we are to sorrowfully admit, if you please, that Mr James is no dramatist, on the general ground that 'the drama's laws the drama's patrons give'. Pray, which of its patrons? – the cultivated majority who, like myself and all the ablest of my colleagues, applauded Mr James on Saturday, or the handful of rowdies who brawled at him? It is the business of the dramatic critic to educate these dunces, not to echo them.

Admitting, then, that Mr James's dramatic authorship is valid, and that his plays are *du théâtre* when the right people are in the theatre, what are the qualities and faults of *Guy Domville*? First among the qualities, a rare charm of speech. Line after line comes with such a delicate turn and fall that I unhesitatingly challenge any of our popular dramatists to write a scene in verse with half the beauty of Mr James's prose. I am not now speaking of the verbal fitness, which is a matter of careful workmanship merely. I am speaking of the delicate inflexions of feeling conveyed by the cadences of the line, inflexions and cadences which, after so long a course of the ordinary theatrical splashes and daubs of passion and emphasis, are as grateful to my ear as the music of Mozart's *Entführung aus dem Serail* would be after a year of *Ernani* and *Il Trovatore*. Second, *Guy Domville* is a story, and not a mere situation hung out on a gallows of plot. And it is a story of fine sentiment and delicate manners, with an entirely worthy and touching ending. Third, it relies on the performers, not for the brute force of their personalities and popularities, but for their finest accomplishments in grace of manner, delicacy of diction, and dignity of style. It is pleasant to be able to add that this reliance, rash as it undeniably is in these days, was not disappointed. Mr Alexander, having been treated little better than a tailor's dummy by Mr Wilde, Mr Pinero, and Mr Henry Arthur Jones successively, found himself treated as an artist by Mr James, and repaid the compliment, not only, as his manager, by charming eighteenth-century stage setting of the piece, but, as actor, by his fine execution of the principal part, which he touched with great skill and judgment. Miss Marion Terry, as Mrs Peveril, was altogether charming, every movement, every tone, harmonized perfectly with the dainty grace and feeling of her lines. In fact, had the second act been equal to the first and third, and the acting as fine throughout as in the scenes between Mr Alexander and Miss Terry (in which, by the way, they were well supported by Mr Waring), the result would have been less doubtful. It will be a deplorable misfortune if *Guy Domville* does not hold the stage long enough to justify Mr Alexander's enterprise in producing it.

Unfortunately, the second act dissolved the charm rather badly; and what was more, the actors felt it. The Falstaffian make-up of Mrs Saker, and the senseless drunken scene, which Mr Alexander played with the sobriety of desperation, made fuss instead of drama; and the dialogue, except for a brief and very pretty episode in which Miss Millard and Mr Esmond took part, fell off into mere rococo. Little of this act can be remembered with pleasure except Miss Millard's 'Forgive me a little', and a few cognate scraps of dialogue. It had better have been left out, and the wanderings of the prodigal taken for

granted. And, to weight it still further, it contained a great deal of the gentleman who played Lord Devenish, and played him just as he might have played
an elderly marquis in a comic opera, grimacing over a snuff-box, and withering
all sense and music out of Mr James's lines with a diction which I forbear to
describe. He was very largely responsible for the irritation which subsequently
vented itself on the author; and I am far from sure that I ought not to borrow
a weapon from the Speaker of the House of Commons, and go to the extreme
length of naming him.

Guy Domville is preceded by a farce (called in the bill a comedy) by Julian
Field, entitled *Too Happy by Half*. It is deftly turned out from old and
seasoned materials, and is capital fun for the audience and for Mr Esmond
and Miss Millard. Miss Millard is not yet quite experienced enough to do
very easy work quite well: she is the least bit crude occasionally.

Mr Oscar Wilde's new play at the Haymarket is a dangerous subject, because he has the property of making his critics dull. They laugh angrily at his
epigrams, like a child who is coaxed into being amused in the very act of
setting up a yell of rage and agony. They protest that the trick is obvious and
that such epigrams can be turned out by the score by any one lightminded
enough to condescend to such frivolity. As far as I can ascertain I am the only
person in London who cannot sit down and write an Oscar Wilde play at will.
The fact that his plays, though apparently lucrative, remain unique under
these circumstances, says much for the self-denial of our scribes. In a certain
sense Mr Wilde is to me our only thorough playwright. He plays with everything: with wit, with philosophy, with drama, with actors and audience, with
the whole theatre. Such a feat scandalizes the Englishman, who can no more
play with wit and philosophy than he can with a football or a cricket bat. He
works at both, and has the consolation, if he cannot make people laugh, of
being the best cricketer and footballer in the world. Now it is the mark of the
artist that he will not work. Just as people with social ambitions will practise
the meanest economies in order to live expensively; so the artist will starve
his way through incredible toil and discouragement sooner than go and earn
a week's honest wages. Mr Wilde, an arch-artist, is so colossally lazy that he
trifles even with the work by which an artist escapes work. He distils the very
quintessence, and gets as product plays which are so unapproachably playful
that they are the delight of every playgoer with twopenn'orth of brains. The
English critic, always protesting that the drama should not be didactic, and
yet always complaining if the dramatist does not find sermons in stones and
good in everything, will be conscious of a subtle and pervading levity in *An
Ideal Husband*. All the literary dignity of the play, all the imperturbable good
sense and good manners with which Mr Wilde makes his wit pleasant to his
comparatively stupid audience, cannot quite overcome the fact that Ireland is
of all countries the most foreign to England, and that to the Irishman (and
Mr Wilde is almost as acutely Irish an Irishman as the Iron Duke of
Wellington) there is nothing in the world quite so exquisitely comic as an
Englishman's seriousness. It becomes tragic, perhaps, when the Englishman
acts on it; but that occurs too seldom to be taken into account, a fact which

intensifies the humour of the situation, the total result being the Englishman utterly unconscious of his real self, Mr Wilde keenly observant of it and playing on the self-unconsciousness with irresistible humour, and finally, of course, the Englishman annoyed with himself for being amused at his own expense, and for being unable to convict Mr Wilde of what seems an obvious misunderstanding of human nature. He is shocked, too, at the danger to the foundations of society when seriousness is publicly laughed at. And to complete the oddity of the situation, Mr Wilde, touching what he himself reverences, is absolutely the most sentimental dramatist of the day.

It is useless to describe a play which has no thesis: which is, in the purest integrity, a play and nothing less. The six worst epigrams are mere alms handed with a kind smile to the average suburban playgoer; the three best remain secrets between Mr Wilde and a few choice spirits. The modern note is struck in Sir Robert Chiltern's assertion of the individuality and courage of his wrongdoing as against the mechanical idealism of his stupidly good wife, and in his bitter criticism of a love that is only the reward of merit. It is from the philosophy on which this scene is based that the most pregnant epigrams in the play have been condensed. Indeed, this is the only philosophy that has ever produced epigrams. In contriving the stage expedients by which the action of the piece is kept going, Mr Wilde has been once or twice a little too careless of stage illusion: for example, why on earth should Mrs Cheveley, hiding in Lord Goring's room, knock down a chair? That is my sole criticism.

The performance is very amusing. The audience laughs conscientiously: each person comes to the theatre prepared, like a special artist, with the background of a laugh ready sketched in on his or her features. Some of the performers labour intensely at being epigrammatic. I am sure Miss Vane Featherstone and Miss Forsyth could play Lady Macbeth and Medea with less effort than Lady Basildon and Mrs Marchmont, who have nothing to do but sit on a sofa and be politely silly for ten minutes. There is no doubt that these glimpses of expensive receptions in Park Lane, with the servants announcing titles *ad libitum,* are enormously attractive to social outsiders (say ninety-nine hundredths of us); but the stage reproduction is not convincing: everybody has an outrageous air of being at a party; of not being used to it; and, worst of all, of enjoying themselves immensely. Mr Charles Hawtrey has the best of the fun among the principals. As everyone's guide, philosopher, and friend, he has moments in which he is, I think, intended to be deep, strong, and tender. These moments, to say the least, do not quite come off; but his lighter serious episodes are excellent, and his drollery conquers without effort. When Miss Neilson sits still and lets her gifts of beauty and grace be eloquent for her, she is highly satisfying; but I cannot say the same for the passages in which she has to take the stage herself and try to act. She becomes merely artificial and superficially imitative. Miss Fanny Brough makes Lady Markby, an eminently possible person, quite impossible; and Miss Maude Millet, playing very well indeed as Mabel Chiltern, nevertheless occasionally spoils a word by certain vowel sounds which are only permissible to actresses of the second rank. As an adventuress who, like the real and unlike the stage adventuress, is not in love with anyone, and is simply selfish, dishonest, and third rate, Miss Florence West is kinetoscopically realistic. The portrait is true to nature; but it has no artistic character: Miss West has not the art of being agreeably disagreeable. Mr Brookfield, a great artist in small things, makes the valet in the third act one of the heroes of the performance. And Mr Waller is handsome and dignified as the ideal husband, a part easily within his means. His management could not have been more auspiciously inaugurated.

The Saturday Review, 12 January 1895

G. B. Shaw
The Notorious Mrs Ebbsmith

MR PINERO'S NEW PLAY

Mr Pinero's new play is an attempt to reproduce that peculiar stage effect of intellectual drama, of social problem, of subtle psychological study of character, in short, of a great play, with which he was so successful in *The Profligate* and *The Second Mrs Tanqueray*. In the two earlier plays, it will be remembered, he was careful to support this stage effect with a substantial basis of ordinary dramatic material, consisting of a well worked-up and well worn situation which would have secured the success of a conventional Adelphi piece. In this way he conquered the public by the exquisite flattery of giving them plays that they really liked, whilst persuading them that such appreciation was only possible from persons of great culture and intellectual acuteness. The vogue of *The Second Mrs Tanqueray* was due to the fact that the commonplace playgoer, as he admired Mrs Patrick Campbell, and was moved for the twentieth time by the conventional wicked woman with a past, consumed with remorse at the recollection of her innocent girlhood, and unable to look her pure step-daughter (from a convent) in the face, believed that he was one of the select few for whom 'the literary drama' exists, and thus combined the delights of an evening at a play which would not have puzzled Madame Celeste with a sense of being immensely in the modern movement. Mr Pinero, in effect, invented a new sort of play by taking the ordinary article and giving it an air of novel, profound, and original thought. This he was able to do because he was an inveterate 'character actor' (a technical term denoting a clever stage performer who cannot act, and therefore makes an elaborate study of the disguises and stage tricks by which acting can be grotesquely simulated) as well as a competent dramatist on customary lines. His performance as a thinker and social philosopher is simply character acting in the domain of authorship, and can impose only on those who are taken in by character acting on the stage. It is only the make-up of an actor who does not understand his part, but who knows – because he shares – the popular notion of its externals. As such, it can never be the governing factor in this success, which must always depend on the commonplace but real substratum of ordinary drama in his works. Thus his power to provide *Mrs Tanqueray* with equal popular successors depends on his freedom from the illusion he has himself created as to his real strength lying in his acuteness as a critic of life. Given a good play, the stage effect of philosophy will pass with those who are no better philosophers than he; but when the play is bad, the air of philosophy can only add to its insufferableness. In the case of *The Notorious Mrs Ebbsmith*,* the play is bad. But one of its defects – to wit, the unreality of the chief female character, who is fully as artificial as Mrs Tanqueray herself – has the lucky effect of setting Mrs Patrick Campbell free to do as she pleases in it, the result being an irresistible projection of that lady's personal genius, a projection which sweeps the play aside and imperiously becomes the play itself. Mrs Patrick Campbell, in fact, pulls her author through by playing him clean off the stage. She creates all sorts of illusions, and gives one all sorts of searching sensations. It is impossible not to feel that those haunting eyes are brooding on a momentous past, and the parted lips anticipating a thrilling imminent future, whilst some enigmatic present must no less surely be working underneath all that subtle play of limb and stealthy intensity of tone. Clearly there must be a great tragedy somewhere in the immediate neighbourhood; and most of my colleagues will no doubt tell us that this imaginary masterpiece is Mr Pinero's *Notorious Mrs Ebbsmith*. But Mr Pinero has hardly anything to do with it. When the curtain comes down, you are compelled to admit that, after all, nothing has come of it except your conviction that Mrs Patrick Campbell is a wonderful woman. Let us put her out of the question for a moment, and take a look at Mrs Ebbsmith.

To begin with, she is what has been called 'a platform woman'. She is the daughter of a secularist agitator – say a minor Bradlaugh. After eight years of married life during which she was for one year her husband's sultana, and for the other seven his housekeeper, she has emerged into widowhood and an active career as an agitator, speaking from the platforms formerly occupied by her father. Although educated, well conducted, beautiful, and a sufficiently powerful speaker to produce a great effect in Trafalgar Square, she loses her voice from starvation, and has to fall back on nursing – a piece of fiction which shews that Mr Pinero has not the faintest idea of what such a woman's career is in reality. He may take my word for it that a lady with such qualifications would be very much better off than a nurse; and that the plinth of the Nelson column, the 'pitch' in the park, and the little meeting halls in poor parishes, all of which he speaks of with such an exquisitely suburban sense of their

* Garrick Theatre.

being the dark places of the earth, enter nowadays very largely into the political education of almost all publicly active men and women; so that the Duke of St Olpherts, when he went to that iron building in St Luke's and saw 'Mad Agnes' on the platform, might much more probably have found there a future Cabinet Minister, a lady of his own ducal family, or even a dramatic critic. However, the mistakes into which Mr Pinero has been led by his want of practical acquaintance with the business of political agitation are of no great dramatic moment. We may forgive a modern British dramatist for supposing that Mrs Besant, for example, was an outcast on the brink of starvation in the days when she graduated on the platform, although we should certainly not tolerate such nonsense from any intellectually responsible person. But Mr Pinero has made a deeper mistake. He has fallen into the common error of supposing that the woman who speaks in public and takes an interest in wider concerns than those of her own household is a special variety of the human species; that she 'Trafalgar Squares' aristocratic visitors in her drawing room; and that there is something dramatic in her discovery that she has the common passions of humanity.

Mrs Ebbsmith, in the course of her nursing, finds a patient who falls in love with her. He is married to a shrew; and he proposes to spend the rest of his life with his nurse, preaching the horrors of marriage. Off the stage it is not customary for a man and woman to assume that they cannot co-operate in bringing about social reform without living together as man and wife; on the stage, this is considered inevitable. Mrs Ebbsmith rebels against the stage so far as to propose that they shall prove their disinterestedness by making the partnership a friendly business one only. She then finds out that he does not really care a rap about her ideas, and that his attachment to her is simply sexual. Here we start with a dramatic theme capable of interesting development. Mr Pinero, unable to develop it, lets it slip through his fingers after one feeble clutch at it and proceeds to degrade his drama below the ordinary level by making the woman declare that her discovery of the nature of the man's feelings puts within her reach 'the only one hour in a woman's life', in pursuance of which detestable view she puts on an indecent dress and utterly abandons herself to him. A clergyman appears at this crisis, and offers her a Bible. She promptly pitches it into the stove; and a thrill of horror runs through the audience as they see, in imagination, the whole Christian Church tottering before their eyes. Suddenly, with a wild scream, she plunges her hand into the glowing stove and pulls out the Bible again. The Church is saved; and our curtain descends amid thunders of applause. In that applause I hope I need not say I did not join. A less sensible and less courageous stage effect I have never witnessed. If Mr Pinero had created for us a woman whose childhood had been made miserable by the gloomy terrorism which vulgar, fanatical parents extract from the Bible, then he might fitly have given some of the public a very wholesome lesson by making the woman thrust the Bible into the stove and leave it there. Many of the most devoted clergymen of the Church of England would, I can assure him, have publicly thanked him for such a lesson. But to introduce a woman as to whom we are carefully assured that she was educated as a secularist, and whose one misfortune – her un-happy marriage – can hardly by any stretch of casuistry be laid to the charge of St Paul's teaching; to make this woman senselessly say that all her misfortunes are due to the Bible; to make her throw it into the stove, and then injure herself horribly in pulling it out again: this, I submit, is a piece of clap-trap so gross that it absolves me from all obligation to treat Mr Pinero's art as anything higher than the barest art of theatrical sensation. As in *The Profligate*, as in *The Second Mrs Tanqueray*, he has had no idea beyond that of doing something daring and bringing down the house by running away from the consequences.

I must confess that I have no criticism for all this stuff. Mr Pinero is quite right to try his hand at the higher drama; only he will never succeed on his present method of trusting to his imagination, which seems to me to have been fed originally on the novels and American humour of forty years ago, and of late to have been entirely starved. I strongly recommend him to air his ideas a little in Hyde Park or 'the Iron Hall, St Luke's', before he writes his next play. I shall be happy to take the chair for him.

I should, by the way, like to know the truth about the great stage effect at the end of the second act, where Mrs Patrick Campbell enters with plain and very becoming dress changed for a horrifying confection apparently made of Japanese bronze wall-paper with a bold pattern of stamped gold. Lest the maker should take an action against me and obtain ruinous damages, I hasten to say that the garment was well made, the skirt and train perfectly hung, and the bodice, or rather waistband, fitting flawlessly. But, as I know nothing of the fashion in evening dresses, it was cut rather lower in the pectoral region than I expected; and it was, to my taste, appalling ugly. So I fully believed that the effect intended was a terrible rebuke to the man's complaint that Mrs Ebbsmith's previous dress was only fit for 'a dowdy demagogue'. Conceive my feelings when everyone on the stage went into ecstasies of admiration. Can Mr Pinero have shared that admiration? As the hero of a recent play observes, 'That is the question that torments me.'

A great deal of the performance is extremely tedious. The first twenty minutes, with its intolerable, unnecessary, and unintelligible explanations about the relationships of the characters, should be ruthlessly cut out. Half the stage business is only Mr Pinero's old 'character actor' nonsense; and much of the other half might be executed during the dialogue, and not between the sentences. The company need to be reminded that the Garrick is a theatre in which very distinct utterance is desirable. The worrying from time to time about the stove should be dropped, as it does not in the least fulfil its purpose of making the Bible incident – which is badly stage managed – seem more natural when it comes.

Mr Hare, in the stalest of parts, gives us a perfect piece of acting not only executed with extraordinary fineness, but conceived so as to produce a strong illusion that there is a real character there, whereas there is really nothing but that hackeyed simulacrum of a cynical and epigrammatic old libertine who has helped to carry on so many plots. Mr Forbes Robertson lent himself to the hero, and so enabled him to become interesting on credit. Miss Jeffreys, miraculously ill fitted with her part, was pleasant for the first five minutes, during which she was suggesting a perfectly different sort of person to that which she afterwards vainly pretended to become. The other characters were the merest stock figures, convincing us that Mr Pinero either never meets anybody now, or else that he has lost the power of observation. Many passages in the play, of course, have all the qualities which have gained Mr Pinero his position as a dramatist; but I shall not dwell on them, as, to tell the truth, I disliked the play so much that nothing would induce me to say anything good of it. And here let me warn the reader to carefully discount my opinion in view of the fact that I write plays myself, and that my school is in violent reaction against that of Mr Pinero. But my criticism has not, I hope, any other fault than the inevitable one of extreme unfairness.

The Saturday Review, 16 March 1895

J. T. Grein
Mrs Dane's Defence

I

Mrs Dane's Defence* is Miss Lena Ashwell's vindications of her claim to rank among the foremost of our contemporary actresses. Her performance in the third act is unforgettable, but from first to last she moulded the character with infinite perspicacity, and with a consistency akin to life itself.

All London will therefore acclaim the actress, and in the midst of the rapture, the author is likely to be relegated to the background. This should not be so, and if I venture to sound this warning note, it is not because I wish to dissent from the praise bestowed on Miss Ashwell, but in order to make it plain that much, in histrionic successes, is due to the author. We in England are apt to forget this; we print the actor's name in gigantic capitals, while the author's comes lower down in tiny letters; many among us who go to the theatre, know the whole playbill by heart except the name of the author. We are mostly not alive to the fact that the author creates, whereas the actor illustrates; that the very existence of the actor is dependent on the author. Sometimes it is the actor that makes the play, but as a rule it is the part that makes the actor.

* Wyndham's Theatre.

Miss Ashwell found such a part in Mrs Dane, and Mr Jones conceived it for her; the honours belong to them both and to Mr Wyndham whose impersonation of the judge was but one more finely-developed character-sketch in the exquisite gallery of his art.

II

The third act of Mr Jones's play is as bold and intense a piece of work as has ever sprung from the prolific mind of this thoughtful dramatist. The great scene is almost primitive in manner – a mere dialogue such as may occur any day in our law courts between counsel and witness. But with what consummate skill the 'moral torture' is used by Mr Jones to let us hear from Mrs Dane's own lips that she has had liaison fraught with scandal; that she is not the widowed woman she pretends to be; that she is by the law of convention not a fit companion for the twenty-year-old son of the judge. It all began as suavely as a drawing-room conversation; every question was satisfactorily answered by Mrs Dane; her lies were well told and made a plausible and harmonious story. Indeed, her battle was almost won, and even the sagacious inquirer felt sure of her innocence, when one little lapse of the tongue spelt perdition. She merely said, 'we' instead of 'I', thereby dragging into the inquiry factors which had hitherto been considered non-existent. The whole aspect of her part changed, as it were, through this solitary word, and, unexpected as the slip was, it led to vacillation, to hopeless hesitation, at last to an ignominious fall. The confidence of the judge once shaken, the *suaviter* changed into the *fortiter in modo*. Question upon question racked the unhappy woman, and the more she answered the worse she grew entangled. Miss Ashwell exhibited this disastrous ride for a fall with marvellous expression – less of voice than of countenance. Now hopeful, now defiant, now wavering, now despondent, with broken breath and restless, erring eyes, she met the charges of her torturer. It was as if the garotte closed round her neck, tighter and tighter and tighter, until, with one last twist when the judge said, 'You are not Mrs Dane, you are the other woman', the soul of Mrs Dane gasped her last, and the phantom of the past instantly took her place.

The effect of this scene is – without exaggeration – colossal; at least such was the impression it made on me. I felt the moral torture so intensely, the cunningly devised phrases of the author, the insinuating force of Wyndham's dulcet manner, of his screwing, digging, exploding voice, the terrible mortified face of Miss Ashwell – all that concentration of influence to destroy the new life of a woman! – it made me almost implore aloud for mercy. It was painful, physically as well as mentally. Yet I do not complain, for author and actors between them had but reproduced an episode of real life, and, in placing it before us, they had, if anything, softened its awful veracity.

III

I wonder how Mr Jones would have constructed this play, if our theatre were ruled by different conditions from those of the present day.

As the play stands, the third act alone is its *raison d'être*; all that precedes is but a lengthy preface of no very deep interest, and the conclusion is like a salon after the ball is over. In fact, as usual, Mr Jones has been too explanatory at the start, and at the finish. He evidently does not place great reliance on our intelligence, or, let me rather say, our quickness of perception. For, really, it was not at all necessary to create an anti-climax by clenching the long pending engagement between the judge and the charming Lady Eastney (nicely acted by Miss Moore), or by foreshadowing that, after all, the lovelorn juvenile wooer of Mrs Dane would ere long be united to his bonnie Scotch lassie of less than twenty summers. We are not so dense as all that, and it worries us to have our noses bumped on the obvious.

Dealing more widely with the drama as a whole, I think that if Mr Jones had not been conscious of writing for a commercial theatre, he would have left out much incident, cut out much (agreeable) cackle, and walked, in all the acts, in the broadway of life, instead of in the tangled lanes of the well-constructed play. There was no need for the slander of the scandal-loving Mrs Porter; for the employment of a private detective who made himself inordinately familiar with the judge, and made a fool of his client; for an enormous scaffolding of collateral situations, all of which tended to discount our belief in the much-vaunted cleverness of a judge in many ways modelled after the august figure of the late Chief Justice when he was Q.C.

I think that, if Mr Jones, with whose gifts of observation and originality of conception one becomes more deeply impressed as play after play leaves his pen, had been untrammelled, he would have built his drama in three (not four) terse straightforward acts. He would have given the situation as it begins now: a woman, about whom one knows little or next to nothing, beloved by a man much younger – as is the fashion nowadays. Then, perfectly naturally, someone would have recognized her, communicated his discovery, and provoked an inquiry. Finally, the judge, who happens to be the lover's adopted father, would, unaided by detectives, documents and what not, but guided solely by his insight into human nature, have forced the secret out of her, and have convinced her of her unsuitability as a mate for his son. Silent departure of the woman would have been the end. Here was the groundwork of a great picture of human battles. A Hauptmann or a François de Curel would have worked on these lines, disregarding all that belongs to the 'manufactured drama'. But, alas! there is no home with us for the drama of life undefiled by considerations of exchequer. And thus Mr Jones had to be content with pleasing himself in one act only, and the exigencies of the system in all the others.

Grave issues are touched upon in Mr Jones's play, and grave words are uttered by the judge, when he pronounces the dread sentence of our conventional laws upon his victim. In his self-defence that it is not he who forbids the woman with a tainted past to enter into an honourable family, but 'the hard law' that governs the life of our community, he refers to a question of immense moment. We might well ask, why is the past of a woman frequently condoned when that woman is a great artist, a member of the aristocracy, or one of 'no class' at all, and why is it irretrievable when she belongs to the middle class? We might go further and discuss whether the judge was right when he prognosticated a hell of unhappiness for his son if he married Mrs Dane, supposing that a few years later a good-looking man came along, with possible consequences which one may guess. For does not the inner meaning of this supposition affect a widow as much as any other woman who enters wedlock unadorned by orange-blossoms? But the play merely throws up these questions, it does not answer them at all, or at least, only in a one-sided manner. We must, therefore, assume that the author had no intention to grapple with these great and grave issues, but that his sole idea was to write an entertaining play with a great part for Mr Wyndham and a good one for a woman. This he has done, and, as it happens, it is the woman who gets the great part, and the actor obtains merely the second best. For, although in the play the judge scores to the detriment of the Magdalen, our sympathies are not with him, but with the sinner. Long after the curtain's fall she stands before us in her pallor, a tearful picture of love, and of the inexorable laws of convention which condones the past of men and is merciless to women.

Dramatic Criticism 1900–1901, 1902

Max Beerbohm
Letty

A MAGNIFICENT DIS-PLAY

If only Mr Pinero would be simple! They say that he took two years to write *Letty** – three thousand hours or so, maybe, of solid labour. And not one too many. The modern form of dramaturgy is the most difficult of all the art-forms. Ibsen himself, even in his prime, was strictly biennial. Let Mr Pinero be quinquennial, if so disposed. It is right for a work of art to be elaborate, in the literal sense of that word. But the elaboration of *Letty* is especially in the other sense. And to this difference I attribute the failure of *Letty* to evoke from me something beyond admiration for the author's amazing skill. An artist should labour to whittle away all that is superfluous to his main theme or idea. Even as an athlete is 'trained' for the annihilation of every ounce of flesh that would impede the strong free play of his muscles, so must the work of art be 'trained', till nothing is left but what is sharply essential to its effect. In Strasbourg there is another mode of 'training'. Certain of the geese there

* Duke of York's Theatre.

are enclosed in hutches, and are given as much food as they want and, having eaten that, are given by force very much more than they want. This system, hideous though it is, produces, at last, pleasant results for the epicure in food. But a similar system applied to works of art will not gratify the artistic epicure. That similar system has been applied by Mr Pinero to *Letty*. The play is too 'rich'.

Using the word in another sense, I declare Mr Pinero himself too 'rich'. It may sound paradoxical, but it is not the less true that Mr Pinero would write better plays if he were a less richly endowed playwright. We all know the danger that lies in actual riches. We all know how the mere possession of fabulous wealth seems to crush the imagination of the millionaire, and to prevent him from regarding his means as a means to an end – except the end of empty ostentation. Tritely, by acquisition of yachts, motors, palaces, picture-galleries, grouse-moors, the millionaire seeks to dazzle us. And dazzled the majority of us is. When we are faced by an exceptional millionaire, who uses his money in pursuit of some ideal, we exchange glances and tap our foreheads significantly. Nobody, so far as I remember, accused 'le petit sucrier' of being a lunatic. He scattered his gold down the customary channels, content with the flash of it, as were also we. But this other M. Lebaudy, who actually eludes our gaze, and will presently sail to a remote part of the world and try to work out an ideal – well, well, well! poor fellow! what a shame that he has no one to look after him! Similarly, there would not be such a general bowing-down to 'our premier dramatist', if Mr Pinero were less eager to dazzle us with a generous display of his perfectly-appointed technique, and more eager to illustrate simply a philosophic idea, or to develop simply a human theme. Just as do very great actual riches, so do very great dramaturgic riches seem to crush originality in their owner, and to foster ostentatiousness. A Henrik Ibsen is as rare as a Jacques Lebaudy – or (since this young man may prove to have not much in him beyond the mere power to break away from tradition) let me say, rather, a Cecil Rhodes. If Mr Pinero were less brilliant in his specific way, there would be more room in him for ideas. As it is, there is no room at all. Mr Archer, rather touchingly, ventures to hope that this absence of ideas is but 'a transient phase of Mr Pinero's development'. As Mr Pinero never has harboured ideas, it is rather too much to expect that he will proceed to do so now. A horse-dealer, commending the points of a pony, does not suggest that the pony is passing through 'a transient phase of development' and will presently be a horse. Even so, Mr Archer should not try to raise hopes that cannot be entertained – much less fulfilled. But, though the smooth and luscious fruit of Mr Pinero's genius can no more prick us with underlying ideas than can thistles be gathered from grapes, there is in Mr Pinero no lack of power for treating a human theme sincerely and fully. Mr Pinero has a keen insight into human nature, more especially into the nature of women. And he might create really great pictures of life if he could but forget to show off his technical skill by bedevilling, as in *Letty* he bedevils, his main theme with a glittering congeries of inessential things. Let Mr Archer concentrate his desires, not on making Mr Pinero think, but on making him make us feel.

A good quality cannot be implanted, but you can sometimes eliminate a bad one.

The essential conflict in *Letty* is strong, and the two conflicting characters are strongly imagined and set forth. On the one hand, we see a rich and rather sentimental profligate; on the other a very sentimental type-writer, rebellious against the shabbiness and drudgery of her existence. He is in love with her, she with him. She has wild hopes that he will marry her. The hopes are dashed: he is already married. There is another rich man, anxious to marry her; but he is definitely 'a bounder', and she is vaguely 'genteel'. Here comes a conflict between her gentility and her desire to do nothing but wear pretty frocks. Gentility wins the day. Then comes a conflict between her inherited sense of propriety with her love of pretty frocks and her love of her lover. Shall she be mistress of the profligate? She wavers, consents, withdraws her consent. Subsequently she marries a 'genteel' person in her own class, bears a child, and is fairly happy. Both she and the profligate are quite real people, behaving quite really. Their story is in itself extremely interesting and moving. And yet, somehow, one is unmoved by it; nor has one a keen sense of the reality of the two persons. This may be partly due to the performance. Miss Irene Vanbrugh catches exactly the tone of the type-writer whom she impersonates – the tone of the partially refined Cockney, 'not quite a lady', but very lady-like indeed. She suggests perfectly the girl's social aspirations; but she does not compass a suggestion that the girl is in love. All the surface is there, but not the romantic soul. Mr H. B. Irving, as the profligate, is ardent enough, but his ardour seems to belong to another time and place. As a fashionable young man of today and of London, he must be taken with several grains of salt. He is too remarkable. Give him a strong and odd character part, and he can be reconciled with modern life. But as young 'Mr Nevill Letchmere', leading in a flat in Grafton Street a life of frivolity, he compels us to remember that he is really a grim visitant from Olympus. We are not quite sure which of the gods he is (Vulcan, perhaps, without the limp). But, whichever he be of them, we are frightened. That high collar round his throat, that hat perched so jauntily upon his head, are, we feel, the work of some practical joker and the Olympian is going to avenge himself on *us*. Outwardly, he still preserves that air of sleek humility which he learnt from the Admirable Crichton; but we can see through it that he is raging within, and we tremble. At least, we should be trembling were not our sense of reality so outraged. Certainly, we must take his performance, and Miss Vanbrugh's, as accounting to some extent for the play's failure to give us so much illusion and emotion as we should expect from a play with so dramatic and so true a motive. But the main reason is that this motive is obscured for us by Mr Pinero's passion for the extraneous. His skill is such that he can handle a whole mass of extraneous things with masterly ease, making them seem, at first glance, quite necessary. And that is the reason why he handles them. He must needs exercise and display his skill, perform feats of which all other men are incapable. Behold how many characters he can manipulate! Behold in how many exciting scenes he can place them without loss of verisimilitude! He will give you almost as much of the cinematographic method as can Mr Cecil Raleigh, yet without the least strain on likelihood. Here is a fashionable restaurant, with waiters, and a manager, and different brands of champagne, and electric lights that can be switched off because it is the midnight of Saturday. And here are the leads of a housetop, with all the chimneys and the soot, and a piano-organ grinding out the latest popular tune from the street below, and a view of various steeples in the West End. And here is the anteroom of a fashionable photographer in Baker Street, with all the details. And every thing seems to be quite relevant. There was one moment, in the crucial scene of the play, when Miss Vanbrugh, rising from a sofa, inclined her body backwards and dangled her hands. I thought there was to be a cake-walk. I had been waiting for it, and I cannot understand the omission. Everything else of up-to-date actuality and 'snap' is introduced so plausibly. Some of the subordinate characters, though all are amusing, are not quite so cinematographic. The tout for an insurance-agency, and the commercial traveller, seem like unpublished fragments of Dickens. The 'bounder', though he is an outside broker, and is admirably played by Mr Fred Kerr, might have stepped out of the pages of Samuel Warren, so remote is he from current reality. He is not a 'bounder' but a 'snob'. It is strange that Mr Pinero should have these lapses into bygone literature; for no one has a keener eye than he in studying from the models of living vulgarity. There is in this play a dressmaker's assistant whose every sentence rings phonographically true. Some of the effect produced by this part is due to the clever acting of Miss Nancy Price; but the part itself is an exquisite one, and only a pedant would grudge the author's extreme elaboration of it. One need not, however, be a pedant to deplore the elaboration of so many other things that are irrelevant to the central scheme of the play. If only, I repeat, Mr Pinero could be simple! Why was it that the first act of *The Finding of Nancy*, wherein we had almost exactly the same situation and problem as we have in *Letty*, gave us so keen an illusion of reality, and moved us to so keen a sense of pity, while *Letty* leaves us cold and critical? It is because Miss Syrett, knowing little about her specific art, went straight to life, and threw us a bit of life, for what it was worth, with no clever superfluities. After the first act, her play fell to pieces, because she had not enough technical skill to carry the tale steadily forward. But that first act, for which little technique was needed, remains with us as a clear memory. And *Letty* shrivels in the light of it. Had Miss Syrett possessed one tithe of Mr Pinero's technical skill, *The Finding of Nancy* would have been a fine whole. And could Mr Pinero have made over to her nine-tenths of his technical skill, *Letty* would have been a fine whole. I have likened Mr Pinero to a plutocrat. And, as erst in Galilee, he who has 'great possessions' will be loth to part with them even for his salvation. But I don't want to dash Mr Archer's hopes.

The Saturday Review, 17 October 1903

A. B. Walkley
His House in Order

When Mr Pinero is at his best you may reckon yourself as close upon the high-water mark of a theatrical enjoyment. In *His House in Order** he is at his very best. His master quality, by which I mean the quality specifically called 'dramatic', is here seen at its *maximum* of energy. This or that playwright may show more 'heart' than Mr Pinero or a more delicate subtlety, a third may easily outclass him in intellectual gymnastic, but in his command of the resources of the stage for the legitimate purposes of the stage he is without a rival. The art of drama is, quintessentially, the art of story-telling, as the sculptors say, 'in the round'. Mr Pinero is supreme as a story-teller of that sort. We are always keenly interested in what his people are doing at the moment; we always have the liveliest curiosity about what they are going to do a moment later. He knows it is the dramatist's main business to 'get along', and he gets along in *His House in Order* at a 'record' pace. The play tells a plain tale plainly, with the directness of a novel of Defoe; there are no suspensions, no digressions. It displays a richly comic invention, it culminates in a situation of tremendous seriousness, it reveals that quasi-clerical element of drama, the 'purging' of a will, and it has a perpetual undertone of almost mocking irony. Not, of course, that this work, any more than any other work, is flawless. Mr Pinero, though he has subdued, has not completely conquered his weakness for talking like a book. And there is one passage which seems to suggest that he has neglected Johnson's advice to Boswell to 'clear his mind of cant'. But, take it for all in all, *His House in Order* is a very choice specimen of Pinero work; in other words a play yielding the highest possible measure of delight.

Distaste for the obvious must not deter me from saying what will be said by everyone – that the play ought to have been called *The Second Mrs Jesson*. That title, indeed, would be far more appropriate for the new play than was *The Second Mrs Tanqueray* for the old. I mean that in the earlier play the contrast between the first and second wife, though indicated, was not worked out; whereas that contrast may be said to be the main *motif* of the new play. The character of the first Mrs Tanqueray had no bearing on the fortunes of the second. The stern lady 'with marble arms' was dead, and there, dramatically, was an end of her. But the first Mrs Jesson, though dead, may be said in a sense to be a protagonist in *His House in Order*; the cult of her memory is what the mathematicians call an 'effective force' in the action; she suffers, posthumously, a change of character which determines the fortunes of the living people in the play. More than that, the evolution in the character of the first wife determines, as by a mathematical law, the evolution of character in the second. It is a case of 'contrary motion'. When wife No. 1 is morally 'up', wife No. 2 is morally 'down' – I do not mean merely seems to others, by dint

* St James's Theatre.

of contrast, but really is an inferior creature. When, through a sudden discovery, wife No. 1 sinks as low as she formerly stood high, wife No. 2 goes up like a rocket – again I do not mean merely in the opinion of the rest, but she actually *becomes* a superior creature. And the very discovery which reveals the inferiority of the dead woman is the means by which the living woman finds her own better self. There is a symmetry about this scheme which should captivate the geometrician in us; it has the 'elegance' of a theorem by Housel or Chasles. But it must not be supposed that there is anything so arid as formal geometry, any suspicion of a blackboard demonstration, in the way Mr Pinero tells his story.

Act I. A journalist who has come to 'interview' Mr Filmer Jesson, M.P. for a Midland county division, on the occasion of his opening a new park, presented to the neighbouring town in memory of his deceased wife Annabel, has a preliminary talk with the M.P.'s private secretary, which is the means of at once bringing the audience acquainted with the names and relationship of all the people in the play. The ceremony is to be graced by the presence of the Ridgeleys, father and mother, brother and sister, of the deceased lady. Geraldine Ridgeley, the sister, is a permanent inmate of the house; is, in fact, its martinet ruler. Then there is little Derek Jesson, the son, and Major Maurewarde, an old friend of the Jesson family. Finally, there is Hilary Jesson, Filmer's elder brother, a diplomat on leave. But, asks the reporter, have you not forgotten the present Mrs Jesson? Oh yes, to be sure! We see at once that Nina, the present Mrs Jesson, counts for nothing in the establishment. A conversation between Filmer and his brother Hilary soon tells us why. Filmer is a prig, whose watchwords are method and order; rigid 'correctness' is his fetish. The late Mrs Jesson lived up to his ideals in these matters; his present wife merely exists to outrage them. In a moment of impulse he has married his child's governess, a clergyman's daughter (note that detail, please), and finds he has made a mistake. Nina smokes cigarettes, brings her dogs into the drawing-room, and is absolutely deficient in those qualities of order which illustrated her dead predecessor. But order is essential to Filmer, and so he has had to call in the dead lady's sister to restore it. Hilary, who has a marked talent for preaching, which, as we shall soon find, is apt to get the better of him, advances the thesis that we should take women as we find 'em, God bless 'em, and not ask from one the virtues special to another. All very well for you, a bachelor, with an easy temper, is Filmer's contemptuous reply. Presently Hilary gets a tête-à-tête with Nina, and learns her side of the story. She recognizes her deficiencies and would have tried to mend them if only she had had a little encouragement. But the Ridgeleys coldly snub her, and have the ear of her husband. The worship of Annabel has got on Nina's nerves. Treated as a naughty child, she can only behave as one. Hilary listens sympathetically; and the pair forthwith become fast friends.

In Act II we make the acquaintance of the Ridgeley family: old Sir Daniel a pompous bore, Lady Ridgeley a dragon, Pryce Ridgely, a solemn ass. Geraldine Ridgeley, the *de facto* ruler of the household, we have already seen. These, with Filmer Jesson, constitute what Nina calls the Society of Annabel

Worshippers. Hilary advises her, for the sake of domestic harmony, to join that society, and she promises to try. An opportunity occurs over the question of the memorial park. There is a suggestion of adding a bandstand (rejected by the Ridgeley family because open-air music is un-English) or a fountain. Nina begs to be allowed to contribute a fountain, an artistic fountain. Artistic fountains are also vetoed as un-English – and Nina flounces out of the room in a rage. Hilary seizes the opportunity to recite to the puzzled Ridgeleys a rather too lengthy apologue about a French cook who succeeded another French cook and, because of unfavourable comparison, blew up the kitchen boiler. Nina returns, and apologizes for her misbehaviour. But the discovery that Annabel's boudoir, reopened today for the first time after its owner's death, is to be realloted to little Derek instead of to herself provokes a more serious outburst of anger. She flatly declines to attend the opening ceremony at the park on the morrow, and is in open revolt. The Ridgeleys throughout this act have been extremely droll. Master Derek has shown himself a charming little boy, and (again, please note) there is an extraordinarily warm affection between him and Major Maurewarde.

Act III. Nina still in full revolt. She defiantly puts on a dress of flaming red, just to scandalize the Ridgeleys, who are all in deep black to celebrate the third anniversary of Annabel's death. To Hilary's friendly remonstrances she turns a deaf ear; with her husband she declares open war. And then, at the moment when Nina's case is touching bottom, comes the great discovery. Little Derek, rummaging in his dead mother's boudoir, has unearthed a handbag from a 'secret' drawer. Nina unsuspectingly opens it – and finds some faded letters from Maurewarde to Annabel. These letters show that Annabel, far from being a saint, was Maurewarde's mistress and that Derek is his child. Annabel was on the point of eloping with Maurewarde when she met her death in a carriage accident. So now the tables are turned! Nina has it in her power to dethrone the sacred image of Annabel, and to humiliate the tyrannical Ridgeleys. She means, she tells Hilary, to use her power. But Hilary also has *his* power, the power of preaching, and he uses – indeed abuses – it. Let her think of Annabel, her remorse, her misery. Why, interjects Nina, she was on the point of eloping when she met her death! Just so, replies Hilary; do you not (being a clergyman's daughter) there recognize the hand of God? And he appeals to her 'belief in the doctrine of Divine interposition in the ordinary affairs of life'. I just quote that phrase – I might quote many more – to support the statement that Mr Pinero has not yet got over his weakness for talking like a book. But Hilary's reference to the 'hand of God' in the carriage accident is an instance of a less venial weakness; it is the lapse, to which I have already alluded, into cant. Hilary is represented as a sensible man of the world, not a fool. Why then is he made to put forward the singular theory of a God who ignores clandestine adultery but intervenes when the secret sin threatens to become an open scandal? And it is done so seriously, with so evident a bid for our 'sympathy'! Mr Pinero should have given us some little sign, at least, to make it clear that he is not the dupe of his own sophistry. Anyhow, he puts a sensible reply into Nina's mouth: 'Oh, yes, and it was also the hand of God that brought the letters to light and delivered them to me.' Thereupon Hilary tries another tack, and this time a successful one. The really heroic people are the people who have learnt to renounce. 'Nina, be among those who wear a halo. Burn Maurewarde's letters, my dear.' After a silent struggle, Nina hands him the letters. What is more, she volunteers to go to the park-opening after all, and rushes off to put on a black dress. And that closes a stirringly dramatic third act.

But we have not yet done with thrills. In Act IV, after Hilary has quietly turned Maurewarde out of the house, the party come back from the ceremony, and the Ridgeleys treat the now submissive Nina more contemptuously than ever. There is a fine irony in the scene to the spectator who knows that the woman is bending her neck to the yoke just when she could, if she chose, turn and rend her persecutors. The sight is, however, too much for Hilary. He resolves that there shall be an end of it – and puts the fatal letters in his brother's hands. Nina, horrified, snatches and burns them. But they have been read, and Filmer Jesson's eyes are at length opened – opened to his own weakness, and his wife's sterling worth. The astounded Ridgeleys are politely bowed out of the house, and Hilary quietly shuts the door as Filmer and Nina sit affectionately, and at last with true understanding, side by side. Hilary's silent exit, by the way, is his best effect – far more eloquent than the prolix speeches which Mr Pinero has lavished upon the part. If Hilary can only be persuaded to be more terse (and to reconsider his 'doctrine of Divine interposition in the ordinary affairs of life') there will be no reasonable fault to find with *His House in Order*. For it would be hypercriticism to object to a certain exaggeration in the handling of the Ridgeley family. Though they exist, dramatically, as a squad, rather than as individual agents, they are cleverly differentiated in details; the slight touch of convention in their treatment is legitimate and indeed inevitable; they remain always in the true key of comedy.

But since there is this trace of exaggeration, however slight, of convention, however legitimate, in the drawing of the Ridgeley family, all the more is it incumbent on the players to go delicately. 'Glissez mais n'appuyez pas' is, the proverb, of which Mlle Thomé, little Derek's French governess, might remind them. Fortunately they need no reminder. It would be difficult to better the tact, the artistic restraint, with which Miss Bella Pateman and Mr Lyall Swete, Miss Beryl Faber and Mr Lowne, present the humorous aspects of this family so monumentally humourless. They all four show triumphantly, as they are intended to show, the vast power for evil, for cruelty, for downright tyranny, of complacent, conscientious narrow-mindedness. Mr Pinero makes, I submit, one little mistake over this group. He allows Hilary, the *raisonneur* of his play, to have an indignant explosion and to declare that the type, as a social pest, ought to be swept off the face of the earth. And this after Mr Pinero has been turning them to such handsome account, forcing them to contribute to the public stock of harmless pleasure! No, Hilary, as a man of the world, ought to have learnt to suffer solemn bores gladly; where would *His House in Order* be without them? And, for that matter, the denunciation of bores comes with a peculiarly ill grace from Hilary. May one whisper it? He comes at times perilously near to being a bore himself. He loves the sound of his own voice. He is a perfect martyr to dictionary English; even in the most intimate tête-à-tête he is careful to 'admit that your allegations are not unfounded', or to 'point out that matters will eventually adjust themselves'. Well, as he himself would say, God bless him; he represents a little weakness of Mr Pinero's, and so we must accept him with philosophic tolerance. Mr Alexander plays him with manifest gusto; the more wordy the speech the more the actor seems to revel in it. Again, God bless him. At any rate, he is an excellent foil to the wayward, impulsive Nina of Miss Irene Vanbrugh, with her rapid staccato utterance, her febrile restlessness. In the great scene of the third act, when the woman stands out for revenge and the man pleads for renunciation, the acting of both rises to a high level of passionate sincerity.

Drama and Life, 1907

Comedy

Charles Lamb
On the Artificial Comedy of the Last Century

The artificial Comedy, or Comedy of manners, is quite extinct on our stage. Congreve and Farquhar show their heads once in seven years only, to be exploded and put down instantly. The times cannot bear them. Is it for a few wild speeches, an occasional licence of dialogue? I think not altogether. The business of their dramatic characters will not stand the moral test. We screw everything up to that. Idle gallantry in a fiction, a dream, the passing pageant of an evening, startles us in the same way as the alarming indications of profligacy in a son or ward in real life should startle a parent or guardian. We have no such middle emotions as dramatic interests left. We see a stage libertine playing his loose pranks of two hours' duration, and of no after consequence, with the severe eyes which inspect real vices with their bearings upon two worlds. We are spectators to a plot or intrigue (not reducible in life to the point of strict mortality) and take it all for truth. We substitute a real for a dramatic person, and judge him accordingly. We try him in our courts, from which there is no appeal to the dramatis personae, his peers. We have been spoiled with – not sentimental comedy – but a tyrant far more pernicious to our pleasures which has succeeded to it, the exclusive and all devouring drama of common life; where the moral point is everything; where, instead of the fictitious half-believed personages of the stage (the phantoms of old comedy) we recognize ourselves, our brothers, aunts, kinsfolk, allies, patrons, enemies – the same as in life – with an interest in what is going on so hearty and substantial, that we cannot afford our moral judgment, in its deepest and most vital results, to compromise or slumber for a moment. What is *there* transacting, by no modification is made to affect us in any other manner than the same events or characters would do in our relationships of life. We carry our fire-side concerns to the theatre with us. We do not go thither, like our ancestors, to escape from the pressure of reality, so much as to confirm our experience of it; to make assurance double, and take a bond of fate. We must live our toilsome lives twice over, as it was the mournful privilege of Ulysses to descend twice to the shades. All that neutral ground of character, which stood between vice and virtue; or which in fact was indifferent to neither, where neither properly was called in question; that happy breathing-place from the burthen of a perpetual moral questioning – the sanctuary and quiet Alsatia of hunted casuistry – is broken up and disfranchised, as injurious to the interests of society. The privileges of the place are taken away by law. We dare not dally with images, or names, of wrong. We bark like foolish dogs at shadows. We dread infection from the scenic representation of disorder; and fear a painted pustule. In our anxiety that our morality should not take cold, we wrap it up in a great blanket surtout of precaution against the breeze of sunshine.

I confess for myself that (with no great delinquencies to answer for) I am glad for a season to take an airing beyond the diocese of the strict conscience – not to live always in the precincts of the law-courts – but now and then, for a dream-while or so, to imagine a world with no meddling restrictions – to get into recesses, whither the hunter cannot follow me –

> – Secret shades
> Of woody Ida's inmost grove,
> While yet there was no fear of Jove –

I come back to my cage and my restraint the fresher and more healthy for it. I wear my shackles more contentedly for having respired the breath of an imaginary freedom. I do not know how it is with others, but I feel the better always for the perusal of one of Congreve's – nay, why should I not add even of Wycherley's – comedies. I am the gayer at least for it; and I could never connect those sports of a witty fancy in any shape with any result to be drawn from them to imitation in real life. They are a world of themselves almost as much as fairy-land. Take one of their characters, male or female (with few exceptions they are alike), and place it in a modern play, and my virtuous indignation shall rise against the profligate wretch as warmly as the Catos of the pit could desire; because in a modern play I am the judge of the right and the wrong. The standard of *police* is the measure of *political justice*. The atmosphere will blight it, it cannot live here. It has got into a moral world, where it has no business, from which it must needs fall headlong; as dizzy, and incapable of making a stand, as a Swedenborgian bad spirit that has wandered unawares into the sphere of one of his Good Men, or Angels. But in its own world do we feel the creature is so very bad? The Fainalls and the Mirabels, the Dorimants and the Lady Touchwoods, in their own sphere, do not offend my moral sense; in fact they do not appeal to it at all. They seem engaged in their proper element. They break through no laws, or conscientious restraints. They know of none. They have got out of Christendom into the land – what shall I call it? – of cuckoldry – the Utopia of gallantry, where pleasure is duty, and the manners perfect freedom. It is altogether a speculative scene of things, which has no reference whatever to the world that is. No good person can be justly offended as a spectator, because no good person suffers on the stage. Judged morally, every character in these plays – the few exceptions only are *mistakes* – is alike essentially vain and worthless. The great art of Congreve is especially shown in this, that he has entirely excluded from his scenes, – some little generosities in the part of Angelica perhaps excepted – not only any thing like a faultless character, but any pretensions to goodness or good feelings what-soever. Whether he did this designedly, or instinctively, the effect is as happy, as the design (if design) was bold. I used to wonder at the strange power which his *Way of the World* in particular possesses of interesting you all along in the pursuits of characters, for whom you absolutely care nothing – for you neither hate nor love his personages – and I think it is owing to this very indifference for any, that you endure the whole. He has spread a privation of moral light, I will call it, rather than by the ugly name of palpable darkness, over his crea-tions; and his shadows flit before you without distinction or preference. Had he introduced a good character, a single gush of moral feeling, a revulsion of the judgment to actual life and actual duties, the impertinent Goshen would have only lighted to the discovery of deformities, which now are none, because we think them none.

Translated into real life, the characters of his, and his friend Wycherley's dramas, are profligates and strumpets – the business of their brief existence, the undivided pursuit of lawless gallantry. No other spring of action, or possible motive of conduct, is recognized; principles which, universally acted upon, must reduce this frame of things to a chaos. But we do them wrong in so translating them. No such effects are produced in *their* world. When we are among them, we are amongst a chaotic people. We are not to judge them by our usages. No reverend institutions are insulted by their proceedings – for they have none among them. No peace of families is violated – for no family ties exist among them. No purity of the marriage bed is stained – for none is supposed to have a being. No deep affections are disquieted – no holy wedlock bands are snapped asunder – for affection's depth and wedded faith are not of the growth of that soil. There is neither right nor wrong – gratitude or its opposite – claim or duty – paternity or sonship. Of what consequence is it to Virtue, or how is she at all concerned about it, whether Sir Simon, or Dapperwit, steal away Miss Martha; or who is the father of Lord Froth's or Sir Paul Pliant's children?

The whole is a passing pageant, where we should sit as unconcerned at the issues, for life or death, as at a battle of the frogs and mice. But, like Don Quixote, we take part against the puppets, and quite as impertinently. We dare not contemplate an Atlantis, a scheme out of which our coxcombical moral sense is for a little transitory ease excluded. We have not the courage to imagine a state of things for which there is neither reward nor punishment. We cling to the painful necessities of shame and blame. We would indict our very dreams.

Amid the mortifying circumstances attendant upon growing old, it is something to have seen the *School for Scandal* in its glory. This comedy grew out of Congreve and Wycherley, but gathered some allays of the sentimental comedy which followed theirs. It is impossible that it should be now *acted*, though it continues, at long intervals, to be announced in the bills. Its hero, when Palmer played it at least, was Joseph Surface. When I remember the gay boldness, the graceful solemn plausibility, the measured step, the insinuat-ing voice – to express it in a word – the downright *acted* villainy of the part, so different from the pressure of conscious actual wickedness – the hypocritical assumption of hypocrisy – which made Jack so deservedly a favourite in that character, I must needs conclude the present generation of play-goers more virtuous than myself, or more dense. I freely confess that he divided the palm with me with his better brother; that, in fact, I liked him quite as well. Not but there are passages – like that, for instance, where Joseph is made to refuse a pittance to a poor relation – incongruities which Sheridan was forced upon by the attempt to join the artificial with the sentimental comedy, either of which must destroy the other – but over these obstructions Jack's manner floated him so lightly, that a refusal from him no more shocked you, than the easy compliance of Charles gave you in reality any pleasure; you got over the paltry question as quickly as you could, to get back into the regions of pure comedy, where no cold moral reigns. The highly artificial manner of Palmer in this character counteracted every disagreeable impression which you might have received from the contrast, supposing them real, between the two brothers. You did not believe in Joseph with the same faith with which you believed in Charles. The latter was a pleasant reality, the former a no less pleasant poetical foil to it. The comedy, I have said, is incongruous; a mixture of Congreve with sentimental incompatibilities: the gaiety upon the whole is buoyant; but it required the consummate art of Palmer to reconcile the discordant elements.

A player with Jack's talents, if we had one now, would not dare to do the part in the same manner. He would instinctively avoid every turn which might tend to unrealize, and so to make the character fascinating. He must take his cue from his spectators, who would expect a bad man and a good man as rigidly opposed to each other as the death-beds of those geniuses are contrasted in the prints, which I am sorry to say have disappeared from the windows of my old friend Carrington Bowles, of St Paul's Church-yard memory (an exhibition as venerable as the adjacent cathedral, and almost coeval) of the bad and good man at the hour of death; where the ghastly apprehensions of the former – and truly the grim phantom with his reality of a toasting fork is not to be despised – so finely contrast with the meek complacent kissing of the rod – taking it in like honey and butter – with which the latter submits to the scythe of the gentle bleeder, Time, who wields his lancet with the apprehensive finger of a popular young ladies' surgeon. What flesh, like loving grass, would not covet to meet halfway the stroke of such a delicate mower? John Palmer was twice an actor in this exquisite part. He was playing to you all the while that he was playing upon Sir Peter and his lady. You had the first intimation of a sentiment before it was on his lips. His unaltered voice was meant to you, and you were to suppose that his fictitious co-flutterers on the stage perceived nothing at all of it. What was it to you if that half-reality, the husband, was over-reached by the puppetry – or the thin thing (Lady Teazle's reputation) was persuaded it was dying of a plethory? The fortunes of Othello and Desdemona were not concerned in it. Poor Jack has passed from the stage in good time, that he did not live to this our age of seriousness. The pleasant old Teazle *King*, too, is gone in good time. His manner would scarce have passed current in our day. We must love or hate – acquit or condemn – censure or pity – exert our detestable coxcombry of moral judgement upon everything. Joseph Surface, to go down now, must be a down-right revolting villain – no compromise – his first appearance must shock and give horror – his specious plausibilities, which the pleasurable faculties of our fathers welcomed with such hearty greetings, knowing that no harm (dramatic harm even) could come, or was meant to come of them, must inspire a cold and killing aversion. Charles (the real canting person of the scene – for the hypocrisy of Joseph has its ulterior legitimate ends, but his brother's professions of a good heart centre in down-right self-satisfaction) must be *loved*, and Joseph *hated*. To balance one disagreeable reality with another, Sir Peter Teazle must be no longer the comic idea of a fretful old bachelor bridegroom, whose teasings (while King acted it) were evidently as much played off at you, as they were meant to concern any body on the stage – he must be a real person, capable in law of sustaining an injury – a person towards whom duties are to be acknowledged – the genuine *crim. con.* antagonist of the villainous seducer Joseph. To realize him more, his sufferings under his unfortunate match must have the downright pungency of life – must (or should) make you not mirthful but uncomfortable, just as the same predicament would move you in a neighbour or old friend. The delicious scenes which give the play its name and zest, must affect you in the same serious manner as if you heard the reputation of a dear female friend attacked in your real presence. Crabtree and Sir Benjamin – those poor snakes that live but in the sunshine of your mirth – must be ripened by this hot-bed process of realization into asps or amphisbaenas; and Mrs Candour – O! frightful! – become a hooded serpent. O! – who that remembers Parsons and Dodd – the wasp and butterfly of the *School for Scandal* – in those two characters; and charming natural Miss Pope, the perfect gentlewoman as distinguished from the fine lady of comedy, in this latter part – would forego the true scenic delight – the escape from life – the oblivion of consequences – the holiday barring out of the pedant Reflection – those Saturnalia of two or three brief hours, well won from the world – to sit instead at one of our modern plays – to have his coward conscience (that forsooth must not be left for a moment) stimulated with perpetual appeals – dulled rather, and blunted, as a faculty without repose must be – and his moral vanity pampered with images of notional justice, notional beneficence, lives saved without the spectator's risk, and fortunes given away that cost the author nothing?

No piece was, perhaps, ever so completely cast in all its parts as this *manager's comedy*. Miss Farren had succeeded to Mrs Abington in Lady Teazle; and Smith, the original Charles, had retired, when I first saw it. The rest of the characters, with very slight exceptions, remained. I remember it was then the fashion to cry down John Kemble, who took the part of Charles after Smith; but, I thought, very unjustly. Smith, I fancy, was more airy, and took the eye with a certain gaiety of person. He brought with him no sombre recollections of tragedy. He had not to expiate the fault of having pleased before-hand in lofty declamation. He had no sins of Hamlet or of Richard to atone for. His failure in these parts was a passport to success in one of so opposite a tendency. But, as far as I could judge, the weighty sense of Kemble made up for more personal incapacity than he had to answer for. His harshest tones in this part came steeped and dulcified in good humour. He made his defects a grace. His exact declamatory manner, as he managed it, only served to convey the points of his dialogue with more precision. It seemed to head the shafts to carry them deeper. Not one of his sparkling sentences was lost. I remember minutely how he delivered each in succession, and cannot by any effort imagine how any of them could be altered for the better. No man could deliver brilliant dialogue – the dialogue of Congreve or of Wycherley – because none understood it – half so well as John Kemble. His Valentine, in *Love for Love*, was, to my recollection, faultless. He flagged sometimes in the intervals of tragic passion. He would slumber over the level parts of an heroic character. His Macbeth has been known to nod. But he always seemed to me to be particularly alive to pointed and witty dialogue. The relaxing levities of tragedy have not been touched by any since him – the playful court-bred spirit in which he condescended to the players in Hamlet – the sportive relief which he threw into the darker shades of Richard – disappeared with him. He had his sluggish moods, his torpors – but they were the halting-stones and resting-places of his tragedy – politic savings, and fetches of the breath – husbandry of the lungs, where nature pointed him to be an economist – rather, I think, than errors of the judgement. They were, at worst, less painful than the eternal tormenting unappeasable vigilance, the 'lidless dragon eyes', of present fashionable tragedy.

The London Magazine, April 1822

G. H. Lewes
Masks and Faces

Go and see *Masks and Faces** for several reasons. You will be amused: that is something. Laughter and the tears of sympathy alternate through the varying scene; bright ingenious dialogue, playing like lambent flame, stimulates the intellect; and homely pathos, homely mirth, kind hearts and loving voices, gently touch the various chords of emotion.

But there are other reasons why you should go. You should go if you are a dramatist or dramatic critic, to learn there the secrets of success and failure.

* Haymarket.

You should go if you are a lover of acting, to learn how truly and artistically Webster, Leigh Murray, Mrs Stirling, and Mrs Leigh Murray can speak behind the Mask when a real Persona is afforded them.

I am not going to tell you the story of this comedy. You have seen or will see it. In the long scene of the second act, where the poor poet is writing his comedy, with a starving family for inspiration, and tears for gaiety – in that touching scene, I say, the dramatic critic will learn the secrets of success and failure. It succeeds because it has the elements of eternal success – character and emotion: the sharpness and individuality of the well-contrasted characters, and the unmistakable reality of the emotion arising out of the circumstance, not artificially brought in for the sake of effect. But then, beside this quality, so precious on the stage and elsewhere, there is a deficiency – felt more on the stage, but felt everywhere – a deficiency of organic construction. All the details of that scene are admirable; and they do *illustrate* the characters of the poor poet, his sick wife, his children, the kind Peg Woffington, and the empty Connoisseurs of Art – but they do no more. They afford the actors good material – they are not built up into a work of art. It is a portfolio of sketches, not a picture. Hence it requires all the resources of the actors to keep up the interest; and even in spite of our laughter and our tears, a sense of weariness ever and anon steals over us. I point out this scene as a study.

Webster surpassed himself in Triplet, the poor poet, painter, and actor. There was an abashed seediness of manner, only half covering the glimmering vanity and hope which shone beneath, as the fire shines through the ashes – a radiant confidence in his own genius, which neglect and failure might sadden, but could not suppress – a contrast between the visionary splendour of hopes formed in the twilight of reverie, which magnifies all things, and the actual poverty which was breaking his heart for the dear ones at the fireless hearth; in a word, there was a picture of the poor poet, such as the stage has never seen before – the eye lighting up its signal of contradiction to the seedy dress and starved sallowness of complexion. In his first scene, where his tragedies are rejected, and where Peg Woffington melts him with her kindness, he was less obviously but as truly a fine actor than in the garret scene, which is more effective on the stage. But go and see him, I say again, and note at the same time the delicate nuances with which Leigh Murray varies his coxcombs. In *Money*, he plays a quiet, selfish coxcomb; in *The Foundlings* he is inimitable as a goodnatured coxcomb, just stepped from the Guard's Club; in *Masks and Faces*, he plays a selfish, but clever, cold, and unscrupulous coxcomb, who is a fine gentleman because he is thrown among fine gentlemen, but whose quiet self-mastery and steady intellect imply that he is capable of playing a part in the world. For gentlemanly ease of bearing and truth of elocution quiet as effective, I commend this to your notice. If he will step aside with me a moment, I will just whisper that he makes rather too frequent use of the snuff-box; but that is the only fault, and a slight one.

Mrs Stirling has not for a long while had a part which shows her off to such advantage, and she evidently resolved not to let a bit of it slip through her fingers. She was gay, natural, touching, loving, throughout, and made one perfectly understand Ernest Vane's infatuation, though *not* his subsequent desertion of her for his wife. There must be some extraordinary charm in 'conjugal love' – some intense fascination in legal happiness which has hitherto escaped my observation; or else no man could possibly, with forty parsons' power of morality, think of quitting such a Peg Woffington for such a Mrs Vane! I must marry, and find out that secret! If I do marry, beloved reader! (I shan't; but I put the extreme hypothesis) I will tell you all about it; isn't that my function in this majestic universe – to tell you 'all about' everything?

I forgot to tell you about Mrs Leigh Murray; but I will not close without a line directing your attention to the truthfulness and pathos with which she plays a very small part, but a part which so many would have *over* played.

The Leader, 27 November 1852

Dutton Cook
School

A German original lies at the foundation of Mr Robertson's comedy of *School*,* which seems, moreover, something indebted to one of those fairy stories which Miss Thackeray has recently translated into everyday incident and modern life. The heroine of the comedy is a Miss Bella Marks, an orphan girl, who occupies the position of pupil teacher in an academy for young ladies, called Cedar-grove House, of which Dr and Mrs Sutcliffe are the proprietors and principals. In the opening scene Bella Marks is discovered reading aloud the story of *Cinderella* to a picturesque group of her fellow pupils, who by-the-by, must be said to be making acquaintance with the old nursery narrative at a somewhat advanced period of their scholastic career. Bella is herself a sort of Cinderella; she is required to perform distinctly menial duties in Mrs Sutcliffe's household, and, on the dispersion of the school girls, owing to the approach of a shooting party of gentlemen and to some alarm as to the presence of an ill-tempered bull in the neighbourhood, she takes to flight, leaving her slipper behind her. The bull is shot by Mr Pointz, and the slipper is found by Lord Beaufoy, two members of the shooting party, who are visitors at the house of Mr Farintosh, the uncle of the young nobleman. Mr Farintosh, a padded, rouged, and bewigged old gentleman, whose attempts

* Prince of Wales's Theatre.

at youthful airiness of manner contrast curiously with his manifold and conspicuous infirmities, is an old college friend of Dr Sutcliffe, and is most
anxious that his nephew, Lord Beaufoy, should marry Miss Naomi Tighe,
an heiress, who is a pupil at Cedar-grove House. The gentlemen obtain
admission to the academy, but it soon becomes apparent that Lord Beaufoy
has fallen in love with Cinderella, and that Miss Tighe's union with Mr Pointz
will certainly happen sooner or later. After this the fairy story is comparatively
neglected until quite the close of the play, and the plot stands still for some
time while the humours of life at a girl's school are being thoroughly investi-
gated and displayed. Certainly the Sutcliffe Academy would seem to have been
an establishment of an exceptional kind. Attached to the educational staff is
an usher, one Mr Krux, who has paid unsuccessful suit to Miss Marks, and
in revenge for his disappointment acts as a spy upon her movements, and
conveys to the heads of the school an unpleasant and unfaithful report of her
relations with Lord Beaufoy. Bella is dismissed the academy with ignominy,
and for some time her fate is uncertain. Meanwhile it has been discovered that
she is in truth the grandchild of wealthy Mr Farintosh, who, after a severe
illness, abandons artifices and cosmetics and presents himself as a very
venerable looking gentleman, freely manifesting the liberal disposition and the
overflowing heart that have throughout been his legitimate if carefully concealed and unsuspected possessions – an incident clearly borrowed from the
dramatic version of George Sand's *Beaux Messieurs de Bois-Doré*, which was
played last year at the Odeon. Finally all uneasiness on account of Bella is
set at rest. She steps from her carriage attended by powdered footmen. She is
the wife of Lord Beaufoy; the prince, marrying Cinderella, has, in fact, given
his hand and his title to his 'first cousin once removed'. The wicked usher is
cudgelled by Mr Pointz, who receives as his reward the love and the fortune
of Miss Naomi Tighe; and, the demands of poetic justice thus thoroughly
satisfied in every respect, the drama ends.

It will be observed that the plot of *School* is of slight substance and that the
events and characters of the comedy are not of a very unfamiliar kind. Yet the
story in representation is far from being without interest, and the quiet vein
of sentiment pervading it, attributable to the old poetic fable with which it
maintains an intermittent sort of alliance, helped to secure for it the approval
of the public. The first act is perhaps the best from a certain freshness of
contrivance which distinguishes it, although the billing and cooing by moonlight of the two pairs of lovers in the third act may find more positive popularity;
the second act, containing an examination of the school-girls in geography
and Roman history, much comicality of a commonplace kind being occa-
sioned by their elaborately erroneous replies, crosses the border-line of farce,
and the concluding act is of too artificial a pattern – the discovery of a long
lost child as the solution of a dramatic dilemma being a somewhat exhausted
device. It may be noted that the limited size of the Prince of Wales Theatre is of
real advantage to the class of plays Mr Robertson is fond of producing; a
story gains in strength and significance by being brought so closely to the view
of the spectators; and the players are not constrained to unnatural shouting

and grimacing in order that their speeches may be heard and the expression of their faces seen from distant portions of the house. Both author and actors are thus enabled to avoid the exaggeration of language and manner which has long been a prominent failing in dramatic writing and representation.

Although it failed, no doubt, to stir the sympathies of the audience so deeply as did the play of *Caste*, which still remains its author's best production, the success of *School* was unquestionable. The general representation was creditable to the Prince of Wales's company. Miss Addison, as the Cinderella of the drama, plays with much delicate pathos. Mr Montague, though he is deficient in tenderness, is easy and agreeable as 'the prince', Lord Beaufoy; the more prosaic and humorous lovers are well represented by Mr Bancroft and Miss Wilton, and Mr Hare provides a very finished presentment of the cosmeticized and decrepit Mr Farintosh.

Nights at the Play, 1883

Joseph Knight
Engaged

13 OCTOBER 1877

In his new comedy of *Engaged*,* Mr Gilbert is on familiar ground. Though no fairy influence or agency surrounds his characters or prompts their actions, the world in which they move is a region of pure fantasy. The idea on which the superstructure rests is kindred to that which forms the basis of *The Palace of Truth*. Each of the various personages he presents is compelled by some mysterious agency to reveal whatever is base in his nature. That species of mental reserve which underlies and qualifies our actions is here brought forward, and our deeds are read by the light of our unconscious avowals. As no one is shocked by the display of folly or meanness on the part of others, and as all seem to pride themselves on their candour, and to anticipate a favourable construction for their actions, the world, though nominally the Scottish border in the first act, and London in the two acts which follow, is, in fact, fairyland. Mr Gilbert's satire is strong and trenchant. Its obvious butt is less the intrinsic baseness of human nature than the falsehood of our social pretences. The one, in truth, includes the other. None except beings influenced by poor and pitiful motives would seek to present themselves to the

* Haymarket.

world as other than they are, and the prolonged existence of social shams affords proof how weak is the society in which they pass current. It is principally by implication, however, that Mr Gilbert attacks human nature in general. What he seeks to do is to supply the kind of reservation we unconsciously place upon our gifts. A man offers a distressed and defenceless woman his assistance. He does not, however, mean in so doing to be out of pocket by his chivalry. Mr Gilbert makes him speak his full thought. 'Count upon any assistance, madam, short of pecuniary aid, that I am able to offer.' The woman proclaims the passion she feels for her lover, and will be his through time and eternity if he will give her the home and comforts she regards as indispensable to her position. With equal frankness every character unburdens his mind, the result being to afford a picture of humanity more cynical than has perhaps been painted since the days of Swift.

It might almost be said, borrowing an illustration from Coleridge, that Mr Gilbert is the soul of Aristophanes *habitans in sicco*. He is as remorseless as the Greek satirist in the application to our sham virtues of the tests which separate the component parts and precipitate the hidden vice. He has, however, no purpose beyond provoking our laughter. That there is no such political significance in the satire as animates the defender of the Athenian republic may be attributed, in part, to changed conditions. There appears, however, to be in Mr Gilbert no moral aim whatever. The lesson, if any, to be extracted from his plays is that our nature is too pitiful to be redeemed, and that it is mere waste of time to sow the seed of virtue or improvement in a soil unfitted to receive it. In this respect he is less like Aristophanes than Swift. These things are not mentioned in condemnation of Mr Gilbert or of his method, but in simple explanation. It is, of course, impossible, in dealing with characters every one of whom is despicable, to count on the slightest manifestation of sympathy from the audience. The experiment has rarely, if ever before, been made of supplying a drama in three acts in which there is not a single human being who does not proclaim himself absolutely detestable. In the present instance it has been made, and it is a success. So witty is the treatment that the piece, to those who are prepared to accept the author's standpoint, is one of the most mirthful and original that has, during late years, been seen on the stage. In using the term 'original' we may make a slight exception: Mr Gilbert has stolen from no one except himself. In the character of Azema in *The Palace of Truth* he has worked to a certain extent the vein he now again explores.

In his exponents he has been fairly happy. Mr Honey who plays the hero, is unsuited to the part. Miss Marion Terry's acting is, however, in its unconsciousness, the perfection of burlesque, and Miss Buckstone, Miss Julia Stewart, Mr Howe, Mr Dewar, and Mr Kyrle realize fully the characters assigned them.

Theatrical Notes, 1893

William Archer
The Case of Rebellious Susan

In *The Case of Rebellious Susan* at the Criterion, Mr Henry Arthur Jones offers us that rarest of commodities in the theatrical market, a pure comedy. There are one or two scenes in which it deflects a little on the side of farce, but they are quite episodic; and where is the comedy-writer who has never availed himself of a little reasonable licence of caricature? English literature, assuredly, knows him not. At no point does Mr Jones's play trend towards drama. Great problems, great passions, great sufferings, do not enter into its scheme. Society is regarded from the ironic point of view, as an amusing game in which nothing very greatly matters, since only vanities and velleities, not love and life and death, are really at stake. It might have for its epilogue this single verse of Heine:

> Vorbei sind die Kinderspiele,
> Und Alles rollt vorbei –
> Das Geld und die Welt und die Zeiten
> Und Glauben und Lieb' und Treu'.

Not a very exhilarating epilogue, certainly, and I am more amused than surprised to observe that one critic at any rate (the only one whose judgment I have as yet seen) is seriously shocked and pained at the cynical 'sermon' which Mr Jones has preached. I think my esteemed colleague ought to look up his Lamb, for this is a case in which the famous plea for the irresponsibility of comedy really applies. If we insist on regarding it from the serious, moral, responsible point of view, we may say (forgive the facile Oscarism) that nothing is so tragic as comedy. Life, once for all, is not a laughing matter, and in the long run there is something essentially melancholy in the hollow pretence that it is. But for once in a way, and in certain moods, this pretence diverts and even delights us: we take our revenge on life by laughing at it: and it is to these moods that comedy appeals. More precisely, it seeks to beget these moods; therein lies its success. Let me say at once that *The Case of Rebellious Susan* succeeded to perfection so far as one, at least, of the audience was concerned. I don't know that the irresponsible mood lies nearer the surface in me than in another, and certainly I am the very last to sympathize seriously with the fireside-and-nursery ideal of womanhood which the play appeared to enforce. 'Nature's darling', says Sir Richard Kato, 'is a stay-at-home woman, a woman who wants to be a good wife and a good mother, *and cares very little for anything else.*' In that case, Nature and I differ, as we do, indeed, on a good many other points. Between ourselves, the woman I sympathize with in this play is Elaine Shrimpton. She happens to be a fool and a vixen; but that is not the fault of her ideas – it is their misfortune. If a creed or opinion were necessarily foolish because it is held by a certain number of fools, which of our world-wisdoms would 'scape whipping? Thus one barrel of the fowling-piece with which Mr Jones sets forth to shoot folly as it flies, is aimed at one of my own little ideals; while the other is levelled point-blank at what the satirist evidently holds to be but a pious opinion – the monogamous ideal of marriage. But what then? What is an ideal worth if you cannot afford to laugh at it once in a while? I laughed, and very heartily, at Mr Jones's banter. It is only when ridicule is stupid and malevolent that one resents it, like any other stupidity. If we decline to laugh at anything that is not wholly and solely and inherently and invariably ridiculous, there is an end of comedy.

The play, then, is a comedy pure and simple. If you chose to call it a comedietta, it would be hard to say you nay, for the whole gist of the matter might have been – nay, has been once and again – compressed into one act. A jealous wife rides the high horse for a certain time, threatens, and even attempts, vengeance in kind, and then climbs down more or less ingloriously – that is the whole story. Dumas eked it out into three acts in *Francillon*, more ingeniously and daringly than Mr Jones; but then Dumas had French society, French manners, to deal with, and that is a great advantage from the theatrical point of view. Mr Jones – I say it without the least impugning his originality – has very skilfully transposed the theme into the key of English life. The simplicity and directness of his handling please me immensely. His technique is really excellent. Note how he plunges straight into the middle of the matter in the first scene, without any tedious and conventional exposition. Dumas could have done no better; Sardou would not have done so well. He would have opened with two servants dusting the furniture and discussing their master and mistress in the intervals of a stereotyped flirtation. As the play goes on, too, we see how Mr Jones is moving with the times. He has no soliloquies, no overhearings; only one coincidence, and that a very simple one. The way in which the affair between Lady Susan and young Edensor is made to leak out is as pretty a piece of theatrical workmanship as heart can desire; and there is genuine and original comedy in the character of the Admiral, who, in the middle of an outpouring of vinous penitence for his conduct towards his 'jewel of a wife', rambles off into a complacent speculation as to why it is that 'the best Englishmen have always been such devils among the women'. Of course there is always a debit side to the account: the play has its weaknesses both of matter and manner. The erring husband, for example, is an inconceivable noodle, without a single convincing touch of character. A strong character he must not be, else the problem could not be worked out 'in committee', so to speak, and the comedy would have become drama. Dumas was confronted with much the same difficulty in *Francillon*, and he too made the husband a noodle; but there are noodles and noodles, and Lucien de Riverolles has ten times more character than Mr Jones's James Harabin. His imbecility reacts upon his wife: we can care very little for a woman who could ever care at all for such a man. Whatever else she forgave him, she ought not to have forgiven his suggestion that she should 'go to Hunt & Roskell's and choose something' – as a memento, it would seem, of this pleasing episode in their married life! On this principle, a lady's jewel-case might come to be a sort of bead-roll of her husband's conquests – a Leporello-register engrossed in gold and diamonds. Again, Mr Jones would have strengthened his last act enormously if he had prepared us for the sentimental passages between Sir Richard Kato and Mrs Quesnel. I confess I was utterly taken aback when Sir Richard began to play the Benedict, and many of the audience must certainly have been in the same case. Pray understand that I am not at all objecting to these love-passages in themselves; they are pleasant, and quite in place; but they would have been much more effective if something in the earlier acts had led us to expect them. Indeed the whole play would have been strengthened if this second, or third, thread of interest had run right through it.

And now we come to a delicate point – delicate, because it is impossible to touch upon it without an appearance of pettifogging and pedantry. Mr Jones, it seems to me, is not sufficiently alive to the value of words and phrases; he is negligent, not to say innocent, of style. It may seem unfair to descend to verbal cavillings which would be impossible if the author himself had not the courtesy to provide us with the printed text of his play; but I promise to adduce no examples which did not strike my ear as I heard the play on the stage, before I had ever set eyes on the book. Not for a moment would I urge Mr Jones to be more 'literary' in his diction: he is already too much inclined, now and then, to sink the dramatist in the essayist. But there is such a thing as style in dialogue, no less than in disquisition; rightly chosen words, and rightly balanced phrases, are just as essential to dramatic as to narrative or expository prose. Mr Jones is careless of these things. He often writes heavy and flaccid sentences which tax the elocution of the actor and the attention of the audience; and when an opportunity offers for some discreet little verbal felicity, he does not always seize it. Take, for instance, this speech of Sir Richard Kato's: 'Well, I can afford to look on with the complacent curiosity of an intelligent rustic who sees the coach rattling down the hill at a devil of a rate with runaway leaders and no break.' Here we have thirty-four words at a stretch, with 'no break', no resting-place for the voice, no opening for light-and-shade of delivery. The actor has simply to reel them out, like a conjuror drawing a ribbon from his mouth. You think this niggling hypercriticism? If you had to listen to a play containing many such phrases, you would alter your opinion, and realize the difference between nervous and flabby dialogue. I do not mean that Mr Jones's dialogue is flabby as a whole, but there are too many soft spots in it. Such, to take another example, is Sir Richard's catalogue of the ladies for whom he has sighed: 'A light girl, a dark girl, a red-haired girl; a tall girl, a short girl; a merry girl, a sad girl', and so forth. There is no trace of wit in any of these antitheses, or in the companion set with which Mrs Quesnel presently responds; and what sense is there in such a passage if it be not witty? Mr Jones may reply that he aims at naturalness, not at artificial wit, and that people in real life do not always talk wittily. No; but clever people, like Sir Richard and Mrs Quesnel, do not talk with this elaborate and long-drawn flatness; and if they did, we would rather not have their conversation reported. Some of the audience laughed, as people always do at mere patter; but this was distinctly one of the languid passages of the play. Yet again, to take a less obvious point, Mr Jones is too fond of allowing his characters, in sentimental passages, simply to echo each other's words. 'All's dull grey with me now', says Lucien, 'for the rest of my life'; and Lady Susan repeats, 'All's dull grey with me for the rest of my life.' Here, for once, the effect is pretty; but the trick is so very easy that it ought to be sparingly employed. A little further on Lucien says, 'I shall hide you in my heart till I die', and Lady Susan again echoes, 'And I shall hide you in my heart till I die.' This identity of phrase grates on the ear; we expect the second line of the couplet, and we have the first repeated instead. It is right that she should echo the sentiment, for that belongs to the amoebean rhetoric of love; but, on pain of mere mawkishness, she ought to vary the expression. She might have said, for instance, 'And I shall treasure you in mine as long as I live.' This is not very famous invention; Mr Jones might easily have hit on something prettier and tenderer; but it will serve to illustrate my meaning. If Mr Jones had worked over his dialogue two or three times, with keen and critical attention to these verbal niceties, *The Case of Rebellious Susan* would have had a much better chance of outlasting its first popularity.

The piece is capitally acted. Mr Wyndham's Sir Richard Kato is a real incarnation; he is the man himself, and could not possibly be better. Miss Mary Moore plays Lady Susan with agreeable vivacity; but the part really requires Miss Ada Rehan to bring out all its possibilities. Mr C. P. Little does what he can with the cruelly 'sacrificed' part of James Harabin; Mr Kemble plays the Admiral in a broadly effective fashion; and Mr Ben Webster is pleasant, if a trifle stiff, in the part of Lucien Edensor. Miss Fanny Coleman plays one of the excellent British matrons who usually fall to her lot, and Miss Gertrude Kingston makes a distinct character of Mrs Quesnel. Mr Fred Kerr and Miss Nina Boucicault enter with excellent spirit into the parts of Pybus and his Pioneering spouse.

The World, 10 October 1894

William Archer
The Importance of Being Earnest

The dramatic critic is not only a philosopher, moralist, aesthetician and stylist, but also a labourer working for his hire. In this last capacity he cares nothing for the classifications of Aristotle, Polonius, or any other theorist, but instinctively makes a fourfold division of the works which come within his ken. These are his categories: (1) Plays which are good to see. (2) Plays which are good to write about. (3) Plays which are both. (4) Plays which are neither. Class 4 is naturally the largest; Class 3 the smallest; and Classes 1 and 2 balance each other pretty evenly. Mr Oscar Wilde's new comedy, *The Importance of being Earnest** belongs indubitably to the first class. It is delightful to see it, it sends wave after wave of laughter curling and foaming round the theatre; but as a text for criticism it is barren and delusive. It is like a mirage-oasis in the desert, grateful and comforting to the weary eye – but when you come close up to it, behold! it is intangible, it eludes your grasp. What can a poor critic do with a play which raises no principle, whether of art or morals, creates its own canons and conventions, and is nothing but an absolutely wilful expression of an irrepressibly witty personality? Mr Pater, I think (or is it some one else?), has an essay on the tendency of all art to verge towards, and merge in, the absolute art – music. He might have found an example in *The Importance of Being Earnest*, which imitates nothing, represents nothing, is nothing, except a sort of rondo capriccioso, in which the artist's fingers run with crisp irresponsibility up and down the keyboard of life. Why attempt to analyse and class such a play? Its theme, in other hands, would have made a capital farce; but 'farce' is far too gross and commonplace a word to apply to such an irridescent filament of fantasy. Incidents of the same nature as Algy Moncrieffe's 'Bunburying' and John Worthing's invention and subsequent suppression of his scapegoat brother Ernest have done duty in many a French vaudeville and English adaptation; but Mr Wilde's humour transmutes them into something entirely new and individual. Amid so much that is negative, however, criticism may find one positive remark to make. Behind all Mr Wilde's whim and even perversity, there lurks a very genuine science, or perhaps I should say instinct, of the theatre. In all his plays and certainly not least in this one, the story is excellently told and illustrated with abundance of scenic detail. Monsieur Sarcey himself (if Mr Wilde will forgive my saying so) would 'chortle in his joy' over John Worthing's entrance in deep mourning (even down to his cane) to announce the death of his brother Ernest, when we know that Ernest in the flesh – a false but undeniable Ernest – is at that moment in the house making love to Cecily. The audience does not instantly awaken to the meaning of his inky suit, but even as he marches solemnly down the stage, and before a word is spoken, you can feel

* St James's Theatre.

the idea kindling from row to row, until a 'sudden glory' of laughter fills the theatre. It is only the born playwright who can imagine and work up to such an effect. Not that the play is a masterpiece of construction. It seemed to me that the author's invention languished a little after the middle of the second act, and that towards the close of that act there were even one or two brief patches of something almost like tediousness. But I have often noticed that the more successful the play, the more a first-night audience is apt to be troubled by inequalities of workmanship, of which subsequent audiences are barely conscious. The most happily-inspired scenes, coming to us with the gloss of novelty upon them, give us such keen pleasure, that passages which are only reasonably amusing are apt to seem, by contrast, positively dull. Later audiences, missing the shock of surprise which gave to the master-scenes their keenest zest, are also spared our sense of disappointment in the flatter passages, and enjoy the play more evenly all through. I myself, on seeing a play a second time, have often been greatly entertained by scenes which had gone near to boring me on the first night. When I see Mr Wilde's play again, I shall no doubt relish the last half of the second act more than I did on Thursday evening; and even then I differed from some of my colleagues who found the third act tedious. Mr Wilde is least fortunate where he drops into Mr Gilbert's Palace-of-Truth mannerism, as he is apt to do in the characters of Gwendolen and Cecily. Strange what a fascination this trick seems to possess for the comic playwright! Mr Pinero, Mr Shaw, and now Mr Wilde have all dabbled in it, never to their advantage. In the hands of the inventor it produces pretty effects enough:

> But Gilbert's magic may not copied be;
> Within that circle none should walk but he.

The acting is as hard to write about as the play. It is all good; but there is no opportunity for any striking excellence. The performers who are most happily suited are clearly Mr Allan Aynesworth and Miss Rose Leclercq, both of whom are delightful. Mr Alexander gives his ambition a rest, and fills his somewhat empty part with spirit and elegance. Miss Irene Vanbrugh makes a charmingly sophisticated maiden of Mayfair, and Miss Evelyn Millard, if not absolutely in her element as the unsophisticated Cecily, is at least graceful and pleasing. Mrs Canninge and Mr H. H. Vincent complete a very efficient cast.

The World, 20 February 1895

J. T. Grein
Trelawny of the 'Wells'

Mr Pinero, with a modesty bordering on humility, calls this delightful play*
a comedietta. He wants us, therefore, to take it lightly, and not to consider it as
a finished picture of some theatrical and non-theatrical folk of the crinoline
and horse-hair sofa days. But however light his touch, however sketchy his
characters, however thin the thread of plot that strings the four acts together,
there is far more depth in this little work than in many volumes of bulky
proportions.

The question is, will the large world of playgoers see and understand the
play as it ought to be seen and understood? Mr Pinero has oftentimes done
things which enchanted the few and bewildered the many; *The Times* is an
example; the memorable *Cabinet Minister* is another; yet another is *The
Amazons*; and all of these, for which he has been sparsely praised, are of his
later and glorious days. Earlier, when he had not yet 'arrived', and wrote in
that same half satirical, half pathetic style which is all his own, he was roundly
abused. No man has encountered more treacherous nails and splinters upon
the ladder of fame than our Pinero. And even now, while we hail him as the
premier playwright of the English-speaking world, it would seem that
the public is slow to appreciate Pinero at his best; it would have little of the
fascinating *Princess and the Butterfly*, and it is by no means certain whether it
will enjoy to the full the exquisite charm of *Trelawny*. For our author leads
us into a sphere which is foreign to most, even though their memory reaches
back to the period when the eccentric theatre – i.e. the theatre on the fringe
of West London – was in the lowest water.

Yet what a field of humour and of true comedy, what a treasure-trove for
an observant man! And Pinero, whose eyes dwell as keenly on the past as
they do on modern society, has drawn a wonderfully vivid picture of the simple-
minded, kind-hearted, rough-and-ready 'cabotins' who flourished at the
'Wells', and of the fossilized gentlefolk who lived in cold monotony in fashionable squares. This Rose, who, like 'bon chien chasse de race', is not happy
when she is taken from the stage to the noble mansion of her fiancé's grandfather, to see how she would acclimatize; this Tom Wrench, sick of stiltedness
and convention, and yearning to give something of his simple, natural self in
a play of unconventional form; this Avonia, common little creature, wont to
please the lowly crowd with her freaks and funny little ways, yet warm-
blooded and kind of heart as the best of women; these mummers all, whose
*H*s rise and fall like the tide, are no mere puppets of the author's conceit.
No; they are sketched from life, and, perhaps, a little rouged and made up for
the purpose of the stage; but, if we try to understand them, we can feel for
them, and live with them. The author is not quite so happy in his portraiture

* Court Theatre.

of the non-theatrical folk; here the satirist is uppermost, and, if young Gower, who wooed Rose, is a normal type of a young gentleman of the sixties, the Vice-Chancellor, Sir William Gower, his sister, and his friends, are more or less caricatures, obviously overdrawn for the purpose of contrast, but, for this reason, the weaker part of the play.

However, it matters little that the collateral characters are more fanciful than real; I would even venture to say that the very exaggeration enhances the charm of the play. It is from beginning to end highly diverting; it is episodically deeply interesting, and, to those who are intimate with the world behind the footlights, it is a conceit of amazing cleverness.

As usual, Mr Pinero has the good fortune to be well interpreted. I have but to take exception to two impersonations. Mr Dion Boucicault is undoubtedly clever, but he seems to forget that our London palate is more sensitive to the condiment of 'overdoing' than colonial taste. His performance as the old Vice-Chancellor constantly reminded us that a comparatively young man endeavoured to embody old age; it reminded us also of how great a loss the Court Theatre sustained in Arthur Cecil. And in the abundantly paragraphed Mr James Erskine, however painstaking he was, I discovered none of those qualifications which justified his being preferred to one of the many tried and hard-working actors who appear to be 'resting' just now. Acting in 'thinking parts' and a thorough training in elocution and deportment, would, I submit, be of greater service to Mr Erskine than his present occupation. Miss Irene Vanbrugh was a charming Rose; the part is long, difficult, and somewhat unsuited to her delicate style, but she conquered the obstacles with flying colours. Miss Hilda Spong had to do what would have been a fitting task for Marie Wilton; that she did not altogether fail is to her credit. Mr Athol Forde as the old actor, Mr Robson as the funny little Colpoys, and Mr Paul Arthur as Wrench, the yearning author, were an admirable triumvirate. But smaller parts were equally well done by Miss Bateman, Miss Le Thiere, Miss Eva Williams, Mr Du Maurier – in fact, I should like to transcribe the whole cast with a menu of fitting adjectives, for Mr Pinero always chooses the right people. On purpose I have not yet named Miss Pattie Browne, who was the joy of the evening as Avonia. True, the part plays itself, as it were; but Miss Pattie Browne endowed it with so much vivacity, so much *savoir faire*, engendered by vast experience, that the character, which is only secondary, stood out in brilliant prominence.

All things considered, *Trelawny of the 'Wells'* will hold its own in the record of Mr Pinero, and if London is to be taken by charm, it will assuredly capitulate.

Dramatic Criticism, 1899

Max Beerbohm
The Admirable Crichton

A WELCOME PLAY

I think *The Admirable Crichton* is quite the best thing that has happened, in my time, to the British stage. New ground has been broken before. But the breakage has ever been made too furtively to attract other miners, or too clumsily not to scare them back to the old congested camp; nor, indeed, has the new ground been invariably of the kind that is worth breaking. Keen, then, in my gladness that Mr Barrie has broken triumphantly, in the eyes of all men, the very ground whose infinite possibilities I have in these columns boomed so long and wistfully. Had the play been written by a tiro, Mr Frohman would have deserved all our thanks for his courage in producing it. But it needed no courage to produce a play by Mr Barrie. Is not he established as the prime purveyor of 'a good cry'? And was not it quite certain that the whole tear-loving public would come flocking from *Quality Street* to *The Admirable Crichton* for long enough to insure the management against actual loss on the production? The only doubt was whether they would catch the intention of the latter play. It was on the cards that they might treat the butler-hero of it as an excruciatingly pathetic figure, and weep floods of tears over his ultimate fate. In that case, so much the better for the box-office. As it happened, the public seemed on the first night really to understand what Mr Barrie was driving at, and seemed to delight in his meaning and his method. Not even the interminable entr'actes, due to a strike of stage carpenters, affected the consensus. Always, when a terrified gentleman in evening dress comes before the curtain and apologizes for delays, and appeals to 'the British love of fair play', he may absolutely rely on a rapturous salvo from the cosmopolosemitics who make up two-thirds of a first-night audience. But the other third, composed of unflattered Britons, is apt to be rather brutal. Not a sound of brutality assailed the apologist at the Duke of York's. Innumerable last trains were lost without a murmur. Thence my glad deduction that the public is ripe for the drama of modern fantasy.

You might, of course, remind me that the public is unripe for any other kind of drama. It is undeniable that the most successful modern plays are those which are most fantastically untrue to real life. But Mr Barrie's play differs from them in that it is frankly, and of a purpose, untrue to life. Here we have impossible people, dressed in the fashion of today doing impossible things, and yet (what a relief!) we are not asked to take them seriously (though, as I shall show, there is quite a serious side to them). In the first act, we are not quite in key. Force of habit is too strong for us, and we object that if a nobleman invited his servants to tea once a month, the good breeding of his sons and daughters would enable them to carry the thing off gracefully: they would not, at least, behave as do the sons and daughters of Lord Loam. Also, we object that all Lord Loam's servants (except Crichton, the philosophic butler) belong to a bygone generation – the generation before board-schools. We are not yet attuned to the fantasy, do not yet see the point of the fable. For the play is fable as well as fantasy. It is not, like the *New Arabian Nights*, which in many ways resembles it, a mere farcical distortion of modern actuality. It is formed and conditioned by a philosophic idea which bears on a problem of modern life – the problem of domestic service. Slavery was justified by Aristotle on the ground that a certain proportion of men are born with servile natures. 'Quite so,' says Mr Barrie, 'but *which* men?' He proceeds to show that servility is merely a matter of environment, and that the most servile of slaves may become, in a place where there is free competition, the most masterly of masters, and vice versa. This may not strike you as in itself a startingly new idea. But it is startingly new for the theatre. It has been circulating in the outer world only during the past five years or so. It never occurred to us before we began to realize the results of compulsory education. Our slaves are still servile enough, superficially, but we know that many of them are in all respects our superiors. And we feel very guilty and uncomfortable in their presence. We have given to them, and cannot now take away from them, the power to meet us and beat us on our own ground; and who knows how soon they will have the courage to exercise that power? Crichton, the butler, is the type – the fantastically faked type – of these potential monsters blindly created by us. So soon as the Loam family is stranded with him on a desert island, he becomes absolute master of them all. He has not changed in any inherent sense, nor have they. The difference is merely the difference of locality. There is no longer that veneer of custom and tradition which alone prevented Crichton from asserting himself at first. Mr Barrie might have made us more uncomfortable if, when the Loam family was rescued by a warship and taken home, Crichton had retained something of his influence. As it is, Crichton retires gracefully to a public house at 'the fashionable end' of the Harrow Road, much as Prince Florizel of Bohemia (whom I hope to see now some day upon the stage) retired to a cigar divan in Rupert Street. Nor does the ironic invention mar the logic of Mr Barrie's lesson. It merely enables even the most thoughtful and nervous of us to smile. Mr Barrie has always been able to amuse us. But this is the first occasion on which he has succeeded in making us also to think. And so he will excuse me for having insisted on the meaning of a play whose chief charm, from first to last, is in the uproarious fun of it.

Bestowing not on Mr Barrie's name (nor, indeed, on his own) the giddy benefit of capital letters or separate line, 'Charles Frohman presents

MISS IRENE VANBRUGH
and
MR H. B. IRVING

in' Mr Barrie's modest little effort. The form of the announcement is roughly significant of the relative commercial value of mimes and dramatists on the other side (perhaps, too, on this side) of the Atlantic Ocean. But it is rather hard on the two 'stars', of whose genial lustre and magnitude Mr Barrie here takes but slight advantage. Neither of them is allowed to shine with more than a modest radiance among the rest, and the authentic 'star' of the evening is a no greater person than small-typed, smuggled-in 'J. M. Barrie' himself. Admirable is Mr H. B. Irving, as Crichton, for his air of dignity and authority, and admirable for the appropriate solemnity with which he takes the ironic humour of the part. He is clearly cut out to play the aforesaid Florizel. The only fault in his present performance is a fault of omission: Crichton ought surely to betray an occasional trace of a cockney accent. That he shall be, in our eyes, socially as inferior to his servants on the island as to his employers in England is not less important a point than that throughout he shall seem to us morally and intellectually superior to them. Mr Irving seems to be socially the equal of the Loam family throughout. And thus something of the irony implicit in the family's subjection is lost for us. His love-scene with Lady Mary, his chivalrous determination to raise her to his own (insular) social position, would be much funnier, and more significant, if there were between the two characters the difference of tone that marks the plebeian from the aristocrat. That Mr Irving made himself too distinguished was the more a pity for that Miss Irene Vanbrugh, as Lady Mary, made herself too little so. When an actress succeeds signally in one part, she is told evermore by the critics that she has not yet ridded herself of that part's influence. Often this charge is quite unjust – a mere parrot-cry. But it does seem to me that Miss Irene Vanbrugh has indeed not yet shed the slough of Miss Sophie Fullgarney. She lacks the repose that once was hers. She is always making little skittish efforts, nodding and becking and wreathing smiles out of season. All these tricks were right and proper in the portrayal of such a young person as Miss Fullgarney. But the part of Lady Mary needs the quietism of good breeding, to bring out its irony and the irony of the whole theme. Miss Vanbrugh should live among poppies for a while.

The Saturday Review, 15 November 1902

Max Beerbohm
Peter Pan

THE CHILD BARRIE

Peter Pan; *or*, adds Mr Barrie, *The Boy Who Wouldn't Grow Up*. And he himself is that boy. That child, rather; for he halted earlier than most of the men who never come to maturity – halted before the age when soldiers and steam-engines began to dominate the soul. To remain, like Mr Kipling, a boy, is not at all uncommon. But I know not any one who remains, like Mr Barrie, a child. It is this unparalleled achievement that informs so much of Mr Barrie's last work, making it unique. This, too, surely, it is that makes Mr Barrie the most fashionable playwright of his time.

Undoubtedly, *Peter Pan* is the best thing he has done – the thing most directly from within himself. Here, at last, we see his talent in its full maturity; for here he has stripped off from himself the last flimsy remnants of a pretence to maturity. Time was when a tiny pair of trousers peeped from under his 'short-coats', and his sunny curls were parted and plastered down, and he jauntily affected the absence of a lisp, and spelt out the novels of Mr Meredith and said he liked them very much, and even used a pipe for another purpose than that of blowing soap-bubbles. But all this while, bless his little heart, he was suffering. It would have been pleasant enough to play at being grown-up among children of his own age. It was a fearful strain to play at being grown-up among grown-up persons. But he was forced to do this; because the managers of theatres, and the publishers of books, would have been utterly dumbfounded if he had asked them to take him as he was. The public, for all its child-worship, was not yet ripe for things not written ostensibly by adults. The managers, the publishers, the public, had to be educated gradually. A stray curl or two, now and again, an infrequent soap-bubble between the fumes – that was as much as could be adventured just at first. Time passed, and mankind was lured, little by little to the point when it could fondly accept Mr Barrie on his own terms. The tiny trousers were slipped off, and under the toy-heap were thrust the works of Mr Meredith. And every one sat around, nodding and smiling to one another rather fatuously, and blessing the little heart of Mr Barrie. All was not yet well, though – not perfectly well. By force of habit, the child occasionally gave itself the airs of an adult. There were such moments even in *Little Mary*. Now, at last, we see at the Duke of York's Theatre Mr Barrie in his quiddity undiluted – the child in a state of nature, unabashed – the child, as it were, in its bath, splashing, and crowing as it splashes.

The first of all the differences between a child's mind and an adult's is the vividness and abundance of a child's fancy. Silently in solitude, or orally among its peers, a child can weave an endless web of romance around itself and around all things. As a child grows into boyhood, this delicate faculty is dimmed. Manhood, in most cases, destroys it utterly. For, as we come to manhood, the logical side of our brain is developed; and the faculty for logic is ever foe to the faculty for romance. It is only in our sleep, when the logical side of our brain is at rest, that the romantic side is at liberty to assert itself. In our dreams we are still fluently romantic, fertile in curious invention. In our dreams romance rises up, laughing, to lord it over logic who lords it over her all day long. She laughs, and leads him a dance all through the night. Sometimes, if we wake suddenly in the night, so suddenly that we remember a dream clearly, logic in us is forced to admit that romance is no mere madcap – that there is, at least, a method in her madness, and that, as man to woman, he is no match for her at her best. Yet, sometimes, remembering a dream, we marvel at the verisimilitude of it, marvel at the soundness of invention in the dialogue that we were waging, or in the adventure that had befallen us. And, with a sigh, we confess that we could not compass consciously so admirable an effect. Even when, as usually happens, the remembered dream is but a tissue of foolishness, how amusing the foolishness is! Why cannot we be amusingly foolish in the manifold follies of our hours of vigil? On the whole, certainly, our minds work to better effect when we sleep than when we wake. Why cannot we sleep for ever? Or, since the mind of a man sleeping is equivalent to a child's mind, why cannot we be for ever children? It is only the man of genius who never experiences this vain regret – never hankers after childhood, with all its material and moral discomforts, for the sake of the spiritual magic in it. For the man of genius is that rare creature in whom imagination, not ousted by logic in full growth, abides, uncramped in unison with full-grown logic. Mr Barrie is not that rare creature, a man of genius. He is something even more rare – a child who, by some divine grace, can express through an artistic medium the childishness that is in him.

Our dreams are nearer to us than our childhood, and it is natural that *Peter Pan* should remind us more instantly of our dreams than of our childish fancies. One English dramatist, a man of genius, realized a dream for us; but the logic in him prevented him from indulging in that wildness and incoherence which are typical of all but the finest dreams. Credible and orderly are the doings of Puck in comparison with the doings of Peter Pan. Was ever, out of dreamland, such a riot of inconsequence and of exquisite futility? Things happen in such wise that presently one can conceive nothing that might not conceivably happen, nor anything that one would not, as in a dream, accept unhesitatingly. Even as in a dream, there is no reason why the things should ever cease to happen. What possible conclusion can inhere in them? The only possible conclusion is from without. The sun shines through the bedroom window, or there is a tapping at the bedroom door, or – some playgoers must catch trains, others must sup. Even as you, awakened, turn on your pillow, wishing to pursue the dream, so, as you leave the Duke of York's, will you rebel at the dream's rude and arbitrary ending, and will try vainly to imagine what other unimaginable things were in store for you. For me to describe to you now in black and white the happenings in *Peter Pan* would be a thankless task. One cannot communicate the magic of a dream. People who insist on telling their dreams are among the terrors of the breakfast table. You must go to the Duke of York's, there to dream for yourselves.

The fact that Mr Barrie is a child would be enough, in this generation which so adores children, to account for his unexampled vogue. But Mr Barrie has a second passport. For he, too, even pre-eminently, adores children – never ceases to study them and their little ways, and to purr sentimental paeans over them, and finds it even a little hard to remember that the world really does contain a sprinkling of adults. In fact, his attitude towards children is the fashionable attitude, struck more saliently by him than by any one else, and with more obvious sincerity than by the average person. It is not to be wondered at that his preoccupation with children endears him to the community. The strange thing is the preoccupation itself. It forces me to suppose that Mr Barrie has, after all, to some extent, grown up. For children are the last thing with which a child concerns itself. A child takes children as a matter of course, and passes on to more important things – remote things that have a glorious existence in the child's imagination. A little boy does not say 'I am a child', but 'I am a pirate', or 'a greengrocer', or 'an angel', as the case may be. A little girl does not say 'I am a little girl, and these are my dolls, and this is my baby brother', but 'I am the mother of this family'. She lavishes on her dolls and on her baby-brother a wealth of maternal affection, cooing over them, and . . . stay! that is just Mr Barrie's way. I need not, after all, mar by qualification my theory that Mr Barrie has never grown up. He is still a child, absolutely. But some fairy once waved a wand over him, and changed him from a dear little boy into a dear little girl. Some critics have wondered why among the characters in *Peter Pan* appeared a dear little girl, named in the programme 'Liza (the Author of the Play)'. Now they know. Mr Barrie was just 'playing at symbolists'.

The Saturday Review, 7 January 1905

The Coming of Ibsen

William Archer
A Doll's House

If we may measure fame by mileage of newspaper comment, Henrik Ibsen has for the past month been the most famous man in the English literary world. Since Robert Elsmere left the Church, no event in 'coëval fictive art' (to quote a modern stylist) has exercised men's, and women's, minds so much as Nora Helmer's departure from her Doll's House. Indeed the latter exit may be said to have awakened even more vibrant echoes than the former; for, while Robert made as little noise as possible, Nora slammed the door behind her. Nothing could be more trenchant than her action, unless it be her speech. Whatever its merits or defects, *A Doll's House* has certainly the property of stimulating discussion. We are at present bandying the very arguments which hurtled around it in Scandinavia and in Germany nine years ago. When the play was first produced in Copenhagen, some one wrote a charming little satire upon it in the shape of a debate as to its tendency between a party of little girls around a nursery tea-table. It ended in the hostess, aged ten, gravely declaring that had the case been hers, she would have done exactly as Nora did. I do not know whether the fame of *A Doll's House* has reached the British nursery, but I have certainly read some comments on it which might very well have emanated from that abode of innocence.

Puerilities and irrelevances apart, the adult and intelligent criticism of Ibsen as represented in *A Doll's House*, seems to run on three main lines. It is said, in the first place, that he is not an artist but a preacher; secondly, that his doctrine is neither new nor true; thirdly, that in order to enforce it, he oversteps the limits of artistic propriety. I propose to look into these three allegations. First, however, I must disclaim all right to be regarded as in any way a mouthpiece for the poet's own views. My personal intercourse with Henrik Ibsen, though to me very pleasant and memorable, has been but slight. I view his plays from the pit, not from the author's box. Very likely – nay, certainly – I often misread his meaning. My only right to take part in the discussion arises from a long and loving study of all his writings, and from the minute familiarity with *A Doll's House* in particular, acquired in the course of translating and staging it.

Is it true, then, that he is a dramatic preacher rather than a dramatic poet?

or, in other words, that his art is vitiated by didacticism? Some writers have assumed that in calling him didactic they have said the last word, and dismissed him for ever from the ranks of the great artists. Of them I would fain enquire what really great art is not didactic? The true distinction is not between didactic art and 'art for art's sake', but between primarily didactic and ultimately didactic art. Art for art's sake, properly so called, is mere decoration; and even it, in the last analysis, has its gospel to preach. By primarily didactic art I mean that in which the moral bearing is obvious, and was clearly present to the artist's mind. By ultimately didactic art I mean that which essays to teach as life itself teaches, exhibiting the fact and leaving the observer to trace and formulate the underlying law. It is the fashion of the day to regard this unconsciously didactic art, if I may call it so – its unconsciousness is sometimes a very transparent pose – as essentially higher than the art which is primarily and consciously didactic, dynamic. Well, it is useless to dispute about higher and lower. From our point of view the Australians seem to be walking head-downwards, like flies on the ceiling; from their point of view we are in the same predicament; it all depends on the point of view. Ibsen certainly belongs, at any rate in his modern prose plays, to the consciously didactic artists whom you may, if you choose, relegate to a lower plane. But how glorious the company that will have to step down along with him! What were the Greek tragic poets if not consciously didactic? What is comedy, from time immemorial, but a deliberate lesson in life? Down Plautus; down Terence; down Molière and Holberg and Beaumarchais and Dumas! Calderon and Cervantes must be kind enough to follow; so must Schiller and Goethe. If German criticism is to be believed Shakespeare was the most hardened sermonizer of all literature; but in this respect I think German criticism is to be disbelieved. Shakespeare, then, may be left in possession of the pinnacle of Parnassus; but who shall keep him company? Flaubert, perhaps, and M. Guy de Maupassant?

The despisers of Ibsen, then, have not justified their position when they have merely proved, what no one disputes, that he is a didactic writer. They must further prove that his teaching kills his art. For my part, looking at his dramatic production all round, and excepting only the two great dramas in verse, *Brand* and *Peer Gynt*, I am willing to admit that his teaching does now and then, in perfectly trifling details, affect his art for the worse. Not his direct teaching – that, as it seems to me, he always inspires with the breath of life – but his proclivity to what I may perhaps call symbolic side-issues. In the aforesaid dramas in verse this symbolism is eminently in place; not so, it seems to me, in the realistic plays. I once asked him how he justified this tendency in his art; he replied that life is one tissue of symbols. 'Certainly,' I might have answered; 'but when we have its symbolic side too persistently obtruded upon us, we lose the sense of reality, which, according to your own theory, the modern dramatist should above all things aim at.' There may be some excellent answer to this criticism; I give it for what it is worth. Apart from these symbolic details, it seems to me that Ibsen is singularly successful in vitalizing his work; in reproducing the forms, the phenomena of life, as well as its deeper meanings. Let us take the example nearest at hand – *A Doll's*

House. I venture to say – for this is a matter of fact rather than of opinion – that in the minds of thousands in Scandinavia and Germany, Nora Helmer lives with an intense and palpitating life such as belongs to few fictitious characters. Habitually and instinctively men pay Ibsen the compliment (so often paid to Shakespeare) of discussing her as though she were a real woman, living a life of her own, quite apart from the poet's creative intelligence. The very critics who begin by railing at her as a puppet end by denouncing her as a woman. She irritates, troubles, fascinates them as no puppet ever could. Moreover, the triumph of the actress is the dramatist's best defence. Miss Achurch might have the genius of Rachel and Desclée in one, yet she could not transmute into flesh and blood the doctrinary doll, stuffed with sawdust and sophistry, whom some people declare Nora to be. Men do not shudder at the agony or weep over the woes of an intellectual abstraction. As for Helmer, I am not aware that any one has accused him of unreality. He is too real for most people – he is commonplace, unpleasant, objectionable. The truth is, he touches us too nearly; he is the typical husband of what may be called chattel matrimony. If there are few Doll's-Houses in England, it is certainly for lack of Noras, not for lack of Helmers. I admit that in my opinion Ibsen has treated Helmer somewhat unfairly. He has not exactly disguised, but has omitted to emphasize, the fact that if Helmer helped to make Nora a doll, Nora helped to make Helmer a prig. By giving Nora all the logic in the last scene (and she is not a scrupulous dialectician) he has left the casual observer to conclude that he lays the whole responsibility on Helmer. This conclusion is not just, but it is specious; and so far, and so far only, I grant that the play has somewhat the air of a piece of special pleading. I shall presently discuss the last scene in greater detail; but even admitting for the moment that the polemist here gets the better of the poet, can we call the poet, who has moved freely through two acts and two-thirds, nothing but a doctrinary polemist?

Let me add that *A Doll's House* is, of all Ibsen's plays, the one in which a definite thesis is most tangibly posited – the one, therefore, which is most exposed to the reproach of being a mere sociological pamphlet. His other plays may be said to scintillate with manifold ethical meanings; here the light is focused upon one point in the social system. I do not imply that *A Doll's House* is less throughly vitalized than *Ghosts*, or *Rosmersholm*, or *The Lady from the Sea*. What I mean is, that the play may in some eyes acquire a false air of being merely didactic from the fortuitous circumstance that its moral can be easily formulated.

The second line of criticism is that which attacks the substance of Ibsen's so-called doctrines, on the ground that they are neither new nor true. To the former objection one is inclined to answer curtly but pertinently, 'Who said they were?' It is not the business of the creative artist to make the great generalizations which mark the stages of intellectual and social progress. Certainly Ibsen did not discover the theory of evolution or the doctrine of heredity, any more than he discovered gravitation. He was not the first to denounce the subjection of women; he was not the first to sneer at the 'compact liberal majority' of our pseudo-democracies. His function is to seize and throw into relief certain aspects of modern life. He shows us society as Kean was said to read Shakespeare – by flashes of lightning – luridly, but with intense vividness. He selects subjects which seem to him to illustrate such and such political, ethical, or sociological ideas; but he does not profess to have invented the ideas. They are common property; they are in the air. A grave injustice has been done him of late by those of his English admirers who have set him up as a social prophet, and have sometimes omitted to mention that he is a bit of a poet as well. It is so much easier to import an idea than the flesh and blood, the imagination, the passion, the style in which it is clothed. People have heard so much of the 'gospel according to Ibsen' that they have come to think of him as a mere hot-gospeller, the Boanerges of some strange social propaganda. As a matter of fact Ibsen has no gospel whatever, in the sense of a systematic body of doctrine. He is not a Schopenhauer, and still less a Comte. There never was a less systematic thinker. Truth is not, in his eyes, one and indivisible; it is many-sided, many-visaged, almost Protean. It belongs to the irony of fate that the least dogmatic of thinkers – the man who has said of himself, 'I only ask: my call is not to answer' – should figure in the imagination of so many English critics as a dour dogmatist, a vendor of social nostrums in pilule form. He is far more of a paradoxist than a dogmatist. A thinker he is most certainly, but not an inventor of brand new notions such as no one has ever before conceived. His originality lies in giving intense dramatic life to modern ideas, and often stamping them afresh, as regards mere verbal form, in the mint of his imaginative wit.

The second allegation, that his doctrines are not true, is half answered when we have insisted that they are not put forward (at any rate by Ibsen himself) as a body of inspired dogmas. No man rejects more consistently than he the idea of finality. He does not pretend to have said the last word on any subject. 'You needn't believe me unless you like,' says Dr Stockmann in *An Enemy of the People*, 'but truths are not the tough old Methuselahs people take them to be. A normally constituted truth lives, let us say, some seventeen or eighteen years; at most twenty.' The telling of absolute truths, to put it in another way, is scarcely Ibsen's aim. He is more concerned with destroying conventional lies, and exorcising the 'ghosts' of dead truths; and most of all concerned to make people think and see for themselves. Here again we recognize the essential injustice of regarding a dramatic poet as a sort of prophet-professor, who means all his characters say and makes them say all he means. I have been asked, for example, whether Ibsen intends us to understand by the last scene of *A Doll's House* that awakened wives ought to leave their husbands and children in order to cultivate their souls in solitude. Ibsen intends nothing of the sort. He draws a picture of a typical household; he creates a man and woman with certain characteristics; he places them in a series of situations which at once develop their characters and suggest large questions of conduct; and he makes the woman, in the end, adopt a course of action which he (rightly or wrongly) believes to be consistent with her individual nature and circumstances. It is true that this course of action is so devised as to throw the principles at stake into the strongest relief; but the object of that is to make people thoroughly realize the problem, not to force upon them the particular solution arrived at in this particular case. No two life-problems were ever precisely alike, and in stating and solving one, Ibsen does not pretend to supply a ready-made solution for all the rest. He illustrates, or, rather, illumines, a general principle by a conceivable case; that is all. To treat Nora's arguments in the last scene of *A Doll's House* as though they were the ordered propositions of an essay by John Stuart Mill is to give a striking example of the strange literalness of the English mind, its inability to distinguish between drama and dogma. To me that last scene is the most moving in the play, precisely because I hold it the most dramatic. It has been called a piece of pure logic – is it not rather logic conditioned by character and saturated with emotion? Some years ago I saw *Et Dukkehjem* acted in Christiania. It was an off season; only the second-rate members of the company were engaged; and throughout two acts and a half I sat vainly striving to recapture the emotions I had so often felt in reading the play. But the moment Nora and Helmer were seated face to face, at the words, 'No, that is just it; you do not understand me; and I have never understood you – till tonight' – at that moment, much to my own surprise, the thing suddenly gripped my heart-strings; to use an expressive Americanism, I 'sat up'; and every phrase of Nora's threnody over her dead dreams, her lost illusions, thrilled me to the very marrow. Night after night I went to see that scene; night after night I have watched it in the English version; it has never lost its power over me. And why? Not because Nora's sayings are particularly wise or particularly true, but because, in her own words, they are so true *for her*, because she feels them so deeply and utters them so exquisitely. Certainly she is unfair, certainly she is one-sided, certainly she is illogical; if she were not, Ibsen would be the pamphleteer he is supposed to be, not the poet he is. 'I have never been happy here – only merry. . . . You have never loved me – you have only found it amusing to be in love with me.' Have we not in these speeches the very mingling of truth and falsehood, of justice and injustice, necessary to humanize the character and the situation? After Nora has declared her intention of leaving her home, Helmer remarks, 'Then there is only one explanation possible – You no longer love me.' 'No,' she replies, 'that is just it.' 'Nora! can you say so?' cries Helmer, looking into her eyes. '*Oh, I'm so sorry, Torvald*,' she answers, '*for you've always been so kind to me.*' Is this pamphleteering? To me it seems like the subtlest human pathos. Again, when she says 'At that moment it became clear to me that I had been living here for eight years with a strange man and had borne him three children – Oh, I can't bear to think of it! I could tear myself to pieces' – who can possibly take this for anything but a purely dramatic utterance? It is true and touching in Nora's mouth, but it is obviously founded on a vague sentiment, that may or may not bear analysis. Nora postulates a certain transcendental community of spirit as the foundation and justification of marriage. The idea is very womanly and may also be very practical; but Ibsen would probably be the first to admit that before it can claim the validity of a social principle we must ascertain whether it be possible for any two human beings to be other than what Nora would call strangers. This further analysis the hearer must carry out for him, or her, self. The poet has stimulated thought; he has not tried to lay down a hard-and-fast rule of conduct. Again, when Helmer says, 'No man sacrifices his honour even for one he loves,' and Nora retorts, '*Millions of women have done that!*' we applaud the consummate claptrap, not on account of its abstract justice, but rather of its characteristic injustice. Logically, it is naught; dramatically, one feels it to be a masterstroke. Here, it is the right speech in the right place; in a sociological monograph it would be absurd. My position, in short, is that in Ibsen's plays, as in those of any other dramatist who keeps within the bounds of his form, we must look, not for the axioms and demonstrations of a scientific system, but simply for 'broken lights' of truth, refracted through character and circumstance. The playwright who sends on a Chorus or a lecturer, unconnected with the dramatic action, to moralize the spectacle and put all the dots on all the *i*s, may fairly be taken to task for the substance of his 'doctrines'. But that playwright is Dumas, not Ibsen.

Lastly, we come to the assertion that Ibsen is a 'coarse' writer, with a morbid love for using the theatre as a physiological lecture-room. Here again I can only cry out upon the chance which has led to so grotesque a misconception. He has written some twenty plays, of which all except two might be read aloud, with only the most trivial omissions, in any young ladies' boarding-school from Tobolsk to Tangiers. The two exceptions are *A Doll's House* and *Ghosts* – the very plays which happen to have come (more or less) within the ken of English critics. In *A Doll's House* he touches upon, in *Ghosts* he frankly faces, the problem of hereditary disease, which interests him, not in itself, but simply as the physical type and symbol of so many social and ethical phenomena. *Ghosts* I have not space to consider. If art is for ever debarred from entering upon certain domains of human experience, then *Ghosts* is an inartistic work. I can only say, after having read it, seen it on the stage, and translated it, that no other modern play seems to me to fulfil so entirely the Aristotelian ideal of purging the soul by means of terror and pity. In *A Doll's House*, again, there are two passages, one in the second and one in the third act, which Mr Podsnap could not conveniently explain to the young lady in the dress-circle. Whether the young lady in the dress-circle would be any the worse for having them explained to her is a question I shall not discuss. As a matter of fact, far from being coarsely treated, they are so delicately touched that the young person suspects nothing and is in no way incommoded. It is Mr Podsnap himself that cries out – the virtuous Podsnap who, at the French theatre, writhes in his stall with laughter at speeches and situations *à faire rougir des singes*. I have more than once been reproached, by people who had seen *A Doll's House* at the Novelty, with having cut the speeches which the first-night criticis pronounced objectionable. It has cost me some trouble to persuade them that not a word had been cut, and that the text they found so innocent contained every one of the enormities denounced by the critics. Mr Podsnap, I may add, has in this case shown his usual alacrity in putting the worst possible interpretation upon things. Dr Rank's declaration to Nora that Helmer is not the only man who would willingly lay down his life for her, has been represented as a hideous attempt on the part of a dying debauchee to seduce his friend's wife. Nothing is further from the mind of poor Rank, who, by the way, is not a debauchee at all. He knows himself to be at death's door; Nora, in her Doll's House, has given light and warmth to his lonely, lingering existence; he has silently adored her while standing with her, as with her husband, on terms of frank comradeship; is he to leave her for ever without saying, as he puts it, 'Thanks for the light'? Surely this is a piece either of inhuman austerity or of prurient prudery; surely Mrs Podsnap herself could not feel a suspicion of insult in such a declaration. True, it comes inaptly at that particular moment, rendering it impossible for Nora to make the request she contemplates. But essentially, and even from the most conventional point of view, I fail to see anything inadmissible in Rank's conduct to Nora. Nora's conduct to Rank, in the stocking scene, is another question; but that is merely a side-light on the relation between Nora and Helmer, preparatory, in a sense, to the scene before Rank's entrance in the last act.

In conclusion, what are the chances that Ibsen's modern plays will ever take a permanent place on the English stage? They are not great, it seems to me. The success of *A Doll's House* will naturally encourage Ibsen's admirers to further experiments in the same direction – interesting and instructive experiments I have no doubt. We shall see in course of time *The Young Men's League, The Pillars of Society, An Enemy of the People, Rosmersholm,* and *A Lady from the Sea* – I name them in chronological order. But none of these plays presents the double attraction that has made the success of *A Doll's House* – the distinct plea for female emancipation which appeals to the thinking public, and the overwhelming part for an actress of genius which attracts the ordinary playgoer. The other plays I cannot but foresee, will be in a measure antiquated before the great public is ripe for a thorough appreciation of them. I should like to see an attempt made to produce one of the poet's historical plays, but that would involve an outlay for costumes and mounting not to be lightly faced. On the other hand I have not the remotest doubt that Ibsen will bulk more and more largely as years go on in the consciousness of all students of literature in general, as opposed to the stage in particular. The creator of *Brand* and *Peer Gynt* is one of the great poets of the world.

The Fortnightly Review, July 1889

A. B. Walkley
Rosmersholm

Ibsen, in the circles of English Podsnappery, is waved aside as a Chimaera, but those of us who are still prepared to erect altars to any sort of unknown god (automatic, of course, in the underground stations – with a slot for the worshipper's penny), think of him rather as a nineteenth-century Sphinx. He has the fascination of the inscrutable, the mysterious, the enigmatic. Now the Sphinx is quite a new Idol of the Theatre. The average modern play, on the psychological side – when it has any psychology at all, which is not often – is as plain as a pikestaff; its moods, its emotions, its currents of thought, are carefully focused to the vision of *l'homme sensuel moyen*, the ten-pound householder, the gentleman who always takes an unfair share of the room on the knifeboard of the omnibus. Ibsen, on the other hand, empties out on the stage a bag of entirely new psychological tricks; with him new-fangled philosophies, religious aspirations, hitherto only dimly perceived by the Englishman in books (mostly 'on grey paper with blunt type'), are for the first time seen in the playhouse; obstinate questionings of invisible things are for the first time heard there. And, along with his new subject-matter, he has brought a new *technique*. It is because, then, of the novelty of his theatre, because he is a 'strong man', an athlete, lifting heavy philosophical weights where such weights have never been lifted before, and because he lifts them in calm contempt of all the old orthodox laws of theatrical gymnastics, that so many of us are attracted to Ibsen; not, as a vain people supposeth, because we approve the conduct of his personages, or regard ourselves as the addressees of his ethical 'message' – whatever that queer missive may be. We take a purely aesthetic delight in him, because he gives us new impressions. There is an impressionist in one of Mr Henry James's novels, whose *animula vagula blandula* is summed up in this way: 'I drift, I float, my feelings direct me – if such a life as mine may be said to have a direction. Where there's anything to feel I try to be there!' Well, dramatic criticism just now is impressionist; it is drifting and floating. There is always something to feel in the playhouse, when Ibsen is being played, and we try to be there.

The novelty of Ibsen's method must have leapt to the eyes of those who visited the Vaudeville Theatre when *Rosmersholm* (translated by Mr Charles Archer) was played for the first time on the English stage. Baldly and brutally stated, the story is by no means new. An adventuress, Rebecca West (not Sharp), establishes her footing in Rosmersholm, a household where the Rosmers, husband and wife, suffer from what the Divorce Court records call incompatibility of temper. By innuendo and suggestion Rebecca succeeds in convincing the wife that she is *de trop*, and that the best thing she can do is to efface herself and so leave her husband free to wed his kindred soul, the adventuress. Brought to this conviction, Mrs Rosmer throws herself into the mill-race at the end of the garden. After living for a while in a Fool's Paradise,

Rosmer learns from external sources that his wife has committed suicide not, as he supposed, in a fit of madness, but in order to make way for Rebecca. That lady's own confession then opens his eyes as to the share she had in the tragedy. Of course, there is only one end to all this. Poetic justice must be done. To expiate their crime, hers of deliberate intention, his of blind folly, they both follow the dead woman into the mill-race.

How this theme would be treated on our native stage it is not difficult to guess. We 'drive at practice', as Jeremy Collier was the first to say, and the material, mechanical side of the tragedy would be the side for the English playwright. The scene of 'the Bridge by Moonlight' (with real water) would be the *clou* of the piece, The adventuress (as Mr Jerome K. Jerome knows) would wear sky-blue satin, smoke cigarettes, with her feet on the table, and probably push Mrs Rosmer into the mill-race *propria manu*, as Lady Audley pushed the gentleman down the well. She herself would be drowned in the mill-race by accident (that time she came down that way to gloat over the late Mrs R.), and Rosmer would be drowned in trying to rescue her. Then an old family servant (or the 'comic man', reformed) would come in with a Bible, and say, 'The wages of sin is death'. Curtain.

In Paris, they would try another way. There would be no 'stupendous mechanical effects'. Everything would be done by talk, and within four walls, as everything is actually done in Ibsen's play. But the personages would not talk much about themselves; they would exchange repartees and listen to a long-haired poet reciting *décadent* or *déliquescent* verses, while they themselves would be explained and commented on by a third person, a sort of lecturer without the wand. But both French and English playwrights, be sure, would have one thing in common: they would both begin at the beginning, i.e., start with Rebecca's entry into Rosmersholm, and show us Mrs Rosmer in the flesh.

Now turn to Ibsen, and see how fresh, how audacious, his treatment is. He starts – where the undergraduate's Ibis walked safest – in the middle, and works backwards. Mrs Rosmer's suicide has occurred some time before the curtain rises, and for a good half of the play 'the enigma of the mill-race', as one of the personages calls it, remains unsolved. Through two entire acts we are left without any hint that Rebecca is not what she seems, that she is other than a 'sympathetic' character. It is not until the third act is nearly over that we discover that it was this apparently harmless young lady, with the mild demeanour and the advanced Liberal opinions, who practically sent Mrs Rosmer headlong into the mill-race. And why she did it we do not learn until just before the curtain finally falls. Note that, whatever we learn, we learn at first hand, from the characters themselves, not from a Dumasian commentator or *raisonneur*. Ibsen's personages always explain themselves, analyse themselves, put themselves under the microscope, pull themselves up by the roots to watch how they are growing, eviscerate themselves to see where the golden eggs come from. They are for ever asking themselves: Why did I come into the world, and what (to speak as M. Paul Bourget doth) is my *état d'âme*? And what a curious, remote 'soul-state' that is! When we come to examine it, we find that the plot of *Rosmersholm*, which I, purposely, began by stating in terms of vulgar melodrama, serves Ibsen as the sub-structure for nothing either vulgar or melodramatic, but for a veritable Soul's Tragedy. Rebecca is found to have established herself in the Rosmersholm household because, if you please, she saw there scope for the development of her 'views', because Rosmer would make her a useful intel-lectual companion – what academic youth calls a 'reading-chum'. 'I wanted to take my share in the life of the new era that was dawning, with all its new ideas. We two, I thought, should march onward in freedom, side by side. But between you and freedom rose that dismal, insurmountable barrier . . .' Mrs Rosmer. Hence the tragedy of the mill-race. Note, too, that the old con-cept of free-will, which had found a last place of refuge in the theatre, is now finally abolished, Rebecca has a metaphysical explanation for her conduct, pat. 'You think I was cool and calculating and self-possessed all the time! I was not then the same woman as I am now, as I stand here relating it all. *And then there are two sorts of will in us, I believe!* I wanted Beata away; but all the same I never believed that it would come to pass. And yet I *could* not stop. I *had* to venture the least little bit further. *That is the way such things come about.*' One cannot listen to that sort of thing without recognizing in Ibsen a new stage-force. All his drama is internal, the evolution of succes-sive 'soul-states'. Even Rebecca's confession is not brought about, as in other hands it assuredly would be, by external means. She simply makes it to restore to Rosmer (whom she has learnt to love) his sense of 'innocence', to lift from his mind the consciousness of guilt which prevents him from continuing his life-work of 'ennobling human souls, making every man in the land a noble man'. Of course she is not troubled by any feeling so old-fashioned and unscientific as mere remorse. There can be no remorse where there has been no free-will. Rosmer, too, has his own soul's tragedy in his conversion, under Rebecca's guidance, from conservatism to liberalism, from orthodoxy (he is a retired clergyman) to free-thought. All this is very piquant, *bizarre*, fresh, of absorbing interest to the serious spectator, and to the more eclectic *dilettante* (say the Des Essarts of M. Huysmans), at least as fascinating as a Japanese curio or the rare edition (uncut) of the *Pastissier Francoys*. One feels that Ibsen's people are ourselves, yet not ourselves. They are intensely human, yet intensely Scandinavian – much farther from us English, with their introspection, their gravity, their melancholy, their morbid intellectuality, than the mere extent of the voyage by steamer from Hull to Bergen. No wonder the blither spirits among them, the Ulric Brendals and the Ejlert Lövborgs, take to drink, for they breathe an atmosphere, in Johnson's phrase, of 'inspissated gloom'.

Playhouse Impressions, 1892

Clement Scott
Ghosts

In the old schoolboy days there existed – and, for aught I know to the contrary, there may exist now – a popular phrase that expressed unfeigned astonishment at almost boundless audacity. We were wont to say to our juniors, 'Well, it is just like your cheek to do so and so.' But in all my experience of the stage, its customs, its changes, and its directors of public taste, I have seldom known a 'cheekier' move than the opening of the Royalty Theatre, already licensed by the Lord Chamberlain to a recognized actress and directress, with a play that has not passed the censorship, and that play none other than the revolting *Ghosts* of the Scandinavian Ibsen. But the 'cheek' does not end there, by any means. It goes on to imply that our poor, neglected, and degraded stage, having no literature of its own, and fettered with the shackles of what the revolutionaries call 'conventionality', is to be taught what literature is with the aid of a dull, verbose preacher, and is to learn what freedom is by means of a play that may be obnoxious to many men, and that cannot possibly be discussed in all its morbid details in any mixed assembly of men and women. Nay, even there the audacity does not stop, for the invited guests to the new Free and Independent Theatre are not permitted to depart home after as wearisome an evening as could well be passed within the walls of a playhouse without being mildly lectured by the founder of the fun, and told that this kind of hospital stuff is art, and that, having no literature of our own, or freedom, or artistic sense, the sooner we fall down and worship at the feet of Ibsen and subscribe to the Independent Theatre the better for ourselves and the future of our poor, convention-bound, commonplace, and unliterary drama.

Whether the Royalty Theatre, licensed by the Lord Chamberlain under given and distinct rules and governed by a definite Act of Parliament, should be used for the purpose to which it is now put is not the affair of anyone but the Lord Chamberlain and his advisers. We have nothing to do with that. It seems even to the uncritical mind to be a little inconsistent and misleading to be told by a legal enactment that when actors play for hire they must be bound by certain rules and regulations, to be informed exactly what playing for hire means, and the penalty to be incurred by any infringement of the law, and then to hear that subscribing for certain seats in a playhouse to see a play is not within the meaning of the Act. By this argument, the Opera in the season, and any theatre that started a subscription list after the plan of the Théâtre Français in Paris, would be free altogether from the censorship. However, there is the law, that anyone, layman or expert, can read for themselves, and there is a precedent, of which advantage will no doubt be taken, to dispense with the control of the censorship altogether. I am not discussing whether the censorship is right or wrong, or whether it benefits or impedes Art. Some think one way, some another. Anyhow Ibsen's *Ghosts* has been played in public, and many people have subscribed to see it. This is admitted by the founders of the Independent Theatre, and it is cordially regretted by all who have the true welfare of the stage at heart.

We next come to the point whether this particular play, *Ghosts*, is so valuable to the well-being of the community that its obviously repulsive subject should be excused under the plea that it contains both literature and art. For my own part, I fail to see the literary excellence of *Ghosts*, or its artistic value. The term 'convention' has become the cant word of a clique. Already we have been asked to admire a stage scene acted in pitch-darkness because it is so unconventional: soon we shall be told it is conventional, and therefore to be reprobated, when people talk at all on the stage. Some of these excellent people, in their desire to be original and revolutionary, are really reducing the thing to an absurdity. They would have us believe that this English stage of ours is the fossil and mummy it was twenty years ago. They would attempt to persuade the younger generation that it is the new prophet Ibsen, and none other than Ibsen, who has discovered that the stage is hampered by conditions inseparable from the freedom and healthy tone of art, and that it is reserved for the Independent Theatre to take credit for the steady work that has been going on in England for a quarter of a century. Convention, indeed! Has there not been a crusade against convention, in its crude, barbarous and unenlightened form, ever since the stage was found sleepy and inert in the interval between the death of Charles Kean and the uprising of Henry Irving? I should like Mr Grein and some of these young gentlemen who talk so airily about convention to have known what our stage was like in the early sixties. Was not Robertson, in his light and delicate way, an opponent of stupid and obstinate convention? Were not the Bancrofts the prime movers of the unconventional school of pleasant comedy? Has not Henry Irving been the most unconventional manager and actor in the century? Have not Hare and a younger generation still carried on the good work of their predecessors to make the stage as unconventional and as natural as the conditions of dramatic effect will allow it to be? Are not Gilbert, Pinero, Henry Arthur Jones, as unconventional and as free in their method as any dramatists in the memory of living man? And now, having attained this important point, after years of struggle and labour, we are to be airily told that Ibsen and the founders of the Independent Theatre are the chosen apostles to free the neglected stage from the fetters and manacles of conventionality! A more stupendous proposition was never offered by misguided men or believed in by masculine women.

These shallow reformers want to kill the goose with the golden eggs. Having gained a drama that is as distinguished in literary excellence as that of any country in the world, our authors are to go, hat in hand, to be taught what literature and what art are by the founders of the Independent Theatre. And *Ghosts* is the first brilliant example! – a play that if presented to the general public would, if not hissed off the stage the first night, close the doors of any London theatre in a fortnight – not mark you, on moral grounds, but on artistic grounds. If people like the discussion of such nasty subjects on the stage, if they care to make the theatre a closed borough and not a free place of assembly, if it is desirable to drive decent-minded women out of the play-house, and to use the auditorium as a hospital-ward or dissecting-room, let it be so. Whatever the people desire they will have, and no talking in the world will prevent it. But in our hurry to dramatize the Contagious Diseases Act let us first set about writing a good play. Who in their senses can say that *Ghosts* is a good play, or is interesting apart from the originality of its subject-matter? If, by the examples we have seen, Ibsen is a dramatist, then the art of the dramatist is dead indeed, and we must all learn our dramatic alphabet and grammar according to a new rule altogether. It is impossible that a dramatist, however earnest or sincere, can carry conviction with him if he only looks at one side of human nature – and that the worst. Shakespeare had a pretty good insight into human nature, and he drew some terrible, often horrible, pictures of humanity. But Shakespeare was too much of an artist, too much of an observer, too full of the milk of human kindness, not to look at the other side of the picture also. A man who says that all human nature is bad says what is untrue. It may be considered smart and original to say so, but it will not command the approbation of the majority, and the majority are not always wrong, as Dr Stockmann insists, in a play that is supposed to present Ibsen as a stage character, and also what he really is, 'an enemy of Society'.

The Illustrated London News, 21 March 1891

G. B. Shaw
Little Eyolf

The happiest and truest epithet that has yet been applied to the Ibsen drama in this country came from Mr Clement Scott when he said that Ibsen was 'suburban'. That is the whole secret of it. If Mr Scott had only embraced his discovery instead of quarrelling with it, what a splendid Ibsen critic he would have made! Suburbanity at present means modern civilization. The active, germinating life in the households of today cannot be typified by an aristocratic hero, an ingenuous heroine, a gentleman-forger abetted by an Artful Dodger, and a parlourmaid who takes half-sovereigns and kisses from the male visitors. Such interiors exist on the stage, and nowhere else: therefore the only people who are accustomed to them and at home in them are the dramatic critics. But if you ask me where you can find the Helmer household, the Allmers household, the Solness household, the Rosmer household, and all the other Ibsen households, I reply, 'Jump out of a train anywhere between Wimbledon and Haslemere; walk into the first villa you come to, and there you are.' Indeed you need not go so far: Hampstead, Maida Vale, or West Kensington will serve your turn; but it is as well to remind people that the true suburbs are now the forty-mile radius, and that Camberwell and Brixton are no longer the suburbs, but the overflow of Gower Street – the genteel slums in short. And this suburban life, except in so far as it is totally vegetable and undramatic, is the life depicted by Ibsen. Doubtless some of our critics are quite sincere in thinking it a vulgar life, in considering the conversations which men hold with their wives in it improper, in finding its psychology puzzling and unfamiliar, and in forgetting that its bookshelves and its music cabinets are laden with works which did not exist for them, and which are the daily bread of young women educated very differently from the sisters and wives of their day. No wonder they are not at ease in an atmosphere of ideas and assumptions and attitudes which seem to them bewildering, morbid, affected, extravagant and altogether incredible as the common currency of suburban life. But Ibsen knows better. His suburban drama is the inevitable outcome of a suburban civilization (meaning a civilization that appreciates fresh air); and the true explanation of Hedda Gabler's vogue is that given by Mr Grant Allen – 'I take her into dinner twice a week.'

Another change that the critics have failed to reckon with is the change in fiction. Byron remarked that

> Romances paint at full length people's wooings,
> But only give a bust of marriages.

That was true enough in the days of Sir Walter Scott, when a betrothed heroine with the slightest knowledge of what marriage meant would have shocked the public as much as the same ignorance today would strike it as tragic if real, and indecent if simulated. The result was that the romancer, when he came to a love scene, had frankly to ask his 'gentle reader' to allow him to omit the conversation as being necessarily too idiotic to interest anyone. We have fortunately long passed out of that stage in novels. By the time we had reached *Vanity Fair* and *Middlemarch* – both pretty old and prim stories now – marriage had become the starting point of our romances. Love is as much the romancer's theme as ever; but married love and the courtships of young people who are appalled by the problems of life and motherhood have left the governesses and curates, the Amandas and Tom Joneses of other days, far out of sight. Ten years ago the stage was as far behind Sir Walter Scott as he is behind Madame Sarah Grand. But when Ibsen took it by the scruff of the neck just as Wagner took the Opera, then, willy nilly, it had to come along. And now what are the critics going to do? The Ibsen drama is pre-eminently the drama of marriage. If dramatic criticism receives it in the spirit of the nurse's husband in *Romeo and Juliet*, if it grins and makes remarks about 'the secrets of the alcove', if it pours forth columns which are half pornographic pleasantry and the other half sham propriety, then the end will be, not in the least that Ibsen will be banned, but that dramatic criticism will cease to be read. And what a frightful blow that would be to English culture!

*Little Eyolf** is an extraordinarily powerful play, although none of the characters are as fascinatingly individualized as Solness or Rosmer, Hedda or Nora. The theme is a marriage – an ideal marriage from the suburban point of view. A young gentleman, a student and an idealist, is compelled to drudge at teaching to support himself. He meets a beautiful young woman. They fall in love with one another; and by the greatest piece of luck in the world (suburbanly considered) she has plenty of money. Thus he is set free by his marriage to live his own life in his own way. That is just where an ordinary play leaves off, and just where an Ibsen play begins. The husband begins to make those discoveries which everybody makes, except, apparently, the dramatic critics. First, that love, instead of being a perfectly homogeneous, unchanging, unending passion, is, of all things the most mutable. It will pass through several well-marked stages in a single evening, and, whilst seeming to slip back to the old starting point the next evening, will yet not slip quite back; so that in the course of years it will appear that the moods of an evening were the anticipation of the evolution of a lifetime. But the evolution does not occur in different people at the same time or in the same order. Consequently the hero of *Little Eyolf*, being an imaginative, nervous, thoughtful person, finds that he has had enough of caresses, and wants to dream alone among the mountain peaks and solitudes, whilst his wife, a warm-blooded creature, has only found her love intensified to a fiercely jealous covetousness of him. His main refuge from this devouring passion is in his peacefully affectionate relations with his sister, and in certain suburban dreams very common among literary amateurs living on their wives' incomes: to wit, forming the mind and character of his child, and writing a great book (on Human Responsibility if you please). Of course the wife, in her jealousy hates the sister, hates the child, hates the book, hates her husband for making her jealous of them, and hates herself for her hatreds with the frightful logic of greedy, insatiable love. Enter then our old friend, Ibsen's divine messenger. The Ratwife, alias the Strange Passenger, alias the Buttom Moulder alias Ulrik Brendel, comes in to ask whether there are any little gnawing things there of which she can rid the house. They do not understand – the divine messenger in Ibsen is never understood, especially by the critics. So the little gnawing thing in the house – the child – follows the Ratwife and is drowned, leaving the pair awakened by the blow to a frightful consciousness of themselves, the woman as a mere animal, the man as a moonstruck nincompoop, keeping up appearances as a suburban lady and gentleman with nothing to do but enjoy themselves. Even the sister has discovered now that she is not really a sister – also a not unprecedented suburban possibility – and sees that the passionate stage is ahead of her too; so, though she loves the husband, she has to get out of his way by the pre-eminently suburban expedient of marrying a man whom she does not love, and who, like Rita, is warm-blooded and bent on the undivided, unshared possession of the object of his passion. At last the love of the woman passes out of the passionate stage; and immediately with the practical sense of her sex, she proposes, not to go up into the

* Avenue Theatre.

mountains or to write amateur treatises, but to occupy herself with her duties as landed proprietress, instead of merely spending the revenues of her property in keeping a monogamic harem. The gentleman asks to be allowed to lend a hand; and immediately the storm subsides, easily enough, leaving the couple on solid ground. This is the play, as actual and near to us as the Brighton and South Coast Railway – this is the mercilessly heart-searching sermon, touching all of us somewhere, and some of us everywhere, which we, the critics, have summed up as 'secrets of the alcove'. Our cheeks, whose whiteness Mr Arthur Roberts has assailed in vain, have mantled at 'the coarseness and vulgarity which are noted characteristics of the author' (I am quoting, with awe, my fastidiously high-toned colleague of the *Standard*). And yet the divine messenger only meant to make us ashamed of ourselves. That is the way divine messengers always do muddle their business.

The performance was of course a very remarkable one. When, in a cast of five, you have the three best yet discovered actresses of their generation, you naturally look for something extraordinary. Miss Achurch was the only one who ran any risk of failure. The Ratwife and Asta are excellent parts; but they are not arduous ones. Rita, on the other hand, is one of the heaviest ever written: any single act of it would exhaust an actress of no more than ordinary resources. But Miss Achurch was more than equal to the occasion. Her power seemed to grow with its own expenditure. The terrible outburst at the end of the first act did not leave a scrape on her voice (which appears to have the compass of a military band) and threw her into victorious action in that tearing second act instead of wrecking her. She played with all her old originality and success, and with more than her old authority over her audience. She had to speak some dangerous lines – lines of a kind that usually find out the vulgar spots in an audience and give an excuse for a laugh – but nobody laughed or wanted to laugh at Miss Achurch. 'There stood your champagne; but you tasted it not', neither shirked nor slurred, but driven home to the last syllable, did not elicit an audible breath from a completely dominated audience. Later on I confess I lost sight of Rita a little in studying the surprising capacity Miss Achurch shewed as a dramatic instrument. For the first time one clearly saw the superfluity of power and the vehemence of intelligence which make her often so reckless as to the beauty of her methods of expression. As Rita she produced almost every sound that a big human voice can, from a creak like the opening of a rusty canal lock to a melodious tenor note that the most robust Siegfried might have envied. She looked at one moment like a young well-dressed, very pretty woman: at another she was like a desperate creature just fished dripping out of the river by the Thames Police. Yet another moment, and she was the incarnation of impetuous, ungovernable strength. Her face was sometimes winsome, sometimes listlessly wretched, sometimes like the head of a statue of Victory, sometimes suffused, horrible, threatening, like Bellona or Medusa. She would cross from left to right like a queen, and from right to left with, so to speak, her toes turned in, her hair coming down, and her slippers coming off. A more utter recklessness, not only of fashion, but of beauty, could hardly be imagined: beauty to Miss Achurch is only one effect among others to be produced, not a condition of all effects. But then she can do what our beautiful actresses cannot do: attain the force and terror of Sarah Bernhardt's most vehement explosions without Sarah's violence and abandonment, and with every appearance of having reserves of power still held in restraint. With all her cleverness as a realistic actress she must be classed technically as a heroic actress; and I very much doubt whether we shall see her often until she comes into the field of repertory as highly specialized as that of Sir Henry Irving or Duse. For it is so clear that she would act an average London success to pieces and play an average actor-manager off the stage, that we need not expect to see much of her as that useful and pretty auxiliary, a leading lady.

Being myself a devotee of the beautiful school, I like being enchanted by Mrs Patrick Campbell better than being frightened, harrowed, astonished, conscience-stricken, devastated, and dreadfully delighted in general by Miss Achurch's untamed genius. I have seen Mrs Campbell play the Ratwife twice, once quite enchantingly, and once most disappointingly. On the first occasion Mrs Campbell divined that she was no village harridan, but the messenger of heaven. She played supernaturally, beautifully: the first notes of her voice came as from the spheres into all that suburban prose: she played to the child with a witchery that might have drawn him not only into the sea, but into her very bosom. Nothing jarred except her obedience to Ibsen's stage direction in saying 'Down where all the rats are' harshly, instead if getting the effect, in harmony with her own inspired reading, by the most magical tenderness. The next time, to my unspeakable fury, she amused herself by playing like any melodramatic old woman, a profanation for which, whilst my critical life lasts, never will I forgive her. Of Miss Robins's Asta it is difficult to say much, since the part, played as she plays it, does not exhibit anything like the full extent of her powers. Asta is a study of a temperament – the quiet, affectionate, enduring, reassuring faithful domestic temperament. That is not in the least Miss Robins's temperament: she is nervous, restless, intensely self-conscious, eagerly energetic. In parts which do not enable her to let herself loose in this, her natural way, she falls back on pathos, on mute misery, on a certain delicate plaintive note in her voice and grace in her bearing which appeal to our sympathy and pity without realizing any individuality for us. She gave us, with instinctive tact and refinement, the 'niceness', the considerateness, the ladylikeness, which differentiate Asta from the wilful, passionate, somewhat brutal Rita. Perhaps only an American playing against an Englishwoman could have done it so discriminately; but beyond this and the pathos there was nothing: Asta was only a picture, and, like a picture, did not develop. The picture, being sympathetic and pretty, has been much admired; but those who have not seen Miss Robins play Hilda Wangel have no idea of what she is like when she really acts her part instead of merely giving an urbanely pictorial recommendation of it. As to Allmers, how could he recommend himself to spectators who saw in him everything that they are ashamed of in themselves? Mr Courtenay Thorpe played very intelligently, which, for such a part, and in such a play, is saying a good deal; but he was hampered a little by the change from the small and intimate auditorium in which he has been accustomed to play Ibsen, to the Avenue, which ingeniously combines the acoustic difficulties of a large theatre with the pecuniary capacity of a small one. Master Stewart Dawson, as Eyolf, was one of the best actors in the company. Mr Lowne, as Borgheim, was as much out of tone as a Leader sunset in a Rembrandt picture – no fault of his, of course (the audience evidently liked him), but still a blemish on the play.

And this brings me to a final criticism. The moment I put myself into my old attitude as musical critic, I at once perceive that the performance, as a whole, was an unsatisfactory one. You may remonstrate, and ask me how I can say so after admitting that the performers shewed such extraordinary talent – even genius. It is very simple, nevertheless. Suppose you take Isaye, Sarasate, Joachim, and Hollman, and tumble them all together to give a scratch performance of one of Beethoven's posthumous quartets at some benefit concert. Suppose you also take the two De Reszkes, Calvé, and Miss Eames, and set them to sing a glee under the same circumstances. They will all shew prodigious individual talent; but the resultant performances of the quartet and glee will be inferior, as wholes, to that of an ordinary glee club or group of musicians who have practised for years together. The Avenue performance was a parallel case. There was nothing like the atmosphere which Lugné Poë got in *Rosmersholm*. Miss Achurch managed to play the second act as if she had played it every week for twenty years; but otherwise the performance, interesting as it was, was none the less a scratch one. If only the company could keep together for a while! But perhaps that is too much to hope for at present, though it is encouraging to see that the performances are to be continued next week, the five matinees – all crowded by the way – having by no means exhausted the demand for places.

Several performances during the past fortnight remain to be chronicled; but Ibsen will have his due; and he has not left me room enough to do justice to any one else this week.

The Saturday Review, 28 November 1896

G. B. Shaw
John Gabriel Borkman

The first performance of *John Gabriel Borkman,** the latest masterpiece of the acknowledged chief of European dramatic art, has taken place in London under the usual shabby circumstances. For the first scene in the gloomy Borkman house, a faded, soiled, dusty wreck of some gay French salon, originally designed, perhaps, for Offenbach's *Favart*, was fitted with an incongruous Norwegian stove, a painted staircase, and a couple of chairs which were no doubt white and gold when they first figured in Tom Taylor's *Plot and Passion* or some other relic of the days before Mr Bancroft revolutionized stage furniture, but have apparently languished ever since, unsold and unsaleable, among secondhand keys, framed lithographs of the Prince Consort, casual fenders and stair-rods, and other spoils of the broker. Still, this scene at least was describable, and even stimulative – to irony. In Act II, the gallery in which Borkman prowls for eight years like a wolf was no gallery at all, but a square box ugly to loathsomeness, and too destructive to the imagination and descriptive faculty to incur the penalty of criticism. In Act III (requiring, it will be remembered, the shifting landscape from *Parsifal*), two new cloths specially painted, and good enough to produce a tolerable illusion of snowy pinewood and midnight mountain with proper accessories, were made ridiculous by a bare acre of wooden floor and only one set of wings for the two. When I looked at that, and thought of the eminence of the author and the greatness of his work, I felt ashamed. What Sir Henry Irving and Mr George Alexander and Mr Wilson Barrett feel about it I do not know – on the whole, perhaps, not altogether displeased to see Ibsen belittled. For my part, I beg the New Century Theatre, when the next Ibsen play is ready for mounting, to apply to me for assistance. If I have a ten-pound note, they shall have it: if not, I can at least lend them a couple of decent chairs. I cannot think that Mr Massingham, Mr Sutro and Mr William Archer would have grudged a few such contributions from their humble cots on this occasion if they had not hoped that a display of the most sordid poverty would have shamed the public as it shamed me. Unfortunately their moral lesson is more likely to discredit Ibsen than to fill the New Century coffers. They have spent either too little or too much. When Dr Furnivall performed Browning's *Luria* in the lecture theatre at University College with a couple of curtains, a chair borrowed from the board room, and the actors in their ordinary evening dress, the absence of scenery was as completely forgotten as if we had all been in the Globe in Shakespear's time. But between that and an adequate scenic equipment there is no middle course. It is highly honourable to the pioneers of the drama that they are poor; but in art, what poverty can only do unhandsomely and stingily it should not do at all. Besides, to be quite frank, I simply do not believe that the New Century Theatre could not have afforded at least a better couple of chairs.

* Strand Theatre.

I regret to say that the shortcomings of the scenery were not mitigated by imaginative and ingenious stage management. Mr Vernon's stage management is very actor-like: that is to say, it is directed, not to secure the maximum of illusion for the play, but the maximum of fairness in distributing good places on the stage to the members of the cast. Had he been selfish enough, as some actor-managers are accused of being, to manage the stage so as to secure the maximum of prominence for himself, the effect would probably have justified him, since he plays Borkman. But his sense of equity is evidently stronger than his vanity; for he takes less than his share of conspicuity, repeatedly standing patiently with his back to the audience to be declaimed at down the stage by Miss Robins or Miss Ward, or whoever else he deems entitled to a turn. Alas! these conceptions of fairness, honourable as they are to Mr Vernon's manhood, are far too simply quantitative for artistic purposes. The business of the stage manager of *John Gabriel Borkman*, is chiefly to make the most of the title part; and if the actor of that part is too modest to do that for himself, some one else should stage-manage. Mr Vernon perhaps pleased the company, because he certainly did contrive that every one of them should have the centre of the stage to himself or herself whenever they had the chance of self-assertion; but as this act of green-room justice was placed before the naturalness of the representation, the actors did not gain by it, whilst the play suffered greatly.

Mr Vernon, I suspect, was also hampered by a rather old-fashioned technical conception of the play as a tragedy. Now the traditional stage management of tragedy ignores realism – even the moderate degree of realism traditional in comedy. It lends itself to people talking at each other rhetorically from opposite sides of the stage, taking long sweeping walks up to their 'points', striking attitudes in the focus of the public vision with an artificiality which, instead of being concealed, is not only disclosed but insisted on, and being affected in all their joints by emotions which a fine comedian conveys by the faintest possible inflexion of tone or eyebrow. *John Gabriel Borkman* is no doubt technically a tragedy because it ends with the death of the leading personage in it. But to stage-manage or act it rhetorically as such is like drawing a Dance of Death in the style of Caracci or Giulio Romano. Clearly the required style is the homely – imaginative, the realistic-fateful – in a word, the Gothic. I am aware that to demand Gothic art from stage managers dominated by the notion that their business is to adapt the exigencies of stage etiquette to the tragic and comic categories of our pseudo-classical dramatic tradition is to give them an order which they can but dimly understand and cannot execute at all; but Mr Vernon is no mere routineer: he is a man of ideas. After all, Sir Henry Irving (in his *Bells* style), M. Lugné Poë, Mr Richard Mansfield, and Mr Charles Charrington have hit this mark (whilst missing the pseudo-classic one) nearly enough to shew that it is by no means unattainable. Failing the services of these geniuses, I beg the conventional stage manager to treat Ibsen as comedy. That will not get the business right; but it will be better than the tragedy plan.

As to the acting of the play, it was fairly good, as acting goes in London now, whenever the performers were at all in their depth; and it was at least lugubriously well intentioned when they were out of it. Unfortunately they were very often out of it. If they had been anti-Ibsenites they would have marked their resentment of and impatience with the passages they did not understand by an irritable listlessness, designed to make the worst of the play as far as that could be done without making the worst of themselves. But the Ibsenite actor marks the speeches which are beyond him by a sudden access of pathetic sentimentality and an intense consciousness of Ibsen's greatness. No doubt this devotional plan lets the earnestness of the representation down less than the sceptical one; yet its effect is as false as false can be; and I am sorry to say that it is gradually establishing a funereally unreal tradition which is likely to end in making Ibsen the most portentous of stage bores. Take, for example, Ella Rentheim. Here you have a part which up to a certain point almost plays itself – a sympathetic old maid with a broken heart. Nineteen-twentieths of her might be transferred to the stage of the Princess's tomorrow and be welcomed there tearfully by the audiences which delight in *Two Little Vagabonds* and *East Lynne*. Her desire to adopt Erhart is plainsailing sentimentalism: her reproach to Borkman for the crime of killing the 'love life' in her and himself for the sake of his ambition is, as a *coup de théâtre*, quite within the range of playwrights who rank considerably below Mr Pinero. All this is presented intelligently by Miss Robins – at moments even touchingly and beautifully. But the moment the dialogue crosses the line which separates the Ibsen sphere from the ordinary sphere her utterance rings false at once. Here is an example – the most striking in the play:

ELLA (*in strong inward emotion*). Pity! Ha ha! I have never known pity since you deserted me. I was incapable of feeling it. If a poor starved child came into my kitchen, shivering and crying and begging a morsel of food, I let the servants look to it. I never felt any desire to take the child to myself, to warm it at my own hearth, to have the pleasure of seeing it eat and be satisfied. And yet I wasn't like that when I was young: *that* I remember clearly. It is you that have created an empty, barren desert within me – and without me too!

What is there in this speech that might not occur in any popular novel or drama of sentiment written since Queen Anne's death? If Miss Millward were to introduce it into *Black-Ey'd Susan*, the Adelphi pit would accept it with moist eyes and without the faintest suspicion of Ibsen. But Ella Rentheim does not stop there. 'You have cheated me of a mother's joy and happiness in life,' she continues, 'and of a mother's sorrows and tears as well. And perhaps that is the heaviest part of the loss to me. It may be that a mother's sorrows and tears were what I needed most.' Now here the Adelphi pit would be puzzled; for here Ibsen speaks as the Great Man – one whose moral consciousness far transcends the common huckstering conception of life as a trade in happiness in which sorrows and tears represent the bad bargains and joys and happiness the good ones. And here Miss Robins suddenly betrays that she is an Ibsenite without being an Ibsenist. The genuine and touching tone of self-pity suddenly turns into a perceptibly artificial snivel (forgive the rudeness of the word); and the sentence, which is the most moving in the play provided it comes out simply and truthfully, is declaimed as a sentimental paradox which has no sort of reality or conviction for the actress. In this failure Miss Robins was entirely consistent with her own successes. As the woman in revolt against the intolerable slavery and injustice of ideal 'womanliness' (Karin and Martha in *Pillars of Society*) or against the man treating her merely as his sexual prey (Mariana in the recital of her mother's fate) her success has had no bounds except those set by the commercial disadvantages at which the performances were undertaken. As the impetuous, imaginative New Woman in her first youth, free, unscrupulous through ignorance, demanding of life that it shall be 'thrilling', and terribly dangerous to impressionable Master Builders who have put on life's chains without learning its lessons, she has succeeded heart and soul, rather by being the character than by understanding it. In representing poignant nervous phenomena in their purely physical aspect, as in *Alan's Wife*, and *Mrs Lessingham*, she has set up the infection of agony in the theatre with lacerating intensity by the vividness of her reproduction of its symptoms. But in sympathetic parts properly so called, where wisdom of heart, and sense of identity and common cause with others – in short, the parts we shall probably call religious as soon as we begin to gain some glimmering of what religion means – Miss Robins is only sympathetic as a flute is sympathetic: that is, she has a pretty tone, and can be played on with an affectation of sentiment; but there is no reality, no sincerity in it. And so Ella Rentheim, so far as she is sympathetic, eludes her. The fact is, Miss Robins is too young and too ferociously individualistic to play her. Ella's grievances come out well enough, also her romance, and some of those kindly amenities of hers – notably her amiable farewell to Erhart; but of the woman who understands that she has been robbed of her due of tears and sorrow, of the woman who sees that the crazy expedition through the snow with Borkman is as well worth trying as a hopeless return to the fireside, there is no trace, nothing but a few indications that Miss Robins would have very little patience with such wisdom if she met it in real life.

Mr Vernon's Borkman was not ill acted; only, as it was not Ibsen's Borkman, but the very reverse and negation of him, the better Mr Vernon acted the worse it was for the play. He was a thoroughly disillusioned elderly man of business, patient and sensible rather than kindly, and with the sort of strength that a man derives from the experience that teaches him his limits. I think Mr Vernon must have studied him in the north of Ireland, where that type reaches perfection. Ibsen's Borkman, on the contrary, is a man of the most energetic imagination, whose illusions feed on his misfortunes, and whose conception of his own power grows hyperbolical and Napoleonic in his solitude and impotence. Mr Vernon's excursion into the snow was the aberration of a respectable banker in whose brain a vessel had suddenly burst; the true Borkman meets the fate of a vehement dreamer who has for thirteen years been deprived of that daily contact with reality and responsibility without which genius inevitably produces unearthliness and insanity. Mr Vernon was as earthly and sane as a man need be until he went for his walk in the snow, and a Borkman who is that is necessarily a trifle dull. Even Mr Welch, though his scene in the second act was a triumph, made a fundamental mistake in the third, where Foldal, who has just been knocked down and nearly run over by the sleigh in which his daughter is being practically abducted by Erhart and Mrs Wilton, goes into ecstasies of delight at what he supposes to be her good fortune in riding off in a silver-mounted carriage to finish her musical education under distinguished auspices. The whole point of this scene, at once penetratingly tragic and irresistibly laughable, lies in the sincerity of Foldal's glee and Borkman's sardonic chuckling over it. But Mr Welch unexpectedly sacrificed the scene to a stage effect which has been done to death by Mr Harry Nicholls and even Mr Arthur Roberts. He played the heartbroken old man pretending to laugh – a descendant of the clown who jokes in the arena whilst his child is dying at home – and so wrecked what would otherwise have been the best piece of character work of the afternoon. Mr Martin Harvey, as Erhart, was clever enough to seize the main idea of the part – the impulse towards happiness – but not experienced enough to know that the actor's business is not to supply an idea with a sounding board, but with a credible, simple, and natural human being to utter it when its time comes and not before. He shewed, as we all knew he would shew considerable stage talent and more than ordinary dramatic intelligence; but in the first act he was not the embarrassed young gentleman of Ibsen, but rather the 'soaring human boy' imagined by Mr Chadband; and later on this attitude of his very nearly produced a serious jar at a critical point in the representation.

Miss Geneviève Ward played Gunhild. The character is a very difficult one, since the violently stagey manifestations of maternal feeling prescribed for the actress by Ibsen indicate a tragic strenuousness of passion which is not suggested by the rest of the dialogue. Miss Ward did not quite convince me that she had found the temperament appropriate to both. The truth is, her tragic style, derived from Ristori, was not made for Ibsen. On the other hand, her conversational style, admirably natural and quite free from the Mesopotamian solemnity with which some of her colleagues delivered the words of the Master, was genuinely dramatic, and reminded me of her excellent performance, years ago, with Mr Vernon, as Lona Hessel. Mrs Tree was clever and altogether successful as Mrs Wilton; and Miss Dora Barton's Frida was perfect. But then these two parts are comparatively easy. Miss Caldwell tried hard to modify her well-known representation of a farcical slavery into a passable Ibsenite parlormaid, and succeeded fairly except in the little scene which begins the third act.

On the whole, a rather disappointing performance of a play which cannot be read without forming expectations which are perhaps unreasonable, but are certainly inevitable.

The Saturday Review, 8 May 1897

Shaw and the New Drama

William Archer
Arms and the Man

No one with even a rudimentary knowledge of human nature will expect me to deal impartially with a play by Mr George Bernard Shaw. 'Jones write a book!' cried Smith, in the familiar anecdote – 'Jones write a book! Impossible! Absurd! Why, *I knew his father!*' By the same cogent process of reasoning, I have long ago satisfied myself that Mr Shaw cannot write a play. I had not the advantage of knowing his father (except through the filial reminiscences with which he now and then favours us), but – what is more fatal still – I know himself. He is not only my old and intimate and valued friend. We have tried our best to quarrel many a time. We have said and done such things that would have sufficed to set up a dozen lifelong vendettas between normal and rightly constituted people, but all without the slightest success, without engendering so much as a temporary coolness. Even now, when he has had the deplorable ill-taste to falsify my frequently and freely-expressed prediction by writing a successful play, which kept an audience hugely entertained from the rise to the fall of the curtain, I vow I cannot work up a healthy hatred for him. Of course I shall criticize it with prejudice, malice, and acerbity; but I have not the faintest hope of ruffling his temper or disturbing his self-complacency. The situation is really exasperating. If only I could induce him to cut me and scowl at me, like an ordinary human dramatist, there would be some chance of his writing better plays – or none at all. But one might as well attempt 'to bully the Monument'.

There is not the least doubt that *Arms and the Man** is one of the most amusing entertainments at present before the public. It is quite as funny as *Charley's Aunt* or *The New Boy*; we laughed at it wildly, hysterically; and I exhort the reader to go and do likewise. But he must not expect a humdrum, rational, steady-going farce, like *Charley's Aunt*, bearing a well-understood conventional relation to real life. Let him rather look for a fantastic, psychological extravaganza, in which drama, farce and Gilbertian irony keep flashing past the bewildered eye, as in a sort of merry-go-round, so quickly that one gives up the attempt to discriminate between them, and resigns oneself to indiscriminating laughter. The author (if he will pardon my dabbling in musical metaphor) is always jumping from key to key, without an attempt at

---

* Avenue Theatre.

modulation, and nine times out of ten he does not himself know what key he is writing in. Here, indeed, lies the whole truth. If one could think that Mr Shaw had consciously and deliberately invented a new species of prose extravaganza, one could unreservedly applaud the invention, while begging him in future to apply it with a little more depth and delicacy. But I more than suspect that he conceives himself to have written a serious comedy, a reproduction of life as it really is, with men and women thinking, feeling, speaking, and acting as they really do think, feel, speak and act. Instead of presenting an episode in the great war between the realms of Grünewald and Gerolstein, or in the historic conflict between Paphlagonia and Crim Tartary, he places his scene in the (more or less) real principality of Bulgaria, dates his action to the year and day (6th March 1886), and has been at immense pains to work-in Bulgarian local colour in the dialogue, and to procure correct Bulgarian costumes and genuine Balkan scenery. It is an open secret, I believe, that Mr Shaw held counsel on these matters with a Bulgarian Admiral – a Bohemian Admiral would scarcely be more unexpected – and that this gallant horse-marine gave him the hints as to the anti-saponaceous prejudices of the Bulgarians, their domestic architecture, their unfamiliarity with electric bells, and the mushroom growth of their aristocracy, which he has so religiously, and in some cases amusingly, utilized. But all this topographical pedantry proves, oddly enough, that "e dunno where 'e are'. By attempting to fix his action down to the solid earth he simply emphasizes its unreality. He is like the young man in *Pickwick* who, having to write an essay on 'Chinese Metaphysics', read up the articles 'China' and 'Metaphysics' in the Encyclopaedia, and combined the two. Mr Shaw went to his Admiral for 'Bulgaria', and to his inner consciousness for 'Psychology', and combined the two in an essay on 'Bulgarian Psychology'. Why confound the issues in this way, my dear G.B.S.? Some critics have assumed, quite excusably, that the play was meant as a satire upon Bulgaria, and I should not be in the least surprised if it were to lead to a 'diplomatic incident' like that which arose from the introduction of the Sultan in *Don Juan*. Of course you really know and care no more about Bulgaria than I do. Your satire is directed against humanity in general, and English humanity in particular. Your Saranoff and Bluntschli and Raina and Louka have their prototypes, or rather their antitypes, not in the Balkan Principalities, but in that romantic valley which nestles between the cloud-capped summits of Hampstead and Sydenham. Why not confess as much by making your scene fantastic, and have done with it?

Having now disentangled 'Bulgaria' and 'Psychology', I put the former article aside as irrelevant, and turn to the latter. Mr Shaw is by nature and habit one of those philosophers who concentrate their attention upon the seamy side of the human mind. Against that practice, in itself, I have not a word to say. By all means let us see, examine, realize, remember, the seamy side. You will never find me using the word 'cynic', as a term of moral reproach. But to say of a man that he is habitually and persistently cynical is undoubtedly to imply an artistic limitation. To look at nothing but the seamy side may be to see life steadily, but is not to see it whole. As an artist, Mr Shaw suffers from this limitation; and to this negative fault, if I may call it so, he superadds a positive vice of style. He not only dwells on the seamy side to the exclusion of all else, but he makes his characters turn their moral garments inside out and go about with the linings displayed, flaunting the seams and raw edges and stiffenings and paddings. Now this simply does not occur in real life, or only to a very limited extent; and the artist who makes it his main method of character-presentation, at once converts his comedy into extravaganza. It is not Mr Shaw's sole method, but he is far too much addicted to it. His first act is genuine fantastic comedy, sparkling and delightful. Here he has set himself to knock the stuffing, so to speak, out of war; to contrast a romantic girl's ideal of battle and heroic raptures, with the sordid reality as it appears to a professional soldier. He has evidently 'documents' to go upon, and he has seized with inimitable humour upon the commonplace and ludicrous aspects of warfare. Of course Bluntschli's picture is not the whole truth any more than Raina's, but it presents a real and important side of the matter, the side which chiefly appeals to Mr Shaw's sceptical imagination. The great and serious artists – Tolstoi, Zola (for I am impenitent in my admiration for *La Débâcle*), Whitman in his *Specimen Days*, Stendhal (I am told) in *La Chartreuse de Parme* – give us both sides of the case, its prose and its poetry. Even Mr Kipling, who also has his 'documents', has found in them a thing or two beyond Mr Shaw's ken. But for the nonce, and in its way, Mr Shaw's persiflage is not only vastly amusing, but acceptable, apposite. So far good. At the end of the first act we do not quite know where the play is coming in, for it is obvious that even Mr Shaw cannot go on through two more acts mowing down military ideals with volleys of chocolate creams. But there are evident possibilities in this generous romantic girl and her genially cynical instructor in the art of war; and we hope for the best. Observe that as yet we have not got upon the ground of general psychology, so to speak; we have had nothing but a humorous analysis of one special phase of mental experience – the sensations of a soldier in battle and in flight. In the second act all is changed. Bluntschli, in whom the author practically speaks in his own person, without any effort at dramatization, has almost disappeared from the scene, and the really dramatic effort commences in the characterization of the Byronic swaggerer, Sergius Saranoff, and the working out of his relation to Raina. At once Mr Shaw's ease and lightness of touch desert him, and we find ourselves in Mr Gilbert's Palace of Truth. The romantic girl is romantic no longer, but a deliberate humbug, without a single genuine or even self-deluding emotion in her bloodless frame. Sergius the Sublime has no sort of belief in his own sublimity, but sets to work before he has been ten minutes on the stage to analyse himself for the entertainment of the maid-servant, and enlarge on the difficulty of distinguishing between the six or seven Sergiuses whom he discovers in his own composition. Petkoff and his wife are mere cheap grotesques, both more or less under the influence of the Palace of Truth. The major-domo, under the same magic spell, affords a vehicle for some of the author's theories as to the evils engendered on both sides by the relation of master and servant. And the most wonderful character of all, perhaps, is the maid Louka, who seems to have wandered in from one of the obscurer of Mr Meredith's novels, so keen is her perception, and so subtle her appreciation, of character and motive. All this crude and contorted psychology, too, is further dehumanized by Mr Shaw's peculiar habit of straining all the red corpuscles out of the blood of his personages. They have nothing of human nature except in pettinesses; they are devoid alike of its spiritual and its sensual instincts. It is all very well for Mr Shaw to be sceptical as to the reality of much of the emotion which passes by the name of love, and over which so much fuss is made both in fiction and in life. For my part, I quite agree with him that a great deal of foolish and useless unhappiness is caused by our habit of idealizing and eternalizing this emotion, under all circumstances and at all hazards. But it is one thing to argue that the exultations and agonies of love are apt to be morbid, factitious, deliberately exaggerated and overwrought, and quite another to represent life as if these exultations and agonies had no existence whatever. Here we have a girl who, in the course of some six hours, transfers her affections (save the mark!) from a man whom she thought she had adored for years, to one whom she has only once before set eyes on, and a young man, who, in the same space of time, quarrels with the mistress about nothing at all, and, for no conceivable reason, makes up his mind to marry the maid. Such instantaneous *chassés croisés* used to be common enough in Elizabethan drama, and are quite the order of the day in Gilbertian extravaganza. In any more serious form of modern drama they would be not only preposterous but nauseous.

It is impossible, in short, to accept the second and third acts of *Arms and the Man* as either 'romantic comedy' or coherent farce. They are bright, clever, superficially cynical extravaganza. In the second act, there are some, not many, intervals of dullness; but with the reappearance of Captain Bernard Bluntschli-Shaw the fun fully revives, and in the third act there are even some patches of comedy, in the author's finer vein. Pray do not suppose, moreover, from my dwelling on the pettiness and sordidness of motive which reign throughout, that the whole effect of the play is unpleasant. Mr Shaw's cynicism is not in the least splenetic; on the contrary, it is imperturbably good-humoured and almost amiable. And amid all his irresponsible nonsense, he has contrived, generally in defiance of all dramatic consistency, to drag in a great deal of incidental good sense. I begin positively to believe that he may one day write a serious and even an artistic play, if only he will repress his irrelevant whimsicality, try to clothe his character-conceptions in flesh and blood, and realize the difference between knowingness and knowledge.

The acting was good from first to last. Mr Yorke Stephens seemed to have cultivated that ironic twist of his lip for the special purpose of creating the 'chocolate-cream soldier'; Mr Bernard Gould played the 'bounder' with humour and picturesqueness; Miss Alma Murray lent her seriousness and charm (invaluable qualities both, as it happened) to the part of Raina; Miss Florence Farr made a memorable figure of the enigmatic Louka; and Mr Welch, Mrs Charles Calvert, and Mr Orlando Barnett were all as good as need be.

The World, 25 April 1894

Max Beerbohm
The Devil's Disciple

For a dramatist who deliberately sits down to write something of a kind which he despises, one would predict failure. For a dramatist who, after two acts, sickens of his task and spends the last act in an endeavour to restore his self-respect by making the other two acts ridiculous, one would predict absolute disaster. Yet *The Devil's Disciple** is not merely a work of extremely fine quality, but a great popular success to boot. I know not which fact surprised me more – the fact that Mr Bernard Shaw has done a romantic melodrama better than it is done by gentlemen with romantic hearts and melodramatic heads, or the fact that the public seemed quite delighted when the play suddenly tumbled into wild frivolity. For my own part, I had been simmering with laughter throughout the first two acts, but the good people of Kennington, not knowing the soul and the creed of Mr Shaw, had been taking his play very seriously. I, in their place, should have done the same, for, I repeat, the play is most excellent. But its very excellence was for me the point of the jest. In a bad melodrama by Mr Shaw there would have been no incongruity. But that he should write a really good one, in spite of himself – that was irresistible! And so I welcomed the farcical last act, not because it amused me more than the other acts, but as an opportunity for unburdening myself of all the laughter which I had been suppressing in deference to a rapt audience. Also, it was a relief to find that Mr Shaw had not imposed too lengthy a strain upon himself, but had broken away just when it was becoming intolerable, none the worse for his penance.

'*Si ipsum audissetis!*' What scorn would Mr Shaw have not poured down these columns on such a play? How he would have riddled the hero, the sympathetic scapegrace (called, of course, 'Dick') who, for all his wickedness, cannot bear to see a woman cry, and keeps a warm corner in his heart for the old horse, Jim, and the old servant Roger, and wishes to be hanged by the English in the place of another man, and tries to throttle the major for calling a lady a woman! What scathing analysis Mr Shaw would have made of this fellow's character, declaring that he, 'G.B.S.', refused to see anything noble in a man who, having lived the life of a wastrel and a blackguard, proposed to commit suicide by imposing on the credulity of a court-martial! Far be it from me to attempt what Mr Shaw would have done with conviction. Indeed, I confess that 'Dick' seemed a very splendid fellow to me, and I rejoice to think that, though he had been so cruelly misunderstood and had lived 'with worthless men, aye! and with worthless women', he had kept his powers of self-sacrifice intact. Yes! 'Dick' thrilled me. At least, he would have done so if any one but Mr Shaw had created him. As it was, I was intolerably tickled by the irony with which Fate contrived that the first really human and convincing char-

* Prince of Wales Theatre, Kennington.

acter drawn by Mr Shaw should be a character which Mr Shaw had drawn quite cynically and with the express intention that it should be absolutely unlike anything in real life. When, as in his serious plays of modern life, Mr Shaw depicts life as he conceives it to be, and men and women as he knows them, the result is not (for me, at least) satisfactory. He imagines emotion to be an unfortunate and not inevitable nuisance, and reason to be the pivot on which the world should go round. His heroes and heroines are, therefore, absolutely rational machines, unclogged by such accessories as flesh and blood. It would be hard to imagine anything less like human beings than they are. To Mr Shaw himself they seem quite real, no doubt. He would probably admit that they are a little in advance of the age, belonging to the twentieth rather than to the nineteenth century. As a matter of fact, there is no reason to suppose that men and women become more rational with the advance of civilization; still less, that they will ever approximate to Vivie Warren or Leonard Charteris. And, incidentally, the fact that Mr Shaw quite honestly believes and hopes that they will, suggests that Mr Shaw himself is born after rather than before his time. His touching faith in the efficacy of reason dates him right back into the eighteenth century. There, had he lived in it, he would have found many supporters – not leaders, of course, but many staunch supporters. As it is, Mr Shaw stands alone, apart from the tendencies of this bustling age, a trifle *rococo*. I would not he were otherwise. I would not play pedagogue to him, as does Mr Archer, trying to persuade him to be this, and to leave off being that, and to beware of becoming the other. On the contrary, I hope Mr Shaw will always be just what he is – as delightful in the defects of his qualities as in the qualities themselves. Nor have I any doubt that my hope will be gratified. You may mould a child, but not, to any appreciable extent, a grown-up man. Mr Archer forgets that. He imagines that there is yet time for what he takes to be Mr Shaw's salvation. But let him cease to trouble. Mr Shaw's salvation, like that of every one else, is in being himself. For the space of two acts, Mr Shaw has pretended – for his own amusement and emolument, not to please Mr Archer – to be not himself. The result is that those two acts are fine and moving drama. But no number of fine and moving dramas to come would compensate me for the permanent obliteration of 'G.B.S.' If Mr Shaw had written his last act in key with the other two, his play would have been a better work of art, but how much less delightful! The success of *The Devil's Disciple* may tempt Mr Shaw to write other melodramas, and I trust that he will never fail to intrude himself in the last act. That he will always be welcome is proved by the attitude of Kennington. I offer Mr Shaw my congratulations on the amazing cleverness with which he has handled the melodramatic form, and on having the loud laugh over the thirty or forty London Managers who have allowed his play to go a-begging. I trust that when, in the fulness of time, I leave off being a dramatic critic and become a dramatist, my successor in these columns may have reason to be half as jealous of me as am I of 'G.B.S.'

The play was admirably performed. Mr Carson, as 'Dick', kept the ball rolling at top speed. His humour and his full-blooded method are peculiarly well suited to the part. Interesting as he always is, I do not think I have ever seen him act better or with more obvious enjoyment. Even Mr Shaw, had he been present at the performance, would have been convinced by 'Dick'. All the other parts seemed to me to be well filled, especially that of General Burgoyne, a part so exquisite in itself that the veriest duffer could not have seemed bad in it. Mr Luigi Lablache played it deliciously. But I am impatient for the publication of the play, in order that I may see how Mr Shaw himself, in accordance with his custom, analyses the General's character in his stage-directions. I hazard, as a conjecture: 'It being his trade to kill off such of his fellow-creatures as do not see their way to being fleeced by his employers, he goes about the job with every desire to speedily bring it to a satisfactory conclusion, but has no enthusiasm, and, if he had, would be careful not to communicate it to his men, knowing well that enthusiasm has been the cause of ninety per cent of his country's defeats. Finding himself outgeneralled, he accepts the situation with perfect good-humour, only regretting that the American climate and the dulness of the American generals prevent him from showing his contempt for his country by going over to the enemy. In fact, a realist, whose only illusion is that he is a very agreeable fellow. This (by any civilized standard) he is not; being, indeed, an aggravated type of English gentleman, whose previous professional success alone prevents him from being cordially disliked by the community which has prostituted him to its own ends, and which his failure as a butcher serves thoroughly well right. Withal . . .' but

> O most presumptuous! lay aside the pipe
> Of that sweet elder shepherd.

The Saturday Review, 7 October 1899

J. T. Grein
Mrs Warren's Profession

I

It was an extremely uncomfortable afternoon. For there was a majority of women to listen to that which could only be understood by a minority of men. Nor was the play fit for women's ears. By all means let us initiate our daughters before they cross the threshold of womanhood into those duties and functions of life which are vital in matrimony and maternity. But there is a boundary line, and its transgression means peril – the peril of destroying ideals. I go further. Even men need not know all the ugliness that lies below the surface of everyday life. To some male minds too much knowledge of the seamy side is poisonous, for it leads to pessimism, that pioneer of insanity and suicide. And, sure as I feel that most of the women, and a good many of the men, who were present at the production of *Mrs Warren's Profession** by the Stage Society, did not at first know, and finally merely guessed, what was the woman's trade, I cannot withhold the opinion that the representation was unnecessary and painful. It is mainly for these reasons that, in spite of my great admiration for Bernard Shaw, the play was not brought out by the late Independent Theatre. As a 'straight talk to men only' it is not sufficiently true to life to be productive of an educational effect. As a drama it is unsatisfactory, because the characters have no inner life, but merely echo certain views of the author. As literature, however, the merits of *Mrs Warren's Profession* are considerable, and its true place is in the study.

II

Mrs Warren's Profession is a 'problem play' in the fullest sense of the word. Mr Shaw will probably deny it, and claim that it is ordinary actable drama, but the text will give evidence in my favour. We hear Mr Shaw all the time, and whatever vitality the characters possess is not their own, but Mr Shaw's. They also own much of his contradictory elements – his depth of observation and thought and his extraordinary 'cussedness'. Here, as in most of G.B.S.'s work, the sublime is constantly spoilt by the ridiculous. It is the author's manner, and his way to express his contempt for the public. But that is a mere side issue. The main point is whether the problem is worth discussing and whether it has been dealt with in an adequate, convincing manner. I say no on both counts. The problem is neither vital nor important. It has none of the *raison d'être* of *Le Fils de Coralie* by Delpit, of *La Dame aux Camélias*, and of *Ghosts*. The case of Mrs Warren has been invented with such ingenuity and surrounded by such impossibilities that it produces revolt instead of reasoning. For Mr Shaw has made the great mistake of tainting all the male characters with a streak of a demoralized tar brush; he has created a cold-

* New Lyric Club.

blooded, almost sexless daughter as the sympathetic element: and he has built the unspeakable Mrs Warren of such motley material that in our own mind pity and disgust for the woman are constantly at loggerheads. If the theme was worth treating at all the human conflict was the tragedy of the daughter through the infamy of the mother. Instead of that we get long arguments – spiced with platform oratory and invective – between a mother really utterly degraded, but here and there white-washed with sentimental effusions, and a daughter so un-English in her knowledge of the world, so cold of heart, and 'beyond human power' in reasoning that we end by hating both; the one who deserves it, as well as the other who is a victim of circumstances. Thus there are false notes all the time, and apart from a passing interest in a few scenes saved by the author's cleverness, the play causes only pain and bewilderment, while it should have shaken our soul to its innermost chords.

It is not so easy to explain this singular effect, or, rather, it would be easy if it did not behove us to touch this work – in a newspaper – with kid-gloved fingers. Mr Shaw, in his attempt to portray a woman of Mrs Warren's type, either lacked the courage to play *misère-ouverte*, or, what is more likely, he had not sufficient knowledge of the monstrosity of such beings. His Mrs Warren is a black soul with spots of human feeling dotted on in whitish chalk. But the real Mrs Warren is the most abject creature in all humanity. I cannot say more. I can but refer Mr Shaw to Parent-Duchatel, to Yves Guyot, to Dr Commange, to Leo Taxil's *Corruption fin de siècle* – to a whole library on the colossal subject of human debasement. If Mr Shaw had fully known the nature of Mrs Warren's profession he would have left the play unwritten, or produced a tragedy of heartrending power. Now he has merely philandered around a dangerous subject; he has treated it half in earnest, half in that peculiar jesting manner which is all his own. He has given free reins to his brain and silenced his heart. He has therefore produced a play of a needlessly 'unpleasant' understructure to no useful end. A play that interests in part, repels in others; a drama that plays fast and loose with our emotions, and will in some awaken a curiosity which had better been left in slumber.

III

It is the fashion in some quarters to express condolence with the actors when a play is of an outspoken unpleasant nature. I see no reason for such uncalled-for patronage. Condolence is in its right place when talent is wasted on futility; but when actors of their own accord choose to appear in works of uncompromising candour, they should be criticized in the ordinary way and not humiliated by doubtful apologies. Artists like Miss Fanny Brough, Miss Madge McIntosh, like Mr Granville Barker and their companions, know full well what they do when they appear in plays like *Mrs Warren's Profession*; they know also that writers like Mr Shaw have no ulterior motives when they deal with strong subjects, and that they afford great chances of distinction to the actor.

The performance of *Mrs Warren's Profession* proved no exception to the rule. In spite of the disadvantage of a cramped stage and impracticable scenery in the theatre of the Lyric Club, the acting reached the highest mark. Miss Fanny Brough, a woman of more brain and heart than half a dozen of our more or less leading ladies *en bloc*, achieved that which had long been predicted by her admirers. She proved that she is not only a splendid comedienne, but that she is endowed with the profounder gifts which characterize tragic actresses. Whatever vitality the character of Mrs Warren now and again seemed to achieve, whatever feeling of sympathy was aroused in the spectator, sprung from Miss Brough's magnificent impersonation. She had to play upon the entire clavier of emotions, and in that exceedingly difficult concerto there was not a wavering note, let alone an inharmonious chord. The younger actress, Miss McIntosh, was also fully equal to her task. She did her best to minimize the frigid side of the daughter's strange character, and to kindle every little spark of womanhood into flame. Her performance betrayed great study and a carefully-planned conception of a part which in less capable hands would seriously try the patience and the sense of humour of the audience.

But the play was admirably cast from first to last, Mr Charles Goodhart and Mr Julius Knight, Mr Granville Barker and Mr Cosmo Stuart, they all worked with an ardour unwonted in any theatre except where 'art for art's sake' is the motto.

Dramatic Criticism 1900–1901, 1902

Desmond MacCarthy
John Bull's Other Island

If *Candida* is one of the best of Mr Shaw's plays for the completeness with which it contains and finishes its story, *John Bull's Other Island** is remarkable for being equally successful for entirely different reasons. It is a play with hardly any story, with no climax, without the vestige of a plot, and without anything like an ending, in fact without one of the qualities of the 'well-constructed' play; yet it is nevertheless an absolute success. The story is simply that of two friends and partners, an Irishman and an Englishman, who visit the former's old home in order to fore-close a mortgage. Incidentally, the Englishman determines to stand for the local seat, and becomes engaged, with his friend's approval, to a young woman with whom the latter had been on rather romantic terms for a short time before starting on his career. That is all; could anything sound more unpromising? There is not even a touch of jealousy to offer a chance of dramatic effect. The interest lies solely in the presentation of character and in the contrast between temperaments; but this is achieved in a masterly fashion. The play has the one aesthetic technical quality, which is necessary to its perfection; the characters are developed by means of a perfectly natural sequence of events; there is no appearance of circumstances being created for the sake of exhibiting them; everything that happens has the air of happening by chance.

Every critic of this play must stop on the threshold of his comments to remark, with whatever emphasis he can command, that the performance itself was one of the best ever given in London. There were faults, of course, but they are only worth mentioning, if this fact is remembered.

Mr Shaw has explained in his preface to the play what he conceives to be the main difference between the Englishman and the Irishman. The Irishman is more imaginative, but he has no illusions about matters of fact; while the Englishman is at the mercy of such imagination as he possesses, and has in consequence a confused sentimental conception of reality. The Duke of Wellington, according to him, is a typical Irishman, while Nelson is typically English. This difference in temperament he attributes not to race (he does not believe in race) but to the climate. These discussions about national characteristics make very good conversation, but it is hard to feel satisfied with the conclusions; for the exceptions are too numerous. For instance, according to Mr Shaw's theory, you would expect to find that such Englishmen as Fielding, Defoe, Cobbett, Gissing, Samuel Butler, had been brought up in the soft moist air and among the brown bogs and heather of Rosscullen, and that such Irishmen as Goldsmith and Steele, who were so full of romantic sentiment about actualities and dearly loved a fool (which Mr Shaw says is almost impossible for an Irishman) had never even been to Ireland. But whether the theory propounded in the preface is true or not, in the play

* Court Theatre.

Larry Doyle and Broadbent are extraordinarily vivid characters, who recall familiar types of Irishmen and Englishmen. The contrast between the two is most striking at the following points. Broadbent is full of 'heart' and takes himself and everything he does and every one he meets absolutely seriously; he has no sense of humour, or of refinement, or of proportion. Larry is discriminative to the point of chilly fastidiousness; he cannot enjoy life and he cannot idealize any human being; he cannot love, though he is found of Tom Broadbent because Tom's warmth of emotion helps him to feel things are worth while at the moment, and because his nature is essentially practical and active, while Larry himself is only capable of being moved by ideals in which he does not believe. He is exasperated by this tendency in himself to feel only the beauty and significance of things which do not exist in any satifying quantities; hence the bitterness of his contempt for romance and mysticism. His life is a perpetual struggle to get used to the world; it is a point of pride with him not to feel an exile here; hence his enthusiasm for the big international world of shipping, engineering and business, into which he has escaped from his dreams and thoughts in poverty-stricken Rosscullen. But business does not really fill him with enthusiasm, and he knows it; hence his fierce dislike of Father Keegan, who, with the same heart-sickness in him, has taken the opposite course, and turned away from reality to live in contemplation of a far-off perfection. Larry feels, as keenly as Father Keegan, the futility and vulgarity of Broadbent's schemes; but he fights fiercely for them because anything seems more tolerable than the helplessness of a visionary's protest against the world.

Mr J. L. Shine's Larry was not so good as many of the other parts; but he did give the impression of loneliness and distraction of heart and of perpetual tension of will to keep turned towards one path in life, which are far the most important characteristics to represent in Larry.

Broadbent, on the other hand, talks with the most reverential enthusiasm of Ruskin and Shelley (whose works he was very fond of reading, he says, as a boy), and he listens in the same spirit to the discourses of Keegan; but there is a profounder disrespect implied in his admiration than in Larry's impatience; for Broadbent is absolutely incapable of really believing in such things; the works of Ruskin and Shelley are merely pots of romantic paint to him, wherein he finds colours with which to daub his own undertakings.

Mr Louis Calvert's Broadbent was a masterpiece of acting. It is seldom that a character so thoroughly homogeneous in gesture, voice, and carriage is seen on the stage. Mr Shaw's description of him runs as follows: 'a robust, full-blooded energetic man in the prime of life, sometimes eager and credulous, sometimes shrewd and roguish, sometimes portentously solemn, sometimes jolly and impetuous, always buoyant and irresistible, mostly likable; and enormously absurd in his most earnest moments.' Mr Calvert was all this to the life. The meeting between Broadbent and Nora Reilly by the round tower, on the first night of his arrival at Rosscullen, when his romantic feelings are so strange to himself, that he accept's Nora's suggestion he is drunk, with shame and conviction, is a delicious bit of comedy. His subsequent wooing of Nora and his easy triumph was a painful spectacle, for Nora is a charming person; but the scene is distressingly plausible.

Mr Barker as Father Keegan did not quite succeed in inspiring the sense of remote dignity which it is important to emphasize in contrast to the eupeptic irreverence of Broadbent and to the squalid go-as-you-please Irish characters. How good they all were! Corney Doyle (Mr F. Cremlin) with his drawling manner and calculating eye; Father Dempsey (Mr Beveridge) with unction, authority and familiarity so perfectly blended in his manner; Barney Doran (Mr Wilfred Shine), the clever sloven with plenty of heartiness and no heart; and Mat Haffigan (Mr A. E. George), that gnarled old stump of dogged density! Miss Ellen O'Mally's Nora had a genuine poetic charm, a quality which hardly ever crosses the footlights.

The Court Theatre, 1904–1907, 1907

A. B. Walkley
The Doctor's Dilemma

'I've lost the thread of my remarks,' says one of Mr Shaw's physicians; 'what was I talking about?' Mr Shaw himself might say this, or something very like it. True, he does not helplessly lose the thread of his play. But he is continually dropping it, in order that he may start a fresh topic. This foible of discursiveness has been steadily gaining on him. *John Bull* was more discursive than *Man and Superman*. *Major Barbara* was more discursive than *John Bull*. *The Doctor's Dilemma** is more discursive than *Major Barbara*. Needless to point out that this discursiveness is not a new method, but a 'throwing back' to a very old method. It was, for instance, the method of Shakespeare. A certain unity of idea does, however, underlie Mr Shaw's new play, and that is to be found in its satire on the medical profession. Therein he has been anticipated by Brieux in his *L'Évasion*. But of course the theme belongs, as of right, to Molière. Is there not something piquant in the spectacle of Mr Shaw applying Shakespearian treatment to a Molièrean theme? After all, there is no such thoroughgoing classicist as your professional iconoclast.

Superficially, no doubt, we seem to have travelled a long way from the buffooneries of M. Purgon and M. Diafoirus. Only superficially, however. For the old mock-Latin, for the instruments which modern delicacy does not

* Court Theatre.

permit to be named, we now have barbarous Greek – opsonin and phago-cytosis – surgical saws and 'nuciform sacs'. *Plus ça change plus c'est la même chose.* That, by the way, is the criticism which, in effect, the oldest of Mr Shaw's physicians, Sir Patrick Cullen, is always applying to the new-fangled dis-coveries of his fellow-practitioners. He has seen all these 'novelties' before; they have their law of periodicity – say, once in every fifteen years – and nothing is altered but the names. Sir Patrick, who stands for bluff cynical comment on scientific affectation, heads a group of half a dozen medical types. There is Sir Ralph Bloomfield Bonnington – familiarly known as 'old B.B.' – Court physician (much liked by what he invariably calls 'the Family') and platitudinously pompous bungler. He is, as you see, an entirely Molièresque figure. Good easy man, he does not know the difference between a vaccine and an antitoxin, and is all for stimulating the phagocytes. There is Sir Colenso Ridgeon – just knighted as the curtain rises for his great 'opsonin' discovery – who is all for buttering the bacilli. There is the great surgeon, Cutler Walpole, who in every human ill sees blood-poisoning, and is all for cutting out the 'nuciform sac'. Physic he bluntly characterizes as 'rot'; the physicians, in return, dismiss surgery as mere 'manual labour'. There remain two types not anticipated by Molière; Leo Schutzmacher, who has made a fortune in the East End by selling advice and drugs for sixpences, under the sign 'cure guaranteed', and Dr Blenkinsop, a hard-working general practitioner who has never succeeded in making both ends meet and begs fashionable consultants for their cast-off frock-coats. All the people display their several humours in a Queen Anne Street consulting-room, whither they have come to congratulate Sir Colenso Ridgeon on his Birthday Honour. The irony of the thing is that Sir Colenso's knighthood is the fruit of one of 'old B.B.'s' most glaring blunders in treating one of 'the Family'. The dis-heartened and disgusted Ridgeon remarks, in an 'aside', 'Ours is not a profes-sion, but a conspiracy.'

Why not call it, rather, a procession? For that is what it turns out to be in the conduct of Mr Shaw's play. Our bevy of doctors career through the play, always together (one wonders what becomes of their unfortunate patients), like the wedding guests in the *Chapeau de Paille d'Italie*. From Queen Anne Street their line of march takes them to the Star and Garter at Richmond, and thence to Louis Dubedat's studio. But who is Louis Dubedat? It is time that he was mentioned here, though it is a whole hour by the clock – an hour devoted to the exhibition and discussion of medical humours – before you hear of him in the theatre. Louis Dubedat is an artist with a tuberculous lung. Please keep one eye fixed on the art and the other on the lung, for these are the two separate elements out of which Mr Shaw makes his play. Examine the lung first, for that *motif* still continues the original thesis – medical humbug. Louis Dubedat is the *corpus vile* on which the medical experiments are to be made. Jennifer Dubedat, Louis's wife, has sought out Sir Colenso Ridgeon, and, with great difficulty, secured his promise to undertake the case. When Ridgeon consents it is really out of his profound (but entirely discreet) admiration for Jennifer, an idealist from Cornwall, a child of nature, to whom belief in Louis's genius is a religion. But Ridgeon's consent at once places him in a dilemma. He has only staff and accommodation for ten cases, and all his beds are full. If he takes in Louis, he must dismiss (practically to certain death) one of the original ten; life for life. Nevertheless, knowing what he does of Jennifer, and knowing as yet nothing of Louis, he consents. As soon as he gets to know Louis the case is altered. Now is the time for you to remember that Louis is an artist as well as a sick man. You find that he is a particular kind of artist – the non-moral artist, a man without any sense of conduct, to whom the words 'right' and 'wrong', as ordinarily understood, have no meaning. Think of him as a Pierrot, or as a Faun. *Imprimis*, he belongs to Elia's great race of borrowers. Invited to meet the doctors (in a body, of course) he 'touches' each of them for a loan. *Item*, he is a bigamist. *Item*, he is a blackmailer. That people should reprobate these practices is a thing he cannot even begin to understand. When the doctors arrive (always in a body) to upbraid him, he sits down and quietly sketches them. He gaily declares himself to be a disciple of Bernard Shaw, a celebrity unknown to Sir Patrick Cullen, who, however, promptly finds in him a moral likeness to John Wesley.

And now Sir Colenso is in a worse dilemma than ever. For he finds that his poor *confrère*, the morally irreproachable Dr Blenkinsop, has also a tuberculous lung. Which is he to save? The good Blenkinsop, who is a social failure, or the bad Dubedat, who paints good pictures? Good men are fairly common, he argues. Good pictures are very rare. And he decides in favour of Dubedat. But here there is a fresh complication. Jennifer Dubedat's whole life consists in the worship of Louis. If Louis ceased to be her hero, she would commit suicide – has, indeed, already marked out a certain cliff in Cornwall for that purpose. To prolong Dubedat's life is to ensure that his wife shall sooner or later find him out, and so have her religion shattered and lose her own life into the bargain. Therefore, for Jennifer's sake (even although, to the vulgar mind, it may look like murdering a man in the hope of marrying his widow) Sir Colenso must let Louis die. 'Rather hard that a lad should be killed because his wife has too high an opinion of him', is old Sir Patrick's comment; 'Fortunately very few of us are in that predicament.'

Killed, however, Louis is. Killed because he is handed over by Sir Colenso, the only man who could save him (with magical opsonin butter for the bacilli), to 'old B.B.', who doesn't know the difference between a vaccine and an antitoxin. Louis dies, or fades away, before our eyes, with his head on Jennifer's breast (as Duse dies on Armand's in the last act of *La Dame*), dies like one of Montaigne's Emperors 'in a jest', chaffing the doctors all round and uttering his artist's *credo* with his last breath – 'I believe in Michael Angelo and Rembrandt and Velasquez and the Message of Art.' Incorrigible Pierrot, unregenerate Faun! *Qualis artifex pereo*, he might have said. But instead of that he says let there be no horrible crape, let not his wife mar her beauty with tears; he hates widows, she must promise him to marry again. Also he gives a plain hint that he understands Sir Colenso's game. So does Jennifer, who coldly dismisses Sir Colenso from the death-chamber. Amateurs of the morbid will revel in this realistic death-scene. Other people will dislike it as bad taste and cheap art. Bad taste in its punctuation of solemnity by jokes (for there is a touch of the Pierrot and the Faun in Mr Shaw himself). Cheap art in its employment of such a fact as death (realistic, not poeticized death) to secure an emotional thrill; a thrill which, from the very constitution of human nature, is bound to come without any reference to the skill of the artist. Mr Shaw made a like mistake in the face 'bashing' scene of *Major Barbara*. But it is useless to argue with him over these things. He will do them. All we can do is to be sorry.

There is a brief, quaint, not entirely comprehensible, epilogue. Jennifer and Sir Colenso meet at Louis Dubedat's posthumous 'one man show'. Sir Colenso, treated with cold disdain, is driven to try and open Jennifer's eyes to the truth about her dead hero. He fails utterly. The secret of his love for her pops out. She mocks at the idea of love in this 'elderly gentleman' – a new view of himself for Sir Colenso. Besides, in deference to her hero's dying injunction, she has already married again. The curtain descends while we are still wondering who is Jennifer's second husband. Can it be the well-groomed manager of the Art Gallery?

A thoroughly 'Shavian' play, this, stimulating and diverting for the most part, occasionally distressing, now and then bewildering. O philosopher! O humorist! you mutter with gratitude. And then you whisper with a half sigh, O Pierrot! O Faun!

Drama and Life, 1907

Max Beerbohm
The Voysey Inheritance

Messrs Vedrenne and Barker have made no more signal discovery than
Mr Barker's new play;* and I hasten to offer my congratulations. I have often
inveighed against the plays written by mimes, and have even asserted that
no mime could possibly write a good play. Mr Barker is an exceptional person,
in whose presence I bow, corrected. On him, somehow, the blight of the theatre
has not fallen. He has continued to keep himself less interested in the
theatre than in life. He is not, and may he never become, 'one o' the boys'.
May he ever continue to be their antithesis, letting his mind range actively
over the actual world, not wallow in that one little weed-covered pond, the
theatre, which reflects nothing. May his very bright intellect never grow dim.
I may have to suggest anon that he is too purely intellectual to be perfect.
For the present, though, let there be nothing but praise.

It is always the most obvious and most promising themes that our playwrights most ostentatiously neglect. One of these themes is the fraudulent
solicitor. Mr Barker's mere choice of this theme is laudable; but far more so is
his treatment of it. Having chosen his type, he has shown it to us from within,
laying bare all its intricacies. Mr Voysey, of Voysey and Son, is no mere
arbitrary figure of a scoundrel. A scoundrel he is, but much besides; and we
are supposed to understand the reason and the exact quality of his scoundrelism, and to gauge the whole of his character 'all round'. In a sense, scoundrelism has been thrust on him. When he inherited his father's business, he found
that it had been based, all the time, on fraud. He threw himself into the task of
setting the business on an honest basis, without doing violence to his filial
instinct by letting the world know about his father. In time, he achieved his
task; but, in doing so, he had acquired a taste for the ingenious manipulation
of funds. He had found that he had a genius for finance. Consequently, he
soon became bored by the humdrum of a well-regulated little business. Moreover, he had begotten a large family, to which he was devoted; and, except by
manipulating his clients' funds, he could not 'provide handsomely' for it. So
he proceeded to manipulate, ministering thus both to his paternal feelings
and to his financial genius. Scruples of conscience troubled him not at all in
his strenuous life. 'Let us realize', he says, 'that religion is one thing, home-
life another, and business another; and that each of these great things in
life is to be practised separately. Then we shall be able to practise them with
all our strength, and to get the full benefit that is in them.' I quote from
memory, and these are not, doubtless, the actual words. But I have preserved
the spirit of the passage well enough to give you a grasp of Mr Voysey's
philosophy, and of the lines along which Mr Voysey's character has developed.
The one cloud on his horizon is that none of his available sons seems fitted
to carry on the business when he dies. Edward, for example, is a prig, and has

* Court Theatre.

steeped himself in various ethical systems. Still, it is on Edward that he must depend. Edward is taken into partnership, and the first scene of the play (for it is only in the play's course, gradually, that one learns what I have told you about Mr Voysey) is concerned with Edward's horror at the revelations that have been made to him, and with the inward conflict in him as to whether he shall desert his father, whom he still loves, or shall become an accessory to, and possibly a scapegoat for, his father's frauds. The conflict is admirably conducted by Mr Barker, who leaves it, however, undecided till the end of the second act. This act is occupied mainly by showing us the family 'interior'. And Mr Barker excels not less in incisive sketches of character than in elaborate portrayals. The Voyseys are a very large family, and a very ordinary family. Yet every one of them is made to stand out distinctly and amusingly. Their very colourlessness becomess lurid through the accuracy with which it is observed by Mr Barker, and through the sharp and subtle irony with which he shows it to us. In the second act we see the Voyseys in their daily round – in all the decent pettiness and dulness of their ordinary selves. In the third act we see them tested by a tragic crisis. Their father has died a death for which the audience was 'prepared' by a queerly felicitous little touch at the end of the third act. After the funeral, Edward, who did finally decide to take up the partnership in his father's business, has to break to the mourning family assembled the news of its founder's nefariousness. A hundred thousand pounds has been left by Mr Voysey; but three hundred thousand would hardly cover the liabilities of the firm to its clients. Edward points out that it is clearly the duty of the various children, married and unmarried, to surrender their legacies. This notion, somehow, does not appeal to the Voyseys; and their attempts to reconcile their distaste for it with the rectitude on which they pride themselves, and their bewildered doubts as to how to reconcile their virtuous indignation against their father with a decorous attitude towards the deceased whom they have been so sincerely mourning, and all the other elements of doubt that are battling in their souls and making them dimly ridiculous even to themselves, suffice to furnish what I am tempted to regard as the finest scene of grim, ironic comedy in modern English drama. Both in conception and in execution, the scene is the work of a master. It is admirably played, too, by the many mimes who figure in it. People often ask, quite innocently, with a genuine desire for information, why the acting at the Court Theatre seems to be infinitely better than in so many other theatres where the same mimes are to be seen. I should have thought that the two reasons were obvious. One is that the mimes at the Court are very carefully stage-managed, every one of them being kept in such relation to his fellows as is demanded by the relation in which the various parts stand to one another – no one mime getting more, or less, of a chance than the playwright has intended him to have. The other reason is that at the Court Theatre are produced only plays written by clever persons who have a sense of character, and who are thus enabled to create characters which are human, and which, therefore, repay the trouble that the mimes take in playing them.

After this conclave scene, which is, I repeat, masterly, comes a scene to remind us that the master is still, to some extent, a pupil – a member of Mr Shaw's academy for young gentlemen. Edward Voysey is tempted to let his father's firm go bankrupt, and so extricate himself from the unpleasant life in which he has become involved. No retrospective blame could be laid on him. Technically, as a member of the firm, he would be responsible. But he could show that since his entry into the firm there had been no fresh irregularities, and that his influence had been all on the side of the clients. On the other hand, if he continued the business, a smash would certainly come sooner or later, and he would be sent to penal servitude. Why should he court imprisonment for doing a thing from which he revolted? There was one highly chivalrous reason. He might, if the smash did not come too soon, gradually rescue the money of the humbler investors. He determines that to this off-chance he will sacrifice himself. I have nothing to urge against this determination in itself. But it is made at the instance of a Miss Alice Maitland, with whom Edward is in love; and Miss Alice Maitland won't do at all. There may, conceivably, be young ladies like her in real life. But the point is that all the young ladies in Mr Shaw's plays are exactly like her; and however appropriate they may sometimes be to their own setting, a replica of them is just what is not needed, and what is injurious, here. Wanted, an ordinary human person, who happens to be in love with Edward Voysey. Miss Maitland has the customary Shavian allowance of coquetry; but she shows no sign that she is in love with Edward, or could possibly be in love with any one except herself. She wants to marry, of course; but whether or not she will marry Edward depends entirely on whether or not he shall startle her by contriving to live up to her own theories of general morality. That she might sympathize with him in his ordeal is the very last thing that would occur to her. She simply waits to see how he will acquit himself. Time passes, and Edward now has managed to rescue some of the money aforesaid, and is in daily risk of exposure and imprisonment. He really has become worthy of her perfect self, and she sets her seal of approval by offering to marry him. 'But what', asks he, 'if I am sent to prison?' 'Then', she says meditatively, 'I shall have to be very careful.' He asks her why. 'Because', she replies, 'my pride will be so great.' I doubt if even a Shavian woman (granted her existence) in real life would, at such a juncture, merely utter this little, dry, academic, all-in-the-air paradox about her own prospective emotions. Certainly, any ordinary woman would shrink with horror from the prospect of her lover being sent to prison, and being parted from her. Master Barker, at his desk in the Shavian academy, has shrunk with not less horror from the notion of admitting an ordinary woman into his play. The British drama has been given over almost exclusively to the portrayal of sentimental emotions, and to false portrayal of them; so that the reaction of a gifted young dramatist against sentimental emotions in any form is quite natural. It is well that we should have a dramatic portrayal of moral enthusiasm. But moral enthusiasm can be distorted even so by Mr Barker. A heroine with nothing in her soul but abstract ethics is just as foolish a contrivance as the heroine of the average conventional play. For Mr Barker's special purpose Miss Maitland ought to have been a woman in whom moral passion was combined with a very strong passion of love for Edward Voysey. Then she would have supplied in herself an interesting conflict that would have added much to the interest of Voysey's own. As it is, she is as undramatic as she is (despite the charm of Miss Mabel Hackney's acting) insufferable; and I cannot imagine a greater tribute to the play than the fact that she doesn't wreck it. If she had not been brought in at all, I should not have lamented the 'lack of feminine interest'. The play would have been quite all right without her. But, as she was brought in, I have to call Mr Barker's attention to her as a warning not to be afraid of sentiment, and ashamed of it, merely because it isn't brain-power. Sentiment is a not uncommon thing in real life. It is a very common and potent thing, and worthy material for even the cleverest of dramatists.

The Saturday Review, 11 November 1905

Max Beerbohm
Justice

We are getting on. Time was when our drama was so utterly divorced from life that the critics never dreamed of condemning a play for artificiality. It is but a few years since they acquired the habit of judging plays in relation to life. And now (so fast has our drama been moving) they are beginning to decry plays on the ground that they are indistinguishable from life. Well, I am not going to join in the doubts expressed by so many critics whether *Justice*, in the repertory at the Duke of York's, be proper art. 'Cinematographic' they call it. So it is, in a sense. We really do, in seeing it, have the sensation of seeing reproduced exactly things that have happened in actual life. Or rather, we feel that we are seeing these things actually happen. If the cinematograph were chromatic and stereoscopic, and free from vibration, and gramophonic into the bargain, Mr Galsworthy might – no, even then, as I shall presently show, he would not have a dangerous rival. In the first act of *Justice* we do not feel that we are seeing an accurate presentment of the humdrum of a lawyer's office: we are *in* a lawyer's office. The curtain rises on the second act; and presently we have forgotten the foot-lights, and are *in* a court of law. At a crucial moment in the cross-examination of a witness, somebody at the reporter's table drops a heavy book on the floor. An angry murmur of 'Sh!' runs round the court, and we ourselves have joined in it. The jury retires to consider its verdict, and instantly throughout the court there is a buzz of conversation – aye, and throughout the auditorium, too: we are all of us, as it were, honorary 'supers'. In the third act, we arrive at a prison. Gloomily producing a special pass signed 'John Galsworthy', we are shown over the interior. We interview the governor, the chaplain, the doctor. Through the wire-blind of the governor's office we have, all the while, a blurred glimpse of certain automata, quickly-revolving – the convicts at exercise. Some of these men we see presently at close quarters in their cells. We are haunted by it all afterwards as by an actual experience, not as by a tragic play. And part of this effect is due, of course, to the excellence of the stage-management and of the acting. But of what avail would these things be if the play itself were not true to life? At the game of producing an absolute illusion of reality a dramatist is heavily handicapped in competition with the cinematograph, undeveloped though that machine still is. What the cinematograph presents to us has happened, is ready-made. What the dramatist presents to us has not happened, has to be specially concocted. Only by constant observation of the surface of things, and by the intuitive sympathy with the soul of things, and then by a laborious process of selection and rejection, can the dramatist evoke in us that absolute illusion. For him there are no happy accidents. Every character must be an amalgam of many actual persons seen from without and within; and every incident must be relevant to these characters, and to the story told through them, and to the idea or ideas through them expressed. Especially such a play as *Justice*, which is the vehicle for criticism of certain conditions of modern life, would be of no value whatsoever if the characters were not types, and if the story were not typical. I think that in *Justice*, as in *Strife*, it is because Mr Galsworthy so carefully eschews any show of sympathy with one character, or of antipathy against another, that the charge of cinematography is preferred against him. In showing us a young criminal caught in the toils of law, he shows us no hero, but a rather uninteresting youth with a tendency to hysteria, who does not, when he is confronted with the cheque that he has forged, hesitate to let suspicion fall on an innocent colleague. There is nothing brutal or vindictive about the young man's employer: he lets the law takes its course, but does so as a matter of principle, and reluctantly. In court, the counsel for the prosecution does not go beyond his duty; and the judge's summing-up is perfectly fair; and the sentence which he passes is according to his sense of duty to the commonweal. The governor of the prison is a very humane and sympathetic man. The chaplain is nothing worse than a prig. The doctor is not only conscientious but intelligent. Mr Galsworthy never takes an unfair advantage. He dispenses with many quite fair advantages. Is this because he is merely a detached and dispassionate observer of life? The reason is the very contrary. It is because he is fulfilled with pity for the victims of a thing he vehemently hates, and because he is consumed with an anxiety to infect his fellow-men with this hatred and this pity, that he strives so unremittingly to be quite impartial. He knows that a suspicion of special pleading would jeopardize his case. He is determined to give us no chance of soothing our nerves by saying to him 'Oh yes, no doubt there is a lot in what you say, but you have let your feelings – which do you great credit – run away with you.' He doesn't mind losing the credit for having fine feelings and being regarded as merely a cold-hearted person who just wants to frighten and depress us, so long as he does succeed in his object of frightening and depressing us. He wants us to have to say 'This is life'; and if we then round on him, saying 'And you're a blooming cinematograph! Yah!' he takes our outburst as rather a compliment than otherwise. He sees that his object is achieved. That we should recognize the passion and the artistry in him is a matter of less importance.

In some of his works he does certainly lay himself open to a (very superficial) charge of inhumanity. In *Strife* he showed us a conflict, and in *Fraternity* a contrast between the poor and the rich; and the implicit moral of the play was that this conflict would be for ever. If things are irremediable, why, it might be asked, harrow us about them? To which, I take it, Mr Galsworthy's answer would be that to recognize the sadness of things is a duty we owe to honesty, and is good for our souls. In *Justice*, however, there is no fundamental pessimism. Mr Galsworthy sees that our criminal law and our penal system are clumsy, mechanical, mischievous. But he sees them as things not beyond redemption. A little spurring of the scientific intelligence in us and of our common humanity is all that is needed to induce reform. Perfect justice there can never be, of course; but the folly and barbarism of our present method – which is far less barbarous and foolish now than it used to be – can be amended. Already it is a universal axiom that society's duty to the criminal lies not in avenging itself on him but reforming him. Let practice be adjusted to theory. At present our practice is mainly in accord with a theory discredited. The method of solitary confinement, for example, is good merely as a torture. And it is against this particular part of our penal system that Mr Galsworthy directs his strongest shafts. No one, nowadays, has a word in defence of solitary confinement. And I shall be surprised if Mr Galsworthy has not delivered its death-blow. The cell-scene in the third act is, for purposes of horror, more effective than tomes of written words, however pungent. When the curtain falls, the auditorium is as silent as the very prison whose silence the convict has just broken by hammering with his fists against his door; and not even when, a moment later, the curtain rises, and we see Mr Dennis Eadie cheerfully bowing his acknowledgment to us, is the horror undone. Cheerfully? No, I am very sure that Mr Eadie is too fine an artist not to shudder at this rising of the curtain – this bland, idiotic attempt, on the part of the management, to undo the horror.

The Saturday Review, 5 March 1910

IV Pantomime and Music Hall

G. B. Shaw
At the Pantomime

When the Superior Person – myself, for instance – takes it upon himself to disparage burlesque, opera bouffe, musical farce, and Christmas pantomime as the mere sillinesses and levities of the theatre, let him not forget that, but for them, our players would have no mimetic or plastic training, and the art of the stage machinist, the costumier, the illusionist scene-painter would be extinct. The late Sir Augustus Harris's description of Wagner's *Das Rheingold* as 'a damned pantomime' was, on its own plane, a thoroughly sound one. For suppose the theatre had been given over entirely throughout this century to plays of the Robertson and Pinero school, performed in the Hare-Bancroft style, in built-in stage drawing rooms, by actors tailored and millinered as they would be for a fashionable At-home, *Das Rheingold* would in that case have been impossible: nobody would have known how to work the changes, to suspend the Rhine maidens, to transform Alberich into a dragon, to assemble the black clouds that are riven by Donner's thunderbolt, or to light up Froh's rainbow bridge. Under such circumstances, some of the most magnificent pages in the *Rheingold* score would not have come into existence; for your great man does not waste his work on the impracticable. And pray how was it that Wagner found the stage machinists ready for the series of landscape and seascape effects which we find in his most characteristic works? Nay, how did the much simpler stage illusions of *Der Freischütz*, *Oberon*, and *Robert le Diable* becomes possible before the Bayreuth epoch? The answer surely is that during all those years which are marked for us in theatrical annals only by events in the careers of great artists, there must have been a continual output of ballets, extravaganzas, and fairy plays of all sorts, in which the phantasma-goric properties of paint and pasteboard, traps and transformations, red fire and green glasses, were studied and cultivated much more practically and incessantly than the five species of counterpoint. To experts in this odd craft, *Das Rheingold* was no impossible dream, but simply 'a damned pantomime'. It is clear to me, then, that we owe the present enormously effective form of the Nibelung tetralogy, a work which towers among the masterpieces of the world's art, to the persistence of just such entertainments as *Aladdin*.

This relationship between Bayreuth and Drury Lane is by no means uncon-scious on the part of Drury Lane. The two are on borrowing terms. Twenty years ago it would have seemed the wildest extravagance to suggest that we should soon have Wagner figuring alongside the music-hall composers in a medley of popular music; but the thing has come to pass for all that. Aladdin's combat with the Slave of the Lamp is accompanied by the heroic strains of the famous *Siegfried* motifs; and the trombones blare out Alberich's curse on the Ring when mention is first made of Abanazar's greed for gold. Such quotations would once have produced the effect of a violently incongruous patch on the rest of the musical fabric, resembling it neither in harmony, melodic intervals, nor instrumental colouring. Today the Wagnerian technique has been so completely assimilated and popularized that the quotations are quite indistinguishable by anyone who does not know the originals. On the other hand, a bar from a minuet by Mozart, Schubert, or Beethoven stands out delicately and elegantly in very notable contrast to the modern style.

As it happens, being no great pantomime goer, I never saw one of Mr Oscar Barrett's pantomimes until I went to *Aladdin*; so I am perhaps unwittingly disparaging his former achievements when I say that it is the best modern Christmas pantomime I have seen. Not that it is by any means faultless. It is much too long, even for the iron nerves of childhood. The first part alone would be a very ample and handsome entertainment. But if thirteen changes and a transformation are *de rigueur*, the surfeit might be lightened by a little cutting; for one or two of the scenes, especially the laundry scene in the first part, are dragged out to a tediousness that defies even Mr Dan Leno's genius. The instrumentation of the ballet in the second part, too, unaccountably discredits the musical taste and knowledge which are so conspicuous in the first part. For here, just at the point when about two and a half hours of orchestration have made one's nerves a little irritable, this big, glittering ballet begins with a reinforcement of two military bands, coarse in tone, and with all the infirmities of intonation produced by valves in brass instruments. The result is a pandemonium which destroys the hitherto admirable balance of sound, and sets up just that perilous worry – the bane of spectacular ballets – which Mr Barrett up to that moment triumphantly avoids. This is the more unexpected because the ballet scene in the first part is a conspicuous example of just the kind of musical judgment that fails him afterwards. In it Mr Barrett fills the back of the stage with trumpets, and overwhelms the house with their ringing clangour, the effect, though of the fiercest kind within the limits of music, being magnificent. But this clarion outbreak is the climax of a long series of effects beginning quietly with a unison movement for the bass strings, and gradually leading up to the *coup de cuivre*. It is astonishing that the same hand that planned the music of this scene should afterwards begin a similar one by flinging those two horrible extra bands at our heads.

Let me add, so as to get my fault finding all together, that I do not see why the traditional privileges of vulgarity in a pantomime should be so scrupulously respected by a manager whose reputation has been made by the comparative refinement of his taste and the superiority of his culture in spectacular and musical matters. Why, for instance, is the 'principal boy' expected to be more vulgar than the principal girl, when she does not want to, and when there is not the slightest reason to suppose that anyone else wants her to? I cannot for the life of me see why Miss Ada Blanche, who at certain moments sings with a good deal of feeling and speaks with propriety, should not be as refined throughout as Miss Decima Moore. But as that would not be customary, Miss Blanche takes considerable trouble, which is probably quite uncongenial to her, to be rowdy and knowing. Again, Mr Herbert Campbell, though he is incapable of the delicate nuances of Mr Leno, is an effectively robust comedian, whose power of singing like a powerful accordion, which some miracle-worker has got into perfect tune, is not unacceptable. But why should it be a point of honour with him to carry the slangy tone and street-corner pronunciation of his music-hall patter into those lines of his part in which he is supposed for the moment to be, not the popular funny man, but the magician of the fairy tale. Mr Campbell can say 'face' instead of 'fice', 'slave' instead of 'slive', 'brain' instead of 'brine', if he likes; and yet he takes the greatest possible pains to avoid doing so lest his occupation as a comically vulgar person should be gone. Naturally, when this occurs in a classic passage, it destroys the effect by suggesting that he mispronounces, not as a comic artist, but because he cannot help it, which I have no doubt is the last impression Mr Campbell would desire to convey. There are passages in his part which should either be spoken as carefully as the speech of the Ghost in Hamlet or else not spoken at all. Pray understand that I do not want the pantomime artists to be 'funny without being vulgar'. That is the mere snobbery of criticism. Every comedian should have vulgarity at his fingers ends for use when required. It is for the business of old Eccles and Perkyn Middlewick to be vulgar as much as it is the business of Parolles and Bobadil to be cowardly or Coriolanus to be haughty. But vulgarity in the wrong place, or slovenliness of speech in any place as a matter of personal habit instead of artistic assumption, is not to be tolerated from any actor or in any entertainment. Especially in a pantomime, where fun, horseplay, and the most outrageous silliness and lawlessness are of the essence of the show, it is important that nothing should be done otherwise than artistically.

Fortunately the Drury Lane pantomime offers more positive than negative evidence under this head. The knockabout business is not overdone; and what there is of it – mostly in the hands of Mr Fred Griffiths as a Chinese policeman – is funny. Mr Leno only falls twice; and on both occasions the gravest critics must shriek with merriment. Mr Cinquevalli's juggling need not be described. It is as well known in London as Sarasate's fiddling; and it fits very happily into the pantomime: indeed, it would be hard to contrive a better pantomime scene of its kind than that in which Cinquevalli, as Slave of the Lamp, appears in the Aladdin household and begins to do impossible things with the plates and tubs. His wonderful address and perfect physical training make him effective even when he is not juggling, as when he is flinging two plates right and left all over the stage, and fielding them (in the cricketing sense) with a success which, though highly diverting, is, no doubt, contemptibly cheap to him. Madam Grigolati's aerial dancing is also, of course, familiar; but it, too, fits perfectly into the pantomime, and is the first exhibition of the kind in which I have seen the aerial device used to much artistic purpose, or maintain its interest after the first novelty of seeing the laws of gravitation suspended in favour of a dancer had worn off. In short, nobody is allowed to take a prominent and independent part in the pantomime without solid qualifications. The second-rate people are not allowed to stand in the corner improvising second-rate tomfooleries. The rank and file are well disciplined; and there is not only order on the stage, but a considerable degree of atmosphere and illusion – qualities which the only Harrisian pantomime I ever saw signally failed to attain. The comedians do not pester you with topical songs, nor the fairy queen (who is only present in a rudimentary form) with sentimental ones. Indeed, the music shews the modern tendency to integrate into a continuous score, and avoid set 'numbers'. The point reached in this respect is not Wagnerian; but it is fairly level with Gounod, who, by the way, is profusely, and sometimes amusingly, quoted. Mr Barrett is catholic in his tastes, and takes his goods where he can find them, Wagner and Bellini being equally at his command. Thus, Abanazar's exhortation to Aladdin to take the magic ring leads to an outburst of 'Prendi l'Anell' ti dono' from *La Sonnambula* (not recognized, I fear, by the present generation, but very familiar to fogies of my epoch); and a capital schoolboy chorus in the second scene is provided by a combination of the opening strains of the Kermesse in Gounod's *Faust* with a tune which flourished in my tenderest youth as Tidd yiddy ido, Chin-Chon-Chino, and which was used freely by Mr Glover in last year's pantomime.

The best scenic effect is that achieved in the last scene of the first part, where the stage picture, at the moment when the procession of bearded patriarchs is passing down from the sun, is very fine. In some of the other scenes, especially those in which a front scene opens to reveal a very luminous distance, the effect is generally to make the foreground dingy and destroy its illusion. No doubt people seldom attend to the foreground under such circumstances: all the same, the effect on them would be greater if the foreground would bear attention; and it seems to me that this could be managed at least as well on the stage as in the pictures of Turner, who also had to struggle with a tradition of dingy foregrounds.

Mr Barrett does not consider the transformation scene and harlequinade out of date. His transformation scene is very pretty; and the harlequinade is of the kind I can remember when the institution was in full decay about twenty-five years ago: that is, the old woman and the swell have disappeared; the policeman has no part; the old window-trap, through which everybody jumped head foremost except the pantaloon (who muffed it), is not used; the harlequin and columbine do not dance; and the clown neither burns people with red-hot poker nor knocks at the baker's door and then lies down across the threshold to trip him up as he comes out. But there *is* a clown, who acts extensively as an advertisement agent, and plays the pilgrims' march from Tannhauser on the trombone until a hundred-ton weight is dropped on his head. His jokes, you see, are faithful to the old clown tradition in being twenty years out of date. His name is Huline; and he is exactly like 'the Great Little

Huline' of my schooldays. And there is a pantaloon, another Huline, whose sufferings and humiliations are luxuries and dignities compared to those which pantaloons once had to undergo.

Let me add, as a touching example of the maternal instinct in Woman (bless her!), that the performance I witnessed was an afternoon one, and that though the house was packed with boys and girls trying to get a good peep at the stage, I never saw the *matinée* hat in grosser feather and foliage. The men, on the other hand, took their hats off, and sacrificed themselves to the children as far as they could. Brutes!

The Saturday Review, 23 January 1897

G. B. Shaw
The Drama in Hoxton

Of late, I am happy to say, the theatres have been so uneventful that I should have fallen quite out of the habit of my profession but for a certain vigorously democratic clergyman, who seized me and bore me off to the last night of the pantomime at 'the Brit.' The Britannia Theatre is in Hoxton, not far from Shoreditch Church, a neighbourhood in which the *Saturday Review* is comparatively little read. The manager, a lady, is the most famous of all London managers. Sir Henry Irving, compared to her, is a mushroom, just as his theatre, compared to hers, is a back drawing-room. Over 4000 people pay nightly at her doors; and the spectacle of these thousands, serried in the vast pit and empyrean gallery, is so fascinating that the stranger who first beholds it can hardly turn away to look at the stage. Forty years ago Mrs Sara Lane built this theatre; and she has managed it ever since. It may be no such great matter to handle a single playhouse – your Irvings, Trees, Alexanders, Wyndhams, and other upstarts of yesterday can do that; but Mrs Lane is said to own the whole ward in which her theatre stands. Madam Sarah Bernhardt's diamonds fill a jewel-box: Mrs Lane's are reputed to fill sacks. When I had the honour of being presented to Mrs Lane, I thought of the occasion when the late Sir Augustus Harris, her only serious rival in managerial fame, had the honour of being presented to me. The inferiority of the man to the woman was manifest. Sir Augustus was, in comparison, an hysterical creature. Enterprise was with him a frenzy which killed him when it reached a climax of success. Mrs Lane thrives on enterprise and success, and is capable, self-contained, practical, vigilant, everything that a good general should be. A West End star is to her a person to whom she once gave so many pounds or shillings a week, and who is now, in glittering and splendid anxiety, begging for engagements, desperately wooing syndicates and potential backers, and living on Alnaschar dreams and old press notices which were unanimously favourable (if you excluded those which were obviously malignant personal attacks). Mrs Lane, well furnished with realities, has no use for dreams; and she knows syndicates and capitalists only as suspicious characters who want her money, not as courted deities with powers of life and death in their hands. The fortune of her productions means little to her: if the piece succeeds, so much the better: if not, the pantomime pays for all.

The clergyman's box, which was about as large as an average Metropolitan railway station, was approached from the stage itself; so that I had opportunities of criticizing both from before the curtain and behind it. I was struck by the absence of the worthless, heartless, incompetent people who seem to get employed with such facility – nay, sometimes apparently by preference – in West End theatres. The West End calculation for musical farce and pantomime appears to be that there is 'a silver mine' to be made by paying several pounds a week to people who are worth nothing, provided you engage enough of them. This is not Mrs Lane's plan. Mr Bigwood, the stage-manager, is a real stage-manager, to whom one can talk on unembarrassed human terms as one capable man to another, and not by any means an erratic art failure from Bedford Park and the Slade School, or one of those beach-combers of our metropolitan civilization who drift to the West End stage because its fringe of short-lived ventures provide congenial liars and imposters with unique opportunities of drawing a few months' or weeks' salary before their preoccupied and worried employers have leisure to realize that they have made a bad bargain. I had not the pleasure of making the prompter's acquaintance; but I should have been surprised to find him the only person in the theatre who could not read, though in the West I should have expected to find that his principal qualification. I made my way under the stage to look at the working of the star-trap by which Mr Lupino was flung up through the boards like a stone from a volcano; and there, though I found eight men wasting their strength by overcoming a counterweight which, in an up-to-date French *théâtre de féerie*, is raised by one man with the help of a pulley, the carpenter-machinist in command was at once recognizable as a well-selected man. On the stage the results of the same instinctive sort of judgment were equally apparent. The display of beauty was sufficiently voluptuous; but there were no good-for-nothings: it was a company of men and women, recognizable as fellow-creatures, and not as accidentally pretty cretinous freaks. Even the low comedians were not blackguards, though they were certainly not fastidious, Hoxton being somewhat Rabelaisian in its ideas of broad humour. One scene, in which the horrors of seasickness were exploited with great freedom, made the four thousand sons and daughters of Shoreditch scream with laughter. At the climax, when four voyagers were struggling violently for a single bucket, I looked stealthily round the box, in which the Church, the Peerage, and the

Higher Criticism were represented. All three were in convulsions. Compare this with our West End musical farces, in which the performers strive to make some inane scene 'go' by trying to suggest to the starving audience that there is something exquisitely loose and vicious beneath the dreary fatuity of the surface. Who would not rather look at and laugh at four men pretending to be sea-sick in a wildly comic way than see a row of young women singing a chorus about being 'Gaiety Girls' with the deliberate intention of conveying to the audience that a Gaiety chorister's profession – their own profession – is only a mask for the sort of life which is represented in Piccadilly Circus and Leicester Square after midnight? I quite agree with my friend the clergyman that decent ladies and gentlemen who have given up West End musical farce in disgust will find themselves much happier at the Britannia pantomime.

I shall not venture on any searching artistic criticism of *Will o' the Wisp*, as the pantomime was called. If it were a West End piece, I should pitch into it without the slightest regard to the prestige and apparent opulence of the manager, not because I am incorruptible, but because I am not afraid of the mere shadow of success. I treat its substance, in the person of Mrs Lane, with careful respect. Shew me real capacity; and I bow lower to it than anybody. All I dare suggest to the Hoxtonians is that when they insist on an entertainment lasting from seven to close upon midnight, they have themselves to thank if the actors occasionally have to use all their ingenuity to spin out scenes of which a judicious playgoer would desire to have at least ten minutes less.

The enthusiasm of the pit on the last night, with no stalls to cut it off from the performers, was frantic. There was a great throwing of flowers and confectionery on the stage; and it would happen occasionally that an artist would overlook one of these tributes, and walk off, leaving it unnoticed on the boards. Then a shriek of tearing anxiety would arise, as if the performer were wandering blindfold into a furnace or over a precipice. Every factory girl in the house would lacerate the air with a mad scream of 'Pick it up, Topsy!' 'Pick it up, Voylit!' followed by a gasp of relief, several thousand strong, when Miss Topsy Sinden or Miss Violet Durkin would return and annex the offering. I was agreeably astonished by Miss Topsy Sinden's dancing. Thitherto it had been my miserable fate to see her come on, late in the second act of some unspeakably dreary inanity at the West End, to interpolate a 'skirt dance', and spin out the unendurable by the intolerable. On such occasions I have looked on her with cold hatred, wondering why the 'varieties' of a musical farce should not include a few items from the conventional 'assault-at-arms', culminating in some stalwart sergeant, after the usual slicing of lemons, leaden bars, and silk handkerchiefs, cutting a skirt-dancer in two at one stroke. At the Britannia Miss Sinden really danced, acted, and turned out quite a charming person. I was not surprised; for the atmosphere was altogether more bracing than at the other end of the town. These poor playgoers, to whom the expenditure of half a guinea for a front seat at a theatre is as outrageously and extravagantly impossible as the purchase of a deer forest in Mars is to a millionaire, have at least one excellent quality in the theatre. They are jealous *for* the dignity of the artist, not derisively covetous of his (or her) degradation. When a white statue which had stood for thirteen minutes in the middle of the stage turned out to be Mr Lupino, who forthwith put on a classic plasticity, and in a series of rapid poses claimed popular respect for 'the antique', it was eagerly accorded; and his demon conflict with the powers of evil, involving a desperate broad-sword combat, and the most prodigious plunges into the earth and projections therefrom by volcanic traps as aforesaid, was conducted with all the tragic dignity of *Richard III* and received in the true Aristotelean spirit by the audience. The fairy queen, a comely prima donna who scorned all frivolity, was treated with entire respect and seriousness. Altogether, I seriously recommend those of my readers who find a pantomime once a year good for them, to go next year to the Britannia, and leave the West End to its boredoms and all the otherdoms that make it so expensively dreary.

The Saturday Review, 9 April 1898

Max Beerbohm
The Older and Better Music Hall

'An octogenarian in the hunting-field' is the title of annual paragraphs in the daily press. Annually one reflects that 'an octogenarian in bed' were better news. One may be wrong. There are men incapable even of growing old – men so insignificant that Time overlooks them. Let such men pursue foxes even to the brinks of their own graves. As with the body so with the mind. There are they who never cease to be intellectually receptive. A new idea, or a new movement, appears in their senile course, and lightly they 'take' it, undaunted by the five bars or so, and gallop on. One admires them as showy exceptions to the law of nature. But one knows that they could not be so receptive if in their youth and prime they had ever deeply understood, or felt strongly, anything. They are shallow, and they are cynics, these genial old souls. What shall be said of those others who, having long ago exhausted their curiosity and keenness, do yet, in sheer vanity, pretend themselves keen and curious? How graceless an eld is theirs! See them riding to the meet, laced and stayed to a semblance of jauntiness! See them furtively leading their horses through the gaps, and piping, at last, a husky 'view holloa' over the fallen fox! (Any reader who is also a sportsman will amend my metaphor if it is wrong.) Such imposters deserve no mercy from us. To us the prejudices of eld are sacred, and should be yet more sacred to their holders. I, for one, in the fulness of time, shall make no secret of them. I am too closely in touch with things now, too glad and eager, to be elastic in the dim future, and as for pretending to be elastic . . . no! I look forward to a crabbed and crusty old age. I mean to be a scourge of striplings.

The history of a keen soul in relation to a live art falls usually into three parts: (1) The soul lives in the future, the art lagging behind. (2) The soul lives in the present, the art having caught it up. (3) The soul lives in the past, left behind by art. My soul, in relation to dramatic art, is still in its first stage. (Or rather, dramatic art, in relation to my soul, is still in its first stage. For the soul itself is always static.) So far as the theatre is concerned, I am still a beckoner, a 'progressive'. But in the matter of music halls, I am already a staunch, even a passionate, reactionary – not a beckoner, but a tugger-back. There never was a time when the music halls lagged behind my soul. To me, as stripling, they seemed perfectly delightful. I dislike the fashion that now dominates not merely the specific 'palaces of varieties' but also such places as the Pavilion, the Tivoli, and even that titular home of lost causes and impossible loyalties, the Oxford. The stripling reader tries politely to repress a sneer. Let him sneer outright. I can justify my prejudice. I may be old-fashioned, but I am right. The music-hall entertainment ought to be stupid, as surely as the drama ought to be intelligent. In every human creature is a mixture of stupidity and cleverness, and for both qualities we need nutrition. How can we satisfy our cleverness in a music hall? What comes to us but a sense of confusion and fatigue from the fashionable gallimaufry of clever poodles, clever conjurers, clever acrobats, clever cinematographs, clever singers and clever elephants? No good can be done to the intellect where no mental effort can be sustained and concentrated. A music hall, by its inherent nature, precludes such good. On the other hand, it can appeal very pleasantly to the stupid, or sensuous, side of us. It did this in the good old days, when there was an unbroken succession of singers, alternate males and females, each singing a couple of songs written and composed in accord to certain traditional conventions. We did not come away wiser and better men; but an inward unity in the entertainment had formed for us a mood. All those so similar songs were merged into our senses, pleasing and amusing, subtly sedative, warm. The old lilt in the veins of us – how bitterly we miss it! Even such songs as are still sandwiched in at the modish halls have lost all their charm. Patter leaves but a corner to tune. Like many other men of original genius, Mr Dan Leno broke the form provided for his expression. We gladly barter tune for a full sense of so delightful a personality and so accomplished an actor as Mr Dan Leno. But the other, the imitators, do not make good our loss. Clever they are, more or less, but we – we who are not of a generation that knows no better – would gladly sacrifice their cleverness in return for straightforward tunes.

Can we anywhere recapture the olden pleasure? Indeed, yes. I have found a place. Let me guide you to it. Half way up the Edgware Road we come to a very signally illuminated building. Nothing could seem more brand-new than the front of this Metropolitan Music Hall; but enter, and you will be transported, deliciously, into the past. The system of ventilation is quite perfect, yet the atmosphere is the atmosphere of a decade since. Look, listen!

> If *you* don't trouble trouble
> Trouble doesn't trouble *you*,
> So don't – you – worry over me!

Is it – no – yes – it must be – it *is* Mr Harry Freeman. That simple, jolly, straightforward singer, dancing as he sings – how long is it since we saw him? We tremble lest he have truckled to changing fashion. Not he! No patter: just a short, sharp phrase uttered through the music between the chorus and the next verse – no more. A thousand memories sweep back to us from the beaming face under the grey bowler hat. That face radiates the whole golden past, and yet, oddly enough, seems not a day older than when last we looked on it. We – we have changed. Our taste, however, is as of yore, and we always did delight in Mr Harry Freeman. We beat time to his familiar music. We sit again at his ever-moving feet. He always was a philosopher, in his way. He was always a Stoic. A Stoic he remains. As of yore, he is overwhelmed with misfortune. Fate still smites him hip and thigh. He has just been robbed by one man and knocked down by another. His home has been broken up. He has been recently in prison. But

> If *you* don't trouble trouble
> Trouble doesn't trouble *you*,

and no sympathy is craved by this joyous dancer. The attitude has a more than personal significance. Not long ago, Mr Arthur Symons wrote an essay about the very thoroughfare whose inhabitants Mr Freeman is now delighting. He suggested that the dominant characteristic of these inhabitants was a dull acquiescence in the sordidness of their lives. Acquiescent they are, but not dully so. Mr Symons, very naturally, cannot imagine a man leading with pleasure their kind of life. They who have to lead it, however, take it as a matter of course and are quite cheerful about it. They are, in fact, Stoics. This is one of the advantages of the old music hall over the new: it does reflect, in however grotesque a way, the characters of the class to which it consciously appeals. And so, after all, accidentally, one gets from it a mental stimulus. . . . Who is this vast man in evening dress? A 'Lion Comique'? Not quite that. But something contemporaneous: a 'Basso Profondo'. He urges us to tak' the high road; he himself is going to tak' the low road. Loch Lomon', in 1903! Delightful! . . . And here is a 'Serio', with the true Serionian voice and method:

> Do not complain,
> I'll single remain,
> Of sweethearts I want no other.

The gallery-boys take the chorus from her, and she sways silently from side to side in measure to the waltz, smiling the smile of triumph. Comes a 'Burlesque Actress', dressed daringly. The diamonds flash, but the heart is in the right place, and the song is about some one whose

Sweet face so glad
Brings smiles to the sad.

Comes a 'Comedienne'. She strikes a rather more modern note. There is, according to her, one, and only one, way of putting the War Office on a sound basis, and that is the instant instalment of Sir Redvers Buller. The audience unanimously endorses her scheme, and she is, no doubt, right; but we regret the introduction of any names that were not names to conjure with in our boyhood: they are anachronisms here. Mr Harry Randall, with his patter, is another anachronism. Several other turns, admirable though they are, we could spare also, for that they interrupt in us the luxurious development of the true music-hall mood.

But, certainly, the Metropolitan is a great discovery, Let us go to it often, magically renewing there our youth. And in those dreary other halls let us nevermore set foot.

The Saturday Review, 14 November 1903

Max Beerbohm
Dan Leno

So little and frail a lantern could not long harbour so big a flame. Dan Leno was more a spirit than a man. It was inevitable that he, cast into a life so urgent as is the life of a music-hall artist, should die untimely. Before his memory fades into legend, let us try to evaluate his genius. For mourners there is ever a solace in determining what, precisely, they have lost.

Usually, indisputable pre-eminence in any art comes of some great originative force. An artist stands unchallenged above his fellows by reason of some 'new birth' that he has given to his art. Dan Leno, however, was no inaugurator. He did not, like Mr Albert Chevalier, import into the music hall a new subject-matter, with a new style. He ended, as he had started, well within the classic tradition. True, he shifted the centre of gravity from song to 'patter'. But, for the rest, he did but hand on the torch. His theme was ever the sordidness of the lower middle class, seen from within. He dealt, as his forerunners had dealt, and as his successors are dealing, with the 'two pair-back', the 'pub', the 'general store', the 'peeler', the 'beak', and other such accessories to the life of the all-but-submerged. It was rather a murky torch that he took. Yet, in his hand, how gloriously it blazed, illuminating and warming! All that trite and unlovely material, how new and beautiful it became for us through Dan Leno's genius! Well, where lay the secret of that genius? How came we to be spell-bound?

Partly, without doubt, our delight was in the quality of the things actually said by Dan Leno. No other music-hall artist threw off so many droll sayings – droll in idea as in verbal expression. Partly, again, our delight was in the way that these things were uttered – in the gestures and grimaces and antics that accompanied them; in fact, in Dan Leno's technique. But, above all, our delight was in Dan Leno himself. In every art personality is the paramount thing, and without it artistry goes for little. Especially is this so in the art of acting, where the appeal of personality is so direct. And most especially is it so in the art of acting in a music-hall, where the performer is all by himself upon the stage, with nothing to divert our attention. The moment Dan Leno skipped upon the stage, we were aware that here was a man utterly unlike any one else we had seen. Despite the rusty top hat and broken umbrella and red nose of tradition, here was a creature apart, radiating an ethereal essence all his own. He compelled us not to take our eyes off him, not to miss a word that he said. Not that we needed any compulsion. Dan Leno's was not one of those personalities which dominate us by awe, subjugating us against our will. He was of that other, finer kind: the lovable kind. He had, in a higher degree than any other actor that I have ever seen, the indefinable quality of being sympathetic. I defy any one not to have loved Dan Leno at first sight. The moment he capered on, with that air of wild determination, squirming in every limb with some deep grievance, that must be outpoured, all hearts were his. That face puckered with cares, whether they were the cares of the small shopkeeper, or of the landlady, or of the lodger; that face so tragic, with all the tragedy that is writ on the face of a baby-monkey, yet ever liable to relax its mouth into a sudden wide grin and to screw up its eyes to vanishing point over some little triumph wrested from Fate, the tyrant; the poor little battered personage, so 'put upon', yet so plucky with his squeaking voice and his sweeping gestures; bent but not broken; faint but pursuing; incarnate of the will to live in a world not at all worth living in – surely all hearts went always out to Dan Leno, with warm corners in them, reserved to him for ever and ever.

To the last, long after illness had sapped his powers of actual expression and invention, the power of his personality was unchanged, and irresistible. Even had he not been in his heyday a brilliant actor, and a brilliant wag, he would have thrown all his rivals into the shade. Often, even in his heyday, his acting and his waggishness did not carry him very far. Only mediocrity can be trusted to be always at its best. Genius must always have lapses proportionate to its triumphs. A new performance by Dan Leno was almost always a dull thing in itself. He was unable to do himself justice until he had, as it were, collaborated for many nights with the public. He selected and rejected according to how his jokes, and his expression of them 'went'; and his best things came to him always in the course of an actual performance, to be incorporated in all the subsequent performances. When, at last, the whole thing had been built up, how perfect a whole it was! Not a gesture, not a grimace, not an inflection of the voice, not a wriggle of the body, but had its significance, and drove its significance sharply, grotesquely, home to us all. Never was a more perfect technique in acting. The technique for acting in a music-hall is of a harder, perhaps finer, kind than is needed for acting in a theatre; inasmuch as the artist must make his effects so much more quickly, and without the aid of any but the slightest 'properties' and scenery, and without the aid of any one else on the stage. It seemed miraculous how Dan Leno contrived to make you see before you the imaginary persons with whom he conversed. He never stepped outside himself, never imitated the voices of his interlocutors. He merely repeated, before making his reply, a few words of what they were supposed to have said to him. Yet there they were, as large as life, before us. Having this perfect independence in his art – being thus all-sufficient to himself – Dan Leno was, of course, seen to much greater advantage in a music-hall than at Drury Lane. He was never 'in the picture' at Drury Lane. He could not play into the hands of other persons on the stage, nor could they play into his. And his art of suggestion or evocation was nullified by them as actualities. Besides, Drury Lane was too big for him. It exactly fitted Mr Herbert Campbell, with his vast size and his vast method. But little Dan Leno, with a technique exactly suited to the size of the average music-hall, had to be taken, as it were, on trust.

Apart from his personality and his technique, Dan Leno was, as I have said, a sayer of richly grotesque things. He had also a keen insight into human nature. He knew thoroughly, outside and inside, the types that he impersonated. He was always 'in the character', whatever it might be. And yet if you repeat to any one even the best things he said, how disappointing is the result! How much they depended on the sayer and the way of saying! I have always thought that the speech over Yorick's skull would have been much more poignant if Hamlet had given Horatio some specific example of the way in which the jester had been wont to set the table on a roar. We ought to have seen Hamlet convulsed with laughter over what he told, and Horatio politely trying to conjure up the ghost of a smile. This would have been good, not merely as pointing the tragedy of a jester's death, but also as illustrating the tragic temptation that besets the jester's contemporaries to keep his memory green. I suppose we shall, all of us, insist on trying to give our grand-children some idea of Dan Leno at his best. We all have our especially cherished recollection of the patter of this or that song. I think I myself shall ever remember Dan Leno more vividly and affectionately as the shoemaker than as anything else. The desperate hopefulness with which he adapted his manner to his different customers! One of his customers was a lady with her little boy. Dan Leno, skipping forward to meet her, with a peculiar skip invented specially for his performance, suddenly paused, stepped back several feet in one stride, eyeing the lady in wild amazement. He had never seen such a lovely child. *How* old, did the mother say? Three? He would have guessed seven at least – 'except when I look at you, ma'am, and then I should say he was one at most.' Here Dan Leno bent down, one hand on each knee, and began to talk some unimaginable kind of baby-language. . . . A little pair of red boots with white buttons? Dan Leno skipped towards an imaginary shelf; but, in the middle of his skip, he paused, looked back, as though drawn by some irresistible attraction, and again began to talk to the child. As it turned out, he had no boots of the kind required. He plied the mother with other samples, suggested this and that, faintlier and faintlier, as he bowed her out. For a few moments he stood gazing after her, with blank disappointment, still bowing automatically. Then suddenly he burst out into a volley of deadly criticisms on the child's personal appearance, ceasing as suddenly at the entrance of another customer. . . . I think I see some of my readers – such of them as never saw Dan Leno in this part – raising their eyebrows. Nor do I blame them. Nor do I blame myself for failing to recreate that which no howsoever ingenious literary artist could recreate for you. I can only echo the old heart-cry 'Si ipsum audissetis!' Some day, no doubt, the phonograph and the bioscope will have been so adjusted to each other that we shall see and hear past actors and singers as well as though they were alive before us. I wish Dan Leno could have been thus immortalized. No actor of our time deserved immortality so well as he.

The Saturday Review, 5 November 1904

Max Beerbohm
At the Gaiety

I am elderly enough to have seen two or three of the old Gaiety burlesques, though I am young enough not to weep bitterly over the reminiscence – young enough not to feel that the Gaiety, as it is today, insults my heart. To me, indeed, the place's main charm seems to be in its abiding likeness to what it was in the dim past. What though 'the Sacred Lamp' has been snuffed out, and the arc-lamp of musical comedy installed? What though the old walls have fallen, and others have arisen on their site? The spell has not been broken. The old traditions still linger. The spirit, the 'note' is as it always was. The temple stands true to its name, and true to that special and peculiar sort of gaiety with which we have always associated it. What though the master-pieces of literature and drama be guyed no more than there? Gone are the rhymed couplets, and the puns, and other things that are sweet in retrospect: what matter? These were but the trappings and gauds that the Muse was decked in. Soul and body, she is her same old self.

It is easy to recognize, hard to define, the 'note' of the Gaiety. One reason why the place is irresistible is that nowhere else do we feel that we are so far away, and so harmlessly and elegantly far away, from the realities of life. We are translated into a sphere where the dwellers have nothing whatever to think about, and would be incapable of thought if there were need for it. Nothing jars there. All the people (except the ladies of the chorus, whose languor is part of the fun) are in the highest spirits, with no chance of a re-action, yet never in the extravagance of their joy do they become loud, or infringe the by-laws of deportment: they are all graceful and tuneful. They are all of them refined, though not in the least like 'ladies' and 'gentlemen' in actual life. They have a school, a higher school, of their own. Some of them are supposed to impersonate the aristocracy, others the proletariat; but in point of refinement there is nothing to choose between them: never a crude word or gesture. And all classes mingle on the easiest of terms. Everyone wants everyone else to have a good time, and tries to make everything easy and simple all round. This good time, as I need hardly say, is of a wholly sexual order. And yet everyone from, the highest to the lowest, is thoroughly 'good'. The most attractive of the men do no harm to the ladies who love them at first sight. Not less instantaneous than theirs are the conquests made by the most unattractive men. A homun-cule, made up to look as absurd as possible, has only to come by and wink at the bevy of lovely ladies to whom he is a perfect stranger, when behold! their arms are about his neck, their eyes devour him, they languish and coo over him, and will follow him to the world's end in deference to his wish for a good time. But be sure he will take no vile advantage. Absurd though he looks, he has his code of honour, like the rest, and never outsteps the bounds of that innocent libertinism which is the rule of Gaiety-land. Evil here is as remote as what we call propriety; and goodness and a good time go hand in hand. Gaiety-land is the Mohammedan paradise, reorganized on a perfectly respectable basis. Emotion is not more alien from its inhabitants than thought. True, there is always a thread of humdrum human love-story woven into the fabric of these plays. In *Our Miss Gibbs* there appears now and again a young man, with a guard's riband round his straw hat, saying, in reference to Miss Gibbs, 'I love her, and want to make her mine', quite soulfully. But who heeds him, or cares twopence whether the marriage will take place? In so far as we notice him at all, we do but deplore that any one so cloddish should have strayed into this ethereal domain.

The fact that in these plays (being what they are, an appeal to our eyes and to our sense of fun) there is no hint of love except 'pour le bon motif', is what most of all bewilders Frenchmen when they visit the Gaiety. They cannot understand how an entertainment of this kind can be kept going without more or less explicit ribaldry; and, when they return to their own shores, it is always the Gaiety that abides in their memory as the most amazing of all our amazing institutions. Also, they never can get over their surprise at the lightness, the vivacity, the exquisite technical accomplishment, of the chief performers. These qualities they had deemed to be inalienably Parisian. And certainly nowhere in London are they to be found in such high degree as at the Gaiety. They are in the air there – have been so since the time of Nellie Farren and Fred Leslie and Kate Vaughan. They are a tradition, handed down through James Lonnen and Lettie Lind. They admirably survive in Miss Gertie Millar, Mr Edmund Payne, and Mr George Grossmith. Miss Millar, though her charm is so distinctly original, is not, certainly, a born comedian; but she has achieved an exquisite style in comedy, of a kind precisely fitted to the tasks laid on it; and this, with her charm, is all-sufficient. One cannot imagine her at any theatre but the Gaiety, nor imagine the Gaiety without her. Mr George Grossmith has brought his innate comedianship to a fine point now; and his singing and dancing are perfect of their kind. I am told that the song 'Yip-i-addy-i-yay' was imported from America; it may have been; but as rendered by Mr Grossmith it becomes a pure symbol of the very spirit of the Gaiety; monumental, in its airy way; banality raised to the sublime. Mr Edmund Payne, by temperament and physique, belongs rather to the music-halls (where he would certainly have outshone all but Dan Leno). But he, too, has schooled himself in the traditions of the Gaiety, and is a worthy *sociétaire*. All the minor parts in *Our Miss Gibbs* are played by people who have been carefully trained to produce the traditional effects. But, as always, the surpassing delight is the chorus. The look of cold surprise that overspreads the lovely faces of these ladies whenever they saunter on to the stage and, as it would seem, behold us for the first time, making us feel that we have taken rather a liberty in being there; the faintly cordial look that appears for the fraction of an instant in the eyes of one of them who happens to see a friend among us – a mere glance, but enough to make us all turn with servile gaze in the direction of the recipient; the splendid nonchalance of these queens, all so proud, so fatigued, all seeming to wonder why they were born, and born so beautiful. . . . I remember that when

The Belle of New York was first produced in London everyone prophesied that the example of that bright, hard-working, athletic American chorus would revolutionize the method of the chorus at the Gaiety. For a while, I think, there was a slight change – a slight semblance of modest effort. But the old local tradition soon resumed its sway, and will never be overthrown; and all the Tory in me rejoices.

The Saturday Review, 30 October 1909

V The Critic on His Craft

Leigh Hunt
Rules for the Theatrical Critic of a Newspaper

In the first place. Never take any notice whatever of the author of a play, or of the play itself, unless it be a new one: if the author be living, it is most probable you will have no reason to speak of him more than once, and if he be not living, you have no reason to speak of him at all, for dead men cannot give dinners.

Secondly. Indulge an acquaintance with every dramatic writer, and with every actor, and you will have a noble opportunity of showing your fine feelings and your philanthropy, for you will praise every play that is acted, and every actor that plays; depend upon it, the world will attribute this praise solely to your undeviating benevolence, which is a great virtue.

Thirdly. If an audience should not possess this virtue equally with your-selves, but should barbarously hiss a new piece merely because it could not entertain them, say in your next day's criticism, that it would have been infinitely more entertaining if a little had been added, or a little had been taken away, a probability which few will dispute with you. No man of real feeling will think of damning another merely because the latter cannot succeed in every attempt to please him. If the exclamation *bravo!* will make a man enjoy his supper and put a few pounds into his pocket every winter, who would not cry out *bravo*? Suppose an ugly, whimsical fellow were to accost you in the streets and to say, 'Sir, I'd thank you to tell me I am handsome, or I shall be miserable for months to come', you would undoubtedly say, 'Sir I am enchanted with your appearance, and entreat you to be perfectly happy.' In the same manner it is easy to say to Mr Reynolds, or Mr Dibdin, or Mr Cherry, 'Your play was excellent', and the poor fellow will be as comfortable as if it were really the case.

Fourthly. If you do not exactly understand how to conceal your evil opinion of men's writing or performances, but find yourself occasionally apt to indulge in maliciously speaking the truth, always say the direct contrary of what you think. The following little glossary, collected from the most approved critics, may be of service to you in this case; you will of course make use of the first column:

A crowded house – a theatre on the night of a performance when all the back seats and upper boxes are empty.

An amusing author – an author whose very seriousness makes us laugh in spite of himself.

A good author – the general term for an author who gives good dinners.

A respectable actor – an insipid actor; one who in general is neither hissed nor applauded.

A fine actor – one who makes a great noise; a tatterdemalion of passions; a clap-trapper: one intended by nature for a town-crier. This appellation may on all occasions be given to Mr Pope, who has the finest lungs of any man on the stage.

A good actor – the general term for an actor who gives good dinners.

A charming play – a play full of dancing, music and scenery; a play in which the less the author has to do the better.

Great applause – applause mixed with the hisses of the gallery and pit.

Unbounded and universal applause – applause mixed with the hisses of the pit only. This phrase is frequently to be found at the bottom of the play house bills in declaring the reception a new piece has met with. The plays announced in these bills are generally printed in red ink, an emblem, no doubt, of the modesty with which they speak of themselves.

There was once a kind soul of an author who could not bear to use a harsh word, even when speaking of villains; he used to call highway-men *tax-gatherers*, pickpockets *collectors*, and ravishers *men of gallantry*. This gentleman would have made an excellent theatrical critic; he would have called Reynolds, Congreve, and Cherry, Shakespeare, and everybody would have admired his invention.

Fifthly and lastly. When you criticize the performance of an old play, never exceed six or seven lines, but be sure to notice by name the fashionables in the boxes, for such notices are indispensably requisite to sound criticism; there is a choice collection of sentences which have been in use from time immemorial with newspaper critics, and are still used by common consent, just as we universally allow one style for a note of hand or a visiting letter. Your observations, therefore, will generally be such as these:

DRURY LANE. Last night the *beautiful* comedy of *The Rivals* was performed with great éclat to an *overflowing* house: Bannister was excellent – Mrs H. Johnston looked *beautiful*. Among the company we observed the Duchess of Gordon, the Duke of Queensbury, Lady Hamilton, and many other *amiable* and *beautiful* personages. There was a quarrel in the pit.

What can be more concise, more explanatory, more critical, than such a criticism? Grammarians undertake to teach a language in five months, musicians, the whole theory of music in five weeks, and dancing-masters all sorts of steps in five hours, but by these rules a man may be a profound critic in five minutes. Let Aristotle and Quintilian hide their huge volumes in dismay, and confess the superiority of a criticism, which, like the magic word *Sesame* in the Arabian Nights, opens to us a thousand treasures in a breath!

Critical Essays on the Performers of the London Theatres, 1807

G. H. Lewes
Vivian in Tears!
(All along of Mr Kean)

What a thing is Life! The remark is novel and profound – its application you
will appreciate on hearing my appeal. Yesterday I was the gayest of the gay,
blithe and joyous as a young bird before family cares perplex it in its calculations of worms; today you see me struck from that sunny altitude into the
gloom of immeasurable despondency! Weep! weep with me, ye that have
any tears! Let me, like a Prometheus of private life, fling my clamorous
agonies upon the winds, and call upon every feeling heart to listen to my
'billowy ecstasy of woe!'.

Hear it, ye winds – Charles Kean has cut me off the Free List!

No more! never never more, am I to enjoy the exquisite privilege of seeing
that poetic eye 'in fine foolishness rolling!' – no more! never never more, am
I to listen to that musical utterance of verse, that delicate expression given to
subtle meanings! I am banished. Charles Kean closes his door upon me!
He courted me, and courted my criticism – then I was happy! then I was
proud! then I knew where to spend an intellectual evening; but now, alas!
that glory is departed; it now appears that he did not like my criticism,
and he cruelly robs me of my only enjoyment – the privilege of seeing him act!
He humbles me, he saddens me, he leaves me no refuge but misanthropy!
Oh, *why* didn't I write more glowingly about his genius; *why* did I not, by
some critical alchemy, convert his peculiarities into talents; *why* did I not
discover eloquence in his pauses, variety and expression in his gestures, and
intelligence in his conceptions? Fool that I was! I might have laughed at him
amongst my friends, as remorselessly as they do, and still have preserved my
precious privilege of free admission to the Princess's Theatre; but now! . . .
As the not more unfortunate Philoctetes, banished from his loved Hellas,
roamed disconsolate about the isle, so I pace Oxford Street with pale wistful
glances, exclaiming:

$$\text{ἀλλ' οἱ μὲν ἐκβαλόντες ἀνοσίως ἐμὲ}$$
$$\text{γελῶσι σῖγ' ἔκοντες ἡ δ'ἐμὴ νόσος}$$
$$\text{ἀεὶ τέθηλε, κἀπὺ μεῖζον ἔρχεται.}$$

(That bit of Greek is especially meant for Mr Kean – the immense intelligence
displayed in his handling of English verse placing beyond question the assumption that he must be very strong indeed upon Greek verse, and, therefore, I
won't translate it.)

Let me for a moment stop the flood of grief and review my position (through
my tears). When Charles Kean was about to take the Princess's Theatre, he
asked me if I would support him; because, he added, it was useless to embark
in such a speculation unless he could get the Press to back him. I gave him the

only promise I could give – I promised to do my best. I was glad to see a gentleman in the position. It looked well for the drama; and no one will dispute that it *has* been a great advantage – that he has made the Princess's a first-class theatre in every respect; and as far as the public is concerned, he has been an excellent manager. Hitherto I have kept my promise; but I told him at the time that it was one thing to support a theatre by all friendly offices, and another to praise actors or pieces which I did not approve. Now mark! because I was silent in a case where, if I had spoken at all, it could only have inflicted a needless wound – because I do *not* think Charles Kean a tragic actor, and never would say I did – because in short, while feeling and (as all who know me will testify) *expressing* a personal liking for him, I exercised towards him a privilege I do not withdraw even with regard to dearest friends – that, namely, of uttering my opinion – because, I say, my friendly articles were not fulsome eulogies, Charles Kean declared me 'one of his bitterest enemies'; and now, I presume, because I said last week that Helen Faucit was the greatest of our tragic actresses (a fact about which there are not two opinions), the 'bitterest enemy' is told he cannot be admitted any more.

Poor fellow! poor fellow! to be so sensitive – and an actor! One hears of hens, in a soil where chalk is deficient, laying eggs without shells – nothing but a thin membrane to protect the embryo chick; how unpleasant to be such a chick.

As for me, I confess that I have long expected to be cut off the free list by some irate manager or other, but do not respect the sagacity which has so exercised the managerial power. Can Mr Kean suppose that by suppressing *free admissions* he suppresses *free speech?* Or does he think that no critic would be mad enough to rush into the utter extravagance of paying for a place to see him act? Let him undeceive himself. I shall be there on first nights as of old; the only difference will be this – that until he declared open war I still preserved my original position; henceforth I shall remember that kindly silence is interpreted as insult, and shall speak out just what I think. In concluding, let me say that whereas I would not suffer my criticism to be eulogistic when urged by *interest* (in the vulgar sense of the term – Mr Kean will understand me), so likewise I have too much pride to allow this last act to *pique* me into injustice.

The Leader, 7 February 1852

G. H. Lewes
Shakspeare as Actor and Critic

Shakspeare was most probably an indifferent actor. If a doubt is permissible on this point, there is none respecting his mastery as a critic. He may not have been a brilliant executant; he was certainly a penetrating and reflective connoisseur.

Modern idolators, who cannot see faults in Shakspeare's plays which are still before us, and which to unbiased eyes present defects both numerous and glaring, may perhaps consider it an impertinence to infer any defects in his acting, which is not before us, which has long ceased to be remembered, and which never seems to have been much spoken of. Why not, with a generous enthusiasm, assume that it was fine? Why not suppose that the creator of so many living, breathing characters must have been also a noble personator? There is nothing to prevent the generous admirer indulging in this hypothesis if he finds comfort in it. I merely remark that it has no evidence in its favour, and a great many points against it. The mere fact that we hear nothing of his qualities as an actor implies that there was nothing above the line, nothing memorable, to be spoken of. We hear of him as wit and companion, as poet and man of business, but not a word of his qualities as an actor. Of Burbage, Alleyn, Tarleton, Knell, Bentley, Miles, Wilson, Crosse, Pope, and others, we hear more or less; but all that tradition vaguely wafts to us of Shakspeare is, that he played the Ghost in *Hamlet*, and Old Knowell in *Every Man in His Humor*, neither of them parts which demand or admit various excellencies.

Like many other dramatists of the early time – Munday, Chettle, Lodge, Kyd, Nash, Ben Jonson, Heywood, Dekker, and Rowley – he adopted sock and buskin as a means of making money; and it is probable that, like actors of all times, he had a favourable opinion of his own performances. He certainly was able to see through the tricks and devices with which more popular players captivated 'the groundlings', and was doubtless one of the 'judicious' whom these devices grieved. But in spite of his marvellous genius, in spite of the large flexibility of mind which could enable him to conceive great varieties of character, it is highly probable that he wanted the mimetic flexibility of organization which could alone have enabled him to *personate* what he conceived. The powers of conception and the powers of presentation are distinct. A poet is rarely a good reader of his own verse, and has never yet been a great personator of his own characters. Shakspeare doubtless knew – none knew so well – how Hamlet, Othello, Richard, and Falstaff should be personated; but had he been called upon to personate them he would have found himself wanting in voice, face, and temperament. The delicate sensitiveness of his organization, which is implied in the exquisiteness and flexibility of his genius, would absolutely have unfitted him for the presentation of characters demanding a robust vigour and a weighty animalism. It is a vain attempt to paint frescoes with a camel's-hair brush. The broad and massive effects necessary to scenic presentation could never had been produced by such a temperament as his. Thus even on the supposition of his having been a good drawing-room mime, he would have wanted the qualities of a good actor. And we have no ground for inferring that he was even a good drawing-room mime.

I dare say he declaimed finely, as far as rhythmic cadence and a nice accentuation went. But his non-success implies that his voice was intractable, or limited in its range. Without a sympathetic voice, no declamation can be effective. The tones which stir us need not be musical, need not be pleasant even, but they must have a penetrating, vibrating quality. Had Shakspeare possessed such a voice he would have been famous as an actor. Without it all his other gifts were as nothing on the stage. Had he seen Garrick, Kemble, or Kean performing in plays not his own he might doubtless have perceived a thousand deficiencies in their conception, and defects in their execution; but had he appeared on the same stage with them, even in plays of his own, the audiences would have seen the wide gulf between conception and presentation. One lurid look, one pathetic intonation, would have more power in swaying the emotions of the audience than all the subtle and profound passions which agitated the soul of the poet, but did not manifestly express itself: the look and the tone may come from a man so drunk as to be scarcely able to stand; but the public sees only the look, hears only the tone, and is irresistibly moved by these intelligible symbols.

That Shakspeare, as a critic, had mastered the principles of the art of acting is apparent from the brief but pregnant advice to the players in *Hamlet*. He first insists on the necessity of a flexible elocution. He gives no rules for the management of voice and accent; but in his emphatic warning against the common error of 'mouthing', and his request to have the speech spoken 'trippingly on the tongue', it is easy to perceive what he means. The word 'trippingly', to modern ears, is not perhaps felicitously descriptive; but the context shows that it indicates easy naturalness as opposed to artificial mouthing. It is further enforced by the advice as to gesture: 'Do not saw the air too much with your hand, but use all gently.'

After the management of the voice, actors most err in the management of the body: they mouth their sentences, and emphasize their gestures, in the effort to be effective, and in ignorance of the psychological conditions on which effects depend. In each case the effort to aggrandize natural expression leads to exaggeration and want of truth. In attempting the ideal they pass into the artificial. The tones and gestures of ordinary unimpassioned moments would not, they feel, be appropriate to ideal characters and impassioned situations; and the difficulty of the art lies precisely in the selection of idealized expressions which shall, to the spectator, be symbols of real emotions. All but very great actors are redundant in gesticulation; not simply overdoing the significant, but unable to repress insignificant movements. Shakspeare must have daily seen this; and therefore he bids the actor 'suit the action to the word, with this special observance, that you overstep not the modesty of nature;

for anything so overdone is from the purpose of playing, whose end, both at first and now, was and is, to hold, as it were, the mirror up to nature.'

It would be worth the actor's while to borrow a hint from the story of Voltaire's pupil, when, to repress her tendency towards exuberant gesticulation, he ordered her to rehearse with her hands tied to her side. She began her recitation in this enforced quietness, but at last, carried away by the movement of her feelings, she flung her arms, and snapped the threads. In tremor she began to apologize to the poet; he, smiling, reassured her that the gesticulation was *then* admirable, because it was irrepressible. If actors will study fine models they will learn that gestures, to be effective, must be significant, and to be significant they must be rare. To stand still on the stage (and not appear a guy) is one of the elementary difficulties of the art – and one which is rarely mastered.

Having indicated his views on declamation, Shakspeare proceeds to utter golden advice on expression. He specially warns the actor against both over-vehemence and coldness. Remembering that the actor is an artist, he insists on the observance of that cardinal principle in all art, the subordination of impulse to law, the regulation of all effects with a view to beauty. 'In the very torrent, tempest, and, as I may say, whirlwind of passion, you must acquire and beget a temperance that may give it smoothness. O! it offends me to the soul to hear a robustious peri-wig-pated fellow tear a passion to tatters, to very rags, to split the ears of the groundlings.' What is this but a recognition of the mastery of art, by which the ruling and creating intellect makes use of passionate symbols, and subordinates them to a pleasurable end? If the actor were really in a passion his voice would be a scream, his gestures wild and disorderly; he would present a painful, not an aesthetic spectacle. He must therefore select from out the variety of passionate expressions only those that can be harmoniously subordinated to a general whole. He must be at once passionate and temperate: trembling with emotion, yet with a mind in vigilant supremacy controlling expression, *directing* every intonation, look and gesture. The rarity of fine acting depends on the difficulty there is in being at one and the same moment so deeply moved that the emotion shall spontaneously express itself in symbols universally intelligible, and yet so calm as to be perfect master of effects, capable of modulating voice and moderating gesture when they tend to excess or ugliness.

'To preserve this medium between mouthing and meaning too little,' says Colley Cibber, 'to keep the attention more pleasingly awake by a tempered spirit than by mere vehemence of voice, is of all the master strokes of an actor the most difficult to reach.' Some critics, annoyed by rant, complain of the ranter being 'too fiery'. As Lessing says, an actor cannot have too much fire, but he may easily have too little sense. Vehemence without real emotion is rant; vehemence with real emotion, but without art, is turbulence. To be loud and exaggerated is the easy resource of actors who have no faculty; to be vehement and agitated is to betray the inexperience of one who has not yet mastered the art. 'Be not too tame neither,' Shakspeare quickly adds, lest his advice should be misunderstood, 'but let your own discretion be your tutor.'

Yes; the actor's discretion must tell him when he has hit upon the right tone and right expression, which must first be suggested to him by his own feelings. In endeavouring to express emotions, he will try various tones, various gestures, various accelerations and retardations of the rhythm; and during this tentative process his vigilant discretion will arrest those that are effective, and discard the rest.

It is because few actors are sufficiently reflective that good acting is so rare; and the tameness of a few who are reflective, but not passionate, brings discredit on reflection. Such study as actors mostly give is to imitation of others, rather than to introspection of their own means; and this is fatal to excellence. 'Nous devons être sensibles,' said Talma 'nous devons éprouver l'émotion; mais pour mieux l'imiter, pour mieux en saisir les caractères par l'étude et la réflexion.'

The anecdotes about Macready and Liston given on page 44* suggest a topic of some interest in relation to the art of acting: In how far does the actor feel the emotion he expresses? When we hear of Macready and Liston lashing themselves into a fury behind the scenes in order to come on the stage sufficiently excited to give a truthful representation of the agitations of anger, the natural inference is that these artists recognized the truth of the popular notion which assumes that the actor really feels what he expresses. But this inference seems contradicted by experience. Not only is it notorious that the actor is feigning, and that if he really felt what he feigns he would be unable to withstand the wear and tear of such emotion repeated night after night; but it is indisputable, to those who know anything of art, that the mere presence of genuine emotion would be such a disturbance of the intellectual equilibrium as entirely to frustrate artistic expression. Talma told M. Barrière that he was once carried away by the truth and beauty of the actress playing with him till she recalled him by a whisper: 'Take care, Talma, you are moved!' on which he remarked, 'C'est qu'en effet de l'émotion nait le trouble: la voix résiste, la mémoire manque, les gestes sont faux, l'effet est detruit'; and there is an observation of Molé to a similar effect: 'Je ne suis pas content de moi ce soir; je me suis trop livré, je ne suis pas resté mon mâitre: j'étais entré trop vivement dans la situation; j'étais le personnage même, je n'étais plus l'acteur qui le joue. J'ai été vrai comme je le serais chez moi; *pour l'optique du théâtre il faut l'étre autrement.*'

Everyone initiated into the secrets of the art of acting will seize at once the meaning of this luminous phrase *l'optique du théâtre*; and the uninitiated will understand how entirely opposed to all the purposes of art and all the secrets of effect would be the representation of passion in its *real* rather than in its *symbolical* expression: the red, swollen, and distorted features of grief, the harsh and screaming intonation of anger, are unsuited to art; the paralysis of all outward expression, and the flurry and agitation of ungraceful gesticulation which belong to certain powerful emotions, may be described by the poet, but cannot be admitted into plastic art. The poet may tell us what is signified by the withdrawal of all life and movement from the face and limbs, describing

* Of *On Actors and the Art of Acting.*

the internal agitations of the deadly calm which disturb or paralyse the sufferer; but the painter, sculptor, or actor must tell us what the sufferer undergoes, and tell it through the symbols of outward expression – the internal workings must be legible in the external symbols; and these external symbols must also have a certain grace and proportion to affect us aesthetically.

All art is symbolical. If it presented emotion in its real expression it would cease to move us as art; sometimes cease to move us at all, or move us only to laughter. There is a departure from reality in all the stage accessories. The situation, the character, the language, all are at variance with daily experience. Emotion does not utter itself in verse nor in carefully chosen sentences, and to speak verse with the negligence of prose is a serious fault. There is a good passage in Colley Cibber's account of Betterton, which actors, and critics who are not alive to the immense effects that lie in fine elocution, would do well to ponder on. 'In the just delivery of poetical numbers, particularly where the sentiments are pathetic, it is scarce credible upon how minute an article of sound depends their greatest beauty or inaffection. The voice of a singer is not more strictly ty'd to time and tune, than that of an actor in theatrical elocution. The least syllable too long, or too slightly dwelt upon in a period, depreciates it to nothing; which very syllable, if rightly touched, shall, like the heightening stroke of light from a master's pencil, give life and spirit to the whole.' It is superfluous to insist on the utter impossibility of attending to such delicate minutiae if the speaker be really agitated by emotion. A similar remark applies to all the other details of his art. His looks and gestures, his position in the picture, all will be out of proportion and fail of their due effect unless he is master of himself.

The reader sees at once that as a matter of fact the emotions represented by the actor are not agitating him as they would agitate him in reality; he is feigning and we know that he is feigning; he is representing a fiction which is to move us as a fiction, and not to lacerate our sympathies as they would be lacerated by the agony of a fellow-creature actually suffering in our presence. The tears we shed are tears welling from a sympathetic source; but their salt bitterness is removed, and their pain is pleasurable.

But now arises the antinomy, as Kant would call it – the contradiction which perplexes judgment. If the actor lose all power over his art under the disturbing influence of emotion, he also loses all power over his art in proportion to his deadness to emotion. If he really feel, he cannot act; but he cannot act unless he feel. All the absurd efforts of mouthing and grimacing actors to produce an effect, all the wearisomeness of cold conventional representation – mimicry without life – we know to be owing to the unimpassioned talent of the actor. Observe, I do not say to his unimpassioned nature. It is quite possible for a man of exquisite sensibility to be ludicrously tame in his acting, if he has not the requisite talent of expression, or has not yet learned how to modulate it so as to give it due effect. The other day in noticing the rare ability of Mlle Lucca in depicting the emotions of Margaret in *Faust*, I had occasion to remark on the surprising transformation which had taken place in two years, changing her from a feeble, conventional, ineffective actress into a passionate, subtle, and original artist. In the practice of two years she had learned the secrets of expression; she had learned to modulate; and having learned this, having felt her way, she could venture to give play to the suggestions of her impulses, which before that had doubtless alarmed her. But although it is quite possible for an actor to have sensibility without the talent of expression, and therefore to be a tame actor though an impassioned man, it is wholly impossible for him to express what he has never felt, to be an impassioned actor with a cold nature.

And here is the point of intersection of the two lines of argument just followed out. The condition being that a man must feel emotion if he is to express it, for if he does not feel it he will not know how to express it, how can this be reconciled with the impossibility of his affecting us aesthetically while he is disturbed by emotion? In other words: how far does he really feel the passion he expresses? It is a question of degree. As in all art, feeling lies at the root, but the foliage and flowers, though deriving their sap from emotion, derive their form and structure from the intellect. The poet cannot write while his eyes are full of tears, while his nerves are trembling from the mental shock, and his hurrying thoughts are too agitated to settle into definite tracks. But he must have felt, or his verse will be a mere echo. It is from the memory of past feelings that he draws the beautiful image with which he delights us. He is tremulous again under the remembered agitation, but it is a pleasant tremor, and in no way disturbs the clearness of his intellect. He is a spectator of his own tumult; and though moved by it, can yet so master it as to select from it only those elements which suit his purpose. We are all spectators of ourselves; but it is the peculiarity of the artistic nature to indulge in such introspection even in moments of all but the most disturbing passion, and to draw thence materials for art. This is true also of the fine actor, and many of my readers will recognize the truth of what Talma said of himself: 'I have suffered cruel losses, and have often been assailed with profound sorrows; but after the first moment when grief vents itself in cries and tears, I have found myself involuntarily turning my gaze inwards ("je faisais un retour sur mes souffrances"), and found that the actor was unconsciously studying the man, and catching nature in the act.' It is only by thus familiarizing oneself with the nature of the various emotions, that one can properly interpret them. But even that is not enough. They must be watched in others, the interpreting key being given in our own consciousness. Having something like an intellectual appreciation of the sequences of feeling and their modes of manifestation, the actor has next to select out of these such as his own physical qualifications enable him to reproduce effectively, and such as will be universally intelligible. To quote Talma once more: 'Oui, nous devons être sensibles, nous devons éprouver l'émotion; mais pour mieux l'imiter, pour mieux en saisir les caractères par l'étude et la réflexion. Notre art en exige de profonds. Point d'improvisation possible sur la scéne sous peine d'échec. Tout est calculé, tout doit être prévu, et l'émotion qui semble soudaine, et le trouble qui paraît involontaire. L'intonation, le geste, le regard qui semblent inspirés, ont été répétés cent fois.'

All this I may assume the reader to accept without dissent, and yet anticipate his feeling some perplexity in reconciling it with the anecdotes which started this digression. Surely, he may say, neither Macready nor Liston could have been so unfamiliar with rage and its manifestations that any hesitation could paralyse their efforts to express these. Why then this preparation behind the scenes? Simply because it was absolutely necessary that they should be in a state of excitement if they were to represent it with truthfulness; and having temperaments which were not instantaneously excitable by the mere imagination of a scene, they prepared themselves. Actors like Edmund Kean, Rachel, or Lemaître found no difficulty in the most rapid transitions; they could one moment chat calmly and the next explode. The imaginative sympathy instantaneously called up all the accessories of expression; one tone would send vibrations through them powerful enough to excite the nervous discharge.

The answer to the question – How far does the actor feel? – is, therefore, something like this: He is in a state of emotional excitement sufficiently strong to furnish him with the elements of expression, but not strong enough to disturb his consciousness of the fact that he is only imagining – sufficiently strong to give the requisite tone to his voice and aspect to his features, but not strong enough to prevent his modulating the one and arranging the other according to a preconceived standard. His passion must be ideal – sympathetic, not personal. He may hate with a rival's hate the actress to whom he is manifesting tenderness, or love with a husband's love the actress to whom he is expressing vindictiveness; but for Juliet or Desdemona he must feel love and wrath. One day Malibran, upbraiding Templeton for his coldness towards her in the love scenes of *La Sonnambula*, asked him if he were not married, and told him to imagine that she was his wife. The stupid tenor, entirely misunderstanding her, began to be superfluously tender at rehearsal, whereupon she playfully recalled to him that it was during the performance he was to imagine her to be Mrs Templeton – at rehearsal Mme Malibran.

We sometimes hear amateur critics object to fine actors that they are every night the same, never varying their gestures or their tones. This is stigmatized as 'mechanical'; and the critics innocently oppose to it some ideal of their own which they call 'inspiration'. Actors would smile at such nonsense. What is called inspiration is the mere haphazard of carelessness or incompetence; the actor is seeking an expression which he ought to have found when studying his part. What would be thought of a singer who sang his aria differently every night? In the management of his breath, in the distribution of light and shade, in his phrasing, the singer who knows how to sing never varies. The *timbre* of his voice, the energy of his spirit, may vary; but his methods are invariable. Actors learn their parts as singers learn their songs. Every detail is deliberative, or has been deliberated. The very separation of art from nature involves this calculation. The sudden flash of suggestion which is called inspiration may be valuable, it may be worthless: the artistic intellect estimates the value, and adopts or rejects it accordingly.

Trusting to the inspiration of the moment is like trusting to a shipwreck for your first lesson in swimming.

A greater master of the art, practical and theoretical, as actor and teacher, the late M. Sanson, of the Théâtre Français, has well said:

> Méditez, réglez tout, essayez tout d'avance;
> Un assidu travail donne la confiance.
> L'aisance est du talent le plus aimable attrait:
> *Un jeu bien préparé nous semble sans apprêt.*

And elsewhere:

> Mais, en s'abandonnat, que l'artiste s'observe;
> De vos heureux hasards sachez vous souvenir:
> Ce qu'il n'a pas produit, l'art doit le retenir,
> L'acteur qui du talent veut atteindre le faîte,
> Quand il livre son coeur doit conserver sa tête.

Shakspeare, who had learned this in his experience as a dramatist, saw that it was equally true of dramatic representation. The want of calculation in actors distressed him. He saw the public applauding players 'who, having neither the accent of Christians, nor the gait of Christian, pagan, nor man, have so strutted and bellowed' that they seemed the products of nature's journeymen. He saw them mistaking violence for passion, turbulence for art, and he bade them remember the purpose of playing, which was to hold the mirror up to nature.

Besides these cardinal directions, Shakspeare gives another which is of minor importance, though it points at a real evil. Avoid gag, he says. It will make some barren spectators laugh, but it shows a pitiful ambition. This, however, is a fault which the audience can correct if it pleases. Generally audiences are so willing to have their laughter excited as to be indifferent to the means employed. Gagging, therefore, is, always was, and always will be popular. I merely allude to it to show how complete is Shakspeare's advice to the players, and how seriously he had considered the whole subject of acting.

On Actors and the Art of Acting, 1875

G. B. Shaw
Problems of Dramatic Criticism

... As it is with the actors and managers, so it is with the critics: the supporters of Ibsen are the younger men. In the main, however, the Press follows the managers instead of leading them. The average newspaper dramatic critic is not a Lessing, a Lamb, or a Lewes: there was a time when he was not necessarily even an accustomed playgoer, but simply a member of the reporting or literary staff told off for theatre duty without any question as to his acquaintance with dramatic literature. At present, though the special nature of his function is so far beginning to be recognized that appointments of the kind usually fall now into the hands of inveterate frequenters of the theatre, yet he is still little more than the man who supplies the accounts of what takes place in the playhouses just as his colleague supplies accounts of what takes place at the police court – an important difference, however, being that the editor, who generally cares little about Art and knows less, will himself occasionally criticize, or ask one of his best writers to criticize, a remarkable police case, whereas he never dreams of theatrical art as a subject upon which there could be any editorial policy. Sir Edwin Arnold's editorial attack on Ibsen was due to the accidental circumstances that he, like Richelieu, writes verses between whiles. In fact, the 'dramatic critic' of a newspaper, in ordinary circumstances, is at his best a good descriptive reporter, and at his worst a mere theatrical newsman. As such he is a person of importance among actors and managers, and of no importance whatever elsewhere. Naturally he frequents the circles in which alone he is made much of; and by the time he has seen so many performances that he has formed some critical standards in spite of himself, he has also enrolled among his personal acquaintances every actor and manager of a few years' standing, and become engaged in all the private likes and dislikes, the quarrels and friendships, in a word, in all the partialities which personal relations involve, at which point the value of his verdicts may be imagined. Add to this that if he has the misfortune to be attached to a paper to which theatrical advertisements are an object, or of which the editor and proprietors (or their wives) do not hesitate to incur obligations to managers by asking for complimentary admissions, he may often have to choose between making himself agreeable and forfeiting his post. So that he is not always to be relied on even as a newsman where the plain truth would give offence to any individual.

Behind all the suppressive forces with which the critic has to contend comes the law of libel. Every adverse criticism of a public performer is a libel, and any agreement among the critics to boycott artists who appeal to the law is a conspiracy. Of course the boycott does take place to a certain extent; for if an artist, manager, or agent shows any disposition to retort to what is called a 'slating' by a lawyer's letter, the critic, who cannot for his own sake expose his employers to the expenses of an action or the anxiety attending the threat of one, will be tempted to shun the danger by simply never again referring to the litigiously disposed person. But although this at first sight seems to sufficiently guarantee the freedom of criticism (for most public persons would suffer more from being ignored by the papers than from being attacked in them, however abusively) its operation is really restricted on the one side to the comparatively few and powerful critics who are attached to important papers at a fixed salary and on the other to those entrepreneurs and artists about whom the public is not imperatively curious. Most critics get paid for their notices at so much per column or per line, so that their incomes depend on the quantity they write. Under these conditions they fine themselves every time they ignore a performance. Again, a dramatist or a manager may attain such a position that his enterprises form an indispensable part of the news of the day. He can then safely intimidate a hostile critic by a threat of legal proceedings, knowing that the paper can afford neither to brave nor ignore him. The late Charles Reade, for example, was a most dangerous man to criticize adversely; but the very writers against whom he took actions found it impossible to boycott him; and what Reade did out of a natural overflow of indignant pugnacity, some of our most powerful artistic entrepreneurs occasionally threaten to do now after a deliberate calculation of the advantages of their position. If legal proceedings are actually taken, and the case is not, as usual, compromised behind the scenes, the uncertainty of the law receives its most extravagant illustration from a couple of lawyers arguing a question of fine art before a jury of men of business. Even if the critic were a capable speaker and pleader, which he is not in the least likely to be, he would be debarred from conducting his own case by the fact that his comparatively wealthy employer and not himself would be the defendant in the case. In short, the law is against straightforward criticism at the very points where it is most needed; and though it is true that an ingenious and witty writer can make any artist or performance acutely ridiculous in the eyes of ingenious and witty people without laying himself open to an action, and indeed with every appearance of good-humoured indulgence, such applications of wit and ingenuity do criticism no good; whilst in any case they offer no remedy to the plain critic writing for plain readers.

All this does not mean that the entire press is hopelessly corrupt in its criticism of Art. But it certainly does mean that the odds against the independence of the Press critic are so heavy that no man can maintain it completely without a force of character and a personal authority which are rare in any profession, and which in most of them can command higher pecuniary terms and prospects than any which journalism can offer. The final degrees of thoroughness have no market value on the Press; for, other things being equal, a journal with a critic who is good-humoured and compliant will have no fewer readers than one with a critic who is inflexible where the interests of Art and the public are concerned. I do not exaggerate or go beyond the warrant of my own experience when I say that unless a critic is prepared not only to do much more work than the public will pay him for, but to risk his livelihood every time he strikes a serious blow at the powerful interests vested in artistic abuses of all kinds (conditions which in the long run tire out the strongest man), he must submit to compromises which detract very considerably from the trustworthiness of his criticism. Even the critic who is himself in a position to brave these risks must find a sympathetic and courageous editor-proprietor who will stand by him without reference to the commercial advantage – or disadvantage – of his incessant warfare. As all the economic conditions of our society tend to throw our journals more and more into the hands of successful moneymakers, the exceeding scarcity of this lucky combination of resolute, capable, and incorruptible critic, sympathetic editor, and disinterested and courageous proprietor, can hardly be appreciated by those who only know the world of journalism through its black and white veil. . . .

Appendix to *The Quintessence of Ibsenism*, 1891

A. B. Walkley
His Difficulties

Despised by the 'serious intellects', the critic turns in vain to the actor. Actors are notoriously shy of critics, because critics wear shocking bad hats; but there are exceptions to every rule, and there is one affable comedian who has consented to overlook my hat. Still, somehow, what is under the bad hats doesn't quite satisfy him. His grievance against the critics is that they should produce so much elaborate criticisms of plays and playwrights, and so little serviceable criticism of players. Why, he asks, are the public treated to whole columns about the piece, and only to a couple of 'sticks' about the acting? Gentlemen of the Press are very fond of teaching the playwrights how to write plays, why don't they tell the actors how to act?

In his last question my friend has fallen into the not uncommon error of supposing criticism to be a didactic art; but there is, perhaps, something in his grievance. There is of dramatic criticism enough and to spare; but there is little, if any, genuine criticism of histrionics. The actors think this is only a part of the general 'cussedness' of their natural enemies, the critics. But let us try to be more sweetly reasonable than the actors, and see if we cannot find a subtler explanation. My first reason may seem whimsical to the matter-of-fact outsider, but all professional scribblers will, I believe, recognize it as a true one. Your critic is a sedentary person with the literary bias. His instinct is to bring to a play the calm lotus-eating mood with which he day-dreams over a book in his library. To this frame of mind the boisterous flesh-and-blood element of the actors comes as a rude distraction. Oxford, said the cynic, would be a delightful place if it were empty of Oxford men; the playhouse, the literary critic feels in his heart of hearts, would be a pleasant place without the players. Here you touch a paradox of the acted drama: the very means that make it possible to judge of it hinder judgment. Of this type of critic Hazlitt is the great example. 'The players', Talfourd records, 'put him out.' Secondly, the critic is tempted to shirk speaking of the actors from a natural delicacy. It is the peculiarity of the actor's art that his artistic materials are composed of his own physical personality. He himself is his own paint and canvas. Hence observations on his acting are bound to verge upon the dangerous ground of 'personal remarks'. Now it irks a gentleman who is probably no Adonis himself (thank goodness, his calling doesn't require that of him!) to have to discuss the tilt of another gentleman's nose. When ladies are concerned, the critic's distress is, of course, much more poignant. I shudder as I think of some fair lady pointing me out to a sister-actress. 'Do you see the sandy, pock-marked little fellow over there in the bad hat? He had the impudence to say of me the other day, that "I was a tolerable Doll Tearsheet; but that my Juliet lacked the indefinable quality known as charm." Now, what can a horrid little wretch like that know about charm?' So the critic naturally prefers to talk about the play, which has no feelings to be hurt.

My thirdly is deducible from the preceding reason. If 'personal remarks' have to be made, there is a tendency to make them agreeable to their subject, and compliments are not criticism. I well remember the advice once given me by the dramatic critic *en titre* of a certain old-fashioned newspaper. 'My boy, your discussions of the Three Unities, your long quotations from Aristotle in the original Greek, your parallels between G. R. Sims and Lope de Vega, are ingenious and scholarly, and all that; but the public don't understand 'em, and our sub-editor has orders to cut 'em out. Write something the actors can quote. Always have a good quotable paragraph.' And now, as I run my eye down the Press notices in the morning papers, I flatter myself I can generally spot the 'quotable paragraph'. Next day out it comes in the advertisement columns – you know the sort of thing –

FRIVOLITY THEATRE – GIGANTIC SUCCESS

The Daily Gazette says:	'Cheered to the echo.'
The Mercury says:	'Will draw all London to the historic little house in Queer-Street.'
The Morning Mail says:	'The most monumental of all Mr Vincent Crummles's colossal creations. Veteran play-goers who had been in the pit that "rose at" Kean, or who had shuddered with awe at Sarah Siddons, wept like children. The whole house one sob', etc., etc.

Another reason why some writers abstain from serious criticism of actors is peculiar to journalism – or was, for even in the most old-fashioned quarters one would not, I suppose, find an editor nowadays instructing his dramatic critic as Delane instructed John Oxenford. An actor whom Oxenford had sharply criticized (the story is told by Mr Edmund Yates) complained in a strong letter to the editor. 'I have no doubt you were perfectly right in all you wrote,' said Delane to his critic, 'but that is not the question. Whether a man acts well or ill is of very little consequence to the great body of our readers, and I could not think of letting the paper become the field for argument on the point. So, in future, you understand, my good fellow, write your notices so as much as possible to avoid this sort of letter being addressed to the office.' And, finally, criticism of acting is shirked because of the critics' lack of technical knowledge. This is not their fault. They are not actors; and how can they be acquainted with even the rudiments of histrionics, when no one will teach them? There is no Conservatoire in London where the conscientious critic could attend a course of lectures, if he would; actors give lessons to would-be actors, but who ever heard of an actor offering to instruct a would-be critic? Our actors and actresses print their reminiscences, or their impressions of foreign travel, or their ideas about plays (which is the critic's affair and not theirs); but plain elementary instruction about their own business – the art of acting – they cannot be induced to print.

Playhouse Impressions, 1892

A. B. Walkley
Dramatic Criticism

... The plain truth is that the playgoer who is merely seeking his pleasure and the playgoer who has to appraise and to justify his pleasure of necessity take somewhat different views. For the one there is the sole question: Am I pleased? For the other there is that question too, but coupled with another question – a question which, by the way, was one of Matthew Arnold's many borrowings from Sainte-Beuve – Am I right to be pleased? Stendhal's precept, 'Interroge-toi quand tu ris', is nothing to the public, but it is everything to the critic. Or the public may say, 'we were bored', and forget the play as quickly as they can. The critics have to say why they are bored, and that is a bore, so that they are sure to be less charitable to a bad play than the public. The wound is kept open. Then it has to be remembered that good plays, plays which rightly please the public, often make bad 'copy' – that is to say, unworkable material – for the critic. A play that presents no variation of type may be interesting enough in itself, but vexes the critic, to whom it offers no 'purchase'. And, to go a little further into technical particulars, there are certain classes of play – for example, melodramas and farces – which always come out worse on paper than on the boards. The critic is generally tempted to describe melodrama by the ironic method – which is a perfidy – and to narrate the plot of a farce is, at the best, to decant champagne. It is for a kindred reason that the 'drama of ideas' is apt to be overpraised in print – which is a good medium for ideas. In brief, criticism, being a form of literature, can do justice to the literary elements in drama; but in drama there are many other elements, and criticism is often at fault with these, because of a purely technical difficulty, the difficulty of transposing the effects of one art into the effects of another. Criticism can give the reader a very fair idea of *Hamlet* or *Paolo and Francesca*, of *Le Demi-Monde* or *A Doll's House*, of *Iris* or *The Admirable Crichton*. It can give only an inadequate account of the pleasure afforded by *A Midsummer Night's Dream* or *La Locandiera* or *L'Enfant Prodigue*. With *Box and Cox* or *Charley's Aunt* it can do nothing.

And we have seen the reason why. It is because the critic, like the piece of furniture in Goldsmith's poem, has 'a double debt to pay'; because he is at once consumer and producer, at once parasite and independent, substantive artist. In the very act of describing and appraising the methods of another art he has to follow the methods, the very different methods, of his own. A criticism is a picture with its own laws of perspective and composition and 'values', and the play which furnishes the subject for this picture has more often than not to be 'humoured' a little, stretched here and squeezed there, in order to fit into the design. The salient points in the pattern of the play may not suit the salient points in the pattern of the criticism – though, no doubt, the good critic is he who most often gets the two sets into perfect coincidence. The critic must have his 'general idea', his leading theme, which gives his criticism its unity, something to hold it together. This general idea, however legitimately it may have been derived from the play criticized, will very likely get exaggerated, will assume a much more important part in the criticism than it actually did in the play itself. Or the critic may take some significant phrase or catchword of the play as a 'refrain' for his article, or he may perform a *fantasia* on some leading theme of the play (for example, the 'nose' theme in *Cyrano de Bergerac*), until he has exhausted all its possible permutations and combinations. These are devices permissible in criticism, because criticism is literature, an art intended to interest, to give pleasure, in itself; but their effect is to warp the genuine first-hand impression of the play, to alter its proportions. Thus criticism tends to systematize what may not be systematic, to follow out its own logic and to expand its own formulas, rather than to conform strictly to the outline and proportions of the thing criticized. That is so, because, in a sense, all art is not only a transformation but a defor-mation of its subject-matter. It is the old difficulty of the portrait painter. The sitter asks, 'Is it like?'; the connoisseur, 'Is it a good piece of painting?' There are whole elements of a play which are ignored by the critic, for the simple reason that they will not work into his scheme. One has even heard of cases where the name of some meritorious actor has been passed over in silence, because mention of it would spoil the hang of the critic's sentence; but that is immoral.

One must not be lured into betraying all the secrets of the craft. Enough has been said, perhaps, to show why the critic and the public differ in their opinions of the same thing, and why this difference is widened in the very process by which the critic records his opinions. It is often widened still further by what may seem a purely mechanical accident – the interval of time which elapses between the critic's impression and his record of it. The objection is often raised against 'first night' criticism, that it is bound to be hasty, undigested, more or less of an improvisation. Apart from the fact that newspaper readers, in any case, insist upon having it, I believe that it is on the whole the criticism most advantageous to the play. The critic's sensations are vivid, his mind is full of his subject, he still has the proportions and details of the play in his eye. Writing after an interval, he is apt to remember his general impression of the play rather than the play itself, and his impression has lost in truth by the fading of minor detail, to the consequent exaggeration of a few prominent features – a process which may lead the most conscientious critic to unconscious caricature.

Now I trust I have not been showing you a glimpse of the critic at work without at the same time suggesting to you his professional drawbacks, his besetting sins. For one thing, I have said that he has often to give an appearance of system to subject-matter which is not really systematic. And so he is apt to become what Joe Gargery would call too 'architectooralooral'. Then again, having to deal perpetually in formulas, he is in danger of becoming their dupe. He is apt to indulge in what another character in Dickens calls 'poll-parrotting'; to repeat mechanically cant phrases – 'objective' and 'subjective', 'classic' and 'romantic', 'organism' and 'reaction'. These are the things which Sir Leslie Stephen, with his wonted manliness and homeliness of sense, brands as 'the mere banalities of criticism. I can never hear them', he says, 'without a suspicion that a professor of Aesthetics is trying to hoodwink me by a bit of technical platitude. The cant phrases which have been used so often by panegyrists, too lazy to define their terms, have become almost as meaningless as the complimentary formulae of society.' And that is just it; the man of letters is here showing the same weakness as the man of the world. For there are fashions in the library just as there are fashions in the *salon*; and the desire for imitation for imitation's sake, is common to all humanity.

And then the critic is apt to theorize 'in the air', because of the constant tendency towards divorce between literature and life. Walter Bagehot makes some characteristic remarks on this point: 'The reason why so few good books are written, is that few people that can write know anything. In general an author has always lived in a room, has read books, has cultivated science, is acquainted with the style and sentiments of the best authors, but is out of the way of employing his own ears and eyes. He has nothing to hear and nothing to see. His life is a vacuum. . . . He sits beside a library-fire, with nice white paper, a good pen, a capital style, every means of saying everything, and nothing to say. . . . How dull it is to make it your business to write, to stay by yourself in a room to write, and then to have nothing to say.' Something like that is very often the fate of the dramatic critic. For there are many plays which are absolutely null and void. The general playgoer settles the matter quite comfortably by falling asleep over them. The critic has to say something, and in reality there is nothing to be said.

So much by way of confession of critical sins. There remain two charges constantly brought against critics which may be admitted to the full, but which, instead of being to their discredit, are really the best evidence of their good faith and their good work. These two charges are: first, lack of unanimity – the critics disagree with one another – and, second, lack of consistency – the critic will often disagree with himself. Critics, it is said, not being unanimous, cannot be representative of public opinion. As though public opinion about a play was ever unanimous! We must not be fooled by a noun of multitude. 'Public' is one word; it does not denote one thing. I know I spoke in my first lecture of the crowd as a whole, and sketched the general aspects of the collective mind. But the public, of course, is extraordinarily disparate in its parts. It comprises the people who applaud a play, the people who hiss it, the people who slumber through it, the people who don't know what to think about it, the people who like it because dear Angelina does, the people who dislike it because they had to forego their after-dinner coffee in order to see it, and the people who would stay away from it if they were not paid to go. So that when criticism is unanimous, then, and only then, shall we be able to say confidently that it is not representative. But fortunately that time – that monotonous time – will never be. For in that time there will have to be absolute rules for judging works of art, applied by everybody in the same way; all critics will possess the same principles, taste, temperament, intellectual education, moral standard, the experience of life. Meanwhile, 'with such a being as man in such a world as the present' – as Bishop Butler used to phrase it – no two critics who are thinking and feeling for themselves can be in complete agreement. We might as well complain that their faces are not alike! There is, no doubt, often a certain appearance of unanimity among critics who are not thinking for themselves but are trying to think what they suppose they ought to think or what they guess other people to be thinking, so as to shout, on Mr Pickwick's principle, with the largest crowd. But these are critics who have mistaken their vocation. So that when Mr Sidney Grundy asks, 'When critics fall out, who shall decide?' and when Sir Henry Irving refers to 'the rapture of disagreement which is served up by the dramatic critics', they ought in reality to have been gratified by the lack of unanimity which they deplore. It is evidence that the plays of the one and the acting of the other are stimulating enough to force the critics into thinking for themselves.

We have seen that while criticism as to its substance is opinion, as to its form it is art. No two opinions can be the same, because no man has the same perceptive apparatus – eye, ear, nerves, brain – as another man. Is it not notorious that no two people will agree in describing the simplest fact, the pace of an omnibus, the number of cats in the back garden? But while criticism is bound to vary, as mere record of fact, its variation is enormously increased because it is an art. Did you ever see two identical pictures of the same subject by different hands? Did you ever hear two pianists play the same sonata in the same way? Of course not, and yet there are people who seem to expect different souls to have the same adventures among the masterpieces. And if they were the same, there would still remain the variations of ability to describe them. The critic's real difficulty is that he never does describe them adequately. To adjust language with exactness to one's thoughts and impressions is an impossible feat; critics, like other writers, spend their lives in practising it, and, like other writers, never bring the feat off.

As to the critic's want of self-consistency, that is apt in this country to bring him into sad trouble. In 1902 a provincial jury mulcted a newspaper in the sum of £100 and costs for a certain theatrical 'notice', and two of the jurors wrote to the newspapers to say that the main ground of their verdict was the consideration that the notice was inconsistent with a former notice of the same play in the same quarter. If these gentlemen had been philosophers – instead of jurymen – they would have congratulated this inconsistent critic on the plain proof that he was not a mechanical recording instrument – a barometer or a pair of scales – a dead thing, but a human being with the principle of growth and life within him. They would have recognized, with a pure natural joy, that the soul never has the same adventures twice over. Nothing – to take perhaps a less humble literary example – nothing could be more interesting than to note the mental development of the well-known Danish critic, Dr George Brandes, in studying the works of Ibsen *pari passu* with their production. He says himself, after noting how Ibsen at different stages of his work was not the same Ibsen: 'But neither was the critic quite the same. He had in the meantime gone through a great deal, and had consequently acquired a larger outlook upon life, and a more flexible emotional nature. He had dropped all the doctrines that were due to education and tradition. He understood the poet better now.' A great historical instance of development in the reverse direction is that of Voltaire in regard to Shakespeare. Voltaire began by blessing Shakespeare (with reservations), and ended by (quite unreservedly) cursing him. That was by no means because he understood the poet better; but for reasons extraneous to his critical development, reasons connected with his objections to the course which he found the French drama was taking without his leave. And the moral of that little affair is that the critic should remain content to be an artist, and not set up for a literary dictator. . . .

Dramatic Criticism: Three Lectures Delivered at the Royal Institution
in February 1903, 1903

Desmond MacCarthy
The Influence of Dramatic Criticism

It may sometimes depress the critic to reflect how little influence he has upon the fate of the plays and books he criticizes, but this fact is the salvation of criticism and often, let me hasten to add, the salvation of art. If the case were otherwise, and the critic knew his opinion had a direct effect upon the commercial success of a play, he could hardly bring himself to point out carefully the defects of a performance, which he thought, nevertheless, far better than its competitors for public favour. He would feel bound, in such a case, to consider the immediate effect of what he wrote, and this pre-occupation would be fatal to criticism. Happily, we need not think of this. It is obvious that success is achieved independently of the opinion of critics; the sky is red with spreading, blazing reputations which their cold water is as powerless to quench as a fire-engine a prairie fire; nor can their unanimous praise always secure even a modicum of success. For instance, in March 1905, the Court Theatre Company produced a translation of Hauptmann's *Bieber Pelz*, called *The Thieves' Comedy*. It was a first-rate performance, and an exceptionally good play. The critics praised it with one accord; not only those who had begun to see in the Vedrenne-Barker management the most notable achievement in modern dramatic production, but also those who were reluctant to admit anything of the kind. They praised the acting, the play, the point; they lavished on it those adjectives which are calculated to rouse curiosity; but the play ran out after nine performances before almost empty houses. It is not likely, in the event of its revival, that it would again fall flat; but that would be due to Messrs Vedrenne and Barker having now gained the confidence of a considerable public, in securing which the support of even the most authoritative critics has only played an ancillary part. If, then, the public do not follow the critics, why do they read them? That they do so is certain, since every daily and weekly paper continues to provide criticism in large quantities.

Dramatic criticism finds two kinds of readers; those who just glance at the plot and the names of the 'stars' to discover whether a play is likely to amuse them, and those who, equally or even more anxious to discover this, are interested at the same time in discussions upon the merits and meanings of plays. To the former, dramatic criticism is simply a species of elaborated, garbled news, less trustworthy than a hint from an acquaintance; to the others it is an expression of opinion upon topics which they are in the habit of discussing themselves. If a critic is interesting they read him, but with no more subservience than they would feel towards a writer who was not a critic; the direct influence of criticism is therefore, in either case, likely to be small. Judging, however, from the prodigious quantity of talk exchanged over plays and novels, readers of the latter kind are numerous enough; even allowing for the fact that conversation upon art and literature is one of the commonest masks that politeness finds for boredom. In France this fact is recognized, and interest at the back of all this general talk about the drama finds a better continuation in the Press. French dramatic critics are allowed at least twenty-four hours during which to examine and express their impressions, while our daily-paper critics are hustled into print an hour or two after leaving the theatre. It is they who are most widely read, while it is their work which is perforce most carelessly done. The deft and spirited *Times* may plunge into his subject at any point, and in a few energetic sentences reach the centre of his theme; but a combination of endowments including logic, quickness, and a fly-paper memory, which catches every telling phrase, is as rare as it is essential under such conditions. On the other hand, a critic may be capable of fathering a fair harvest of observation, without having the high-pressure mental machinery to reap and thresh it within a couple of hours, and such critics have now no chance of doing their best. Consequently they are in disgrace in all quarters; managers talk as though they would gladly be rid of them; actors are sick of finding their acting dismissed in a few vague phrases at the end of an account of the plot, their strokes of imagination unnoticed, their bungling carelessly praised; authors complain that their plays are misunderstood – Mr Shaw frequently writes prefaces to show they are dunderheads; their editors cut them down, their readers think they could do better themselves. All this would surprise nobody who had seen a first-night rush back to newspaper offices, where copy is often snatched away in the writing, and the time allowed commonly varies from forty to a hundred minutes. So driven, a man will usually find himself writing, not what he would most like to express, but whatever he can put down quickest. The remedy is simple; the editors must be persuaded to accept a brief 'report' of the first night and to hold over the critical account of the play till the following issue; or, better still for a weekly *feuilleton*. It would pay them well; they would be getting far better copy; they would please a section of the public they never cease to cater for by literary articles and reviews of all kinds, while they would be providing the people, who choose their plays by rules of thumb, just the prompt, ungarnished news they require on the following morning. That it would be an advantage, from the point of view of the theatres, if critics were enabled to write their best, may seem in contradiction with the fact that criticism has little direct influence; for it is certainly true that the sale of tickets depends upon the taste of the public, and not upon the taste of the critic; but criticism has nevertheles s a strong direct influence; an example can be taken from the history of the Court Theatre.

In accounting for its success, after you have pointed to the originality and power of Mr Shaw's plays and the intelligence and naturalness of the acting, further explanations may seem as superfluous as Harlequin's thirty-six reasons why his dead master could not appear; yet if we do seek further, the influence of ten years' criticism upon public sentiment, during which the most entertaining critics assaulted the stock London play, laughed at its hackneyed situations, its vapid sentiments, exposed its reach-me-down solutions and superficial problems, must be taken into consideration in accounting for the difference between the success of Messrs Vedrenne and Barker and that of such intermittent enterprises, so similar in spirit, as the Independent and New Century Theatres.

Beside the comparatively few people who knew all along what they wanted from the theatre, there were a large number who knew vaguely what they did not want, but were inclined to explain their constant dissatisfaction by telling themselves that they were not naturally fond of the drama. The few who knew what they wanted went to the Independent and New Century Theatres, or joined the Stage Society; the others, without being convinced completely, began to be persuaded, by such critics as 'G.B.S.', 'Max', Mr William Archer and Mr Walkley, that there might be the best reasons for their lack of interest in the average play. When in 1904 the Court Theatre started under a new management, the enterprise this time did not wear the truculent, propagandist aspect of the Independent Theatre; Ibsen was no longer a bugbear, though he was far from being a draw; the plays of Mr Shaw had been widely read, and there was considerable curiosity to see them; *Arms and the Man* and the few performances already given of *You Never Can Tell, The Devil's Disciple* and *Candida* had been remembered and talked about; and moreover, Messrs Vedrenne and Barker had the good fortune to produce, as their second play, *John Bull's Other Island*, which attracted all sorts and conditions of men. Society, on the eve of a general election, came to laugh at Broadbent, and to listen to brilliant discussions upon Irish and English character. They sat enthralled through a play with no vestige of a plot, delighted by acting unlit by the light of 'a star', which was obviously and incomparably the better for that. Here, too, they found a play the roots of which struck among the interests of the time, which presented types of character delightfully recognizable, yet new to the stage, in which a most natural sequence of events carried them along like a series of ingeniously contrived surprises, and left them with plenty to think over, laugh over, and dispute over when the curtain fell; in short, here was a new play full of qualities which the critics had been arraigning the London stage for not possessing. No wonder when the question of going to the theatre next came up people should ask themselves what was being done at the Court.

Thus in an indirect way these critics, who were so amusing to read, had prepared the public to see the significance of the new management; and though it cannot be supposed that were this suggestion, for giving the majority of critics more time, taken up, the result would be a rich crop of remarkable criticisms, certainly the discussions upon the merits and defects of plays would be henceforward much closer, and the articles proportionately more interesting to numbers of people. It is of small consequence that a critic should damn a good play; but it is of consequence that the feeling which criticism promotes should be that plays are well worth discriminating upon, since only in such an atmosphere can drama flourish. Criticism may miss the point again and again; but provided it is of the kind which stimulates impartial scrutiny and interest in the minds of those who concern themselves with works of art, it has fulfilled its main function both as regards art and the public.

Introduction to *The Court Theatre 1904–1907*, 1907